Family Measurement Techniques

Family Measurement Techniques
Abstracts of Published Instruments, 1935-1974

Revised Edition

Murray A. Straus and Bruce W. Brown

UNIVERSITY OF MINNESOTA PRESS □ MINNEAPOLIS

Library of Congress Cataloging in Publication Data

Straus, Murray Arnold, 1926-
    Family measurement techniques.

    Includes bibliographies and indexes.
    1. Family — Abstracts. 2. Psychometrics — Abstracts.
I. Brown, Bruce W., joint author. II. Title.
HQ728.S86 1978   301.42'08   78-14598
ISBN 0-8166-0799-0

Preface to First Edition

This book is a part of the Inventory of Published Research in Marriage and the Family of the Minnesota Family Study Center in more than a formal administrative sense. The work was begun at Cornell University as a subsidiary part of a program to develop new techniques for measuring characteristics of families. However, it was Reuben Hill who suggested its expansion and suggested that I apply to the National Institute of Mental Health for funds to do so. The first phase of the work was subsequently carried out with support from that Institute under Grant No. M-5147A. After I joined the faculty of the University of Minnesota, the work was supported by the Minnesota Family Study Center, in part with funds made available by a grant from the Institute for Life Insurance.

Many people have assisted me in the task of searching for and abstracting the family measurement literature. First drafts of a number of the abstracts were originally prepared by students at Cornell University in my research practicum on methods for studying the family. In revising these student-prepared abstracts, I have in all cases read the original work on which they report in its entirety, so that any errors which appear are my responsibility. The work at Cornell was greatly facilitated by the diligence and skill of my research assistant Miss Janice Feldtmose.

v

At the University of Minnesota a number of people helped bring the project to completion. I am particularly indebted to Joan Aldous, Cecilia Sudia, and Richard Devine. In addition to searching the literature and abstracting, Mr. Devine was in charge of the final editing of the manuscript. Finally, I am indebted to Mrs. Barbara B. Rutledge for indexing.

University of New Hampshire   M.A.S.
Durham
May 1969

Preface to Second Edition

There has been an exponential growth in the number of techniques for measuring characteristics of the family. Specifically, the first edition covered a thirty-year period and included abstracts of 319 measures. But the second edition, which adds abstracts of instruments published in just a ten-year span, contains 494 additional measures, or a total of 813. Because the number of instruments has more than doubled, it was not possible for the two of us alone to search the hundreds of journals in which these measures appear and to abstract all 494 instruments. Fortunately, it was possible to draw on two sources of help. First, about 150 authors of tests were generous enough to prepare draft abstracts of their measures. We are deeply grateful to them and hope that they will accept our thanks and will be pleased with the changes we have sometimes had to make in their abstracts. Second, we want to express our appreciation to the devoted staff of assistants at the University of New Hampshire who wrote about 100 of the asbtracts: Bonnie Cobb, Joyce Foss, Susan Murray, Blair Nelson, Thomas Sparhawk, and Kersti Yllo.

It is hard to describe the amount of correspondence and record keeping which was involved in the compilation of this book. Looking back, we ourselves find it difficult to believe that so much time and care was necessary for this aspect of the work. But it was, and we want to express our appreciation to Sieglinde Fizz for this aspect of the work.

The equivalent of setting the type for the book was done on the University of New Hampshire DEC-10 computer. The input of the text was done by Lee Aldrich, Valerie Harrington, Marcia Richardson, and Tamy Van Slooten, working under miserable conditions in the windowless hot room where our computer terminals are located. Their patience with this and with the many frustrations of an often balky computer was truly remarkable.

Finally, we are grateful to the University of New Hampshire Library and Computer Center. The staff of the library must have at times wondered what was going on when they were deluged with inquiries and requests for inter-library loans from six or seven of us during the final cleanup work in the summer of 1976. The Computer Center, however, was already familiar with the demands that we often make on their services, and as usual took it in their stride. Without their help, and the grant of free computer time, it would not have been possible to produce the book with the same efficiency.

University of New Hampshire   M.A.S.
Durham   B.W.B.
January, 1978

Contents

Family Measurement Techniques

Chapter I

Introduction

The rapid expansion of research dealing with the family has heightened the need for a means by which researchers can efficiently locate techniques for measuring the aspect of the family of concern to their studies. It is hoped that the descriptions of the 813 measurement techniques in this volume will fill this need. If our search has been effective, the book provides a comprehensive inventory of techniques that have been developed for quantitatively expressing the properties of the family or the behavior of people in family roles.

A. THE IMPROVEMENT OF FAMILY MEASUREMENT

In addition to its convenience for individual investigators, it is also hoped that this volume will make a more general contribution to research on the family by encouraging the further development and standardization of many promising techniques. The cumulative nature of science is nowhere more apparent than in such a development of measurement technology. A brief consideration of measures of length illustrates the point. The system of inches, feet, and miles is terribly cumbersome, yet rigorous scientific work is possible with this ancient system because it is a standardized measure. Similarly, despite the rationality of the length of the meter, it is essentially an arbitrary unit--the other characteristics which make the metric system so convenient would be of no value were there not consensus on this system and familiarity with its use.

In the case of measures of relatively intangible variables such as are common in research on the family, the importance of cumulative use and standardization is even greater since only with repeated use can the characteristics, limits, and correlates of a test become known. In short, measurement instruments become more valuable with each use. Similarly, as Campbell and Fisk (1959) make clear in their discussion of the Washburn "Social Intelligence" test, it is largely through repeated use that an apparently promising technique can be invalidated.

Obviously, if such a process of cumulative development is to take place, a minimum essential is for investigators to be aware of the range of possibilities at their disposal. The fact that this minimum condition has not been met was apparent in the development of this book. When the process of abstracting existing techniques was first begun, it was thought that there would be only twenty-five to fifty instruments in the literature. The actual total described in this book is 813, and some have surely been overlooked. Conversation with a number of other researchers suggests that a similar ignorance of the work already done on family measurement is probably widespread, even among methodologically sophisticated investigators. Among the reasons for this failure of scientific communication may be, first, the fact that family research is carried out primarily in two disciplines (psychology and sociology), the practitioners of which tend not to read one another's journals; and second, the fact that a large part of the research and writing on the family is done by sociologists, who, historically, have devoted relatively little attention to problems of standardized measurement as compared with psychologists. Both these facts point to the need for a comprehensive list of existing instruments and to the need for a critical evaluation of these instruments. This abstract series is primarily intended to meet the first of these needs.

1.   Abstracts Versus Reviews

The fact that one of us (Straus) was an associate editor of Sociological Abstracts, no doubt influenced the decision to present material on existing instruments in the tradition of an abstract journal, where the objective is simply to make material conveniently available, in brief form. Unlike a book review, no critique is made--at least not in the abstract of an instrument. Instead, the critical and the abstracting role have been segregated, with the former in another publication (Straus, 1964a). Other critiques are also available, such as that by Hoffman and

Lippitt (1960). This separation of the critical and abstracting roles contrasts with the organization of the Mental Measurements Yearbooks (Buros, 1969, 1972a, 1972b), where each test entry is a critical review.

The introduction to the first edition expresses the hope that ". . . in the future, combining the abstracting and critical functions will be a fruitful approach. . .but the present inadequacy of the available instruments would make such a system repetitious." Unfortunately, the situation has not changed. A tabulation of a random sample of 100 of the instruments in this book reveals figures almost identical to those of ten years ago: more than half (58%) give no evidence of reliability. In respect to validity, the situation is even less adequate. Almost three-quarters (65%) did not even mention the concept of validity, much less offer any evidence. This may seem like a worsening of the situation because the first edition indicated that a little over half of the instruments were without evidence of validity. But there has virtually been no change. The seeming discrepancy between "half" and "three-quarters" is due to a change in procedures. From the sample of instruments added to this edition, a measure was counted as having some evidence of validity only if the author claimed this. If there was no mention of validity, then it was included in the three-quarters without such evidence. By contrast, for the first edition certain types of data were construed as evidence of construct validity, even if the test author did not make this claim. Specifically, we took as evidence of construct validity any correlation between the test and some other variable with which (on theoretical grounds) the test should be associated. Although this was described as grossly stretching the idea of construct validity (Straus, 1964:367), and in the introduction to the first edition as "a liberal, or loose criterion [which]. . . might even be considered a travesty on the notion of construct validity, especially by comparison with such rigorous criteria as Campbell and Fiske's Multitrait-Multimethod technique (1959)," it seemed reasonable at the time as an educational step. The intention was to encourage the authors and users of these tests to confront the problem of validity by showing them that the situation was not hopeless. We still think that the situation is not hopeless, but we now believe that stretching the idea of construct validity in this way may have been misleading and done more harm than good by suggesting that an instrument is valid when, in fact, there is no firm evidence of this.

2. Modification of Tests

It should be clear, then, that the inclusion of a technique in this set of abstracts in no way constitutes an endorsement, approval, or recommendation. In fact, there is

even a danger that this compilation might encourage the use
of invalid or inappropriate instruments just because they
are conveniently available. But though this danger exists,
it is felt that most investigators will not view the
instruments abstracted as packages to be bought and used
blindly, but rather as something to be modified as needed,
or as a source of leads for creating entirely new
instruments, taking advantage of the experiences, mistakes,
and findings of the prior investigator.

Among the many modifications which researchers might
make to adapt one of the instruments described in this
volume are the following:

(1) Add or eliminate items, preferably on the basis of
a pilot study in which some empirical criterion such as item
analysis or factor analysis is used as part of the decision
process.

(2) Modify instruments designed for one age or sex of
respondent to fit another age or sex (for example;
instruments developed for use with children might be
modified for use with adults and the reverse).

(3) Modify self-administered questionnaires for use as
interview guides, or the reverse.

(4) Use self-rating questions or scales as
observer-rating scales or the reverse.

(5) Secure social desirability ratings on test items as
outlined by Edwards (1957) in order to form them into
"forced-choice" pairs or Q-sort sets.

(6) Administer the instrument with different response
instructions: For example, one can often change a "role
prescription"--many so-called attitude tests--to a role
performance measure by asking for responses in terms of
actual past actions rather than likes or preferences.

3. Comparative Validity Studies

The two-fold increase in the number of instruments
abstracted, combined with the topical arrangement of the
revised edition, highlights the fact that many of the
instruments which are separately abstracted may differ in
only minor respects from other similar instruments. For
example, Chapter II, Section B.2, dealing with husband-wife
role differentiation in family task performance, contains 25
instruments. Many of them in one way or another use a
somewhat similar list of activities indicating who does each
of the activities. Moreover, the equivalent section of
Chapter IV contains additional instruments which differ
primarily in including children as well as the spouses.

This raises the question (and also facilitates research to answer the question) of whether the seemingly small differences in lists of activities and in response format make a difference. One instrument, for example, may include lawn mowing and clothes washing; another may include taking out garbage and dishwashing. What difference does the specfic list of household tasks make? One instrument may ask how often the wife does each task and how often the husband does each; another may ask for only one response to each item, with responses on a scale ranging from "Wife always" through "Both equally" to "Husband always." What difference, if any, does this make?

Since one of the outstanding characteristics of family measures is that with rare exceptions they are not based on methodological studies exploring such issues, there is at present no way of deciding among these similar instruments except on the basis of such factors as the testing time and the stylistic preferences of the person making the choice of techniques from among those abstracted. Perhaps the accessibility of already developed instruments made possible by this book will encourage researchers to build on the existing work where appropriate, rather than duplicating it with further minor variations. Obviously, one of the important ways of building on the existing instruments would be conducting research to determine if seemingly minor variations of the type just described (to say nothing of major differences in measurement approaches) produce important differences in validity and reliability.

4. Sexism in Family Measures

The sexist structure of a society, almost by definition, is manifest in all the institutions of such a society, including science. This is clearly illustrated by many of the instruments in this compendium. Thus, the measures of household task performance in this book often assume that most of these tasks are the province of women and paid employment is the province of men. Even when the objective is to measure shared or joint activities, biases creep in. For example, one instrument counts as an indicator of "joint" activities instances in which the husband "sometimes" cooks and "rarely" does laundry.

In a test designed to measure accuracy of nonverbal communication, the situations are highly sex stereotyped; for example, "You come home to the dinner table as your wife begins to serve chicken..." Another instrument makes use of data from both the husband and the wife. The wife's section of the interview is used to obtain the data on who does each of the listed tasks. But the data on norms--on who should do what--are obtained from the interview with the husband! Finally, it should be noted that biases of this type are not limited to measures of role differentiation and power. They creep in in many, often subtle, ways. For example, one of the techniques abstracted is a procedure for measuring the accuracy of nonverbal communication. The situations used for this, however, are highly sex stereotyped, for example: "You come home to the dinner table as your wife begins to serve chicken. . . ." One could go on at some length documenting the numerous instances of how the sexist organization of the society is built into these measurement techniques.

Of course, it can be argued that it is the task of science to find out about the nature of society, not to change the society. Indeed one can go further and argue that it would be bad science to build into these measures an equalitarian or any other ideology. But that is a false dichotomy. What is needed are measures which do not assume either a sexist or an equalitarian family system, measures which allow for the tremendous range of variation existing in all societies, and measures which are capable of producing data unbiased by either the existing ideology or by ideology concerning alternative modes of social relationships. A first step in this direction would be a systematic analysis of the nature and extent of sexist bias in the instruments included in this book. Obviously, we hope that some readers will take this step, and that all users of this book will examine the instruments they choose for possible sexist bias and make whatever modifications are needed.

B. CLASSIFICATION OF MEASURES

The classification of abstracts was begun with what we thought of as a purely empirical approach. That is, the abstracts were first divided into the major role relationships (husband-wife, parent-child). We then sorted through the husband-wife abstracts and grouped those which measured the same or closely related variables.

1. A Latent Theory

The main outline of the classification which was finally adopted emerged within an hour or so of the first attempt at such grouping. At first, this seemed to be a purely empirical phenomenon, merely reflecting the topics on which marriage and family research had focused over the past 40 years. But when the parent-child measures were sorted and the same categories emerged, it became clear that there is an implicit theory underlying the A and B sections of the classification scheme. Specifically, students of the family, whether they are sociologists or anthropologists studying family interaction per se, or psychologists

studying socialization patterns, have over and over again
found that there are two main axes of family structure which
are critical for understanding what goes on in the family:
(A) an interpersonal support or love axis, and (B) authority
or power axes. Since the fundamental importance of the
power and support dimensions was the focus of a theoretical
paper some years back (Straus, 1964b), and since power and
support are a continuing theme in Straus' theoretical
analysis of the family and in the work of others (see
Thomas, Gecas, Weigert, and Rooney, 1974), it seems that the
taxonomy used in this book reflects both these pre-existing
theoretical ideas as well as the empirically found
similarity in variables measured.

There are several implications of the above. First, it
shows that much family research has been guided by a concern
for a theoretical model, even if not always explicitly.
Second, it helps explain the placement of certain
instruments. That is, our theoretical commitments may have
pushed us to place an instrument in a particular category
when from the point of view of some other theory, a
different category would be more appropriate (See for
example the classification system of Cromwell, Olson, and
Fournier, 1976). Third, it explains why a separate category
was created for instruments which provide a score for both
the power and the support axes: the combinations of power
and support (such as high power and low support, or high
power and high support) interact and serve as powerful
elements of family structure. Fourth, the classification
system used in this book is not intended to be logically
exhaustive. Rather, it represents the combination of
variables reflecting one particular conceptual focus
together with such additional categories as were suggested
by the instruments included in this compilation.

2. Browsing Versus Searching

The arrangement of abstracts just described facilitates
browsing through the book. However, it does not provide the
reader with a means of tracking down all instruments
measuring a specific variable. This is because many
instruments do not clearly fit one or the other headings. A
number provide measures of from two to dozens of variables.
If there were two headings under which an abstract could be
classified, we picked one of the two. If there were more
than two, then it is classified in a residual heading such
as "other," except if, despite covering a number of
variables, the predominant flavor or emphasis of the
instrument leaned toward one specific classification.

To deal with the problem of multiple classification a
complete subject index has been prepared. Thus, if one
wants to get a general idea of instruments measuring
husband-wife power, then going through the "Power" section

is probably best. But if one wants to be sure to have
considered every instrument in the book which measures some
aspect of husband-wife power, then the subject index must be
used.

C. ABSTRACTING PROCEDURE

1. Literature Searched for First Edition

     The sociological and psychological literature from 1935
to 1965 was searched for techniques employed to measure
family behavior, with the objective of obtaining exhaustive
coverage starting with 1935. In addition, techniques
published before 1935 uncovered in the course of other
aspects of this work are also included. Certain journals,
such as American Sociological Review, Marriage and Family
Living, and Child Development, were searched thoroughly.
For most other journals primary reliance was placed on
citations in other references and on Psychological Abstracts
and Sociological Abstracts to locate books and articles that
might contain a family measurement technique.

2. Literature Searched for Second Edition

     The greater financial resources available and the
shorter time span to be covered for the second edition
enabled a somewhat more comprehensive search of the
literature. Specifically, instead of doing a complete
search of only a selected set of journals and depending on
citations and reference works for the remainder, it was
decided to check every social science journal in the
University of New Hampshire Library for the period 1965
through 1974. Altogether, some 130 different journals were
searched, issue by issue. A list of these journals is at
the end of the Introduction.

     In addition to a complete search of these journals, the
second edition also had the advantage of the recent
publication of a number of measurement compendia. These are
all both more complete and less complete than the present
volume. They are more complete in the sense of including
techniques for measuring variables covering the entire range
of social science, not just research on the family. They
are less complete in their coverage of family measures.
Moreover, the work which has the most material dealing with
the family (Chun, Cobb, and French, 1975) provides only a
list of variables and references.

     We do not wish to disparage any of these compendia. In
fact, together they consitute an invaluable resource for the
social scientist. A particularly important work for users
of this book is Cromwell, Olson, and Fournier's chapter on

"Diagnosis and Evaluation in Marital and Family Counseling"
(1976). In fact, since readers of this book are likely to
be interested in these related compendia, and since some are
difficult to locate, 21 of them are included in the
reference list for this Introduction. All of these
compendia were searched to find instruments which our search
may have missed.

At the time the final text of this book was being
edited, Johnson's Tests and Measurements in Child
Development: Handbook II, became available. A comparison
of the instruments abstracted there and in our book showed
that only 28 of the 813 instruments abstracted in our book
are also abstracted in Johnson's. However, there are also
40 instruments abstracted in Johnson's book which meet our
criteria, but which somehow escaped our search. Since the
format of Johnson's work is very similar to ours, it seemed
unwise to delay publication just to prepare parallel
abstracts for these 40 tests. Instead, we included them in
this book by adding a brief listing of author, test title,
and the variables measured by these 40 tests, together with
a statement referring the reader to Johnson for the
abstract. A further examination of the 40 tests indicated
the reason why most were omitted from this book: they are
tests which must be obtained by writing to the author. In
several cases we had written to the author for a copy of the
test and received no reply. It is precisely to save readers
this frustration that (with a few exceptions) unpublished
tests are not included in this book unless the author has
supplied a copy to be deposited with the National Auxiliary
Publications Service (NAPS). This resulted in the exclusion
of 49 measures, plus those in the Johnson book which
indicate that the test must be obtained from the author.

We hope that users of this volume will suggest
techniques or instruments which they do not find listed.
This will greatly facilitate the development of a more
comprehensive set of abstracts. We will be even more
grateful if the authors of any such instruments could
prepare an abstract of their instrument for inclusion, or at
the least, send reprints and other materials needed to
prepare an abstract.

3. Criteria for Inclusion

The relatively undeveloped state of family measurement
techniques has necessitated liberal criteria for inclusion
in the book. These criteria were:

1. The technique must provide a classification or
numerical score based on the use of three or more
"indicators" or determinations (such as questions,
observations, events) of the property being measured.

2.   The behavior measured must refer to the   subject's
action   or   disposition to act in a family role (or
proto-family role, as in the case of courtship measures).

3.   The instrument must be described in some published
source so that it is available to users of this volume. If
the instrument is not contained in full in a published
source, we obtained a copy from the author and deposited it
with the National Auxiliary Publications Service (NAPS).
Directions for obtaining copies of such tests are given
below.

4.   Measurement of reproductive behavior in the sense
of fertility is omitted, since these measures are well
covered in such works as Barclay (1958), Spiegelman (1955),
and Shryock and Siegel (1976). However, as explained below,
some instruments dealing with attitudes toward contraception
and family planning are included.

These criteria are somewhat arbitrary.   They evolved
from a combination of practical considerations, such as
availability of the instrument to readers of the book, and
scientific   commitments.   The   most   important of the
scientific considerations is the belief that quantification
is a critical step in the development of any field of
science, both basic science and applied science. One result
of this is that an important class of instruments has been
omitted: clinical interview forms and other diagnostic
techniques which do not provide a numerical score, as for
example, Charny's "Individual and Family Development Review"
(1969).

The inclusion of instruments to measure favorability or
opposition to abortion, sexual knowledge and values, and
contraceptive knowledge and values posed a problem. Insofar
as   the   instrument covered what is known as "family
planning," it clearly fell within the scope of this book,
and some of these instruments are included.   However,
knowledge of contraceptive techniques or of sexual
physiology, although important for the family, is also
important for single persons. The decision to include a few
such measures (we have not aimed at complete coverage) was
based on the fact that these are topics of concern to
"family life educators" and those who do research on family
life education.

The instruments to measure sex roles and feminist
versus traditional orientation also posed a problem. The
ones included are a somewhat arbitrary selection from the
large number of such instruments. Our selection was based
on the extent to which the items in the instrument referred
to values about sex roles or interaction within the family.
We chose those instruments which either contained many such
items or provided family subscores.

Finally, we included abstracts of several widely used personality tests. Some are included because they have specific subscales referring to family relationships. Others are included because the test has been used in family research to measure such things as husband-wife similarity in personality, perceptions of an ideal spouse, or "empathy" between husband and wife (in the sense of the extent to which the responses of a spouse under the instruction to answer as the spouse would, actually corresponds with the responses of the spouse). The list of references for such general tests includes only those studies in which the instrument was used to measure some family property per se. However, if more general use of the test is covered in compendia such as Buros' Personality Tests and Reviews (1969), the compendium is included in our list of references.

This edition is composed of all the instruments which were in the first edition and the newly abstracted instruments. The latter include a few which were published before 1965 but were missed in the first edition. The reasons for retaining the first edition measures (in addition to the fact that the first edition is no longer in print) are: (1) The abstracts have been brought up to date by including new references to the use of each measure. In some cases the test description was also revised to include descriptions of modifications or revisions by the test author(s) or by others. (2) Instruments in the first edition have continuing utility and are of roughly the same average quality as those more recently produced. (3) It is a major convenience for the reader to have all the instruments together and included in a single subject index. (4) The topical arrangement of this edition facilitates browsing through sections of interest--something which is not possible with the purely alphabetical arrangement of the first edition.

4. Differences between First and Second Edition Abstracts

The abstracts in this edition differ from those in the first edition in two ways: They are shorter and a number were written by the authors of the tests themselves. These changes are due to a combination of scientic and practical reasons. First is the doubling of the number of new instruments published from 1965 through 1974. To adhere to the original format would have meant a volume of such bulk that the cost would have been excessive. The time needed to prepare these abstracts would also have meant a three-year delay in publication with the resulting book out of date by the time of publication.

The abstracts are shorter because some sections have been omitted. These are the sections on validity, reliability, norms, and the description of the normative

population.   Since   authors of measurement instruments
dealing with the family rarely carry out standardization and
validation   studies, the abstractor must infer such material
from the information the author does present.   For example,
if a contingency table is presented relating scores on the
instrument to some other variable, the marginal frequencies
can   be considered normative data, insofar as the population
studied is a useful reference point.   The same contingency
table (or correlation coefficient) can be used to infer the
presence or absence of construct validity.   But this is
time-consuming and lacks precision.   Moreover, reporting
such information takes up as much space as the rest of the
abstract.   Consequently, because of the space required for
presentation, the time required for extracting the needed
information, and the fact that such information is often of
dubious accuracy (see section B), it was decided to omit
these elements from the abstracts.   This means that users of
this book must examine the materials on each test and come
to a judgment themselves about whether it meets their
standards for reliability and validity.   In view of the many
factors entering into such a decision, we feel that the
omission of the brief, nonevaluative, and   sometimes
questionable sections on reliability and validity is a step
toward higher standards.

     One possible way out of the dilemma posed by the
question   of   whether   or not to include material on
reliability, validity, and norms might have been to include
such information only when the test authors themselves
provide it.   At first this seemed like an ingenious
solution.   However, it soon became apparent that those
instruments for which such information is reported are not
necessarily more adequate in these respects than those for
which information is not reported.   But if we were to enter
"none" after the headings for reliability, validity, and
norms, it could create a subtle implication of their being
less adequate than the instruments for which the test author
discussed validity, etc.

     This somewhat paradoxical situation occurs in part
because authors of family measures generally do not include
sections on reliability, validity, and norms in their
reports;   and in part because test authors who do include
such information (who are often the authors of commercially
published tests) sometimes provide inadequate and misleading
information.   This problem is discussed and illustrated in
the   American   Psychological   Association's Standards for
Educational and Psychological Tests (1974).   Consequently,
to accurately present information on these aspects of the
tests abstracted would require editorial judgments which are
contrary to the principles of abstracting followed by the
editors of abstract journals the world over.

To a limited extent the need for a critical evaluation of family measures is admirably met by Buros' Mental Measurements Yearbooks (See Section F). However, as valuable as are the reviews in those volumes, they are limited to instruments available through test publishers; and that leaves out all but a small percentage of family measures. Evaluative reviews of some family instruments may also be found in Lake, Miles, and Earle (1973). For general discussions cf problems of validity and reiability of family measures, the reader can consult works such as those of Hoffman and Lippitt (1960), Straus (1964a), and Yarrow (1968). Finally, although the primary focus of Robinson, Rusk, and Head's Measures of Social Psychological Attitudes (1968c) is reporting rather than evaluating, much useful evaluative information is given; but again the number of family measures is extremely limited. An Oscar Buros of family measurement is needed, but that, unfortunately, is not the present authors.

A second change from the first edition is that about 150 of the abstracts were written by the test authors themselves. This procedure was followed because of limits on the time available for this work and the funds available to employ abstractors. However, every abstract written by a test author has been carefully gone over by Straus. It is believed that fifteen years of writing these abstracts enabled him to almost intuitively recognize places where there might be errors or omissions. In all such cases, the original sources have been consulted and the abstract modified or amplified as necessary. If no abstractor is named, it means that the abstract is one carried over from the first edition (with updating as needed), or an abstract written for this edition by Straus.

5. Journals Searched (1965 through 1974 unless other years are noted in parentheses).

Adolescence (66-74)
Aggressive Behavior (74)
Albion (73-74)
American Anthropologist (74)
American Behavioral Scientist
American Ethnologist (74)
American Journal of Psychology
American Journal of Sociology
American Psychologist
American Sociological Review
American Sociologist
Australian and New Zealand Journal of Sociology (71-74)
Behavior Therapy (71-72)
Behavioral Science
British Journal of Criminology (66-74)
British Journal of Social and Clinical Psychology
British Journal of Sociology (65-73 except 70)

Canadian Review of Sociology and Anthropology
Child Development
Child Psychiatry and Human Development (70-74)
Developmental Psychology (69-74)
Educational and Psychological Measurement
Ethnology
Family Coordinator (68-74)
Family Process
Genetic Psychology Monographs
Graduate Research in Education and Related Disciplines
Human Development (70-74)
Human Organization
Human Relations
Impact of Science on Society
Indian Journal of Psychology (73-74)
Insight and Opinion (70-71)
The Insurgent Sociologist (74)
Interchange (70-74)
International Journal of Comparative Sociology
International Journal of Criminology and Penology (73-74)
International Journal of Psychology (66-74)
International Journal of Social Psychiatry (68-74)
International Journal of Sociology (71-74)
International Social Science Journal (66-74)
Japanese Psychological Research (65-73)
Journal for the Theory of Social Behavior (71-74)
Journal of Abnormal Child Psychology (73-74)
Journal of Abnormal Psychology
Journal of Anthropological Research (73-74)
Journal cf Applied Psychology
Journal of Applied Social Psychology (71-74)
Journal of Biosocial Science (69-74)
Journal of Child Psychology and Psychiatry
Journal of Clinical Psychology
Journal of Community Psychology (74)
Journal of Consulting and Clinical Psychology (68-74)
Journal of Consulting Psychology (65-67)
Journal of Counseling Psychology
Journal of Cross-Cultural Psychology (70-74)
Journal of Experimental Child Psychology
Journal of Experimental Social Psychology
Journal of Health and Human Behavior (65-66)
Journal of Health and Social Behavior (67-74)
Journal of Homosexuality (74-75)
Journal of Individual Psychology
Journal of Marriage and the Family
Journal of Personality
Journal of Personality and Social Psychology
Journal of Personality Assessment (71-74)
Journal of Projective Techniques and Personality
    Assessment (65-70)
Journal of Psychology
Journal of Research in Crime and Delinquency
Journal of Research in Personality (73-74)
Journal of School Psychology

Journal of Social Issues (except 70, V28)
Journal of Youth and Adolescence (72-74)
Manchester School cf Economic and Social Studies
Maternal-Child Nursing Journal (72-74)
Mental Hygiene
Merrill-Palmer Quarterly
Minnesota Symposia on Child Psychology (66-74)
Modern Age (64-74)
Multivariate Behavioral Research (66-74)
Nebraska Symposium on Motivation
Occupational Mental Health (71-73)
Occupational Psychology (65-73)
Organizational Behavior and Human Performance (66-74)
Organizational Dynamics (73-75)
Pacific Sociological Review
Philippine Sociological Review (65-71)
The Polish Sociological Bulletin (68-73)
Politics and Society (71-74)
Population Studies
Professional Psychology (69-74)
The Psychoanalytic Quarterly
Psychoanalytic Review (69-74)
Psychologia
Psychological Bulletin (65-73)
Psychological Monographs (65-66)
The Psychological Record
Psychological Reports
Psychological Review
Psychology in the Schools
Quality and Quantity (67-74)
Quarterly Journal of Experimental Psychology
The Rocky Mountain Social Science Journal (70-74)
Rural Sociology
Social Forces
Social Problems
Social Research (66-74)
Social Science
Social Science and Medicine (67-74)
Social Science Information
Social Science Research (72-74)
Society for Research in Child Develoment-Monographs
Sociological Analysis
Sociological Bulletin
Sociological Inquiry
Sociological Methods and Research (72-74)
Sociological Quarterly
Sociological Review (65-73)
Sociology and Social Research
Sociolcgy of Education
Sociometry
Southern Quarterly
Soviet Sociology
Teaching Sociology (73-74)
Theory and Society (74)
Urban Affairs Quarterly

Urban Life and Culture (72-74)
Urban Studies
Youth and Society (69-74)

D. OUTLINE OF ABSTRACT CONTENTS

The abstracts are based on reports (both published and unpublished) by all the authors of the measures, plus all references to the use of the technique that could be located. Each abstract conforms to the following outline:

AUTHORS AND TEST NAMES. [If the test is unnamed in the book or article, an appropriate name has been supplied.]

VARIABLES MEASURED. [Each variable has been given an arabic numeral. If there are groups of variables, a combination of arabic numerals and letters has been used.]

TEST DESCRIPTION. [This section describes the type of questions, observations, or other data used in the measure, the method of obtaining such data, and the method of combining these indicators to form the measure. The test description is written in the present tense, irrespective of the way it was presented in the source documents.]

SAMPLE ITEM. [The first item in the test, unless it is atypical in content or length.]

LENGTH. [Time, number of items.]

AVAILABILITY. [The main reference in which the entire test is printed--for example, "in Jones, 1948." If published by a commercial test publisher, the name and address are given. In some cases, the test is available from the ADI or NAPS.]

REFERENCES. [References include studies by the author of the test and other studies that have made use of the instrument.]

E. OBTAINING TESTS FROM THE ADI OR NAPS

A number of the instruments described in this book are not printed in full in the published sources from which the abstract was prepared. In most such instances, a copy of the complete instrument has been obtained from the author and deposited with the National Auxiliary Publications Service (NAPS) of the American Society for Information Science--formerly the American Documentation Institute (ADI). A copy of instruments deposited with NAPS may be

secured by citing the document number given below. Order
from ASIS/NAPS, Microfiche Publications, P.O.Box 3513, Grand
Central Station, New York, New York 10017. Remit in advance
$3.00 for microfiche copy or for photocopy, $5.00 up to 20
pages plus 25 cents for each additional page. All orders
must be prepaid. Institutions and organizations may order
by purchase order. However, there is a billing and handling
charge for this service of $5.00. Foreign orders add $3.00
for postage and handling.

1. Availability "From NAPS"

      These are instruments which were deposited at the time
the first edition was published. Order the document number
which includes the needed test.

Doc. No.	Pages	Authors' Last Names
00390	60	Adams to Bowerman and Kinch
00391	59	Bronfenbrenner and Devereux to Buerkle and Badgley
00392	61	Chang and Block to Goodrich, Boomer, and Ryder
00393	60	Harris, Clark, Rose, and Valasek to Jansen
00394	42	Kirkpatrick and Hobart to Lyle and Levitt
00395	74	Morgan
00396	60	Pikas to Roe and Siegelman
00397	60	Samenfink to Stryker
00398	60	Tyler, and Rafferty to Walters
00399	60	Williams to Zuk, Miller, Bartram, and Kling

2. Availability "From NAPS-2"

      These are instruments deposited for the first time as
supplement to this edition. Order the document number which
includes the needed test.

Doc. No.	Pages	Author's Last Names	
03122	86	Adamek to Beier-Sternberg	$21.50
03123	95	Berardo	$23.75
03124	45	Biller to Bowerman	$11.25
03125	62	Bronfenbrenner	$15.50
03126	77	Bruce to Cvetkovich	$19.25
03127	76	Danziger to DeLamater	$19.00
03128	96	Fink	$24.00
03129	63	Edwards and Golightly	$15.75
03130	174	Gottman	$43.50
03131	72	Hawkins to Holroyd	$18.00
03132	73	Hurley to Kahn	$18.25

03133	98	Kieren and Tallman	$24.50
03134	75	Kando to Khatri	$18.75
03135	68	Kogan to Leton	$17.00
03136	81	Levinger	$20.25
03137	68	Leventhal and Stollak to Linden and Hackler	$17.00
03138	72	Lindholm and Touliatos to Lytton	$18.00
03139	49	Marwell to McDaniel	$12.25
03140	88	McLeod	$22.00
03141	87	Meadow and Schlesinger to Meltzer	$21.75
03142	91	Nakamura to Oppenheim	$22.75
03143	81	Orden and Bradburn to Pless and Satterwhite	$20.25
03144	74	Pratt to Reiss	$18.50
03145	85	Riskin	$21.25
03146	68	Rothbart and Maccoby to Schulman	$17.00
03147	54	Schwarzweller and Lyson to Stollack	$13.50
03148	93	Straus	$23.25
03149	62	Straus and Cytrynbaum to Szyrynski	$15.50
03150	98	Tallman, Marotz-Baden, Straus, Wilson to Weiss et. al.	$24.50
03151	77	Wells to Winch	$19.25
03152	66	Winder and Rau to Zigler, Butterfield and Goff	$16.50

3. Availability When Document Number Is Given in the Abstract

If the abstract itself contains an ADI or NAPS document number, the author himself has deposited a copy of the test. In such cases the number indicated in the abstract, rather than the number indicated above, should be used in ordering. These instruments, all deposited before June 30, 1968, should be ordered from the American Documentation Institute, Auxiliary Publications Project, c/o Library of Congress, Washington, D.C. 20540. Advance payment is required. Make checks or money orders payable to: Chief, Photoduplication Service, Library of Congress.

F. REFERENCES

American Psychological Association, American Educational Research Association, and National Council on Measurements in Education, Joint Committee. Technical Recommendations for Psychological Tests And Diagnostic Techniques, Washington, D.C.: American Psychological Association, 1974.

Barclay,G.W. Techniques of Population Analysis. New York: Wiley, 1958.

Bodin,A.M. Conjoint family assessment: an evolving field. In McReynolds,P. (Ed.) Advances in Psychological Assessment. Palo Alto, California: Science and Behavior Books, 1968, 223-243.

Bonjean,C.M.   Hill,R.J.   and   McLemore,S.D. Sociological Measurement: An Inventory of Scales and Indices. San Francisco: Chandler, 1967.

Buros,O.K. Personality Tests and Reviews. New York: The Psychological Corporation, 1969.

Buros,O.K. Tests in Print. Revised Edition. New York: The Psychological Corporation, 1972a.

Buros,O.K. The Seventh Mental Measurements Yearbook. New Brunswick, New Jersey: Rutgers University Press, 1972b. (There are six previous editions covering different tests.)

Campbell,D.T.   and   Fiske,D.W.   Convergent and discriminant validation by the multitrait-multimethod matrix. Psychological Bulletin, 1959, 56, 81-105.

Cattell,R.B. and Warburton,F.W. Objective Personality and Motivation Tests: A Theoretical Introduction and Practical Compendium. Chicago: University of Illinois Press, 1967.

Charny,I. Individual and Family Development Review. Los Angeles: Western Psychological Services, 1969.

Chun,K.T. Cobb,S. and French,J.R.P.Jr. Measures for Psychological Assessment: A Guide to 3,000 Original Sources and Their Applications. Ann Arbor: University of Michigan, 1975.

Comrey,A.L. Backer,T.E. and Glaser,E.M. A Sourcebook for Mental Health Measures. Los Angeles: Human Interaction Research Institute, 1973.

Cromwell,R.E.   Olson,D.H.L.   and   Fournier,D.G. Diagnosis and evaluation in marital and family counseling. Chapter 22 in Olson,D.H.L. (Ed.) Treating Relationships. Lake Mills, Iowa: Graphic Publications, 1976.

Edwards,A.L. The Social Desirability Variable in Personality Assessment and Research. New York: Dryden, 1957.

Goldman,B.A.   and   Saunders,J.L.   Directory   of Unpublished Experimental Mental Measures: Volume 1. New York: Behavioral Publications, 1974.

Hersen,M. and Bellack,A. Eds. Behavioral Assessment: A Practical Handbook. New York: Pergamon Press, 1976.

Hoffman,L.W. and Lippitt,R. The measurement of family life variables. In Mussen,P.H. (Ed.) Handbook of Research Methods in Child Develoment. New York: Wiley, 1960, 945-1014.

Jchnson,O.G.   Tests   and   Measurements   in   Child Development: Handbook II. San Francisco: Jossey-Bass, 1976.

Jchnson,O.G.   and   Bommarito,J.W.   Tests   and Measurements in Child Development: A Handbook. San Francisco: Jossey-Bass, 1971.

Lake,D.G. Miles,M.B. and Earle,R.B.Jr. Measuring Human Behavior: Tools for the Assessment of Social Functioning. New York: Teachers College Press, 1973.

Miller,D.C. Handbook of Research Design and Social Measurement. New York: David McKay, 1970.

Rabin,A.I.   and   Haworth,M.R.   eds.   Projective Techniques With Children. New York: Grune and Stratton, 1960.

Robinson,J. Rusk,J.G. and Head,K.B. Measures of Occupational Attitudes. Ann Arbor: Institute for Social Research. University of Michigan, 1968a.

Robinson,J. Rusk,J.G. and Head,K.B. Measures of Political Attitudes. Ann Arbor: Institute for Social Research. University of Michigan, 1968b.

Robinson,J. Rusk,J.G. and Head,K.B. Measures of Social Psychological Attitudes. Ann Arbor: Institute for Social Research. University of Michigan, 1968c.

Shaw,M.E. and Wright,J.M. Scales for the Measurement of Attitudes. New York: McGraw-Hill, 1967.

Shryock,H.S.   and   Siegel,J.S.   The   Methods   and Materials of Demcgraphy, Condensed Edition.   Edited by Edward G. Stockwell. New York: Academic Press, 1976.

Spiegelman,M. Introduction to Demography.   Chicago, Ill.: Society of Actuaries, 1955.

Straus,M.A. Measuring families.   In Christensen,H.T. (Ed.) Handbook of Marriage and the Family. Chicago: Rand, 1964a, 335-400.

    Straus,M.A. Power and support structure of the family
in relation to socialization. Journal of Marriage and the
Family, 1964b, 26, 318-326.

    Thomas,D.L.   Gecas,V.   Weigert,A.   and   Rooney,E.
Family Socialization and the Adolescent. Lexington, Mass:
D.C. Heath-Lexington Books, 1974.

    Walker,D.K. Socioemotional Measures for Preschool and
Kindergarten Children. San Francisco: Jossey-Bass, 1973.

    Yarrow,M.R.   Campbell,J.D.   and Burton,R.V.   Child
Rearing: An Inquiry into Research Methods. San Francisco:
Jossey-Bass, 1968.

Chapter II

Husband-Wife Relationship Measures

A. Conflict and Integration

1. Adjustment, Agreement, Integration, Satisfaction, Solidarity (See also subject index)

ARNOTT,C.C. Homemaking Comparison Level of Alternatives

VARIABLE MEASURED. Extent of satisfaction (profit) in the fulltime homemaker role as compared with profit (experienced or anticipated) in an alternative role.
TEST DESCRIPTION. The index consists of 14 items, each consisting of three questions. The items refer to such factors as: satisfying use of time, relationship with husband and children, companionship, financial rewards, preparation for the future, and achievement. Question A in each item set measures the respondent's profit in the fulltime homemaker role, Item B measures the profit in the dual role (e.g. homemaker and volunteer worker, homemaker and student, or homemaker and employee). Item C measures the importance of saliency of the role. The score for each item is obtained as follows: (Item A Score - Item B Score) X (Item C Score). The sum of the scores on each item set produces the Index. A plus score indicates greater profit in a dual role.
SAMPLE ITEM. A. How costly or rewarding is your fulltime homemaker (or dual) role in terms of your relationship with your husband? Very costly = -3 to Very rewarding = 3.   B.

How costly or rewarding would a dual (or fulltime homemaker)
role be in terms of your relationship with your husband?
Very costly = -3 to Very rewarding = 3. C. How important
is your relationship with your husband? Extremely = 4 to
Not at all = 0.
LENGTH. Time: One hour total for CLALT index and CL index
(Arnott, 1972). Items: 14
AVAILABILITY. In Arnott, 1972.
REFERENCES.
    Arnott,C.C. Married women and the pursuit of profit:
an exchange theory perspective. Journal of Marriage and the
Family, 1972, 34, 122-131.
    Arnott,C.C. and Bengston,V.L. Only a homemaker:
distributive justice and role choice among married women.
Sociology and Social Research, 1970, 54, 495-507.

ARNOTT,C.C. Marital Role Comparison Level Index

VARIABLE MEASURED. The extent to which the female marital
role has fulfilled the wife's expectations with reference to
such salient factors as housekeeping, children, husband, and
friends.
TEST DESCRIPTION. The index consists of nine items, each
consisting of three questions. Each item set refers to a
particular role, for example "understanding expected from
husband." Item A in each set measures the respondent's
expectations concerning the role. Item B measures the
actual role performance. Item C measures the importance or
saliency of the role. Each item is scored as follows:
(Item A Score - Item B Score) X (Item C Score). The results
for each of the item sets are summed to produce the Index.
SAMPLE ITEM. A. Before you married, how much understanding
did you expect from your husband? Very much = 4 to None =
0. B. How much understanding have you received from your
husband? Very much = 4 to None = 0. C. How important is
your husband's understanding to you? Extremely = 4 to Not
at all = 0.
LENGTH. Time: One hour total for this index and the
Homemaker Comparison Level of Alternatives Index (CLALT)
(Arnott, 1972) Items: 9.
AVAILABILITY. In Arnott, 1972.
REFERENCE.
    Arnott,C.C. Married women and the pursuit of profit:
an exchange theory perspective. Journal of Marriage and the
Family, 1972, 34, 122-131.

AZRIN,N.H. NASTER,B.J. JONES,R. Marital Happiness Scale

VARIABLES MEASURED. Current happiness in each of the
following areas of married life: household
responsibilities, child-rearing, social activities, money,
communication, sex, academic or occupational progress,
personal independence, spouse independence, and general

happiness.
TEST DESCRIPTION. Spouses rate their current happiness with
each area of their marriage along a ten point continuum
ranging from 1 (completely unhappy) to 10 (completely
happy). The items may be combined for an overall marital
happiness score.
SAMPLE ITEM. Household responsibility: Completely Unhappy
1 2 3 4 5 6 7 8 9 10 Completely Happy.
LENGTH. Items: 10.
AVAILABILITY. From NAPS-2
ABSTRACTED BY: Bruce Brown
REFERENCE.
        Azrin,N.H.   Naster,B.J.   and Jones,R.   Reciprocity
counseling: a rapid learning-based procedure for marital
counseling. Behavior Research and Therapy, 1973, 11,
365-382.

BALSWICK,J. Spouse Participation Support Scale

VARIABLES MEASURED. Spouse participation support.
TEST DESCRIPTION. The Spouse Participation Support Scale is
a Likert-type scale based upon the following three items:
        (1) How often do you attend events like fairs, movies,
athletics, games, church, etc. with your spouse? Every
week; several times a month; several times a year; never;
does not apply.
        (2) How often do you engage in relaxing activities such
as playing cards, watching television, going to a tavern,
bowling, etc. with your spouse: Very often, often, not
very often, never; does not apply.
        (3) How many meals do you usually eat together with
your spouse: Almost all; about one a day; several times a
month; several times a year; never; does not apply.
SAMPLE ITEM. See above.
LENGTH. Time: 1 minute. Items: 3.
AVAILABILITY. In Balswick, 1970 and above.
ABSTRACTED BY: Jack Balswick
REFERENCE.
        Balswick,J. The effect of spouse companionship support
on employment success. Journal of Marriage and the Family
(May) 1970, 212-215.

BARRETT-LENNARD,G.T. Barrett-Lennard Relationship Inventory

VARIABLE MEASURED. Emotional satisfaction with the marital
relationship.
TEST DESCRIPTION. Self-administered questionnaire where
subjects are asked to indicate the degree to which they feel
that the statement is true of their spouse. Ratings are
done on a six-point scale (-3, -2, -1, +1, +2, +3). Items
are combined into five subscales: Level of regard, Empathy,
Congruence, Unconditionality of regard, and Willingness to
be known. In scoring, the signs of some items are reversed,

so that a low score is always indicative of disturbances.
SAMPLE ITEM. My husband respects me. My wife pretends to
understand me or like me more than she really does.
LENGTH. Items: 92.
AVAILABILITY. In Barrett-Lennard, 1962;   modified version
by Quick and Jacob, 1973, from NAPS-2.
ABSTRACTED BY. Thomas G. Sparhawk
REFERENCES.
     Barrett-Lennard,G.T. Dimensions of therapist response
as causal factors in therapeutic change. Psychological
Monographs, 1962, 76.
     Quick,E. and Jacob,T. Marital disturbance in relation
to role theory and relationship theory. Journal of Abnormal
Psychology, 1973, 82, 309-316.

BERNARD,J.   Success in Marriage Instrument

VARIABLE MEASURED. Success in marriage.
TEST DESCRIPTION. Success in marriage is defined as "A
marriage which builds and stabilizes and integrates the
personalities of its members--the degree of satisfaction
which each spouse feels in the other is taken as an index of
the satisfaction his or her personality is receiving from
the marriage." The test consists of an alphabetical list of
qualitative terms. Subjects check all terms that apply to
their spouse, double check the very characteristic, and
triple check the most characteristic. On a second copy of
the test the subject checks, double checks, and triple
checks traits considered necessary, very necessary, and
extremely necessary for success in marriage. On a third
copy the same is done for traits considered harmful to
success in marriage. Two scores can be obtained: (1) The
inclusive method: The sum of the percentages of traits
marked as desirable but not checked as characteristic of the
spouse, plus the percentage of traits marked as unfavorable
and checked as characteristic of the spouse. This is
subtracted from the percentage of desirable traits that were
attributed to the spouse plus the percentage of unfavorable
traits marked not present.   Then 100 is added to .this
number, and the result is divided by 2 to get the score.
Scores range from 0 to 100; (2) The exclusive method: the
percentage of favorable traits marked present is obtained;
the result is reduced to a scale of 0-100 by the method
described above.
SAMPLE ITEMS. Abusive, affectionate.
LENGTH. Items: 100.
AVAILABILITY. Bernard (personal communication) writes:
"the precise list of traits used in the instrument was not
crucial; any list would do--the more, within limits, the
better;   half positive, half negative, or a third positive,
a third negative, a third neutral."
REFERENCES.
     Bernard,J. The distribution of success in marriage.
American Journal of Sociology, 1933, 39, 194-203.

Bernard,J. An instrument for measurement of success in marriage. Publications of the American Sociological Society, 1933, 17, 94-106.

Bernard,J. Factors in the distribution of success in marriage. American Journal of Sociology, 1934, 40, 49-60.

BLOOD,R.O.Jr. and WOLFE,D.M. Marital Satisfaction Index

VARIABLE MEASURED. Marital satisfaction of the wife.
TEST DESCRIPTION. The original version uses four questions, one each dealing with the areas of standard of living, spousal understanding, love and affection, and companionship. For each of these questions the subject may reply with one of five weighted responses ranging from disappointed to enthusiastic. The index is the sum of the responses.
SAMPLE ITEM. How do you feel about your standard of living? Responses--(weight given each response is in parentheses) (1) Pretty disappointed--I'm really missing out on that; (2) It would be nice to have more; (3) It's all right, I guess--I can't complain; (4) Quite satisfied I'm lucky the way it is; (5) Enthusiastic--it couldn't be better.
LENGTH. Items: U.S., Greek and French studies = 4; Yugoslavian study = 7.
AVAILABILITY. In Blood and Wolfe, 1960, and from NAPS-2.
REFERENCES.
   Blood,R.O.Jr. and Wolfe,D.M. Husbands and Wives: The Dynamics of Married Living. New York: Free Press of Glencoe, 1960.
   Blood,R.O.Jr. and Wolfe,D.M. Negro-white differences in blue-collar marriages in a northern metropolis. Social Forces, 1969, 48, 59-64.
   Buric,O. and Zecevic,A. Family authority, marital satisfaction, and the social network in Yugoslavia. Journal of Marriage and the Family, 1967, 29, 325-336.
   Michel,A. Comparative data concerning the interaction in French and American families. Journal of Marriage and the Family, 1967, 29, 337-344.
   Rollins,B.C. and Cannon,K.L. Marital satisfaction over the family life cycle: a reevaluation. Journal of Marriage and the Family, 1974, 36, 271-282.
   Safilios-Rothschild,C. A comparison of power structure and marital satisfaction in urban Greek and French families. Journal of Marriage and the Family, 1967, 29, 345-352.

BOWERMAN,C.E. Bowerman Marital Adjustment Scales

VARIABLES MEASURED. Adjustment in marriage: (1) family expenditures, (2) recreation, (3) relations with in-laws, (4) relations with friends, (5) religious beliefs and practices, (6) sexual relations, (7) homemaking duties and responsibilities, (8) philosophy of life, (9) child-rearing, and (10) general evaluation of marriage.

TEST DESCRIPTION.   Each specific area of adjustment is
measured by 6 parallel questions (one each for husband-wife
similarity   in   attitude,   disagreement,   intensity   of
disagreement, tolerance of disagreement, satisfaction with
this aspect of the relationship, and satisfaction with the
dominance pattern).   General evaluation of marriage scale
has 13 items. Scales form 3 groups: family activities and
values variables (1, 7, 8, 9); personal-centered
(2, 6); external relations of the family (3, 4).
SAMPLE ITEM. How much difference is there between you and
your husband (wife) in your attitudes about how your money
should be spent?
LENGTH. Items: 67.
AVAILABILITY. From NAPS.
REFERENCES.
     Bowerman,C.E. Adjustment in marriage: Overall and in
specific areas.   Sociology and Social Research, 1957, 41,
257-263.
     Burr,W.R. An expansion and test of a role theory of
marital satisfaction.   Journal of Marriage and the Family,
1971, 33, 368-372.

BURGESS,E.W.   COTTRELL,L.S.   and   WALLIN,P.
Burgess-Cottrell-Wallin Marital Adjustment Scale

VARIABLE MEASURED. Marital adjustment or success.
TEST DESCRIPTION. Multiple-choice questions in 3 groups:
(1) self-ratings of satisfaction with various aspects of
marriage, including affection, confiding,   methods   of
settling   disagreement, loneliness, and so forth;   (2)
frequency of disagreement over family life matters;   (3)
checklist of sources of unhappiness in the marriage. Score,
based on either husband's or wife's responses, is derived by
adding weights for test items.
SAMPLE ITEM. State approximate extent of agreement or
disagreement on the following items: Handling family
finances: (+2) always agree, (+1) almost always agree, (0)
occasionally disagree, (-1) frequently disagree, (-2) almost
always disagree, (-3) always disagree. A modification of
the test was used by Hill (1949) in a study of the impact of
wartime separation on the family.
LENGTH. Items: 130.
AVAILABILITY. In Burgess and Cottrell, 1939; Burgess and
Wallin, 1953; and from Family Life Publications, Inc., Box
6725 College Station, Durham, N.C.   27708
REFERENCES.
     Burgess,E.W. and Cottrell,L.S. Predicting Success or
Failure in Marriage.   New York: Prentice- Hall, 1939,
58-74.
     Burgess,E.W. and Wallin,P. Engagement and Marriage.
New York: Lippincott, 1953.
     Buros,O.K. (ed.) Personality Tests and Reviews.
Highland Park, N.J.: Gryphon Press, 1970.
     Clark,A.L.   and   Wallin,P.   Women's   sexual

responsiveness and duration and quality of their marriages. American Journal of Sociology, 1965, 1, 187-196.

Crouse,B. Karlins,M. and Schroder,H.M. Conceptual complexity and marital happiness. Journal of Marriage and the Family, 1968, 30, 643-646.

Edmonds,V.H. Marital conventionalization: definition and measurement. Journal of Marriage and the Family, 1967, 29, 681-688.

Hill,R.L. Families under Stress: Adjustment to the Crises of War Separation and Reunion. New York: Harper, 1949.

King,C.E. The Burgess-Cottrell method of measuring marital adjustment applied to a nonwhite southern urban population. Marriage and Family Living, 1952, 14, 280-285.

Lewis,R.A. Social reaction and the formation of dyads: an interactionist approach to mate selection. Sociometry, 1973, 36, 409-418.

Mathews,V.D. and Mihanovich,C.S. New orientations on marital maladjustment. Marriage and Family Living, 1963, 25, 300-304.

McHugh,G. Counselor's Guide to Administration, Scoring and Interpretation of Scores for Use with a Marriage Prediction Schedule and a Marital Adjustment Form. Durham, N.C.: Family Life Publications, n.d.

Pickford,J.H. Signori,E.I. and Rempel,H. Similar or related personality traits as a factor in marital happiness. Journal of Marriage and the Family, 1966, 28, 190-192.

Price-Bonham,S. Student husbands versus student couples. Journal of Marriage and the Family, 1973, 35, 33-37.

Smythe,L.C.S. The success of Chinese families as families. Marriage and Family Living, 1952, 14, 286-294.

Terman,L.M. and Wallin,P. The validity of marriage prediction and adjustment tests. American Sociological Review, 1949, 14, 497-504.

BURR,W.R. Marital Satisfaction Indexes

VARIABLE MEASURED. Six aspects of marital satisfaction: handling of finances, the couple's social activities, the way the spouse performs his or her household tasks, companionship, sexual interaction, and relationships with the children.
TEST DESCRIPTION. A separate index for each of the above six aspects of marital satisfaction is formed by summing the scores on the applicable items. An overall index is not developed by the author, but such an index is possible. Each index consists of 3 items with a range of responses indicating degree of satisfaction. A high score indicates high satisfaction.
SAMPLE ITEM. (Handling of finances) How often do I get mad or angry at something in regard to the way money is handled in our family? Very frequently, Frequently, Occasionally, Seldom, Very seldom, Never.

LENGTH. Items: 18.
AVAILABILITY. From NAPS-2.
REFERENCE.
    Burr,W.R. Satisfaction with various aspects of marriage over the life cycle: a random middle-class sample. Journal of Marriage and the Family, 1970, 32, 1, 29-37.

CARLAN,R.W.   REYNOLDS,R.   GREEN,L.W.   and   KHAN,N.I.
Interspousal Agreement Index

VARIABLES MEASURED. Extent to which husband and wife agree on eight family-related areas.
TEST DESCRIPTION. Identical questionnaires are given separately to husbands and wives. Eight items are used to index interspouse agreement. These eight items deal with decision-making, financial condition, religious views, attitudes toward moving, and qualities sought in selecting a son's wife. Interspousal agreement scores are given for a couple on each of the eight items, scoring 2 for strongly agree, 1 for mildly agree, and 0 for disagree.
SAMPLE ITEM. Who is the general decision-maker in the home?
LENGTH. Items: 8
AVAILABILITY. In Carlan, et al., 1971.
ABSTRACTED BY: Bruce Brown
REFERENCE.
    Carlan,R.W.   Reynolds,R.   Green,L.W.   and   Khan,N.I.
Underlying sources of agreement and communication between husbands and wives in Dacca, East Pakistan. Journal of Marriage and the Family, 1971, 33, 571-583.

CORSINI,R.J. Similarity of Self-Perception Index

VARIABLE MEASURED. Similarity in self-perception of husband and wife.
TEST DESCRIPTION. 50 adjective items are Q-sorted by husband and by wife (10 piles). The sort of the husband is correlated with that of the wife. The resulting coefficient is taken as the Similarity of Self-Perception Index.
SAMPLE ITEM. NR
LENGTH. Items: 50.
AVAILABILITY. From Psychometric Affiliates, Box 1625, Chicago, Ill. 60690.
REFERENCE.
    Corsini,R.J. Multiple predictors of marital happiness. Marriage and Family Living, 1956, 18, 240-242.

DYER,E.D. Marital Agreement and Adjustment Measures

VARIABLES MEASURED. (1) Perception of agreement between husband and wife and (2) Marital adjustment.

TEST DESCRIPTION. There are 11 questions on wife's
perception of the agreement between her husband and herself,
and one each on success in solving family problems and
wife's marital happiness. These indices are combined into a
six-point marital adjustment measure ranging from excellent
to very poor.
     "The wife's perception of the agreement between her
husband and herself was sought on the handling of family
finances, matters of recreation, religious matters,
conventionality and etiquette, moral problems, philosophy of
life, the wife's working, child-rearing. The husband's
sharing household tasks, political issues, and ways of
dealing with each other's families. Five choices were given
ranging from 'Always agree' to 'Always disagree'."
SAMPLE ITEM. See above.
LENGTH. Items: 13.
AVAILABILITY. In Dyer, 1970.
ABSTRACTED BY: Thomas G. Sparhawk
REFERENCE.
     Dyer,E.D. Upward social mobility and nuclear family
integration as perceived by the wife in Swedish urban
families. Journal of Marriage and the Family, 1970, 32,
341-350.

ESHLEMAN,J.R. Marital Integration Mean

VARIABLE MEASURED. "Marital integration is the extent to
which the husband and wife get from one another the
attitudes, services and goods they learn to need and to
expect from marriage."
TEST DESCRIPTION. Each subject is asked what needs should
be filled by a marital partner and to what extent each of
these needs is being met in the marriage. Responses for
each need are rated for fulfillment, totaled and divided by
the number of needs mentioned.
SAMPLE ITEM. In your estimation, what are the most
important things that is, satisfactions or needs, that a
man expects from a wife (if wife, that a woman expects from
a husband). For each need the respondent is then asked:
Would you say that your marriage: entirely provides, very
much provides, somewhat provides, provides very little or
does not provide at all for......?
LENGTH. Time: average interview = 2 1/2 hours. Items:
10.
AVAILABILITY. In Eshleman, 1965.
REFERENCES.
     Eshleman,J.R. Mental health and marital integration in
young marriages. Journal of Marriage and the Family, 1965,
27, 255-262.
     Gurin,G. Veroff,J. and Feld,S. Americans View
Their Mental Health. New York: Basic Books, 1960.

FARBER,B. Marital Integration Index

VARIABLE MEASURED. Marital integration as measured by a combination of Role Tension Index and Value Consensus Index.
TEST DESCRIPTION. The index of marital integration is formed by adding scores on the Role Tension Index and the Value Consensus Index. The 2 are given equal weight. "In order to assign tentative weights, data on consensus and role tension for the first 200 cases to be interviewed in this study for which this index was developed were arranged in quartiles. The lowest quartile received a 0 weight, and the top quartile a weight of 3 for each of the two indices.... A case falling into the top quartile for both consensus and role-tension indices received a marital integration score of 6; a case in the lowest quartile for both indices received a score of 0."
SAMPLE ITEM. See Farber's Role Tension Index. and Value Consensus Index.
LENGTH. Items: 20 (10 each in two parts).
AVAILABILITY. Value Consensus Index is in Farber, 1957; Role Tension Index in Farber and Blackman, 1956.
REFERENCES.

Crain,A.J. Sussman,M.B. and Weil,W.B.Jr. Effects of a diabetic child on marital integration and related measures of family functioning. Journal of Health and Human Behavior, 1966, 7, 122-127.

Dryer,A.S. and Wells,M.B. Parental values, parental control, and creativity in young children. Journal of Marriage and the Family, 1966, 28, 83-88.

Farber,B. An index of marital integration. Sociometry, 1957, 20, 117-134.

Farber,B. and Blackman,L.S. Marital role tensions and number and sex of children. American Sociological Review, 1956, 21, 596-601.

Kerckhoff,A.C. and Bena,F.D. Role-related factors in person perception among engaged couples. Sociometry, 1967, 30, 176-186.

Levinger,G. Senn,D.J. and Jorgensen,B.W. Progress toward permanence in courtship: a test of the Kerckhoff-Davis hypotheses. Sociometry, 1970, 33, 427-443.

FINK,S.L. SKIPPER,J.K.Jr. and HALLENBECK,P.N. Marital Satisfaction Scale

VARIABLES MEASURED. Marital satisfaction, subdivided into seven "clusters" of items: companionship, social status, power, understanding, affection, esteem, and sex.
TEST DESCRIPTION. A 26-item interview schedule. Judges listen to a taperecorded protocol and rate each item on a seven-point scale, ranging from "very dissatisfied" to "very satisfied." Raters are instructed to follow the subject's subjective feelings about the issues to determine the rating, rather than their own feelings. Possible total marital satisfaction scores range from 52 to 364. The 26

items are grouped into the "clusters" referred to above and
weighted so that scores will be comparable.
SAMPLE ITEM. Companionship cluster: Are you satisfied with
the number of things you do and the amount of time you spend
with your husband?
LENGTH. Items: 26.
AVAILABILITY. From NAPS-2.
REFERENCES.
   Fink,S.L.   Skipper,J.K.Jr.   and   Hallenbeck,P.N.
Marital Satisfaction Scale. Journal of Marriage and the
Family, 1968, 30, 64-73.
   Hallenbeck,P.N. Skipper,J.K.Jr. and Fink,S.L.   Final
Report of VRA Project, RD-1584, Cleveland, Vocational
Guidance and Rehabilitation Services, July, 1966.

FINK,S.L.   SKIPPER,J.K.Jr.   and   HALLENBECK,P.N.
Satisfaction of Needs Scale

VARIABLE MEASURED.   Need satisfaction at five levels:
Physiological, safety, love and belongingness, esteem, and
self-actualization, from Maslow's (1954) hierarchy of needs.
TEST DESCRIPTION. A 25-item interview schedule, five items
for each need level. Judges listen to a tape recording of
the interview and rate each item on a seven-point scale,
ranging from "very dissatisfied" to "very satisfied." Raters
are instructed to follow the respondent's subjective
feelings about the issues to determine the rating. Scores
range from 50 to 350 for the total need satisfaction scale,
and from 10 to 70 for each of the five need levels. The
items are adapted for use with the disabled; items
pertaining to illness are omitted for husbands. Not all
items refer to husband-wife need satisfaction.
SAMPLE ITEM. Love and belongingness: Some married couples
get along by admiring each other and some get along by
criticizing each other and some just accept one another for
what they are. How is it in your family? Is it different
from how it was before your disability?   How do you feel
about this?
LENGTH. Items: 25.
AVAILABILITY. From NAPS-2.
REFERENCES.
   Fink,S.L.   Skipper,J.K.Jr.   and   Hallenbeck,P.N.
Physical disability and problems in marriage. Journal of
Marriage and the Family, 1968, 30, 64-73.
   Hallenbeck,P.N. Skipper,J.K.Jr. and Fink,S.L.   Final
Report of VRA Project, RD-1584, Cleveland, Vocational
Guidance and Rehabilitation Services, July, 1966.

HAMILTON,G.V. Marital Adjustment Test

VARIABLES MEASURED. Satisfaction or dissatisfaction with
marriage.

TEST DESCRIPTION. A series of open-ended questions with responses recorded verbatim. Comparison with an answer key indicating responses representing marital satisfaction is used for scoring. The number of such responses is summed to get the marital satisfaction score.
SAMPLE ITEM. What is there in your marriage that is especially unsatisfactory to you?
LENGTH. Items: 13.
AVAILABILITY. In Hamilton, 1929.
REFERENCE.
     Hamilton,G.V. A Research in Marriage. New York: Boni, 1929, 59-83; 532-542.

HAWKINS,J.L. Marital Companionship Scale

VARIABLES MEASURED. Marital companionship on an expressive level, as indicated by "mutual expression by the spouses of affective behavior, self-revelatory communication, and mutual participation in other informal non-task recreational activities."
TEST DESCRIPTION. A questionnaire which both spouses fill out together in the presence of a third party (interviewer). Spouses are instructed to discuss each question and then check the answer which they both agree on. Questions generally refer to behavior during the four weeks prior to the test date. The questionnaire is administered conjointly in order to minimize distortions by either spouse and to maximize recall.
SAMPLE ITEM. In the last four weeks, did you take a little time during the day or evening to affectionately caress and kiss each other? At least once a day, Several times a week, Once or twice a week, A few times in the last four weeks, Less often.
LENGTH. Items: 43.
AVAILABILITY. From NAPS-2.
ABSTRACTED BY: James L. Hawkins
REFERENCE.
     Hawkins,J.L. Associations between companionship, hostility and marital satisfaction. Journal of Marriage and the Family, 1968, 30, 647-650.

HAWKINS,J.L. and JOHNSEN,K.P. Current Marital Satisfaction Test

VARIABLE MEASURED. Current and recent marital satisfaction.
TEST DESCRIPTION. A four-item test referring to recent and present satisfaction. Each item has seven responses ranging from "completely dissatisfied" to "completely satisfied." The total scores range from 4 to 28, a high score indicating high satisfaction.
SAMPLE ITEM. Everything considered, how happy are you with your marriage as it is right now?

LENGTH. Items: 4.
AVAILABILITY. In Hawkins and Johnsen, 1969.
REFERENCES.

Hawkins,J.L.   and   Johnsen,K.P.   Perception   of
behavioral conformity, imputation of consensus, and marital
satisfaction. Journal of Marriage and the Family, 1969, 31,
507-511.

Ort,S.A.   A study   of   role   conflicts   as   related   to
happiness in marriage. Journal of Abnormal and Social
Psychology, 1950, 45, 691-699.

INSELBERG,R.M.   Marital Satisfaction Sentence Completions

VARIABLES MEASURED. Marital satisfaction; subject's fears,
wishes, and feelings.
TEST DESCRIPTION. "The Sentence Completion Blank included
13 sentence stems.   Subjects were asked to complete a
sentence, the first few words being furnished.   It was
assumed that the subject's fears, wishes and feelings,
reflected in his responses, were associated with his
satisfaction in married life." Ratings were 0-4, with 4
indicating the highest satisfaction and 2 indicating an
ambivalent or neutral response.
SAMPLE ITEM. "In-laws are. . ."
LENGTH. See test description.
AVAILABILITY. In Inselberg, 1961.
REFERENCES.

Inselberg,R.M.   Social   and   psychological   factors
associated with high school marriages.   Journal of Home
Economics, 1961, 53, 766-772.

Inselberg,R.M. The sentence completion technique in
the   measurement   of   marital satisfaction.   Journal of
Marriage and the Family, 1964, 26, 339-341.

Sheinbein,M.L.   Multiplicity of marital adjustment
ratings: a suggestion. Journal of Family Counseling, 1974,
2, 49-52.

Swensen,C.H.   A scale for measuring the behavior and
feelings of love. In Pfeiffer,K.W. and Jones,J.E.   (Eds.)
The 1973 Annual Handbook for Group Facilitators. Iowa City:
University Associates.

JANSEN,L.T.Jr.   Family Solidarity Scales

VARIABLES MEASURED. Family solidarity or integration, as
indicated by: (1) Husband-wife agreement, (2) Cooperation,
(3) Concern for others' welfare, (4) Enjoyment of
association with others, (5) Affection; (6) Esteem or
admiration: (7) Interest in each other; (8) Confidence or
trust.
TEST DESCRIPTION.   5 multiple-choice questions for each
dimension, each forming a Guttman scale when questions are
dichotomized. The 7 scales correlate .56-.74 with each
other, justifying "using a sum of the scores . . . as a

family solidarity score."
SAMPLE ITEM. Are the members of your family ashamed of each
other? never, very seldom, sometimes, quite often.
LENGTH. Items: 40.
AVAILABILITY. From NAPS.
REFERENCES.
    Browning,C.J.   Differential   impact   of   family
disorganization cn male adolescents. Social Problems, 1960,
8, 37-44.
    Jansen,L.T.Jr. Measuring family solidarity. American
Sociological Review, 1952, 17, 727-733.

KIRKPATRICK,C. Family Interests Scale

VARIABLES MEASURED.   Shared family interests, marital
adjustment.
TEST DESCRIPTION. A series of short phrases which the
subject answers by indicating whether he/she enjoys the
activity. The same items are repeated on the reverse side
of the form, but refer to activities enjoyed in the spouse's
company. By placing the form over a light, the number of
activities enjoyed alone and in company with the spouse can
be determined. Two scores are computed: (1) individual
family interests score (IFI)-- percentage of personal
interests checked on Part A which are also checked as family
interests on Part B; (2) relationship family interests
score (RFI)--percentage of all different personal interests
which are interests of both spouses.
SAMPLE ITEM. Exchanging visits with old friends.
LENGTH. Items: 6.
AVAILABILITY. In Kirkpatrick, 1937.
REFERENCES.
    Kirkpatrick,C.   Community of interest and the
measurement of marriage adjustment. The Family, 1937, 18,
133-137.
    Taves,M.J. A direct versus an indirect approach in
measuring marital adjustment. American Sociological Review,
1948, 13, 538-541.

LOCKE,H.J. Marital Adjustment Test

VARIABLE MEASURED. Marital adjustment.
TEST DESCRIPTION. Multiple-choice items including 19 items
from the Burgess-Cottrell Marriage Adjustment Form, 2 items
adapted from Terman, and 8 items formulated by Locke.
Scores are derived by adding the weights assigned to the
test answers. There are separate systems of weights for men
and women. Maximum score is 194. Karlsson (1951) used most
of Locke's items for an index of marital satisfaction he
gave to Swedish couples.
SAMPLE ITEM. Have you ever wished you had not married?
Frequently (2 men, 2 women), occasionally (2, 2), rarely (6,
5).

LENGTH. Items: 29.
AVAILABILITY. In Locke, 1951.
REFERENCES.

Buxbaum,J. Effects of nurturance of wives' appraisals of their marital satisfaction and the degree of their aphasia. Journal of Consulting Psychology, 1967, 31, 240-243.

Cone,J.D. Social desirability, marital satisfaction and concomitant perceptions of self and spouse. Psychological Reports, 1971, 28, 173-174.

Hawkins,J.L. The Locke Marital Adjustment Test and social desirability. Journal of Marriage and the Family, 1966, 22, 387-395.

Johnson,S.M. and Lobitz,G.K. The personal and marital adjustment of parents as related to observed child deviance and parenting behaviors. Journal of Abnormal Child Psychology, 1974, 2, 193-207.

Kahn,M. Non-verbal communication and marital satisfaction. Family Process, 1970, 9, 449-456.

Karlsson,G. Adaptability and Communications in Marriage: A Swedish Predictive Study of Marital Satisfaction. Uppsala: Almquist and Wiksells, 1951.

Kimmel,D. and Van-der-Veen,F. Factors of marital adjustment in Locke's Marital Adjustment Test. Journal of Marriage and the Family, 1974, 36, 57-63.

Locke,H.J. Predicting Adjustment in Marriage: A Comparison of a Divorced and a Happily Married Group. New York: Holt, 1951, 42-66.

Locke,H.J. Sabagh,G. and Thomes,M.M. Correlates of primary communication and empathy. Research Studies of the State College of Washington, 1956, 24, 116-124.

Luckey,E.B. Number of years married as related to personality perception and marital satisfaction. Journal of Marriage and the Family, 1966, 28, 44-48.

Murphy,D.C. and Mendelson,L.A. Use of observational method in the study of live marital communication. Journal of Marriage and the Family, 1973a, 35, 256-263.

Murphy,D.C. and Mendelson,L.A. Communication and adjustment in marriage: investigating the relationship. Family Process, 1973b, 12, 317-326.

Navran,L. Communication and adjustment in marriage. Family Process, 1967, 6, 173-184.

Paris,B.L. and Luckey,E.B. A longitudinal study in marital satisfaction. Sociology and Social Research, 1966, 50, 212-222.

Spanier,G.B. Romanticism and marital adjustment. Journal of Marriage and the Family, 1972, 34, 481-487.

Van-der-Veen,F. The parent's concept of the family unit and child adjustment. Journal of Counseling Psychology, 1965, 12, 196-200.

Whitehurst,R.N. Premarital reference-group orientations and marriage adjustment. Journal of Marriage and the Family, 1968, 30, 397-401.

LOCKE,H.J. and WALLACE,K.M. Short Marital Adjustment Test

VARIABLE MEASURED. Marital adjustment.
TEST DESCRIPTION. A questionnaire of 15 multiple-choice items from previous studies that had the highest level of discrimination. Weighted linear combination.
SAMPLE ITEM. Do you confide in your mate? Almost never, Rarely, In most things, In everything.
LENGTH. Items: 15.
AVAILABILITY. In Locke and Wallace, 1959.
REFERENCES.
    Buxbaum,J. Effect of nurturance on wives' appraisals of their marital satisfaction and the degree of their husbands' aphasia. Journal of Consulting Psychology, 1967, 31, 240-243.
    Cole,C.L. A symbolic interactionist perspective on marital adjustment. Social Science, 1974, 44, 234-237.
    Edmonds,V.H. Withers,G. and Dibatista,B. Adjustment, conservatism, and marital conventionalization. Journal of Marriage and the Family, 1972, 34, 96-103.
    Hawkins,J.L. The Locke marital adjustment test and social desirability. Journal of Marriage and the Family, 1966, 28, 193-195.
    Hooper,D. and Sheldon,A. Evaluating newly-married couples. British Journal of Social and Clinical Psychology, 1969, 8, 169-182.
    Hurley,J.R. and Palonen,D.P. Marital satisfaction and child density among university student parents. Journal of Marriage and the Family, 1967, 29, 483-484.
    Kotlar,S.L. Middle-class marital role perceptions and marital adjustment. Sociology and Social Research, 1965, 49, 283-293.
    Lewis,R.A. A longitudinal test of a developmental framework for premarital dyadic formation. Journal of Marriage and the Family, 1973, 35, 16-25.
    Locke,H.J. and Wallace,K.M. Short marital adjustment and prediction tests: their reliability and validity. Marriage and Family Living, 1959, 21, 251-255.
    Matteson,R. Adolescent self-esteem, family communication, and marital satisfaction. Journal of Psychology, 1974, 86, 35-47.
    Murstein,B.I. The complementary need hypothesis in newlyweds and middle-aged married couples. Journal of Abnormal and Social Psychology, 1961, 63, 194-197.
    Murstein,B.I. and Glaudin,V. The use of the MMPI in the determination of marital adjustment. Journal of Marriage and the Family, 1968, 30, 651-655.
    Rollins,B.C. and Cannon,K.L. Marital satisfaction over the family life cycle: a reevaluation. Journal of Marriage and the Family, 1974, 36, 271-282.
    Russell,C.S. Transition to parenthood: problems and gratifications. Journal of Marriage and the Family, 1974, 36, 294-302.
    Ryder,R.G. Longitudinal data relating marriage satisfaction and having a child. Journal of Marriage and

the Family, 1973, 35, 604-606.
    Spanier,G.B.   Whose marital adjustment?   A research
note. Sociological Inquiry, 1973, 43, 95-96.
    Speer,D.C. Variations of the prisoner's dilemma game
as measures of marital interaction: sequential dyadic
measures.   Journal of Abnormal Psychology, 1972, 80,
287-293.
    Sporakowski,M.J. Marital preparedness, prediction and
adjustment. The Family Coordinator, 1968, 17, 155-161.
    Taylor,A.B.   Role perception empathy and marriage
adjustment. Sociology and Social Research, 1967, 52, 22-34.
    Thomas,M.M.   Children with absent fathers. Journal of
Marriage and the Family, 1968, 30, 89-96.
    Wallace,K.M. Construction and validation of marital
adjustment and prediction scales.   Ph.D.   dissertation,
University of Southern California, 1947.

LOCKE,H.J. and WILLIAMSON,R.C. Marital Adjustment Scale

VARIABLES   MEASURED.   Component factors in marital
adjustment: (1) companionship or couple-sufficiency, (2)
agreement or consensus, (3) affectional intimacy or
emotional adjustment, (4) masculine interpretation or wife
accommodation, (5) euphoria or halo effect.
TEST DESCRIPTION. 20 multiple-choice items from Peterson
and Williamson's test, which was taken from Locke's test of
marital adjustment.   Factor scores can be obtained by
assigning each item to the factor with the highest loading
and summing the values for that factor.
SAMPLE ITEM. Check the place on the scale which best
describes the degree of happiness of your present marriage.
1 (very unhappy), 2, 3 (happy), 4, 5 (very happy).
LENGTH. Items: 20.
AVAILABILITY. In Locke and Williamson, 1958.
REFERENCES.
    Browning,C.J.   Differential   impact   of   family
disorganization cn male adolescents. Social Problems, 1960,
8, 37-44.
    Figley,C.R.   Child   density   and   the   marital
relationship. Jcurnal of Marriage and the Family, 1973, 35,
272-282.
    Johnson,S.M. and Lobitz,G.K. The personal and marital
adjustment of parents as related to observed child deviance
and parenting behaviors. Journal of Abnormal Child
Psychology, 1974, 2, 193-207.
    Kahn,M.   Non-verbal communication and marital
satisfaction. Family Process, 1970, 9, 449-456.
    Locke,H.J. and Williamson,R.C. Marital adjustment: a
factor analysis study. American Sociological Review, 1958,
23, 562-569.
    Luckey,E.B.   Marital satisfaction and personality
correlates of spouse. Journal of Marriage and Family
Living, 1964, 26, 217-220.
    Murphy,D.C.   and Mendelson,L.A.   Communication   and

adjustment in marriage: investigating the relationship. Family Process, 1973, 12, 317-325.

Peterson,J.A. The relation of objective and subjective factors to adjustment and maladjustment in marriage. Ph.D. dissertation, University of Southern California, 1951.

Spanier,G.B. Romanticism and marital adjustment. Journal of Marriage and the Family, 1972, 34, 481-487.

Speer,D.C. Marital dysfunctionality and two-person non-zero-sum game behavior; cumulative monadic measures. Journal of Personality and Social Psychology, 1972, 21, 18-24.

Sporakowski,M.J. Marital preparedness, prediction and adjustment. The Family Coordinator, 1968, 17, 155-161.

Williamson,R.C. Socioeconomic factors in marital adjustment in an urban setting. Ph.D. dissertation, University of Southern California, 1951.

Williamson,R.C. Socioeconomic factors and marital adjustment in an urban setting. American Sociological Review, 1954, 19, 213-216.

MANSON,M.P. and LERNER,A. Marriage Adjustment Inventory (MAI)

VARIABLES MEASURED. Self-evaluation and evaluation of spouse in terms of: (1) family relationships (liking for immediate and extended family), (2) dominance, (3) immaturity, (4) neurotic traits, (5) sociopathic traits, (6) money management, (7) children, (8) interests, (9) physical, (10) abilities, (11) sex, (12) incompatibility.
TEST DESCRIPTION. A booklet with 157 descriptive statements, all negative or undesirable, in which the subject circles the letters H or W or both to indicate if it is a problem of the husband, the wife, or both. The total number of traits marked is summed to obtain the score for each variable for husband, for wife, and for both. These 3 scores are then added for a Total Evaluation Score. A low score indicates few problems.
SAMPLE ITEM. Is unfair in many ways. (Scored under immaturity.)
LENGTH. Items: 157.
AVAILABILITY. From Western Psychological Services, Box 775, Beverly Hills, CA 90213.
REFERENCE.
Buros,O.K. (ed.) Personality Tests and Reviews. Highland Park, N.J.: Gryphon Press, 1970.
Manson,M.P. and Lerner,A. The Marriage Adjustment Inventory Manual. Beverly Hills, California: Western Psychological Services, 1962.

MANSON,M.P. and LERNER,A. Marriage Adjustment Sentence Completion Survey (MASCS)

VARIABLES MEASURED. (1) Needs--conscious and unconscious

needs to grow, develop, fulfill oneself; (2) Problems--both
recognized and unrecognized; (3) Maturity level--physical,
emotional, intellectual, cultural, spiritual, and economic;
(4) Goals--immediate and future in various areas; (5)
Values-- individual economic gain versus family group goals.
TEST DESCRIPTION. A total of 100 sentence-completion items.
There are separate forms for husband and wife, but the items
are the same except for pronouns and substitution of the
words husband and wife. Each item is rated on a 5-point
scale for each variable. Four profiles can be constructed:
husband's description of self and of wife; wife's
description of self and husband. Suggestions for
interpretating omitted items, cynical responses, and so
forth are given.
SAMPLE ITEM. (Needs:) I am very unhappy because. . .
LENGTH. Time: 20-40 minutes. Items: 100.
AVAILABILITY. From Western Psychological Services, Box 775,
Beverly Hills, CA 90213.
REFERENCE.
     Manson,M.P. and Lerner,A. The marriage adjustment
sentence completicn survey manual. Beverly Hills,
California: Western Psychological Services, 1962.

NYE,F.I. and MacDOUGALL,E. Nye-MacDougall Marital
Adjustment Scale

VARIABLE MEASURED. Marital adjustment.
TEST DESCRIPTION. A questionnaire of 9 items, 1 for each of
the following: happiness, satisfaction, quarreling
frequency, considering a divorce, living apart following a
quarrel, and argument--on house and furniture, recreation,
money, and children. Response categories from never to very
often are dichotcmized to form a Guttman scale.
SAMPLE ITEM. Have you ever lived apart from your husband
following a quarrel? Once or more often; never.
LENGTH. Items: 9.
AVAILABILITY. In Nye and MacDougall, 1959.
REFERENCES.
     Axelson,L.J. The marital adjustment and marital role
definitions of husbands of working and nonworking wives.
Marriage and Family Living, 1963, 25, 189-195.
     Buros,O.K. (ed.) Personality Tests and Reviews.
Highland Park, N.J.: Gryphon Press, 1970.
     Dean,D.G. Emotional maturity and marital adjustment.
Journal of Marriage and the Family, 1966, 28, 454-457.
     Dean,D.G. Alienation and marital adjustment.
Socological Quarterly, 1968, 9, 186-192.
     Nye,F.I. Employment status of mothers and marital
conflict, permanence, and happiness. Social Problems, 1958,
6, 260-267.
     Nye,F.I. and MacDougall,E. The dependent variable in
marital research. Pacific Sociological Review, 1959, 2,
67-70.
     Ridley,C.A. Exploring the impact of work satisfaction

and involvement on marital interaction when both partners are employed. Journal of Marriage and the Family, 1973, 35, 229-237.

Weller,L. Natan,O. and Hazi,O. Birth order and marital bliss in Israel. Journal of Marriage and the Family, 1974, 36, 794-797.

ORDEN,S.R. and BRADBURN,N.M. Marriage Adjustment Balance Scale

VARIABLES MEASURED. Marriage sociability, marriage companionship and marriage tensions.
TEST DESCRIPTION. The scale consists of an inventory of activities that husbands and wives might do together and of common topics about which they might argue. Respondents are asked to report which activities they have done together with their spouses during the past few weeks and which topics they have argued about. The items are scored into 3 separate subscales: sociability, companionship and tensions. An overall adjustment scale is constructed by summing the positive items and subtracting the sum of the negative items.
SAMPLE ITEM. I am going to read you some things about which husbands and wives sometimes agree and sometimes disagree. Would you tell me which ones caused differences of opinion or were problems in your marriage during the past few weeks: First, how about--. . .time spent with friends.
LENGTH. Time: 5 minutes. Items: 18.
AVAILABILITY. In Bradburn, 1969.
ABSTRACTED BY: N.M. Bradburn
REFERENCES.
Bortner,R.W. A cross-cultural study of the effects of children on parental assessment of past, present and future. Journal of Marriage and the Family, 1974, 36, 370-378.
Bradburn,N.M.   The Structure of Psychological Well-Being. Chicago: Aldine, 1969.
Corrales,R.G. Power and satisfaction in early marriage, 197-216. Cromwell,R.E. and Olson,D.H. (Eds.) Power in Families, New York: Wiley, 1975.
Lurie,E.E. Sex and stage differences in perceptions of marital and family relationships. Journal of Marriage and the Family, 1974, 36, 260-269.
Orden,S.R. and Bradburn,N.M. Dimensions of marital happiness. American Journal of Sociology, 1968, 73, 715-731.
Orden,S.R. and Bradburn,N.M. Working wives and marriage happiness. American Journal of Sociology, 1969, 74, 392-407.
Otto,L.B. and Featherman,D.L. A critique of the Marital Adjustment Balance Scale in the context of couple data. Center for Demography and Ecology, University of Wisconsin, mimeographed paper, 1972.

PETERMAN,D.J. RIDLEY,C.A. and ANDERSON,S.M.   Relationship
Quality Index

VARIABLES MEASURED. The   quality   of   a   heterosexual
relationship.
TEST DESCRIPTION. Responses to five rating scales used for
description of a respondent's most significant heterosexual
relationship are combined to form the Relationship Quality
Index.   This index consists of a sum of scores on the
closeness to ideal partner, openness of communication, need
satisfaction, sexual attractiveness, and sexual satisfaction
rating scales. Each rating scale is scored from 1 to 5.
Therefore, the Relationship Quality Index could range from 5
to 25, with a high score indicating a "high quality"
relationship.
SAMPLE ITEM. See above.
LENGTH. Items: 5.
AVAILABILITY. In Peterman, Ridley, and Anderson, 1974.
ABSTRACTED BY: Bruce Brown
REFERENCES.
     Peterman,D.J.   Ridley,C.A.   and   Anderson,S.M.   A
comparison of cohabitating and noncohabitating college
students. Journal of Marriage and the Family 1974, 36,
344-354.

POULSON,J. WARREN,R. and KENKEL,W.F. Goal Agreement Score

VARIABLES MEASURED.   (1) Family goals, (2) Extent   of
agreement   of spouses on family goals, (3) Change in
agreement of spouses on family goals.
TEST DESCRIPTION. Each husband and each wife select from a
list of 15 goals the 5 most important goals and rank them in
order of importance.   Each also answers an open-ended
question about their goals. Three methods of relating the
goal-choices of a husband-wife pair to one another to
produce goal agreement scores are available: (A) The number
of goals listed by the husband which are also listed by the
wife.   (B) The goals that appeared on the lists of husbands
and wives and the order of choice. (C) The lower of the
ranks indicated (by either husband or wife) is subtracted
from the higher. If the goal is selected by one spouse and
not the other, the rank of the goal assigned is subtracted
from six, on the basis that the goal was beyond the fifth in
importance in the hierarchy of the mate not mentioning it.
     To measure agreement between spouses elicited by the
open-ended item, a count is made of the number of goals that
appeared on both the list of the husband and the list of the
the wife. The number of agreed upon goals is divided by the
total number of goals listed by husband and wife.
SAMPLE ITEM. "Learn to be a better manager of money and
time."
LENGTH. Items: 15.

AVAILABILITY. In Poulson, Warner, Kenkel, 1966.
ABSTRACTED BY: William F. Kenkel
REFERENCES.
     Poulson,J.   Warren,R. and Kenkel,W.F. The measurement
of goal agreement between husbands and wives. Sociological
Quarterly, 1966, 7, 480-488.

RENNE,K.S.   Index of Marital Satisfaction

VARIABLE MEASURED. Marital satisfaction.
TEST DESCRIPTION. A series of pre-coded questions dealing
with   satisfaction   with   spouse's   "understanding"   and
"affection" and frequency of problems in "getting along with
spouse." Score depends on the number of answers to items
that indicate unhappiness or dissatisfaction.   Individuals
are   classified   as   "dissatisfied" if they gave one or more
negative (i.e., indicating dissatisfaction) responses to the
three   most   extreme   items   (e.g.,   seriously   considered
separation or divorce recently), or if they have negative
responses to two or more of the three less extreme items.
SAMPLE ITEM. Do you ever regret your marriage?   Often,
Sometimes, Never.
LENGTH. Time: 2 minutes. Items: 6.
AVAILABILITY. In Renne, 1970.
ABSTRACTED BY: Karen S. Renne
REFERENCES.
     Renne,K.S.   Correlates cf marital   dissatisfaction.
Journal of Marriage and the Family, 1970, 32, 54-67.
     Renne,K.S. Health and marital experience in an urban
population.   Journal of Marriage and the Family, 1971, 33,
338-350.
     Renne,K.S. Measurement of social health in a general
population survey. Social Science Research, 1974, 3, 25-44.

SAFILIOS-ROTHSCHILD,C. Marital Satisfaction of Couples with
Mentally Ill Partner

VARIABLES MEASURED. (1) Quality of the marital relationship
and (2) Spouse's satisfaction with the marital relationship.
TEST DESCRIPTION. "Normal" spouses are interviewed, and are
asked to rate their marriages as very happy, happy, fair, or
poor. These subjects are also asked to rate ten areas of
marital relations with their mentally ill spouses, for
degree of satisfaction. Items dealing with the presence or
absence of infidelity and presence or absence of separations
(regardless of divorce intentions) are rated 0 or 1 (0 =
presence, 1 = absence).   Other items are rated 0 if the
"normal" spouse is dissatisfied, 1 if he or she is fairly
satisfied, and 2 if he or she is satisfied or very
satisfied.
SAMPLE ITEM.   Degree of conflict between spouses:
Dissatisfied, Fairly satisfied, Satisfied, Very satisfied.

LENGTH. Items: 11.
AVAILABILITY. In Safilios-Rothschild, 1968.
ABSTRACTED BY: Blair Nelson
REFERENCE.
    Safilios-Rothschild,C. Deviance and mental illness in
the Greek family. Family Process, 1968, 7, 100-117.

SAFILIOS-ROTHSCHILD,C. Marital Satisfaction Index

VARIABLE MEASURED. Wife's marital satisfaction.
TEST DESCRIPTION. The wife's satisfaction from the marital
relationship, measured by summing the degree of satisfaction
expressed for: (1) Husband's understanding of his wife's
problems, (2) Tenderness shown by the husband toward his
wife, (3) Standard of living, (4) Wife's comparison of her
marriage with those of her friends and relatives, (5)
Husband's help in domestic chores, (6) Use of leisure time,
(7) Authority and esteem enjoyed by wife in the family, (8)
Intensity and content of marital communication.   Items are
scored: Very satisfied = 5, Satisfied = 4, I cannot
complain = 3, It could be better = 2, and I am disappointed
= 1.
SAMPLE ITEM. How satisfied are you with your standard of
living, that is, the available money for food, clothing,
rent and entertainment?
LENGTH. Items: Yugoslavian: 7;   Greek and French: 4.
(Item 1 is unique to the Greek and French studies. Items 2,
3, and 4 were used in all studies. Items 5 through 8 are
unique to the Yugoslavian study.)
AVAILABILITY. In Safilios-Rothschild, 1967.
REFERENCES.
    Michel,A. Comparative data concerning the interaction
in French and American families. Journal of Marriage and
the Family 1967, 29, 337-345.
    Neubeck,G. (ed.) Extramarital Relations.   Englewood
Cliffs, N.J.: Prentice-Hall, Inc., 1969.
    Safilios-Rothschild,C. A comparison of power structure
and marital satisfaction in urban Greek and French families.
Journal of Marriage and the Family, 1967, 29, 345-352.
    Safilios-Rothschild,C.   Sociopsychological   factors
affecting fertility in urban Greece: a preliminary report.
Journal of Marriage and the Family, 1969, 31, 595-606.
    Safilios-Rothschild,C. The influence of the wife's
degree of work commitment upon some aspects of family
organization and dynamics. Journal of Marriage and the
Family, 1970, 32, 681-691.
    Zecevic,A. Family authority, marital satisfaction, and
the social network in Yugoslavia. Journal of Marriage and
the Family, 1967, 29, 325-336.

SCHLEIN,S. GUERNEY,B.G.Jr.   and STOVER,L.   Interpersonal
Relationship Scale

VARIABLES MEASURED. Trust and intimacy in interpersonal
relationships.
TEST DESCRIPTION. The test seeks to measure the quality of
an interpersonal relationship as it exists at the time of
testing. Respondents are asked to rate each item on a
five-point Likert scale ranging from Strongly agree to
Strongly disagree. Items are arranged to avoid direction of
wording effects.   Scores range from 52 to 260; the higher
the score, the greater the level of trust and intimacy. The
test items were selected from an initial pool of 106 items.
There were presented to eight judges in the field of
interpersonal relationships who were asked to rate each item
as a measure of trust, intimacy or both.   Items were
eliminated when rejected by more than 25% as a valid measure
of these concepts.
SAMPLE ITEM. I share and discuss my problems with my
partner.
LENGTH. Items: 52.
AVAILABILITY. In B. Guerney, Jr. Relationship Enhancement
Skill Training Programs for Therapy, Prevention, and
Enrichment. San Francisco: Jossey-Bass, 1977.
ABSTRACTED BY: Carole Hatch
REFERENCES.
      Guerney,B.G.Jr.   Relationship   Enhancement   Skill
Training Programs for Therapy, Prevention, and Enrichment.
San Francisco: Jossey-Bass, 1977.
      Rappaport,A.F.   The   effects   of   an   intensive
relationship modification program.   Ph.D. dissertation,
Pennsylvania State University, 1971.
      Schlein,S. Training dating couples in empathic and
open communication: an experiment evaluation of a potential
preventative mental health program.   Unpublished Doctoral
Dissertation, Pennsylvania State University, 1971. As cited
in the chapters 3 and 8 in Olson,D.H.L.   (Ed.)   Treating
Relationships.   Lake Mills, Iowa: Graphic Publishing Co.,
1976.

SHEINBEIN,M.L. Marital Satisfaction Direct-Report

VARIABLE MEASURED. Subjective self-report of marital
satisfaction.
TEST DESCRIPTION. Spouses independently of each other rate
their marital satisfaction on a scale from 1 (Highly
dissatisfied) to 5 (Highly satisfied). They then write a
short paragraph which mentions the points of satisfaction
and the points of dissatisfaction in their marriage.   The
examiner or judge scores the protocol by reading the rating
and the paragraph and making his own rating of the same
scale.   The couple's score is the average of the three
ratings.

SAMPLE ITEM. How satisfied are you with your marriage on the following five-point scale, and why? Compare yourself with your married friends. (Highly dissatisfied) 1, 2 (Average) 3 (Highly satisfied) 4, 5.
LENGTH. Time: 1-2 minutes.
AVAILABILITY. From NAPS-2.
ABSTRACTED BY: Marc Sheinbein (modified)
REFERENCE.
     Sheinbein,M.L. Multiplicity of marital adjustment ratings: a suggestion. Journal of Family Counseling, 1974, 2, 49-52.

STINNETT,N. COLLINS,J. and MONTGOMERY,J.E. Marital Need Satisfaction Scale

VARIABLES MEASURED. The extent of satisfaction which older husbands and wives (60 years of age or over) express concerning the fulfillment of certain needs involved in the marriage relationship during the later years.
TEST DESCRIPTION. The Marital Need Satisfaction Scale is a Likert-type scale of 24 statements which represent six developmental needs basic in the marital relationship among older couples: (a) love, (b) personality fulfillment, (c) respect, (d) communication, (e) finding meaning in life, and (f) integration of past life experiences. The items and the need categories were developed from a review of literature and in part from a factor analysis. All items are characterized by five degrees of response ranging from very satisfactory to very unsatisfactory. A favorable response is given the highest score.
SAMPLE ITEM. Rate your spouse's performance in each of the following areas of your marital relationship: Being a good listener (a) Very satisfactory, (b) Satisfactory, (c) Undecided, (d) Unsatisfactory, (e) Very unsatisfactory.
LENGTH. Items: 24.
AVAILABILITY. In Stinnett, Collins, and Montgomery, 1970.
REFERENCE.
     Stinnett,N. Collins,J. and Montgomery,J.E. Marital need satisfaction of older husbands and wives. Journal of Marriage and the Family, 1970, 32, 428-434.

TERMAN,L.M. Marital Happiness Index

VARIABLE MEASURED. Marital happiness.
TEST DESCRIPTION. "The marital happiness score. . .is based upon information regarding communality of interests, average amount of agreement or disagreement between spouses in 10 different fields, customary methods of settling disagreements, regret of marriage, choice of spouse if life were to be lived over, contemplation of separation or divorce, subjective estimates of happiness, direct admission of unhappiness, and a complaint score based upon domestic grievances checked in a long list presented." The total

happiness score of a given subject is the sum of the weights corresponding to his/her individual responses. Items were selected and weighted on the basis of an internal consistency item analysis. Kelly (1939) found Terman's weights and questions to be valid for a population in New England (Terman's was from California).
SAMPLE ITEM. Do you or your wife engage in outside interests together? (7) all of them, (5) most of them, (3) some of them, (1) very few of them, (0) none of them.
LENGTH. Items: 19 (1 is the sum of 10 separate questions, 1 obtained by summing 53 questions).
AVAILABILITY. In Terman, et al., 1938.
REFERENCES.
        Hardyck,C.D. Chun,K.T. and Engel,B.T. Personality and marital adjustment differences in essential hypertension in women. Journal of Consulting Psychology, 1966, 30, 459.
        Kelly,E.L. Concerning the validity of Terman's weights for predicting marital happiness. Psychological Bulletin, 1939, 36, 202-203.
        Luckey,E.B. Marital satisfaction and parent concepts. Journal of Consulting Psychology, 1960, 24, 195-204.
        Luckey,E.B. Number of years married as related to personality perception and marital satisfaction. Journal of Marriage and the Family, 1966, 28, 44-48.
        Paris,B.L. and Luckey,E.B. A longitudinal study in marital satisfaction. Sociology and Social Research, 1966, 50, 212-222.
        Terman,L.M. assisted by Buttenwieser,P. Ferguson,L.W. Johnson,W.B. and Wilson,D.P. Psychological Factors in Marital Happiness. New York: McGraw-Hill, 1938.
        Terman,L.M. and Wallin,P. The validity of marriage prediction and marital adjustment tests. American Sociological Review, 1949, 14, 497-504.

WHITE,J.G. Marriage Scale

VARIABLE MEASURED. Agreement between husband and wife on numerous aspects of married life.
TEST DESCRIPTION. Couples seeking pre-marital or marital counseling respond to 21 statements which are concerned with the "essentials" of a happily married life. Items are rated on a continuum from 1 to 10 from both partners. The husband's and the wife's ratings of each item are compared to obtain the discrepancy score.
SAMPLE ITEM. How essential are <u>children</u> (own cr adopted) to a happy home?

Never   Seldom   Sometimes   Usually   Absolutely
Essential Essential Essential   Essential   Essential

--1------2------3----4----5----6----7----8----9----10--

LENGTH. Time: 10-15 minutes. Items: 21.
AVAILABILITY. From NAPS-2.
ABSTRACTED BY: Gwen Pearson
REFERENCE.
     White,J.G.   Marriage   Scale.   Jacksonville,   Ill.:
Psychologists and Educators, Inc., 1970.

2. Love (See also Subject Index)

BARDIS,P.D. Erotometer

VARIABLE MEASURED. Heterosexual love.
TEST DESCRIPTION. 50 items, selected from approximately 500
initial statements, dealing with aspects of heterosexual
love. Since the subject responds to each item by means of a
3-point scale (0, Absent; 1, Weak; 2, Strong), the entire
Likert-type scale gives scores whose theoretical range is 0
(Ideal-typical absence of love) to 100 (Strongest possible
love).
SAMPLE ITEM. Feeling as if we were one person.
LENGTH. Time: 12 minutes. Items: 50.
AVAILABILITY. In Bardis, 1971;   from Panos D.   Bardis,
University of Toledo, Toledo, Ohio; or from NAPS-2.
ABSTRACTED BY: Panos D. Bardis
REFERENCE.
     Bardis,P.D.   Erotometer: a   technique   for   the
measurement cf heterosexual love. International Review of
Sociology, 1971, 1, 71-77.

BAUM,M. Goals In Marriage Scale

VARIABLES MEASURED.   (1) Romantic love, defined as a
powerful attraction: unique, compelling, unpredictable.
(2) Companionate love, defined as sharing and reciprocity:
understanding, mutuality of life goals, giving of mutual
support and affection.
TEST DESCRIPTION. Three different tests of romantic or
companionate objectives: The first test utilizes 15 brief
marital goal statements to be rated from Extremely important
to Extremely unimportant (7-point scale). The second test
employs 15 Likert-type items (4-point scale) asking about
situations in which people should not marry, seeking to
establish the extent to which engaged persons sought common
ground in marriage. The third test offers 10 descriptions
of desirable marital partners to be ranked in order of
respondent's choice.
SAMPLE ITEM. (First Test). To find lasting love; to gain
affection and understanding.

LENGTH. Items: 40.
AVAILABILITY. Test Three reproduced in full in Baum, 1971;
full scale available on request or from NAPS-2.
ABSTRACTED BY: Martha Baum
REFERENCE.
        Baum,M. Love, marriage, and the division of labor.
Sociological Inquiry, 1971, 41, 107-116. Also reprinted in
Dreitzel,H.P. (Ed.) Family, Marriage and the Struggle of
the Sexes. New York: MacMillan,1972, 83-106.

DAVIS,K.E. and LIPETZ,M.E. (1) Feelings Questionnaire and
(2) Parental Interference Scale

VARIABLES MEASURED. Husband-wife: (1) Love, (2) Trust, (3)
Criticalness, and (4) Expression of concern about parental
interference.
TEST DESCRIPTION. (1) Feelings Questionnaire: Each subject
rates self and partner on a 6-point scale. The measures are
designed to assess feelings in as straightforward and
undisguised a manner as possible. (2) Parental Interference
Scale: assesses the extent to which spouses inform each
other about difficulties they perceive from the parents
interfering in the couple's relationship.
SAMPLE ITEM. (1) My spouse loves me. 1 = Not at all, 2 =
Slightly, 3 = Somewhat, 4 = Moderately, 5 = Very much, 6 =
Completely (or extremely, or always). (2) I tell my spouse
that his/her parents interfere in our family affairs. Same
response scale.
LENGTH. Items: Love scale = 4; Trust scale = 5;
Criticalness Scale = 5; Parental Interference Scale = 6.
AVAILABILITY. From NAPS-2.
ABSTRACTED BY: Richard Driscoll
REFERENCE.
        Driscoll,R. Davis,K.E. and Lipetz,M.E. Romantic
love: the Romeo and Juliet effect. Journal of Personality
and Social Psychology, 1972, 24, 1-10.

KNOX,D. Love Attitude Inventory

VARIABLE MEASURED. Romantic vs. conjugal love.
TEST DESCRIPTION. The Inventory consists of 29 items on a
Likert scale which view love as ranging on a continuum from
extreme romanticism (there is only one love; true love is
eternal) to extreme realism. The latter referred to as
conjugal love. Two hundred items were constructed on the
basis of a review of the literature on love in the fields of
sociology, psychology, family relationships, adolescent
behavior, and psychiatry. The items were submitted to 10
professionals in the field of marriage and family.
Eighty-five items were retained, based on 70 percent or
greater agreement per item when asked to classify them as
being "romantic" or "conjugal" in nature. An item analysis
yielded 29 items statistically significant at the .01 level.

Scoring of the instrument uses a five-point continuum. A value of one is given to responses which indicate the most romantic attitude, and a value of five is assigned to the most conjugal response.
SAMPLE ITEM. When you are really in love, you just aren't interested in anyone else. Strongly agree (definitely yes) = 1, Mildly agree (I believe so) = 2, Undecided (not sure) = 3, Mildly disagree (probably not) = 4, Strongly disagree (definitely not) = 5.
LENGTH. Time: 15 minutes. Items: 29.
AVAILABILITY. Family Life Publications, Inc., P.O.Box 427, Saluda, N.C. 28773.
ABSTRACTED BY: David Knox
REFERENCES.
    Knox,D. Conception of love at three developmental levels. The Family Coordinator, 1970, 19, 151-157.
    Knox,D. Conceptions of love of married college students. College Student Survey, 1970, 4, 28-30.
    Knox,D. Attitudes toward love of high school seniors. Adolescence, 1970, 5, 89-100.
    Knox,D. and Sporakowski,M.J. Attitudes of college students toward love. Journal of Marriage and the Family, 1968, 30, 638-642.

RUBIN,Z. Love Scale and Liking Scale

VARIABLES MEASURED. The respondent's degree of "love" and of "liking" for another person. Love is defined as an interpersonal attitude including components of attachment, caring, and intimacy. "Liking" emphasizes admiration and respect for the other person.
TEST DESCRIPTION. Each scale consists of 9 items (reduced from original 13-item forms) on which the respondent indicates his or her degree of agreement with a particular statement of his or her feelings toward the other person. The scales have been used mainly in research on male-female dating couples. The scales have also been used with married couple samples, but are probably less valuable for this purpose. In administering the scales, items from the two scales should be interspersed.
SAMPLE ITEM. (From Love Scale) If I could never be with _, I would feel miserable.

1	2	3	4	5	6	7	8	9
Not at all true			Moderately true				Completely true	

LENGTH. Items: 9 items per scale.
AVAILABILITY. In Rubin, 1970 and 1973, p.216 (see note on 9-item versions).
ABSTRACTED BY: Zick Rubin
REFERENCES.
    Rubin,Z. The social psychology of romantic love. Ph.D. dissertation. University of Michigan, 1969.

University Microfilms, Ann Arbor, Michigan, No. 70-4179.
       Rubin,Z. Measurement of romantic love. Journal of
Personality and Social Psychology, 1970, 16, 265-273.
       Rubin,Z. Liking and Loving: An Invitation to Social
Psychology. New York: Holt, Rinehart and Winston, 1973,
Chapter 10.

RUBIN,Z. Romantic Love Scale

VARIABLE MEASURED. Feeling of love toward a specified
individual (physical attraction, idealization, a
predisposition to help, the desire to share emotions and
experiences, feelings of exclusiveness and absorption, felt
affiliative and dependent needs, the holding of ambivalent
feelings, and the relative unimportance of universalistic
norms in the relationship).
TEST DESCRIPTION. Couples rate both their partner and a
close, same-sex friend. Responses can range from
"Definitely true; agree completely" (scored 9) to "Not at
all true; disagree completely" (scored 1). Scores are
summed.
SAMPLE ITEM. If _____ were feeling badly, my first duty
would be to cheer him (her) up.
LENGTH. Items: 13.
AVAILABILITY. In Rubin, 1970.
ABSTRACTED BY: Thomas G. Sparhawk
REFERENCE.
       Rubin,Z. Measurement of romantic love. Journal of
Personality and Social Psychology, 1970, 16, 265-273.

RYDER,R.G. Lovesickness Scale

VARIABLE MEASURED. "Lovesickness," i.e., the degree to
which a person reports wanting more attention or caring from
his/her spouse.
TEST DESCRIPTION. Test items inquire about the amount of
attention or concern shown one by the spouse. Items are
scored True, Partly true, or False, and the test score is
summed over all items. This is an experimental testing
procedure not designed for general use without further
statistical refinement. It is designed to quantify one
particular aspect of marriage, "satisfaction," namely the
popular report that one's spouse "does not pay enough
attention."
SAMPLE ITEM. I know my spouse loves me but I wish he/she
would show it more.
LENGTH. Items: 32.
AVAILABILITY. From NAPS-2.
ABSTRACTED BY: Robert Ryder
REFERENCE.
       Ryder,R.G. Longitudinal data relating marriage
satisfaction and having a child. Journal of Marriage and
the Family, 1973, 35, 604-606.

SHOSTROM,E. and KAVANAUGH,J. Abridged Love Attraction
Inventory.

VARIABLES MEASURED. Type and extent of relationship held
between individual and "significant other."
TEST DESCRIPTION. Self-administered questionnaire requiring
true or false answers to each item. Scores are provided for
seven types of relationships between two individuals: (1)
mother/son pair, (2) daddy/doll pair, (3) bitch/nice-guy
pair, (4) master/servant pair, (5) hawk pair, (6) dove pair,
and (7) rhythmic pair. The higher the score in each
category the more the relationship is like that category,
the lower the less.
SAMPLE ITEM. Male: When things get tough, I turn to her
for help. Female: When things get tough, he turns to me
for help.
LENGTH. Time: 20 minutes. Items: 112.
AVAILABILITY. In Shostrom and Kavanaugh, 1971.
ABSTRACTED BY: Thomas G. Sparhawk
REFERENCE.
    Shostrom,E. and Kavanaugh,J. Between Man and Woman.
Los Angeles: Nash Publishing, 1971.

3. Conflict, Discrepancy, Hostility, Problems, Tension (See
also Subject Index)

BEIER,E.G. and STERNBERG,D.P. Beier-Sternberg Marital
Discord Scale

VARIABLE MEASURED. Marital Discord: Defined as the
distance between husband and wife in their perceptions of
how much disagreement and resultant unhappiness exists in
their marriage.
TEST DESCRIPTION. Husbands and wives individually rate 10
important topics in marriage on two, seven-point scales.
The first scale asks each spouse to rate how much
disagreement there is on each of the topical items. The
second scale asks each spouse to rate how much unhappiness
occurs as a result of the disagreement on each of the
topical items. The two discord scores are the differences
between husband and wife on the disagreement scale and the
unhappiness scale.
SAMPLE ITEM. (Scale 1) Money: Agree 1 2 3 4 5 6 7 Disagree
(Scale 2) Results of Agreement or Disagreement: Happy 1 2 3
4 5 6 7 Unhappy.
LENGTH. Time: 15 minutes. Items: 10.
AVAILABILITY. In Beier and Sternberg, 1971 and from NAPS-2.
ABSTRACTED BY: David M. Young
REFERENCES.
    Beier,E.G. and Sternberg,D.P. Interaction patterns in
newlywed couples. Paper presented at the meeting of the

Rocky Mountain Psychological Association, Denver, Colorado, May, 1971.
    Sternberg,D.P. and Beier,E.G.   Changing patterns of conflict in marriage: a follow-up study of 51 newlywed couples. Paper presented at the meetings of the Western Psychological Association, Portland, Oregon, April, 1972.
    Young,D.M. Korner,K.M. Gill,J.D. and Beier,E.G. Relationship of game aggression to quality of marriage. Paper presented at the meeting of the Western Psychological Association, Sacramento, April, 1975.
    Young,D.M. Korner,K.M. Gill,J.D. and Beier,E.G. Aggression as communication in marital interaction. Journal of Communication, in press.

BRIM,O.G.JR. FAIRCHILD,R.W. and BORGATTA,E.F.   Family Problems Index

VARIABLES MEASURED. Twenty-five family problem areas grouped into five major and 10 minor factors. The five major factors as revealed by factor analysis are: (1) Child-rearing, (2) Husband-wife relations, (3) Style of life (SES), (4) Community involvement (5) Religion.
TEST DESCRIPTION.   A 25-item checklist questionnaire of problem areas in family life. Subjects check those items they see as a problem needing solution in the past year. Factor analysis revealed five major problems. Items are summed to indicate high problem families. This can also be done for specific factors.
SAMPLE ITEM. TV and radio listening habits.
LENGTH. Time: 2 hours (for interview and questionnaire). Items: 25.
AVAILABILITY. In Brim et al., 1961.
REFERENCES.
    Brim,O.G.Jr.   Fairchild,R.W.   and   Borgatta,E.F. Relations between family problems. Marriage and Family Living, 1961, 23, 219-226.
    Petersen,D.M. Husband-wife communication and family problems. Sociology and Social Research, 1969, 53, 375-384.

BURR,W.R. Marital Role Discrepancy Index

VARIABLE MEASURED. Marital role discrepancy: the amount of congruence between the role expectations someone has for his or her spouse and the behavior of the spouse. This is a continuous variable ranging from low discrepancy when expectations and behavior are congruent, to a high amount of "role discrepancy" when most behavior is different from expectations.
TEST DESCRIPTION. Subjects first complete a 65-item, multiple choice questionnaire describing how much it would "bother" or "please" them if their spouse were to act in a variety of ways. Subjects then complete a second 65-item questionnaire that deals with the same behaviors but asks

how the spouse behaves. The score is the number of areas where the behavior is different from the desires. The expectations questionnaire includes a scale to measure how "important" the discrepancies are, since behavior could bother or please in varying degrees.
SAMPLE ITEMS. (A) Item for Expectations:

It would please me...   It would bother me...

	Ex-treme-ly	Quite a bit	A little	None	A little	Quite a bit	Ex-treme-ly
1. If he were moody:	3	2	1	0	0	1	2	3

All of the time .   .   .   .
Most of the time .   .   .   .
Some of the time .   .   .   .
None of the time .   .   .   .

(B) Item for Behavior:

2. He is moody...
( ) very frequently
( ) frequently
( ) occasionally
( ) seldom
( ) very seldom
( ) never

LENGTH. Time: 60 minutes. Items: 65 twice.
AVAILABILITY. From NAPS-2.
ABSTRACTED BY: Wesley R. Burr
REFERENCES.
Burr,W.R. Marital satisfaction: a conceptual reformulation, theory and partial test of the theory. Ph.D. dissertation, University of Minnesota, 1967. Order No. 68-7284. Available on microfilm.
Burr,W.R. An expansion and test of a role theory of marital satisfaction. Journal of Marriage and the Family, 1971, 33, 368-372.

ELSENOUSSI,A. ElSenoussi Multiphasic Marital Inventory (SMMI)

VARIABLES MEASURED. (1) Predisposition to marital discord. (2) Existing marital discord. (3) "Factor Profiles" indicative of marital discord. These three variables use scores for the following nine factors: a. frustration and chronic projection, b. cumulative ego strain, c. adolescent "hangover" or immaturity, d. revolt against

femininity,   e.   flight   into   rejection,   f.   early
conditioning   against   marriage,   g.   "will o'-the-wisp", h.
sex dissatisfaction and projection.
TEST DESCRIPTION. The questionnaire consists of 360 brief
questions, each answered by a Yes or No response. The test
is divided into five chronological periods: (1) Early
childhood to 10 years, (2) Later childhood from 10 years to
15 years, (3) Adolescence and early adulthood from 16 years
to 21 years, (4) Time prior to the first marriage and, (5)
First marriage. The first four periods include questions
about "premarital experiences, impressions, attitudes" and
measure predisposition and marital discord. The fifth
period measures the marital relationship. Clusters of
questions in each of these periods are combined to obtain
scores on the nine factors listed above.
SAMPLE ITEM. Were your parents separated during your
childhood? Yes, No.
LENGTH. Time: 30-50 minutes. Items: 360.
AVAILABILITY. Western Psychological Services, Box 775,
Beverly Hills, California.
ABSTRACTED BY: E. Cobb
REFERENCES.
        Buros,O.K.   (Ed.) Personality Tests   and   Reviews.
Highland Park, N.J.: Gryphon Press, 1970.
        ElSenoussi,A.   The   ElSenoussi   Multiphasic   Marital
Inventory   Manual.   California: Western   Psychological
Services, 1973.

ERON,L.D.   WALDER,L.O.   and   LEFKOWITZ,M.M.   Parental
Disharmony Scale

VARIABLE MEASURED. "The extent of disharmony in the home as
measured by disagreement about various specific matters of
importance in a family."
TEST DESCRIPTION. In a structured interview, parents are
asked 13 questions concerned with family disharmony. Each
question has two to four response categories, coded 0 to 3.
A total disharmony score is obtained by summing item scores.
A high score reveals great disharmony.
SAMPLE ITEM. Do you and your spouse have serious
disagreements about raising NAME? 2 = Yes; 1 = Sometimes
or don't know; 0 = No.
LENGTH. Items: 13.
AVAILABILITY. In Eron, et al., 1971.
ABSTRACTED BY: Kersti Yllo
REFERENCE.
        Eron,L.D.   Walder,L.O.   Lefkowitz,M.M.   Learning of
Aggression in Children. Boston: Little, Brown and Co.
1971, 194, 201-202.

FARBER,B.   Role Tension Index

VARIABLES MEASURED. (1) Family Role Tension Index (sum of

role tension ratings by husband of self, husband of wife, wife of self, and wife of husband); (2) Perceived similarity in role tension.
TEST DESCRIPTION. Husband and wife rate themselves and each other on 10 personality traits indicative of role tension.
SAMPLE ITEM. Stubborn: (-2) Very much, (-1) Considerably, (0) Somewhat, (+1) A little, (+2) Hasn't the trait at all.
LENGTH. Items: 10.
AVAILABILITY. In Farber and Blackman, 1956.
REFERENCES.
        Burgess,E.W. and Wallin,P. Engagement and Marriage, New York: Lippincott, 1953.
        Dryer,A.S. and Wells,M.B. Parental values, parental control, and creativity in young children. Journal of Marriage and the Family, 1966, 28, 83-88.
        Farber,B. An index of marital integration. Sociometry, 1957, 20, 117-134.
        Farber,B. and Blackman,L.S. Marital role tensions and number and sex of children. American Sociological Review, 1956, 21, 596-601.
        Hill,R.L. Family Development in Three Generations. Cambridge, Mass: Schenkman Publishing Co., Inc., 1970.
        McKain,J.L. Relocation in the military: alienation and family problems. Journal of Marriage and the Family, 1973, 35, 205-209.
        Srole,L. Social integration and certain corollaries, American Sociological Review, 1956, 21, 709-716.
        Tallman,I. Working-class wives in suburbia: fulfillment or crisis? Journal of Marriage and the Family, 1969, 31, 65-72.

GOODRICH,D.W. and BOOMER,D.S. Color-Matching Technique

VARIABLES MEASURED. Conflict resolution behavior in terms of such dimensions as activity level, involvement in discussion, effectiveness of communication, perspective on the situation, capacity to reach agreement, dominance-submission, and maintenance of esteem.
TEST DESCRIPTION. The husband and wife are seated with an easel between them which prevents them from seeing each other, although both can see the E. Each subject has a numbered display cf small, colored paper cards, arranged in five vertical columns of six cards each. Each column contains cards of varying shades of a basic color. The task is ostensibly a test of the subject's ability to discriminate slight gradations of color. (Color blindness is irrelevant since the conflict items involve differences in shading only. The Isihara test of color blindness is, however, given before the test so that the subject's attention can be called to the fact that color blindness is irrelevant since all the colors are labeled.) The subjects are told to look at their cards and see which most closely matches the test card that the experimenter puts on the easel. After they have independently decided this, the

experimenter puts the sample card away. The couple then attempts to agree on which of the numbered cards is the best match. The motivation to agree is heightened by the instructions that the score consists of the number of cards agreed upon. The first few cards are legitimate. Then the experimenter puts up a card to which the husband's and wife's matching copies have different numbers (e.g., her card is numbered 12, his is 19). The modes of conflict resolution arising from these conflict cards are the foci of the experiment -- 10 of the 20 matches have these built-in contradictions. The entire proceeding is tape-recorded, and interaction scores are coded from the protocols. The dominance score is the number of times each person's color number is chosen as the correct answer.
SAMPLE ITEM. See Test Description.
LENGTH. Time: 10-20 minutes. Items: 20 matches.
AVAILABILITY. From NAPS.
REFERENCES.
         Goodrich,D.W. and Boomer,D.S. Experimental assessment of modes of conflict resolution. Family Process, 1963, 2, 15-24.
         Goodrich,D.W. Ryder,R.G. and Raush,H.L. Patterns of newlywed marriage. Journal of Marriage and the Family, 1968, 30, 383-389.
         Hooper,D. and Sheldon,A. Evaluating newly-married couples. British Journal of Social and Clinical Psychology, 1969, 8, 169-182.
         Ryder,R.G. Two replications of color matching factors. Family Process, 1966, 5, 43-48.
         Ryder,R.G. Husband-wife dyads versus married strangers. Family Process, 1968, 7, 233-238.
         Ryder,R.G. Dimensions of early marriage. Family Process, 1970, 9, 51-68.
         Ryder,R.G. and Goodrich,D.W. Married couples' responses to disagreement. Family Process, 1966, 5, 30-42.

HAWKINS,J.L. and JOHNSEN,K.P. Perceived Role Discrepancy (PRD) And Imputed Role Consensus (IRC) Scores.

VARIABLES MEASURED. (1) Perceived Role Discrepancy is the degree to which a subject sees the role performance in his marriage as deviating from his role expectations. (2) Imputed role consensus is the "degree to which the role expectations which a subject imputes to his/her spouse deviate from his/her own expectations." Content areas are expression of affection, expression of hostility, companionship, communication and sexual relations; items on the division of household tasks and decision-making power are not included.
TEST DESCRIPTION. The test is constructed similarly to the Marital Role Conflict Score (Ort,1950). A list of 48 items with responses which include a range of possible behavior is presented to the respondent. Subjects are asked first to indicate for each item the response they prefer, any other

acceptable responses, any responses about which they are ambivalent, and any objectionable responses. Second, respondents indicated what they think their spouse's most preferred response would be. Third, the items are reworded so that respondents are asked to indicate which response best describes actual behavior in the past four weeks. The PRD score is "the number of items where the perceived performance lies outside the range of acceptable behaviors," using only the 37 items which correlated .20 or higher with the PRD score. A high score indicates high discrepancy. The IRC score is the number of items where the expectations imputed to the spouses deviate from the respondents' expectations. The sum is then reversed so that a high score indicates high consensus.
SAMPLE ITEM. (Expectation): How often should the husband and wife take a little time during the day or evening to kiss and caress each other? More than once a day; Once a day; Several times a week; Once or twice a week; A few times a month; Less often. (Actual recent behavior): In the last four weeks, how often did the husband and wife actually take a little time...? Same responses.
LENGTH. Items: 37.
AVAILABILITY. From NAPS-2.
REFERENCES.
       Hawkins,J.L. and Johnsen,K.P. Perception of behavioral conformity, imputation of consensus, and marital satisfaction. Journal of Marriage and the Family, 1969, 31, 507-511.
       Ort,S.A. A study of role conflicts as related to happiness in marriage. Journal of Abnormal Social Psychology, 1950, 45, 691-699.

HOBART,C.W. Criticism Of Parents' Marriage Score

VARIABLE MEASURED. Evaluation of parents' marriage.
TEST DESCRIPTION. A checklist of items which subject's would want to see different in their marriage as compared with that of their parents. Score is number of items checked.
SAMPLE ITEM. I would want my married life to differ from that of my parents in the following ways: In my marriage I want: Father to participate more in family life with wife and children.
LENGTH. Items: 10.
AVAILABILITY. From NAPS.
REFERENCE.
       Hobart,C.W. Emancipation from parents and courtship in adolescents. Pacific Sociological Review, 1958, 1, 25-29.

HOBBS,D.F.Jr. Crisis Rating for First-Time Parents

VARIABLE MEASURED. Parental perceptions of the birth of the first child as a crisis.

TEST DESCRIPTION. A four-category scale used to rate
tape-recorded interview material concerning the degree of
difficulty parents have in adjusting to the birth of the
first child. The scale positions are defined as follows:

Degree of Difficulty	Code	Selected Responses from Interview Protocols
None	1	Baby has been no problem at all. No known trouble adjusting. No particular difficulties.
Slight	2	Had to cut down on some of our activities. It took a couple of days to get used to her. It was certainly necessary to adjust, but adjustment wasn't difficult.
Moderate	3	I was worried whether I could hear her at night, whether she would wake me up. I wasn't sure the baby was doing all right, whether she was getting enough to eat, whether sleeping normally, whether crying meant she was hurting or sick or something.
Severe	4	The baby hampers me and I haven't adjusted to that; if I'm in the middle of something I don't want to be interrupted to go and do something for the baby. The first few weeks were terrible. I was so tired, so weak, and getting up at night was so terrible. We had a difficult time. It was hard to get adjusted to all his crying. We had trouble with his formula and he had colic.

Interviewers listen to the tape recordings and assign the
subject parent to one of the four levels of adjustment
difficulty. Spouses are rated independently and the judges
are unaware of which subject they are rating. If the two
judges disagree on the rating, a third judge rates the
respondent.
SAMPLE ITEM. (Interview schedule) Starting with the time
you (your wife) came home from the hospital, would you
describe how the first day and night went?
LENGTH. Depends on length of the interview protocol.
AVAILABILITY. See above.
REFERENCE.
    Hobbs,D.F.Jr. Transition to parenthood: a replication
and an extension. Journal of Marriage and the Family, 1968,
30, 413-417.

HURVITZ,N. Marital Roles Inventory

VARIABLES MEASURED. (1) Role performance of husband and
wife;   (2)   Role expectations which husband has of wife and
wife has of husband;   (3)   Index of marital role strain
(IMS)--the degree to which the performance of the husband
(wife) differs from the expectations of the spouse;   (4)
Index of deviation of role performance (IDRP)--degree to
which the role performance of the husband (wife) differs
from the model role performance of all husbands (wives) of
the group; (5) Index of deviation of role expectations
(IDRE)--degree to which the role expectations of the husband
(wife) differ from the model role expectations of all
husbands (wives) of the group;   (6) Corrected index of
marital strain (C-IMS)--the index of marital strain
corrected for the deviations from the modes of the group.
TEST DESCRIPTION. Each spouse is given a list of 11 role
activities. Each is asked to rank his own role set in order
of importance in which he carries out these activities in
his family at present.   Then, each is asked to rank his
spouse's role set in the way that he would prefer his mate
to carry out functions. The various indexes are the sums of
the numerical differences between the rank orders that
spouses assign to particular role activities and that of the
other spouse or the model assignment of the total group of
husbands and wives.
SAMPLE ITEM. I do my (he does his) jobs around the house.
I am (he is) a ccmpanion to my (his) wife.
LENGTH. Time: 20 minutes. Items: 11 items, ranked twice.
AVAILABILITY. From Western Psychological Services, Box 775,
Beverly Hills, California 90213.

REFERENCES.
        Buros,O.K.   (Ed.) Personality Tests   and   Reviews.
Highland Park, N.J.: Gryphon Press, 1970.
        Hooper,D.   and Sheldon,A.   Evaluating newly-married
couples. British Journal of Social and Clinical Psychology,
1969, 8, 169-182.
        Hurvitz,N. The index of strain as a measure of marital
satisfaction.   Sociology   and   Social   Research, 1959, 44,
106-109.
        Hurvitz,N.   The marital roles inventory and the
measurement of marital adjustment.   Journal of Clinical
Psychology, 1960, 16, 377-380.
        Hurvitz,N.   The   measurement   of   marital   strain.
American Journal of Sociology, 1960, 65, 610-615.
        Hurvitz,N. The components of marital roles. Sociology
and Social Research, 1961, 45, 301-309.
        Hurvitz,N.   Marital Roles Inventory   Manual.   Beverly
Hills, California: Western Psychological Services, 1961.
        Hurvitz,N. The marital roles inventory as a counseling
instrument.   Journal of Marriage and the Family, 1965a, 27,
492-501.
        Hurvitz,N.   Marital roles strain as a sociological
variable. Family Life Coordinator, 1965b, 14, 39-42.

LOEVINGER,J. and SWEET,B. Family Problems Scale

VARIABLES MEASURED. Authoritarian family ideology, conventionality anxiety, orderliness, rejection of women's biological role, masochism.
TEST DESCRIPTION. A personality inventory consisting of forced choice questions (paired items of equal social desirability). The test measures the personality patterns of women in terms of their family role opinions. Items were culled from case histories, conversations, and so forth, and were constructed to sample systematically the day's activities from morning through night and the life cycle from infancy through grandparenthood. The variables are the content clusters derived with the use of factor analysis. Homogeneous keys of clusters of items were constructed by factor analysis.
SAMPLE ITEM. From authoritarian family ideology: 68a. No child should be permitted to strike his mother. 68b. A mother should not be harsh with a small child who strikes her.
LENGTH. Items: 86 pairs of questions.
AVAILABILITY. In Loevinger, 1962; later edition from NAPS.
REFERENCES.
     Ernhart,C.B. Changes in authoritarian family ideology with child-rearing experience. Psychological Reports, 1975, 37, 567-570.
     Ernhart,C.B. Jordan,T.E. and Spanier,S.D. Maternal Quick Test (QT) scores in child development research. Psychological Reports, 1971, 28, 669-670.
     Ernhart,C.B. and Loevinger,J. Authoritarian family ideology: a measure, its correlates, and its robustness. Multivariate Behavioral Research Monographs, 1969, 1, 3-82.
     Hurley,J.R. and Hohn,R.L. Shifts in child-rearing attitudes linked with parenthood and occupation. Developmental Psychology, 1971, 4, 324-328.
     Johns,B.L. Maternal childrearing attitudes: identification, measurement, and relation to parity and other variables. Ph.D. dissertation. Hofstra University, Hempstead, New York, 1975.
     Jordan,T.E. The influence of age and social class on authoritarian family ideology. Multivariate Behavioral Research, 1970, 5, 193-201.
     Loevinger,J. and Sweet,B. Construction of a test of mothers' attitudes. In J.C.Glidewell, (Ed.) Parental Attitudes and Child Behavior. Springfield, Ill.: Charles C Thomas, 1961. Pp.110-123.
     Loevinger,J. Measuring personality patterns of women. Genetic Psychology Monographs, 1962, 65, 53-136.

MATHEWS,V.D. and MIHANOVICH,C.S. Marital Problems Checklist

VARIABLES MEASURED. Marital problems: needs, decision-making or interaction, personality, social

relations, and sexual relations.
TEST DESCRIPTION. The above five variables are measured by
a checklist consisting of 400 problems: 40 problems for
each of 10 areas, half the problems refer to the self and
half to the spouse. The problem areas are: (1) Basic human
needs; (2) Financial; (3) Home life and children; (4)
Job; (5) Family and in-laws; (6) Religion; (7) Sex; (8)
Decision-making; (9) Personality; and (10) Social
activities. These 10 areas are subsumed under the five
variables, but the classification of areas by variable is
not explicated.
SAMPLE ITEMS. Needs: Often feel unloved. Decision-making:
Don't think alike on many things. Personality: Keep things
to myself. Social: Mate does not like to do same things.
Sexual: Mate thinks only of his (her) own pleasure.
LENGTH. Items: 400.
AVAILABILITY. The 50 items which best differentiate between
happy and unhappy couples are given in Mathews and
Mihanovich, 1963.
REFERENCE.
     Mathews,V.D. and Mihanovich,C.S. New orientations on
marital maladjustment. Marriage and Family Living, 1963,
25, 300-304.

MOST,E. Rating of Marital Satisfaction and Friction

VARIABLES MEASURED. Satisfaction with spouse and marital
interaction in respect to: (1) Personality, (2)
Companionship, (3) Sex relationship, (4)
Job/household/finances, (5) Family/children/in-laws, (6)
Activities/interests/friends. Norms in behavior or absolute
functioning are excluded; consideration is only of
perception or attitudes in the above areas.
TEST DESCRIPTION. A list of 42 items related to traits such
as affection, ambition, steadiness of work, cleanliness,
self-confidence, sense of humor, loyalty, desire for
children, frequency of sex, discipline of the children, and
so on; and a list of 22 areas of potential friction such as
sexual adjustment, husband's family finances, wife's
employment, and recreation. All the items are listed in
"jumbled order to prevent contamination or 'halo' effects."
Each item is checked by the subject as Very satisfied,
Moderately satisfied, Somewhat dissatisfied, or Very
dissatisfied. The items are scored with a value for each
reply ranging from a minimum of 1 point to a maximum of 4.
The highest possible score for the items related to
satisfaction is 168, for the items related to friction, 88.
There are also 4 points for a final global question on the
extent of happiness in the marriage. The test was
originally constructed to measure movement during social
casework counseling.
SAMPLE ITEM. In Most, 1960.

LENGTH. Items: 65.
AVAILABILITY. In Most, 1960.
REFERENCES.
     Most,E. Casework results among married couples in
conflict: a device to measure attitudinal change. Ph.D.
dissertation,, Columbia University, 1960.
     Most,E. Measuring change in marital satisfaction.
Journal of Social Work, 1964, 9, 64-70.

NEVILL,D. and DAMICO,S. Role Conflict Questionnaire For
Women

VARIABLES MEASURED. Role Conflict in relation to: (1) Time
management, (2) Relations with husband, (3) Household
management, (4) Financial, (5) Child care, (6) Expectations
for self, (7) Expectations of others, and (8) Guilt.
TEST DESCRIPTION. A questionnaire containing eight conflict
situations dealing with the above variables. Responses are
scored on a Likert-type scale, with 7 being the response of
most stress.
SAMPLE ITEM. Frequently there are disagreements about how
money is spent. How much does this affect you? Does not
apply = 0, Not at all = 1, 2, 3, 4, Extremely = 5.
LENGTH. Items: 8.
AVAILABILITY. From NAPS-2.
ABSTRACTED BY: Thomas G.Sparhawk
REFERENCE.
     Nevill,D. and Damico,S. Development of a role
conflict questionnaire for women: some preliminary
findings. Journal of Consulting and Clinical Psychology,
1974, 42, 743.

NYE,F.I. and MacDOUGALL,E. Spousal Argument Scale

VARIABLE MEASURED. Husband-wife arguing.
TEST DESCRIPTION. Six questions dealing with frequency of
arguments about money, children, recreation, use of house
and furniture, TV and radio, and an open-ended "other." Five
response categories from Never to Very often. Responses are
dichotomized to form a Guttman scale.
SAMPLE ITEM. How often do you and your husband argue about
money? Very often, Frequently, Sometimes, Rarely, Never.
LENGTH. Items: 6.
AVAILABILITY. In Nye and MacDougall, 1959.
REFERENCE.
     Nye,F.I. and MacDougall,E. The dependent variable in
marital research. Pacific Sociological Review, 1959, 2,
67-70.

ORT,R.S.   Marital Role Conflict Score

VARIABLES MEASURED.   Role conflicts in marriage.   Role
conflicts are seen as a way to measure marital happiness
that is unbiased by SES.
TEST DESCRIPTION.   An interview schedule of 22 questions
presented in four sets.   Each question is in four forms:
(1) an inquiry into the various aspects of the subject's
role expectations in marriage;   (2) the roles played by the
subject in marriage;   (3) the subject's expectations of the
mate's role in marriage; and (4) the roles played by the
subject's mate.   Each discrepancy between role expectations
for the self and role played by the self, and between role
expectations for the mate and role played by the mate is
counted as an indication of role conflict and summed.
SAMPLE ITEM.   Should a husband expect to win most arguments?
LENGTH. Items: 88.
AVAILABILITY.   From ADI, Doc. No. 2908. $.50 for
microfilm or photocopy.
REFERENCE.
    Ort,R.S. A study of role conflicts as related to
happiness in marriage.   Journal of Abnormal Social
Psychology, 1950, 45, 691-699.

PARKER,S.   and   KLEINER,R.J.   Husbands'   Marital   Role
Discrepancy Index.

VARIABLE MEASURED.   The discrepancy between the husband's
perception of the actual marital role performance and the
perception of the ideal marital role performance.
TEST DESCRIPTION.   A test consisting of four items, two of
which refer to the parental role and two to the spousal
role, taken from a larger index of general role discrepancy.
As part of a larger interview schedule, subjects are
presented with a series of descriptions of role behavior all
preceded by the statement "I am a person who..." The
response categories (Almost never, Occasionally, Usually,
Almost always) are scored from 1 to 4.   Later in the
interview, the same items and response categories are
presented again, but are preceded by the statement "I would
like to be a person who..." The sum of the numerical
differences between a subject's responses for the two
presentations is the role discrepancy index.
SAMPLE ITEM.   I am a person who/I would like to be a person
who makes the decisions on money and other important family
matters.
LENGTH.   Items: 8 (4 ideal and 4 actual role performance.)
AVAILABILITY.   In Parker and Kleiner, 1969.
REFERENCES.
    Parker,S. and Kleiner,R.J.   Mental Illness in the
Urban Negro Community. New York: The Free Press, 1966.
    Parker,S. and Kleiner,R.J. Social and psychological
dimensions of the family role performance of the Negro male.
Journal of Marriage and the Family, 1969, 31, 500-506.

RYDER,R.G.   Problem Inventory

VARIABLES MEASURED.   Yielding or stand pat behavior in
hypothetical marital disputes, as self reported.
TEST DESCRIPTION. Two hypothetical disputes for each of
seven content areas (food, sex, occupation, housekeeping,
relatives, parenthood, friends). The response alternatives
for each item let S agree with modifying reasons, agree flat
out, disagree with modifying reasons, and disagree flat out,
after the model presented in the Yale Marital Interaction
Battery (Buerkle, et al., 1959). The brief form of this
scale is designed to fit into a comprehensive testing
battery. In Ryder (1970) PI was scored by dividing items
into areas of conventional husband concern and areas of
conventional wife concern, and then into stems in which the
husband complained and stems in which the wife complained,
generating four scores of self-reported yielding behavior.
Only the two referring to areas of conventional wife concern
seemed worth using.
SAMPLE ITEM. Suppose you and your wife are shopping at a
supermarket. Both pick out groceries, but when you are
finished you notice your wife has gotten some things you do
not want. What would you tell her? (a) I'd tell her to
keep them. She probably knows more about grocery shopping
than I do. (b) To take them back. There's no reason to buy
things I don't want. (c) Her choices may be all right, but
I'd like her to take them back. (d) What she chose might
not be what I want, but still she doesn't have to take them
back.
LENGTH. Items: 14.
AVAILABILITY. From NAPS-2.
ABSTRACTED BY: Robert G. Ryder
REFERENCES.
       Buerkle,J.V. and Badgley,R.F. Couple role-taking:
the Yale Marital Interaction Battery. Marriage and Family
Living, 1959, 21, 53-58.
       Ryder,R.G. Profile factor analysis and variable factor
analysis. Psychological Reports, 1964, 15, 119-127.
       Ryder,R.G. The factualizing game: a sickness of
psychological research. Psychological Reports, 1966, 19,
563-570.
       Ryder,R.G. Rotating principal axis into approximately
mutually exclusive categories. In the Final Report:
Conference on Cluster Analysis of Multivariate Data, New
Orleans, December 1966.
       Ryder,R.G. Two replications of color matching factors.
Family Process, 1966, 5, 43-48.
       Ryder,R.G. Compatibility in marriage. Psychological
Reports, 1967, 20, 807-813.
       Ryder,R.G. Husband-wife dyads versus married
strangers. Family Process, 1968, 7, 233-238.
       Ryder,R.G. Dimensions of early marriage. Family
Process, 1970, 9, 51-68.
       Ryder,R.G. and Goodrich,D.W. Married couples'
responses to disagreements. Family Process, 1966, 5, 30-42.

SCANZONI,J. Perceived Hostility Score

VARIABLE MEASURED. Hostility between husband and wife.
TEST DESCRIPTION. Subjects are asked to respond to
questions dealing with hostility toward their spouse.
Response categories are: Very often = 7, Often = 5,
Sometimes = 3, Seldom = 1, Never = 0. The weights are added
to obtain a "total perceived hostility score."
SAMPLE ITEM. How often do you get so angry with your
husband (wife) that you refuse to talk?
LENGTH. Items: 4.
AVAILABILITY. Scanzoni, 1970 and 1972.
ABSTRACTED BY: Kersti Yllo
REFERENCES.
    Scanzoni,J. Opportunity and the Family. New York:
The Free Press, 1970, p. 137.
    Scanzoni,J. Sexual Bargaining. Englewood Cliffs,
N.J.: Prentice-Hall, Inc., 1972, 99.

SMITH,J.R. Perception of Interpersonal Hostility Scale and
Perception of Marital Interaction Scale

VARIABLES MEASURED. Perception of interpersonal relations
and hostility in a marriage relationship.
TEST DESCRIPTION. Each spouse responds to a series of
statements about the marriage, including areas in dispute,
and then responds to a parallel list about the spouses'
perceptions. The male's perception is subtracted from the
female's.
SAMPLE ITEM. My husband thinks my family causes our
quarrels versus I think my husband's family causes our
quarrels.
LENGTH. Time: 5 minutes. Items: 20 for each scale.
AVAILABILITY. From NAPS-2.
ABSTRACTED BY: J. Rex Smith
REFERENCE.
    Smith,J.R. Suggested scales for prediction of client
movement and the duration of marriage counseling. Sociology
and Social Research, 1967, 52, 63-71.

WEISS,R.L. PATTERSON,G.R. HOPS,H. Pleasurable and
Displeasurable Behavior Checklist

VARIABLES MEASURED. (1) Actions of a spouse which please or
displease (positive and negative reinforcement), grouped
under the following headings: finances-money management,
and decision making, meals and shopping, household chores
and cleaning, automobile and transportation, management of
leisure time, care of children, personal habits and
appearance, sex, shared recreational events. (2) Conflicts.
(3) Constructive problem solving sessions.

TEST DESCRIPTION. Each heading contains from 5 to 25 items which a spouse might find pleasurable or displeasurable, and space to write in additional items. All items must have a definite beginning and end and must be countable. The subject completes the check list once each day, recording for each relevant item the frequency with which it occurred and whether it is pleasurable or displeasurable. Pleasurable events are those "...which make life easier for you (e.g. 'spouse picked me up on time'), which involve things you particularly like to have done for you (e.g. 'spouse fixed a favorite food or dessert'), or which involve actions you consider necessary in the role of a good husband or wife (e.g. 'spouse played with the children')." In addition, the subject also is asked to circle the most intensely pleasing and intensely displeasing item which occurred during the day.

The last page consists of a list of areas of potential conflict or problems. The subject records the number of times a conflict occurred that day for each item (including space for write-in items) and also the number of times that a "constructive problem solving session" occurred. The latter is defined as "discussions during which some agreement is reached about a specific change to be made by one or both of you."

The above data, together with the data on the amount of time the couple spent together each day, enables the computing of rates of positive and negative reinforcement and of conflict.

SAMPLE ITEM. Spouse helped in planning a budget.

LENGTH. See above.

AVAILABILITY. In Patterson, 1976. A modification for use with parents and children is available from Elaine Blechman-Beck, Department of Psychiatry, Yale University or from NAPS-2.

REFERENCES.

Birchler,G.R. Differential patterns of instrumental affiliative behavior as a function of degree of marital distress and level of intimacy. Ph.D. dissertation. University of Oregon, 1972.

Birchler,G.R. and Weiss,R.L. Instrumental affiliative behavior and self-awareness. Paper presented at the meeting of the Western Psychological Association, Los Angeles, April 1970.

Birchler,G.R. Weiss,R.L. and Vincent,J.P. A multi-method analysis of social reinforcement exchange between maritally distressed and nondistressed spouse and stranger dyads. Journal of Personality and Social Psychology, 1975, 31, 349-360.

Birchler,G.R. Weiss,R.L. and Wampler,L.D. Differential patterns of social reinforcement as a function of degree of marital distress and level of intimacy. Paper presented at the meeting of the Western Psychological Association, Portland, Oregon, April 1972.

Patterson,G.R. Some procedures for assessing changes in marital interaction patterns. Oregon Research Institute

Research Bulletin, 1976, 16.
     Patterson,G.R. and Hops,H. Coercion, a game for two:
intervention techniques for marital conflict. In
Ulrich,R.E. and Mountjoy,P. (Eds.). The Experimental
Analysis of Social Behavior. New York:
Appleton-Century-Crofts 1972.
     Vincent,J.P. Problem-solving behavior in distressed
and non-distressed married and stranger dyads. Ph.D.
dissertation. University of Oregon, 1972.
     Weiss,R.L. Birchler,G.R. and Vincent,J.P.
Contractual models for negotiating training in marital
dyads. JOurnal of Marriage and the Family, 1974, 36,
321-330.
     Weiss,R.L. Hops,H. and Patterson,G.R. A framework
for conceptualizing marital conflict, a technology for
altering it, some data for evaluating it. In
Hamerlynck,L.A. Handy,L.C. and Mash,E.J. (Eds.) Behavior
Change: Methodology Concepts and Practice. Champaign,
Illinois: Research Press, 1972, 309-342.
     Wills,T.A. The measurement of pleasurable and
displeasurable events in marital relationships. Unpublished
Master's Thesis. University of Oregon, 1972.
     Wills,T.A. Weiss,R.L. and Patterson,G.R. A
behavioral analysis of the determinants of marital
satisfaction. Journal of Consulting and Clinical
Psychology, 1974, 42, 802-811.

WYER,R.S.Jr. Parental Differences Score

VARIABLES MEASURED. Differences between the parents'
attitudes and behaviors toward the child, and the
differences in their perceptions of the child's responses to
them.
TEST DESCRIPTION. The first part of this questionnaire
consists of 63 items modified from the Parental Attitude
Research Instrument (Schaefer and Bell, 1957) to establish
parental attitudes. The second part contains 54 items
selected from Radke (1946). Of these, 34 items assess
parental behaviors toward the child, and 20 items assess
parents' interpretations of their child's responses toward
them. All responses are rated on a six-point scale.
Differences between parents' general attitude, behaviors
toward the child, and interpretations of the child's
responses are assessed by summing the absolute differences
between parents' responses to each of the sections of the
questionnaire.
SAMPLE ITEM. I play with my child. My child is easy to
manage.
LENGTH. Items: 117.
AVAILABILITY. From NAPS-2.
ABSTRACTED BY: Thomas G. Sparhawk
REFERENCES.
     Radke,M. Relation of parental authority to children's
behavior and attitudes. University of Minnesota, Institute

of Child Welfare Monographs, 1946, 22.
     Schaefer,E.S. and Bell,R.Q.   Patterns of attitudes
toward child rearing and the family. Journal of Abnormal
and Social Psychology, 1957, 54, 391-395.
     Wyer,R.S.Jr. Effects of child-rearing attitudes and
behavior
on children's responses to hypothetical social situations.
Journal of Personality and Social Psychology, 1965, 2,
480-486.

WYER,R.S.Jr.   Parental Perception of Child Check List

VARIABLES   MEASURED.   Discrepancy   between   parents'
perceptions of a child.
TEST DESCRIPTION. Respondents estimate the amount of time
they feel each adjective on a list is descriptive of their
son or daughter, using a five-point scale ranging from
Seldom to Most of the time. They then rate their feelings
about their child in that respect, using a five-point scale
ranging from Dislike very much to Like very much.
     "For each adjective, the absolute difference between
the rating by the mother and that by the father was used as
an indication of parental discrepancy in perceiving or
evaluating their child along this dimension."
SAMPLE ITEM. Acceptable, Alert, Ambitious.
LENGTH. Items: 24.
AVAILABILITY. In Wyer, 1965.
ABSTRACTED BY: Thomas G. Sparhawk
REFERENCE.
     Wyer,R.S.Jr. Self acceptance, discrepancy between
parents' perceptions of their children, and goal-seeking
effectiveness.   Journal   of   Personality   and   Social
Psychology, 1965, 2, 311-316.

                B. Role Differentiation and Performance

1. Authority and Power (See also Subject Index)

ALDOUS,J.   Adult Role Perception Index

VARIABLES MEASURED. The extent to which the father is
perceived as a (1) Powerful leader, (2) Expressive leader,
(3)   Authority-disciplinarian   for   boys,   (4)
Authority-disciplinarian for girls, and (5) Responsible
earner. Scores are obtainable for all five of these in
respect to a "pretend family"; for 1 and 2 for the
man-woman comparisons; and for 1, 2, and 5 for "real family
comparisons."

TEST DESCRIPTION. Instrument designed for 4 to 5 year olds.
For the "pretend family" scores, the child is asked to
indicate which members of a "pretend family" display various
behaviors such as "Who is boss in this family." The child
can respond by naming a person or by pointing to a picture
of an adult male, female, or child. For the "real family"
the child is asked the same questions about his own family.
The score for each variable consists of the number of times
the father is designated as the person characterized by the
items in the variable. Thus, for "power leader" in the
"pretend family" reference, the scores can range from 0 to
5.
SAMPLE ITEM. From "real family" section: Who is the boss
in your family?
LENGTH. Items: 55.
AVAILABILITY. In Aldous, 1972.
REFERENCE.
     Aldous,J.   Children's perceptions of adult role
assignment: father-absence, class, race and sex influences.
Journal of Marriage and the Family, 1972, 34, 55-65.
     Aldous,J. and Kamiko,T. A cross-national study of the
effects of father absence: Japan and the United States. In
Sussman,M.B. and Cogswell,B.E. (Eds.) Cross National
Family Research. Leiden: E.J.Brill, 86-101.
     Sussman,M.B. and Cogswell,B.E. Cross-National Family
Research. Leiden, Netherlands: E.J. Brill, 1972.

BAHR,S.J. BOWERMAN,C.E. and GECAS,V. Adolescent
Perception of Conjugal Power Index

VARIABLE MEASURED. Adolescent perception of which parent
has the most influence or the final say in decisions upon
which they initially disagree.
TEST DESCRIPTION. A structured questionnaire containing
eight items is administered to adolescent subjects. Items
are concerned with parental decision-making in a variety of
areas. There are seven possible responses to each question:
(1) Mother, almost always; (2) Mother, much more often;
(3) Mother, little more often; (4) About equal; (5)
Father, little more often; (6) Father, much more often;
(7) Father, almost always. The first three are combined to
form the Mother-Dominant category, the fourth response is
labeled Equalitarian, and responses five through seven are
combined into the Father-Dominant category. There were five
responses to the remaining questions, the responses ranging
from Father usually to Mother usually. These are collapsed
in a similar manner with the middle response being labeled
Equalitarian and the two responses on each end being labeled
Father Dominant and Mother Dominant respectively.
SAMPLE ITEM. When important family problems come up, which
parent usually has the most influence in making the
decision?

LENGTH. Items: 8.
AVAILABILITY. In Bahr, Bowerman and Gecas, 1974.
ABSTRACTED BY: Kersti Yllo.
REFERENCES.
     Bahr,S.J.   Bowerman,C.E.   and   Gecas,V.   Adolescent
Perceptions of Conjugal Power.   Social Forces, 1974, 52,
357-367.

BILLER,H.B. Father Dominance Index

VARIABLES MEASURED.   Children's   perception   of   father
dominance.
TEST DESCRIPTION. Five questions in each of four areas are
asked   of   kindergarten   children.   These   are   (1)
Decision-making (which   parent   makes   decisions),   (2)
Competence (which parent "knows" the most), (3) Nurturance
(which parent provides the most), and (4) Limit setting
(which parent has authority).   If father is named in any
question, four points are scored, if mother, zero points.
If the answer is "both" or "don't know," the child is asked
who does it the most, and three points are scored for
answering father and one point for answering mother. If
still no distinction is made, two points are scored.
SAMPLE ITEMS. (1) Who says which TV program your family
watches?   (2) Who in your family knows most about animals?
(3) Who gives you the most gifts and toys?   (4) Who tells
you what time to go to bed?
LENGTH. Items: 20.
AVAILABILITY. From NAPS-2.
ABSTRACTED BY: Thomas G. Sparhawk.
REFERENCES.
     Biller,H.B. Father dominance and sex-role development
in kindergarten-age boys. Developmental Psychology, 1969,
1, 87-94.
     Freedheim,P.K. An investigation of masculinity and
parental role patterns.   Unpublished Ph.D. dissertation,
Duke University, 1960.

BILLER,H.B. Paternal Dominance and Conflict Situational
Task

VARIABLES MEASURED. Father's dominance in father-mother
interaction.
TEST DESCRIPTION.   Interviews are conducted with both
parents individually in which they are asked how they would
respond to certain hypothetical situations concerning child
behavior.   They are again interviewed on the same questions
together, and asked to come to joint agreements.   These
interviews are recorded. Each time the father speaks first,
speaks most, or speaks last, a point is scored.   Each time
the mother passively accepts the father's decision, a point
is scored, and each time the father passively accepts the
mother's decision, a point is subtracted. Each time the

mother moves closer to the father in terms of a final
decision, a point is scored.
SAMPLE ITEM. Twice in the last hour you have told your son
to pick up his toys. As you look around now you see that
he's stopped working and is now looking off into the air.
You ask him a third time, but he refuses to pick up his
toys.
LENGTH. Items: 12.
AVAILABILITY. From NAPS-2.
ABSTRACTED BY: Thomas G. Sparhawk.
REFERENCES.
     Biller,H.B. Father dominance and sex-role development
in kindergarten-age boys. Developmental Psychology, 1969,
1, 87-94.
     Farina,A. Patterns of role dominance and conflict in
parents of schizophrenic patients. Journal of Abnormal and
Social Psychology, 1960, 61, 31-38.

BLOOD,R.O.JR. and HAMBLIN,R.L. Decision Role Performance
(Power) Index

VARIABLES MEASURED. Power in family decisions.
TEST DESCRIPTION. Husbands and wives are asked "The last
time you decided --, who first suggested what you decided to
do?" 18 questions about selecting a home, having a baby,
buying a car, etc.
SAMPLE ITEM. See Test Description.
LENGTH. Items: 18.
AVAILABILITY. From NAPS.
REFERENCE.
     Blood,R.O.JR. and Hamblin,R.L. The effect of the
wife's employment on the family power structure. Social
Forces, 1958, 36, 347-352.

BLOOD,R.O.JR. and HAMBLIN,R.L. Marital Authority
Expectations Scale

VARIABLE MEASURED. Husband-dominant role prescription.
TEST DESCRIPTION. Statements of what husband and wife
should do, from Jacobson (1951) are used to form a
cumulative scale.
SAMPLE ITEM. Husbands should be more strict with their
wives: Strongly disagree, Disagree, Uncertain, Agree,
Strongly agree.
LENGTH. Items: 8.
AVAILABILITY. In Blood and Hamblin, 1958.
REFERENCES.
     Blood,R.O.Jr. and Hamblin,R.L. The effect of the
wife's employment on the family power structure. Social
Forces, 1958, 36, 347-352.
     Jacobson,A.H. Attitudes toward the role of husband and
wife in marriage. Research Studies of the State College of
Washington, 1951, 19, 103-106.

BLOOD,R.O.JR. and WOLFE,D.M.   Decision Power Index

VARIABLE MEASURED. Relative decision power of husband and
wife, expressed either as a score or as a taxonomy of four
family power types: husband-dominant, wife-dominant,
autonomic, and syncratic.
TEST DESCRIPTION. Subject is asked to indicate "who has the
final say" in respect to eight family decisions (what job
the husband should take, what car to get, whether or not to
buy life insurance, where to go on vacation, what house or
apartment to take, whether or not the wife should go to work
or quit work, what doctor to have, how much money to spend
on food).   Response alternatives are weighted from   5
(husband always) to 1 (wife always) and summed to obtain the
Decision Power Index.
     The four family power types are described in Wolfe
(1959).   They are determined by first obtaining a Shared
Power Index consisting of the number of decisions for which
subject indicated "husband and wife exactly the same."
Syncratic families are those in which half or more of the
decisions are reported as being shared. Husband-dominant
families are those with Shared Power Index scores below four
and Decision Power Index scores of 29 or above;
wife-dominant families have low Shared Power Index scores
and Decision Power Index scores of 19 or less. Finally,
autonomic families assign equal numbers of separate
decisions to both partners. The husband has the final say
for some, and the wife for others.   Such families are
identified by having a Decision Power Index in the middle
(scores of 20-28) together with a low Shared Power Index (3
or less).
     There have been many revisions and modifications of the
basic procedure of this instrument, most of them consisting
of adding, deleting, or modifying the list of decisions.
For example, Centers, Raven, and Rodrigues (1971) added six
items to make the list of decisions more representative.
Others have modified the items to make them more appropriate
for specific populations, especially for use in other
societies (Blood and Takeshita, 1964; Straus and Winkelman,
1969). Safilios-Rothschild's version (1970) used open-ended
responses and classifies the responses into the same five
interval categories as the Blood and Wolfe multiple choice
answers.
SAMPLE ITEM. In every family somebody has to decide such
things as where the family will live and so on. Many
couples talk such things over first, but the final decision
often has to be made by the husband or the wife. For
instance, who usually makes the final decision about what
car to get? Husband always, Husband more than wife, Husband
and wife exactly the same, Wife more than husband, Wife
always.
LENGTH. Items: 8.
AVAILABILITY. In Blood and Wolfe, 1960; Wolfe, 1959.

REFERENCES.
Aldous,J. Wives' employment status and lower-class men as husband-fathers: support for the Moynihan thesis. Journal of Marriage and the Family, 1969, 31, 469-476.
Aldous,J. and Straus,M.A. Social networks and conjugal roles: a test of Bott's hypothesis. Social Forces, 1966, 44, 576-580.
Bahr,S.J. The internal consistency of Blood and Wolfe's measure of conjugal power: a research note. Journal of Marriage and the Family, 1973, 35, 293-295.
Blood,R.O.Jr. The husband-wife relationship. In Nye,F.G. and Hoffman,L.W. The Employed Mother in America. Chicago: Rand McNally, 1963a, 282-305.
Blood,R.O.Jr. The measure and bases of family power: a rejoinder. Marriage and Family Living, 1963b, 25, 475-477.
Blood,R.O.Jr. and Takeshita,Y.J. Development of cross-cultural equivalence of measures of marital interaction for U.S.A. and Japan. Transactions of the Fifth World Congress of Sociology, 1964, 4, 333-344.
Blood,R.O.Jr. and Wolfe,D.M. Husbands and Wives: The Dynamics of Married Living. Glencoe, Illinois: Free Press, 1960.
Blood,R.O.Jr. and Wolfe,D.M. Negro-white differences in blue-collar marriages in a northern metropolis. Social Forces, 1969, 48, 59-64.
Buric,O. and Zecevic,A. Family authority, marital satisfaction, and the social network in Yugoslavia. Journal of Marriage and the Family, 1967, 29, 325-336.
Centers,R. Raven,B.H. and Rodrigues,A. Conjugal power structure: a re-examination. American Sociological Review, 1971, 36, 264-277.
Davis,H.L. Measurement of husband-wife influence in consumer purchase decisions. Journal of Marketing Research, 1971, 8, 305-312.
Granbois,D.H. and Willett,R.P. Equivalence of family role measures based on husband and wife data. Journal of Marriage and the Family, 1970, 32, 68-72.
Heer,D.M. The measurement and bases of family power: an overview. Marriage and Family Living, 1963a, 25, 133-139.
Heer,D.M. The measurement and bases of family power: reply. Marriage and Family Living, 1963b, 25, 477-478.
Hill,R.L. Family Development in Three Generations. Cambridge, Mass: Schenkman Publishing Company, Inc., 1970.
Kandel,D.B. and Lesser,G.S. The internal structure of families in the United States and Denmark. In Sussman,M.B. and Cogswell,B.E. (Eds.) Cross-National Family Research. Leiden, Netherlands: E.J.Brill, 1972, 70-85.
Kandel,D.B. and Lesser,G.S. Marital decision-making in American and Danish urban families: a research note. Journal of Marriage and the Family. 1972, 34, 134-138.
Kandel,D.B. and Lesser,G.S. Youth in Two Worlds. San Francisco: Jossey-Bass, 1972.
Lamouse,A. Family roles of women: a German example.

Journal of Marriage and the Family, 1969, 31, 145-152.

Michel,A. Comparative data concerning the interaction in French and American families. Journal of Marriage and the Family, 1967, 29, 337-344.

Michel,A. Wife's satisfaction with husband's understanding in Parisian urban families. Journal of Marriage and the Family, 1970, 32, 351-359.

Mishler,E.G. and Waxler,N.E. Interaction in Families. New York: John Wiley and Sons, Inc., 1968, 317.

Rodman,H. Marital power in France, Greece, Yugoslavia, and the United States: a cross-national discussion. Journal of Marriage and the Family, 1967, 29, 320-324.

Safilios-Rothschild,C. A comparison of power structure and marital satisfaction in urban Greek and French families. Journal of Marriage and the Family, 1967, 29, 345-352.

Safilios-Rothschild,C. Family sociology or wives' family sociology? A cross-cultural examination of decision-making. Journal of Marriage and the Family, 1969, 31, 290-301.

Safilios-Rothschild,C. The influence of the wife's degree of work commitment upon some aspects of family organization and dynamics. Journal of Marriage and the Family, 1970, 32, 681-691.

Sawer,B.J. Predictors of the farm wife's involvement in general management and adoption decisions. Rural Sociology, 38, 1973, 412-426.

Straus,M.A. and Winkelmann,D. Social class, fertility, and authority in nuclear and joint households in Bombay. Journal of Asian and African Studies, 1969, 9, 61-74.

Straus,M.A. Exchange and power in marriage in cultural context: a multimethod and multivariate analysis of Bombay and Minneapolis families. Paper read at the 1977 meeting of the Association for Asian Studies, New York.

Turk,J.L. and Bell,N.W. Measuring power in families. Journal of Marriage and the Family, 1972, 34, 215-222.

Weller,R.H. Female work experience and fertility in San Juan, Puerto Rico: a study of selected lower and middle income neighborhoods, Unpublished Ph.D. dissertation, Cornell University, 1967.

Weller,R.H. The employment of wives, dominance, and fertility. Journal of Marriage and the Family, 1968, 39, 437-442.

Wolfe,D.M. Power and authority in the family. In Cartwright,D. (Ed.) Studies in Social Power. Ann Arbor, Michigan: Institute for Social Research, 1959, 99-117.

FOX,G.L. Power Index

VARIABLE MEASURED. Husband's marital power.
TEST DESCRIPTION. A set of five questions deal with the husband's relative power in making final decisions about a series of family-linked matters. A second set of questions focuses on different activities of the wife which are either

forbidden or not forbidden by the husband. The "decision" set might be seen as a measure of the husband's power in bargaining situations; the "forbids" set assesses his "right to decree," or the extent to which the husband exercises power absolutely.

The response to each item is coded as either a husband-dominant or non-husband-dominant. Husband-dominant responses indicate that decisions are usually or always made by the husband or that given activities are forbidden by the husband. Decisions that are shared equally or made by the wife and activities not forbidden are coded as non-husband-dominant responses. A score of one is assigned to husband-dominant responses while zero is given to non-husband-dominant responses. The scores are totaled over the 13 items to form the power index of husband's power.

SAMPLE ITEM. Does your husband forbid you to talk to men your husband doesn't know? Yes, No.

LENGTH. Items: Decision Set: 5; Forbids Set: 8.

AVAILABILITY. In Fox, 1973.

ABSTRACTED BY: Greer Litton Fox.

REFERENCES.

Fox,G.L. Some determinants of marital behavior in Ankara, Turkey. Ph.D. dissertation, University of Michigan, 1970.

Fox,G.L. Another look at the comparative resources model: assessing the balance of power in Turkish marriages. Journal of Marriage and the Family, 1973, 35, 718-730.

GREENSTEIN,J.M. Father Dominance Rating

VARIABLE MEASURED. Decision-making dominance relative to the wife.

TEST DESCRIPTION. During an interview, with both spouses, the interviewer considers seven questions dealing with the interaction of the spouses during the interview. When the interview is completed, a single global rating of father dominance is arrived at. This is a six-point rating scale ranging from "Father is very clearly and strongly the dominant partner; mother has very little say in things" to "Mother is very clearly and strongly the dominant partner; father has very little to say in things."

SAMPLE ITEM. Who appears to take charge in asking questions, making demands, or relating events?

LENGTH. Items: 7.

AVAILABILITY. In Greenstein, 1966.

ABSTRACTED BY: Thomas G. Sparhawk

REFERENCE.

Greenstein,J.M. Father characteristics and sex typing. Journal of Personality and Social Psychology, 1966, 3, 271-277.

HAAVIO-MANNILA,E.   Equality of the Sexes in the Family Scale

VARIABLES MEASURED.   The scale combines two aspects of
equality: (1) Division of household tasks between men and
women, and (2) Equality in decision-making.
TEST DESCRIPTION. Expectations concerning men's and women's
roles in the family are measured by four attitude questions
presented in a personal interview on the basis of which an
additive scale is constructed. The alternatives available
in replying are: Absolutely agree, Almost agree, Cannot
say, Almost disagree, and Absolutely disagree. In a study
conducted in the Tornio River Valley in Northern Sweden and
Finland (N=750), the scale has a reliability of .66 on the
Swedish side and .58 on the Finnish side of the border
according to the Spearman-Brown formula.
SAMPLE ITEM. Men should not participate in housework.
LENGTH. Time: 3-5 minutes. Items: Four.
AVAILABILITY. In Haavio-Mannila, 1972.
ABSTRACTED BY. Elina Haavio-Mannila.
REFERENCES.
      Haavio-Mannila,E. Suomalainen nainen ja mies, Porvoo:
Werner Soderstrom Oy, 1968.
      Haavio-Mannila,E.   Cross-national   differences   in
adoption of new ideologies and practices in family life.
Journal of Marriage and the Family, 1972a, 34, 525-537.
      Haavio-Mannila,E.   Sex-role attitudes   in   Finland,
1966-1970. Journal of Social Issues, 1972b, 28, 2, 93-210.

HILL,R.L.   Family Control Type Classification

VARIABLE MEASURED.   Family power typology ranging from
patriarchal to wife-dominant.
TEST DESCRIPTION. A technique of classifying families into
six   types   on   the   basis   of   four   variables:
Dominance-submission, Social role played by   wife   in
marriage,   Method of handling family purse, Method of
settling disagreements.   Subjects answer four questions
corresponding to these four variables. The pattern of their
answers is used as the basis for classifying types of family
control: (1)   Patriarchal,   (2)   Husband-dominant,   (3)
Equalitarian, (4) Husband-wife equal, (5) Matriarchal, and
(6) Wife-dominant.
SAMPLE ITEM. Dominance-submission in husband-wife relation
-- that is, Who is most frequently the boss? Husband much
stronger, assertive, dominant, leading,   responsibility
assuming;   Husband somewhat stronger; Husband and wife
equal;   Husband somewhat weaker; Husband much weaker,
nonassertive, passive, dependent.
LENGTH. Items: 4.
AVAILABILITY. In Hill, 1949.
REFERENCE.
      Hill,R.L. Families under Stress: Adjustment to the
Crises of War Separation and Reunion. New York: Harper,
1949.

HILL,R.L.   STYCOS,J.M.   and BACK,K.W.   Familism Typology

VARIABLES MEASURED.   (1) Activities prohibited to the wife,
(2) Dominance index, (3) Wife working or home. Results are
combined   to   give   a   profile   of   eight
familistic-person-centered organization types.
TEST DESCRIPTION. (1) Activities prohibited to the wife is
a   list of five items dichotomized into high or low
prohibitions   on   her   activities.   Responses   are
Guttman-scaled.   (2) Dominance index is a list of three
questions answered by the wife on whether she gives in to
her husband, with scores weighted 1 for Wife gives in, 0 for
No.   Total scores range from 3 (high dominance) to 0 (low
dominance).   These   are   combined   with the objective
information on whether or not the wife is employed outside
the   home   to   give a profile of eight types of family
organization (wife at home,   husband high-dominance, high
prohibitions, etc.).
SAMPLE ITEM.   Uses make-up. Prohibited = 1.   Do you ever
refuse to have sex relations with your husband apart from
the times when you are sick or menstruating?   Never = 1;
Yes = 0.
LENGTH.   Items: 3.
AVAILABILITY.   In Hill et al., 1959, 426-428.
REFERENCE.
        Hill,R.L.   Stycos,J.M. and Back,K.W. The Family and
Population Control: A Puerto Rican Experiment in Social
Change. Chapel Hill: University of North Carolina Press,
1959.

HOFFMAN,L.W.   Male-Dominance Ideology

VARIABLE MEASURED.   Traditional-equalitarian male dominance
ideology.
TEST DESCRIPTION.   Four-item list to be answered on a
four-point scale: Agree a lot, Agree, Disagree, Disagree a
lot. The greater the agreement, the greater the endorsement
of traditional male-dominance ideology.
SAMPLE ITEM.   Some equality in marriage is a good thing, but
by and large the husband ought to have the main say-so in
family matters.
LENGTH.   Items: 4.
AVAILABILITY.   In Hoffman, 1960.
REFERENCES.
        Hoffman,L.W.   Effects of the employment of mothers on
parental power relations and the division of household
tasks. Marriage and Family Living, 1960, 22, 27-35.
        Turk,J.L. and Bell,N.W. Measuring power in families.
Journal of Marriage and the Family, 1972, 34, 215-222.

HOFFMAN,L.W.   Marital Power and Task Participation Measures

VARIABLES MEASURED. Power and participation in tasks of
husband and wife.
TEST DESCRIPTION. Thirty-three paired items (after Herbst)
which   ask   the   subject who does a particular routine
household activity and which members of the family decide
about that activity.   Three types of scores are obtained:
(1) Task participation scores are computed for mothers and
fathers by scoring 2 points when the parent was reported to
have a major role in doing a given household activity,   1
point for a minor role, and 0 for no role.   These scores can
be computed separately by area--tasks usually done by
husband,   tasks   usually   done by wife, and so forth.   (2)
Activity control scores are computed for the wife and the
husband.   The number of items about which the wife decides
is her activity control score.   (3) Power scores are
obtained by weighting and summing the responses for each
task: Mother decides, father does (3);   Mother decides,
both do (2); Both decide, father does (1); Mother decides,
Mother does--father decides, father does--both decide, both
do--neither parent decides, neither parent does (0);   Both
decide, mother does (1);   Father decides, both do (2);
Father decides, mother does (3).
SAMPLE ITEMS. Who cooks the evening meal? Who decides what
to cook for the evening meal?
LENGTH. Items: 33 pairs.
AVAILABILITY. In Hoffman, 1960.
REFERENCE.
     Hoffman,L.W. Effects of the employment of mothers on
parental power relations and the division of household
tasks. Marriage and Family Living, 1960, 22, 27-35.

HURVITZ,N. Control Roles Attitude Scale

VARIABLES MEASURED.   Superordinate versus subordinate
marital role prescriptions (attitudes) in six areas of
marital   interaction: Source   of   recognized   family
leadership, attitudes toward a working wife, Attitudes
toward the amount of activity a woman should undertake
outside   her   home,   Source of decisions regarding the
children, Attitudes toward the father in decision-making,
General questions about the relationship between men and
women.
TEST DESCRIPTION. Each subscale is represented by either
three or four intensity of agreement-disagreement items.   A
total score may be obtained by summation of subscores.   A
low   score   indicates   companionship,   equalitarian and
democratic roles in marriage; a high score indicates
traditional,   authoritarian,   and male superordinate and
female subordinate control roles in marriage.   Separate
scales, based upon Guttman Scalogram Analyses, for husbands
and wives.

SAMPLE ITEM. If we think of the family as a team, the husband is the captain. (1) Strongly disagree, (2) Disagree, (3) Undecided, (4) Agree, (5) Strongly agree.
LENGTH. Items: 19.
AVAILABILITY. In Hurvitz, 1958; 1959.
REFERENCES.
    Hurvitz,N. Marital roles and adjustment in marriage in a middle-class group. (Unpublished Ph.D. dissertation, University of Southern California, 1958.
    Hurvitz,N. A scale for the measurement of superordinate-subordinate roles in marriage. American Catholic Sociological Review, 1959, 20, 234-241.
    Hurvitz,N. Control roles, marital strain, role deviation, and marital adjustment. Journal of Marriage and the Family, 1965, 27, 29-31.

JACOBSON,A.H. Marriage Role Attitude Inventory

VARIABLES MEASURED. Male-dominant versus equalitarian marital role attitudes (prescriptions).
TEST DESCRIPTION. Linear summation of intensity of agreement weights for single sentence statements of what husbands and wives should do. The 28 items included are those from an original 50-item test which were found to significantly differentiate divorced couples from still married couples who were married on the same date.
SAMPLE ITEM. The husband should decide whether or not to have children. Strongly agree, Agree, Uncertain, Disagree, Strongly disagree.
LENGTH. Items: 28.
AVAILABILITY. In Jacobson, 1950; 1951.
REFERENCES.
    Arkoff,A. Meredith,G. and Dong,J. Attitudes of Japanese-American and Caucasian-Japanese-American students toward marriage roles. Journal of Social Psychology, 1963, 59, 11-15.
    Gardiner,H.W. Attitudes of Thai students toward marriage roles. Journal of Social Psychology, 1968, 75, 61-65.
    Gardiner,H.W. Singh,U.P. and D'Orazio,E. The women in three cultures: marital role preferences in Thailand, India and the United States. Human Organization, 1974, 33, 413-415.
    Jacobson,A.H. A study of conflict in attitudes toward the roles of the husband and wife in marriage. Unpublished Ph.D. dissertation, Ohio State University, 1950.
    Jacobson,A.H. Attitudes toward the role of husband and wife in marriage. Research Studies of the State College of Washington, 1951, 19, 103-106.
    Jacobson,A.H. Conflict of attitudes toward the roles of the husband and wife in marriage. American Sociological Review, 1952, 17, 146-150.
    Kalish,R.A. Maloney,M. and Arkoff,A. Cross-cultural comparisons of college student marital-role preferences.

Journal of Social Psychology, 1966, 68, 41-47.
        Sharma,K.L.   Attitudes of Indian students   towards
marriage roles.   Journal of Social Psychology, 1971, 83,
299-300.

KERCKHOFF,A.C.   Dimensions of Husband-Wife Interaction

VARIABLES MEASURED. Positive, neutral and negative control
(dominance-submission), and Positive, neutral and negative
inclusion (integration-division) are used to classify molar
acts into the nine categories formed by viewing the two
dimensions as orthogonal. Only four of these categories
were found sufficiently often to permit analysis:
Leadership (positive control, positive inclusion), Assertion
(positive control, neutral inclusion), Cooperation (negative
control, positive inclusion), and Dependence   (negative
control, neutral inclusion).
TEST DESCRIPTION. Task-oriented conversations of husbands
and wives are recorded and transcribed. Each unit act is
independently coded (by two separated coders) on each of the
two basic dimensions.   A unit act is defined as a whole,
separate idea--usually a whole sentence.
SAMPLE ITEM. See above.
LENGTH. Items: 2 behavior coding scales.
AVAILABILITY. In Kerckhoff, 1972.
ABSTRACTED BY: Alan C. Kerckhoff.
REFERENCE.
        Kerckhoff,A.C.   Two   dimensions   of   husband-wife
interaction. The Sociological Quarterly, 1972, 13, 49-60.

LUPRI,E. Farm Husband Power Questionnaire

VARIABLE MEASURED. Husband's marital power as perceived by
wife.
TEST DESCRIPTION. An interview schedule for wives listing
six decision-making areas: (1) What farm machinery to buy;
(2) Whether to use new seeds; (3) What livestock to sell;
(4) Whether or not to remodel the home; (5) What household
goods to buy; (6) How much money the family should spend on
food.   For each area the wife chooses among five methods of
how decisions are reached in the family, ranging from
"Husband always decides" to "Wife always decides." Each
method is weighted, and the husband's mean power score is
computed from the particular decision-making methods
indicated by the wife.
SAMPLE ITEM. Decision-making area: What farm machinery to
buy.   Decision-making methods: Wife always = 1; Wife more
than husband = 2; Husband and wife decide together = 3;
Husband more than wife = 4; Husband always = 5.
LENGTH. Items: 6.
AVAILABILITY. In Lupri, 1969.

REFERENCES.
     Lupri,E. The German family today and yesterday: A
study in changing authority patterns. (Unpublished Ph.D.
dissertation,   University   of   Wisconsin.)   Ann   Arbor:
University Microfilms, 1967.
     Lupri,E. Contemporary authority patterns in the West
German family: A study in cross-national validation.
Journal of Marriage and the Family, 1969, 31, 134-144.

LUPRI,E.   Urban Husband Authority Questionnaire

VARIABLE MEASURED.   Husband's marital authority as perceived
by wife.
TEST DESCRIPTION.   An   interview   schedule   for   wives
containing four normative statements about family authority.
There are six response categories ranging from "Agree very
strongly" to "Disagree very strongly." There is also a
question about how family finances are handled with four
possible answers. The responses are transformed into a mean
power score for the husband.
SAMPLE ITEM. Authority pattern statement: (1) The husband
is master of the home; the wife should act accordingly.
AGREE: Very strongly, Strongly, Mildly.   DISAGREE: Very
strongly, Strongly, Mildly. Family finance question: Every
family handles things differently. Who takes care of the
finances and money in your family? (1) Husband handles
money; (2) Wife handles money; (3) Money is handled
jointly; (4) Money is handled by each partner individually.
LENGTH. Items: 4.
AVAILABILITY. In Lupri, 1969.
REFERENCES.
     Lupri,E. The German family today and yesterday: A
study in changing authority patterns. (Ph.D. dissertation,
University of Wisconsin.) Ann Arbor: University Microfilms,
1967.
     Lupri,E. Contemporary authority patterns in the West
German family: a study in cross-national validation.
Journal of Marriage and the Family, 1969, 31, 134-144.

McKINLEY,D.   Source of Authority Measure

VARIABLE MEASURED. The relative authority of the mother and
father.
TEST DESCRIPTION.   Subjects are asked three questions
concerning general authority, discipline and decision-making
in their family. The total score for authority is relative.
That is, subjects may respond "Father mostly" for all three
questions, or, at the other extreme, "Mother mostly" for all
three.   The total score is the sum of item scores. The
lower the score, the more authority lies with the father.
SAMPLE ITEM. Who is the main scource of authority regarding
most matters in the family? Nearly always my father = 1, A
little more often = 4, Generally my mother = 5, Nearly a

little more often = 4, Generally my mother =5, Nearly always
my mother = 6.
LENGTH. Items: 3.
AVAILABILITY. In McKinley, 1964.
ABSTRACTED BY: Kersti Yllo
REFERENCE.
     McKinley,D. Social Class and Family Life.   New York:
The Free Press, 1964.

MILLER,S. and WACKMAN,D.   Word Ranking Instrument

VARIABLE MEASURED. Relative Control of Husband and Wife.
TEST DESCRIPTION. Each subject is given a list of ten words
which presumably reflect important substantive aspects of
marriage and family. Each member of the dyad is given a
copy of the list and asked to "pick the five most important
words and rank them in order of importance (to you) in the
past year." After individually ranking words from the list,
the spouses are brought together and left alone for five
minutes with instructions to negotiate a joint list of words
important to them as a couple. The individual lists are
then compared to the joint list.   The changes from the
individual list to the joint list are assumed to capture the
relative control of husband and wife as they negotiate to
have their choices represented.   Operationally, the
variables are described as follows by Corrales (1975): "(1)
Husband's control: similarity of H's own individual list
with the joint list. (2) Wife's control: Similarity of W's
own individual list with the joint list.   (3) Balance of
control: creation of ordinal categories depicting HW, H=W,
H<W, by using the formula: Balance of control equals H's
control minus W's control." The method for comparing one
list to another is given in Corrales, 1975.
SAMPLE ITEM. Word list: Housing, friends, personality,
career, religion, communication, individuality, relatives,
sex, and children.
LENGTH. Items: 10.
AVAILABILITY. In Corrales, R., in Cromwell and Olson, 1975.
ABSTRACTED BY: Kersti Yllo.
REFERENCES.
     Corrales,R.G.   Power and satisfaction in early
marriage.   In Cromwell,R. and Olson,D. eds. Power in
Families. New York: John Wiley and Sons, 1975, 197-216.
     Miller,S. and Wackman,D.   Word ranking instrument.
Unpublished instrument, Minneapolis: University of
Minnesota, Minnesota Family Study Center, 1970.

OLSON,D.H.L. and RYDER,R.G. Inventory of Marital Conflicts

VARIABLES MEASURED. The outcome and process of decision
making, problem-solving and conflict-resolution behavior in
married couples. (1) Relevancy: the perceived closeness of
test items to typical problems encountered in marriage, (2)

Win scores: whose final decision was accepted on items of
disagreement, (3) Interactional behavior: derived from
coding tape-recorded or videotaped interaction sequences. A
Marital   and   Family Interaction Coding System (MFICS),
composed of 35 content and process codes, has been developed
for coding the interaction, although other coding systems
could also be used.   (4) Relationship typology: based on
unique styles of interaction when resolving conflict.
TEST DESCRIPTION. The test consists of 18 vignettes that
describe various types of marital conflicts. Couples are
separated and each individually responds to the vignettes by
identifying "who is primarily responsible for the problem"
and by indicating if they agree or disagree with the
proposed solution.   The test is structured so that there
will be agreement between the couple (6 vignettes) or
disagreement (12 vignettes).   Disagreement is accomplished
by slanting information on the husband's form to make the
wife appear at fault and, conversely, making the husband
appear guilty on the wife's vignettes. After each partner
has completed his/her forms, they are brought together and
asked to discuss each conflict and jointly decide who is
guilty and the best way to resolve the problem. This
procedure allows marital interaction to be observed under
conflict and non-conflict situations.
     An interaction. Relevancy scores and win scores are
recorded   on   individual and joint answer sheets and
behavioral interaction is tape-recorded and coded using a
specially designed coding system.   In addition to its
research uses (Birchler et. al., 1975;   Olson and Ryder,
1970; and Vincent et. al., 1975) the IMC has demonstrated
diagnostic potential by identifying ten unique styles of
couple interaction that are readily useful as relationship
typologies (Miller, 1975).
SAMPLE ITEM. Husband's vignette: A conflict has arisen
between Jack and Colleen following a party with friends.
During the party Jack talked to another woman, resulting in
his wife becoming very angry. Following the party, Colleen
angrily accuses Jack of intentionally ignoring her for the
entire evening and becomes argumentative.
     Wife's vignette: A conflict has arisen between Jack
and Colleen following a party with friends. During the
party, Jack becomes involved with another woman and ignores
his wife.   Colleen feels hurt and attempts to discuss her
feelings of being neglected but feels that she is not
understood.
     Questions: (a) Who is primarily responsible for the
problem?   (b) Have you had a similar problem? (c) Have you
known other couples who have similar problems?   (d) (for
husband) Should Jack be permitted to talk to another woman
at a party without Colleen becoming upset? (d) (for wife)
Should Jack be more attentive to his wife at parties?
LENGTH. Time: Individual Form 30 minutes, Joint Form 30
minutes. Items: 18.

AVAILABILITY. From NAPS-2 or from David Olson.
ABSTRACTED BY: David H. Olson
REFERENCES.

Birchler,G.R.   Weiss,R.L.   and   Vincent,J.P.
Multimethod   analysis   of   social   reinforcement   exchange
between maritally distressed and nondistressed spouse and
stranger   dyads.   Journal   of   Personality   and   Social
Psychology, 1975, 31, 349-360.

Gottman,J. Motarius,C. Markman,H. Bank,S. Voppi,B.
and Rubin,M.E. Phenomenological behavior-exchange models of
marital success.   Unpublished paper, Indiana University,
Department of Psychology, 1974.

Miller,B. Types of marriage interaction and their
relation to contextual characteristics in a sample of young
married   couples.   Unpublished   Ph.D.   dissertation,
University of Minnesota, 1975.

Olson,D.H.L.   and Ryder,R.G.   Inventory of marital
conflicts (IMC):   An experimental interaction procedure.
Journal of Marriage and the Family, 1970, 32, 443-448.

Shoemaker,M.E.   and Paulson,T.L.   Group   Assertive
Training for Mothers: A Family Intervention Strategy.
Unpublished manuscript, 1975.

Vincent,J.P.   Weiss,R.L.   and   Birchler,G.R.   A
behavioral analysis of problem solving in distressed and
non-distressed married and   stranger   dyads.   Behavior
Therapy, 1975, 6, 475-487.

POLGAR,S. and ROTHSTEIN,F. Conjugal Role Index

VARIABLES MEASURED.   Jointness and spouse dominance of
conjugal role relationship.
TEST DESCRIPTION. Six task participation questions, six
decision-making questions, and three social participation
questions. The measure combines two distinct components:
joint   versus   separated   roles, and among the latter,
husband-dominant   vs.   wife-dominant   relationships.
Jointness of roles is determined by the extent to which the
husband helps with household chores, on frequency of talking
to each other about their activities, and on the frequency
of making decisions jointly.
SAMPLE ITEM. I want you to tell me whether your (husband)
(boyfriend) ever helps you do any of these things. The
first one is the cooking. 0 = Does not help, 1 = Once in a
while 2 = Often.
LENGTH. Items: 15.
AVAILABILITY. From NAPS-2.
ABSTRACTED BY: Steven Polgar
REFERENCE.

Polgar,S.   and Rothstein,F.   Family   planning   and
conjugal roles in New York City poverty areas. Social
Science and Medicine, 1970, 4, 135-139.

PRATT,L.   Conjugal Organization Index

VARIABLES MEASURED.   (1)   Husband-wife companionship;   (2)
Conjugal power;   (3) Sex role differentiation.
TEST DESCRIPTION.   Data are obtained through personal
interview or questionnaire from husbands and wives, using a
pre-coded instrument with fixed answer categories.   The
coded responses are summed for each of the three dimensions
of conjugal organization.
SAMPLE ITEM. Who in your family has the responsibility for
each of the following: Is it the husband entirely, the
husband somewhat more than the wife, equally both the
husband and wife, the wife somewhat more than the husband,
the wife entirely, or neither the husband nor the wife?   A
list of seven areas of decision follows.
LENGTH.   Time: 10-15 minutes. Items: 24.
AVAILABILITY.   From NAPS-2.
ABSTRACTED BY: Lois Pratt
REFERENCES.
    Pratt,L. Conjugal organization and health. Journal of
Marriage and the Family, 1972, 34, 85-95.
    Pratt,L.   Family Structure and Effective Health
Behavior: The Energized Family. Boston: Houghton Mifflin
Company, 1976.

RAVICH,R.A.   Ravich Interpersonal Game/Test (RIG/T)

VARIABLES MEASURED. Patterns of husband-wife interaction:
competitive, alternating, dominant-submissive, and mixed.
TEST DESCRIPTION. The RIG/T is a simulation game consisting
of two model trains, each under the control of a member of
the couple. Points are scored by getting the trains to the
destination at the partner's end of the table in the
shortest possible time. The shortest route is partly over a
single track, so couples must coordinate their trains to
prevent them meeting head on. The alternate route is three
times longer than the direct route. Since each person's
decisions are interrelated with those of the other "...this
is not a psychological test, but an interactive test of
individuals as members of specific dyads." A computer
program is available to transform the raw data on route
selection, direction of motion, barrier use, and time per
trial onto a profile chart for the couple, from which each
of the patterns listed under Variables Measured can be
discerned.
SAMPLE ITEM. See above.
LENGTH. Time: 45 minutes. Items: 20 trips.
AVAILABILITY. Interpersonal Testing Corporation, 55 East
87th Street, New York, New York.
ABSTRACTED BY: Bruce Brown
REFERENCES.
    Liebowitz,B. and Black,M. The structure of the Ravich
Interpersonal Game/Test. Family Process, 1974, 13, 169-183.
    Ravich,R.A.   Game-testing in conjoint marital

psychotherapy. American Journal of Psychotherapy, 1968, 12, 29-38.

Ravich,R.A. The use of an interpersonal game test in conjoint marital psychotherapy. American Journal of Psychotherapy, 1969, 23, 217-229.

Ravich,R.A. A system of notation of dyadic interaction. Family Process, 1970, 9, 297-300.

Ravich,R.A. The marriage/divorce paradox. In Sager,C.W. and Kaplan,H.S. (Eds.) Progress in Group and Family Therapy. New York: Brunner/Mazel, 1972.

Ravich,R.A. Deutsch,M. and Brown,B. An experimental and clincial study of family decision-making processes. American Psychiatric Association: Psychiatric Report 20, 1966.

Ravich,R.A. Deutsch,M. and Brown,B. An experimental and clinical study of family decision-making processes. In Winter, W. and Ferreira,A. eds. Research in Family Interaction. Palo Alto, California: Science and Behavior Books, Inc., 1969, 302-303.

ROMAN,M. and BAUMAN,G. Interaction Testing

VARIABLES MEASURED. (1) Marital intelligence: defined as "the ability of the couple to solve problems drawn from an individual intelligence test;" (2) Marital decision-making e.g. dominance: defined as "the presence (selection) of one member's individual response in the absence of the other member's individual response."

TEST DESCRIPTION. Each member of the couple is tested individually in the standard manner; the couple is then brought together and the same items are re-administered to them jointly. To derive the marital intelligence (Interaction I.Q.), the Comprehension and Similarities subtests of the Wechsler-Bellevue Intelligence Scale (combining items from Forms I and II) are administered, and the protocol of the couple is scored as if it had been obtained from one individual. In addition to obtaining individual I.Q.s and an Interaction I.Q., a Potential I.Q. is derived which represents the maximum I.Q. the couple would have achieved had they consistently utilized the better of the two responses received in the individual spouse testings; and a Task Efficiency score is calculated by subtracting the Interaction I.Q. from the Potential I.Q. The reliability of Interaction I.Q. (using a split-half method) = .85.

Data on qualitative and quantitative marital decision-making processes are derived from comparing the Interaction I.Q. items with the individual I.Q. items. Dominance is scored when the couple response contains one member's individual response in the absence of the other's individual response. Combination is scored when elements of both members' responses, in whole or in part, are found in the interaction response. Emergence is scored for the presence of a new idea in the interaction response.

Reinforcement occurs when the same response is given by each individual and by husband and wife together.

The outcome of the decision-making process is also scored by assigning the symbols +, -, and 0 to each response: Plus is scored when the couple score for the item compares favorably with the individual scores. It is, therefore, used when the interaction score is better than one or both individual scores, and is at least as good as the better of the individual scores. The minus score is assigned when the interaction response is poorer than the better individual response.

SAMPLE ITEM. (Similarities Series): How are a cat and a mouse alike? (Comprehension Series): Why are shoes made of leather?

LENGTH. Time: 1 1/2 to 2 hours. Half-hour per each spouse (can be administered simultaneously if two testers), 3/4 to one hour per couple. Items: 44 (3 administrations).

AVAILABILITY. In Roman and Bauman, 1966b and from NAPS-2.

ABSTRACTED BY: Betty C. Meltzer

REFERENCES.

Bauman,G. and Roman,M. Interaction testing in the study of marital dominance. Family Process, 1966, 5, 230-242.

Bauman,G. et al. Interaction testing in the measurement of marital intelligence. Journal of Abnormal Psychology, 1967, 72, 489-495.

Bauman,G. Roman,M. Borello,J. and Meltzer,B. Interaction testing in the measurement of marital intelligence, in Grey,A. (Ed.) Man, Woman and Marriage. New York: Atherton Press, 1970. (Originally published in Journal of Abnormal Psychology, 1967, 72.)

Borello,J. Psychosocial factors related to reported marital adjustment and task efficiency. Ph.D. dissertation, Yeshiva University, 1966.

Horowitz(Ehrenberg),D. The relevance of individual interpersonal expectations, styles of response to provocation, and interaction factors to interpersonal behavior and satisfaction in marriage. Unpublished Ph.D. dissertation, New York University, 1969.

Roman,M. and Bauman,G. Interaction testing: a technique for the psychological evaluation of small groups, in Harrower,M. et al. Creative Variations in the Projective Techniques. Charles C Thomas, 1960.

Roman,M. and Bauman,G. Interaction Testing: Administration and Scoring Manual. (Mimeo), 1966.

Roman,M. Bauman,G. Borello,J. Meltzer,B. and Ehrenberg,D. Effect of change in patient status on marital interaction. Family Process, 1976, 12.

SCHNAIBERG,A. Nuclear Family Role Structure Index

VARIABLE MEASURED. Egalitarianism in nuclear family role structure.

TEST   DESCRIPTION.   The   index   covers   both
normative-attitudinal   and   behavioral   aspects   of   the
husband-wife relationship. The first portion of the index
covers the wife's acceptance or rejection of traditional
male-female   role   segregation   within   the   nuclear
family--e.g., on male decision-making, work separation,
irresponsibility of women, external working of women, etc.
The last portion deals with behavioral dimensions, relating
to the freedom of wives to engage in various non-traditional
activities: e.g., wearing of short dresses, shopping alone,
talking to strange men/women, going to parties alone, etc.
SAMPLE ITEM. Disapproves or mildly approves that males
should make decisions versus strongly approves that males
should make decisions.
LENGTH. Items: 19.
AVAILABILITY. In Schnaiberg, 1970a, 1970b, 1971.
ABSTRACTED BY: Allan Schnaiberg
REFERENCES.
    Schnaiberg,A. Rural-urban residence and modernism: a
study of Ankara province, Turkey. Demography, 1970a, 7,
71-85.
    Schnaiberg,A. Measuring modernism: theoretical and
empirical explorations. American Journal of Sociology,
1970b, 76, 399-425.
    Schnaiberg,A. The modernizing impact of urbanization:
a   causal   analysis.   Economic   Development and Cultural
Change, 1971, 20, 80-104.

STOKES,C.S. Family Role Structure

VARIABLES MEASURED. Conjugal role segregation (joint vs.
segregated role relations).
TEST DESCRIPTION. Subjects respond to 17 questions dealing
with   family   activities   and   decisions.   Five   response
categories are employed: Husband always, Husband more than
wife, Husband-wife the same, Wife more than husband, and
Wife always. Replies of Husband always or Wife always
represent a segregated reply and are assigned a weight of 3;
Husband more or wife more is given a score of 2;   Husband
and wife the same (a joint reply) is scored 1. Summing the
replies to all 17 items yields scores ranging from 17 to 51.
SAMPLE ITEM. Who keeps track of money and bills?
LENGTH. Time: 3-4 minutes. Items: 17.
AVAILABILITY. From NAPS-2.
ABSTRACTED BY: C. Shannon Stokes
REFERENCES.
    Stokes,C.S. Family structure and fertility: a social
demographic   study.   Ph.D.   dissertation, University of
Kentucky, 1969.
    Stokes,C.S. Family structure and socio-economic
differentials in fertility. Population Studies, 1973, 27,
295-304.

TOOMEY,D.M. Marital Power and Decision-Making Index

VARIABLES MEASURED. Marital power and decision-making.
TEST DESCRIPTION. Replies indicating that decisions are
shared are classified as joint. An affirmative response to
the question of whether the wife knows the husband's weekly
earnings is classified as joint. The score is the number of
joint responses.
SAMPLE ITEM. Who has control of the financial affairs of
the family?
LENGTH. Items: 3.
AVAILABILITY; In Toomey, 1971.
ABSTRACTED BY: Blair Nelson
REFERENCE.
     Toomey,D.M. Conjugal roles and social networks in an
urban working class sample. Human Relations, 1971, 24,
417-431.

WILKENING,E.A. Father-Centered Decision-Making Index

VARIABLES MEASURED. The extent to which family decisions
and behavior are controlled by the father.
TEST DESCRIPTION. Nine attitudinal and behavioral questions
pertaining to chores for children; age at which boys should
be free to make own decisions; extent to which husband
discusses certain farm matters with wife; extent to which
husband is influential in decisions to buy farm equipment,
household appliances and automobile; whether husband or
wife decides on children's spending money and recreation,
with or without consulting the children; whether children
have a separate bank account; and whether deed to farm is
in husband's name only. Some questions are asked of the
husband, some of the wife, and some of both.
SAMPLE ITEM. At what age should boys be entirely free to
make their own decisions?
LENGTH. Items: 12.
AVAILABILITY. In Wilkening, 1953, Appendix Table 5; also
see Wilkening, 1954.
REFERENCES.
     Wilkening,E.A. Adoption of improved farm practices as
related to family factors. Madison: University of
Wisconsin Agricultural Experimental Station Bulletin 183,
1953.
     Wilkening,E.A. Change in farm technology as related to
familism, family decision-making, and family integration.
American Sociological Review, 1954, 19, 29-36.

WILKENING,E.A.   and   BHARADWAJ,L.K.
Husband-Wife-Decision-Making Indexes

VARIABLES MEASURED. Decision making or power in respect to:
(1) Farm resource, (2) Farm operations, (3) Household
furnishing and maintenance, (4) Food and entertainment, (5)

Children's socialization.
TEST DESCRIPTION. A list of 18 test decisions covering farm
and household matters; five variables were obtained. The
wife is asked how the decisions were actually made and the
husband is asked how the decisions ought to be made. The
husbands' responses are designed to tap the norms of the
family and the wives' responses are designed to tap how
decisions are actually made.
SAMPLE ITEM.   Whether to buy or rent more farm land?
Husband decides and seldom discusses with wife, Husband
decides and usually discusses with wife, Husband and wife
usually decide together, Wife decides and usually discusses
with husband, Wife decides and seldom discusses   with
husband.
LENGTH. Time: 7 minutes. Items: 15.
AVAILABILITY. In Wilkening and Bharadwaj, 1967.
ABSTRACTED BY: Eugene A. Wilkening (modified)
REFERENCES.
       Wilkening, E.A.   and Bharadwaj, L.K.   Dimensions of
aspirations, work roles and decision-making of farm husbands
and wives in Wisconsin. Journal of Marriage and the Family,
1967, 29, 701-706.
       Wilkening, E.A.   and Bharadwaj, L.K.   Aspirations and
task involvement as related to decision-making among farm
husbands and wives. Rural Sociology, 1969, 33, 30-45.

WOLFE, D.M. Marital Authority Index

VARIABLES MEASURED. (1) Relative authority of husband and
wife, (2) Degree of shared authority in the family, (3)
Family authority types: autonomic, syncratic,   husband
dominant, wife dominant.
TEST DESCRIPTION. Eight questions concerning who makes the
final decision about: buying a car, buying life insurance,
buying a house, husband's job, wife's working, money spent
on food, what doctor to see, and where to go on a vacation.
The relative authority score is obtained by summation of the
numerical   codes   (see   sample item) across the eight
questions. The lower the relative authority score, the
greater the husband's authority; the higher the score, the
greater the wife's authority.   The degree of   shared
authority score is the number of questions answered "husband
and wife exactly the same." The family power typology is
obtained by cross tabulating the relative authority scores
by the shared authority scores. All families with scores
below 19 are classified as husband dominant, those with
scores above 29 as wife dominant. Of the remaining families
(those with relative authority scores in the middle or
equalitarian range), those with shared authority scores of 4
or more are classified as syncratic, whereas those with
shared authority scores of 3 or less (those who have equal
relative authority, but who do not share decisions) are
classified as autonomic.

SAMPLE ITEM. In every family somebody has to decide such
things as where the family will live and so on. Many
couples talk things over first, but the final decision often
has to be made by the husband or wife. For instance, who
usually makes the final decision about what car to get? (1)
Husband always, (2) Husband more than wife, (3) Husband and
wife exactly the same, (4) Wife more than husband, (5) Wife
always.
LENGTH. Items: 8.
AVAILABILITY. In Wolfe, 1959.
REFERENCE.
     Wolfe,D.M. Power and authority in the family. In
Cartwright,D. (Ed.) Studies in Social Power. Ann Arbor,
Michigan: Institute of Social Research, 1959, 99-117.

2. Task Performance (See also Subject Index)

ABELL,H.C. Homemaking Practices Adoption Scales

VARIABLES MEASURED. Adoption of scientific homemaking
practices.
TEST DESCRIPTION. Scalogram analysis is used to rank
housewives on a scale of homemaking practice adoption and
knowledge in four areas: (1) Foods and food groups that
homemakers felt should be included in family meals; (2)
Knowledge of foods that compose the basic seven food groups;
(3) Protective foods named in (2); (4) Foods and food
groups included in a 24-hour menu that had been served to
families. In addition, it was attempted to measure use of
food preservation methods, growing of vegetables at home,
and use of certain child-rearing, sewing, and nutritional
practices, but these were found not to scale.
SAMPLE ITEM. What types of food or foods do you feel should
be included in family meals?
LENGTH. Items: 7 for each of the four scales.
AVAILABILITY. In Abell, 1951.
REFERENCES.
     Abell,H.C. The differential adoption of homemaking
practices in four rural areas. Ph.D. dissertation, Cornell
University, 1951.
     Abell,H.C. The use of scale analysis in a study of the
differential adoption of homemaking practices. Rural
Sociology, 1952, 17, 161-167.

ALDOUS,J. and STRAUS,M.A. Task Differentiation Index

VARIABLES MEASURED. Relative extent to which husband or
wife performs household tasks.

TEST DESCRIPTION. Respondents indicate whether the husband
or the wife usually performs each of a list of 16 household
tasks. These tasks are divided between child-care tasks,
traditionally male tasks, and traditionally female tasks.
The respondent chooses one of the following response
categories: Wife only = 3; Wife, but husband sometimes
does = 2; Both, but wife more often than husband = 1; Both
exactly the same = 0; Both, but husband more often than
wife = 1; Husband, but wife sometimes does = 2; Husband
only = 3. The index is scored by adding the weights shown
in parenthesis and dividing by the number of items answered.
SAMPLE ITEM. See to it (or saw to it) that the children get
out of bed at the right time.
LENGTH. Items: 16.
AVAILABILITY. From NAPS-2.
ABSTRACTED BY: Bruce Brown.
REFERENCE.
    Aldous,J.   and   Straus,M.A.   Social   networks   and
conjugal roles: a test of Bott's hypothesis. Social
Forces, 1965, 44, 576-580.

ANGRIST,S.S. Wife's Post-Hospital Role Performance Measures

VARIABLES MEASURED. (1) Performance of the wife in the
following roles as reported by the husband: (a) Domestic
activity (5 items); (b) Social participation (9 items);
(c) Psychological behavior (32 items); (2) Husband's
expectations of wife's performance in social and domestic
behavior (10 items); and (3) The same questions answered by
the wife.
TEST DESCRIPTION. Interview questions asked of former
mental patients and their husbands. Scores are additive,
using arbitrary weights not reported. There are separate
scores for perfcrmance in each role and a total performance
index.
SAMPLE ITEM. NR.
LENGTH. Items: 50.
AVAILABILITY. In Angrist, 1960.
REFERENCES.
    Angrist,S.S. Some factors in the outcome of mental
hospitalization. Unpublished Ph.D. dissertation, Ohio
State University, 1960.
    Lefton,M. Angrist,S.S. Denitz,S. and Pasamanick,B.
Social class, expectations and performance of mental
patients. American Journal of Sociology, 1962, 68, 79-87.

BALLWEG,J. Household Task Performance Index

VARIABLE MEASURED. The extent to which selected household
tasks are performed by the husband, the wife, or hired help.
TEST DESCRIPTION. Respondents indicate the extent to which
12 household tasks are performed by the wife, husband, or
hired help within their own homes. Possible responses are:

Never,   Rarely,   Sometimes,   Frequently,   or   Always.   The
scoring procedure is designed to determine the percentage of
the   12   household tasks which receives each of the possible
responses. This is done individually for each of the task
performers,   i.e.,   wife,   husband,   or hired help.   For
example, what percentage of the household tasks does the
husband perform frequently?
SAMPLE ITEM. Household dusting.
LENGTH. Items: 12.
AVAILABILITY. In Ballweg, 1967.
ABSTRACTED BY: Bruce Brown
REFERENCE.
     Ballweg,J.   Resolution of conjugal role adjustment
after retirement. Journal of Marriage and the Family, 1967,
29, 277-281.

BLOOD,R.O.JR.   Division of Labor Index

VARIABLES MEASURED. Husband's and wife's household roles.
TEST DESCRIPTION. Subject is asked who does each of the
following household tasks: grocery shopping, getting the
husband's breakfast on weekdays, doing the evening dishes,
straightening the living room when company is coming,
repairing things around the house, mowing the   lawn,
shoveling the walk, keeping track of money and bills.
Scored by summation of response category weights. The lower
the score, the greater the tendency for the husband to do
household tasks.
SAMPLE ITEM. We should like to know how you and your
husband divide up some of the family jobs. Who does the
grocery shopping? (1) Husband always, (2) Husband more than
wife, (3) Husband and wife exactly the same, (4) Wife more
than husband, (5) Wife always.
LENGTH. Items: 8.
AVAILABILITY. In Blood, 1958.
REFERENCES.
     Hill,R.L. Family Development in Three Generations.
Cambridge, Massachusetts: Schenkman Publishing Company,
Inc., 1970.
     Michel,A. Working wives and family interaction in
French and American families.   International Journal of
Comparative Sociology, 1970, 11, 157-165.
     Silverman,W. and Hill,R.L.   Task   allocation   in
marriage in the U.S. and Belgium. Journal of Marriage and
the Family, 1967, 353-359.

BLOOD,R.O.JR. and HAMBLIN,R.L. Household Task Performance
Index

VARIABLE MEASURED. Proportion of household tasks performed
by husband and wife.
TEST DESCRIPTION. Husbands estimate how many hours a week
they spend doing each household task on a list of 12. Wives
make the same estimate for themselves.

SAMPLE ITEM. Doing the dishes; cooking meals.
LENGTH. Items: 12.
AVAILABILITY. From NAPS.
REFERENCES.
    Blood,R.O.Jr. and Hamblin,R.L.   The effect of the
wife's employment on the family power structure. Social
Forces, 1958, 36, 347-352.
    Mishler,E.G. and Waxler,N.E.   Interaction in Families.
New York: John Wiley and Sons, Inc., 1968.

BLOOD,R.O.JR. and WOLFE,D.M.   Task Participation Index and
Role Specialization Index.

VARIABLES MEASURED.   Relative extent of performance and the
division of labor in household task performance by husband
and wife.
TEST DESCRIPTION. Subject is asked who does each of a set
of eight tasks that most families perform (repair things
around the house, mow the lawn, shovel the sidewalk, keep
track of money and pay the bills, grocery shopping, make
husband's breakfast on workdays, straighten up the living
room when company is coming, wash dishes in the evening)
with response categories weighted from Husband always = 1 to
Wife always = 5. The Task Participation Index consists of
the sum of the responses to these eight items.   The Role
Specialization Index consists of the number of tasks
performed exclusively by the husband or the wife.
SAMPLE ITEM. We would like to know how you and your husband
divide up some of the family jobs. Here is a list of
different ways of dividing up jobs (subject is handed card
with the following response categories: (1) Husband always,
(2) Husband more than wife, (3) Husband and wife exactly the
same, (4) Wife more than husband, (5) Wife always).
LENGTH. Items: 8.
AVAILABILITY. In Blood and Wolfe, 1960.
REFERENCES.
    Aldous,J.   and Straus,M.A.   Social   networks   and
conjugal roles: a test of Bott's hypothesis. Social
Forces, 1966, 44, 576-580.
    Blood,R.O.Jr. The division of labor in city and farm
families. Marriage and Family Living, 1958, 20, 170-174.
    Blood,R.O.Jr.   Kinship   interaction   and   marital
solidarity. Merrill-Palmer Quarterly, 1969, 15, 171-184.
    Blood,R.O.Jr. and Wolfe,D.M. Husbands and Wives: The
Dynamics of Married Living. New York: Free Press of
Glencoe, 1960.
    Blood,R.O.Jr. and Wolfe,D.M. Negro-white differences
in blue-collar marriages in a northern metropolis. Social
Forces, 1969, 48, 59-64.
    Campbell,F.L. Family growth and variation in family
role structure.   Journal of Marriage and the Family, 1970,
31, 45-53.
    Granbois,D.H. and Willett,R.P. Equivalence of family
role measures based on husband and wife data. Journal of

Marriage and the Family, 1970, 31, 68-72.
    Michel,A.   Wife's   satisfaction   with   husband's
understanding   in   Parisian   urban   families.   Journal   of
Marriage and the Family, 1970, 32, 351-359.
    Mishler,E.G.   and Waxler,N.E.   Interaction in Families.
New York: John Wiley and Sons, Inc., 1968.
    Silverman,W.   and   Hill,R.L.   Task   allocation   in
marriage   in   the   United   States   and   Belgium.   Journal of
Marriage and the Family, 1967, 29, 353-359.

BURNS,M.S.A.   Women's Life Style Attitude Scale

VARIABLES MEASURED. Feelings with respect to a career or
traditional (motherhood) orientation.
TEST DESCRIPTION.   Females   are   asked   to   answer   for
themselves   and   males are asked to answer the statements as
they would prefer their future wife   or   living   partner   to
answer them.   The scale uses five-point Likert items.
SAMPLE ITEM. I would have a great deal of difficulty being
a mother and housewife 24 hours a day. Strongly agree = 1;
Agree = 2; Undecided = 3; Disagree = 4; Strongly disagree
= 5.
LENGTH. Items: 20.
AVAILABILITY. In Burns, 1974.
ABSTRACTED BY: Kersti Yllo
REFERENCE.
    Burns,M.S.A. Life styles for women, an attitude scale.
Psychological Reports, 1974, 35, 227-230.

BUXBAUM,J.   Marital Roles Questionnaire

VARIABLES MEASURED.   (1) Role changes after husband's
disability. (2) Degree of liking or disliking of role.
TEST DESCRIPTION. The same 15 items used to assess role and
role changes are also used to assess liking or disliking of
particular items. They are answered four times, once to
rate   frequency   of role performance of an item in a
retrospective report before disability and again to rate the
item after disability, and then once each for liking an item
before and after disability.   Each item is rated on a
7-point scale.   The role changes score is the sum of the
before-after differences. The liking score is the sum of
the relevant items.
SAMPLE ITEM. Fixing things around the house.
LENGTH. Items: 15.
AVAILABILITY. From NAPS-2.
ABSTRACTED BY: Thomas G. Sparhawk
REFERENCE.
    Buxbaum,J. Effect of nurturance of wives' appraisals
of their marital satisfaction and the degree of their
husbands' aphasia. Journal of Consulting Psychology, 1967,
31, 240-243.

DOWDALL,J.A.   Attitudes Toward   Married   Women's   Employment Scale

VARIABLE MEASURED.   Attitudes toward   the   employment   of married women under a variety circumstances.
TEST DESCRIPTION.   Five questionnaire items ask   whether   or not   and to what degree the respondent approves of a married woman holding a job under   each   of   five   conditions.   The conditions   specified   are   related   to   familial role obligations   (e.g.,   if   the   woman   has   small   children), economic   factors   (e.g.,   to   get   extra money to pay large expenses), and the woman's own needs (e.g.,   if   she   really wants   a   job).   Guttman scale analysis produced a scale in which respondents' scores range from zero to five, based   on the number of items approved.
SAMPLE ITEM.   Do you think it is all   right   for   a   married woman to have a job instead of only taking care of the house and the children while her husband provides for   the   family Yes,   No,   Unsure;   Do you feel strongly about it or not so strongly?
LENGTH.   Items: 5.
AVAILABILITY.   In Dowdall, 1974a and 1974b.
ABSTRACTED BY: Jean A.   Dowdall
REFERENCES.
    Dowdall,J.A.   Structural   and   attitudinal   factors associated   with   female   labor force participation.   Social Science Quarterly, 1974a, 55, 121-130.
    Dowdall,J.A.   Women's attitudes toward   employment   and family roles.   Sociological Analysis, 1974b, 35, 251-262.

HALLIDAY,J.R.   Home Management Goals Inventory

VARIABLES MEASURED.   The relative strength of four goals   in home management: (1) Social approval;   (2)Self-realization, to meet own expectations;   (3)   Happiness   and   harmony   in family   life;   (4)   Conditions   for   optimum development of individuals in family group.
TEST DESCRIPTION.   A forced-choice instrument which aims   to control the social desirability effect by arranging items in sets of four (tetrads).   Each tetrad consists of   two   pairs of   items   matched   on   an   empirically   determined   social desirability index.   The subjects are asked to   choose   from each tetrad one phrase which is most like themselves and one which is least like themselves.   Thus, the subjects who want to present themselves in a favorable light cannot merely say yes to all socially desirable statements   and   no   to   all undesirable ones as in a Yes, No, test.   Since the items are matched in social desirability, the subjects are   forced   to choose in terms of their end goal rather than their prestige value.   The test is scored   by   subtracting   the   number of "least   like"   answers   from   the   number   of   "most   like" responses for each goal.   Scores   for   any   one   goal   can therefore range from -16 to +16.

SAMPLE ITEM. Check which one of the following statements is most like you and which one is least like you: Would like people to think that I make the house look attractive. When I tidy things, I enjoy the sense of order even though I know they won't stay that way long. Think if all of us keep things where we can find them easily, there is less friction and unpleasantness generally. Think neatness and orderliness in the house contribute to our emotional well being.
LENGTH. Time: 10-20 minutes. Items: 16 tetrads.
AVAILABILITY. In Halliday, 1960.
REFERENCES.
    Halliday,J.R. A study to explore the goals of students taking a home management course (HMCD 332A) at Michigan State University and the development of an instrument for comparing goals among selected groups. M.A. Thesis, Michigan State University, 1960.
    Halliday,J.R. and Paolucci,B. An exploration of home management goals. Marriage and Family Living, 1962, 24, 68-73.

HECKSCHER,B.T. Mother's Housework Score

VARIABLE MEASURED. Mother's degree of involvement in housework.
TEST DESCRIPTION. A list of household tasks (excluding child rearing) is presented to the mother. The mother's housework score is the number of tasks performed only by herself out of 14 household tasks. The higher the number of tasks selected, the higher the mother's degree of involvement in housework.
SAMPLE ITEM. Who does the cooking? Mother = 1; Someone else = 0.
LENGTH. Items: 14.
AVAILABILITY. In Tancock, 1961 and from NAPS-2.
ABSTRACTED BY: Eruce Brown
REFERENCES.
    Heckscher,B.T. Household structure and achievement orientation in lower class Barbadian families. Journal of Marriage and the Family, 1967, 29, 521-526.
    Tancock,C.B. A study of household structure and child training in a lower class Barbadian group. Ph.D. dissertation, Graduate School of Education, Harvard University, 1961, 42-64.

KATELMAN,D.K. and BARNETT,L.D. Favorableness to Wife Working Index

VARIABLES MEASURED. Favorableness toward paid employment for married wcmen. Respondents are labelled either as traditional-oriented (not approving of employment)or as modern-oriented (approving).

TEST DESCRIPTION. An 11-item Likert scale.
SAMPLE ITEM. Gainful employment gives more prestige to a
woman than being a housewife. Five possible responses
ranging from "Strongly agree" to "Strongly disagree."
LENGTH. Items: 11.
AVAILABILITY. In Katelman and Barnett, 1968.
REFERENCE.
      Katelman,D.K. and Barnett,L.D. Work orientations of
urban, middle-class, married women. Journal of Marriage and
the Family, 1968, 30, 80-88.

KELLAR,B. Attitude Toward Any Homemaking Activity

VARIABLE MEASURED. Liking or favorableness toward any
activity which might be carried out in the house.
TEST DESCRIPTION. A generalized Thurstone-type attitude
scale which can be used to measure favorableness toward a
specific activity (for example, meal preparation, caring for
children) selected by the user of the test. Subjects are
asked to put a plus sign before each statement that
expresses their feeling about the referent activity. The
score assigned to a subject is the median of the scale
values of the items checked. There are two 45-item
alternate forms with equivalent scale and Q values. There
are also two parallel short forms, the items for which are
indicated by an asterisk in Exhibit 3-33 of Shaw and Wright
(1967).
SAMPLE ITEM. I like to do this better than anything else I
can think of (Scale value, 10.9).
LENGTH. Items: Form A, 45; Form B, 45.
AVAILABILITY. In Kellar, 1934; Shaw and Wright, 1967.
REFERENCES.
      Kellar,B. The construction and validation of scale for
measuring attitude toward any homemaking activity. Purdue
University Studies in Higher Education, 1934, 35, 47-63.
      Shaw,M.E. and Wright,J.M. Scales for the Measurement
of Attitudes. New York: McGraw-Hill, 1967, 126-129.

KING,K.   McINTYRE,J.   and   AXELSON,L.J.   Adolescent
Perception of Maternal Employment Scale

VARIABLE MEASURED. Adolescents' perceptions of maternal
employment as a threat to marital relationships.
TEST DESCRIPTION. A five-item Guttman scale derived from
earlier work by Axelson (1963). Scores range from 1 to 6;
a low score represents agreement with the items and
indicates that maternal employment is perceived as a threat
to the marital relationship.
SAMPLE ITEM. If a working wife earns more than her husband,
the husband should feel like a failure.
LENGTH. Items: 5.

AVAILABILITY. In King, McIntyre, and Axelson, 1968.
REFERENCES.
    Axelson,L.J. The marital adjustment and marital role
definition of husbands of working and non-working wives.
Journal of Marriage and the Family, 1963, 25, 189-195.
    King,K. McIntyre,J. and Axelson,L.J.   Adolescents'
views cf maternal employment as a threat to the marital
relationship. Journal of Marriage and the Family, 1968, 30,
633-637.

LAMOUSE,A.   Family Division of Labor Scale

VARIABLE MEASURED. Division of relative participation in
family tasks between husband and wife.
TEST DESCRIPTION. An interview schedule listing 14 family
tasks.   Those tasks are grouped into three areas:
traditional female tasks, traditional male tasks, and
"household tasks of a more technical kind or which need some
effort and thus may be more easily done by men." There are
six possible responses to each task item, and the possible
responses are scaled from 1 (Wife always performs task) to 5
(Husband always performs task). Mean scores are figured for
each of the three general areas.
SAMPLE ITEM.   Area: traditional female tasks.   Item:
shopping. Wife always = 1; Wife mostly but sometimes
husband = 2; Husband and wife alternately = 3; Both = 3;
Husband mostly but sometimes wife = 4; Husband always = 5.
LENGTH. Items: 14.
AVAILABILITY. In Lamouse, 1969.
REFERENCE.
    Lamouse,A. Family roles of women: a German example.
Journal of Marriage and the Family, 1969, 31, 145-152.

MARSHALL,H.R. and MAGRUDER,L. Family Practices in Areas of
Money Management Interview

VARIABLES MEASURED. Family practices in areas of money
management: (1) Planning the use of the family income; (2)
Decisions for and selection of purchases, (3) Control of the
family purse, (4) The use of banks and commercial financing;
(5) Financial records; (6) Provisions for the future;   (7)
Use of money to reward and punish children's behavior; (8)
Talking to children about money.
TEST DESCRIPTION. An open-ended interview form.   Weighted
scores are assigned to the responses on the basis of the
desirability of the practice. The possible range of scores
is 9 to 77 points.
SAMPLE ITEM.   Responses to the questions on planning
expenditures are given 2 to 5 points. "More points are
given for (a) a written plan, (b) covering most
expenditures, (c) planned by all family members, (d) that
was acceptable and was followed."

LENGTH. Time: 45 minutes. Items: 11 pages of interview
schedule.
AVAILABILITY. From authors.
REFERENCE.
     Marshall,H.R. and Magruder,L.   Relations between
parent money education practices and children's knowledge
and use of money. Child Development, 1960, 31, 253-284.

MCDONALD,A.P.Jr. Social-Domestic Work Factor of the Sex
Role Survey (SRS)

VARIABLE MEASURED. Support for the notion that men and
women should be involved in both domestic and social work.
TEST DESCRIPTION. A questionnaire where subjects "indicate
their agreement or disagreement with each item by circling a
number from +3 (I agree very much) to -3 (I disagree very
much). Ratings were converted to a 1 to 7 scale by adding a
constant of +4. No response and responses between +1 and -1
were assigned a score of 4."
SAMPLE ITEM. The ideal marriage is one in which the husband
and wife share equally in housework and outside work.
LENGTH. Items: SRS = 53, of which 11 deal with this
variable.
AVAILABILITY. In McDonald, 1974.
ABSTRACTED BY: Thomas G. Sparhawk
REFERENCE.
     McDonald,A.P.Jr. Identification and measurement of
multidimensional attitudes toward equality between the
sexes. Journal cf Homosexuality, 1974, 1, 165-182.

NELSON,H.Y. Wife Works Scale

VARIABLE MEASURED. Favorability towards wife working.
TEST DESCRIPTION. Subjects respond to the questionnaire by
circling Yes, No, or Undecided in response to nine
statements describing situations in which a wife might work
at each of three different stages of the family life cycle.
The situations of pressing economic necessity; raising
family standard of living modestly and educating children;
buying luxuries for the family; buying luxuries for the
wife; wife's skills needed in community; wife finds
housework boring, unfulfilling. A score is accumulated over
the 27 responses: 3 points for Yes; 2 points for
Uncertain; 0 points for No. Forms are worded differently
for males and females.
SAMPLE ITEM. If I find housework boring and monotonous I
think it is all right for me to find diversion in paid
employment outside our home: As long as we had no children
- Yes, No; After we had children but before they went to
school - Yes, Nc; After all our children were in school -
Yes, No.

LENGTH. Items: 27.
AVAILABILITY. From NAPS-2.
ABSTRACTED BY: Helen Y. Nelson
REFERENCES.
     Dennis,K. and Nelson,H.Y. Report of testing programs
1958-1960, Linton High School, Schenectady, 1959-1960 North
Syracuse and Spencerport Central Schools.   Unpublished
report to the Bureau of Home Economics Education, State
Education Department, Albany, New York, Undated.   The
Department of Community Service Education, Cornell
University, Ithaca, New York.
     Nelson,H.Y. and Goldman,P.R. Attitudes of high school
students and young adults toward the gainful employment of
married women. The Family Coordinator, 1969, 18, 251-255.

PROPPER,A.M. Household Chores Scale

VARIABLES MEASURED.   Frequency of performing household
chores.
TEST DESCRIPTION. Questionnaire respondents indicate how
frequently they perform common household chores by checking
one of three columns: (1) Once every two weeks, (2) Once or
twice a week, and (3) Once every day or two. If the chore
is performed less frequently than once every two weeks, no
column is checked. A score is calculated for each chore by
summing a 3-2-1-0 rating such that a high score indicates
high performance of household chores.
SAMPLE ITEM. Care for children, wash floor, vacuum.
LENGTH. Items: 23 items and blank spaces to list three
other chores.
AVAILABILITY. From NAPS-2.
ABSTRACTED BY: Alice M. Propper
REFERENCE.
     Propper,A.M. The relationship of maternal employment
to adolescent roles, activities, and parental relationships.
Journal of Marriage and the Family, 1972, 34, 417-421.

SEARLS,L.G. Enjoyment of Homemaking Tasks Rating Scale

VARIABLES MEASURED. Enjoyment of homemaking tasks.
TEST DESCRIPTION. Items on this scale are adapted from
those on the Perceived Mastery of Homemaking Scale. The
respondent indicates the extent of her enjoyment in the
performance of each task. The instrument is scored with a
weight of from 1 to 4 for each item.
SAMPLE ITEM. NR
LENGTH. NR.
AVAILABILITY. In Searls, 1965.
REFERENCES.
     Searls,L.G. Leisure role emphasis of college graduate
homemakers. M.S. Thesis, Carnegie Institute of Technology,
1965.
     Searls,L.G. Leisure role emphasis of college graduate

homemakers.   Journal of Marriage and the Family, 1966, 28,
77-82.
    Weigand,E. The use of time by full-time and part-time
homemakers in relationship to household ma ragement.   Cornell
Agricultural Experiment Station, 1954, memoir 330.

SEARLS,L.G. Perceived Mastery of Homemaking Rating Scale

VARIABLE MEASURED. Perceived mastery of homemaking.
TEST DESCRIPTION. A list of homemaking tasks covering the
following areas: family meals;   marketing and budgeting;
housing and furnishings; family clothing;   and child-care
and family relationships. A number of the task items are an
adaptation of items from Weyland's study of use of time for
homemaking activities (1954). For each task, the respondent
indicates the extent to which she desires improvement in her
homemaking activities, how close she approaches her "ideal
homemaker". The instrument is scored with a weight of from
one to four for each item.
SAMPLE ITEM. Planning well-balanced meals. Respondent
checks one of the following: Considerable improvement
desirable; Some improvement desirable;   Close to ideal;
Same as ideal.
LENGTH. Items: 18.
AVAILABILITY. In Searls, 1965 and from L.G. Searls.
REFERENCES.
    Searls,L.G. Leisure role emphasis of college graduate
homemakers.   Journal of Marriage and the Family, 1966, 28,
77-82.
    Weigand,E. The use of time by full-time and part-time
homemakers in relationship to household ma ragement.   Cornell
Agricultural Experiment Station, 1954, memoir 330.

TOOMEY,D.M. Domestic Tasks Performance Index

VARIABLES MEASURED. Sharing of domestic tasks.
TEST DESCRIPTION. Each spouse is asked whether he or she
carried out particular activities normally defined within
the cther's role. For wives, responses of Very often and
Often are classified as joint. For husbands, responses of
Sometimes are also tabulated as joint for ironing and
cooking and Rarely for doing the laundry. Scores are joint
responses.
SAMPLE ITEM. Wife does painting inside the house: Very
often, Often, Sometimes, Rarely, Never.
LENGTH. Items: Wife = 3; Husband = 6.
AVAILABILITY. In Toomey, 1971.
ABSTRACTED BY: Blair Nelson
REFERENCE.
    Toomey,D.M. Ccnjugal roles and social networks in an
urban working class sample. Human Relations, 1971, 24,
417-431.

UDRY,J.R. and HALL,M.   Role Segregation Index

VARIABLE MEASURED.   Marital role segregation.
TEST DESCRIPTION. A schedule of 25 items asking who does
various family activities. Husband and wife schedules are
scored separately and then summed.
SAMPLE ITEM. Who determines what job the husband should
take?   Husband always = 3; Wife always = 3; Husband more
than wife = 2; Wife more than husband = 2; Either husband
or wife, but separately = 1; Neither husband nor wife = 1;
Husband and wife together = 1.
LENGTH. Items: 25.
AVAILABILITY. In Udry, 1965.
REFERENCES.
     Bott,E. Family and Social Network. London: Tavistock
Publications, 1957.
     Udry,J.R. and Hall,M. Marital role segregation and
social networks in middle-class, middle-aged couples.
Journal of Marriage and the Family, 1965, 27, 392-395.

WILKENING,E.A.   and   BHARADWAJ,L.K.   Husband-Wife   Task
Involvement Indexes

VARIABLE MEASURED. Specialization of tasks or role
differentiation in farm families.
TEST DESCRIPTION. The wife is asked how the tasks are
actually allocated while the husband is asked how they
should be allocated between husband and wife.   Factor
analysis yielded five factors: (1) Field work and barn
chores, (2) Farm and home money matters, (3) Household
maintenance,   (4)   Domestic   tasks, and (5) Children's
socialization.
SAMPLE ITEM. Milking: Only the husband, Husband more than
wife, Husband and wife exactly the same, Wife more than
husband, and Only the wife.
LENGTH. Time: 7 minutes. Items: 15.
AVAILABILITY. In Wilkening and Bharadwaj, 1967.
ABSTRACTED BY: Eugene A. Wilkening (modified)
REFERENCES.
     Wilkening,E.A.   and Bharadwaj,L.K.   Dimensions   of
aspirations, work roles and decision-making of farm husbands
and wives in Wisconsin. Journal of Marriage and the Family,
1967, 29, 701-706.
     Wilkening,E.A.   and Bharadwaj,L.K.   Aspirations and
task involvement as related to decision-making among farm
husbands and wives. Rural Sociology, 1969, 33, 30-45.

3.   Sex Roles in General (See also Subject Index)

CAMERON,C.   Autonomy For Women Attitude Inventory

VARIABLE MEASURED.   Belief in women's right to be in charge
of   (to determine)   their own lives in areas such as
socialization, maternal and husband-wife   relationships,
vocational .choice and extent of involvement, sexuality and
legal matters.
TEST DESCRIPTION.   The inventory consists of 10 items (5
positive and 5 negative) on attitude toward autonomy for
women.   Respondents mark each item Strongly agree, Mildly
agree, Mildly disagree, and Strongly disagree.   Scoring is
on a seven-point scale (from Strong agreement = 7 to Strong
disagreement = 1).   Reverse scoring is used on anti-Autonomy
items and scores are summed.   Scores of 10-25 are called
conservative in attitude toward autonomy for women, 55-70
are liberal and 33-47 are moderate.   The test can be used on
males or females, and is especially useful for comparing the
attitudes of husbands and wives.
SAMPLE ITEM.   Women should subordinate their career to home
duties to a greater extent than men.   (Respondent indicates
extent of agreement/disagreement; this item is negative on
Autonomy.)
LENGTH.   Time: 5 minutes.   Items: 10.
AVAILABILITY.   In Arnott, 1972.
ABSTRACTED BY: Catherine Cameron   (formerly   Catherine
Cameron Arnott)
REFERENCES.
     Arnott,C.C.   Husbands' attitude and wives' commitment
to employment.   Journal of Marriage and the Family, 1972,
34, 673-684.
     Arnott,C.C.   Feminists and anti-feminists.   Sociology
and Social Research, 1973, 57, 300-306.

FAND,A.B.   Feminine Role Inventory

VARIABLE MEASURED.   Other (or traditional) orientation to
the feminine sex role versus self (or liberal) orientation.
TEST DESCRIPTION.   A series of role prescription and
performance statements dealing with women's needs, rights,
and obligations, to which subject responds on a 5-point
scale ranging from Strong agreement to Strong disagreement.
The other-oriented woman is defined as one who conceives of
herself primarily as the counterpart of the "significant
others" (husband and children) in her life, and who realizes
herself indirectly by fostering fulfillment of the others.
The self-oriented woman represents the achievement
orientation of American culture and strives to fulfill
herself directly by realizing her own potential.
     Half of the items represent other-orientation and half
self-orientation.   The   weighted   scores   for   the

self-orientation items are subtracted from the scores for the other-orientation items to obtain the total score. Consequently, negative total scores indicate self-orientation, positive scores, other-orientation. The test can also be administered with instructions to respond in terms of the "ideal woman," the "average woman," and "men's ideal woman," thus permitting the calculation of various self-ideal discrepancy scores.

SAMPLE ITEM. A husband who insists on being the sole provider will be more ambitious and responsible. Strongly agree, Agree, Don't know, Disagree, Strongly disagree.

LENGTH. Items: 34.

AVAILABILITY. In Fand, 1955.

REFERENCES.

Fand,A.B. Sex role and self concept. Ph.D. dissertation, Cornell University, 1955.

Steinmann,A. The vocational roles of older married women. Journal of Social Psychology, 1961, 54, 93-100.

Steinmann,A. A study of the concept of the feminine role of 51 middle-class American families. Genetic Psychology Monographs, 1963, 67, 275-352.

Steinmann,A. Levi,J. and Fox,D.J. Self-concept of college women compared with their concept of Ideal Woman and Men's Ideal Woman. Journal of Counseling Psychology, 1964, 11, 370-374.

GREENBERG,H. STRAIGHT,B. HASSENGER,W. and RASKA,W. Female Equalitarian Scale

VARIABLE MEASURED. Favorableness toward female equality.

TEST DESCRIPTION. A series of prescriptive statements concerning the status and roles of women. The subject is required to indicate extent of agreement on a five-point scale from Strongly agree to Strongly disagree. The item scores are summed to obtain a total score.

SAMPLE ITEM. Successful careers and successful homes cannot mix.

LENGTH. Items: 6.

AVAILABILITY. In Greenberg et al., 1961.

REFERENCE.

Greenberg,H. Straight,B. Hassenger,W. and Raska,W. Personality attitudinal differences between employed and unemployed married women. Journal of Social Psychology, 1961, 53, 87-96.

HILL,R.L. STYCOS,J.M. and BACK,K.W. Male Anxiety (Machismo) Index

VARIABLE MEASURED. Desire to prove masculinity.

TEST DESCRIPTION. A series of paired statements from which S chooses the more self-descriptive. High anxiety responses are given a score of 1. Low anxiety responses a score of 0. The index is computed by summing the scores--from 0 (low

machismo) to three (high machismo).
SAMPLE ITEM. Which of these 3 types of men would you like
to be?   A man who is lucky with women (first or second
choice, score 1), respected for religious faith (score 0),
or who can have many sons (score 0).
LENGTH. Items: 3.
AVAILABILITY. In Hill et al., 1959, 428-429.
REFERENCE.
    Hill,R.L. Stycos,J.M. and Back,K.W. The family and
population control: A Puerto Rican experiment in social
change. Chapel Hill: University of North Carolina Press,
1959.

HOFFMAN,L.W.   Traditional Sex Role Ideology Index

VARIABLE MEASURED.   Traditional-equalitarian   sex   role
ideology.
TEST DESCRIPTION. Role prescription items answered on a
four-point scale: Agree a lot, Agree, Disagree, Disagree a
lot. The greater the agreement, the greater the endorsement
of traditional sex role ideology.
SAMPLE ITEM. Raising children is much more a mother's job
than a father's.
LENGTH. Items: 5.
AVAILABILITY. In Hoffman, 1960.
REFERENCES.
    Angrist,S.S. Role conception as a predictor of adult
female roles. Sociology and Social Research, 1966, 50,
448-459.
    Hoffman,L.W. Effects of the employment of mothers on
parental power relations and the division of household
tasks. Marriage and Family Living, 1960, 22, 27-35.

KAMMEYER,K. Feminine Role Attitudes

VARIABLES MEASURED. Feminine role attitudes: (1) Normative
role behavior, (2) Beliefs concerning female personality
traits.
TEST DESCRIPTION. Attitudes toward normative role behavior
are described as attitudes toward "the proper kinds of
behavior for women in various spheres of life";   beliefs
concerning female personality traits are described as
"beliefs about the personality characteristics   of
psychological traits of women vis-a-vis men." There are two
scales; one for each of the above variables. (1) The first
scale is a set of five statements about feminine role
behavior (cut of eight items in the original questionnaire).
The scale was cut between scale types two and three; the
top three scale types are characterized as statements
endorsing   the   traditional feminine role   (Kammeyer
substituted the term traditional for Komarovsky's feminine
sex role, using feminine sex role as the generic term). For
this scale the response categories are combined uniformly

for all items in the scale analysis. (2) The second scale
is a set of eight items which form a Likert-type scale.
Subjects are given a total score by summing the arbitrary
weights assigned to the response categories: 1 for Agree, 2
for Somewhat agree, 3 for Disagree somewhat, and 4 for
Disagree. The range of total scores is from 8 to 32:
agreement with all items gives a score of 8; disagreement
with all equals 32. The traditional category includes
scores 8-20; the modern category includes scores 21-32.
SAMPLE ITEM. Normative role attitudes scale: In marriage,
the major responsibility of the wife is to keep her husband
and children happy. Personality traits belief scale: Women
are more emotional than men.
LENGTH. Items: 13.
AVAILABILITY. In Kammeyer, 1964.
REFERENCE.
    Kammeyer,K. The feminine role: An analysis of
attitude consistency. Journal of Marriage and the Family,
1964, 3, 295-305.

KANDO,T.M. Sex Role Strain Scale

VARIABLE MEASURED. Sex role strain, measured as the
discrepancy between (1) The extent of an individual's
support of traditional sex ascriptions and (2) The extent to
which individuals in fact abide by these ascriptions.
TEST DESCRIPTION. The items in this scale represent six
different aspects of traditional sex roles: (1) Attitudes,
(2) Personality characteristics, (3) Skills and
responsibilities, (4) Occupations, (5) Structural roles, (6)
Gender attributes. The scale is divided into two parts.
The first part is designed to measure the extent of an
individual's endorsement of traditional sex ascriptions (the
"ought" scale). The subject's responses are scored on a
disagree-agree continuum with a higher score indicating
greater endorsement of traditional sex ascriptions. The
second part (the "fact" scale) refers to the individuals
report of his actual behavior. Scoring for this part of the
scale is the same as for the first part with a high score
indicating high masculinity and a low score indicating
femininity. Sex role strain is measured by the discrepancy.
between the subject's average scores on the two parts of the
scale.
SAMPLE ITEM. From the "ought" scale: Women must have a
greater desire tc have children than men. Strongly Agree =
4, Agree = 3, Disagree = 2, and Strongly disagree = 1. From
the "fact" scale: I (would) love to have children.
Strongly Agree = 4, Agree = 3, Disagree = 2, and Strongly
Disagree = 1.
LENGTH. Items: 84.
AVAILABILITY. Twenty items in Kando, 1972, and from NAPS-2.
REFERENCE.
    Kando,T.M. Role strain: a comparison of males,
females, and transexuals. Journal of Marriage and the

Family, 1972, 34, 459-464.
    Kando,T.M.   Males,   females,   and   transexuals: a
comparative study of sexual conservatism. Journal of
Homosexuality, 1974, 1, 45-64.

KIRKPATRICK,C.   Feminism Scale

VARIABLE MEASURED.   Attitudes toward feminism.
TEST DESCRIPTION.   Subject   checks   the   statements   he/she
agrees with, and double-checks statements he/she accepts and
feels strongly about.   A score is derived by assigning a
weight   of   +1   to a feminist proposition, -1 to an
anti-feminist proposition.   The score is the sum of the
feminist and anti-feminist propositions accepted.   Scores
can be computed for four categories of feminist belief
(economic,   domestic,   political-legal,   and conduct and
status) as well as the total score.
SAMPLE ITEM.   Women have the right to compete with men in
every sphere of economic activity.
LENGTH. Items: 80.
AVAILABILITY.   In Kirkpatrick, 1936b;   Shaw   and   Wright,
1967.
REFERENCES.
    Kirkpatrick,C.   A comparison of generations in regard
to   attitudes   toward   feminism.   Journal   of   Genetic
Psychology, 1936a, 39, 343-361.
    Kirkpatrick,C.   The construction of a belief-pattern
scale for measuring attitudes toward feminism. Journal of
Social Psychology, 1936b, 7, 421-437.
    Kirkpatrick,C.   An   experimental   study   of   the
modification of social attitudes.   American Journal of
Sociology, 1936c, 41, 649-656.
    Kirkpatrick,C.   Inconsistency in attitudinal behavior
with   special   reference   to   attitudes   towards   feminism.
Journal of Applied Psychology, 1936d, 20, 535-552.
    Kirkpatrick,C.   The   measurement   of   ethical
inconsistency in marriage.   International Journal of Ethics,
1936e, 46, 444-460.
    Kirkpatrick,C.   Measuring attitudes toward feminism.
Sociology and Social Research, 1936f, 20, 512-526.
    Shaw,M.E. and Wright,J.M. Scales for the Measurement
of Attitudes. New York: McGraw-Hill, 1967.

LAKIN,M.   Female Role Attitudes Test

VARIABLES MEASURED.   Positive or negative attitude toward
five   aspects   of   the   female   role: (1)   Parental
relationships, (2) Role acceptance, (3) Felt adequacy, (4)
Psychosexual adjustment, (5) Motherliness.
TEST DESCRIPTION.   Ten picture interpretation cards (two for
each   role   aspect).   Stories   are   scored   either: (1)
plus--positive, affectively toned interaction depicted; (2)
zero--neutral or ambivalent, affectively toned interaction

depicted, or irrelevance; (3) minus--negative, affectively
toned interaction depicted. Thematic interpretation is also
possible.
SAMPLE ITEM. Card 2. A young woman sits knitting upon a
park bench. She is usually seen as pregnant. The
expression on her face is open to diverse interpretation.
LENGTH. Items: 10.
AVAILABILITY. Cards are described in Lakin, 1957.
REFERENCE.
    Lakin,M. Assessment of significant role attitudes in
primiparous mothers by means of a modification of the TAT.
Psychosomatic Medicine, 1957, 19, 50-60.

LAUMANN,E.O. Traditional Marital Role Relations Index

VARIABLE MEASURED. Traditionalism of sex roles within
marriage.
TEST DESCRIPTION. "Traditionalism" in marital roles is
measured by the sum of a respondent's responses to three
attitudinal questions. The respondent is asked to rate each
question on a four-point scale: Disagree strongly, Disagree
somewhat, Agree somewhat, Agree strongly. The test is
designed to separate out those individuals who see clearly
defined roles for each sex within marriage from those who do
not sex-type familial tasks.
SAMPLE ITEM. Most of the important decisions in the life of
the family should be made by the man of the house.
LENGTH. Items: 3.
AVAILABILITY. In Laumann, 1973.
ABSTRACTED BY: Lynn Pettler
REFERENCES.
    Laumann,E.O. Bonds of Pluralism. New York:
Wiley-Interscience, 1973.
    Laumann,E.O. and House,J.S. Living room styles and
social attributes: the patterning of material artifacts in
a modern urban community. Sociology and Social Research,
1970, 54, 321-342.

MEIER,H.C. Feminine Social Equality H-Scale (FSE)

VARIABLE MEASURED. Favorable attitude toward equalitarian
feminine social roles.
TEST DESCRIPTION. The scale was developed from data
obtained in two survey samples. The scale consists of seven
contrived items each of which consists of three response
items. Each response item is dichotomously coded 1 or 0
(Agree-Disagree or Approve-Disapprove), then each contrived
item is coded 1 or 0 based on the majority of 1's or 0's in
the response set. The respondent's scale score is the sum
of coded scores for the contrived items in the scale. Scale
scores may vary from 0 to 7.

SAMPLE ITEM. It is all right for women to participate in
local politics, such as in precinct work; but they should
not hold the more important offices in government. Agree =
1, Disagree = 0.
LENGTH. Items: 18, combined into 7 contrived items.
AVAILABILITY. In Meier, 1972.
REFERENCE.
     Meier,H.C.   Mother-centeredness and college youths'
attitudes toward social equality for women: some empirical
findings. Journal of Marriage and the Family, 1972, 34,
115-121.

STEINMANN,A.   and FOX,D.J.   Maferr Inventory of Female
Values

VARIABLE MEASURED. Relative importance of familistic as
compared to individualistic values.
TEST DESCRIPTION. The Inventory consists of 34 statements
to which the respondent indicates the strength of his or her
agreement or disagreement on a five-point scale ranging from
Completely agree to Completely disagree. The midpoint is I
have no opinion.
     Seventeen of the 34 items are considered to allow a
respondent to delineate a family-oriented woman who sees her
own satisfaction taking second place to that of her husband,
and family responsibilities taking precedence over any
potential personal occupational activity.   The other 17
items delineate a self-achieving woman who considers her own
satisfactions equally important with those of her husband
and family.   The score on the inventory represents the
difference in strength of agreement to the intra-family and
extra-family items.   Scores range from -68 (passive
position) to +68 (active position).
     The Inventory may be given in several forms: the
respondent's own feelings about self, ideal woman, man's
ideal woman as perceived by a woman, and man's ideal woman
as perceived by a man.
SAMPLE ITEM. Unless single, women should not crave personal
success but be satisfied with their husbands' achievements.
LENGTH. Items: 34.
AVAILABILITY. In Steinmann and Fox, 1966.
ABSTRACTED BY: Blair Nelson
REFERENCES.
     Steinmann,A. and Fox,D.J. Male-female perceptions of
the female role in the United States. Journal of
Psychology, 1966, 64, 265-276.
     Steinmann,A. and Fox,D.J.   Attitudes toward women's
family role among black and white undergraduates. The
Family Coordinator, 1970, 19, 363-368.

C. INTERPERSONAL COMPETENCE

1. Adaptability, Creativity, Flexibility (See also Subject Index)

ALDOUS,J.   Husband's and Wife's Communication Index

VARIABLES MEASURED.   (1) Extent to which the husband talked
with his wife about a series of problems and (2) Husbands'
reports on how often their wives talked with them about a
series of problems.
TEST DESCRIPTION. Long, semi-structured interviews produce
indications of the extent to which the husband talks with
his wife about a series of problems: feeling depressed,
health problems, work problems, money problems, and problems
with relatives.   The Wife's Communication Index   also
includes an item on problems with children. The index is
the summed weights of the responses divided by the number of
problems the respondent is reported to have had.
SAMPLE ITEM. Work problems: Never = 0, Seldom = 1, Half
the time = 2, Usually = 3, Always = 4.
LENGTH. Items: Husband Index = 5, Wife Index = 6.
AVAILABILITY. See Aldous, 1969.
REFERENCE.
      Aldous,J. Wives' employment status and lower-class men
as husband-fathers: support for the Moynihan thesis.
Journal of Marriage and the Family, 1969, 31, 469-476.

BRIM,O.G.JR. GLASS,D.C. and LAVIN,D.E.   Parent Decision
Process Test

VARIABLE MEASURED. Decision or problem-solving processes.
TEST DESCRIPTION. The theoretical rationale underlying this
test views problem-solving decisions as having the following
phases: (1) Identification of the problem, (2) Obtaining
information, (3) Producing solutions, (4) Evaluation of
solutions, (5) Strategy selection, and (6) Execution of the
strategy and subsequent reformulation. The test measures
behavior in phases 4, 5, and 6. Measures for phase 4
(evaluation) are called matrix variables, and those for
phases 5 and 6 (selection of strategy) are called strategy
variables.
      The matrix variables are: (1) Number of outcomes
perceived for each possible action, (2) Desirability of
outcomes as viewed by subject, (3) Extremity of   the
desirability rating (either highly desirable or highly
undesirable), (4) Probability of the outcome occurring, (5)
Extremity of probability of occurrence, (6) Temporal range
of results (whether long- or short-range outcomes are
anticipated), (7) Extremity of temporal range, (8) E,

expected utility of alternatives (product of the desirability of alternatives and their subjective probability of occurrence), (9) E', a modified expected utility of alternatives index, which includes time (rapidity) of expected occurrence of the effect in the equation, (10) Content of outcome alternatives (three content analysis variables are suggested: internal versus external results, originality, and global versus specific results).

The strategy variables are: (1) number of alternatives selected for performance, (2) rank order of the alternative actions, (3) sequence of performance of alternatives selected, (4) contingency of actions (according to success or failure of prior actions).

A third group of scores relates the rank order of alternative actions to the expected utility measures: (1) Agreement score (S) -- a measure of agreement (Kendall's S) between the rank order of alternatives selected for action and the rank order of the individual's expected utility indices for the alternatives; (2) Agreement score (S') -- identical with subject except for use of E' to rank the expected utilities of alternatives.

The test is usable in a variety of decision areas, such as interpersonal problems, economic decisions, career choices, and family planning. This abstract refers to its use in assessing parental decisions in four child-rearing problems of deviations from socialization norms by a 10-year-old son: masturbation, disobedience, refusal to do homework, and stealing. In this form, it consists of four eight-page booklets, one for each problem. Page 1 of each booklet describes the problem. Each of the next six pages presents a possible action; the subject is asked to list the possible consequences of the six actions and to rate each consequence for desirability, probability, and time of occurrence. On the eighth page, subject is asked to state which of the six actions he/she believes best and to rank the six actions in order of preference.
SAMPLE ITEM. Description of stealing problems and one alternative action.

SAMPLE ITEM: For some time now in a certain family a boy about 10 years old has been stealing things from the local five-and-ten. No one but his parents knows about it. Suppose that you were the parent faced with this situation. On the following pages are 6 different actions which you as a parent might take. Each action is listed on a separate page. You are asked to do 2 things: (1) evaluate each action by filling in the boxes on that page, (2) when you have evaluated all 6 actions, decide which action is best.

This is an ACTION a parent might take . . . NUMBER 1. IGNORE IT: DO NOTHING ABOUT IT.

	(i)	(ii)	(iii)

A. What would be some of the *results* if you took this action? Space is provided on the right to write in as many as three results if you wish to. Write only one result in each box.

B. What are the *chances* that the results written in above would happen?

(i)
___Highly probable
___Probable
___About half and half
___Improbable
___Highly improbable

(ii)
___Highly probable
___Probable
___About half and half
___Improbable
___Highly improbable

(iii)
___Highly probable
___Probable
___About half and half
___Improbable
___Highly improbable

C. How much would you *want* these results to happen?

(i)
___Strongly desire
___Desire
___Don't care either way
___Do not desire
___Strongly do not desire

(ii)
___Strongly desire
___Desire
___Don't care either way
___Do not desire
___Strongly do not desire

(iii)
___Strongly desire
___Desire
___Don't care either way
___Do not desire
___Strongly do not desire

D. How soon would these results *begin to happen?*

(i)
___Within a week
___A week to 6 months
___6 months to 1 year
___1–5 years
___5 years or more

(ii)
___Within a week
___A week to 6 months
___6 months to 1 year
___1–5 years
___5 years or more

(iii)
___Within a week
___A week to 6 months
___6 months to 1 year
___1–5 years
___5 years or more

LENGTH. Time: 1 1/2 hours for one S, 2 hours when filled
out jointly by couple. Items: 84-228, depending on the
number of consequences listed by S.
AVAILABILITY. In Brim et al., 1962.
REFERENCE.
    Brim,O.G.Jr. Glass,D.C. and Lavin,D.E. Personality
and Decision Process: Studies in the Social Psychology of
Thinking. Stanford, California: Stanford University Press,
1962.

CROUSE,B.   KARLINS,M.   and   SCHRODER,H.M.   Integrative
Complexity In Marriage Index.

VARIABLE MEASURED. Integrative complexity within the domain
of marriage, or "the ability of the individual to be
adaptive and flexible in dealings with his/her spouse."
TEST DESCRIPTION. A three-item sentence completion test,
modeled after Schroder's Paragraph Completion Inventory
(1967), which is a measure of integrative complexity at a
general interpersonal level. The items in the present
measure are specific to the husband-wife relationship. The
subject is asked to write three sentence responses to each
of the three sentence stems, each of which is presented for
90 seconds. Responses are scored on a seven-point scale.
The scale represents a continuum of low to high levels of
integrative complexity, as given in Schroder, Driver, and
Streufert, 1967.
    Responses are scored along a seven-point scale. "The
scale represents a continuum from low to high levels of
integrative complexity." Four nodal points (1, 3, 5, and 7)
and three transitional points (2, 4, and 6) are used. The
rater assigns a score value of 1 (low integration) if he
feels "that the response could be generated by a single
fixed rule, that no alternative interpretations were
considered, and that subtle conditional changes would
produce no changes in the response." A value of 3 (medium
low integration) is assigned to a response that clearly
represents the availability of alternate rule structures for
perceiving that event. To be assigned a value of 5 (medium
high integration) the response "must give evidence not only
of alternative interpetations but also of the use of
comparison rules for considering the joint as opposed to the
conditional outcome of these different perceptions."
Finally, responses are given a 7 rating (high integration)
if they state or imply that alternative perceptions occurred
and were compared, and also "indicate that the outcomes of
various comparisons can be considered in producing causal
statements about the functional relations between 'ways of
viewing the world.'"
SAMPLE ITEMS. (Sentence stems) When a husband and wife
quarrel...; Marital doubt...; When my mate does not agree
with me, I...

LENGTH. Items: 3; Responses: 9.
AVAILABILITY. In Crouse, Karlins, and Schroder, 1968.
REFERENCES.
    Crouse,B. Karlins,M. and Schroder,H.M. Conceptual
complexity and marital happiness. Journal of Marriage and
the Family, 1968, 30, 643-646.
    Schroder,H.M. Driver,M. and Streufert,S. Human
Information Processing. New York: Holt, 1967.

DENTLER,R.A. and PINEO,P. Personal Growth in Marriage
Index

VARIABLE MEASURED. Personal growth in marriage.
TEST DESCRIPTION. Subject responds to a checklist of items
under the general question: What have you gained from the
marriage? Nine-item index gives equal weight to each part
of the checklist.
SAMPLE ITEM. Made my life more interesting.
LENGTH. Items: 9.
AVAILABILITY. In Dentler and Pineo, 1960.
REFERENCES.
    Burgess,E.W. and Wallin,P. Engagement and Marriage,
2nd ed. New York: Lippincott, 1953, 507-557.
    Dentler,R.A. and Pineo,P. Sexual adjustment, marital
adjustment and personal growth of husbands: a panel
analysis. Marriage and Family Living, 1960, 22, 45-48.

FELDMAN,H. and RAND,M.E. Egocentrism-Altercentrism Rating
Scale for Husband-Wife Interaction.

VARIABLES MEASURED. Egocentrism (self-concern with no
concern for the other), cocentrism (concern for self and
other), altercentrism (denial of self in concern for needs
of the other), and outcome (win, lose, or compromise) of a
contrived conflict situation.
TEST DESCRIPTION. Husband and wife participate in a six
minute tape-recorded role-playing situation. Instructions
are given separately and spouses are unaware of the
conflicting nature of the instructions. Subject's
statements are categorized as being egocentric, cocentric or
altercentric. A scorable unit is defined as a statement by
P (person) preceded and succeeded by a scorable statement by
O (other). Since improvisations yield from three to fifteen
scorable statements, the percentage of statements in each
category is reported rather than the number.
SAMPLE ITEM. See above.
LENGTH. Time: 6 minutes. Items: 1 role-playing
situation.
AVAILABILITY. In Feldman and Rand, 1965.
REFERENCE.
    Feldman,H. and Rand,M.E. Egocentrism-altercentrism in
the husband-wife relationship. Journal of Marriage and the
Family, 1965, 27, 386-391.

HILL,R.L. Wife's Self-Sufficiency Score

VARIABLE MEASURED. Self-sufficiency of the wife while her
husband was in the army.
TEST DESCRIPTION. Responses to open-ended questions about
life during the separation are categorized and assigned
weights. Scores derived by summing the weights of the items
subject mentions.
SAMPLE ITEM. Managed well without a husband.   (weight, 1)
LENGTH. Items: 6.
AVAILABILITY. In Hill, 1949.
REFERENCE.
      Hill,R.L. Families under Stress: Adjustment to the
Crises of War Separation and Reunion. New York: Harper,
1949.

KARLSSON,G. Adaptability Indexes

VARIABLE MEASURED. Adaptability, defined as the ability to
adjust to different situations without difficulties.
TEST DESCRIPTION. A multiple-choice questionnaire.   There
are three types of items: (1) Items on adjustment in life
situations other than marriage -- childhood, work, and so
forth; (2) Items from the psychopathic deviate scale of the
MMPI; (3) Ratings of self and mate on personality and
interactional traits thought to be related to adaptability.
Scoring weights take into account the relation between the
various items and the marital satisfaction scores; items
are weighted differently for men and women. The items are
combined into three indexes: (1) Limited adaptability
index, composed of items generally agreed to be indicative
of adaptability;   (2) Extended adaptability index, composed
of items about which there was some doubt of their relation
to adaptability;   (3) Combined adaptability index, the sum
of (1) and (2).
SAMPLE ITEM. Type 3: Demonstrative, spouse: Has the trait
markedly;   Has the trait considerably;   Has the trait
somewhat; Has the trait a little; Has the trait not at
all.
LENGTH. Items: Limited adaptability, 8;   Extended
adaptability; 4; Combined adaptability, 12.
AVAILABILITY. In Karlsson, 1951, 126-127.
REFERENCE.
      Karlsson,G.   Adaptability and Communication in
Marriage: A Swedish Predictive Study of Marital
Satisfaction. Uppsala: Almquist and Wiksells, 1951.

KIEREN,D. and TALLMAN,I. Spousal Adaptability Index

VARIABLE MEASURED. Adaptability (ability to cope) in
spousal relations. Adaptability is composed of three
components: flexibility, empathy, and motivation.

TEST   DESCRIPTION.   The   instrument   consists   of   18
problem-solving   situations.   The   situations   are:
disagreements about television, use of the car, getting
things done around the house, children's schoolwork, bedtime
for spouses, church attendance, amount of affection
expressed   to   or   by   spouse,   unwillingness to discuss
problems, irritating personal habits of self or spouse,
husband's behavior at social gatherings, sexual relations,
saving money, balancing the checkbook, and wife's cooking.
The subject is asked to recall or is asked a question about
one of the problem-solving situations. The subject is then
asked questions designed to elicit responses which are rated
according to the three adaptability components. Scores for
each of the component parts range from 1 to 4 with the final
score representing a mean for all answered questions.
SAMPLE ITEM. Do you ever disagree about your husband's
behavior at social gatherings? What happened the last time?
Flexibility: a. What did you do? b. Do you always do the
same thing when this happens? c. What other things do you
do? Empathy: Why do you think your husband/wife acted the
way he/she did? Motivation: a. How would you like to have
your husband/wife act when this occurs? b. What can you do
to get him/her to act this way? c. Is there anything else
you think can be done?
LENGTH. Items: 18.
AVAILABILITY. From NAPS-2.
REFERENCES.
     Henton,J.   Problem   Solving   through   Conflict   in
Marriage.   Ph.D.   dissertation,   University   of Minnesota,
1970.
     Kieren,D. and Tallman,I. Adaptability: a measure of
spousal problem-solving. Technical Report No. 1, Minnesota
Family Study (mimeographed), 1971.
     Kieren,D. and Tallman,I. Spousal adaptability: an
assessment of marital competence. Journal of Marriage and
the Family, 1972, 34, 247-256.
     Tallman,I. Adaptability: a problem-solving approach
to assessing child-rearing practices. Child Development,
1961, 32, 651-668.
     Tallman,I. Spousal role differentiation and the
socialization of severely retarded children. Journal of
Marriage and the Family, 1965, 27, 37-42.

STANTON,H.R.   and LITWAK,E.   Interpersonal Competence I.
(Short Form). Autonomy

VARIABLES MEASURED. Interpersonal competence, specifically,
autonomy, empathy, and creativity.
TEST DESCRIPTION. A series of role-playing scenes with the
E playing one of the roles. Raters score subject on 20
specific points (e.g., dogmatic -- None, Maybe, Some, Much).
Ratings for each aspect of interpersonal competence are
summed.

SAMPLE ITEM. Parrying an interfering parent. Autonomy:
The E acts role of parent. Spouse of subject is criticized.
subject is treated like a child, and is put in the wrong.
LENGTH. Items: 3 role-playing scenes.
AVAILABILITY. From authors.
REFERENCES.
        Back,K.W. and Stycos,J.M. The survey under unusual
conditions.   Monographs   of   the   Society for Applied
Anthropology, 1959, Whole No. 1.
        Stanton,H.R. Back,K.W. and Litwak,E. Role playing in
survey research.   American Journal of Sociology, 1956, 62,
172-176.
        Stanton,H.R. and Litwak,E. Toward the development of
a short form test of interpersonal competence. American
Sociological Review, 1955, 20, 668-674.

STANTON,H.R. and LITWAK,E.   Interpersonal Competence II.
Creativity

VARIABLE MEASURED. Creativity, defined as novelty   of
response, in two standardized role-playing situations.
TEST DESCRIPTION. Role-playing situations used to elicit
behavior scored for creativity: (1) Husband and wife
attempt to make a bashful country cousin feel at home, (2)
Couple attempt to keep boss near them at a party and away
from a competitor. A creative or novel response requires
that they ask the cousin for help in scene (1) and that they
remain silent in (2). The E played the role of the third
person in both cases, and rewarded the novel response and
indicated unrest with all other more conventional responses.
Os score the number of appropriate responses made by husband
and wife. The couple is scored in two ways: (1) Addition
of the husband's and wife's creativity scores for a total
score, and (2) Relational measure of creativity for the
couple computed by dividing the wife's creativity score into
the husband's to give an index or relative score of the
relative dominance of husband's creativity over that of the
wife.
SAMPLE ITEM. Entertaining a bashful young cousin just
arrived from the ccuntry.
LENGTH. Time: 8 minutes per scene. Items: 2 scenes.
AVAILABILITY. Frcm authors.
REFERENCES.
        Back,K.W. and Stycos,J.M. The survey under unusual
conditions.   Monographs   of   the   Society for Applied
Anthropology, 1959, Whole No. 1.
        Burgess,E.W. and Wallin,P. Engagement and Marriage.
New York: Lippincott, 1953.
        Litwak,E. Count,G. and Haydon,E.M.   Group structure
and interpersonal creativity as factors which reduce errors
in the prediction of marital adjustment.   Social Forces,
1960, 38, 308-315.
        Stanton,H.R. Back,K.W. and Litwak,E. Role playing in
survey research.   American Journal of Sociology, 1956, 62,

172-176.

2. Empathy, Identification (See Also Subject Index)

BUERKLE,J.V. and BADGLEY,R.F.   Yale Marital Interaction Battery

VARIABLES MEASURED. (1) Reciprocal role-taking (i.e., viewing the situation from spouse's position), (2) Sympathy for spouse's expectations, (3) Actual role-playing in conformity with spouse's desires, (4) Altruism.
TEST DESCRIPTION. Forty behavior sequences involving role conflict, with four choices for each, whose order indicates: (1) Absence of all variables, (2) The spouse's role is taken but no sympathy is expressed and action is in terms of subject's own set, (3) Role-taking and qualified sympathy for position so that action is in compliance with spouse's set, and (4) Symbolically taking spouse's role, full sympathy with spouse's set, and role-playing in terms of spouse's expectation. Parallel forms for husband and wife.
    Responses can be dichotomized into "egoistic" (choices 1, 2) and "altruistic" (choices 3, 4) answers. Factor analysis of 17 items using this classification revealed the following factors:

	Factor No.	
Factor	H	W
Resistance to W's dominance	I	
Deference and respect for H's Judgement		II
Not named (no manifest under- lying dimension)	II	II
Mutual altruism	III	I
Conformity to middle-class ref- erence groups	IV	III

    Levinger (1965) revised the battery. Each of the 12 new items had four possible responses; two are presumably altruistic and two are egoistic. One altruistic and one egoistic response is relatively matter-of-fact (nonempathic) expressions, while the other expresses concern for the other's feelings (empathic).
SAMPLE ITEM. Suppose your new baby wakes up several times each night. Your wife is tired because she gets up at night and cares for the baby during the day while you work. She says that you should take turns getting up at night, but you know that you have to get up at 5:30 a.m. and go to work every morning. What would you tell her? (check one) (1) It's her place to get up with the baby. (2) I know she's

very tired, but it's really more important that I get my
sleep. (3) I need that extra sleep badly, but she is tired
too, so I'd get up half the time. (4) I'd get up half the
time. I want to help her all I can.
LENGTH. Items: 40.
AVAILABILITY. From NAPS. Levinger revision from NAPS-2.
REFERENCES.
       Buerkle,J.V.   Anderson,T.R.   and   Badgley,R.F.
Altruism, role conflict, and marital adjustment: a factor
analysis of marital interaction. Marriage and Family
Living, 1961, 23, 20-26.
       Buerkle,J.V. and Badgley,R.F.   Couple role taking:
the Yale Marital Interaction Battery. Marriage and Family
Living, 1959, 21, 53-58.
       Levinger,G. Altruism in marriage: a test of the
Buerkle-Badgley   battery.   Journal of Marriage and the
Family, 1965, 27, 32-34.

CLEMENTS,W.H. Interspouse Sensitivity Rating Scale

VARIABLES MEASURED. (1) General sensitivity (awareness of
general   areas   of   upset)   and   (2)   Specific   sensitivity
(awareness of effects of specific behaviors). Both refer to
the subject's awareness of the effects of his or her
behavior on the spouse, especially the degree to which
various general areas of behavior (affection, communication,
finances, responsibility, sex, and understanding) as well as
specific acts are upsetting to the spouse.
TEST DESCRIPTION. Couples from two groups (unstable and
stable marriages) rank order a series of specific behaviors
from most to least upsetting to themselves and, in the
second section of the scale, upsetting to their spouse. The
sensitivity measure is the rank order correlation (rho)
between the ranking of the items for the spouse and that
spouse's ranking of his or her own behavior.
       The scale uses items which refer to six areas of
interaction: affection,   communication,   finances,
responsibility, sex and understanding. Under each of these
areas, four representative behaviors are listed. Couples
are required to rank order the four specific behaviors under
each general area from 1 to 4 (from most to least upsetting)
and to rank order the general areas themselves from 1 to 6
(most to least upsetting).
SAMPLE ITEM. General area: Affection.   Specific behavior
item: Seems to care for others more than for me.
LENGTH. Items: 24.
AVAILABILITY. In Clements, 1967.
REFERENCE.
       Clements,W.H.   Marital   interaction   and   marital
stability: a point of view and a descriptive comparison of
stable and unstable marriages. Journal of Marriage and the
Family, 1967, 29, 697-702.

COUCH,C.J.   Role Concept Questionnaire

VARIABLES MEASURED.   (1) Marital role presciption, (2)
Husband-wife consensus in role prescription, (3) Evaluation
of adequacy of role performance, (4) Role-taking accuracy.
TEST DESCRIPTION. Open-ended questionnaire with parallel
forms for husband and wife. Each subject is asked to list
the five most important obligations of a husband and a wife,
to estimate his spouse's answers to these questions, and to
evaluate how adequately S and his spouse perform the marital
obligations   which   were   listed.   Consensus scores are
obtained by judging (on a 1 to 5 scale) extent of agreement
between   subject's   and   spouse's definitions of the marital
roles.
SAMPLE ITEM. In the five blanks below, please list the five
most   important   obligations   you   think   a   wife   has   in
fulfilling her duties as a wife. To what extent does your
wife   fulfill   the   obligations   you   feel   she   has?   (1)
Completely, (2) Most of the time, (3) Sometimes, (4) Seldom
or never.
LENGTH. Items: 30.
AVAILABILITY. In Couch, 1958.
REFERENCE.
       Couch,C.J.   The use of the concept "role" and its
derivatives in a study of marriage. Marriage and Family
Living, 1958, 20, 353-357.

FARBER,B.   Value Consensus Index

VARIABLES   MEASURED.   (1) Value Consensus   Index;   (2)
Social-Emotional Valuation Index.
TEST DESCRIPTION. Husband and wife are asked separately to
rank 10 value standards in order of their importance for
success in marriage.   Rank order   correlation   between
husband's and wife's rankings (rho) constitutes the Value
Consensus Index. Rho with a predetermined ranking in order
of   social-emotional   orientation   constitutes   the
Social-Emotional Valuation Index.
SAMPLE ITEM. Health and happy children. _Rank.
LENGTH. Items: 10.
AVAILABILITY. In Farber, 1957.
REFERENCES.
       Capubianco,R.J. and Knox,S.   IQ estimate and the index
of   marital   integration.   American Journal of Mental
Deficiency, 1964, 68, 718-721.
       Crain,A.J.   Sussman,M.B. and Weil,W.B.Jr. Effects of
a diabetic child on marital integration and related measures
of family functioning. Journal of Health and Human
Behavior, 1966, 7, 122-127.
       Dryer,A.S. and Wells,M.B. Parental values, parental
control, and creativity in young children. Journal of
Marriage and the Family, 1966, 28, 83-88.
       Farber,B.   An   index   of   marital   integration.
Sociometry, 1957, 20, 117-134.

Farber,B. Effects of a severely mentally retarded child on family integration. Monographs of the Society for Research in Child Development, 1959, 24, No. 2 (Serial No. 71).

Farber,B. Family organization and crisis: maintenance of integration in families with a severely mentally retarded child. Monographs of the Society for Research in Child Development, 1960, 25, No. 1 (Serial NO. 75).

Farber,B. Marital integration as a factor in parent-child relations. Child Development, 1962, 33, 1-14.

Farber,B. and McHale,J. Marital integration and parents; agreement on satisfaction with their child's behavior. Marriage and Family Living, 1959, 21, 65-69.

Hill,R.L. Family Development in Three Generations. Cambridge, Massachusetts: Schenkman Publishing Co., Inc., 1970.

Kerckhoff,A.C. and Bean,F.D. Role-related factors in person perception among engaged couples. sociometry, 1967, 30, 176-186.

Kerckhoff,A.C. and Davis,K.E. Value consensus and need complementarity in mate selection. American Sociological Review, 1962, 27, 295-303.

Levinger,G. Senn,D.J. and Jorgensen,B.W. Progress toward permanence in courtship: a test of the Kerckhoff-Davis hypotheses. Sociometry, 1970, 33, 427-443.

Murstein,B.I. Who Will Marry Whom? New York: Springer Publishing Co., Inc., 1976, 328.

GOODMAN,N. and OFSHE,R. Empathy Test

VARIABLE MEASURED. Empathic accuracy.
TEST DESCRIPTION. Subjects rate 12 "goal words" (see Goodman and Ofshe Communication Efficiency Test) on 10 bipolar semantic differential scales (Osgood, Suci and Tannenbaum, 1957). After a brief pause, during which background data are collected, subjects are asked to rate the same words a second time as they think their partner has. The score is the difference between the response of the subject to a word on a given set of scales when asked to act as the partner and the actual response of the partner to the same word, specifically the mean absolute squared difference between the two ratings of the same words. For example, if a female rated the word "birth" as very pleasurable and the male rated it as moderately painful, he is given a score of 16, the square of the number of steps is given a score of 16, the square of the number of steps (in this case, four) that separates the two ratings.
SAMPLE ITEM. Goal words: Family related word--birth; General word--beef.
LENGTH. Items: 12.
AVAILABILITY. In Goodman, 1968.
REFERENCES.
Goodman,N. and Ofshe,R. Empathy, communication efficiency, and marital status. Journal of Marriage and the

Family, 1968, 30, 597-603.
    Osgood,C.E.   Suci,G.J.   and   Tannenbaum,P.   The
Measurement of Meaning.   Urbana, Illinois: University of
Illinois Press, 1957.

KIRKPATRICK,C. and HOBART,C.W. Family Opinion Survey

VARIABLES MEASURED. (1) Role prescriptions (attitudes) for
husband and   wife   in   14 areas of family life (numbers in
parentheses indicate number of items for each area):
personal freedom (10), sex and affection (4), relative
dominance (4), economic roles (9), marital roles (3), having
children (5), child-rearing (8), in-laws (6), religion (8),
intellectual values (2), neatness values (4), savings values
(2), home life valuation (8), divorce (8). (2) Disagreement
score between responses of partners to the same items.   (3)
Non-empathy score--the discrepancy between the response
imputed to a partner and the actual response of that person.
(4) Disagreement estimate score--the discrepancy between a
person's own response and that imputed to the partner.
TEST   DESCRIPTION.   Multiple-choice   intensity   of
agreement-disagreement items.   Questions are worded to be
appropriate for both sexes and for single as well as married
Ss.
SAMPLE ITEM. In my marriage, I would want to make whatever
family sacrifices are necessary in order to have several
children. Strongly agree, Agree, No opinion, Disagree,
Strongly disagree.
LENGTH. Items: 81.
AVAILABILITY. From NAPS.
REFERENCES.
    Ater,E.C.   and Deacon,R.E.   Interaction of family
relationship qualities and managerial components. Journal
of Marriage and the Family, 1972, 33, 257-263.
    Hobart,C.W.   Disillusionment   in   marriage   and
romanticism. Marriage and Family Living, 1958, 20, 156-162.
    Hobart,C.W.   Attitude change during courtship and
marriage. Marriage and Family Living, 1960, 22, 352-359.
    Hobart,C.W.   and   Klausner,W.J.   Some   social
interactional correlates of marital role disagreement and
marital adjustment. Marriage and Family Living, 1959, 21,
256-263.
    Kirkpatrick,C.   and   Hobart,C.W.   Disagreement,
disagreement estimate, and non-empathetic imputations for
intimacy groups varying from favorite date to married.
American Sociological Review, 1954, 19, 10-19.

3. Communication (See also Subject Index)

BIENVENU,M.J.Sr.   Marital Communication Inventory

VARIABLE MEASURED. Communication between husband and wife
defined as the verbal and nonverbal exchange of feelings and
meanings as husbands and wives try to understand one another
and to see their problems and differences from both a man's
and a woman's point of view.
TEST DESCRIPTION. The 46 items refer to the characteristic
styles, degrees, and patterns of communication between
marriage partners. Elements of communication include the
handling of anger and differences, tone of voice,
understanding and empathy, self-disclosure, listening
habits, nagging, conversational discourtesies, and
uncommunicativeness. The items were formulated from a
review of the literature and from the author's experience in
marriage and family couseling. In earlier pilot work the
instrument was subjected to a quartile comparison between
the top scores and the lower scores and later underwent
further validity and reliability studies.
SAMPLE ITEM. Does your spouse let you finish talking before
saying what he/she has to say? Possible responses:
Frequently, Sometimes, Seldom, Never.
LENGTH. Time: 15 minutes. Items: 46.
AVAILABILITY. Family Life Publications, Inc., Box 427,
Saluda, N.C. 28773
ABSTRACTED BY: Millard J. Bienvenu, Sr.
REFERENCES.
    Bienvenu,M.J.Sr. Measurement of marital communication.
The Family Coordinator, 1970 19, 26-31.
    Bienvenu,M.J.Sr. An interpersonal communication
inventory. The Journal of Communication, 1971, 21, 381-388.
    Matteson,R. Adolescent self-esteem, family
communication, and marital satisfaction. Journal of
Psychology, 1974, 86, 35-47.

GOODMAN,N. and OFSHE,R. Communication Efficiency Test

VARIABLE MEASURED. Communication efficienncy: ability of
subject to give cues which will aid the "other" in
identifying the object of his cues.
TEST DESCRIPTION. A variation of the parlor game
"Password." The game requires one member of the dyad to give
"cue words" to the other in order to suggest to him/her each
of the 12 "goal words." The unit of communication consists
of one English word. No other talking is permitted.
    The subjects continue the cue-response sequence in each
case until the goal word is correctly identified. Each dyad
is given a mean communication efficiency score based on the
average number of incorrect responses to cue words for the
12 words. Therefore, a low score indicates greater

communicative efficiency.

In order to vary the relevance of the words to the interactive situation, the goal words are divided into two classes: Family-related words designate objects the authors believed to be relevant to the activities of a family of procreation and hence are salient to engaged and married couples. The second type consists of more general words that could not be so easily classified as either related to courtship and marriage or used more frequently in these kinds of relationships.

SAMPLE ITEM. Family-related word: birth.   General word: beef.

LENGTH. Items: 12.

AVAILABILITY. In Goodman and Ofshe, 1968.

REFERENCE.

Goodman,N. and Ofshe,R. Empathy, communication efficiency, and marital status. Journal of Marriage and the Family, 1968, 30, 597-603.

HILL,R.L. STYCOS,J.M. and BACK,K.W. Marital Communication and Agreement Test

VARIABLES MEASURED. Communication about and agreement on a variety of topics by husband and wife.

TEST DESCRIPTION. Members of a couple are given separate structured questionnaires listing a series of topics. They are asked to indicate how often they discuss each topic and how closely they think they agree on it even if they do not discuss it.

SAMPLE ITEM. a. Handling family finances: We discuss - Often, Once in a while, Never; I think we - Always agree, Almost always agree, Occasionally disagree, Frequently disagree, Always disagree.

LENGTH. Items: 13.

AVAILABILITY. In Hill, R., 1970.

ABSTRACTED BY: Kersti Yllo

REFERENCE.

Hill,R.L. Family /Development in Three Generations. Cambridge, Mass.: Schenkman Publishing Co., Inc., 1970.

HILL,R.L. STYCOS,J.M. and BACK,K.W. Spousal Communication Scale

VARIABLE MEASURED. Communication with spouse.

TEST DESCRIPTION. Multiple-choice questions which require the S to indicate the frequency with which he or she discusses each of the following topics with spouse: religion, how to discipline children, future plans, sexual relations, birth control, and ideal family size. Responses are dichotomized for purposes of forming Guttman scales. The wife's scale omits the item for ideal family size. The husband's scale omits items for children's discipline and sexual relations.

SAMPLE ITEM. As you know, there are married couples who
discuss things other married couples do not discuss. In
general, do you cr do you not discuss religion with your
husband? If yes: Would you say that you discuss such
things often or once in a while?
LENGTH. Items: 5 (wife scale), 4 (husband scale).
AVAILABILITY. In Hill, et al., 1959.
REFERENCE.
    Hill,R.L. Stycos,J.M. and Back,K.W. The Family and
Population Control: A Puerto Rican Experiment in Social
Change. Chapel Hill: University of North Carolina Press,
1959.

HOBART,C.W. and KLAUSNER,W.J. Communication Between
Husband and Wife Score

VARIABLES MEASURED. (1) Barriers to communication; (2)
Non-verbal (empathic) communication.
TEST DESCRIPTION. Communication is defined as "the exchange
of meaningful symbols, both words and gestures." Three
scores are obtained: (1) The "barriers to communication"
score consists of 19 questions concerning issues and
relationships taboo in husband-wife verbal interaction
scored by frequency of occurrence response categories. (2)
The empathic communication score consists of seven items
dealing with nonverbal communication situations in which the
husband or wife can anticipate the other's response; also
with frequency of response categories. (3) Total
communication score is the sum of (1) and (2).
SAMPLE ITEMS. Barriers: Do you and your mate talk over
things you disagree about or have difficulties over?
Nonverbal: When you start to ask a question does your mate
know what it is before you ask it? Very frequently = 4,
Frequently = 3, Occasionally = 2, Seldom = 1, Never = 0.
LENGTH. Items: 26.
AVAILABILITY. From Hobart and Klausner.
REFERENCES.
    Hobart,C.W. and Klausner,W.J. Some social
interactional correlates of marital role disagreement and
marital adjustment. Marriage and Family Living, 1959, 21,
256-263.
    Petersen,D.M. Husband-wife communication and family
problems. Sociology and Social Research, 1969, 53, 375-384.

KAHN,M. Marital Communication Scale

VARIABLE MEASURED. Accuracy of nonverbal communication
between marriage partners.
TEST DESCRIPTION. The test is an objective, behavioral
measure of accuracy of marital nonverbal communication
consisting of 16 items. Each item involves a typical
marital situation in which one spouse must communicate one
of three alternative intentions to his/her partner in a

face-to-face arrangement. The communicating subject
verbalizes a standard message which was designed so that it
could mean any of the three intentions for a given
situation. The receiver's only means of discriminating
among the alternative intentions are the communicator's
nonverbal cues such as facial expression and vocal
intonation. Eight items are designed for the wife to
communicate and eight items are designed for the husband to
communicate. There are also three preliminary sample items
for each spouse to act as communicator.

The score is obtained from the number of items in which
the receiver selects the intention which the communicator
attempted to convey. (A Spearman-Brown split-half
reliability coefficient of .87 was obtained.)
SAMPLE ITEM. You come to the dinner table as your wife
begins to serve chicken, a main course you recall having had
four days ago for dinner too. __a. You are irritated with
her for preparing the same meal again and are warning her
that she had better not make the same mistake in the future
of a closely repeated meal. __b. You do not mind but are
curious to see if your memory for meals is accurate. __c.
You are elated because chicken is one of your favorites and
you are not accustomed to her graciousness of serving it so
often for you. "Didn't we have chicken for dinner a few
nights ago?"
LENGTH. Items: 16 plus 6 sample items which must be
administered.
AVAILABILITY. From NAPS-2 or in Kahn,M.L. Nonverbal
communication .as a factor in marital satisfaction. (Ph.D.
dissertation, Southern Illinois University, 1969) University
Microfilms Ann Arbor, Michigan No. 70-7292.
ABSTRACTED BY: Malcolm Kahn
REFERENCES.
        Kahn,M. Non-verbal communication and marital
satisfaction. Family Process, 1970, 9, 449-546.
        Murphy,D.C. and Mendelson,L.A. Communication and
adjustment in marriage: investigating the relationship.
Family Process,1973, 12, 317-326.
        Nadeau,K.G. An examination of some effects of the
Marital Enrichment Group. Ph.D. dissertation, University
of Florida, 1970.

KARLSSON,G. Spousal Communication Indexes

VARIABLES MEASURED. Communication (1) Frequency of "talking
things over" and self-ratings of spouses' understanding each
other; communication (2) Frequency of correctly estimating
spouse's wishes.
TEST DESCRIPTION. (1) Multiple-choice items with weighted
answers summed to obtain a score. (2) A checklist for the
extent to which the subject would like to see the listed
behavior in the spouse, and for the extent the subject
thinks the spouse wants this of him or her. The score is
the number of correct identifications of mate's wishes.

SAMPLE ITEM. Communication (1): Do you in general talk things over with your spouse: Never or Almost never (3 weight for husband's score, 2 weight for wife's score); Sometimes (3, 3); Almost always (4, 4); Always (5, 6). (2) Discuss the education of the children with you (him): Would you like your mate to more, less, as now. Do you think your mate would like you to more, less, as now, don't know.
LENGTH. Items: 38.
AVAILABILITY. In Karlsson, 1951.
REFERENCE.
    Karlsson,G.   Adaptability   and   Communication   in Marriage: A   Swedish   Predictive   Study   of   Marital Satisfaction. Uppsala: Almquist and Wiksells, 1951.

LOCKE,H.J.   SABAGH,G.   AND   THOMES,M.M.   Primary Communication Inventory (PCI).

VARIABLES MEASURED. Primary communication, defined as communication in the primary group, between husbands and wives.
TEST DESCRIPTION. Subjects rate the frequency with which 25 kinds of communication take place between themselves and their spouses. Responses are: Very frequently, Frequently, Occasionally, Seldom and Never, with point values ranging from 0 to 5. Higher scores indicate greater frequency of communication. Navran (Navran, 1967; Kahn, 1970) adapted the PCI by eliminating one item and changing the scoring system to measure each spouse's individual communication.
SAMPLE ITEM. "Does your mate explain or express himself to you through a glance or gesture?"
LENGTH. Items: 25.
AVAILABILITY. From NAPS-2 for 12-item version.
ABSTRACTED BY: Blair Nelson
REFERENCES.
    Ely,A.L. Guerney,B.G.Jr. and Stover,L.   Efficacy of the training phase of conjugal therapy. Psychotherapy: Theory, Research, and Practice, 1973, 10, 201-207.
    Kahn,M.   Nonverbal   communication   and   marital satisfaction. Family Process, 1970, 9, 449-456.
    Locke,H.J. Sabagh,G. and Thomes,M.M.   Correlates of primary communication and empathy. Research Studies of the Statz College of Washington, 1956, 24, 116-124.
    Navran,L. Communication and adjustment in marriage. Family Process, 1967, 6, 173-184.

MICHEL,A. Husband-Wife Communication Index

VARIABLE MEASURED. Husband-wife communication, defined as a reciprocal communication in which there is a dialogue between the two members of the couple.

TEST DESCRIPTION. The index refers to communication about
the wife's problems which are hidden from the husband, the
financial difficulties related to management of the home,
the wife's emotional disturbances, the husband's worries,
and his daily attitude toward his wife when he returns home.
The index is obtained by summing the responses to the five
questions.
SAMPLE ITEM. Does your husband ask you how you spent your
day when he returns home?: Usually, Sometimes, Never.
LENGTH. Time: 5 minutes. Items: 5.
AVAILABILITY. In Michel, 1970.
ABSTRACTED BY: Andree Michel
REFERENCES.
    Michel,A. Interaction and family planning in the
French urban families. Deomograph, 1967a, 4, 615-625.
    Michel,A. Le planning familial en France. Economie et
Humanisme, 1967b, 176, 29-41.
    Michel,A. Wife's satisfaction with husband's
understanding in Parisian urban families, Journal of
Marriage and the Family, 1970, 32, 351-359.
    Michel,A. Interaction and goal attainment in Parisian
working wives' families. In Michel,A. (Ed.) Family Issues
of Employed Women in Europe and America. Leiden: E.J.
Brill, 1971a.
    Michel,A. Roles masculins et feminins dans la famille:
un examen de la theorie classique. Informations sur les
Sciences Sociales (Social Science Information), 1971b, 10,
113-135.
    Michel,A. and Picard-Laliberte,F. Some differentials
of the marital satisfaction of French working wives in the
Paris area. International Journal of Sociology of the
Family, 1971, 1, 1-17.

SAFILICS-ROTHSCHILD,C. Level of Communication Measure

VARIABLE MEASURED. The degree of communication between
spouses.
TEST DESCRIPTION. In an interview subjects are asked about
communication with their husband or wife. The degree of
communication is measured on the basis of: (1) The number
of 'taboo' subjects between husband and wife; (2) The
frequency of communication of worries, problems, and
troubles; (3) The frequency of exchange of everyday routine
happenings; (4) The frequency of joint discussions of
financial difficulties; and (5) The frequency of joint
discussion of emotional (sentimental) problems and
preoccupations. If there is no taboo subject for the
spouses they are coded as 3; if some taboo subjects, 2; if
many taboo subjects, 1. In the other questions, if the
answer was Usually it is scored as 4; if Sometimes as 3;
if Rarely as 2; and if Never as 1. A cumulative score of
communication is then calculated.

SAMPLE ITEM. "When your husband has problems, worries, or troubles, do you try to talk to him in order to find out what is the matter or help him if you can? How Often? Usually, Sometimes, Seldom, Never.
LENGTH. Items: 8.
AVAILABILITY. In Neubeck, 1969.
ABSTRACTED BY: Kersti Yllo
REFERENCE.
      Safilios-Rothschild,C. Attitudes of Greek spouses toward marital infidelity. In Neubeck,G. (Ed.) Extramarital Relations. Engelwood Cliffs, N.J.: Prentice-Hall, Inc., 1969, 77-93.

D. Family Planning, Sex, Abortion (See also Subject Index)

BARDIS,P.D. Abortion Scale

VARIABLE MEASURED. Attitudes toward induced abortion.
TEST DESCRIPTION. The criterion of internal consistency was applied to approximately 1,500 initial statements dealing with attitudes toward induced abortion, and covering both familial and nonfamilial phenomena. The resulting final scale, a Likert-type instrument, consists of 25 items. Since each of them is responded to on the basis of a five-point scale (Strongly disagree = 0 to Strongly agree = 4), the theoretical range of scores on the Abortion Scale is 0 (typical disapproval of abortion) to 100 (ideal-typical approval).
SAMPLE ITEM. Abortion is all right during the first three months of pregnancy.
LENGTH. Time: 12 minutes. Items: 25.
AVAILABILITY. In Bardis, 1972a; 1972b; 1975a; 1975b; and from Panos D.Bardis, University of Toledo, Toledo, Ohio; Blasi et al., 1975; Norman and Sekhon, 1973.
ABSTRACTED BY: Panos D. Bardis
REFERENCES.
      Bardis,P.D. Abortion and public opinion: a research note. Journal of Marriage and the Family,1972a, 34, 111.
      Bardis,P.D. A technique for the measurement of attitudes toward abortion. International Journal of Sociology of the Family, 1972b, 2, 1-7.
      Bardis,P.D. Abortion attitudes among Catholic college students. Adolescence, 1975a, 10, 433-441.
      Bardis,P.D. Abortion attitudes among university students in India. International Journal of Sociology of the Family, 1975b.
      Blasi,A. et.al. Abortion attitudes. Social Science, 1975.
      Norman,C. and Sekhon,G. Attitudes toward abortion. Social Science, 1973, 48, 234-235.

BARDIS,P.D. Pill Scale

VARIABLE   MEASURED.   Favorable   attitude   toward   oral
contraception.
TEST DESCRIPTION.   A 25-item questionnaire.   Items are
scored Strongly disagree = 0; Disagree = 1; Undecided = 2;
Agree = 3; Strongly agree = 4.   Possible total scores,
therefore, range from 0 (least liberal) to 100 (most
liberal).
SAMPLE ITEM. The pill should be sold to single adults
without any restrictions.
LENGTH. Items: 25.
AVAILABILITY. In Bardis, 1969.
REFERENCE.
     Bardis,P.D.   A pill scale: a technique for   the
measurement of attitudes toward oral contraception. Social
Science, 1969, 44, 35-42.

CVETKOVICH,G.T.   and   LONNER,W.J.   Hypothetical Family
Questionnaire (HYFAM)

VARIABLES MEASURED.   The importance of the following
variables for birth planning: Number of children in family,
age of youngest child, length of marriage, health of wife,
age of husband, age of wife, total annual income, wife's
working status.
TEST DESCRIPTION. The instrument consists of a set of case
studies depicting 40 hypothetical families.   Each case
varies in the above eight characteristics. Respondents are
required to state whether they personally believe each
family should have another (or first) child.   A regression
of these responses against the values for each of the eight
family characteristics is computed.   The resulting beta
coefficients provide the scores for each respondent on the
eight characteristics.
SAMPLE ITEM. Should this family have another child?   The
family has the following characteristics: (1) Number of
children in family: boys 2, girls 0.   (2) Age of youngest
child: 1 year.   (3) Length of marriage: 5 years.   (4)
Health of wife: average. (5) Age of husband: 46.   (6) Age
of wife: 47.   (7) Total annual income: very high. (8)
Wife's working status: not employed.
LENGTH. Items: 40.
AVAILABILITY. From NAPS-2.
ABSTRACTED BY: Susan Murray.
REFERENCE.
     Cvetkovich,G.T.   and Lonner,W.J.   A   transnational
comparison of individual birth planning decisions for
hypothetical families.   Journal of Cross-Cultural
Psychology, 1973, 4, 470-480.

FINNER,S.L. and GAMACHE,J.D.   Attitude Towards Induced
Abortion Scale

VARIABLE MEASURED. Approval of induced abortion.
TEST DESCRIPTION.   Each item of the test describes
circumstances surrounding a specific pregnancy and asks the
respondent to indicate approval/disapproval, assuming no
legal prohibitions.   The respondent may select: Approves;
Approves with reservations; Is sympathetic but does not
approve; Disapproves. The responses are summed as a Likert
scale, with a sccre ranging from liberal = 0 to conservative
= 21.
SAMPLE ITEM. An 18-year-old girl becomes pregnant by her
father.   She applies for an abortion. Do you...Approve;
Approve with reservations; Sympathetic but do not approve;
Disapprove.
LENGTH. Items: 7.
REFERENCE.
        Finner,S.L. and Gamache,J.D.   The relation between
religious commitment and attitudes toward induced abortion.
Sociological Analysis, 1969, 30, 1-12.

FISCHER,E.H. Birth Planning Attitudes

VARIABLES MEASURED. Concern about population growth,
intention to limit own family size, nontraditional view of
procreation, and birth planning attitude.
TEST DESCRIPTION. A questionnaire and attitude items
concerning various aspects of birth planning. There are
three attitude scales, derived by factor analysis: (1)
Concern about population growth/intention to limit family
size, (2) Nontraditional view of procreation, and (3)
Attitude toward birth control. Scale scores were derived by
summing item ratings.
SAMPLE ITEM. It would be a good idea if the government
offered rewards (such as tax reductions) to couples who
limit their families to two or fewer children.   Agree,
Probably agree, Probably disagree, or Disagree.
LENGTH. Time: 15 minutes. Items: 26.
AVAILABILITY. In Fischer, 1972.
REFERENCE.
        Fischer,E.H. Birth planning of youth: ccncern about
overpopulation and intention to limit family size. American
Psychologist, 1972, 27, 951-958.

GRINDER,R.E. and SCHMITT,S.S.   Contraceptive Information
Rating Scale

VARIABLES MEASURED. Extent of knowledge of condom, rhythm,
diaphragm and douche contraceptive techniques.
TEST DESCRIPTION. To assess knowledge of the rhythm method,
respondents mark a calendar as to which days a hypothetical
woman might become pregnant. For each of the three other

techniques, series of five multiple choice questions are
asked. Subjects are credited with knowledge of the rhythm
method if the day or days circled are among the ten days on
which conception is likely to occur. For the other
techniques, respondents are regarded as knowledgeable if
they know when the method should be used, who should use it,
and where it should be worn.
SAMPLE ITEM. How does .... (method) prevent pregnancy?   (a)
Preventing the woman from having a menstrual flow, (b)
Preventing the woman from producing an egg, (c) Causing the
woman's body to expel the fertilized egg, (d) Preventing the
sperm from reaching the egg, and (e) I don't know.
LENGTH. Items: 15 multiple choice questions.
AVAILABILITY. In Grinder and Schmitt, 1966.
REFERENCE.
    Grinder,R.E. and Schmitt,S.S. Coeds and contraceptive
information. Journal of Marriage and the Family, 1966,
28, 471-479.

HILL,R.L.   Stycos,J.M.   and   BACK,K.W.   Contraceptive
Information Index

VARIABLE MEASURED. Knowledge of contraceptive techniques.
TEST DESCRIPTION. Responses to three questions are weighted
and summed to give a score--from Little information = 0 to
Much information = 16.
SAMPLE ITEM. Subject knows where to obtain free birth
control materials. Yes = 2, No = 0.
LENGTH. NR.
AVAILABILITY. In Hill et al., 1959, p.260.
REFERENCE.
    Hill,R.L. Stycos,J.M. and Back,K.W. The Family and
Population Control: A Puerto Rican Experiment in Social
Change. Chapel Hill: University of North Carolina Press,
1959.

HILL,R.L.   STYCOS,J.M.   and   BACK,K.W.   Family Size
Preference Index

VARIABLE MEASURED. Size of family desired.
TEST DESCRIPTION. "This index is based on four pairs of
items, each having a possible score from 0 to 3. A score of
0 meant that both questions were answered consistently
toward the small family alternative, 3 that both were
answered consistently toward the large family alternative.
Intermediate scores reflect inconsistency, the score being
chosen according to the direction in which the inconsistency
was resolved. The total possible score of the index thus
could range between 0 (desire for small family) and 12
(desire for large family)."
SAMPLE ITEMS. Generally speaking, one of the most important
things in life is to have children (large family
alternative). Generally speaking, there are many more

important things in life than having children (small family
alternative).
LENGTH. Items: 4.
AVAILABILITY. In Hill et al., 1959, p. 429.
REFERENCE.
    Hill,R.L. Stycos,J.M. and Back,K.W. The Family and
Population Control: A Puerto Rican Experiment in Social
Change. Chapel Hill: University of North Carolina Press,
1959.

JACCARD,J.J. and DAVIDSON,A.R. Orientation to Family
Planning Indexes

VARIABLES MEASURED. Family Planning: (1) Beliefs about
what birth control is related to, (2) Evaluation of beliefs,
(3) Evaluative attitudes toward birth control, (4) Normative
beliefs about what others expect one to do in respect to
birth control, (5) Motivation to comply with the norms, (6)
Behavioral intention tc use birth control, and (7) Various
combinations of the above.
TEST DESCRIPTION. A series of measures constructed to
operationalize the Fishbein model of attitude measurement
(1967,1972). There are 15 questions dealing with beliefs
and 15 with evaluation of beliefs. The normative beliefs
and motivation to comply questions are repeated for 12
referent persons. Each item is scored from +3 through 0 to
-3.
SAMPLE ITEM. (Beliefs) Using birth contrcl pills would
affect my sexual mcrals.
LENGTH. Items: 56.
AVAILABILITY. In Jaccard and Davidson, 1972.
ABSTRACTED BY: Thomas G. Sparhawk
REFERENCES.
    Fishbein,M. An investigation of the relationship
between beliefs about an object and attitudes toward that
object. Human Relations, 16, 1963, 233-240.
    Fishbein,M. Toward an understanding of family planning
behaviors. Journal of Applied Social Psychology, 1972, 2,
214-227.
    Jaccard,J.J. and Davidson,A.R. Toward an
understanding of family planning behaviors: an initial
investigation. Journal of Applied Social Psychology, 1972,
2, 228-235.

LINDHOLM,B.W. and TOULIATOS,J. Motivation and Potential
for Adoptive Parenthood

VARIABLES MEASURED. (1) Motivation for adoptive parenthood,
and (2) Potential for adoptive parenthood.
TEST DESCRIPTION. A 72-item rating scale that is designed
to quantify and summarize the evaluation by caseworkers of
male and female applicants for adoptive parenthood. The
measure consists of two subscales: (1) Motivation for

Adoptive Parenthood and (2) Potential for Adoptive
Parenthood. The Motivation and the Potential subscales
include 2 and 10 factors, respectively, which were derived
from factor analysis. Factors subsumed under Motivation
are: (1) positive reasons for wanting to adopt, and (2)
lack of negative reasons for wanting to adopt; and under
Potential are: (1) attitudes toward adoption and the
natural parents of adopted children, (2) acceptance and
flexibility toward the children that the parents were
willing to adopt, (3) ability to use help, (4) relationships
with one's family, (5) relationships with one's spouse, (6)
relationships with one's friends, (7) positive experiences
with children, (8) being able to enjoy and have a
relationship with a child, (9) being able to assume
responsibility for others, and (10) dealings with previous
life situations. The caseworker determines whether the
applicant is different from or similar to the characteristic
described in the item, using a frame of reference that is
based on past experience and that includes applicants who
have been successful and unsuccessful in having children
placed. A value of 1 to 4 is assigned to each item
indicating the degree cf difference or similarity. Scores
for the Motivation subscale and for the Potential subscale
are obtained by adding the ratings for each. A total score
for Motivation and Potential for Adoptive Parenthood is
obtained by adding the scores for the two subscales.
SAMPLE ITEM. Motivation for adoption is based on
emotionally healthy needs. Very different = 1, Somewhat
different = 2, Somewhat similar = 3, Very similar = 4.
LENGTH. Time: 20 minutes. Items: 72.
AVAILABILITY. From Monitor, P.O.Box 2337, Hollywood,
California 90028 and from NAPS-2.
ABSTRACTED BY: B.W. Lindholm
REFERENCES.
      Lindholm,B.W. and Touliatos,J. Development of a
Motivation and Potential for Adoptive Parenthood Scale.
Psychological Reports, (in press).
      Lindholm,B.W. and Touliatos,J. A factor analytic
study of motivation and potential for adoptive parenthood.
Psychological Reports, (in press).
      Touliatos,J. and Lindholm,B.W. Use of standardized
measures in child placement. Paper presented at the annual
meeting of the National Council on Family Relations, Salt
Lake City, August, 1975.

MAXWELL,J.W. and MONTGOMERY,J.E. Timing of Parenthood
(ATOP) Scale

VARIABLE MEASURED. Belief in the responsibility of a young
married couple to have a child within the first two years of
marriage.
TEST DESCRIPTION. Ten self-administered questionnaire items
constitute a Likert-type scale which contains five degrees
of response from Strongly agree to Strongly disagree.

Responses most favoring early parenthood are given the
highest scores and those favoring delayed parenthood the
lowest scores. Possible scores range from 10 to 50.
SAMPLE ITEM. The best time to begin having children is
usually within the first two years of marriage--Strongly
Agree, Agree, Undecided, Disagree, Strongly Disagree.
LENGTH. Items: 10.
AVAILABILITY. In Maxwell and Montgomery, 1969.
ABSTRACTED BY: Blair Nelson
REFERENCE.
     Maxwell,J.W. and Montgomery,J.E. Societal pressure
toward early parenthood. The Family Coordinator, 1969, 18,
340-344.

MILLER,K.A. and INKELES,A. Acceptance of Family Limitation
Scale

VARIABLE MEASURED. Verbal acceptance of family size
limitation.
TEST DESCRIPTION. The items are dichotomous forced-choice
questions measuring whether the respondent is favorable or
unfavorable to: (1) family size limitation as a general
value, (2) medical means of contraception, and (3)
government campaigns advising limitation of family size.
The mean score is obtained.
SAMPLE ITEM. With which of these opinions do you agree:
(1) Some people think that it is necessary for a man and his
wife to limit the number of children they have so that they
can take better care of those they do have. (2) Others say
that it is wrong for a man and wife ever to purposely limit
the number of children they have.
LENGTH. Items: 3.
AVAILABILITY. In Miller and Inkeles, 1974. Originally
presented in slightly different form by Williamson, 1970.
ABSTRACTED BY: Karen A. Miller
REFERENCES.
     Miller,K.A. and Inkeles,A. Modernity and acceptance
of family limitation in four developing countries. Journal
of Social Issues, 1974, 30, 167-188.
     Williamson,J.B. Subjective efficacy and ideal family
size as predictors of favorability toward birth control.
Demography, 1970, 7, 329-339.

MIRANDE,A.M. Premarital Abortion Permissiveness Scale

VARIABLE MEASURED. Acceptance of abortion.
TEST DESCRIPTION. A list of items representing hypothetical
conditions under which a respondent would view abortion as
an acceptable alternative to an unwanted pregnancy was
compiled. Respondents are asked to indicate their level of
agreement (ranging from Strongly agree to Strongly
disagree). The items are dichotomized into agree and
disagree for purposes of forming a Guttman scale.

The results yielded a 13-item Guttman Scale with a CR
of .91 in Virginia and .92 in North Dakota and an MMR of .63
in Virginia and .68 in North Dakota.
SAMPLE ITEM. I would never have an abortion for any reason.
Agree--Strong, Medium, Slight; Disagree--Strong, Medium,
Slight.
LENGTH. Items: 13.
AVAILABILITY. In Mirande and Hammer, 1974.
ABSTRACTED BY: Alfred M. Mirande
REFERENCES.
        Mirande,A.M.   and   Hammer,E.L.   Premarital   sexual
permissiveness and abortion: standards of college women.
Pacific Sociological Review, 1974, 17, 485-503.
        Mirande,A.M.   and   Hammer,E.L.   Love,   sex,
permissiveness and abortion: a test of alternative models.
Archives of Sexual Behavior. In Press.

MYERS,G.C. and ROBERTS,J.M. Preferential Family Size and
Composition Scale

VARIABLES MEASURED. Preferred family size and composition.
TEST DESCRIPTION. Subjects choose, in terms of personal
preference on a nine-point scale, between two distinct sets
of female and male children combinations ranging in number
from 0 to 6, or 1,176 pairs of boy-girl combinations in all.
This selection process reveals preference and contrast
patterns for each boy-girl combination. Preference scores
(the choice of 2 girls, 2 boys over 5 girls, 4 boys, for
example)   are   computed,   following   Torgerson, by the
constant-sum method to obtain ratio-scale values.   The use
of logarithms simplifies this process. The contrast scores,
a measure of the preference rather than the direction of the
choice, are calculated in a similar manner. The overall
preference and contrast scores for different combinations
are the geometric means of the column entries in the n x n
matrix of the different scores. At a later point in the
interview, respondents are also asked independently about
their ideal family size and composition for comparison with
the scaling technique.
SAMPLE ITEM. Which family would you prefer, (2 girls, 1
boy) (1 girl, 2 boys)?
LENGTH. Items: 1,178.
AVAILABILITY. In Myers and Roberts, 1968.
ABSTRACTED BY: Carolyn E. Dean
REFERENCE.
        Myers,G.C. and Roberts,J.M. A technique for measuring
preferential   family   size   and   composition.   Eugenics
Quarterly, 1968, 15, 165-172.

RABIN,A.I. and GREENE,R.J. The Child Study Inventory (CSI)

VARIABLE MEASURED. Motivation for parenthood.
TEST DESCRIPTION. The Child Study Inventory (CSI) is
composed of 14 sentence stems related to motivation for
parenthood. In addition, four filler items are included.
Each stem is followed by four completion choices which are
categorized into one of the basic CSI motivational
categories: Altruistic, Narcissistic, Fatalistic, and
Instrumental. Scoring consists of summing the rankings of
each category--frcm Fits best = 1 to Least = 4.
SAMPLE ITEM. Parents expect their children: ( ) To fulfill
the purpose of life, ( ) To strengthen the family, ( ) To be
healthy and happy, ( ) To follow in their footsteps.
LENGTH. Time: 10 minutes. Items: 18.
AVAILABILITY. From NAPS-2.
ABSTRACTED BY: A.I. Rabin. State University, E. Lansing,
Michigan.
REFERENCES.
    Greene,R.J. Motivation for parenthood in mothers of
disturbed and mothers of normal children: an exploratory
study.   Unpublished   M.A.   thesis.   Michigan   State
University, 1967.
    Major,M.A. Assessment of motivation for parenthood in
parents of disturbed and normal children.   Ph.D.
dissertation, Michigan State University, 1967.
    Rabin,A.I. Motivation for parenthood. Journal of
Projective Techniques and Personality Assessment, 1965, 29,
405-411.
    Rabin,A.I. and Greene,R.J. Assessing motivation for
parenthood. Journal of Psychology, 1968, 69, 39-46.

ROBERTO,E.L. Belief about Vasectomy Index

VARIABLES MEASURED. Beliefs concerning the significance of
a vasectomy for (1) Self-actualization, (2) Family, (3)
Contraception, (4) Paternal role, (5) Sexual pleasure, (6)
Population control and child care.
TEST DESCRIPTION. Each of the 19 statements about vasectomy
is presented three times: (A) To measure "Expectancy
Belief" operationalized as what it would be like to obtain
the vasectomy operation; (B) To measure "Value Importance"
by asking subjects to rate each item on a five-point scale
from Very Unimportant to Very Important; (C) To measure
"Vasectomy Attitude" by rating the items on six evaluative
semantic differential scales.
SAMPLE   ITEM.   Gives   a   man   a   feeling   of
responsibility_ _ _ _ Gives a man a feeling of guilt.
LENGTH. Time: 10 minutes. Items: 19.
AVAILABILITY. In Roberto, 1974.
REFERENCE.
    Roberto,E.L. Marital and family planning expectancies
of men regarding vasectomy. Journal of Marriage and the
Family, 1974, 36, 698-706.

SCHNAIBERG,A.   Child-Years-of-Dependency Measure (CYD)

VARIABLES MEASURED. This measure incorporates both "tempo" (child-spacing) and "quantity" (numbers of children) dimensions of standard fertility measures used in social demographic research.
TEST DESCRIPTION. This measure cumulates the total number of "child-years" for a given woman/couple, as an approximation to the past dependency burden of the woman/couple. It requires raw data on the dates of birth and/or adoption of all children, and the date of marriage/sexual union of the woman/couple. Unlike conventional demographic measures, the CYD measure can incorporate such "deviations" from normal family formation processes as (1) the deaths of children, (2) pre-marital pregnancies/birth, (3) divorce and separation of spouses, and (4) any assumptions about age-sex-class gradients in the time/fiscal costs of child-rearing. It is intended to broaden conventional bio-demographic measures so as to more closely approximate a socially meaningful measure of dependency burden, which may influence future couple child-bearing. The measure can be used to compute dependency burdens over any _segment_ of the woman's/couple's life cycle (e.g., by five-year marriage intervals, etc.), as well as provide a cross-sectional measure at any given point in the life cycle.
SAMPLE ITEM. See above.
LENGTH. See above.
AVAILABILITY. Schnaiberg, 1973; Schnaiberg, 1974.
ABSTRACTED BY: Allan Schnaiberg
REFERENCES.
     Schnaiberg,A. The concept and measurement of child dependency: an approach to family formation analysis. Population Studies, 1973, 27, 69-84.
     Schnaiberg,A. Children versus fertility: a social revision of demographic approaches. Comparative Family and Fertility Research. In Tien,H.Y. and Bean,F.D. (Eds.) Leiden: E.J.Brill,1974, 127-157.

STOLKA,S.M. and BARNETT,L.D. Childbearing Motivation Scales

VARIABLES MEASURED. (1) Whether a married couple's prestige is increased by having children; (2) Whether a woman's most important role and main responsibility in life is being a mother; (3) Whether childbearing is a religious duty; (4) Whether marital happiness is contingent upon having children.
TEST DESCRIPTION. Four Guttman scales using 11 items: three each for the "prestige," "woman's role," and "religious duty" scales and two for the "marital happiness" scale. The respondent chooses between Strongly Agree, Agree, Don't know, Disagree, and Strongly disagree. Response to one statement must be in the opposite direction

from the response(s) to the other statement(s) in order for
the respondent to be consistent.
SAMPLE ITEM. Strongly Agree, Agree, Don't know, Disagree.
The more children a couple has, the greater is their social
prestige.
LENGTH. Time: 5 minutes. Items: 11.
AVAILABILITY. In Stolka and Barnett, 1969.
ABSTRACTED BY: Larry D. Barnett
REFERENCE.
        Stolka,S.M. and Barnett,L.D. Education and religion
as factors in women's attitudes motivating childbearing.
Journal of Marriage and the Family, 1969, 31, 740-750.

TROST,J.   Abortion Scale

VARIABLE MEASURED. Favorability to abortion.
TEST DESCRIPTION. Subjects disagree or agree (five stages
of disagreement-agreement) to attitude statements about
legal abortions and how liberal the laws should be.
SAMPLE ITEM. Abortion should be granted only if serious
medical reasons exist.
LENGTH. Items: 3.
AVAILABILITY. In Trost, 1967, and with original Swedish
items from NAPS-2.
ABSTRACTED BY: Jan Trost
REFERENCE.
        Trost,J. Some data on mate selection: Homogomy and
perceived homogomy.   Journal of Marriage and the Family,
1967, 29, 739-755.

WANT,C.K.A. and THURSTONE,L.L.   Attitude Toward Birth
Control Scale

VARIABLE MEASURED. Favorableness toward or acceptance of
birth control.
TEST DESCRIPTION. A Thurstone-type equal-appearing interval
scale.   The subject is asked to put a check next to those
items with which he/she agrees, a double check next to those
with which he/she emphatically agrees, and an X beside those
with which he/she disagrees. There are two alternate forms
of the scale. The score is the median of the scale values
of items double checked by S.
SAMPLE ITEM. Birth control is a legitimate health measure
(scale value, 7.6).
LENGTH. Items: 20 items each in forms A and B.
AVAILABILITY. In Shaw and Wright, 1967; Thurstone, 1931.
REFERENCES.
        Carlson,H.B.   Intellectuals' and students' attitudes.
Psychological Bulletin, 1933, 30, 578.
        Carlson,H.B.   Attitudes of undergraduate students.
Journal of Social Psychology, 1934, 5, 202-213.
        Diggory,J.C. Sex differences in the organizaticn of
attitudes. Journal of Personality, 1953, 22, 89-100.

Ferguson,L.S.   A revision of the primary social attitude scales. Journal of Psychology, 1944, 17, 229-241.

Likert,R.   Roslow,S. and Murphy,G.   A simple and reliable method of scoring the Thurstone attitude scales. Journal of Social Psychology, 1934, 5, 228-238.

Lorge,I.   The   Thurstone   attitude   scales.   I. Reliability and consistency of rejection and acceptance. Journal of Social Psychology, 1939, 10, 187-198.

Shaw,M.E. and Wright,J.M. Scales for the Measurement of Attitudes. New York: McGraw-Hill, 1967. Pp. 134-136.

Smith,M. Change of attitude with reference to birth control. School and Society, 1942, 56, 25-28.

Smith,M. On the increase and homogeneity of attitudes during a sociology course: Second report. School and Society, 1946, 64, 223-225.

Thurstone,L.L. The Measurement of Social Attitudes. Chicago: University of Chicago Press, 1931.

WILKE,W.H.   Birth Ccntrol Scale

VARIABLE MEASURED. Favorableness toward birth control.
TEST DESCRIPTION. A series of items to which the subject indicates   whether   he/she Strongly agrees, Agrees, Is undecided, Disagrees, or Strongly disagrees. Half the items represent statements favorable to birth control, half indicate disapproval of it. The test is scored by summing weights of from 5 (for Strongly agree) to 1 (Strongly disagree) for the positive items and the reverse for the negative items.
SAMPLE ITEM. We should be absolutely opposed to birth control.
LENGTH. Items: 22.
AVAILABILITY. In Shaw and Wright, 1967; Wilke, 1934.
REFERENCES.

Shaw,M.W. and Wright,J.M. Scales for the Measurement of Attitudes. New York: McGraw-Hill, 1967, Pp. 136-137.

Wilke,W.H. An experimental comparison of the speech, the radio, and the printed page as propaganda devices. Archives of Psychology, New York, 1934, 169, 32.

WILLIAMSON,J.B.   Favorability Toward Birth Control Index

VARIABLE MEASURED. Favorability toward birth control.
TEST DESCRIPTION. The scale is composed of three items. Each question is dichotomized into categories indicating a favorable versus unfavorable attitude toward birth control. Positive responses are summed to form the favorability index.
SAMPLE ITEM. Suppose the government of the country recommended to people to limit the size of their family and showed them how to do it. Should people then follow this advice?

LENGTH.   Items: 3.
AVAILABILITY. In Williamson, 1970.
ABSTRACTED BY: Kersti Yllo
REFERENCE.
    Williamson,J.B.   Subjective efficacy and   ideal   family
size   as   predictors   of   favorability toward birth control.
Demography, 1970, 7, 329-339.

E.   Values and Ideology (See also Subject Index)

CUBER,J.F.   and PELL,B.   Family Moral Judgments Technique

VARIABLE MEASURED.   Conformity to traditional sex morals.
TEST DESCRIPTION.   Brief "cases" and "situations" involving
what are thought to be controversial moral issues. Subjects
judge the behavior of   the characters   as   morally right,
wrong, or "uncertainty of opinion." Summation of item scores
is not suggested, but since all items reflect conformity to
traditional sexual morality a summary score is possible.
SAMPLE ITEM. Glenna has been married almost a decade.
There are two children. Her husband's work takes him away
from home often during the evening. Glenna does not object
to this but is annoyed by neighborhood gossip regarding a
friend of hers and her husband's who often comes to spend
the evening with Glenna while her husband is away. This man
has been a good friend of hers and of her husband. "In
fact," she says, "my husband often asks me why I don't
invite Dale to come over oftener. Dale seems just like one
of the family. He's alone much of the time himself and
seems to appreciate coming over. He writes a great deal and
likes to read to me what he has written--says I can give him
a great deal of much-needed criticism, understanding, and
encouragement to go on. That's about all we ever do." (a)
Is this wrong for Glenna? Yes.   No.   Uncertain.   (b) Is
this wrong for Dale? Yes. No. Uncertain.
LENGTH. Items: 12.
AVAILABILITY. In Cuber and Pell, 1941.
REFERENCE.
    Cuber,J.F.   and Pell,B.   A method for studying moral
judgments relating to the family. American Journal of
Sociology, 1941, 47, 12-23.

FENGLER,A.P. Marital Ideology Scales

VARIABLE MEASURED. The extent to which marital commitment
is   based   upon   "economic   security,"   "expressive
companionship" or "parental responsibility."

TEST DESCRIPTION. The test items incorporate instrumental
and expressive attitudes toward marriage. These attitudes
were factor analyzed to identify the major orientations or
ideological commitments of subjects toward marriage. Most
of the explained variance could be accounted for by three
major factors mentioned under "variable measured" above.
Five-point response categories from Strongly agree to
Strongly disagree are used for all items.
SAMPLE ITEM. Except when children are very young both
husband and wife should share responsibility for the
financial support of the family. Strongly agree, Agree,
Agree-Disagree, Disagree, Strongly disagree.
LENGTH. Items: 20.
AVAILABILITY. In Fengler, 1973.
ABSTRACTED BY: A. Fengler
REFERENCE.
      Fengler,A.P. The effects of age and education on
marital ideology. Journal of Marriage and the Family, 1973,
35, 264-271.

FORER,B.R. Forer Sentence Completion Test

VARIABLES MEASURED. Attitudes toward sex, love, and
marriage.
TEST DESCRIPTION. A special rating scale for the eight
items in a 100-item sentence-completion test which refer to
sex, love, and marriage. Items are scored 3 for positive
response, 2 for ambiguous or including both positive and
negative elements, and 1 for negative.
SAMPLE ITEM. After a year of marriage, he/she...
LENGTH. Items: 8 sentence completions.
AVAILABILITY. 8 items in Karen, 1961; complete test in
Forer, 1950.
REFERENCES.
      Forer,B.R.   Structured   sentence   completion   test
responses. Journal of Projective Techniques and Personality
Assessment, 1950, 14, 15-30.
      Karen,R.L. A method for rating sentence completion
test responses. Journal of Projective Techniques and
Personality Assessment, 1961, 25, 312-314.
      VanSlyke,V. and Leton,D.A. Children's perception of
family relationships and their school adjustment. Journal
of School Psychology, 1965, 4, 19-28.

HARDY,K.R. Divorce Opinionaire

VARIABLE MEASURED. Favorableness toward divorce.
TEST DESCRIPTION. A series of Likert-type items, half of
which express attitudes favorable toward divorce and half
unfavorable toward divorce. The subject indicates whether
he/she Strongly agrees (marked with a ++), Mildly agrees
(+), Is more or less neutral or indifferent (0), Mildly
disagrees (-), or Strongly disagrees (--).

SAMPLE ITEM. I feel that divorce is a sensible solution to
many unhappy marriages.
LENGTH. Items: 12.
AVAILABILITY. In Shaw and Wright, 1967.
REFERENCES.
       Hardy,K.R. Determinants of conformity and attitude
change.   Journal of Abnormal Social Psychology, 1957, 54,
289-294.
       Shaw,M.E. and Wright,J.M. Scales for the Measurement
of Attitudes. New York: McGraw-Hill, 1967, 106-108.
       Snow,C. Differential marriage and family perceptions
and attitudes of adolescents living in child care
institutions and adolescents living in intact families.
Adolescence, 1973, 8, 373-378.

HILL,R.J. Favorableness of Attitude to Marriage Scale

VARIABLE MEASURED. Favorableness of attitude toward
marriage.
TEST DESCRIPTION. Multiple-choice items scored to form a
Guttman scale.
SAMPLE ITEM. If you were to marry, to what extent will you
miss the life you have had as a single person? Not at all,
Very little, To some extent, Very much.
LENGTH. Items: 9.
AVAILABILITY. In Hill, 1951; Wallin, 1954.
REFERENCES.
       Hill,R.J. Attitude toward marriage. M.A.   Thesis,
Stanford University, 1951.
       Snow,C. Differential marriage and family perceptions
and attitudes of adolescents living in child care
institutions and adolescents living in intact families.
Adolescence, 1973, 8, 373-378.
       Wallin,P. Marital happiness of parents and their
children's attitude to marriage. American Sociological
Review, 1954, 19, 20-23.

HILL,R.L. STYCOS,J.M. and BACK,K.W. Modesty Scale

VARIABLE MEASURED. Modesty of the spouse.
TEST DESCRIPTION. Responses to items concerning six
activities are dichotomized into positive and negative
answers to form a Guttman Scale.
SAMPLE ITEM. Informing daughter on sex (scale value, 1).
LENGTH. Items: 6.
AVAILABILITY. In Hill et al., 1959, 426.
REFERENCE.
       Hill,R.L. Stycos,J.M. and Back,K.W. The Family and
Population Control: A Puerto Rican Experiment in Social
Change. Chapel Hill: University of North Carolina Press,
1959.

MOTZ,A.B.   Role Conception Inventory

VARIABLES MEASURED. The extent to which the subject
endorses "traditional" and "companionship" marital roles for
himself/herself (personal roles) and in general (public).
TEST DESCRIPTION. The subject is presented with a
random-appearing assortment of statements and is asked to
check those statements which most nearly agree with or
reflect his/her own views. The questions refer to six areas
of behavior: housework, employment, financial support, care
of children, participation in community activities, and
schooling. Within each area the items reflect either a
traditional or a companionship role prescription. Items are
further classified according to whether they indicate
prescriptions for self (personal role), or a general feeling
about the roles of others (public). For example, the sample
item below is classified: financial support, traditional,
public. Scores are the number of traditional-public,
traditional-personal, companionship-public, and
companionship-personal items endorsed. The inventory was
originally devised for women but has been adapted for
husbands (Guerrero, 1965).
SAMPLE ITEM. The wife should help support the family only
when it is absolutely necessary.
LENGTH. Items: 24 for husband, 24 for wife.
AVAILABILITY. 24 sample items are given in Motz, 1952.
REFERENCES.
      Guerrero,S.H. An analysis of husband-wife roles among
Filipino professionals at U.P. Los Banos Campus.
Philippine Sociological Review, 1965, 13, 275-281.
      Motz,A.B. The role conception inventory: a tool for
research in social psychology. American Sociological
Review, 1952, 17, 465-471.
      Weil,M.W. An analysis of the factors influencing
married women's actual or planned work participation.
American Sociological Review, 1961, 26, 91-96.

NELSON,L.W.   Survey of Attitudes and Beliefs

VARIABLE MEASURED. Attitude toward sex, marriage, and
family.
TEST DESCRIPTION. One scale from an attitude test. The
"sex, marriage, and family area" (Area 3) is defined: "A
high score here indicates that the student has knowledge of
accepted sexual behavior and understanding of the social
role of the family; he looks ahead to marriage
realistically and is likely to feel secure in his present
home situation. The low-scoring student indicates poor
understanding of the reasons for conventional sexual
behavior; he is apt to have a negative attitude toward
marriage and family responsibilities." (Nelson, 1955, 5).
      The subject indicates whether he/she agrees, disagrees,
or is undecided about each statement on the survey by
punching a hole in the appropriate circle on the answer

sheet.   The instrument is scored by comparing a scoring key
which is printed in the test booklet to the pattern of holes
punched by the S.
SAMPLE ITEM. A wife should never date men other than her
husband. Agree, Disagree, Undecided.
LENGTH. Items: 49.
AVAILABILITY. From Science Research Associates, 259 East
Erie Street, Chicago, Illinois 60611. 20 tests, $2.75. 20
profiles, $1.20. Specimen set, $.75.
REFERENCE.
     Nelson,L.W. Survey of Attitudes and Beliefs.   Grades
9-12. Form AH. Chicago: Science Research Associates,
1955.

SAMENFINK,J.A. Catholic Sexual and Family Ideology Test

VARIABLES MEASURED. Catholic dogma and ideology concerning
sex and family roles.
TEST   DESCRIPTION.   Forty   statements   considered
representative of Catholic dogma and contra-dogma relative
to sexual behavior;   and 18 attitudinal and factual
questions considered by Catholic authorities to express the
practical ideology of behavior in the marriage of a
Catholic.
SAMPLE ITEM. Both husband and wife should jointly be head
of the family. Agree, Disagree.
LENGTH. Items: 40; 18.
AVAILABILITY. From NAPS.
REFERENCE.
     Samenfink,J.A. A study of some aspects of marital
behavior as related to religious control. Marriage and
Family Living, 1958, 20, 163-169.

STINNETT,N. and MONTGOMERY,J.E.   Perception of Older
Marriages Scale (POM)

VARIABLE MEASURED. Favorableness toward marriage of persons
over age 65.
TEST DESCRIPTION. A six-item Likert-type scale with five
degrees of responses.   The answers are scored so that the
most favorable response is given the highest score and the
least favorable, the lowest. Maximum possible score is 30.
SAMPLE ITEM. Persons aged 65 and over should not enter into
marriage.   (a) Strongly agree, (b) Agree, (c) Neutral, (d)
Disagree, (e) Strongly disagree.
LENGTH. Items: 6.
AVAILABILITY. In Stinnett and Montgomery, 1968.
REFERENCE.
     Stinnett,N. and Montgomery,J.E.   Youth's perceptions
of marriage of older persons. Journal of Marriage and the
Family, 1968, 30, 392-396.

THURSTONE,L.L.   Attitude Toward Divorce Scale

VARIABLE MEASURED. Favorableness toward divorce.
TEST DESCRIPTION. An equal-appearing interval scale.
Subjects check items with which they agree, put an X next to
items with which they disagree. Subject's score is the
median of the scale values of the items checked. The
original scale values computed by Thurstone are not
reported; however, a new set of values was computed by Shaw
and Wright (1967).
SAMPLE ITEM. Divorce is justifiable only after all efforts
to mend the union have failed (scale value, 3.7).
LENGTH. Items: 22.
AVAILABILITY. In Shaw and Wright, 1967; Thurstone, 1931.
REFERENCES.
     Shaw,M.E. and Wright,J.M. Scales for the Measurement
of Attitudes. New York: McGraw-Hill, 1967, 104-106.
     Thurstone,L.L. The Measurement of Social Attitudes.
Chicago: University of Chicago Press, 1931.

WILKENING,E.A.   and BHARADWAJ,L.K.   Husband and Wife
Aspirations Indexes

VARIABLES MEASURED. Level of striving in respect to: (1)
Home improvement, (2) Farm improvement, (3) Community
participation, and (4) Child development.
TEST DESCRIPTION. Four to six items to measure the level of
striving in each of four areas, as viewed by both husband
and wife in questionnaires administered individually.
Factor analysis yielded four clearly defined factors from a
set of 29 items. A fifth factor including leisure items had
items which loaded on other factors so was not used. The
items are scored from 1 to 5 on level of striving.   Scores
of husbands and wives are moderately correlated.
SAMPLE ITEM. Compared with most other families I know, our
family is: Trying much less, Trying somewhat less, Trying
about the same, Trying somewhat more, or Trying much more to
have modern conveniences in the home.
LENGTH. Time: 7 minutes. Items: 19.
AVAILABILITY. In Wilkening and Bharadwaj, 1967.
ABSTRACTED BY: Eugene A. Wilkening
REFERENCES.
     Bharadwaj,L.K. and Wilkening,E.A. Canonical analysis
of farm satisfaction data. Rural Sociology, 1973, 38,
159-173.
     Bharadwaj,L.K.   and   Wilkening,E.A.   Occupational
satisfaction of farm husbands and wives. Human Relations,
1974, 27, 739-753.
     Wilkening,E.A.   and Bharadwaj,L.K.   Dimensions of
aspirations, work roles and decision-making of farm husbands
and wives in Wisconsin. Journal of Marriage and the Family,
1967, 29, 701-706.
     Wilkening,E.A.   and Bharadwaj,L.K.   Aspirations and
task involvement as related to decision-making among farm

husbands and wives. Rural Sociology, 1969, 33, 30-45.
     Wilkening,E.A.   and   VanEs,J.C.   Aspirations   and
attainments among German farm families. Rural Sociology,
1967, 32, 446-455.

F. Other

BACH,G.R.   Father-Typing Rating Scales

VARIABLES MEASURED. The conception of the father which the
mother present to the child in the father's absence. The
scales measure the following: (1) Degree he is idolized or
criticized, (2) His social prestige, (3) Position as a
provider, (4) Devction and interest in the family, and (5)
Aggressive or submissive.
TEST DESCRIPTION. Five rating scales patterned after the
Fels scales, with descriptions at each of five cue points.
Ratings are made on the basis of home interview and
observation.
SAMPLE ITEM.   First cue point: F idol; overimitated.
Second: F worthy; appreciated.   Third: F taken for
granted. Fourth: F criticized;   imitation   reproved.
Fifth: F image taboo.
LENGTH. Items: 5.
AVAILABILITY. In Bach, 1946.
REFERENCE.
     Bach,G.R.   Father-fantasies and father-typing in
father-separated children.   Child Development, 1946, 17,
63-79.

BLAZIER,D.C. and GOOSMAN,E.T.   A Marriage Analysis

VARIABLES MEASURED. Seven aspects of married life: role
concept ideal; feelings toward marriage partner; emotional
openness; knowledge of husband/wife; sexual adjustment and
security; activities, beliefs, and interests in common;
and the meaning cf marriage.
TEST   DESCRIPTION.   A   forced-choice   questionnaire
administered separately to the husband and wife. Questions
are answered according to the respondents' present
attitudes, judgments, and
concepts.   The questionnaire is not designed to be a
fact-finding device, but rather it is intended to reveal
attitudes and feelings of marital partners in terms of the
seven aspects of married life mentioned above.
SAMPLE ITEM. My husband/wife should place my needs above
his/her own desires.
LENGTH. Time: 30 minutes. Items: 113.

AVAILABILITY. From Family Life Publications, Inc., P.O.
Box 6725, College Station, Durham, N.C. 27708.
ABSTRACTED BY: Bruce W. Brown
REFERENCES.
    Araoz,D.L.   Thematic   apperception   test   in
marital-therapy. Journal of Contemporary Psychiatry, 1972,
5, 41.
    Blazier,D.C. and Goosman,E.T. A Marriage Analysis and
Marriage Counselor's Guide. Durham, N.C.: Family Life
Publications, 1966.
    Buros,O.K. (Ed.), Personality Tests and Reviews.
Highland Park, N.J.: Gryphon Press, 1970.

DRISCOLL,R. DAVIS,K.E. LIPETZ,M.E. Feelings Questionnaire

VARIABLES MEASURED. Love, trust, and criticalness between a
couple.
TEST DESCRIPTION. Each member of a couple rates on a
six-point scale how he/she feels about his/her spouse (or
"steady") and how he/she perceives the other feels toward
him/her on key aspects of the relationship. (1) The love
score is based on items concerning: love, care about, need,
and relationship more important than anything else. (2) The
trust scale has five items concerning areas of trust and
being able to count on, considerateness. (3) The
criticalness scale has five items: criticalness,
disappointment, and seeing spouse as uninteresting, not
developing, too dependent.
SAMPLE ITEM. I love my spouse: (6) Completely; (5) Very
much; (4) Moderately; (3) Somewhat; (2) Slightly; (1)
Not at all; (0) Not applicable.
LENGTH. Items: 14.
AVAILABILITY. From NAPS-2.
ABSTRACTED BY: Susan Murray
REFERENCE.
    Driscoll,R.   Davis,K.E.   Lipetz,M.E.   Parental
interference and romantic love: the Romeo and Juliet
effect. Journal of Personality and Social Psychology, 1973,
24, 1-10.

DUNN,M.S. Marriage Role Expectation Inventory

VARIABLES MEASURED. Equalitarian versus traditional
husband-wife role expectations for seven areas: (1)
Authority, (2) Homemaking, (3) Care of children, (4)
Personal characteristics, (5) Social participation, (6)
Education, (7) Employment and support.
TEST DESCRIPTION. The test consists of a series of
statements all starting with "In my marriage, I expect..."
The subject indicates agreement or disagreement on a
five-point scale. Each subscore is represented by 7-12
items, approximately evenly divided between statements
reflecting an equalitarian or a traditional role

expectation. There are parallel forms for boys and girls.
The inventory is scored by assigning +1 for an agreement
with an equalitarian item, -1 for agreement with a
traditional item, and 0 for disagreement or uncertainty on
any item.
SAMPLE ITEM. In my marriage, I expect: That if there is a
difference of opinion, I will decide where to live.
Strongly agree, Agree, Undecided, Disagree, Strongly
disagree.
LENGTH. Time: 20-50 minutes. Items: 71.
AVAILABILITY. In Dunn, 1960.
REFERENCES.
        Buros,O.K.   (Ed.), Personality Tests and Reviews.
Highland Park, N.J.: Gryphon Press, 1970.
        Busdice,J.J.   Marriage   role   expectations   and
personality adjustments. Master's thesis, Northwestern
State College, 1962.
        Dunn,M.S. Marriage role expectations of adolescents.
Ph.D. dissertation, Florida State University, 1959.
        Dunn,M.S. Marriage role expectations of adolescents.
Marriage and Family Living, 1960, 22, 99-111.
        Geiken,K.F.   Expectations   concerning   husband-wife
responsibilities in the home. Journal of Marriage and the
Family, 1964, 26, 349-352.
        Gould,N.S.   Marriage role expectations of single
college students as related to selected social factors.
Ph.D. dissertation, Florida State University, 1961.
        Hobart,C.W. Attitudes toward parenthood among Canadian
young people. Journal of Marriage and the Family, 1973, 35,
71-82.
        Moser,A.J. Marriage role expectations of high school
students. Master's Thesis, Florida State University, 1960.
        Moser,A.J. Marriage role expectations of high school
students. Marriage and Family Living, 1961, 23, 42-43.
        Rooks,E. and King,K. A study of the marriage role
expectations of black adolescents. Adolescence, 1973, 8,
317-324.
        Snow,C. Differential marriage and family perceptions
and attitudes of adolescents living in child care
institutions and adolescents living in intact families.
Adolescence, 1973, 8, 373-378.
        Sterrett,J.E. and Bollman,S.R. Factors related to
adolescents' expectations of marital roles. The Family
Coordinator, 1970, 19, 353-356.

EDMONDS,V.H. Marital Conventionalization Scale

VARIABLE MEASURED. Marital conventionalization: defined as
"the extent to which a person distorts the appraisal of his
marriage in the direction of social desirability."
TEST DESCRIPTION. The test items refer to the most highly
valued aspects of marriage such as happiness, harmony, love,
presence or absence of regret, etc.
        The test is disguised to prevent subjects from

ascertaining by inspection that it is designed to measure
conventionalization. 16 items from the Burgess-Wallin
Marital Happiness Scale are randomly interspersed with the
34 marital conventionalization items.
A short form was developed by using the 15 most
discriminating items with weights assigned according to each
item's contribution to the total variance. (A
product-moment correlation coefficient of .99 was obtained
when the long and short forms were compared.)
SAMPLE ITEM. T F There are times when my mate does things
that make me unhappy.
LENGTH. Items: Long form, 34; short form, 15.
AVAILABILITY. In Edmonds, 1967.
REFERENCES.
      Edmonds,V.H. Marital conventionalization: definition
and measurement. Journal of Marriage and the Family, 1967,
29, 681-688.
      Edmonds,V.H. Withers,G. and Dibatista,B. Adjustment,
conservatism, and marital conventionalization. Journal of
Marriage and the Family, 1972, 34, 96-103.

GLAZER-MALBIN,N. Intimacy Index

VARIABLES MEASURED. (1) Conflict, (2) Dependency, (3)
Confidence sharing, (4) Emotional involvement, and (5)
Relationship primacy within the marital dyad.
TEST DESCRIPTION. A 25-item questionnaire with five factor
scores, one for each of the variables. The seven items in
the Conflict factor are concerned with quarrels, fights, and
other conflict between spouses, and with decreasing
self-disclosure, which is considered concomitant with much
conflict. The eight Dependency items are concerned with the
respondent's views about how necessary the other partner is
for enjoyment of life, satisfaction with activities,
feelings of stability, and other dependency indicators. The
three Confidence sharing items are concerned with the
respondents' view of mutual sharing of feelings and
activities with their marital partner and the extent the
twosome treat each other as trustworthy and dependable in
interpersonal functioning. The five emotional involvement
items are concerned with whether or not the respondent sees
the relationship itself as the central bond in the twosome
relative to common interests and activities. The scoring
consists of summing the factor weighted response category
values.
SAMPLE ITEM. (Conflict factor) When my mate and I are not
quarreling, we seem to have hardly anything to say to each
other. 1 = Very much describes my relationship, 2 =
Somewhat describes my relationship, 3 = Does not describe my
relationship very much, 4 = Does not describe my
relationship at all.
LENGTH. Items: 25.

AVAILABILITY. In Glazer-Malbin, 1975.
ABSTRACTED BY: Susan Murray
REFERENCE.
    Glazer-Malbin,N. (Ed.) Old Family/New Family. New
York: D. Van Nostrand co., 1975, 27-66.

HILL,R.L. Husband-Wife Interaction Index

VARIABLES MEASURED. The relative role of each spouse in
husband-wife interaction on the following dimensions:
amount   of   talking;   domination-subordination   in
decision-making; contribution of ideas; initiative vs.
passivity; degree of partnership; companionate vs.
segregated roles; harmony vs. conflict; face-saving and
smoothing over differences; affection-hostility.
TEST DESCRIPTION. Several questions, designed to generate
discussion between spouses by revealing differences, are
posed to a couple by the interviewer. The interviewer rates
the husband-wife interaction on a structured coding form as
the couple arrive at consensus on the questions.
SAMPLE ITEM. Do you feel that husband and wife should each
have their own circle of friends?
LENGTH. Items: 6.
AVAILABILITY. In Hill, 1970.
ABSTRACTED BY: Kersti Yllo
REFERENCE.
    Hill,R.L.   et al. Family Development in Three
Generations.   Cambridge,   Massachusetts: Schenkman
Publishing Company, 1970.

HUNTINGTON,R.M. The Marital Projection Series (MPS)

VARIABLE MEASURED. The marital relationship sector of each
partner's personality.
TEST DESCRIPTION. The MPS consists of 10 pictures of
couples in various situations which are presented to each
partner separately. Then, the partners are brought
together, again presented the pictures, and asked to make up
stories they can agree on. Sessions with the subjects are
recorded and later transcribed. The resulting protocols can
be analyzed by: (1) Use of Bales's categories (Bales,
1950);   (2) Quantitative ratings on needs (following Murray
et al., 1938); and (3) A qualitative, case-study method.
Huntington believes that this method has the advantage of
more intensive analysis.
SAMPLE ITEM. Picture of male and female sitting at table
with plates, cups and saucers, silverware, other eating
materials, newspaper, empty chair. Window behind them with
half-lowered venetian blinds.
LENGTH. Items: 10 pictures.
AVAILABILITY. From NAPS.

REFERENCES.
     Bales,R.F. Interaction Process Analysis: A Method for
the Study of Groups. Cambridge, Mass: Addison-Wesley,
1950.
     Huntington,R.M.   II.   The   personality-interaction
approach to study of the marital relationship. Marriage and
Family Living, 1958, 20, 43-46.
     Murray,H.A. Explorations in Personality. New York:
Oxford University Press, 1938.

HUTTER,M. Husband Role Attitude Index and Father Role
Attitude Index.

VARIABLE MEASURED. Favorability towards husband and father
roles by married college students.
TEST DESCRIPTION. The tests are Likert-type summated score
indexes. Response categories and scoring are not indicated.
SAMPLE ITEM. Based on your experience, do you think that
being married is a good idea for others who are pursuing the
same educational objectives as you are?
LENGTH. Items: 3 for each index.
AVAILABILITY. In Hutter, 1974.
ABSTRACTED BY: Pam Rosenberg
REFERENCE.
     Hutter,M. Significant others and married student role
attitudes. Journal of Marriage and the Family, 1974, 36,
31-36.

KAUFFMAN,J.H. Traditional-Emergent Family Traits Index

VARIABLES MEASURED. Traditional family traits.
TEST DESCRIPTION. The index consists of 22 questionnaire
items intended to reflect traditional family traits in nine
classes of behavior: authoritarian behavior norms,
patriarchal authority, little open demonstration of
affection, strict discipline and obedience of children,
husband seldom helps with housework, wife seldom works
outside the home, children rarely consulted on major family
decisions, family finances are managed by the husband, and
little sex education received by children from parents. The
weight for each item is the average score for that item.
Total scores below 54 (the median) are categorized as
emergent, those above as traditional.
SAMPLE ITEM. NR.
LENGTH. Items: 22.
AVAILABILITY. In Kauffman, 1960.
REFERENCES.
     Kauffman,J.H. A comparative study of traditional and
emergent family types among midwest Mennonites. Ph.D.
dissertation, University of Chicago, 1960.
     Kauffman,J.H. Interpersonal relations in traditional
and emergent families among midwest Mennonites. Marriage
and Family Living, 1961, 23, 247-252.

KOMISAR,D.D. Marriage Problem Story Completion Test

VARIABLES MEASURED. Marital roles and attitudes, and
related personality characteristics.
TEST DESCRIPTION. A projective technique designed for
individual oral administration. Five cards, each with a
brief summary of a problem facing a married couple, are
presented in sequence to the S. The task is to create a
dialogue between husband and wife which would follow from
the situation, and to supply an ending to each problem.
Designed for marriage counseling interview. No scoring
system.
SAMPLE ITEM. Mr. and Mrs. V. have been married for two
weeks. They have just returned from their honeymoon and are
planning the financial arrangements for their household.
LENGTH. Time: Unlimited, but averages less than 30
minutes. Items: 5.
AVAILABILITY. In Komisar, 1949.
REFERENCE.
    Komisar,D.D. A marriage problem story completion test.
Journal of Consulting Psychology, 1949, 13, 403-406.

KUHN,M.H. and McPARTLAND,T.S. Twenty Statements Test

VARIABLE MEASURED. Salience of family role
self-conceptions.
TEST DESCRIPTION. In adaptation by Buerkle (1960), the S is
asked to ask himself/herself, Who am I? and then to list
the first 20 answers that come to mind. Salience of
self-reference to the state of being married (or being a
member of a nuclear family) is measured by the rank of the
reference, if any is made. If the subject's first
self-reference is that he/she is married (or a member of a
nuclear family), this is scored 20, a high salience for that
category; if the last item, it is scored 1; and if
omitted, 0. Salience may also be measured by the frequency
of family role self-conceptions on the list of 20.
SAMPLE ITEM. Sample responses: I am a father, I am a
husband, I am religious, I am bored.
LENGTH. Time: 12-minute limit. Items: 20 statements
about self.
AVAILABILITY. In Buerkle, 1960; Kuhn and McPartland, 1954.
REFERENCES.
    Buerkle,J.V. Self-attitudes and marital adjustment.
Merrill-Palmer Quarterly, 1960, 6, 114-124.
    Couch,C.J. Family role specialization and
self-attitudes in children. Sociological Quarterly, 1962,
3, 115-121.
    Edwards,R.C. Letter to the editor. Sociological
Quarterly, 1965, 6, 180.
    Gecas,V. Karwin,T.L. and Weigert,A.J. Social
identities in Anglo and Latin adolescents. Social Forces,
1973, 51, 477-484.
    Kuhn,M.H. and McPartland,T.S. An empirical

investigation of self attitudes. American Sociological
Review, 1954, 19, 68-76.
    Mulford,H.A. and Salisbury,W.W. Self-conceptions in a
general population. Sociological Quarterly, 1964, 5, 35-46.
    Scwirian,K.P. Variations in structure of the
Kuhn-McPartland Twenty Statements Test and related response
differences. Sociological Quarterly, 1964, 5, 47-60.
    Stewart,R.L. and Vernon,G.M. Four correlates of
empathy in the dating situation. Sociology and Social
Research, 1959, 43, 279-285.

LAING,R.D. PHILLIPSON,H. and LEE,A.R. Interpersonal
Perception Method (IPM)

VARIABLES MEASURED. Interpersonal perceptions in dyads
concerning the following areas: (1) Interdependence and
autonomy, (2) Warm concern and support, (3) Disparagement
and disappointment, (4) Contentions: fight/flight, (5)
Contradiction and confusion, (6) Extreme denial of autonomy.
TEST DESCRIPTION. The IPM is made up of 60 dyadic issues
around each of which 12 questions must be answered. The 60
issues are presented as phrases that express interaction and
interexperience and deal with the six areas listed above.
The IPM makes provisions for three levels of perspective for
each issue. That is, if (X) stands for any issue:
husband's view of (X) is the direct perspective; husband's
view of wife's view of (X) is the metaperspective; and
husband's view of wife's view of his view of (X) is the
meta-metaperspective. Three similar levels apply to the
wife for each issue. The coding and scoring of responses
and the construction of the IPM profile for a dyad are
explained in Laing, et al., 1966.
SAMPLE ITEM. How true do you think the following are? (1)
She understands me; (2) I understand her; (3) She
understands herself; (4) I understand myself. If you feel
the statement is very true, put a mark in column ++; if it
is slightly true, put a mark in column +; if it is slightly
untrue, put a mark in column -; if it is very untrue, put a
mark in column --.
LENGTH. Time: 70 minutes. Items: 720.
AVAILABILITY. In Laing, et al., 1966.
ABSTRACTED BY: Kersti Yllo
REFERENCE.
    Laing,R.D. Phillipson,H. and Lee,A.R. Interpersonal
Perception. New York: Springer Publishing Company, 1966.

LEVINGER,G. Task and Social-Emotional Marriage Behaviors
(Instrumental and Expressive Marital Behaviors)

VARIABLES MEASURED. (1) Task performance and (2)
Social-emotional behavior--supportiveness, frequency of
communication, sexual relationship.

TEST DESCRIPTION. Task behavior is defined as a subject-object activity and social-emotional behavior as a subject-subject activity. The 10 task items ask who performs tasks associated with the family and with what frequency; the 6 social-emotional items include 4 referring to frequency of communication, 1 referring to praise of the other, and 1 referring to frequency of kissing the spouse when leaving for or coming from work. The items are separately analyzed by means of husband-wife comparisons, and no summed score is derived although this is possible. (Several other measures were used to gather data for comparison with the responses on the task and social-emotional items.)
SAMPLE ITEM. Task: Who (how frequently do you) repairs things around the house? Social-emotional: (How often) do you (does spouse) talk about feelings with (other) when...bothered or upset?
LENGTH. Items: 16.
AVAILABILITY. In Levinger, 1964.
REFERENCE.
        Ater,E.C. and Deacon,R.E. Interaction of family relationship qualities and managerial components. Journal of Marriage and the Family, 1972, 34, 257-263.
        Levinger,G. Task and social behavior in marriage. Sociometry, 1964, 27, 433-448.
        Levinger,G. Systematic distortion in spouses' reports of preferred and actual sexual behavior. Sociometry, 1966, 29, 291-299.
        Levinger,G. and Breedlove,J. Interpersonal attraction and agreement: a study of marriage partners. Journal of Personality and Social Psychology, 1966, 3, 367-372.
        Levinger,G. and Senn,D.J. Disclosure of feelings in marriage. Merrill-Palmer Quarterly, 1967, 13, 237-249.

MURSTEIN,B.I. Attitude of Mother of Hospitalized Child Toward Husband

VARIABLE MEASURED. Perception of husband by mothers of hospitalized children.
TEST DESCRIPTION. 20 single-sentence items. Response format and scoring system are not specified.
SAMPLE ITEM. Husbands are of little help when a child is ill.
LENGTH. Items: 20.
AVAILABILITY. In Murstein, 1958.
REFERENCE.
        Murstein,B.I. Attitudes of parents of hospitalized children toward doctors, nurses, and husbands: the construction of three scales. Journal of Clinical Psychology, 1958, 14, 184-186.

NEUBECK,G.   and SCHLETZER,V.   Extramarital Involvement
Interview

VARIABLES MEASURED. Actual and fantasy involvement with
persons other than spouse.
TEST DESCRIPTION. Open-ended interview questions designed
to elicit information concerning: (1) Actual involvement,
including emotional as well as sexual involvement, and (2)
Fantasy involvement which includes potential and projective
involvement. Two judges divide the subjects into groups,
using a three-part rating scale: Involved, Somewhat
involved, Not involved.
SAMPLE ITEM. (Fantasy:) Suppose you were living next door
to people with whom you had become very close friends. As
it happened, your wife (husband) has gone on a visit in
another part of the country, to her (his) folks perhaps, and
she (he) has the children with her (him). Also, the husband
(wife) next door is away on a business trip, and the wife
(husband) is by herself (himself). How would you feel about
(1) going out to dinner with her (him); (2) spending an
evening or evenings in your or their living room with her
(him); (3) dancing with her (him) to the radio.
LENGTH. NR.
AVAILABILITY. From Neubeck and Schletzer.
REFERENCE.
     Neubeck,G. and Schletzer,V. A study of extra-marital
relationships. Marriage and Family Living, 1962, 24,
279-281.

NYE,F.I. and GECAS,V. The Washington Family Role Inventory

VARIABLES MEASURED. Role norms, sanctions to inforce norms,
role enactment (including role sharing), role strain, role
conflict, role power, role identification, and role
competence, for each of the following roles: provider,
housekeeper, child care, child socialization, kinship,
recreational, sexual and therapeutic.
TEST DESCRIPTION. A 10-page self-administered booklet.
Each item is considered to measure a variable rather than to
be accumulated into a scale. For example, conflict in the
child socialization role may be frequent, occasional or
absent. However, one would likely want to compare it with
conflict in the other seven roles and a conflict index may
be devised by adding conflict across roles. Other similar
indexes may also be computed.
SAMPLE ITEM. Do you ever worry about how you do each of the
following activities? Housekeeping: Never = 1; Seldom =
2; Sometimes = 3; Frequently = 4; Very frequently = 5;
I've never done this = 6.
LENGTH. Time: 30-60 minutes. Items: 120.
AVAILABILITY. Single copies free from: Department of Rural
Sociology, 27 Wilson Hall, Washington State University,
Pullman, Washington 99163. Also available from NAPS-2.

ABSTRACTED BY: F.   Ivan Nye and Viktor Gecas
REFERENCES.
      Gecas,V. and Nye,F.I. Sex and class differences in
parent-child interaction: a test of Kohn's hypothesis.
Journal of Marriage and the Family, 1974, 36, 742-749.
      Nye,F.I. Emerging and declining family roles. Journal
of Marriage and the Family, 1974, 36, 238-245.
      Nye,F.I. Role Structure and Analysis of the Family.
Beverly Hill, CA: Sage Publications, 1976.

PAIGE,K.E. and PAIGE,J.M. Birth Practices Indexes: Scale
1, Maternal Restrictions During Pregnancy Scale; Scale 2,
Husband Involvement During Pregnancy Scale

VARIABLES MEASURED. (1) Societal restriction of women's
behavior during pregnancy.   (2) Societal norms requiring
changes in men's behavior during pregnancy of spouse.
TEST DESCRIPTION: The customary birth practices of a
society are coded from ethnographic sources to determine the
presence or absence of each custom on the scale, which is
ordered into a Guttman-type scale.   Scale 1 measures
maternal restriction during pregnancy. Societies with high
scores have close monitoring and control of the birth
process, and indicate the presence of significant maternal
restriction.   Scale 2 measures societal norms requiring
change in men's behavior during pregnancy of spouse.   The
lowest scale category indicates the absence of any change in
husband behavior.   The three highest categories include
behavior which could be called couvade. The scale indicates
the presence or absence of couvade.
SAMPLE ITEM. Scale 1: Eating certain foods during either
pregnancy or post-partum is restricted. Scale 2: Minor
ritual observances, such as seeking a vision, performs
birth-related sacrifices. May help wife with daily chores.
LENGTH. Items: 5 for each scale.
AVAILABILITY. From Paige and Paige, 1973.
ABSTRACTED BY: Susan Murray
REFERENCE.
      Paige,K.E.   and Paige,J.M.   The politics of birth
practices: a strategic analysis, The American Sociological
Review, 1973, 38, 663-677.

PATTERSON,G.R. RAY,R.S. SHAW,D.A. and COBB,J.A.   Marital
Interaction Coding System (MICS)

VARIABLES MEASURED. Verbal and nonverbal behaviors that
occur as marriage partners attempt to negotiate resolution
of a problem, as follows: Agree, Approve, Accept
responsibility, Assent, Attention, Command, Compliance,
Complain,   Criticize,   Compromise,   Disagree,   Deny
responsibility, Excuse, Humor, Interrupt, Laugh,
Noncompliance, Normative, No response, Negative solution,
Not tracking, Problem description, Positive physical

contact, Positive solution, Put down, Question, Talk, Turn
off.
TEST DESCRIPTION. MICS consists of two basic types of
behavior codes: verbal categories to code the content of a
speaker's statements, and nonverbal categories to record
such behaviors as facial expressions and eye contact. In
the majority of cases one sentence will be coded as one
behavior unit. Observers use a coding form divided into ten
30-second lines, for a total of five minutes of recorded
behavior per coding sheet. Each 30-second line is, in turn,
divided horizontally into two parts, the upper half of the
line being used for recording the husband's behavior and the
lower half being used for recording the wife's behavior. At
the beginning of each line the coder records the appropriate
verbal code for the person who is talking (and a nonverbal
code if necessary) and just to the right of this, on the
other half of the time line, records a nonverbal code for
the behavior of the listener. This process continues
throughout the 30-second line, with every change in behavior
unit being indicated by the recording of a new behavior
code(s). The effect is that of a time line in which the
behavior that takes place is recorded in sequence from left
to right. By looking at a completed coding sheet the reader
can determine for any given moment (a) who was speaking and
who was listening, (b) the content of the speaker's
statement and any nonverbal concomitants, and (c) the
nonverbal behavior of the listener.
SAMPLE ITEM. Agree: Situations where one person expresses
or advances an opinion and the other's verbal response
indicates that the two parties are in agreement on the
issue.
LENGTH. Items: 28 coding categories.
AVAILABILITY. In Hops, Wills, Weiss, and Patterson, 1972;
and Patterson, Ray, Shaw, and Cobb, 1969. The 28 category
version is in Patterson, 1976.
REFERENCES.
    Gonzalez,J. Martin,S. and Dysart,R. Comparison of
various methods of recording behavior. Proceedings, 81st
Annual Convention, APA.
    Hops,H. Wills,T.A. Weiss,R.L. and Patterson,G.R.
Marital interaction coding system (MICS). Unpublished
manuscript, University of Oregon and Oregon Research
Institute, 1972. See NAPS Document 02077 for 29 pages of
suplementary material. Order from ASIS/NAPS, c/o Microfiche
Publications, 440 Park Avenue South, New York, N.Y. 10016.
Remit in advance for each NAPS accession number $1.50 for
microfiche or $5.00 for photocopies. Make checks payable to
Microfiche Publications.
    Jacobsen,N.S. The effects of behavioral treatment
program on troubled marriages: a pilot study. Unpublished
Master's Thesis, University of North Carolina, Chapel Hill,
1974.
    Johnson,S.M. and Lobitz,G.K. The personal and marital
adjustment of parents as related to observed child deviance
and parenting behaviors. Journal of Abnormal Child

Psychology, 1974, 2, 193-207.
    Lerner,L.F. Actual versus expected compatibility in
the   problem-solving   dyad.   Unpublished   Doctoral
Dissertation. University of Oregon, 1973.
    Patterson,G.R. Some procedures for assessing changes
in marital interaction patterns. Oregon Research Institute
Research Bulletin, 1976, 16, No. 7.
    Patterson,G.R. and Hops,H. Coercion, a game for two:
intervention   techniques   for   marital   conflict.   In
Ulrich,R.E.   and Mountjoy,P.   (Eds.)   The   Experimental
Analysis   of   Social   Behavior.   New   York:
Appleton-Century-Crofts, 1972, 424-440.
    Patterson,G.R. Hops,H. and Weiss,R.L. Interpersonal
skills training for couples in the early stages of conflict.
Journal of Marriage and the Family, 1975, 37, 295-303.
    Patterson,G.R.   Hops,H.   and Weiss,R.L.   A   social
learning approach to reducing rates of marital conflict. In
Stuart,R. Liberman,R. and Wilder,S. (Eds.) Advances in
Behavior Therapy. New York: Academic Press, 1976.
    Patterson,G.R.   Ray,R.S.   Shaw,D.A.   and   Cobb,J.A.
Manual   for   coding   family   interaction,   1969.   Document
 01234. Order from ASIS/NAPS, c/o Microfiche Publications,
440 Park Avenue South, New York, N.Y. 10016. Remit in
advance $5.45 for photocopies, $1.50 for microfiche. Make
checks payable to Microfiche Publications.
    Patterson,G.R. Weiss,R.L. and Hops,H.   Training of
marital   skills: some   problems   and   concepts.   In
Leitenberg,H. (Ed.) Handbook of Behavior Modification. New
York: Prentice-Hall, 1976.

PODELL,L. Familial Role Expectation Scale

VARIABLES   MEASURED.   Specificity-diffuseness   and
neutrality-affectivity in family role prescriptions.
TEST DESCRIPTION. Two six-item Guttman scales, one for
specificity-diffuseness and one for neutrality-affectivity.
SAMPLE ITEM. Specificity-diffuseness: To be a good father,
I should be successful in my occupation: Agree-Disagree.
Neutrality-affectivity: Too much emotional involvemment in
a   marriage   can   lead   to   unrealistic   planning:
Agree-Disagree.
LENGTH.   Items: Specificity-diffuseness: 4;
Neutrality-affectivity: 5.
AVAILABILITY. In Podell, 1967.
REFERENCE.
    Podell,L. Occupational and familial role-expectations.
Journal of Marriage and the Family, 1967, 29, 492-493.

ROLFE,D.J.   Financial Priorities Inventory

VARIABLES MEASURED.   (1)   Financial   priorities: the
individual rank crdering of preferences for money use. (2)
Couple's financial priorities consensus: the degree of
similarity between couple member's financial priorities.
TEST DESCRIPTION.   The test consists of 10   sections.
Section 1 is a listing of 36 categories often found in
family budgets. Subjects individually choose which they
feel are the 10 most important categories, and rank order
their choices. The rank ordering can be compared with that
derived from test populations (Rolfe, 1974 and 1975a) or
with the rank ordering of the subject's partner. Scoring is
accomplished by comparing partner A's rank ordering with
partner B's. Any items in A's rank not common to B are
scored 10.   Items in common are scored 0, with any rank
order difference added to the score. The sum of these 10
comparisons is subtracted from 100 to find the couple's
consensus score.   (See   Rolfe,   1975a   for   percentile
comparison rankings.)
     Sections 2 through 10 ask the subject to estimate the
net monthly income needed for comfortable married living;
expectations about the cost of purchasing a car;   rent or
mortgage costs;   and debt accumulation. The subject is also
instructed to indicate who will be primarily responsible for
paying bills and handling the checkbook; and how much say
each partner will have in budget planning. These last two
items are forced-choice items: there is no allowance for
the socially desirable response of "we do everything
together."
SAMPLE ITEM. Some people feel uncomfortable when they use
credit cards or charge items at stores. How much total debt
(everything except house mortgage) could you have in the
first year of your marriage WITHOUT feeling anxious or
uncomfortable? $____
LENGTH. Items: 10.
AVAILABILITY. In Rolfe, 1975b or from author.
ABSTRACTED BY: David J. Rolfe
REFERENCES.
     Rolfe,D.J.   The financial priorities inventory.   The
Family Coordinator, 1974, 23, 139-141.
     Rolfe,D.J.   Marriage adjustment of couples: a
pre-marriage assessment, and follow-up in marriage. Ph.D.
Dissertation, Michigan State University, (East Lansing,
Michigan), 1975a.
     Rolfe,D.J. Marriage Preparation Manual. New York:
Paulist Press, 1975b.

SCHLEIN,S. and GUERNEY,B.G.Jr.   The Relationship Change
Scale

VARIABLES MEASURED. Change in the quality of a relationship
such as satisfaction, communication, trust, intimacy,
sensitivity, openness, and understanding.

TEST DESCRIPTION. Respondents are asked to respond to a series of items which assess how they feel about the quality of their relationship in comparison with a specific time in the past on a four-point scale. Scores range from 27 to 108; the higher the score, the greater the satisfaction with the relationship. The time interval can be varied to suit the needs of the investigation.
SAMPLE ITEM. In comparison with___ago, my satisfaction with my partner as a person has become: (a) Much less; (b) Less; (c) Unchanged; (d) Greater; (e) Much greater.
LENGTH. Items: 27.
AVAILABILITY. In Guerney, 1977.
ABSTRACTED BY: Carole Hatch
REFERENCES.
    Guerney,B.G.Jr.   Relationship   Enhancement   Skill Training Programs for Therapy, Prevention, and Enrichment. San Francisco: Jossey-Bass, 1977.
    Rappaport,A.F.   The   effects   of   an   intensive relationship modification program.   Ph.D.   Dissertation, Pennsylvania State University, 1971.
    Schlein,S. Training dating couples in empathic and open communication: an experiment evaluation of a potential preventative mental health program.   Ph.D.   Dissertation, Pennsylvania State University, 1971. As used in Chapters 3 and 8 in Olson,D.H.L. (Ed.) Treating Relationships. Lake Mills, Iowa: Graphic Publications.

STUART,R.B. and STUART,F. Marital Pre-Counseling Inventory

VARIABLES MEASURED; (1) Assets of spouses. (2) Behavior change targets. (3) Perceived and ideal decision making power of both spouses. (4) Self-ratings and ratings of spouse's perceived satisfaction in 12 areas of functioning, with subsequent detailed assessment of these aspects of satisfaction in the areas of communication, sexual experience, and child management. (5) Commitment to the marriage. (6) Understanding of each other's evaluation.
TEST DESCRIPTION. The Inventory is for use both as a clinical and research tool. Beginning with demographic information, it leads couples through a self-assessment of major areas of their marital experience with each sub-section both measuring satisfaction in its area and delineating targets for change.
    The Inventory consists of six Likert-type scales with additional open response items. The scales are scored to measure the level of satisfaction of each spouse, their agreement on their reciprocal functioning, and their understanding of each other's evaluation. Open-ended items are scored both quantitatively and qualitatively. For example, answers to the question: "Please list ten things which your spouse does which please you" are scored as follows: the number of entries is counted; and entries are then coded for instrumental or expressive focus and for their egocentric, alterocentric or cocentric importance.

The Inventory is suitable for use as an aid to treatment planning, as a means of assessing changes in couples over time and as a means of comparing the marital experience of cohorts of couples at any given time.
SAMPLE ITEM. See above.
LENGTH. 6 scales, 11 pages.
AVAILABILITY. Research Press, 2612 N. Mattis Avenue, Champaign, Illinois 61820.
ABSTRACTED BY: Richard B. Stuart (modified)
REFERENCE.
     Stuart,R.B. and Stuart,F. Marital Precounseling Inventory and Guide. Champaign, Illinois: Research Press, 1972.

THARP,R.G. Marriage Role Dimensions

VARIABLES MEASURED. Role expectations and role enactments for 22 factors grouped under five classes: (1) External relations--social activity, community affairs; (2) Internal instrumentality--wife adequacy, work performance; (3) Division of responsibility--role-sharing, social influence, masculine authority, division of influence; (4) Sexuality--premarital chastity, sexual fidelity, sexual gratification; (5) Solidarity--intimacy, social and emotional integration, togetherness, understanding, companionship.
TEST DESCRIPTION. A 98-item questionnaire--the first 50 items refer to marriage role expectations, the next 48 refer to marriage role enactments. The questionnaire is given separately to husband and wife. Each item is checked by a Likert-type rating (e.g., How important for the ideal marriage is it...? Very essential, Usually desirable, Makes little or no difference, Usually not desirable, Decidedly not desirable). There are nine other types of response categories used for various questions--for example, Disagree much to Agree very much, Wife much more to Husband much more. Factor analyses were conducted separately for men and for women to determine the variables listed. Factors for the husband's expectations are: intimacy, sexual gratification, social influence, wife role adequacy, role-sharing, sexual fidelity, premarital chastity, social intellectual equality, and parental adequacy. The wife's factors are the same except that parental adequacy and role sharing are not important and the factors for participation in community affairs and desire for masculine dominancy are added. For role enactments, the factors which appear for both husband and wife are: intimacy, social activity, participation in community affairs, social integration, social influence, division of influence, understanding, and work performance. Factors for husbands only are wife role adequacy and nonsexual companionship; factors for wives only are sexual gratification and masculine authority role.

SAMPLE ITEM. (Role expectations:) How important for the
ideal marriage is it: that the husband should be the social
equal of his wife? (Role enactments:) How well do you (your
spouse) play the following parts: housekeeper?
LENGTH. Items: 98
AVAILABILITY. In Tharp, 1963.
REFERENCES.
    Amanat,E. and Able,S. Marriage role conflicts and
child psychopathology. Adolescence, 1973, 8, 575-588.
    Barton,K. and Cattell,R.B. Marriage dimensions and
personality. Journal of Personality and Social Psychology,
1972, 21, 369-375.
    Barton,K. Kawash,G. and Cattell,R.B. Personality,
motivation, and marital role factors as predictors of life
data in married couples. Journal of Marriage and the
Family, 1972, 34, 474-480.
    Crago,M. and Tharp,R.G. Psychopathology and marital
role disturbance: a test of the Tharp-Otis descriptive
hypothesis. Journal of Consulting and Clinical Psychology,
1968, 32, 338-341.
    Kelly,E.L. Consistency of the adult personality.
American Psychologist, 1955, 10, 659-681.
    Quick,E. and Jacob,T. Marital disturbance in relation
to role theory and relationship theory. Journal of Abnormal
Psychology, 1973, 82, 309-316.
    Tharp,R.G. Dimensions of marriage roles. Marriage and
Family Living, 1963, 25, 389-404.
    Tharp,R.G.   Meadow,A.   Lennhoff,S.G.   and
Satterfield,D. Changes in marriage roles accompanying the
acculturation of the Mexican-American wife. Journal of
Marriage and the Family, 1968, 30, 404-412.

VEROFF,J. and FELD,S. Marriage Restrictiveness Index

VARIABLES MEASURED. Subject's perception of marriage or the
change from the single to the married status as being
restricting or burdensome upon his/her life style.
TEST DESCRIPTION. Subjects are asked to discuss how a man's
or a woman's life is changed by being married. Each
response is coded for whether or not it indicates that the
subject views "the changes accompanying marriage as
restricting one's life or
burdening a man or a woman with new responsibilities." The
final index is a three-point scale summarizing across all
responses: it indicates whether (1) No, (2) Some, or (3)
All responses indicate that the respondent saw marriage as
restrictive.
SAMPLE ITEM. Thinking about a man's (woman's) life--how is
a man's (woman's) life changed by being married?
LENGTH. NR.
AVAILABILITY. In Veroff and Feld, 1970.
ABSTRACTED BY: Kersti Yllo

REFERENCE.
   Veroff,J. and Feld,S. Marriage and Work in America.
New York: Van Nostrand Reinhold Co., 1970, 86.

Chapter III

Parent-Child and Sibling to Sibling Relationship Measures

A. Conflict and Integration

1. Acceptance-Rejection, Adjustment, Satisfaction (See also Subject Index)

AUSUBEL,D.P.   BALTHAZAR,E.E.   ROSENTHAL,I.   BLACKMAN,L.S.
SCHPOONT,S.H.   and   WELKOWITZ,J.   Perceived Parent Attitude Rating

VARIABLES MEASURED. Child's perceptions of parental role prescriptions and behavior-- (1) Parental acceptance-rejection and (2) Parental Intrinsic-extrinsic valuation of child.
TEST DESCRIPTION. Items rated by child on five-point scales to indicate his/her parents' attitudes and behavior; 18 items each correspond to acceptance-rejection and intrinsic-extrinsic valuation.
SAMPLE ITEM. No matter what happens, I know that I can always turn to my parents for help.
LENGTH. Items: 36.
AVAILABILITY. From NAPS.
REFERENCE.
    Ausubel,D.P.   Balthazar,E.E.,   Rosenthal,I.
Blackman,L.S.   Schpoont,S.H.   and   Welkowitz,J.   Perceived parent attitudes as determinants of children's ego

structure. Child Development, 1954, 25, 173-183.

AUSUBEL,D.P.   BALTHAZAR,E.E.   ROSENTHAL,I.   BLACKMAN,L.S.
SCHPOONT,S.H. and WELKOWITZ,J. Thematic Materials Test

VARIABLES MEASURED. (1) Parental acceptance-rejection and
(2) Intrinsic-extrinsic valuation of child.
TEST DESCRIPTION. Sixteen selected pictures from the TAT,
Children's Apperception Test, Blacky Pictures, Symonds
Adolescent Fantasy Test, and the Lydia Jackson Projection
Test, and 16 brief uncompleted stories. Half the pictures
and half the stories illustrate acceptance-rejection, the
other half intrinsic-extrinsic valuation. All pictures and
stories are presented individually to the child. After
presentation subject is given two alternative
interpretations, one indicating acceptance and the other
rejection, or one indicating intrinsic and the other
extrinsic valuation. Subject is requested to choose the
alternative he/she thinks most in accord with the situation
in the picture or story. Scores are the number of choices
in each category.
SAMPLE ITEM. NR.
LENGTH. Items: 16 pictures and 16 stories.
AVAILABILITY. From authors.
REFERENCE.
     Ausubel,D.P.   Balthazar,E.E.   Rosenthal,I.
Blackman,L.S. Schpoont,S.H. and Welkowitz,J. Perceived
parent attitudes as determinants of children's ego
structure. Child Development, 1954, 25, 173-183.

BRUNKAN,R.J. Family Relations Inventory.

VARIABLES MEASURED. (1) Mother avoidance, (2) Mother
acceptance, (3) Mother concentration, (4) Father avoidance,
(5) Father acceptance, (6) Father concentration.
     An abstract of this test is given in Johnson,O.G.
Tests and Measurements in Child Development: Handbook II.
San Francisco: Josey-Bass, 1976.

CASSEL,R.N. Child Behavior Rating Scale

VARIABLE MEASURED. Home adjustment.
TEST DESCRIPTION. Twenty statements (of a total of 78 in a
general child behavior instrument) which a teacher or other
rater checks on a six-point scale from 1 (yes) to 6 (no).
The scale values are added to give a total score for each
area with low scores indicating undesirable home adjustment.
For kindergarten and grades 1-3.
SAMPLE ITEMS. Often expresses strong dislike for home and
family. There is evidence of overdominance by parents (do
too much of child's thinking). There is evidence of
excessive bad habits in home.

LENGTH. Time: 5-10 minutes. Items: 20.
AVAILABILITY. From Western Psychological Services, Box 775,
Beverly Hills, California 90213. Manual and sample test,
$10.00.
REFERENCES.
        Buros,O.K.   (Ed.) Personality Tests and Reviews
Highland Park, N.J.: Gryphon Press, 1970.
        Cassel,R.N.   Child Behavior Rating Scale Manual.
Beverly Hills, California: Western Psychological Services,
1962.
        Cassel,R.N. A comparison of teacher and parent ratings
on the Child Behavior Rating Scale for 800 primary pupils.
Journal of Educational Research, 1964, 57, 437-439.

COOPER,J.B. and BLAIR,M.A. Parent Evaluation Scale

VARIABLE MEASURED. Child's evaluation of his/her parents on
a diverse series of items.
TEST DESCRIPTION. Subject checks all items which are like
his/her parents on a list of 25 positive and 25 negative
statements about parental attributes. The statements are
grouped as follows: (1) Statements describing relations
with child: (a)   positive   statements--acceptance,
comradeship, helpfulness, consistency, reasonableness,
assurances of love and affection, confidence in child's good
judgment, acceptance of parental role, and wholesomeness of
attitudes   toward   sex   and   dating;   (b)   negative
statements--favoritism for a sibling, rejection, neglect,
punitiveness, overprotection, martyrdom, nagging, scolding,
ridicule, coldness, lack of confidence in the child's
authoritarian control, and unwholesomeness of attitudes
toward   sex   and   dating.   (2)   Statements describing
personality traits: (a) positive statements--cheerfulness,
friendliness, hospitality, optimism, self-confidence, and a
sense of humor;   (b)   negative   statements--pessimism,
irritability, stinginess, insecurity, quarrelsomeness, and
unfriendliness. The original list of 85 statements for each
parent was reduced to 50 statements by using only items with
small judge deviation scores.
SAMPLE ITEM. (A filler statement:) I have felt closer to my
mother than to my father.
LENGTH. Items: 50.
AVAILABILITY. In Cooper, 1966.
REFERENCES.
        Cooper,J.B. Parent evaluation and social ideology.
Psychological Reports, 1960, 7, 414.
        Cooper,J.B. Two scales for parent evaluation. Journal
of Genetic Psychology, 1966, 108, 49-53.
        Cooper,J.B. and Blair,M.A. Parent evaluation as a
determiner of ideology. Journal of Genetic Psychology,
1959, 94, 93-100.
        Cooper,J.B.   and Lewis,J.H.   Parent evaluation as
related   to social ideology and academic achievement.
Journal of Genetic Psychology, 1962, 101, 135-143.

Schultz,J.P.   Firetto,A.   and   Walker,R.E.   The
relationship of parental assessment and anxiety in high
school freshmen. Psychology in the Schools, 1969, 6,
311-312.

FARBER,B. Material Involvement with Retarded Child Scale

VARIABLE MEASURED. Current personal impact of the retarded
child on the mother.
TEST DESCRIPTION. Each respondent is asked the extent to
which the following items are descriptive of the situation:
(a) Our retarded child needs patience and understanding.
(b) Our retarded child is hard to handle. (c) I feel worn
out from taking care of our retarded child.   (d) My life
revolves around our retarded child. Response categories are
combined to form dichotomies. The range for scores is 0 to
4, with 4 indicating great stress.
SAMPLE ITEM. Our retarded child needs patience and
understanding.
LENGTH. Items: 4.
AVAILABILITY. In Farber, 1959 and Meyerowitz, 1966.
ABSTRACTED BY: Bruce Brown
REFERENCES.
Barsch,R.H.   The   Parent   of   the   Handicapped   Child.
Springfield, Illinois: Charles C Thomas, Publisher, 1968.
Farber,B. Effects of a Severely Retarded Child on
Family Integration. Monographs of the Society for Research
in Child Development, 1959, 24, 2.
Farber,B. Perceptions of crisis and related variables
in the impact of a retarded child on the mother. Journal of
Health and Human Behavior, 1960, 1, 108-118.
Farber,B. Jenne,W.C. and Toigo,R. Family crisis and
the decision to institutionalize the retarded child, Council
for Exceptional Children Research Monograph Series, 1960, 1.
Meyerowitz,J.H. Maternal involvement and educational
retardation. Journal of Marriage and the Family, 1966, 28,
87-93.

FARBER,B. Satisfaction with Family Role Performance Indexes

VARIABLES MEASURED.   (1)   Father's   and   (2)   Mother's
satisfaction with child's performance of social-emotional
activities; (3) Father's and (4) Mother's satisfaction with
child's performance of instrumental activities; (5) Child's
perception of Father's and (6) Mother's satisfaction with
social-emotional activities; (7) Child's perception of
father's and (8) Mother's satisfaction with instrumental
activities.
TEST DESCRIPTION. A list of 50 activities which the subject
(mother, father, child) is asked to rate: Much less, A
little less, As I do now, A little more, Much more, or Does
not apply. Factor scores provide the weight for each item
in the total score. The instrumental index is a contrived

scale with items from the list of 50 activities; this scale
ranges from a minimum of parental satisfaction with the
child's conformity to conventional behavior to a maximum of
parental satisfaction with the child's performance of
specific tasks.
SAMPLE ITEM. If your mother could change the following
things about you, which cf them do you think she would like
to have you do more often, less--and which do you think she
would like you to do as you do now? Show affection toward
father. Show affection toward mother. Be friendly to
people.
LENGTH. Items: 50.
AVAILABILITY. In Farber and Jenne, 1963, 21-28 and
Appendixes A and B.
REFERENCES.
     Farber,B.   Marital integration as a factor in
parent-child relations. Child Development, 1962, 33, 1-14.
     Farber,B.   and Jenne,W.C. Family organization and
parent-child communication: parents and siblings of a
retarded child. Monographs of the Society for Research in
Child Development, 1963, 28, No. 7 (Serial No. 91).

HAAS,M.B. and BRITTON,J.H. (1) Acceptance Scale; (2)
Parent for Child Understanding Scale

VARIABLES MEASURED. (1) Acceptance of the child (14 items);
(2) Understanding of the child and his needs (14 items);
(3) Overprotective acceptance (7 items); (4) Overprotective
understanding (7 items).
TEST DESCRIPTION. The scale for each variable consists of a
seven-point continuum. Scores on the first two scales are
the sums of the rating of the items; scores on the second
two scales are weighted values which reduce the score of the
overprotective, overindulgent mother. A trained O makes the
ratings based on interview material from the mother.
SAMPLE ITEMS. Loving 7 6 5 4 3 2 1 Resentful. Indifferent
1 2 3 4 5 6 7 Laudatory.
LENGTH. Items: 42.
AVAILABILITY. From authors.
REFERENCE.
     Haas,M.B. and Britton,J.H. Competition in children as
related to maternal acceptance. Journal of Home Economics,
1961, 53, 179-184.

HESTON,J.C. Heston Personal Adjustment Inventory

VARIABLE MEASURED. Satisfaction of child with family.
TEST DESCRIPTION. A personality inventory requiring Yes-No
responses to each item. A high home satisfaction score
denotes the following: pleasant family relations; an
appreciation of desirable home conditions; a feeling of
mutual understanding and respect; freedom from emotion
breeding home ccnflict; and a healthy recognition of one's

obligation to home and family.
SAMPLE ITEM. Do you find less appreciation at home than
elsewhere? Yes, No.
LENGTH. Items: 270.
AVAILABILITY. See Heston, 1949.
REFERENCES.
      Auble,D. Validity indices for the Heston personal
adjustment inventory. Journal of Applied Psychology, 1957,
41, 79-81.
      Heston,J.C. Heston Personal Adjustment Inventory.
Yonkers, N.Y.: World Book, 1949.
      Tindall,R.H. Relationships among indices of adjustment
status. Educational and Psychological Measurement, 1955,
15, 152-162.

HURLEY,J.R. Child Behavior Inventory

VARIABLES MEASURED. (1) Active (manifest) rejection of the
child by the parent, (2) Overprotection, (3) Achievement
pressure on the child, (4) Passive-rejection of the child by
the parent, and (5) Over-indulgence of the child by the
parent.
TEST DESCRIPTION. Self-administered questionnaire based on
Shoben (1949) and Mark (1953). There are 36 manifest
rejection items, a 30-item overprotection cluster, 29
achievement pressure items, 33 passive rejection items, and
25 over-indulgent items. Five response categories are given
for each item: Strongly agree, Mildly agree, Neutral,
Mildly disagree and Strongly disagree. These are scored
from 0 to 4. Each scale is balanced by nearly equal numbers
of "Agreement" and "Disagreement" items.
SAMPLE ITEM. It is better for children to play at home than
to visit other children.
LENGTH. Time: 45 minutes. Items: 178.
AVAILABILITY. From NAPS-2.
ABSTRACTED BY: Thomas G. Sparhawk and J.R.Hurley
REFERENCES.
      Hurley,J.R. Achievement pressure: an attitudinal
correlate of college course grades. Psychological Reports,
1962, 10, 695-702.
      Hurley,J.R. and Hohn,R.L. Shifts in child-rearing
attitudes linked with parenthood and occupation.
Developmental Psychology, 1971, 4, 324-328.
      Hurley,J.R. and Laffey,J.J. Influence of a
conventional child psychology course upon attitudes toward
children. Collected Papers of the Michigan Academy of
Science, Arts, and Letters, 1957, 42, 299-306.
      Mark,J.C. Attitudes of mothers of male schizophrenics
toward child behavior. Journal of Abnormal and Social
Psychology, 1953, 48, 185-190.
      Shoben,E.J.Jr. The assessment of paternal attitudes in
relation to child adjustment. Genetic Psychology
Monographs, 1949, 39, 101-148.

HURLEY,J.R. Child Relations Inventory

VARIABLES MEASURED. (1) Manifest rejection of the child by
the adult or parent, (2) Achievement pressure exerted toward
the child, (3) Overprotection of the child.
TEST DESCRIPTION. Self-administered questionnaire derived
from the prior Child Behavior Inventory used in the Hurley
and Hohn (1971) study. There are 45 items, 30 concerned
with manifest rejections, 10 with achievement pressure, ancd
5 with overprotection. Five response categories (Strongly
agree, Tend to agree. Neither agree nor disagree, Tend to
disagree, and Strongly disagree) are used for all items.
The manifest rejection scale contains equal numbers of
"agree" and "disagree" items. Strongly agree responses are
scored 4 points for "agree" items but 0 points for
"disagree" items; tend to agree responses are scored 3
points for "agree" items but 1 point for "disagree" items,
neither agree or disagree responses are scored 2 points for
all items, etc.
SAMPLE ITEM.   (1) It is hard to make some children really
"feel bad."
LENGTH. Time: 10 to 15 minutes. Items: 45.
AVAILABILITY. From NAPS-2.
ABSTRACTED BY: J.R. Hurley
REFERENCES.
        Hurley,J.R.   Achievement   pressure: an   attitudinal
correlate of college course grades. Psychological Reports,
1962, 10, 695-702.
        Hurley,J.R.   Parental   acceptance-rejection   and
children's intelligence.   Merrill-Palmer Quarterly, 1965,
11, 19-31.
        Hurley,J.R. and Hohn,R.L.   Shifts in child-rearing
attitudes   linked   with   parenthood   and   occupation.
Developmental Psychology, 1971, 4, 324-328.
        Hurley,J.R. and Randolph,C.C.   Behavioral attributes
preferred in eight-year-olds. JSAS Catalog of Selected
Documents in Psychology, 1971, 1, 10.

HURLEY,J.R. Manifest Rejection (MR) Index

VARIABLE MEASURED. Acceptance-Rejection.
TEST DESCRIPTION. The items concern the general inclination
of parents to endorse a tough disciplinary policy toward
children. To restrain the influence of the acquiescence
response sets, extreme scores can be obtained only by
agreeing with certain items and disagreeing with their
counterparts.
SAMPLE ITEM. See test description. All items use the
following respcnse categories: Strongly agree, Mildly
agree, Neither agree nor disagree, Mildly disagree, Strongly
disagree.
LENGTH. Items: 30 (for the MR Index).

AVAILABILITY. From ADI, Doc. No. 8146. Cost $1.25.
REFERENCES.
     Eron,L.D.   Progress report: Psychosocial development
of aggressive behavior. Project M1726 USPHS. October 31,
1961.
     Eron,L.D.   and   Walder,L.O.   Test   burning: II.
American Psychology, 1961, 16, 237-244.
     Eron,L.D.   Walder,L.O.   Toigo,R.   and Lefkowitz,M.M.
Social class, parental punishment for aggression, and child
aggression. Child Development, 1963, 34, 849-868.
     Hurley,J.R.   Parental   acceptance-rejection   and
children's intelligence. Merrill-Palmer Quarterly, 1965,
11, 19-31.

KAUFFMAN,J.H. Child-Parent Relations Index

VARIABLE MEASURED. Satisfactory parent-child relations as
perceived by the child.
TEST DESCRIPTION. A 36-item questionnaire for adolescents.
A high score indicates the subject feels his/her parents
treat him/her fairly, understand him/her, love him/her, and
so forth.   A low score indicates the subject feels his/her
parents are often unfair, irritable, critical, and hard to
please. Scoring technique is not reported.
SAMPLE ITEM: NR.
LENGTH. Items: 36.
AVAILABILITY. In Kauffman, 1960.
REFERENCES.
     Kauffman,J.H. A comparative study of traditional and
emergent family types among midwest Mennonites.   Ph.D.
dissertation, University of Chicago, 1960.
     Kauffman,J.H. Interpersonal relations in traditional
and emergent families among midwest Mennonites. Marriage
and Family Living, 1961, 23, 247-252.
     Kauffman,J.H. Family relations test responses of
disturbed and normal boys: additional comparative data.
Journal of Personality Assessment, 1971, 35, 128-138.
     Kauffman,J.H.   Weaver,S.J.   and   Weaver,A.   Family
relations test responses of retarded readers: comparative
and reliability data. Journal of Personality Assessment,
1972, 36, 358-360.

LINDEN,E. and HACKLER,J. Family Closeness Index

VARIABLE MEASURED. Closeness of an adolescent's ties to
his/her parents.
TEST DESCRIPTION. The test items include such elements as
the amount of communication between a subject and his/her
parents, their supervision of his/her behavior, the parents'
interest in the subject's problems, strictness of
discipline, etc. Scores for each item are summed and
averaged.

SAMPLE ITEM. Do you enjoy telling your parents about your good times? Yes, No.
LENGTH. Items: 25.
AVAILABILITY. From NAPS-2.
ABSTRACTED BY: Eric Linden
REFERENCES.
    Linden,E. and Hackler,J. Affective ties and delinquency. Pacific Sociological Review, 1973, 16, 27-46.

LYNN,D.B. and DEPALMA-CROSS,A. Parent-Preference Play Situations

VARIABLE MEASURED. The choice or preference by a child of a particular parent tc participate in play situations.
TEST DESCRIPTION. A male and female experimenter present the child with seven play activities. The parents meanwhile remain in the waiting room. The parent chosen is then summoned into the play room, engages in the activity with the child, and returns to the waiting room. Each activity is thoroughly demonstrated so that the child knows what is involved before choosing a parent. Scoring involves recording the parent choice for each of the seven situations. The activities themselves have no purpose other than giving reality to the choices. Father or mother preference is operationally defined as choosing that parent four times or more out of the seven.
SAMPLE ITEM. Catwalk. The subject is shown a raised plank with blocks nailed in a staggered line upon it. The child is tcld that he/she is to balance a block on his/her head as he/she walks across the board. He is asked, "Who do you want to help keep the block from falling off your head; your Mommy or your Daddy?"
LENGTH. Time: 30-40 minutes. Items: 7 items and 6 filler items.
AVAILABILITY. In Lynn and DePalma-Cross, 1974.
ABSTRACTED BY: David B. Lynn
REFERENCE.
    Lynn,D.B. and DePalma-Cross,A. Parent preference of preschool children. Journal of Marriage and the Family, 1974, 36, 555-559.

McCLEERY,R.L. McCleery Scale of Adolescent Development

VARIABLE MEASURED. Adjustment of the adolescent in respect to family life and preparing for marriage and family life.
TEST DESCRIPTION. Multiple-choice, pencil and answer sheet personality inventory. Scored manually or by IBM machine. S tells how important the problem is to him. Items are based on a definition of adjustment as "harmonious relationship between needs and the cultural restrictions and requirements which impinge upon him. The attainment of the harmonious relationships is equivalent to the possession of a mature personality...[a] normally developing person is one

who is successfully solving his developmental tasks."
SAMPLE ITEM. Parents making too many decisions for me. (1)
Important, (2) Of little importance, (3) Of no importance.
LENGTH. Items: 150 (16 in family life scale).
AVAILABILITY. In McCleery, 1955.
REFERENCES.
        McCleery,R.L.   McCleery   Scale   of   Adolescent
Development. Lincoln: University of Nebraska Press, 1955.
        Nelson,S. Changes in the solution of adolescent tasks
by eleventh grade boys during one year and in terms of
socio-economic status. Ph.D. dissertation, University of
Nebraska, 1957.

MUSSEN,P.H. and DISTLER,L. Child's Perception of Parental
Behavior

VARIABLES MEASURED. Nurturant, rewarding, punitive, and
threatening parents, as perceived by the child.
TEST DESCRIPTION. A structured doll play session. Child is
told nine incomplete family situation stories which he/she
completes in doll play. If subject fails to indicate how
the father acts, he/she is prodded to do so. The recorded
stories are scored for presence of nurturance or punishment
by father, mother or "they" (parents undifferentiated).
Father nurturance score is determined by the number of
stories in which the father helped, comforted, or reassured
the child character in the story. Mother nurturance score
is the number of stories in which the mother was nurturant.
The "they" nurturance score is the number of stories in
which parents as a unit were nurturant. Total nurturance
score is the mother nurturance score, the father nurturance
score, and the "they" nurturant scores. Similarly, father
punishment scores, mother punishment scores, "they"
punishment scores, and total punishment scores are
determined by the number of stories in which the respective
actors disciplined, spanked, criticized, or admonished the
child.
SAMPLE ITEM. The child wants a certain toy. He/she can't
reach it. He/she goes into the living room to get help.
Both Mommy and Daddy are busy reading. What happens?
LENGTH. Items: 9.
AVAILABILITY. Partly described in Mussen and Distler, 1959.
REFERENCE.
        Mussen,P.H.   and   Distler,L.   Masculinity,
identification, and father-son relationships. Journal of
Abnormal Social Psychology, 1959, 59, 350-356.

NYE,F.I. Adolescent-Parent Adjustment Measure

VARIABLES MEASURED. Adjustment as reflected in feeling of
being loved and accepted by the parents, parents' trust and
confidence in the child, and child's feeling about the
personalities of parents, socialization of child, and

adjustment to groups outside the family.
TEST DESCRIPTION. Thirty-one adolescent-mother items, 31
adolescent-father items, and 6 adolescent-parent items.
Each item is scored from Always = 5 to Never = 1.   Factor
analysis revealed only one factor, hence no subscales are
used.
SAMPLE ITEM. When my father makes me do something, he tells
me why it is necessary. Always, Almost always, Sometimes,
Seldom, Never.
LENGTH. Items: 68.
AVAILABILITY. In Nye, 1950.
REFERENCES.
     Nye,F.I.   Adolescent adjustment to parents.   Ph.D.
dissertation, Michigan State College, 1950.
     Nye,F.I.   Adolescent-parent adjustment: age, sex,
sibling number, broken homes, and employed mothers as
variables. Marriage and Family Living, 1952, 14, 327-332.

OFFER,D. Family Relations Segment of the Self Image
Questionnaire

VARIABLE MEASURED. Child's degree of adjustment in family
relationships.
TEST DESCRIPTION. Respondents answer questions on a six-
point scale, ranging from Describes me very well = 6 to Does
not describe me at all = 1. Some items are scored in the
opposite direction. Scores for each questionnaire are
summed. The higher the score, the higher the family
adjustment.
SAMPLE ITEM. I can count on my parents most of the time.
LENGTH. Items: 20.
AVAILABILITY. In Offer, 1969.
ABSTRACTED BY: Thomas G. Sparhawk
REFERENCES.
     Bledsoe,J.C. and Wiggins,R.G. Self concepts and
academic aspirations of "understood" and "misunderstood"
boys and girls in ninth grade. Psychological Reports, 1974,
35, 57-58.
     Ingersoll,G.M. Effects of age, form class and word
frequency on homogeneous word associations. Psychological
Reports, 1974, 35, 59-64.
     Offer,D. The Psychological World of the Teen-Ager.
New York: Basic Books, 1969.

PIETY,K.R. Piety Parent Perception Questionnaire.

VARIABLES MEASURED. (1) Inappropriate parent perception,
(2) Consistency of discrimination between parents.
     An abstract of this test is given in Johnson,O.G.
Tests and Measurements in Child Development: Handbook II.
San Francisco: Jossey-Bass, 1976.

PORTER,B.M. Parental Acceptance Scale

VARIABLES MEASURED. Parental acceptance of the child as
indicated by: (1) Respect for child's feelings and right to
express them; (2) Appreciation of the child's unique
make-up; (3) Recognition of the child's need for autonomy
and independence; (4) Unconditional love.
TEST DESCRIPTION. Each of the four aspects of parental
acceptance is measured by 10 multiple-choice items. Items
describe situations in which children express behavior and
verbalizations or unique characteristics indicating
becoming, or attempting to become independent. Each item is
repeated twice--inquiring (1) How the parent feels about the
situation and (2) What the parent does about the situation.
SAMPLE ITEM. When my child says angry and hateful things
about me to my face, it: (1) Makes me feel like punishing
him. (2) Makes me feel like telling him not to talk that
way to me. (3) Makes me annoyed. (4) Makes me feel that I
will be glad when he is past this stage. (5) Pleases me
that he feels free to express himself.
LENGTH. Items: 40.
AVAILABILITY. In Porter, 1952.
REFERENCES.
        Burchinal,L.G. Hawkes,G.R. and Gardner,B. The
relationship between parental acceptance and adjustment of
children. Child Development, 1957, 28, 65-77.
        Crain,A.J. Sussman,M.B. and Weil,W.B.Jr. Effects of
a diabetic child on marital integration and related measures
of family functioning. Journal of Health and Human
Behavior, 1966, 7, 122-127.
        Hawkes,G.R. Burchinal,L.G. Gardner,B. and
Porter,B.M. Parents' acceptance of their children. Journal
of Home Economics, 1956a, 48, 195-200.
        Hawkes,G.R. Burchinal,L.G. Gardner,B. and
Porter,B.M. Marital satisfaction, personality
characteristics, and parental acceptance of children.
Journal of Counseling and Psychology, 1956b, 3, 216-221.
        Johnson,O.G. and Bommarito,J.W. Tests and
Measurements in Child Development: A Handbook. San
Francisco: Jossey-Bass, Inc., 1971, 365.
        Porter,B.M. The relationship between marital
adjustment and parental acceptance of children. Ph.D.
dissertation, Cornell University, 1952.
        Porter,B.M. Measurement of parental acceptance of
children. Journal of Home Economics, 1954, 46, 176-182.

PURCELL,K. and CLIFFORD,E. Story Completion Test

VARIABLES MEASURED. Child's perception of parents as
nurturant or punitive. Perceived power of parents is also
determined.
TEST DESCRIPTION. Children are asked to complete 12 stories
each of which involves a child in an interpersonal situation
with his/her parents (there are two parallel forms of the

test--one for each sex). Each story completion is scored for the presence of nurturance and/or punishment by the parent or parents. The nurturance score is the number of stories in which the child character received help, comfort, reassurance or attention. Corresponding punitive scores are recorded for the number of stories in which the child is spanked, warned, reprimanded, criticized or disciplined. Several outcomes are possible: (1) Mother-nurturant (MN); (2) Mother-punitive (MP); (3) Father-nurturant (FN); (4) Father-punitive (FP); (5) Both parents nurturant (BN); and (6) Both parents punitive (BP). The scoring categories are not mutually exclusive. A child's score is the sum of each categorized response across all 12 story completions. A number of derived scores including Mother power, Father power and Relative power can also be obtained.
SAMPLE ITEM. A boy and his mother and father are eating breakfast. The boy doesn't like his cereal and asks for something else. What happens?
LENGTH. Items: 12 stories.
AVAILABILITY. Three of the stories are in Purcell and Clifford, 1966.
ABSTRACTED BY: Kersti Yllo
REFERENCE.
    Purcell,K. and Clifford,E. Binocular rivalry and the study of identification in asthmatic and nonasthmatic boys. Journal of Consulting Psychology, 1966, 30, 388-394.

RABIN,A.I. Sentence Completion Test of Children's Views of Parents

VARIABLES MEASURED. Adjustment of child to (1) Family, (2) Mother, (3) Father.
TEST DESCRIPTION. A 12-item sentence-completion test which is an adaptation in an abbreviated form of the 36-item test devised by Sacks and Levy (1950) for use with adults. The items are divided equally into three relevant areas: family, mother, and father. In classification of the various responses, the guiding principle is that of "positiveness" of attitude revealed; two judges dichotomize the responses into Positive and Other.
SAMPLE ITEM. Compared with most families, Mine...My mother...If only my father were...
LENGTH. Items: 12.
AVAILABILITY. In Rabin, 1959.
REFERENCES.
    Johnson,O.G. and Bommarito,J.W. Tests and Measurements in Child Development: A Handbook. San Francisco: Jossey-Bass, Inc., 1971, 165.
    Rabin,A.I. Attitudes of kibbutz children to family and parents. American Journal of Orthopsychiatry, 1959, 29, 172-179.
    Sacks,J.M. and Levy,S. The sentence completion test. In Abt,L.E. and Bellak,L. (Eds.), Projective Psychology. New York: Knopf, 1950, 357-402.

RADKE,M.J.   Radke Projective Pictures

VARIABLES MEASURED.   (1) Child's relation to mother, (2)
Child's relation to father, (3) Child's perception of
mother, (4) Child's perception of father, (5) Child's
perception of father-mother relations, (6) Child's
perception of home atmosphere.
TEST DESCRIPTION. Thirty-four paired pictures, matched in
all but one feature, are mounted in pairs on white
backgrounds. The subject responds to consecutive pairs of
pictures. The subject is asked to tell the experimenter
which of the pictures are "most like you or your mother and
father." A weight of +1 is assigned to pictures showing a
pleasant situaticn, of -1 to pictures showing an unpleasant
situation. The score of each subject on each of the
variables is determined by counting the number of plus or
minus responses given.
SAMPLE ITEM.   Picture of a child with a parent under
pleasant circumstances versus a picture of a child with a
parent under unpleasant circumstances. "Which one is most
like you?" "Which one feels or acts like you?"
LENGTH. Items: 34 paired pictures.
AVAILABILITY. Scoring procedures in Radke, 1946; pictures
no longer available.
REFERENCE.
     Radke,M.J.   The relation of parental authority to
children's behavior and attitudes. University of Minnesota
Child Welfare Monographs, 1946, No. 22.

ROGERS,C.R.   A Test of Personality Adjustment

VARIABLES MEASURED.   The extent to which a child is
satisfactorily adjusted to his/her fellows, his/her family,
and himself/herself.
TEST DESCRIPTION. A paper-and-pencil multiple-choice
personality test, with forms for boys and girls. A score
for family maladjustment is derived by comparing Subject's
responses with scoring instructions in the test manual.
SAMPLE ITEM. (Boy's form:) Part I: Suppose that just by
wishing you could change yourself into any sort of person.
Which of these people would you wish to be? Write a 1 in
front of your first choice, a 2 in front of your second
choice, and a 3 in front of your third choice: a teacher.
Part II: Suppose you could have just three of the wishes
below, which would you want to come true? Put a 1 in front
of your biggest wish, a 2 in front of your second biggest
wish, and a 3 in front of your third: I would like to be
stronger than I am now. Part III: Suppose you were going
away to live on a desert island, and could take only three
people with you. Write here the names of the three people
you would choose. Part IV: Peter is a big strong boy who
can beat any of the other boys in a fight. Am I just like
him? Yes, No. Do I wish to be just like him? Yes, No.
Part V: Check the true answer: How well can you play ball?

Can't play ball at all, Can play pretty well, Best player in
my class.
LENGTH. Time: 40-50 minutes. Items: 18.
AVAILABILITY. From Association Press, 291 Broadway, New
York, N.Y.   10007.
REFERENCES.
        Babcock,M.E.   A   Comparison   of   Delinquent   and
Non-Delinquent Boys by Objective Measures of Personality.
Honolulu, H.I.: The Author, 1932, 74.
        Boynton,P.L.   and Walsworth,B.M.   Emotionality test
scores of delinquent and nondelinquent girls. Journal of
Abnormal and Social Psychology, 1943, 38, 87-92.
        Burchinal,L.G. Parents' attitudes and adjustment of
children. Journal of Genetic Psychology 1958, 92, 69-79.
        Burchinal,L.G. Gardner,B. and Hawkes,G.R. Children's
personality adjustment and the socio-economic status of
their families. Journal of Genetic Psychology, 1958a, 92,
149-159.
        Burchinal,L.G.   Gardner,B.   and   Hawkes,G.R.   A
suggested   revision   of   norms   for   the Rogers Test of
Personality Adjustment.   Child Development, 1958b,   29,
135-139.
        Burchinal,L.G.   Hawkes,G.R.   and   Gardner,B.   The
relationship between parental acceptance and adjustment of
children. Child Development, 1957, 28, 65-77.
        Buros,O.K.   (Ed.) Personality Tests and   Reviews.
Highland Park, N.J.: Gryphon Press, 1970.
        L'Abate,L.   The effect of paternal failure to
participate during the referral of child psychiatric
patients. Journal of Clinical Psychology 1960, 16, 407-408.
        Rogers,C.R. Test of Personality Adjustment. New York:
Association Press, 1931.

ROTH,R.M. The Mother-Child Relationship Evaluation

VARIABLES MEASURED. 1. Acceptance; 2.   Nonacceptance in
the forms of (a) overprotection, (b) overindulgence, (c)
rejection;   3.   Confusion-Dominance, a continuum   which
"expresses the degree to which the relationship between
mother and child is dominated by an attitude, a combination
of attitudes, or by confusion."
TEST DESCRIPTION. A booklet containing 48 statements about
mother-child relationships about which the mother expresses
her opinion on a five-point Likert-type scale (Strongly
agree to Strongly disagree). Variables 1 and 2 are scored
by summing the weighted item. Variable 3 is determined by
the number of scores on the first four scales which reach
the 75th percentile or higher.
SAMPLE ITEM. If possible, a mother should give her child
all those things the mother never had (overprotection).
LENGTH. Time: "Can be completed, scored, and profiled in
approximately 30 minutes or less." Items: 45.

AVAILABILITY. From Western Psychological Services, Box 775, Beverly Hills, California 90213.
REFERENCES.
    Buros,O.K. (Ed.) Personality Tests and Reviews. Highland Park, N.J.: Gryphon Press, 1970.
    Roth,R.M. The Mother-Child Relationship Evaluation. Beverly Hills, California: Western Psychological Services, 1961.

RUNDQUIST,E.A. and SLETTO,R.F. Family Scale

VARIABLE MEASURED. Satisfaction with family relationships.
TEST DESCRIPTION. A Likert-type scale containing items primarily reflecting parent-child relationships, especially satisfactions and tensions. The family scale items are interspersed among items for the five other scales making up the Survey of Opinions. Each item is answered Strongly agree, Agree, Undecided, Disagree, or Strongly disagree (weighted 1 to 5 or 5 to 1 depending on whether item indicates satisfactory or unsatisfactory family relationship). All items included are those which significantly discriminated between extreme quartiles for the total score.
SAMPLE ITEM. Home is the most pleasant place in the world.
LENGTH. Items: 22.
AVAILABILITY. In Rundquist and Sletto, 1936; Shaw and Wright, 1967.
REFERENCES.
    Ramsey,C.E. and Nelson,L.W. Change in values and attitudes toward the family. American Sociological Review, 1956, 21, 605-609.
    Rundquist,E.A. and Sletto,R.F. Personality in the Depression. Minneapolis: University of Minnesota Press, 1936.
    Shaw,M.E. and Wright,J.M. Scales for the Measurement of Attitudes. New York: McGraw-Hill, 1967, 418-420.

SCHWARZWELLER,H.K. and LYSON,T.A. Perceived Parental Interest Scale (PPI)

VARIABLE MEASURED. Perceived parental interest: a child's general feelings about parents' responsiveness to needs, interests and problems.
TEST DESCRIPTION. A brief, self-administered questionnaire. Test items refer to perception of parents' readiness to "praise," to "listen," to "discuss" problems and career plans, and to "help" with things related to school. The items are derived from focused interviews and extensive pre-testing in Norway and Kentucky. Each item is scored as a trichotomy and, summed, the combined items yield an 11-point scale.

SAMPLE ITEM. My parents are ready to listen when I need them. Always, Usually, Sometimes, Never.
LENGTH. Items: 5.
AVAILABILITY. From NAPS-2.
ABSTRACTED BY: Harry K. Schwarzweller
REFERENCE.
    Schwarzweller,H.K. and Lyson,T.A. Social class, parental interest and the educational plans of American and Norwegian rural youth. Sociology of Education, 1974, 47, 443-465.

SEATON,J.K. Incomplete Story Test

VARIABLE MEASURED. Parental acceptance-rejection.
TEST DESCRIPTION. A series of brief, incomplete stories with multiple-choice endings. Subjects are instructed to choose the alternatives which seem most like what the person in the story would do. There are forms for boys and for girls. Endings are classified as Accepting weight (3), Neutral (2), or Rejecting (1), according to explicit definitions of these terms. These weights are based on prior evaluation of the items by a pool of judges.
SAMPLE ITEM. Peter's mother gave Peter a dollar bill and sent him to the store to buy some groceries. When he got to the store Peter found that he had lost the money. He looked everywhere along the sidewalk but could not find the dollar. Finally he went home and told his mother, "I have bad news. When I got to the store, I found that I had lost the money, I've looked everywhere but I cannot find it." What did Peter's mother say? (1) You should have been more careful but I know everyone could lose money. Are you sure you looked everywhere for it? (2) I don't understand how you could do such a thing. Go out and look some more. (3) Such carelessness. Either you find that money or you will get punished and have nothing to spend until you have made up what you lost.
LENGTH. Items: 15.
AVAILABILITY. In Seaton, 1949.
REFERENCE.
    Seaton,J.K. A projective experiment using incomplete stories with multiple-choice endings. Genetic Psychology Monographs, 1949, 40, 149-228.

SIMMONS,R.G. ROSENBERG,F. and ROSENBERG,M. Perceived Opinion of Parents Scale

VARIABLES MEASURED. Children's perceptions of parent's opinion of them.
TEST DESCRIPTION. The child is asked two multiple choice, close-ended questions and one opened-ended question which are combined into a score to determine how favorably the child sees parents rating him/her as a person. It is a global measure, rather than a specific evaluation. The

child is asked whether each of his/her parents rates him/her
as A wonderful person, A pretty nice person, A little bit of
a nice person, or Not such a nice person. He/she is asked
how his/her parents would describe him/her, and the
resultant answer is coded as Favorable, Unfavorable,
Neutral, or Mixed and scored accordingly. These items have
been used without problem on children from grades 3 to 12,
on healthy and physically ill youngsters, and on blacks and
whites.
SAMPLE ITEM. Would you say your mother thinks you are (1) A
wonderful person, (2) A pretty nice person, (3) A little bit
of a nice person, or (4) Not such a nice person.
LENGTH. Number of items: 3.
AVAILABILITY. In Simmons, et al., 1973.
ABSTRACTED BY: Roberta G. Simmons.
REFERENCES.
      Klein,S.D. and Simmons,R.G. Chronic disease and
childhood development: kidney disease and transplantation.
Abstract to be published in International Medical News
Service.
      Rosenberg,M. and Simmons,R.G. Black and White
Self-Esteem: The Urban School Child. Arnold M. and
Caroline Rose Mcnograph Series, American Sociological
Association, 1972.
      Simmons,R.G. Rosenberg,F. and Rosenberg,M.
Disturbance in the self-image at adolescence. American
Sociological Review, 1973, 38, 553-568.

STOGDILL,R.M. Attitudes Toward Child Behavior Scale

VARIABLES MEASURED. Parental approval or disapproval of an
introverted or an extroverted social adjustment for
children.
TEST DESCRIPTION. Parent and child role prescription
statements to be answered on a seven-point scale, from
Extreme agreement through Neutral to Extreme disagreement.
Each item of the scale scored 0 to 6.
SAMPLE ITEM. A child should feel bashful about putting
himself/herself forward. Very strongly agree, Strongly
agree, Agree, Neutral or undecided, Disagree, Strongly
disagree, Very strongly disagree.
LENGTH. Time: 15 minutes. Items: 99 reported in Stogdill
(1936). Printed test form supplied by author contains 20
items.
AVAILABILITY. From NAPS.
REFERENCES.
      Brown,F. An experimental study of parental attitudes
and their effect on child adjustment. American Journal of
Orthopsychiatry, 1942, 12, 224-231.
      Buros,O.K. (Ed.) Personality Tests and Reviews.
Highland Park, N.J.: Gryphon Press, 1970.
      Coost,L.C. A study of the knowledge and attitudes of
parents of preschool children. University of Iowa Studies
in Child Welfare, 1939, 17, 157-181.

Read,K.H.   Parents' expressed attitudes and children's behavior.   Journal of Consulting Psychology, 1945, 9, 95-100.

Stedman,L.A.   An investigation of knowledge of and attitudes toward child behavior. Remmers,H.H.   (Ed.), Purdue University, Division of Educational Reference, Studies in Higher Education [No.] 62. Lafayette, Indiana: The Division, 1948, 66.

Stogdill,R.M.   The measurement of attitudes toward children. Ph.D. dissertation, Ohio State University, 1934.

Stogdill,R.M.   The measurement of attitudes toward parental control and the social adjustments of children. Journal of Applied Psychology, 1936, 20, 359-367.

STOTT,D.H.   and SYKES,E.G.   Bristol   Social   Adjustment Guides, No. 4: The Child in the Family

VARIABLES MEASURED. (1) Child's attitudes toward mother; (2) Mother's attitudes toward child; (3) Child's attitudes toward father; (4) Father's attitudes toward child. Within these   general   variables,   the   following   types   of maladjustment are scored: X, Anxious overconcern; HX, Hostility-anxiety   conflict;   E,   Estrangement;   DI, Irritable-depressive nontolerance; L, Lack of parental feeling; UP, Child's general family insecurity--seeking parent-substitute, anxiety for two-role acceptance by other children, avoidance, and miscellaneous symptoms of family insecurity.
TEST DESCRIPTION. A series of descriptive statements organized as paragraphs under major headings and subheadings (such as parent-child relationship, or child's behavior toward mother).   The rater underlines those phrases in the paragraph which apply to subject or his/her family situation.   Underlined items are then compared with a diagnostic key to determine the number of underlined items falling into each of the variables measured by the test. "The teacher... needs no expert knowledge or insight beyond... his or her professional training and experience. The practitioner is not asked to make interpretations of the observed behavior or estimate its gravity..." Approximately half of the items in each paragraph represent normal behavior and are therefore not used in scoring.
SAMPLE ITEM. Child's behavior toward mother (older child): Doesn't   display   much feeling, Seems sulky to mother; Doesn't spend much time in same room...Never lets mother forget he's about...Takes advantage, Makes a slave of her...Normal for age.
LENGTH. Items: 221 (estimated).
AVAILABILITY.   From University of London Press, Little Paul's House, Warwick Square, London E.C. 4, England.
REFERENCES.
Stott,D.H.   Unsettled Children and Their Families. London: University of London Press, 1956.
Stott,D.H.   and Sykes,E.G.   Manual   to   the   Bristol

Social Adjustment Guides. London: London University Press, 1958.

SWANSON,G.E. Child-Parent Relationship Scale (CPRS)

VARIABLES MEASURED. Child's feelings of happiness and satisfaction in his/her relationships with his/her parents.
TEST DESCRIPTION. Linear combination of single-sentence Yes-No items. Vocabulary level does not exceed seventh grade. Items included were selected by item analysis (extreme quartiles) from a 90-item pool.
SAMPLE ITEM. It is hard for me to feel pleasant at home. Yes, No, Uncertain.
LENGTH. Items: 50.
AVAILABILITY. In Swanson, 1950.
REFERENCES.
    Serot,N.M. and Teevan,R.C. Perception of the parent-child relationship and its relation to child development. Child Development, 1961, 32, 373-378.
    Swanson,G.E. The development of an instrument for rating child-parent relationships. Social Forces, 1950, 29, 84-90.
    VanSlyke,V. and Leton,D.A. Children's perception of family relationships and their school adjustment. Journal of School Psychology, 1965, 4, 19-28.

THORPE,L.P. CLARK,W.W. and TIEGS,E.W. California Test of Personality

VARIABLES MEASURED. A general personality test. Of 12 scores, one is family relations, defined as measuring the extent to which "the pupil exhibits desirable family relationships, is the one who feels that he is loved and well treated at home, and who has a sense of security and self-respect in connection with the various members of his family. Superior family relations also include parental control that is neither too strict nor too lenient."
TEST DESCRIPTION. A self-report personality inventory providing for Yes or No responses. The test is published in five parallel forms for ages from kindergarten to adulthood. Each form has an accompanying test manual.
SAMPLE ITEM. (Adult form:) Is your family interested in becoming acquainted with your problem? Yes, No.
LENGTH. Time: 45-60 minutes. Items: 96-180, depending on grade level.
AVAILABILITY. From California Test Bureau, 5916 Hollywood Boulevard, Los Angeles, California 90028.
REFERENCES.
    Aikman,A.L. An analytical study of attitudes and other selected measures of economically depressed children in grades five and six. Ph.D. dissertation, Southern Illinois University, 1965.
    Baker,L.S. The relationship of maternal understanding

of the child and attitudes toward the child to the adjustment of the child. Ph.D. dissertation, New York University, 1955.

Brown,L.P. Gates,H.D. Nolder,E.L. and VanFleet,B. Personality characteristics of exceptional children and of their mothers. Elementary School Journal 1952, 52, 286-290.

Brownstein,J.B. A study of children with contrasting records of social adjustment in relation to certain school, home and community factors. Ph.D. dissertation, Indiana University, 1958.

Burchinal,L.G. Parents' attitudes and adjustment of children. Journal of Genetic Psychology, 1958, 92, 69-79.

Buros,O.K. (Ed.), The Nineteen Forty Mental Measurements Yearbook. Highland Park, N.J.: Gryphon Press, 1941.

Buros,O.K. (Ed.), The Third Mental Measurements Yearbook. Highland Park, N.J.: Gryphon Press, 1949.

Buros,O.K. (Ed.), The Fourth Mental Measurements Yearbook. Highland Park, N.J.: Gryphon Press, 1953.

Buros,O.K. (Ed.), The Fifth Mental Measurements Yearbook. Highland Park, N.J.: Gryphon Press, 1959.

Buros,O.K. (Ed.), The Sixth Mental Measurements Yearbook. Highland Park, N.J.: Gryphon Press, 1965.

Buros,O.K. (Ed.), Personality Tests and Reviews. Highland Park, N.J.: Gryphon Press, 1970.

Haller,A.O. and Shailer,T. Personality correlates of the socioeconomic status of adolescent males. Sociometry 1962, 25, 398-404.

Inselberg,R.M. and Burke,L. Social and psychological correlates of masculinity in young boys. Merrill-Palmer Quarterly, 1973, 19, 41-47.

Jackson,V.B. Successful and unsuccessful elementary school children: a study of some of the factors that contribute to school success. Ph.D. dissertation, Ohio State University, 1962.

Kemp,C.G. Parents' and adolescents' perceptions of each other and the adolescents' self-perception. Personnel and Guidance Journal, 1965, 44, 58-62.

Langford,L.M. and Alm,O.W. A comparison of parent judgments and child feelings concerning the self adjustment and social adjustment of 12-year-old children. Journal of Genetic Psychology, 1954, 85, 39-46.

Lessing,E.E. and Oberlander,M. Developmental study of ordinal position and personality adjustment of the child as evaluated by the California Test of Personality. Journal of Personality, 1967, 35, 487-497.

Leukel,D.A. The psychogenic tic in childhood. Ph.D. dissertation, University of Washington, 1962.

Martin,M.F. Personality development and social adjustment of mentally retarded children. American Journal of Mental Deficiency, 1941, 46, 94-101.

Ratliff,J.A. A comparison of mothers' estimates with the measured adjustments of their junior high school children. Ph.D. dissertation, University of Houston, 1957.

Rouman,J. School children's problems as related to

parental factors.   Journal of Educational Research, 1956, 50, 105-112.

Serot,N.M. and Teevan,R.C. Perception of the parent-child relationship and its relation to child adjustment. Child Development, 1961, 32, 373-378.

Sewell,W.H. Infant training and the personality of the child. American Journal of Sociology, 1952, 58, 150-159.

Sewell,W.H. and Haller,A.O. Social status and the personality adjustment of the child. Sociometry, 1956, 19, 114-125.

Sewell,W.H. and Haller,A.O. Factors in the relationship between social status and the personality adjustment of the child. American Sociological Review, 1959, 24, 511-520.

Skidmore,R.A. and McPhee,W.M. The comparative use of the California Test of Personality and the Burgess-Cottrell-Wallin Schedule in predicting marital adjustment. Marriage and Family Living, 1951, 13, 121-126.

Smith,P.M.Jr. Personal and social adjustment of Negro children in rural and urban areas of the South. Rural Sociology, 1961, 26, 73-77.

Stott,L.H. Family prosperity in relation to the psychological adjustment of farm folks. Rural Sociology, 1945a, 10, 256-263.

Stott,L.H. Some environmental factors in relation to personality adjustment of rural children. Rural Sociology, 1945b, 10, 394-403.

Straus,M.A. Child Training and Child Personality in a Rural and Urban Area of Ceylon. Ph.D. dissertation, University of Wisconsin, Madison, 1956.

Straus,M.A. Anal and oral frustration in relation to Sinhalese personality. Sociometry, 1957, 20, 21-31.

Thorpe,L.P. Clark,W.W. and Tiegs,E.W. California Test of Personality. Los Angeles: California Test Bureau, 1953.

Turner,A. Personality adjustment of children of employed and home-making mothers. M.A. Thesis, University of Missouri, 1954.

WEINSTEIN,L.   Parental Acceptance Measure

VARIABLE MEASURED. Parental acceptance as experienced by the child.
TEST DESCRIPTION. A twelve-item scale asks about issues such as skill in playing ball, grades and behavior in school, getting angry easily, etc. Each item describes a child ("Johnny gets good grades in school") and is followed by three questions: "How much like Johnny are you?"; "How much like Johnny does your mother want you to be?"; "How much like Johnny does your father want you to be?" Responses are "Not at all," "Not much," "Pretty much," and "Very much," with scores ranging from 0 to 3. Parental acceptance is the discrepancy between self-concept and maternal (paternal) expections: the sum over items of the absolute

difference between the responses to "How much like Johnny are you?" and "How much like Johnny does your mother (father) want you to be?". A low discrepancy score indicates high acceptance. A parental discrepancy score may be obtained by summing the mother's discrepancy score and the father's discrepancy score.
SAMPLE ITEM. See test description.
LENGTH. Time: 10 minutes. Items: 12.
AVAILABILITY. From NAPS-2.
ABSTRACTED BY: Blair Nelson
REFERENCE.
    Weinstein,L. Social experience and social schemata. Journal of Personality and Social Psychology, 1967, 6, 429-434.

2. Love, Nurturance, Support, Involvement (See also Subject Index)

BOWERMAN,C.E. and IRISH,D.P. Child-Parent Adjustment Scales

VARIABLES MEASURED. (1) Affection for and by parents. (2) Association between parents and child. (3) Congruence of values and norms between parent and child.
TEST DESCRIPTION. Three Guttman scales based on items from a longer questionnaire completed by the child.
SAMPLE ITEM. Do you talk over your personal matters with your mother (father)?
LENGTH. Items: Affection = 9, Association = 8, Norms and Values = 8.
AVAILABILITY. From NAPS-2.
REFERENCES.
    Bowerman,C.E. Family background and parental adjustment of step-children. Research Studies of the State College of Washington, 1956, 24, 181-182.
    Bowerman,C.E. and Irish,D.P. Some relations of stepchildren to their parents. Marriage and Family Living, 1962, 24, 113-121.
    Irish,D.P. The parental preferences of Kitsap County youth. Ph.D. dissertation, University of Washington, 1957.
    Irish,D.P. The adolescent project: Parental preference patterns of adolescents from broken homes. Research Review, 1961, 8, 1-10.

DUBERMAN,L. Stepparent-Stepchild Relationship Score

VARIABLES MEASURED. Stepparent's affection for and interest in stepchildren.

TEST DESCRIPTION. Both interview and written questionnaire
items are included. The stepparent is asked to evaluate his
or her relationship with each stepchild, and the parent
evaluates the spouse's relationship with each stepchild.
These ratings produce an index of self-rated steprelations
for a family. The investigator also evaluates and scores
the relationships based on comments made during the
interview and on observation of the interaction between the
stepparent and the child. The mean of the self-ratings and
the investigator's rating is combined for a
Stepparent-Stepchild Relationship Score, ranging from 1
(Very close) to 5 (Very distant).
SAMPLE ITEM. Write the name of one of your stepchildren on
each line on the left side. Then place an X on the right
hand line to indicate how you feel about this child.
   /_____/   /_____/
      Name/
LENGTH. Time: depends on number of children. Items: Two
questions per child. Approximate length of time for two
children from each parent: 10 minutes.
AVAILABILITY. In Duberman, 1975.
REFERENCE.
     Duberman,L.   Stepkin   relationships.   Journal   of
Marriage and the Family, 1973, 35, 283-284.
     Duberman,L.   The   Reconstituted   Family,   Chicago:
Nelson-Hall, 1975.

ERON,L.D.   WALDER,L.O.   and   LEFKOWITZ,M.M.   Nurturance
Scales

VARIABLES MEASURED. Part A, Punishment for Nurturance
Signals, measures "rewards and punishment of various
intensities administered to child by socializing agent in
situations which might tend to lead to nurturant behavior on
part of agent." Part B, Nonrecognition of Child's Needs
Scale, measures "an aspect of nonnurturant behavior."
TEST DESCRIPTION. Part A: During an interview parents are
asked how they would respond to their child in various
situations. Three judges code the responses on a scale from
1 to 4 (1 = Giving nurturance; to 4 = Punishing the child).
These scores are added. Part B: Parents are asked
questions with regard to their child's needs. The response
categories are limited and coded from 0 to 2, with 0 being
the most nurturant answer and 2 showing a lack of
nurturance. Item scores are added.
SAMPLE ITEM. Part A: What do you usually do when NAME is
afraid? Part B: Do you usually have time so that NAME can
talk to you about things that interest him?
LENGTH. Items: Part A = 5, Part B = 6.
AVAILABILITY. In Eron, et al., 1971.
ABSTRACTED BY: Kersti Yllo
REFERENCE.
     Eron,L.D.   Walder,L.O.   and Lefkowitz,M.M.   Learning of
Aggression in Children. Boston: Little, Brown and Co.,

1971, 193-194, 208.

FLOYD,H.H.Jr. and SOUTH,D.R. Parent-Peer Need Satisfaction Scale

VARIABLE MEASURED. Need satisfaction: the relative degree to which youths see parents or peers as meeting their social-psychological needs.
TEST DESCRIPTION. The scale consists of 12 specific types of needs which are considered to be salient for youth (i.e. grades, companionship, acceptance by others, etc.). With regard to each item, the respondent indicates: (1) The degree (high, moderate, or low) to which he perceives he needs the item; (2) The degree to which he perceives his parents help him satisfy his need for the item and (3) The degree to which he perceives his peers help him satisfy his need for the item.
    In scoring this scale a response of high is assigned 3, a response of moderate 2, and a response of low 1. A summated score for each respondent is derived in the following manner: (a) For each item, the difference between the degree to which parents, as opposed to peers, helped the respondent to meet his needs is calculated. (b) This difference is multiplied by the score indicating the degree of need which the respondent had indicated that he had for the item and the 12 items were summed.
SAMPLE ITEM. (I) Usually, I have a High (H), or Moderate (M), or Low (L) degree of need; (II) My parents help me to meet the needs listed in Column I to a High (H) or Moderate (M), or Low (L) degree; (III) My friends help me to meet the needs listed in Column I to a High (H), or Moderate (M), or Low (L) degree.

    To make good grades: I__ II__ III__

LENGTH. Time: 10 minutes. Items: 12.
AVAILABILITY. From NAPS-2.
ABSTRACTED BY: H. Hugh Floyd, Jr.
REFERENCES.
    Floyd,H.H.Jr. and South,D.R. Parent or peer orientation? Options and implications for youth and parents. Southern Quarterly, 1971, 49-62.
    Floyd,H.H.Jr. and South,D.R. Dilemma of youth: a choice of parents or peers as a source of orientation. Journal of Marriage and Family, 1972, 34, 627-634.

GREENBERG,M. Greenberg First-Father Engrossment Survey.

VARIABLES MEASURED. Paternal feelings and involvement with the newborn.
    An abstract of this test is given in Johnson,O.G. Tests and Measurements in Child Development: Handbook II. San Francisco: Jossey-Bass, 1976, 781.

GREENSTEIN,J.M.   Father-Closeness Rating

VARIABLE MEASURED.   Closeness of father to son.
TEST DESCRIPTION.   Father and son are interviewed together
and the interviewer observes seven aspects of father-child
relations.   At the end of the interview, a global rating of
father closeness is obtained, ranging on a six-point scale
from Father is obviously very warm towards, involved with,
and emotionally close to son" to "Father is obviously cold
towards, uninvolved with, and emotionally distant from son."
SAMPLE ITEM.   Does he show ease or discomfort in talking to
his son?
LENGTH.   Items: 7.
AVAILABILITY.   In Greenstein, 1966.
ABSTRACTED BY: Thomas G. Sparhawk
REFERENCE.
     Greenstein,J.M.   Father characteristics and sex typing.
Journal of Personality and Social Psychology, 1966, 3,
271-277.

HEILBRUN,A.B.JR.   Parent-Child Interaction Rating Scales

VARIABLE MEASURED.   Nurturance of child by parent.
TEST DESCRIPTION.   A questionnaire presented to adolescents
intended to measure the following kinds of nurturant
behavior: (1) Degree of affection felt for subject by
parent;   (2) Degree of affection physically expressed toward
subject;   (3) Approval of subject and his behavior;   (4)
Sharing of personal feelings and experiences;   (5) Concrete
giving (gifts, money, etc.) to subject;   (6) Encouragement
of subject in meeting responsibilities and pursuing personal
interests;   (7) Trust placed in subject;   (8) Sense of
security felt by subject in relation to parents.   Each item
is presented with a five-point rating scale, with each point
designated by a descriptive phrase;   5 is the highest score
for all items although the direction of scoring is varied by
page to avoid a position responseset.   The subject rates
father and mother for each item.
SAMPLE ITEM.   NR.
LENGTH.   Time: 10 minutes.   Items: 8 for each parent.
AVAILABILITY.   In Heilbrun, 1964.
REFERENCES.
     Calonico,J.M.   and Thomas,D.L.   Role-taking as a
function of value similarity and affect in the nuclear
family.   Journal of Marriage and the Family, 1973, 35,
655-665.
     Doster,J.A.   and   Strickland,B.R.   Perceived
child-rearing practices and self-disclosure patterns.
Journal of Consulting and Clinical Psychology, 1969, 33,
382.
     Heilbrun,A.B.Jr.   Parental model attributes, nurturant
reinforcement, and consistency of behavior in adolescents.
Child Development, 1964, 35, 151-167.
     Heilbrun,A.B.Jr.   Perceived maternal childrearing

patterns   and   subsequent   deviance   in   adolescence.
Adolescence, 1966, 1, 152.

Heilbrun, A. B. Jr.   Cognitive   sensitivity   to   aversive
maternal   stimulaticn   in   late-adolescent males.   Journal of
Consulting and Clinical Psychology, 1968, 32, 326-332.

Heilbrun, A. B. Jr.   Parental   identification   and   the
patterning   of   vocational   interests   in   college males and
females.   Journal   of   Counseling   Psychology,   1969,   16,
342-347.

Heilbrun, A. B. Jr.   Perceived maternal child rearing   and
effects   of delayed reinforcement upon constant acquisition.
Developmental Psychology, 1969, 1, 605-612.

Heilbrun, A. B. Jr.   Perceived   maternal   child-rearing
experience   and   the   effects   of   vicarious   and   direct
reinforcement   on   males.   Child   Development,   1970,   41,
253-262.

Heilbrun, A. B. Jr.   Style   of   adaptation   to   perceived
aversive   maternal   ccntrol   and internal scanning behavior.
Journal of Consulting and Clinical Psychology, 1972, 39,
15-21.

Heilbrun, A. B. Jr.   Adaptation   to   aversive   maternal
control   and   perception   of   simultaneously   presented
evaluative cues;   a further test of a developmental model of
paranoid   behavior.   Journal   of   Consulting   and   Clinical
Psychology, 1973, 41, 301-307.

Heilbrun, A. B. Jr.   Gillard, B. J.   and   Harrell, S. N.
Perceived   maternal   rejection   and   cognitive interference.
Journal   of   Child   Psychology   and   Psychiatry,   1965,   6,
233-242.

Heilbrun, A. B. Jr.   and Harrell, S. N.   Perceived   maternal
child-rearing   patterns   and   the   effects   of   social
nonreactions   upon   achievement   motivation.   Child
Development, 1967, 38, 267-281.

Heilbrun, A. B. Jr.   and   Norbert, N. A.   Maternal
childrearing   experience   and   self-reinforcement
effectiveness.   Developmental Psychology, 1970, 3, 81-87.

Heilbrun, A. B. Jr.   and Orr, H. K.   Maternal   childrearing
control   history   and   subsequent cognitive and personality
functioning of the cffspring.   Psychological Reports,   1965,
17, 259-272.

Heilbrun, A. B. Jr.   Orr, H. K.   and Harrell, S. N.   Patterns
of   parental   child-rearing   and subsequent vulnerability to
cognitive disturbance.   Journal   of   Consulting Psychology,
1966, 30, 51-59.

Heilbrun, A. B. Jr.   and Waters, D. B.   Underachievement   as
related   to   perceived   maternal   child rearing and academic
conditions of reinforcement.   Child Development,   1968,   39,
913-921.

Magaro, P. A.   and   Hanson, B. A.   Perceived   maternal
nurturance   and   control of process schizophrenics, reactive
schizophrenics,   and   normals.   Journal   of   Consulting and
Clinical Psychology, 1969, 33, 507.

Nowicki, S. Jr.   and   Segal, W.   Perceived   parental
characteristics, locus of control orientation and behavioral
correlates of locus of control.   Developmental Psychology,

1974, 10, 33-37.

HOLLENDER,J.W.   Parental Contact Scale.

VARIABLES   MEASURED.   Affectionate   physical   contact   with
parents.
     An abstract of this test is given in Johnson,O.G.
Tests and Measurements in Child Development: Handbook II.
San Francisco: Jossey-Bass, 1976, 834.

KING,D.L.   Contact Comfort Ratings

VARIABLE MEASURED.   Contact comfort initiated by the mother.
TEST DESCRIPTION.   Each subject is asked to complete one of
the 16 possible combinations of two paragraphs.   The extent
of contact comfort expressed in the paragraph completion is
rated on a six-point scale: 1 = Extensive contact comfort
is initiated by the mother ("picks up the child," "takes the
child in her arms,") to 6 = Negative physical contact is
initiated by the mother ("hits the child," "slaps his
hands").   "If behaviors belonging to more than one rating
category are indicated, the score closer to 1 was always
given."
SAMPLE ITEM.   A mother turns toward (away from)   her
two-year-old child.   She then says a few words to her child
in a pleasant (harsh) tone of voice.   The child then walks
toward the mother.   The mother approaches the child (remains
where she is), smiles (grimaces), and...
LENGTH.   Items: 16 variations (see item in parenthesis in
Sample Item) for each of the paragraphs, making a total of
32.
AVAILABILITY.   In King, 1973.
ABSTRACTED BY: Thomas G. Sparhawk.
REFERENCES.
     Arrington,B.V. and King,D.L.   Expectations concerning
children's obtaining contact comfort following parents'
interpersonal behaviors.   Psychological Reports, 1974, 34,
455-460.
     King,D.L.   Expectations of behaviors of   mothers
preceding initiation of contact comfort with their children.
Psychological Reports, 1973, 33, 131-137.
     King,D.L.   and Marcus,M.   Expectations of parents'
behaviors preceding initiation of contact comfort with their
children: an extension. Psychological Reports, 1974, 35,
795-801.

LEIDERMAN,P.H.   and LEIDERMAN,G.F.   Attachment Index

VARIABLE MEASURED.   Infant's affective response to mother,
to a caretaker, and to a stranger.

TEST DESCRIPTION.   An observer hides from the infant's
sight, and records reactions to the following situation: A
stranger approaches the infant, who is with the mother,
stops about 10 feet away, then approaches and offers to pick
up the infant.   At this point the mother goes out of
infant's sight for about two minutes, then approaches using
the above procedure.   The same procedure is carried out with
a caretaker and the infant.
     Infant reactions are scored from Positive = 1 to
Negative = 2 at specified times throughout the procedure,
and summed for each individual responded to.
SAMPLE ITEM: Positive, "Lifts arms to be picked up."
LENGTH.   NR.
AVAILABILITY.   In Leiderman and Leiderman, 1974.
ABSTRACTED BY: Thomas G. Sparhawk
REFERENCE.
     Leiderman,P.H.   and   Leiderman,G.F.   Affective   and
cognitive consequences of polymatric infant care in the East
African highlands.   In Pick,A.D.   (Ed.)   Minnesota Symposia
on   Child   Psychology, Vol.   8.   Minneapolis: University of
Minnesota Press, 1974.

McKINLEY,D.   Source of Emotional Support Measure

VARIABLE MEASURED.   Which parent is the major source of
affection and support?
TEST DESCRIPTION.   Subjects are asked   four   questions
concerning   their   relationship with   their parents.   Total
scores can vary from the arithmetic sum of the answers of
the subjects who chose their mother in three questions and
listed her as Very affectionate to the other extreme where
the   father is chosen in all and rated as Very affectionate.
The score is relative in that "it does not measure absolute
emotional   support given by the   parents but the relative
importance of the father and mother."
SAMPLE ITEM.   In your family when both your parents are
around, who do you usually talk over your worries with?   (1)
Nearly always with mother;   (2) Generally with my mother;
(3)   A little more often with my mother;   (4) A little more
often with my father;   (5) Generally with my father;   (6)
Nearly always with my father.
LENGTH.   Items: 4.
AVAILABILITY.   In McKinley, 1964.
ABSTRACTED BY: Kersti Yllo
REFERENCE.
     McKinley,D.   Social Class and Family Life.   New   York:
The Free Press, 1964.

MILLER,B.B.   Perceived Closeness-To-The-Mother Scale.

VARIABLES MEASURED.   Perceived closeness to the mother.

An abstract of this test is given in Johnson,O.G. Tests and
Measurements in Child Development: Handbook II. San
Francisco: Jossey-Bass, 1976, 626.

ROBERTSON,L.S. and DOTSON,L.E. Parental Expressivity Scale

VARIABLE MEASURED. Expressivity of parents as perceived by
adolescents.
TEST DESCRIPTION. Eight questionnaire items are each asked
separately regarding father's and mother's behavior
indicative of warmth, rejection, indulgence, concern, and
love. Answers range over five points from completely true
to completely false. Scores are obtained by Guttman
scaling.
SAMPLE ITEM. My father is not very warm and affectionate
toward me. (keyed false)
LENGTH. Time: 5 minutes. Items: 8 for each parent.
AVAILABILITY. In Robertson and Dotson, 1969.
ABSTRACTED BY: L.S.Robertson
REFERENCE.
        Robertson,L.S. and Dotson,L.E. Perceived parental
expressivity, reaction to stress, and affiliation. Journal
of Personality and Social Psychology, 1969, 12, 229-234.

ROSENBERG,M. Parental Interest Index

VARIABLE MEASURED. Parents' interest in their child.
TEST DESCRIPTION. A Guttman scale made up from seven
questions concerned with the interest their parents
displayed in their friends, report cards and in what they
had to say. The total score is obtained by adding the
number of items checked which are indicative of low
interest. The more such items are checked, the lower the
level of parental interest.
SAMPLE ITEM. When you were about 10 to 11 years old, did
mother know most of your friends? (1) Knew who all were;
(2) Knew who most were; (3) Knew who some were; (4) Knew
none, almost none.
LENGTH. Items: 7.
AVAILABILITY. In Rosenberg, 1965.
ABSTRACTED BY: Kersti Yllo
REFERENCE.
        Rosenberg,M. Society and the Adolescent Self-Image.
Princeton, N.J.: Princeton University Press, 1965, 316.

ROSENBERG,M. Relationship with Father Score

VARIABLE MEASURED. The quality of relationship with father.
TEST DESCRIPTION. Subjects are asked six questions
concerned with their relationship with their father. Total
score is obtained by summing item scores. Scores may range
from 6 to 31. A low score indicates a good relationship

with father.
SAMPLE ITEM. Which parent is it easier for you to talk to?
(1) Father much more; (2) Father somewhat more; (3) Both
about same; (4) Mother somewhat more; (5) Mother much
more.
LENGTH. Items: 6.
AVAILABILITY. In Rosenberg, 1965.
ABSTRACTED BY: Kersti Yllo
REFERENCE.
    Rosenberg,M. Society and the Adolescent Self-Image.
Princeton, N.J.: Princeton University Press, 1965, 318.

RUBENSTEIN,J.L. Maternal Attentiveness Scale

VARIABLE MEASURED. Maternal attentiveness: The extent to
which the mother provides auditory, visual, or tactile
stimulation to the young infant in the natural environment.
TEST DESCRIPTION. Maternal locking at, touching, holding,
and talking to the infant are time sampled in the home
during three hours of infant awake time. A time sampling
unit consists of 10 seconds for recording. A daily
attentiveness score for mother is the number of observations
during which any form of attentiveness occurred. Two days
of observation are recommended for reliable assessment. The
Day 1 by Day 2 correlation is, 91 (N=13).
SAMPLE ITEM. Mother holds infant (checked or not checked on
a checklist).
LENGTH. Three hours of time-sampling on each of two days.
Two hours per day may suffice for an infant under 5 months.
AVAILABILITY. In Rubenstein, 1967.
ABSTRACTED BY: Judith L. Rubenstein
REFERENCE.
    Rubenstein,J.L. Maternal attentiveness and subsequent
exploratory behavior in the infant. Child Development,
1967, 38, 1089-1100.

SEVERY,L.J. Value Parent Scale

VARIABLES MEASURED. Value placed on association with
parents.
TEST DESCRIPTION. A questionnaire consisting of True-False
and multiple-choice items on various aspects of parent-child
relations. The score is the sum of the items.
SAMPLE ITEM. Have you defied your parent's authority to
their face? Very often = 1, Several times = 2, Once or
twice = 3, No = 4.
LENGTH. Items: 11.
AVAILABILITY. FROM NAPS-2.
ABSTRACTED BY: Susan Murray
REFERENCES.
    Severy,L.J. Exposure to deviance committed by valued
peer group and family members. Journal of Research in Crime
and Delinquency, 1973, 10, 35-46.

STRYKER,S.   Married Offspring-Parent Adjustment Checklist

VARIABLES MEASURED. Married child-parent relations in: (1)
Affection,   (2)   Intimacy,   (3)   Tension,   (4) Sympathy
(ego-involvement), (5) Dependency.
TEST DESCRIPTION. Ten items in each variable which   require
accepting or   rejecting the statement as applying to
relationship with a parent. The score is the number of
positive adjustment items minus the negative.
SAMPLE ITEM. We have little in common.
LENGTH. Items: 50.
AVAILABILITY. From NAPS.
REFERENCES.
     Komarovsky,M.   Functional analysis of sex   roles.
American Sociological Review, 1950, 15, 508-516.
     Stryker,S.   The adjustment of married offspring to
their parents.   American Sociological Review, 1955, 20,
149-154.

UTTON,A.C.   Childhood Experience Rating Scales

VARIABLE MEASURED. Warmth of childhood home environment as
assessed in the following areas: Acceptance, direction of
criticism,   child   centeredness,   rapport,   and
affectionateness.
TEST DESCRIPTION. Subjects are given a   questionnaire made
up of five scales (one for each of the areas listed above).
The items in each of the scales range along a continuum
reflecting a warm to cold family environment. Subjects are
directed to check each item as "More true than false" or
"More false than true," and then draw a circle around the
number in front of the one item which most accurately
reflects their recollected feelings.   The items on each
scale are weighted on a warm-to-cold continuum. The average
weight of the   "More true than false" items checked is the
total score.
SAMPLE ITEM. Your welfare got slightly more attention   than
the welfare of others.
LENGTH. Items: 30.
AVAILABILITY. The five scales are slightly modified
versions of the five scales used by Baldwin, et al. in the
more comprehensive "Parent Behavior Rating Scale." The
original versions of the five scales are available in
Baldwin, et al., 1949.
ABSTRACTED BY: Kersti Yllo
REFERENCES.
     Baldwin,A.L.   Kalhorn,J.C.   and   Breese,F.H.   The
appraisal of parent behavior.   Psychological Monographs,
1949, 63, whole no. 299.
     Utton,A.C.   Childhood Experience Rating Scales.
Recalled   parent-child   relations   as   determinants   of
vocational choice. Journal of Counseling Psychology, 1962,
9, 49-53.

VEROFF,J. and FELD,S. Parental Distancing Index

VARIABLE MEASURED. Whether the parent is actively involved
in the obligations of the parental role or distances
him/herself from the role.
TEST DESCRIPTION. Answers to the questions, "What would you
say is the nicest thing about having children? and What
other kinds of things do you think of?" are coded for
whether the satisfaction described shows the parent as
actively involved in his/her role or distancing him/herself
from the role. Those replies which mention things the
parent does in relationship to his/her children fall into
the first category. Those replies which focus on the
characteristics of the children which are seen as gratifying
fall into the second. The index is "a three-point scale
based on the frequency of distancing vs. actively involved
replies": (1) None of the satisfactions are coded as
indicating distancing from the parental role; (2) The
satisfactions mentioned include both distancing and
self-involved role behaviors; (3) All satisfactions are
coded as indicating distancing from the parental role.
SAMPLE ITEM. See above.
LENGTH. NR.
AVAILABILITY. In Veroff and Feld, 1970.
ABSTRACTED BY: Kersti Yllo
REFERENCE.
     Veroff,J. and Feld,S. Marriage and Work in America.
New York: Van Nostrand Reinhold, Co., 1970, 139-140.

3. Aggression, Conflict, Disapproval, Problems, Rejection

AUSUBEL,D.P.   BALTHAZAR,E.E.   ROSENTHAL,I.   BLACKMAN,L.S.
SCHPOONT,S.H.   AND WELKOWITZ,J. Disagreement with Perceived
Parent Opinion Test

VARIABLES MEASURED. Degree of divergence of child's
opinions with those he/she perceives his/her parents to have
on various topics concerning parent-child
relationships--such as home, chores, discipline, privileges,
spending money.
TEST DESCRIPTION. Five-point intensity of agreement scales
rated by the subject as he/she believes his/her parents
would answer. One week later the subject rates them
according to his/her own opinions. Scores are the sums of
all disagreements, regardless of direction.
SAMPLE ITEM. Do your parents think that a child should have
enough spending money so that he can pay for his own movies,
ice cream cones, etc.?
LENGTH. Items: 41.

AVAILABILITY. From NAPS.
REFERENCE.
      Ausubel,D.P.   Balthazar,E.E.   Rosenthal,I.
Blackman,L.S.   Schpoont,S.H.   and Welkowitz,J. Perceived
parent attitudes as determinants of children's ego
structure. Child Development, 1954, 25, 173-183.

BAKER,H.J. Detroit Adjustment Inventory ("Telling What I
Do")

VARIABLES MEASURED. The problems of junior and senior high
school pupils. There are four family-related scores: (1)
Home status, (2) Home atmosphere, (3) Home attitudes, and
(4) Growing up.
TEST DESCRIPTION. A self-administered, multiple-choice
test. A score is derived by summing the weights of the
answers indicated. There are five items for each variable.
SAMPLE ITEM. (Home status:) About speaking English at home:
A. My parents speak fairly well [weight 4], B. My parents
don't speak much English [2], C. No one speaks much English
in our home [1], D. We all speak English all the time [5],
E. We speak English cnly part of the time at home [3].
LENGTH. Items: 120.
AVAILABILITY. From Bobbs-Merrill Co., 4300 East 62nd
Street, Indianapolis, Indiana 46206.
REFERENCE.
      Baker,H.J. Detroit Adjustment Inventory. Teacher's
Handbook for the Detroit Adjustment Inventory. Record blank
and scoring key for Detroit Adjustment Inventory.
Indianapolis: Bobbs- Merrill, 1942.

BLOCK,V.L. Conflicts with Mother Checklist

VARIABLE MEASURED. Conflicts between mother and adolescent
child.
TEST DESCRIPTION. Subject checks problems with mother
perceived as seriously disturbing from a list.
SAMPLE ITEM. Insists on nagging me regarding what I wear
and how I dress.
LENGTH. Items: 50.
AVAILABILITY. In Block, 1937.
REFERENCE.
      Block,V.L. Conflicts of adolescents with their
mothers. Journal of Abnormal Social Psychology, 1937, 32,
193-206.

BOOCOCK,S.S. and SCHILD,E.O. Generation Gap Simulation
Game

VARIABLES MEASURED. The simulation involves players in
decision-making and conflict resolution in relationships
involving trust and differential authority.

TEST DESCRIPTION. Simulates the interaction between a
parent and an adolescent son or daughter. Each pair of
players consists of one parent and one teenager, but parents
compete against each other and teens compete against each
other. The game concerns five issues, such as how late the
teen comes home at night, or how much homework she/he does.
The teen has two behavior alternatives on each issue--one
gives the score to the parent, the other to the teen. The
strength of preference varies from issue to issue. Each
round of the simulation begins with a few minutes of
discussion during which parent and teen try to reach
agreement. On any issue where agreement is not reached, the
parent gives an order to the teen. The teen then selects
his or her behavior (she/he may violate agreements or
disobey orders). The parent can, within certain
constraints, punish the teen by subtracting points from the
teen's score. Winners in each group are the players with
the highest satisfaction score after a designated number of
rounds.
SAMPLE ITEM. Issues for discussion involve (1) doing
homework, (2) helping around the house, (3) going to a show,
(4) physical appearance, (5) going on a date.
LENGTH. Time: less than one hour. Number of items:
Decisions about 5 conduct issues.
AVAILABILITY. From Bobbs-Merrill Co. Inc., 4300 West 62nd
Street, Indianapolis, Indiana 46206.
ABSTRACTED BY: Sarane S. Boocock
REFERENCE.
    Stoll,C.S. and McFarland,P.T. Player characteristics
and interaction in a parent-child simulation game.
Sociometry, 1969, 3, 259-272.

BROUSSARD,E.R. Broussard Neonatal Perception Inventory
(BNPI)

VARIABLES MEASURED. Maternal rejection of the neonate.
An abstract of this test is given in Johnson,O.G. Tests and
Measurements in Child Development: Handbook II. San
Francisco: Jossey-Bass, 1976, 745.

CUMMINGS,J.D. Family Pictures Test

VARIABLES MEASURED. "The child's attitude to his home and
parents;...his conscious feelings...and fantasies of
parental anger and punishment."
TEST DESCRIPTION. A projective technique using line
drawings (head and shoulders) showing: (1) A child of the
same sex; (2) The parents with neutral and (3) With
frowning expressions; (4) Same sex child crying and (5)
Frightened; (6) Opposite sex child if subject has brother
or sister; and finally, (7) A baby picture.
    For the first picture the subject is asked, "What shall
we call him?" and "What is he like?--tell me about him." The

latter instructions are repeated for each picture. In
addition, for each picture depicting a fearful, frowning, or
crying person, the subject is asked, "Why? What has
happened?"
SAMPLE ITEM. Figure 1: A boy of about 6 or 7. Full-face
head and shoulders, neutral facial expression. (First item
should show child of same sex as S.)
LENGTH. Time: 10 minutes. Items: 11 pictures (not all
are used with each S).
AVAILABILITY. In Cummings, 1952.
REFERENCE.
        Cummings,J.D. Family pictures: a projection test for
children. British Journal of Psychology, 1952, 43, 53-60.

DARLEY,J.G. and MCNAMARA,W.J. Minnesota Personality Scale

VARIABLES   MEASURED.   Friendly-healthy   or
conflict-maladjustment in parent-child relations.
TEST DESCRIPTION. A personality test with a family
relations section. Subjects answer: Almost always,
Frequently, Occasionally, Rarely, or Almost never. There
are different forms of the test for men and women.
SAMPLE ITEM. Are the members of your family too curious
about your personal affairs?
LENGTH. Time: 30-40 minutes. Items: 30 (male form), 36
(female form).
AVAILABILITY. From Psychological Corporation, 304 East 45th
Street, New York, N.Y. 10017. $.60 per sample set of test
form, IBM answer sheet, hand-scoring stencils, manual.
REFERENCES.
        Darley,J.G. and McNamara,W.J. Minnesota Personality
Scale. New York: Psychological Corporation, 1941.
        Johnson,B. Family relations and social adjustment
scores on the Minnesota Personality Scale as related to home
and school backgrounds of a selected group of freshman
women. Ph.D. dissertation, Florida State University, 1956.

DENTLER,R.A. and MONROE,L.J. Interpersonal Relations Scale

VARIABLE MEASURED. Subjectively experienced strain in
parent-child relations.
TEST DESCRIPTION. Some items were selected from Nye, 1958,
but "emphasis is on scaling a cluster of items which provide
a general measure of subjective quality of parent-child
relations," along a continuum from smooth (balanced) to
strained. Items are dichotomized and formed into a Guttman
scale.
SAMPLE ITEM. Do you confide in your father? Answers of
Some to Never are counted as "strained."
LENGTH. Items: 9.
AVAILABILITY. In Dentler and Monroe, 1961.

REFERENCES.
    Dentler,R.A. and Monroe,L.J.   The family and early
adolescent conformity and deviance.   Journal of Marriage and
the Family, 1961, 23, 241-247.
    Nye,F.I. Family Relationships and Delinquent Behavior.
New York: Wiley, 1968.

DOLL,R.C. and WRIGHTSTONE,J.W.   Life Adjustment Inventory

VARIABLES MEASURED.   Area E, boy-girl relations;   Area J,
education for family living.
TEST DESCRIPTION.   A list of problem statements with 1, 2,
and 3 printed alongside them.   Subject circles 1 if the
statement represents a big problem to him/her, 2 if a
problem of medium importance, and 3 if of small or no
importance. Scores for each area are derived by counting
the number of 1's circled.
SAMPLE ITEM. (Area E:) I'd like to know more about dating.
(Area J:) I wish the school would do more to help me
understand and appreciate my parents.
LENGTH. Time: 20-25 minutes for whole test, 180 items.
Items: (1) 12, (2) 12.
AVAILABILITY. From Psychometric Affiliates, 1743 Monterey,
Chicago, Illinois, 60643.
REFERENCE.
    Doll,R.C.   and   Wrightstone,J.W.   Life   Adjustment
Inventory Manual, Tabulation Sheet. Rockville Center, N.Y.
1951.

DYER,E.D. Parenthood Crisis Scale

VARIABLE MEASURED.   Family crisis manifested at the arrival
of the first child.
TEST DESCRIPTION. A questionnaire administered separately
to the husband and wife, based on Hill's definition of
crisis: "Any sharp or decisive change for which old
patterns are inadequate...A crisis is a situation in which
the usual behavior patterns are found unrewarding and new
ones are called for immediately." The following areas of
family life were chosen as probable channels through which
crisis would be manifested: (1) Husband-wife division of
labor;   (2) Husband-wife division of authority;   (3)
Husband-wife companionship patterns; (4) Family income and
finances; (5) Homemaking and housework;   (6) Social life
and recreational patterns;   (7) Husband-wife mobility and
freedom of action; (8) Child care and rearing; (9) Health
of husband, wife, and child; and (10) Extra-family
interests and activities. There were originally 26 items
for the crisis scale; 10 of them were dropped, since they
failed to show a discriminative power of .50 or higher.
Each of the remaining items represents a five-point
continuum with values 0-4--the largest indicating the
greatest degree of crisis. Each couple's crisis score is

the average of the summed items for both husband and wife.
Five crisis categories are distinguished: (1) No crisis,
score of 0; (2) Slight crisis, 1-16; (3) Moderate crisis,
17-32; (4) Extreme crisis, 33-48; (5) Severe crisis,
49-64.
SAMPLE ITEM. Did you feel tired and exhausted after the
arrival of your child? (0) Never, (1) Seldom, (2) Quite
often, (3) Very frequently, (4) All the time.
LENGTH. Items: 6.
AVAILABILITY. In Dyer, 1963.
REFERENCES.
      Dyer,E.D. Parenthood as crisis: a re-study. Marriage
and Family Living, 1963, 25, 196-201.
      LeMasters,E.E. Parenthood as crisis. Marriage and
Family Living, 1957, 17, 352-355.

EDWARDS,J.N. and ERAUBURGER,M.B. Parent-Youth Conflict
Scale

VARIABLE MEASURED. Degree of conflict between parents and
adolescent youth.
TEST DESCRIPTION. Subjects respond to nine Likert-type
items, ranging in content from the general (the frequency of
arguments with parents) to the specific (disagreements with
parents over the choice of friends, fads, the political
situaticn, what is learned in school, the choice of a future
vocation, etc.).
SAMPLE ITEM. How often in the past few months have you
argued with either one or both of your parents over what you
should do and where you should go? (1) Frequently, more
than once a week (2) Often, about once a week (3) Sometimes,
about once every few weeks (4) Seldom, less than once a
month (5) Never.
LENGTH. Time: 5 minutes. Items: 9.
AVAILABILITY. From NAPS-2.
ABSTRACTED BY: John N. Edwards
REFERENCE.
      Edwards,J.N. and Brauburger,M.B. Exchange and
parent-youth conflict. Journal of Marriage and the Family
1973, 35, 101-107.

ERON,L.D. BANTA,T.J. WALDER,L.O. and LAULICHT,J.H.
Aggression Scales for Child in Home

VARIABLES MEASURED. (1) Approval of aggression (by parent),
(2) Confessing by child, (3) Dependence avoidance of child,
(4) Ethnicity (generational level of parents), (5,6)
Father's and mother's aggression, (7) Home aggression of
child, (8) Lack of social participation (of parents), (9)
Nonrecognition cf child's needs, (10) Parental aspirations
for child, (11) Parental aspirations for self, (12) Parental
disharmony, (13) Parental rejection, (14) Parental
restrictiveness, (15) Punishment for aggression, (16)

Punishment for dependency, (17) Punishment for nurturance signals, (18) Residential mobility (of parents), (19) Rural background (of parents) (20,21) Shame out of home and shame at home (choice of places where parent would shame child), (22) Social isolation of child.

TEST DESCRIPTION. Information about the above variables is obtained by means of a separate interview with each parent. The interview is "almost entirely precoded." The variables were chosen in order "to get at the sociocultural and psychological antecedents of aggression as they are mediated by child-parent interaction"; variables included were "suggested as important by both general behavior theory and clinical hunches."

Each variable is based on 1 to 20 indicators which can presumably be summed to yield a score for each S. Some questions are rated by judges--for example, punishment for nurturance signals is rated 1 to 4 by three judges, according to subject's verbatim response. On other questions, the parent's responses are checked by the E along a rating scale--that for approval of aggression is: Strongly disapprove = 0, Mildly disapprove = 1, Don't care (and don't know) = 2, Mildly approve = 3, Strongly approve = 4. In a later study, open-ended responses were translated to an objective format (Eron et al., 1963).

No definition for any of these variables was accepted until items could be written which were judged by a number of experts to fit the definition. The homogeneity of the variables was increased by eliminating all items which correlated less than 30 with the total scale score of which it was a part.

A listing of variables and sample items is available in Eron et al. (1961). The scales for variables 3, 5, 6, 7, 12, 13, 14, 15, and 22 are discussed in Banta et al. (1963), and their discriminant and convergent validity is examined. Eron et al. (1963) and Lefkowitz et al. (1963) discuss the punishment indexes; Hurley (1965) reports on a different aspect of the punishment indexes. See also other abstracts by Eron.

SAMPLE ITEM. Suppose NAME gets very mad. Would you: Strongly disapprove = 0; Mildly disapprove = 1; Not care and don't know = 2; Mildly approve = 3; Strongly disapprove = 4.

LENGTH. Time: 1-1/2 hours. Items: Total is not reported by variables 2 to 7, 12 to 15 and 22 amount to a total of 60 items; "the median number of items for each variable was 10 with a range from 1 to 20."

AVAILABILITY. From ADI, Doc. No. 7660. Many of the scales are also in Eron et al, 1971.

REFERENCES.

Banta,T.J. Walder,L.O. and Eron,L.D. Convergent and disciminant validation of child-rearing survey questionnaire. Journal of Social Psychology, 1963, 60, 115-125.

Eron,L.D. Banta,T.J. Walder,L.O. and Laulicht,J.H. Comparison of data obtained from mothers and fathers on

childrearing practices and their relation to child
aggression. Child Development, 1961, 32, 457-472.
        Eron,L.D. Walder,L.O. and Lefkowitz,M.M. Learning of
Aggression in Children. Boston: Little-Brown, 1971.
        Eron,L.D. Walder,L.O. Toigo,R. and Lefkowitz,M.M.
Social class, parental punishment for aggression, and child
aggression. Child Development, 1963, 34, 849-868.
        Hurley,J.R. Parental acceptance-rejection and
children's intelligence. Merrill-Palmer Quarterly, 1965,
11, 19-32.
        Lefkowitz,M.M. Walder,L.O. and Eron,L.D. Punishment,
identification and aggression. Merrill-Palmer Quarterly,
1963, 9, 159-174.
        Walder,L.O. Abelson,R.P. Eron,L.D. Banta,T.J. and
Laulicht,J.H. Development of a peer-rating measure of
aggression. Psychological Reports Monograph Suppliment,
1961, 9, 497-556.

ERON,L.D. WALDER,L.O. and LEFKOWITZ,M.M. Approval of Home
Aggression Scale

VARIABLE MEASURED. Parental standard for aggressive
behavior stated in terms of approval or disapproval of
specific items of aggressive behavior of their child.
TEST DESCRIPTION. Parents are given a list of 13 aggressive
acts which their child might perform. For each item, the
respondent is asked to indicate whether he or she would:
Strongly disapprove = 0; Mildly disapprove = 1;Not care and
don't know = 2; Mildly approve = 3; Strongly approve = 4.
The numerical scores for each item are added to obtain the
total approval score. The higher the score, the greater the
tendency to approve of aggressive behavior in the child.
SAMPLE ITEM. Suppose NAME gets very mad. Would you: (see
response categories listed above).
LENGTH. Items: 13.
AVAILABILITY. In Eron, et al., 1971.
ABSTRACTED BY: Kersti Yllo
REFERENCE.
        Eron,L.D. Walder,L.O. and Lefkowitz,M.M. Learning of
Aggression in Children. Boston: Little, Brown and Co.,
1971, 193, 203.

ERON,L.D.   WALDER,L.O.   and   LEFKOWITZ,M.M.   Parental
Rejection Scale

VARIABLES MEASURED. "The number of changes in the child's
behavior...and characteristics desired by the socializing
agent. The parent is considered to be accepting when he
indicates that his needs are satisfied by the child: 'I
like you the way you are.'"
TEST DESCRIPTION. Parents are asked to respond to 10
questions dealing with the child's behavior and
characteristics. There are three response categories per

item, coded 0 to 2. Item scores are added to form a total score. A high score implies rejection of child.
SAMPLE ITEM. Do you think NAME wastes too much time?   2 = Yes;   1 = Sometimes and Don't know;   0 = No.
LENGTH. Number of items: 10.
AVAILABILITY. In Eron, et al., 1971.
ABSTRACTED BY: Kersti Yllo
REFERENCE.
      Eron,L.D. Walder,L.O. and Lefkowitz,M.M. Learning of Aggression in Children. Boston: Little, Brown and Co. 1971, 194, 202.

ERON,L.D. WALDER,L.O. and LEFKOWITZ,M.M.   Sanctions for Aggression Scale

VARIABLES MEASURED. "Rewards and punishments of various intensities administered by socializing agents contingent upon the child's aggressive behavior"
TEST DESCRIPTION. Parents are asked what they do when their child displays various aggressive behaviors. The questions are opened-ended and a panel of three judges code each response on a scale from 1 to 7 (1 = Rewarding aggression; 2 = Don't do anything; 3-7 = Mildest to severe punishment for aggression). The numerical scores for each item are summed to obtain a total score.
SAMPLE ITEM. What do you usually do when NAME is rude to you?
LENGTH: Number of Items: 11.
AVAILABILITY. In Eron, et al., 1971.
ABSTRACTED BY: Kersti Yllo
REFERENCES.
      Eron,L.D. Walder,L.O. and Lefkowitz,M.M. Learning of Aggression in Children. Boston: Little, Brown and Co., 1971, 194, 207-8.

FARBER,B. and JENNE,W.C. Index of Parental Dissatisfaction with Social-Emotional Behavior

VARIABLES MEASURED.   Four measures of parental satisfaction-dissatisfaction: the child's perception of mother's and father's satisfaction, and the perception of satisfaction by each parent for the child's behavior.
TEST DESCRIPTION. The social-emotional index measures interactional patterns in the family that express a concern for other members. The separate scales for each parent consist of seven items with the highest factor loadings from an original test of 21 items. The items from the father's scale, for example, are as follows (Farber and Jenne, 1963): Show affection toward father (highest loading) [.71]; Show affection toward mother [.71]; Be friendly to people [.61]; Trust people [.53]; Feel sorry for those in trouble [.44]; Show feelings toward friends [.40]; Show care in picking out friends [.36].   Details are provided on all items

selected to represent the factors, the procedure for
determining the weighted factor scores, and the range of the
weighted scores (Farber and Jenne, 1963).
SAMPLE ITEM.   See above.
LENGTH.   Items: 1.
AVAILABILITY.   In Farber and Jenne, 1963.
ABSTRACTED BY: Kersti Yllo based on Johnson and Bommarito,
1971, 347.
REFERENCE.
     Farber,B.   and Jenne,W.C.   Family organization and
parent-child communications. Monographs of the Society for
Research in Child Development, 1963, 28 (Whole Monograph,
No. 7).

FARBER,B. and JENNE,W.C.   Scale of Parental Dissatisfaction
with Instrumental Behavior

VARIABLES MEASURED. Instrumental activities are defined as
activities directed to goals external to the family but that
are conducive to maintaining the family as a social system.
The scale measures behavior along a dimension of external
constraint or conventionality versus internalization of
norms.   More precisely, the scale measures the parents'
estimate of the extent to which the child has behaved to the
degree expected by them, and the child's estimate regarding
the degree to which he has abided by these parental
expectations.
TEST DESCRIPTION. In the scale, scores of four contrived
items are derived from fourteen subitems. The contrived
items include conformity to conventional behavior,
definition of his "world" as serious, propensity toward task
performance, and performance of specific tasks. Since each
contrived item is scored as 0 or 1, the range of the total
scores is from 0 to 4.   Agreement on a subitem between
parental and child's dissatisfaction is scored plus,
disagreement as minus. A contrived item is scored as 1 when
two or three of the subitems are scored plus. The subitems
for the contrived item of conformity to conventional
behavior follow (Farber and Jenne, 1963): Go to church or
Sunday School; Stay out late at night; Go along with fads
(rock'n'roll, hot rods, and so on).
     Four scores are obtained on the child's perception of
mother's and father's satisfaction and the perception of
satisfaction by each parent for the child's behavior.   The
child is requested to answer each item in terms of the
mother's (or father's) desire to change the frequency of
behavior or her(his) satisfaction with its present form.
Appropriate changes in wording were made in the directions
for parents.
SAMPLE ITEM. See above.
LENGTH. Items: 14.
AVAILABILITY. In Farber and Jenne, 1963.

ABSTRACTED BY: Kersti Yllo based on Johnson and Bommarito, 197, 368.
REFERENCE.
    Farber,B. and Jenne,W.C. Family organization and parent-child communications. Monographs of the Society for Research in Child Development, 1963, 28 (Whole Monograph No. 7).

GARDNER,R.A. Conscious Affection-Hostility Scale

VARIABLES MEASURED. Parental affection-hostility toward a child.
    An abstract of this test is given in Johnson,O.G. Tests and Measurements in Child Development: Handbook II. San Francisco: Jossey-Bass, 1976, 761.

GRACE,H.A. and LOHMANN,J.J. Parent-Child Conflict Stories

VARIABLES MEASURED. The child's reactions to parent-child conflict situations: (1) Emotional, (2) Constructive, (3) Active opposition, (4) Simple compliance.
TEST DESCRIPTION. Stories appropriate for 5- to 9-year-olds, involving common home conflict situations in which the parent is the frustrating agent through command, punishment, or threat of withdrawal of affection. In addition, there is one control situation in which the parent is a rewarding agent. Mother and father appear alternately as the frustrating parent in the stories. An alternate form reverses the parents in the situations. There are also separate forms for boys and girls in which the child in the stories is given the sex of the subject. The subject is given a standardized introduction to the task in which he/she is asked to choose a name for the child in the stories. The subject is then instructed, upon presentation of each story, to complete the story, telling how the child reacts to the situation. Responses are categorized as emotional, constructive, active opposition, or simple compliance. In case of more than one type of response for a story, priority is given to the emotional category, then constructive, then opposition and finally compliance. Each story is categorized only once. The reward situation is not categorized. Final scores are percentages of responses for each category.
SAMPLE ITEM. One day __'s mother goes downtown shopping. She promises to bring __ a surprise when she comes back. As soon as school is out, __ runs all the way home to see what the surprise is. But when he gets there, mother doesn't have a surprise for him.
LENGTH. Items: 10 (9 of which were scored).
AVAILABILITY. In Grace and Lohmann, 1952.
REFERENCE.
    Grace,H.A. and Lohmann,J.J. Children's reactions to stories depicting parent-child conflict situations. Child

Development, 1952, 23, 61-74.

HOBBS,D.F.Jr.   Difficulty Index for First-time Parents

VARIABLES MEASURED.   Parent's perception of difficulties
engendered by the birth of the first child.
TEST DESCRIPTION. An objectively scored checklist of 23
items is completed by subject to index the extent of
difficulty associated with the birth of the first child.
Subjects indicate degree to which they have been "bothered"
by each item (None = 0, Somewhat = 1, Very much = 2).
Possible scores range from zero (No difficulty) through 46
(Severe difficulty).
SAMPLE ITEM.   Interruption of routine habits of sleeping,
going places, etc.
LENGTH.   Items: 23.
AVAILABILITY.   From NAPS-2.
REFERENCES.

        Beauchamp,D.   Parenthood as crisis: an additional
study.   1968 Independent study of Masters degree.
University of North Dakota.
        Bogdanoff,K.P.   Method of childbirth and its
relationship to marital adjustment and parental crisis.
Unpublished Master's Thesis, Virginia Polytechnical
Institute and State University, 1974.
        Hobbs,D.F.Jr. Parenthood as crisis: a third study.
Journal of Marriage and the Family, 1965, 27, 367-372.
        Hobbs,D.F.Jr.   Transition to parenthood: a replication
and extension.   Journal of Marriage and the Family, 1968,
30, 413-417.
        Hobbs,D.F.Jr. and Cole,S.P. Transition to parenthood:
a decade replication. Journal of Marriage and the Family,
1976, In Press.
        LeMasters,E.E. Parenthood as crisis.   Marriage and
Family Living, 1957, 19, 352-355.
        Locke,H.J. and Wallace,K.M. Short marital adjustment
and prediction tests: their reliability and validity.
Marriage and Family Living, 1959, 21, 251-255.
        Mace,D.R. Can a baby break up a marriage?   McCalls,
1959, 50ff.
        Meyerowitz,J.H.   and Feldman,H.   Transition to
parenthood. Psychiatric Research Report, 1966, 20, 78-84.
        Mudd,E.   Children almost wrecked our marriage.
Redbook, 1953, September, 35ff.
        Rossi,A.S.   Transition to parenthood.   Journal of
Marriage and the Family 30, 26-39.
        Russell,C.S. Transition to parenthood: problems and
gratifications.   Journal of Marriage and the Family, 1974,
36, 294-302.
        Tooke,S. Adjustment to parenthood among a select group
of disadvantaged parents.   Unpublished Master's Thesis,
Montana State University, 1974.
        Uhlenberg,B.T.   Crisis factors in transition of college
students to parenthood. Unpublished Master's Thesis, Ohio

State University, 1970.

JOHNSON,S.M. and LOBITZ,G.K.   Parental Negativeness Measure

VARIABLE MEASURED. Behavior which conveys a negative
communication to the child.
TEST DESCRIPTION. Families are observed in their homes
under semi-restricted conditions. Negative communications
to the child are coded, and their sum is the measure of
parental negativeness. Behaviors designated as negative are
threatening command, negative command, crying, ignoring,
noncompliance, negativism, physical negativism, smart talk,
teasing, tantrums, whining, yelling, and demanding
attention.
SAMPLE ITEM. See above.
LENGTH. Time: 45 minutes.
AVAILABILITY. In Johnson and Lobitz, 1974.
ABSTRACTED BY: Thomas G. Sparhawk
REFERENCE.
     Johnson,S.M. and Lobitz,G.K. The personal and marital
adjustment of parents as related to observed child deviance
and parenting behaviors. Journal of Abnormal Child
Psychology, 1974, 2, 193-207.

LEVENTHAL,T. and STOLLAK,G.E.   Child Problem List

VARIABLES MEASURED. Problems in various areas of child's
physical and psychosocial functioning, including: eating
and sleeping, soiling, sex, school, self-concept, emotional,
anti-social, physical habits, and parent-child and sibling
relationships.
TEST DESCRIPTION. The list consists of 237 different items
referring to problems. Directions are: "This is a list of
problems that children often have and need help for. Pick
out the problems or difficulties that the child has. Read
every line on the list, without skipping any, and draw a
line under any problems that the child has which trouble
you. For example, if you are quite worried about the
child's lack of eating, underline the first item, like this,
"Eats too little." If you are concerned about your child's
behavior, such as running away from home without permission,
you would underline number 73, like this, "Runs away from
home."
SAMPLE ITEM. (1) Eats too little.
LENGTH. Time: 30 minutes. Number of items: 237 different
items.
AVAILABILITY. From Gary E. Stollak or NAPS-2.
ABSTRACTED BY: Gary E. Stollak
REFERENCES.
     Leventhal,T. and Stollak,G.E. The Problem List of the
Children's Psychiatric Center. Eatontown, N.J.: Children's
Psychiatric Center, 1963.
     Stollak,G.E.   An   integrated   graduate-undergraduate

program in the assessment, treatment, and prevention of child psychopathology. Professional Psychology, 1973, 4 158-169.

Stollak,G.E. Scholom,A. Green,L. Schreiber,J. and Messe,L. The process and outcome of play encounters between undergraduates and clinic-referred children. Psychotherapy: Theory, Research and Practice, 1975, 12, 257-261.

LOSCIUTO,L.A. and KARLIN,R.M. Child-Parent Dissidence Scale

VARIABLE MEASURED. Dissidence, defined as "perceived extent of agreement with parents."
TEST DESCRIPTION. Test items are 15 social issues assumed relevant to adolescents. Items are self-administered and rated on a four-point scale of perceived agreement with parents. A dissidence score is computed by summing the item scores.
SAMPLE ITEM. Your choice of friends: Do you and your parents feel Exactly, Much, Somewhat, or Not at all the same about this subject?
LENGTH. Number of items: 15.
AVAILABILITY. In LoSciuto and Karlin, 1972.
ABSTRACTED BY: Leonard A. LoSciuto.
REFERENCE.
LoSciuto,L.A. and Karlin,R.M. Correlates of the generation gap. The Journal of Psychology, 1972, 81, 253-262.

LYLE,W.H.JR. and LEVITT,E.E. Problem Situation Test

VARIABLES MEASURED. Child punitiveness in situations of (1) Aggression among siblings, peers, and authority figures; (2) Moral transgressions such as stealing or cheating; (3) Personal problems such as shyness.
TEST DESCRIPTION. A measure of the child's willingness to be punitive where punitiveness is hypothetical and no retaliation can be anticipated. Situations are presented to Ss, and responses are scored by two independent judges. A response is counted as punitive if it recommends deprivation, coercion, or physical or verbal abuse. The test can be used in two forms: a 32-item open-ended form or a 14-item multiple-choice form. Correlation between forms is .56.
SAMPLE ITEM. Multiple-choice form: Sandra is sitting at home in the living room playing with her paper dolls. Her little sister runs overand grabs one of the dresses for her paper dolls and tears it to pieces. Sandra cries and runs to tell her mother. What should her mother do? (a) Scold her sister. (b) Send her sister to her room and make her stay there. (c) Give Sandra's sister some paper dolls of her own. (d) Give her sister a whipping and tell her not to do it anymore. (e) Tell Sandra to play where the little

sister can't reach the dolls. (f) Explain to Sandra that
her sister doesn't know because she is just young.
LENGTH. Items: 32 open-ended; 14 multiple choice.
AVAILABILITY. From NAPS.
REFERENCES.
        Lyle,W.H.Jr. and Levitt,E.E. Situational differences
in punitiveness of Iowa school children. Proceedings of the
Iowa Academy of Science, 1954, 61, 378-381.
        Lyle,W.H.Jr.   and   Levitt,E.E.   Punitiveness,
authoritarianism, and parental discipline of grade school
children. Journal of Abnormal Social Psychology, 1955, 51,
42-46.

MAXWELL,P.H.   CCNNOR,R.   and WALTERS,J.   Perception   of
Parent Role Performance Questionnaire

VARIABLES MEASURED. (1) Role performance of parents;   (2)
Discrepancy between child's and parent's report of parental
role performance.
TEST DESCRIPTION. Each subject responds individually to a
questionnaire with 17 items concerning the mother-child
relationship and 17 items concerning the   father-child
relationship.   There are parallel forms for adolescents and
for their parents. The subjects respond to the items on a
variety of five-point continua-- for example, Always, Almost
always, Usually, Sometimes, Seldom or never;   Always fair,
Almost always fair...
SAMPLE ITEM. Parent item: I nag my child...   Child item:
My father nags me...; My mother nags me...
LENGTH. Items: 34.
AVAILABILITY. In Maxwell et al., 1961.
REFERENCE.
        Maxwell,P.H. Ccnnor,R. and Walters,J.   Family member
perception of parent role performance.   Merrill-Palmer
Quarterly, 1961, 7, 31-37.

MCDILL,J.A. Emancipation from Parents Scale

VARIABLES MEASURED.   (1) Emancipation from parents, (2)
Conflict with parents, (3) Self-conflict, (4) Conflict in
desires.
TEST DESCRIPTION. A series of 120 questions about
adolescent decisicns and activities for ages 13-16, which
the boy answers in three ways: (1) What I do, (2) What I
want to do, (3) What my parents want me to do. Each
category is answered by circling Yes, No, or ?   The
emancipation measure is scored by answers from the "what I
do" column. Items are scored +1 for those indicating
emancipation, -1 for dependence. The other variables listed
above are combinations of the other columns.
SAMPLE ITEMS. Decide things for myself.   Depend on my
parents to buy all my things for me.

LENGTH. Items: 120 (each answered three times).
AVAILABILITY. From McDill.
REFERENCE.
     Dimock,H.S. Emancipation from parents. In Dimock,H.S.
Rediscovering the Adolescent. New York: Association Press,
1937, 141-151.

McKINLEY,D. Father's Hostility Measure

VARIABLE MEASURED.   General hostility of father toward
child.
TEST DESCRIPTION.   Subjects are given a list of four
hypothetical ways a father can act toward his son. They are
then asked how closely their own father's behavior resembled
that in the hypothetical case. Response categories are: My
father is: 1 = Very much like this; 2 = Quite a bit like
this; 3 = Somewhat like this; 4 = Very slightly like this;
5 = Not at all like this. The points for each item are
summed to form the total hostility score. The lower the
score, the greater the father's hostility.
SAMPLE ITEM. This father often makes his son feel bad by
ignoring or refusing to talk to him and by acting cold and
distant.
LENGTH. Items: 4.
AVAILABILITY. In McKinley, 1964.
ABSTRACTED BY: Kersti Yllo
REFERENCE.
     McKinley,D. Social Class and Family Life.   New   York:
The Free Press, 1964.

MORGAN,P.K.   and   GAIER,E.L.   Punishment   Situation   Index
(PSI)

VARIABLES MEASURED. Direction of aggression in mother-child
punishment   situations   scored   according   to Rosenzweig's
(1947) categories for reactions to frustrations--that is,
extrapunitiveness, intropunitiveness, and impunitiveness.
When used with both mothers and their children, four
concepts of the punishment situation are obtained: from the
child, (1) His concept of himself (CC) and (2) Of his mother
(CM); and from the mother, (3) Her concept of herself (MM)
and (4) Of her child (MC).
TEST DESCRIPTION.   Projective device consisting of   10
pictures.   Each picture depicts a child and his mother in a
situation commonly followed by a punishment.   Spaces are
provided above the figures (as in a comic strip) for the
subject to fill in what each character is saying. There are
separate forms for boys and girls. For each picture, an
individual inquiry consisting of seven questions   is
conducted (see Morgan and Gaier, 1956, for format), and
answers are recorded verbatim by the E.   Responses are
scored using a system developed by Rosenzweig.

SAMPLE ITEM. Card I: Situations involving possible physical injury. Male: boy is shown emerging from fight with two other boys. Female: girl is hanging by her knees from a tree.
LENGTH. Items: 10.
AVAILABILITY. Plates are described in Morgan and Gaier, 1956; Scoring is described in Morgan and Gaier, 1956; 1957. Also, from NAPS.
REFERENCES.
     Morgan,P.K. and Gaier,E.L. The direction of aggression in the mother-child punishment situation. Child Development, 1956, 27, 447-457.
     Morgan,P.K. and Gaier,E.L. Types of reactions in punishment situations in the mother-child relationship. Child Development, 1957, 28, 161-166.
     Rosenzweig,S. Fleming,E.E and Clarke,H.J. Revised scoring manual for the Rosenzweig Picture-Frustration Study. Journal of Psychology, 1947, 24, 165-208.

MOSYCHUK,H. Differential Environmental Process Variables (DEPVAR) Scale

VARIABLES MEASURED. (1) Academic and vocational aspirations and expectations of parents, (2) Knowledge of, and interest in, child's academic and intellectual development, (3) Material and organizational opportunities for the use and development of language, (4) Quality of language in the home, (5) Female dominance in child rearing, (6) Planfulness, purposefulness, and harmony in the home, (7) Dependency-fostering overprotection, (8) Authoritarian home, (9) Interaction with physical environment (visual and kinesthetic experiences), and (10) Opportunity for, and emphasis on, initiating and carrying through tasks.
     An abstract of this test is given in Johnson,O.G. Tests and Measurements in Child Development: Handbook II. San Francisco: Jossey-Bass, 1976, 765.

PERDUE,O.R. and SPIELBERGER,C.D. Disapproval of Childhood Behavior Index

VARIABLE MEASURED. Extent to which parents expressed disapproval for various childhood behaviors.
TEST DESCRIPTION. Ten questions from a Childhood Experiences Questionnaire. Subjects rate degree of disapproval for 10 types of frequently punished child behaviors.
SAMPLE ITEM. Fighting with other children. Did not disapprove = 0, Slightly disapprove = 1, Moderately disapprove = 2, Strongly disapprove = 3, or Very strongly disapprove = 4.
LENGTH. Items: 10.

AVAILABILITY. In Perdue and Spielberger, 1966.
ABSTRACTED BY: Thomas G. Sparhawk
REFERENCE.
Perdue,O.R.   and   Spielberger,C.D.   Anxiety   and   the
perception   of   punishment.   Mental   Hygiene,   1966,   50,
390-397.

REMMERS,H.H. and BAUERNFEIND,R.H.   SRA Junior Inventory

VARIABLE MEASURED. Problems bothering schoolchildren.
TEST DESCRIPTION. A list of problems on which subjects in
grades 4-8 check their problems. Of the five sections, one
is titled "about me and my home"; the number of problems
checked is the score.   Scores are intended to indicate
relative frequency, not intensity, of problems.
SAMPLE ITEM. I wish we had more money.
LENGTH. Time: 40 minutes. Items: 46.
AVAILABILITY. From Science Research Associates, 259 East
Erie Street, Chicago, Illinois 60611.
REFERENCE.
      Remmers,H.H.   and   Bauernfeind,R.H.   SRA   Junior
Inventory. Chicago: Science Research Associates, 1951.

REMMERS,H.H. and SHIMBERG,B.   SRA Youth Inventory

VARIABLES MEASURED.   Family and heterosexual   relations
problems of adolescents.
TEST DESCRIPTION. A list of problems to be checked by high
school   students   (grades 9-12).   Of eight areas, two are
"home and family" and "boy meets girl." For Form A, the
number of problems checked in each area gives an area
score--scores indicate   frequency,   not   intensity,   of
problems. Form S of the test is answered according to
intensity of the problem (most serious problem, moderate
problem, small problem, not applicable).
SAMPLE ITEM. A. I have no quiet place at home where I can
study. S. I seldom have dates.
LENGTH. Time: 30-40 minutes. Items: A, 52; S, 31.
AVAILABILITY. Frcm Science Research Associates, 259 East
Erie Street, Chicago, Illinois 60611.
REFERENCE.
      Remmers,H.H. and Shimberg,B.   SRA Youth Inventory.
Chicago: Science   Research   Associates, 1949(Form A), 1956
(Form S).

RULE,B.G. AND DUKER,P. Moral Judgments of Aggression

VARIABLES MEASURED. Moral judgment of aggressive behavior:
defined as the degree to which the act is judged as naughty
by parents.

TEST DESCRIPTION. The test items describe several situations of unjustified aggression in which the consequences of (mild versus severe), and the intentions (good versus bad) underlying, the aggressive act are varied. Research participants are asked to rate on a four-point scale the aggressor's degree of naughtiness.
SAMPLE ITEM. During physical education class, Jan and Wim are playing with the ball. Jan plays mean. Wim tackles Jan to punish Jan for his dirty play. Jan is never supposed to do it again. Then Jan falls and has two scratches on his leg. Response: Which circle do you want to make red? I think Wim very naughty; I think Wim naughty; I don't think Wim naughty; I don't think Wim naughty at all. (Translated from Dutch)
LENGTH. Time: 5 minutes per story. Items: 12 stories.
AVAILABILITY. In Rule and Duker, 1973.
REFERENCE.
        Rule,B.G. and Duker,P. Effects of intentions and consequences on children's evaluations of aggressors. Journal of Personality and Social Psychology, 1973, 27, 184-189.

SEARS,R.R. Mother Attitude Scales for Sex and Aggression

VARIABLES MEASURED. Parent attitudes concerning training for sex and aggression control in young children: (1) Permissiveness for (a) nudity, (b) masturbation, (c) social sex play, (d) aggression toward parents;(2) punishment for aggression toward parents.
TEST DESCRIPTION. Items were derived from mother interviews of Patterns of Child Rearing (Sears, Maccoby and Levin, 1957). They are expressions of attitudes on a permissiveness-restrictiveness dimension, and a punitiveness dimension for aggression. Each of 79 items is to be checked in one of five boxes labeled from "Strongly agree" to "Strongly disagree. Scoring: a permissive answer is scored 5, etc. Score for each of the five scales is raw sum of items for a given scale. They are presented in blocks of items by scale.
SAMPLE ITEM. (Nudity) I just tell our daughter that neither her father nor I take our clothes off so she mustn't take hers off either. (Strongly disagree = 5).
LENGTH. Time: 30 minutes. Items: 79.
AVAILABILITY. Document No. 8381, ADI Auxiliary Publication Project, Library of Congress.
ABSTRACTED BY: Robert R. Sears
REFERENCES.
        Lynn,R. and Gordon,I.E. Maternal attitudes to child socialization. British Journal of Social and Clinical Psychology, 1962, 1, 52-55.
        Sears,R.R. Comparison of interviews with questionnaires for measuring mothers' attitudes toward sex and aggression. Journal of Personality and Social Psychology, 1965, 2, 37-44.

Sears,R.R. Maccoby,E.E. and Levin,H. Patterns of Child Rearing. Evanston, Illinois: Row, 1957.
Sears,R.R. Rau,L. and Alpert,R. Identification and Child Training. Stanford, Calif.: Stanford University Press, 1965.

SEARS,R.R. PINTLER,M.H. AND SEARS,P.S. Doll Play Family Aggression Measure

VARIABLES MEASURED. Degree to which separate family members give and receive aggression in doll play, as well as a total aggression measure.
TEST DESCRIPTION. Symbols for recording doll play acts in terms of aggression agents and direction of aggression. Symbols refer to each of the doll family members as well as others--S, E, equipment, imaginary characters, or impersonal agents. Direction of aggression is indicated by an arrow. Aggression is defined as "having the intent to injure, punish, destroy, or generally disparage and depreciate. If a doll character was described as having an aggressive-hostile nature, attitude, or mood, such descriptions were recorded as aggressive units." An aggressive act is considered a unit of aggression with no definite change "in person or method of expressing aggression...or a definite break in the sequence of aggression..." Aggressive acts are recorded for two 20-minute sessions. Scores are number of aggressive acts initiated and received by each family member, as well as a total number of aggressive acts.
SAMPLE ITEM. "The boy fighting the girl" is written "B--- G."
LENGTH. Time: two 20-minute sessions. Items: 10 scoring symbols.
AVAILABILITY. In Sears et al., 1946.
REFERENCE.
Sears,R.R. Pintler,M.H. and Sears,P.S. Effect of father separation on preschool children's doll play aggression. Child Development, 1946, 17, 219-243.

SINES,J.O. PAUKER,J.D. SINES,L.K. and OWEN,P.R. Missouri Childrens Behavior Checklist

VARIABLES MEASURED. Aggressive behavior, inhibition, and sociability exhibited by the child and noticed by the mother in the previous six months.
TEST DESCRIPTION. A questionnaire with 70 items, 43 of which have factor loadings on the above variables. The mother indicates by a yes or no response whether or not her child has shown the described behavior. The total of positive responses is summed for each of the behavior dimensions, and divided by the total number of items in the dimension.

SAMPLE ITEM. Says for instance, I'll get even, You won't get away with that, I'll show him, expresses desire for revenge.
LENGTH. Items: 43.
AVAILABILITY. In Sines, Pauker, Sines, and Owen, 1969.
ABSTRACTED BY; Thomas G. Sparhawk
REFERENCES.
    Sines,J.O. and Pauker,J.D. Identification of clinically relevant dimensions of children's behavior. Journal of Consulting and Clinical Psychology, 1969, 33, 728-734.
    Sines,J.O. Pauker,J.D. and Sines,L.K. The development of an objective, nonverbal, personality test for children. Paper presented at the meeting of the Midwestern Psychological Association, Chicago, May 1966.

WEATHERLY,D. Mother's Responses to Childhood Aggression

VARIABLE MEASURED. Tolerance of child's aggression.
TEST DESCRIPTION. A permissiveness score is the average value of alternatives, weighted in terms of the permissiveness implied on two items of the questionnaire. A punitiveness score is obtained from the response to an item concerning the severity of punishment the children received for expressing prohibited aggression. The permissiveness score is subtracted from the punitiveness score to yield a sternness score as an index of disciplinary attitudes toward aggression. High sternness scores indicate relatively high punitiveness combined with relatively low permissiveness.
SAMPLE ITEM. NR.
LENGTH. Items: 3.
AVAILABILITY. From NAPS-2.
ABSTRACTED BY: Blair Nelson
REFERENCE.
    Weatherly,D. Maternal response to childhood aggression and subsequent anti-semitism. Journal of Abnormal and Social Psychology, 1963, 66, 183-185.

        B.   Role Differentiation and Performance

1.   Authority, Control, Discipline, Punishment, Authoritarianism (See also Subject Index)

ACKERLEY,L.A. Ackerley Parental Attitude Scales

VARIABLES MEASURED. (1) Belief in use of fear as a means of controlling children's behavior; (2) Favorable attitude toward giving children sex information; (3) Disapproval of

older children's telling lies.
TEST DESCRIPTION. A set of three Thurstone-type scales.
Subject is asked to check each statement he/she wishes to
endorse; the score assigned is the median of the scale
values of the items endorsed, with high scores indicating,
respectively: unfavorable attitude toward the use of fear
as a means of controlling children's behavior; unfavorable
attitude toward giving children sex information; and
unfavorable attitude toward children's telling lies. The
values for items in the fear scale are based on scores
assigned by 60 judges, the sex information scale values are
based on 55 judges' ratings, and the lie-telling scale
values are based on 20 judges' ratings.
SAMPLE ITEM. Fear scale: I feel that scaring a child now
and then by a promise of whipping doesn't hurt the child in
any way (scale value=3.5). Sex information scale: I feel
that much unhappiness in adult life is caused by parents
failing to give their children adequate sex information
(scale value=1.9). Lie-telling scale: I feel that lying is
dishonorable, never justifiable, and detrimental to the
child's morals (scale value=10.1).
LENGTH. Fear scale, 32 items; sex information scale, 33
items; lie-telling scale, 9 items.
AVAILABILITY. In Ackerley, 1934; Shaw and Wright, 1967.
REFERENCES.
    Ackerley,L.A. The information and attitudes regarding
child development possessed by parents of elementary school
children. University of Iowa Study of Child Welfare, 1934,
10, 113-167.
    Shaw,M.E. and Wright,J.M. Scales for the Measurement
of Attitudes. New York: McGraw-Hill, 1967, 60-66.

ANDERS,S.F. Anders' Child-Rearing Attitude Survey

VARIABLES MEASURED. Permissiveness in socialization
(infancy through adolescence).
An abstract of this test is given in Johnson,O.G. Tests and
Measurements in Child Development: Handbook II. San
Francisco: Jossey-Bass, 1976, 737.

BLOCK,J.H. Child-Rearing Attitude Scale

VARIABLE MEASURED. Fathers' disposition to act in a
restrictive manner in child-rearing situations.
TEST DESCRIPTION. Four-interval intensity-of-agreement
statements, ranging from Strongly agree to Strongly
disagree.
SAMPLE ITEM. Children should not argue with their parents:
Agree very much, very true for me; Agree pretty much, true
for me; Disagree pretty much, not true for me; Disagree
very much, Not true at all for me.

LENGTH. Items: 20.
AVAILABILITY. In Block, 1955.
REFERENCES.
    Block,J.H. Personality characteristics associated with
fathers' attitudes toward child-rearing. Child Development,
1955, 26, 41-48.
    Feshbach,N.D. Cross-cultural studies of teaching
styles in 4-year-olds and their mothers. Minnesota Symposia
on Child Psychology, 1972, 7, 87-116.

BORDIN,D.S. Parents Questionnaire

VARIABLE MEASURED. Parental control over activities of
teen-age child.
TEST DESCRIPTION. Parents are asked to indicate on a
five-point scale the degree of choice they give their
offspring for each of a list of 29 behavioral areas such as
clothes, dating, and drinking. The response can be analyzed
item by item or summed to provide an overall ccntrol-freedom
scale.
SAMPLE ITEM. Traveling, overnight: No choice = 1, Little
choice = 2, Considerable choice = 3, Mostly free = 4,
Completely free choice = 5.
LENGTH. Items: 29
AVAILABILITY. In Bordin, Shaevitz and Lacher, 1970.
REFERENCE.
    Bordin,E.S. Shaevitz,M.H. and Lacher,M. Entering
college student's preparation for self-regulatioon. Journal
of Counseling Psychology, 1970, 17, 291-298.

BRUCE,J.A. Maternal Involvement in the   Courtship of
Daughters Scale

VARIABLES MEASURED. Mother's encouragement of the courtship
of her daughter by promoting the attentions and
accessibility of desirable and appropriate males.
TEST DESCRIPTION. Likert-type responses to 12 of 16
empirically derived items are summed to yield a score for
things a mother does when she approves of potential suitors
for her daughter, as represented by the daughter. The items
were derived from a much larger pool, and subjected to
observer and statistical tests of validity and reliability
(Bruce, 1972).
SAMPLE ITEM. Make a special effort to get to know him well
(have personal conversations of greater length than usual;
ask about his interests, job, school, hobbies, etc.):   (4)
Nearly all the time; (3) Pretty often; (2) Hardly ever;
(1) Never. (The 12 scale items omit items 1, 3, 4, 7 of the
16 approved items found in the original instrument.)
AVAILABILITY. In Bruce, 1972 or from NAPS-2.
REFERENCES.
    Bruce,J.A. Maternal Involvement in the Courtship of
Daughters. Ph.D. dissertation, University of Minnesota,

1972.
        Bruce,J.A.   Influence parentale sur le choix des
frequentations et d'un conjoint aux Etats-Unis, Recherches
Sociologiques, Universite Catholique de Louvain, Belgique,
1973, 4, 219-245.
        Bruce,J.A. The role of mothers in the social placement
of daughters: marriage or work? Journal of Marriage and
the Family, 1974, 36, 492-497.
        Bruce,J.A.   Intergenerational   solidarity   versus
progress for women?   Journal of Marriage and the Family,
1976, 38, 519-524.

CICCHETTI,D.V.   The Child Rearing Attitude Scale (CRAS)

VARIABLES MEASURED.   (1) Dominance;   (2) Overprotection;
and (3) Rejection.
TEST DESCRIPTION.   Extent of parental dominance,
overprotection, and rejection (or ignoring) is measured by
responses to questionnaire items on the Child Rearing
Attitude Scale (CRAS) of Garmezy, Clarke, and Stockner,
1961. Data are obtained by asking the subject to think back
to the time when he/she was about 13 or 14 years old and try
to remember his/her mother as she was at that time.   The
interviewer reads each of 63 items (typed separately on a 4"
X 6" card, and ordered randomly); hands the card to the
subject, who then reads it again. The subject then decides
whether his mother would have agreed or disagreed with the
statement at that time. The same items and procedure are
then used to obtain a measure of the father's attitudes.
The scale is keyed so that "Agree" is always considered a
deviant response. Each subject receives three scores: the
proportion of items which endorse parental dominance,
overprotection, or rejection.
SAMPLE ITEM.   (Parental Dominance) Children who always obey
grow up to be the best adults. Agree, Disagree.
LENGTH.   Items: 63 in all;   27 measure dominance;   25
assess overprotection; and 12 measure rejection.
AVAILABILITY. From NAPS-2.
ABSTRACTED BY: Domenic V. Cicchetti
REFERENCES.
        Cicchetti,D.V.   and Ornston,P.S.   Reliability of
reported parent-child relationships among neuropsychiatric
patients. Journal of Abnormal Psychology, 1968, 73, 15.
        Garmezy,N. Clarke,A.R. and Stockner,C. Child-rearing
attitudes of mothers and fathers as reported by
schizophrenic and normal patients. Journal of Abnormal and
Social Psychology, 1961, 63, 176-182.
        Johnson,O.G.   and Bommarito,J.W.   Tests and
Measurements in Child Development: A Handbook.   San
Francisco: Jossey-Bass, Inc., 1971, 267.

CLIFFORD,E.   Reward and Punishment Preferences Evaluation

VARIABLES MEASURED. Rank order of child's preferences for
eight types of punishment (P) and eight types of reward (R).
These types are roughly equated in two scales for "social
value" as follows: supernatural force (P), supernatural
force (R); desertion (P), visiting (R); deprivation (P),
material reward (R); spanking (P), physical affection (R);
scolding (P), praise (R); shaming (P), emotional appeal
(R);   isolation (P), centrality (R); withdrawal of love,
(P), verbal love (R).
TEST DESCRIPTION.   After an initial introductory story
(different for the punishment and the reward scales)
structuring the task, the child is presented with 28 paired
items for each of which he/she must state his/her preference
(which punishments would be worse).
SAMPLE ITEM. Punishment Scale: Which would be worse...If
his/her mother said, "I'll send the bogeyman after you."
(Supernatural force.) If his/her mother said, "I'll drive
off in the car and leave you all alone in the house."
(Desertion.)
LENGTH. Items: 8 items, or 28 paired comparisons for each
scale.
AVAILABILITY.   In Clifford, 1959.
REFERENCES.
      Clifford,E.   Ordering of phenomenon in   a   paired
comparisons   procedure.   Child   Development,   1959, 30,
381-388.
      Clifford,E. and Wischner, G.J. The relative severity
of different kinds of parental punishments as evaluated by
preschool children. Paper read at Midwestern Psychological
Association meeting, Chicago, April, 1951.

COUCH,A.S.   Authoritarian Child Attitudes Scale

VARIABLE MEASURED. Authoritarian attitude in child-rearing.
TEST DESCRIPTION. Subjects are asked to respond to three
statements concerning child-rearing. Further explanation of
the scale and the scoring method is available from American
Documentation Institute.
SAMPLE ITEM. The daughter in a family should realize that
it is her job to help every day with the cooking.
LENGTH. Items: 3.
AVAILABILITY. From ADI. Order Document No. 7860.
ABSTRACTED BY: Kersti Yllo
REFERENCES.
      Nuttall,R.L.   Some correlates of high need for
achievement among northern Negroes. Journal of Abnormal and
Social Psychology, 1964, 68, 593-600.

CRANDALL,V.J. ORLEANS,S. PRESTON,A. and RABSON,A. Rating
Scales for Child-tc-Parent Compliance

VARIABLES MEASURED. (1) Compliance with commands and
suggestions,   (2) Degree that mother rewards compliant
behavior,   (3) Amount of punishment mother employs for
noncompliance.
TEST DESCRIPTION. Rating scales with verbal definitions and
descriptive cue points constructed in the same fashion as
the Fels Parent Behavior Scales. Ratings are made on the
basis of home observation of mother-child interaction.
SAMPLE ITEM. NR.
LENGTH. Items: Three rating scales.
AVAILABILITY. From Fels Research Institute, Yellow Springs,
Ohio 45387.
REFERENCE.
     Crandall,V.J. Orleans,S.   Preston,A.   and Rabson,A.
The development of social compliance in young children.
Child Development, 1958, 29, 429-443.

DLUGOKINSKI,E.L.   Parent Discipline Inventory

VARIABLES MEASURED.   Children's perceptions of maternal
induction in peer-conflict situations.
An abstract of this test is given in Johnson,O.G. Tests and
Measurements in Child Development: Handbook II.   San
Francisco: Jossey-Bass, 1976, 622.

DREYER,A.S. AND HAUPT,D. Adult Authority Story Completions

VARIABLES MEASURED. Parental: (1) Power, (2) Pressure, (3)
Arbitrariness, and (4) Immediacy.
TEST DESCRIPTION. Eleven (reduced to five for analysis)
brief story completion situations of children's behavior to
which mother or another adult gives replies indicating what
she would do. Answers are rated on a five-point scale for
the four variables and summed.
SAMPLE ITEM. Some people expect children to show adult
table manners when they are around 4 years old. Others feel
this is an area which should be left alone until later. For
example, how would you usually handle it if your child
spilled his/her juice on the table?
LENGTH. Items: 11 story completion situation.
AVAILABILITY. From Dreyer and Haupt.
REFERENCES.
     Dreyer,A.S. and Haupt,D. The assertion of authority:
differences between teachers, student teachers, and mothers
of young children. Journal of Educational Research, 1960,
54, 63-66.
     Harrison,H.K.   An investigation of transfer from
children''s expectations of teachers.   Psychological
Newsletter, 1956, 7, 107-120.

EPSTEIN,R. AND KOMORITA,S.S. Parental Punitiveness Scale
(PPS)

VARIABLE MEASURED. Severity of parental discipline for
aggressive behavior (as perceived by child).
TEST DESCRIPTION. Subject fills out the questionnaire by
circling in the left column the letter best representing the
punishment his/her father would use in a series of different
misbehaviors.   He/she also circles (in the right-hand
column) the punishment his/her mother would use. There are
four alternatives for each item.   In increasing order of
severity, they are: have a long talk with me, take away my
TV, send me to bed without supper, and whip me. The
categories are given arbitrary integral weights of 1, 2, 3,
and 4 respectively.   The score is computed separately for
father and mother and consists of the sum of the weighted
item scores. The response alternatives are randomly ordered
on the questionnaire.
SAMPLE ITEM. If I put paint on someone's house...my father
would...my mother would (the four responses follow).
LENGTH. Items: 45.
AVAILAILITY. In Epstein and Komorita, 1965a.
REFERENCES.
        Epstein,R. and Komorita,S.S.   The development of a
scale of parental punitiveness toward aggression. Child
Development, 1965a, 36, 129-142.
        Epstein,R. and Komorita,S.S.   Parental discipline,
stimulus characteristics of outgroups, and social distance
in children. Journal of Personality and Social Psychology,
1965b, 2, 416-420.
        Epstein,R. and Komorita,S.S. Childhood prejudice as a
function of parental ethnocentrism, punitiveness, and
outgroup characteristics. Journal of Personality and Social
Psychology, 1966, 3, 259-264.
        Epstein,R. and Komorita,S.S.   Prejudice among Negro
children as related to parental ethnocentrism and
punitiveness. Journal of Personality and Social Psychology,
1966, 4, 643-647.
        Johnson,O.G. and Bommarito. Tests and Measurements in
Child   Development: A   Handbook.   San   Francisco:
Jossey-Bass, Inc., 1971, 267.

ERON,L.D. WALDER,L.O.   AND LEFKOWITZ,M.M.   Judgement of
Punishment Scale (JUP)

VARIABLE MEASURED. The tendency to use harsh or mild
punishments on a child.
TEST DESCRIPTION. Respondents are given a list of 40
punishment items to judge for harshness as it might be
experienced by their children. For each item, the subject
is asked to circle a number from zero to eight on a line,
eight indicating that the punishment is very harsh and zero
indicating that the punishment is very mild. It is assumed
that respondents reveal indirectly their tendency to use

harsh or mild punishments by their average placement of
items along this intensity continuum.
SAMPLE ITEM. Sending NAME to his/her room without supper.
LENGTH. Items: 40.
AVAILABILITY. In Eron, et al., 1971.
ABSTRACTED BY: Kersti Yllo
REFERENCE.
      Eron,L.D. Walder,L.O. and Lefkowitz,M.M. Learning of
Aggression in Children. Boston: Little, Brown and Co.,
1971, 273-274.

ERON,L.D. WALDER,L.O. AND LEFKOWITZ,M.M. Shaming Index

VARIABLE MEASURED. Tendency to punish in public assessed by
items involving different kinds of punishment and different
publics.
TEST DESCRIPTION. Parents are given a list of four
different punishments which they may feel their child
deserves for being naughty. In each case they are asked if
they would do it when: (1) Your spouse and other children
could hear it; (2) One of NAME's friends could hear; (3)
One of your close friends or relatives could hear; (4) A
close neighbor or acquaintance could hear; (5) You were in
public and someone else might hear. The response categories
for each of the twenty situations are: 0 = No; 1 =
Sometimes and don't know; 2 = Yes.
SAMPLE ITEM. Suppose NAME was naughty and you felt he
deserved a scolding. Would you do it when: (See above
listing).
LENGTH. Number of items: 20.
AVAILABILITY. In Eron, et al., 1971.
ABSTRACTED BY: Kersti Yllo
REFERENCE.
      Eron,L.D. Walder,L.O. and Lefkowitz,M.M. Learning of
Aggression in Children. Boston: Little, Brown and Co.,
1971, 195-205.

ERON,L.D. WALDER,L.O. TOIGO,R. AND LEFKOWITZ,M.M.
Punishment Indexes

VARIABLES MEASURED. (1) Physical and (2) Psychological
punishment by the parents for: (a) child's aggression
toward the parent and (b) child's aggression toward peers.
TEST DESCRIPTION. The punishment scale is part of an
objective, precoded interview of 286 items. The punishment
items consist of questions concerning the parents' likely
responses to four kinds of aggressive behavior by the child,
two toward his parents, two toward his peers. Two specific
punishments from each of three levels of intensity are
assigned to each of the four items--24 punishments in all.
Each item receives a weighted score (3 for high, 2 for
medium, 1 for low intensity) if the subject agrees that
he/she would be likely to administer that punishment for a

given behavior. The sum of all 24 items is the score used.
The physical punishment part of this index is reported
separately in Lefkowitz et al. (1963).
SAMPLE ITEM. If __ were rude to you, would you: Tell him,
"I will give you something you like if you act differently"?
Wash out his mouth with soap? Remind __ of what others will
think of him? Say, "Get on that chair and don't move until
you apologize"? Tell __ that young men/ladies don't do this
sort of thing? Spank __ until he cries.
LENGTH. Items: 24 (4 are physical punishment items).
AVAILABILITY. In Eron, et al., 1963.
REFERENCES.

Bronfenbrenner,U. Freudian theories of identification
and their derivatives. Child Development, 1960, 31, 15-40.
Eron,L.D. Walder,L.O. Toigo,R. and Lefkowitz,M.M.
Social class, parental punishment for aggression, and child
aggression. Child Development, 1963, 34, 849-868.
Friedland,H.A. Aggressive behavior in children and
reported discipline practices of their parents. Graduate
Research in Education and Related Disciplines, 1966, 2,
29-48.
Hurley,J.R.   Parental   acceptance-rejection   and
children's intelligence. Merrill-Palmer Quarterly, 1965,
11, 19-32.
Hurley,J.R. Parental malevolence and children's
intelligence. Journal of Consulting Psychology, 1967, 31,
199-204.
Kohn,M.L. Social class and the exercise of parental
authority. American Sociological Review, 1959, 24, 352-366.
Lefkowitz,M.M. Walder,L.O. and Eron,L.D. Punishment,
identification and aggression. Merrill-Palmer Quarterly
1963, 9, 159-174.
Sears,R.R. Maccoby,E.E. and Levin,H. Patterns of
Child Rearing. Evanston, Illinois: Row, 1957.
Toigo,R. Parental social status as a contextural and
individual determinant of aggressive behavior among
third-grade children in the classroom situation. Ph.D.
dissertation, Columbia University, 1962.
Walder,L.O. Abelson,R.P. Eron,L.D. Banta,T.J. and
Laulicht,J.H. Development of a peer-rating measure of
aggression. Psychological Reports and Monographs
Supplement, 1961, 9, 497-556.

GLASSER,P.H. AND RADIN,N. Glasser-Radin Revision of the
Parental Attitude Research Instrument

VARIABLES MEASURED. Child rearing attitudes, which includes
the following factors: (1) Authoritarian-control; (2)
Democratic sharing or equalitarianism; (3) Rejection of the
homemaker role: and (4) Strictness.
TEST DESCRIPTION. Thirty-six from among the original 113
items developed by Schaefer and Bell were selected on the
basis of one of three criteria: ability to differentiate
sharply between lower-class and middle-class respondents;

inability to differentiate social classes; and likelihood
of eliciting a response of "disagree." This permits control
for the "acquiescence response set," making the test much
more valid for use with low-income parents.
Each of   the   statements   uses   a   Likert-type,
forced-choice scale, and the items are scored 4, 3, 2, 1,
respectively. All items are stated in a single direction,
and totals can be obtained for each of the four factors by
simple addition. Thus, the greater the agreement with each
statement on any factor, the higher the sub-scale or factor
score.
Respondents   are   generally   asked   to   read   the
questionnaire and respond by circling their preferred
response.   However, for respondents who have literacy
problems, extensive use of the test has been made by
administering it orally.
SAMPLE ITEM. A child who is "on the go" all the time will
most likely be happy. A=Strongly agree; a=Mildly agree;
d=Mildly disagree; and D=Strongly disagree.
LENGTH. Time: 20-40 minutes. Items: 36.
AVAILABILITY. From NAPS-2.
ABSTRACTED BY: Paul H. Glasser and Norma Radin
REFERENCES.
Navarre,E.   Glasser,P.H.   and   Costabile,J.   An
evaluation of group work practice with AFDC mothers. In
Glasser,P.H. Sarri,R. and Vinter,R. (Eds.) Individual
Change through Small Groups. New York: Free Press, 1974,
387-403.
Radin,N. Three degrees of maternal involvement in a
preschool program: impact on mothers and children. Child
Development, 1972, 43, 1355-1364.
Radin,N. and Glasser,P.H.   The use of parental
attitude questionnaires with culturally disadvantaged
families. Journal of Marriage and the Family, 1965, 27,
373-382.
Radin,N. and Glasser,P.H. The utility of the Parental
Attitude Research Instrument for intervention programs with
low-income families. Journal of Marriage and the Family,
1972, 34, 448-458.
Radin,N. and Wittes,G. Integrating divergent theories
in a compensatory preschool program. In Glasser,P.H.,
Sarri,R. and Vinter,R. (Eds.) Individual Change through
Small Groups. New York: Free Press, 1974a, 420-430.
Radin,N. and Wittes,G.   Integrating Skinnerian and
Piagetian concepts in a compensatory preschool program.
Ferenders,N.W., Jr. and VanHandel,D.   (Eds.) Handbook of
School Social Work. Linden, N.J.: Remediation Associates,
Inc., 1974b, 15-34.
Wittes,G. and Radin,N. Two approaches to group work
with parents in a compensatory preschool program. Social
Work, 1971, 16, 42-50.

GORDON,T. Parental Authority Index

VARIABLE MEASURED. Extent to which parents use punishment and incentives to control their children's behavior.
TEST DESCRIPTION. Parents respond to each of 40 "typical" things which parents do in their relationships with their children in one of the following three ways: Unlikely for you to do this or something similar (U), Likely for you to do this or something similar (L), or Uncertain or do not understand (?). The test score is the number of items which are responded to according to the (L) category.
SAMPLE ITEM. Praise your child for being consistently prompt in coming home to dinner. U, L, ?.
LENGTH. Items: 40.
AVAILABILITY. In Gordon, 1970.
ABSTRACTED BY: Bruce Brown
REFERENCE.
    Gordon,T. Parent Effectiveness Training. New York: Peter H. Wyden, 1970.

HART,I. Child Disciplining Practices Score

VARIABLES MEASURED. Love-oriented discipline (serving to maintain child's striving for parental love by denial of love, threats of denial of reward, and threatened ostracism) versus nonlove-oriented discipline (by physical punishment, ridicule, or threats of physical punishment which make child tend to avoid parents).
TEST DESCRIPTION. Structured interviews in which mothers indicated their most probable response to their child's behavior in specific situations. Child behavior situations depicted in six areas: feeding and oral activities, cleanliness-toilet training, sex, aggression, dependence, and independence. The subject is also asked two projective questions, and is asked to describe her three biggest problems concerning her child. The number of situations for which subject selects nonlove-oriented disciplinary techniques is the nonlove-oriented discipline score. A love-oriented discipline technique score is computed by counting the number of times the subject selects a love-oriented discipline technique.
SAMPLE ITEM. Insists on eating with fingers.
LENGTH. Items: 38.
AVAILABILITY. From NAPS.
REFERENCE.
    Hart,I. Maternal child-rearing practices and authoritarian ideology, Journal of Abnormal Social Psychology, 1957, 55, 232-237.

HAWKES,G.R. AND LEWIS,D.B.   Hawkes-Lewis Family Control
Scale

VARIABLES MEASURED.   Children's perceptions of parental
control of their behavior.
TEST DESCRIPTION.   Multiple-choice questions, scored by
linear summation using either: (1) Judges' weights:
assigned to response categories by 13 judges, so that
parental controls judged to be most conducive to mental
health receive the highest score; or (2) subjects' weights:
percentage choosing each answer, rounded to the nearest
single digit (1, 2, 3, etc.), are used as weights to
indicate typicality of perception of parental control.
SAMPLE ITEM. How much do your parents discuss with you what
your family is going to do? Always, Often, Sometimes,
Seldom, Never.
LENGTH. Items: 59, children's form; 37, judges' form.
AVAILABILITY. From NAPS.
REFERENCES.
      Hawkes,G.R.   Burchinal,L.G.   and   Gardner,B.
Measurement of pre-adolescents' views of family control of
behavior. Child Development, 1957a, 28, 387-392.
      Hawkes,G.R.   Burchinal,L.G.   and   Gardner,B.
Pre-adolescents' views of some of their relations with their
parents. Child Development, 1957b, 28, 393-399.
      Hawkes,G.R.   Burchinal,L.G.   Gardner,B.   and
Porter,B.M. Parents' acceptance of their children. Journal
of Home Economics, 1956, 48, 195-200.
      Lewis,D.B.   Relation between selected variables of
family living and personal and social behavior of childhood.
I. Children's perceptions of certain family controls of
behavior. M.A. Thesis, Iowa State University, 1953.

HOEFLIN,R. AND KELL,L.   Kell-Hoeflin Incomplete Sentence
Blank: Youth-Parent Relations

VARIABLES MEASURED. Developmental (democratic) versus
traditional (autocratic) family relationships.
TEST DESCRIPTION. There are two forms, a parent form and a
youth (teen-age) form, each containing 20 sentence stems.
The stems are designed to elicit responses concerning
intra-familial affect and parent-child roles, with special
emphasis on authority patterns. Responses are categorized
under eight headings: categories a, b, and c denote three
degrees of positive feelings (equated with description of
developmental or democratic home); category d denotes mixed
or neutral feelings; categories e, f, and g denote negative
feelings (reflecting traditional or autocratic homes); and
a final category for factual statements. This last category
is not used in scoring. Scoring is done by weighting
categories 1-7: category a responses (positive end of
continuum) are multiplied by 1, category b responses are
multiplied by 2, and so forth. Weighted scores are added
and divided by the number of sentences completed to obtain a

mean rating, which constitutes the raw score.
SAMPLE ITEM. Parent: As a parent I enjoy...Youth: As a
child I enjoyed...
LENGTH. Time: 30 minutes. Items: 20.
AVAILABILITY. In Hoeflin and Kell, 1959.   Scoring guide
included.
REFERENCES.
    Buros,O.K.   (ed.) Personality Tests and Reviews.
Highland Park, N.J.: Gryphon Press, 1970.
    Hoeflin,R. and Kell,L.   The Kell-Hoeflin Incomplete
Sentence Blank: Youth-Parent Relations. Monographs of the
Society for Research in Child Development, 1959, 24, (Serial
No. 72).
    Kennedy,W.A. and Willcutt,H. Youth-parent relations
of mathematically gifted adolescents. Journal of Clinical
Psychology, 1963, 19, 400-402.
    Searles,W.B. The relationship between the perceived
emotional climate of the home of college students and
certain variables in their functioning related to
self-concept and academic functioning. Ph.D. dissertation,
University of Maryland, 1963.

HOFFMAN,L.W.   ROSEN,S.   AND   LIPPITT,R.   Parental
Coerciveness and Child Autonomy Questionnaire

VARIABLES MEASURED. (1) Parental coerciveness, (2) Child
autonomy.
TEST DESCRIPTION. A two-part questionnaire. In Part I the
child indicates from his/her experience the person or
persons who fit each of a series of behaviors such as
punishes and threatens. Weighted responses are combined
into an overall parental coerciveness score; the top
quartile is taken as the high coerciveness group. Part II
is composed of four questions with the responses Quite
often, Sometimes, and Hardly ever; for the fourth question
an additional response is included--Never have to ask.   The
responses to the first three questions are assigned scores
2, 1, and 0. For the fourth question, the response Never
have to ask is scored 2 points and any other answer, 0. The
top quartile is defined as the high autonomy group.
SAMPLE ITEM. Autonomy: How often do you go some place in a
bus or streetcar without a grown-up along with you?
LENGTH. NR.
AVAILABILITY. Part II in Hoffman, et al., 1960. A complete
copy of Part I is no longer available.
REFERENCE.
    Hoffman,L.W.   Rosen,S.   and   Lippitt,R.   Parental
coerciveness, child autonomy, and child's role at school.
Sociometry, 1960, 23, 15-22.

HOFFMAN,M.L. Parental Influence Techniques

VARIABLES MEASURED. Parental influence techniques used by
the mother: (1) Acceptance, (2) Consequence orientation,
(3) Other orientation.
TEST DESCRIPTION. A technique for coding detailed interview
protocols   using   the   same   method as in the author's
Unqualified Power Assertion Index, but for the following
categories: (1)   Acceptance of the child--pleasurable
interaction between mother and child involving no attempt to
change the child's behavior against his/her will (e.g.,
playing,   reading   to   the   child,   conversation   on
child-centered   topics);   (2)   Consequence-oriented
discipline--influence techniques containing reference to the
direct consequences of the child's behavior (e.g., "You'll
drop it and it'll break if you run so fast," "Don't walk
where   it's   muddy.   You'll   slip   and   fall.");
(3) Other-oriented
discipline--techniques   containing   reference   to   the
implications of the child's behavior for another person
(e.g., referring to the direct consequences of the behavior
for another; pointing out the relevant needs or desires of
another, or explaining the motives underlying another's
behavior toward the child--"Don't yell at him. He was only
trying to help."). Each of the three variables is measured
in terms of the ratio of each type of interaction to the
total number of interactions reported in the interview.
SAMPLE ITEM. See test description.
LENGTH. NR.
AVAILABILITY. In Hoffman, 1963.
REFERENCE.
      Hoffman,M.L.   Parent discipline and the child's
consideration for others.   Child Development, 1963, 34,
573-587.

HOFFMAN,M.L. Unqualified Power Assertion Index (UPA)

VARIABLES   MEASURED.   (1)   Initial   unqualified   power
assertion, (2) Reactive unqualified power assertion.
TEST DESCRIPTION. Parents are interviewed separately about
all   contacts   with their child on the previous day.
Interviews are recorded and transcribed. All purely overt
behaviorial interaction sequences between parent and child
are abstracted from the protocols, and all situations in
which the parent attempts to change the behavior of the
child are coded. In unqualified power assertion the parent
does not attempt to explain or justify his/her demand
(direct commands, threat, deprivations, and physical force).
Initial UPA differs from reactive UPA in that in the latter
case the child has refused to comply with the initial
demand, and the parent asserts his/her power a second time.
In order to control for volume, both initial and reactive
UPA scores are recorded as the percentage of influence
technique fitting the category of unqualified   power

assertion. Hoffman (1963) reports on the other category of
influence techniques, of which unqualified power assertion
is one type. The other category is qualified power
assertion and contains techniques of influence qualified by
explanations referring to nonarbitrary conditions (i.e.,
conditions outside the parent's control). Reference to
another's welfare, the demands of the situation, or socially
prescribed norms qualify power assertion.
SAMPLE ITEM. NR (but a description of the influence
techniques is available from the author).
LENGTH. Time: Interviews lasted from 30 minutes to 1 hour.
AVAILABILITY. In Hoffman, 1957; 1960.
REFERENCES.
    Hoffman,M.L. An interview method for obtaining
descriptions of parent-child interaction. Merrill-Palmer
Quarterly, 1957, 4, 76-83.
    Hoffman,M.L. Power assertion by the parent and its
impact on the child. Child Development, 1960, 31, 129-143.
    Hoffman,M.L. Personality, family structure, and social
class as antecedents of parental power assertion. Child
Development, 1963, 34, 869-884.

HONIG,A.S. and CALDWELL,B.M. Implicit Parental Learning
Theory Interview (IPLET)

VARIABLES MEASURED. The methods and techniques a parent
uses to deal with typical child behaviors which the parent
wants to encourage or discourage for preschool children.
TEST DESCRIPTION. The first four IPLET forms, available
with coding instruction booklet, each consist of a 45-item
inventory. The parent is assured of the experimenter's
interest in the variety of methods parents have found useful
in bringing up children. Each inventory, with separate
forms available for parents of children 1, 2, 3, 4, and 5-6
years of age, is administered as a structured interview
which assesses via verbal report (a) the array of behaviors
likely to appear at least fleetingly in a child's repertoire
that a parent would either encourage or discourage, and (b)
the type of teaching technique which would be employed to
produce either response stabilization or change. Data from
(a) give some indication of parental values for
developmental achievements and also provide an index of
indifference about the child's performance. Data from (b)
reflect the type of teaching techniques likely to be used by
the parent and thus indirectly the parent's implicit theory
about how children learn.
    Coding of the responses involves a determination of
whether a parent tends to rely on (1) Direct manipulation of
the environment (such as provision or deprivation of
privileges, physical punishment, provision of behavioral
models), (2) Symbolic manipulations (promises or threats,
deprivation of privileges, provision of cultural
expectations or expected consequences of behaviors, and
commands), or (3) absence of response. The scoring results

in a profile of the frequency with which the different types of teaching techniques are employed.
SAMPLE ITEMS. Tries new foods. Asks you to read to him. Takes a special blanket to go to sleep. When he can't get his own way, tries to hit or fight. Is thoughtful when someone is ill or sleeping.
LENGTH. Time: 45 minutes. Items: 45 for IPLETs 1-4; 20 for IPLETs 5-6.
AVAILABILITY. Copies of each of the five IPLET inventories are available for purchase through the Family Development Research Program: Syracuse University, College for Human Development, Syracuse, NY 13210. IPLETS 1 and 2--$1.40; IPLETS 3 and 4--$1.40; IPLET 5--$.80; Scoring Booklet--$.70.
ABSTACTED BY: Alice S. Honig.
REFERENCES.

Alamprese,J. Maternal child-rearing practices: a contrast study of families participating or not participating in an intervention program for five years. Ph.D. dissertation, Syracuse University, 1977.

Caldwell,B.M. Mozell,C.J. and Honig,A.S. The Implicit Parental Learning Theory. Paper presented at the annual meeting of the American Psychological Association, New York City, 1966.

Chung,M. Child-rearing practices in the first five years of life by urban mothers in five cultures. M.A. thesis, Syracuse University, 1973.

Honig,A.S. Maternal behaviors in childrearing among poor urban mothers in five cultures. Unpublished manuscript. Syracuse University, Syracuse, New York, 1973.

Honig,A.S. Caldwell,B.M. and Tannenbaum,J.A. Patterns of information processing used by and with young children in a nursery school setting. Child Development, 1970, 41, 1045-1065.

Honig,A.S. Caldwell,B.M. and Tannenbaum,J.A. Maternal behavior in verbal report and in laboratory observation: a methodological study. Child Psychiatry and Human Development, 1973, 3, 216-230.

Matthieson,D. Child-rearing practices in the pre-school years by lower-social class--urban mothers in five cultures. Master's thesis, Syracuse University, 1976.

HUNT,D.G. Child's Perception of Parental Permissiveness Scale

VARIABLE MEASURED. Child's perception of parental permissiveness: defined as "offspring perception of the extent of parent-child participation in decision making and parents' tolerance of offspring behavior."
TEST DESCRIPTION. Two scales are used. The first, a 16-item Participation in Decision-Making is modified from a study by Burgess and Cottrell. A modified 22-item intolerant-tolerant scale by Prentice comprises the second scale. The two scales are cross-tabulated, yielding four

types of the child's perception of parental permissiveness:
laissez-faire, autocratic, quasi-democratic and democratic.
SAMPLE ITEM. Degrees of Tolerance: My parents never
punished me for misbehavior.
LENGTH. Items: Decision-making, 16; tolerance, 22.
AVAILABILITY. In Hunt, 1972.
ABSTRACTED BY: Deryl G. Hunt.
REFERENCES.
      Hunt,D.G. Parental permissiveness as perceived by the
offspring and the degree of marijuana usage among offspring,
Ph.D. dissertation, University of Michigan, 1972.
      Hunt,D.G. Parental permisiveness as perceived by the
offspring. Human Relations, 1974, 27, 267-285.

JACKSON,P.W. Child-Rearing Situation Questionnaire

VARIABLE MEASURED. Coerciveness in solving child-rearing
problems.
TEST DESCRIPTION.   Eleven hypothetical child-rearing
situations are presented to parents who independently write
solutions to the various misbehaviors. Responses are scored
along a 17-category continuum of coercion from acceptance to
creation of fear. Since more than one solution is often
given, scores may be given as (1) The numerical score of the
most coercive method suggested (high coercion score) and the
numerical value of the least coercive method (low coercion
score), (2) The sum of these two scores, and (3) The
difference between the high and low coercion scores or
coercion range. Categories are also provided for responses
involving elaboration of situation and negation of
situation, but these are not used in determining the
coercion scores.   Garmezy et al.   (1960) adapted these
situations for use in the Parental Domination and Conflict
Situational Task.
SAMPLE ITEM. You are seated in your living room when your
12-year-old son enters. As he takes off his jacket, a pack
of cigarettes falls from his pocket.
LENGTH. Items: 11.
AVAILABILITY. In Jackson, 1956.
REFERENCES.
      Becker,J. and Iwakami,E. Conflict and dominance with
families of disturbed children.   Journal of Abnormal
Psychology, 1969, 74, 330-335.
      Becker,J.   and Siefkes,H.   Parental   dominance,
conflict, and disciplinary coerciveness in families of
female schizophrenics.   Journal of Abnormal Psychology,
1969, 74, 193-198.
      Garmezy,N. Farina,A. and Rodnick,E.H.   Direct study
of child-parent interactions: the structured situational
test.   A method for studying family interaction   in
schizophrenia.   American Journal of Orthopsychiatry, 1960,
30, 445-452.
      Jackson,P.W. Verbal solutions to parent-child problems
and reports of experiences with punishment.   Ph.D.

dissertation, Columbia University, 1955.
    Jackson,P.W.   Verbal   solutions   to   parent-child
problems. Child Development 1956, 27, 339-349.

JOHNSEN,K.P. Johnson's Parental Permissiveness Scales

VARIABLES MEASURED.   (1) Generalized concept of what a
parent should do, (2) Tolerance for deviant behaviors, (3)
Usual parental response to specific actions depicting the
behavioral categories.
An abstract of this test is given in Johnson,O.G.   Tests and
Measurements   in   Child Development: Handbook II.   San
Francisco: Jossey-Bass, 1976, 800.

KLEIN,M.M.   PLUTCHIK,R.   AND CONTE,H.R.   Parental   Patterns
Inventory

VARIABLES   MEASURED.   Parental: (1)   Dominance,   (2)
Passivity.
TEST DESCRIPTION. As used in family therapy, a family
therapist checks each of 22 behavioral items, separately for
the mother and the father, on a three-point scale of
occurrence: Rarely cr never; Sometimes; or Often. The
overall score on these items for each parent provides a
measure of the degree of dominance-passivity, with the
higher score dencting a higher degree of dominance.   Items
1-11 denote passivity, and hence are weighted 2, 1, 0.
Items 12-22 denote dominance, and hence the three-point
scale is weighted 0, 1, 2, respectively.
SAMPLE ITEM. Passivity: Is unusually quiet during family
therapy sessions.   Dominance: Interrupts others during
family therapy sessions.
LENGTH. Items: 22.
AVAILABILITY. In Klein, Plutchik, and Conte, 1973.
ABSTRACTED BY; Hope R. Conte
REFERENCE.
    Klein,M.M.   Plutchik,R.   and   Conte,H.R.   Parental
dominance-passivity and behavior problems of children.
Journal of Consulting and Clinical Psychology, 1973, 40,
416-419.

KOHN,M.L. and CLAUSEN,J.A.   Parental Authority Behavior
Checklist

VARIABLES MEASURED.   (1) Parental decision-making;   (2)
Parental authority behavior.
TEST DESCRIPTION. Twenty-five traits or descriptions which
the child marks as describing his/her mother, father, both
parents, or neither parent.   In addition, there is a
question relating to who makes various decisions in the
family and a final question concerning punishing agent and
type of punishment inflicted when the subject is punished

for misbehavior. Various questions might be grouped to
measure broader variables. For example, Kohn and Clausen
group stricter, made day-to-day decisions, restrictive of
the children's freedom, and dominating into a parental
authority behavior scale. Guttman scaling was applied to
these items, and separate scales emerged for mother and
father. These resulted in naming strong, moderate, and weak
authority behavior types. Presumably this could be done for
other items.
SAMPLE ITEM. Stricter--mother, father, both, neither.
LENGTH. Items: 28.
AVAILABILITY. From NAPS.
REFERENCE.
     Kohn,M.L.   and   Clausen,J.A.   Parental   authority
behavior   and   schizophrenia.   American   Journal   of
Orthopsychiatry, 1956, 26, 297-313.

LARSEN,K.S.   AND   SCHWENDIMAN,G.   Parental   Aggression
Training Scale (PAT)

VARIABLE MEASURED. Severity of parent aggression training
as perceived by the child.
     An abstract of this test is given in Johnson,O.G.
Tests and Measurements in Child Development: Handbook II.
San Francisco: Jossey-Bass, 1976, 832.

LI,A.K-F. Parental Attitude Scale in Chinese

VARIABLE MEASURED. Parental attitudes toward childrearing:
(1) Dominance and harshness; (2) Obedience, strictness and
fostering dependency; and (3) Communication, comradeship
and sharing.
TEST DESCRIPTION. The scale consists of 18 statements, in
Chinese, about various aspects of childrearing practices.
Subjects are asked to indicate whether they Strongly agree,
Agree, Disagree, or Strongly Disagree, and the responses are
scored 1, 2, 3, or 4 correspondingly. The three scores are
based on a principal component factor analysis. The scale
items were derived from the Parent Attitude Research
Instrument (Schaefer and Bell, 1958), and the Parent
Attitude Survey (Shoben, 1949), and a few items written by
the author.
SAMPLE ITEM. (in English) Quiet children are much nicer
than chatter boxes: Strongly agree, Agree, Disagree,
Strongly disagree.
LENGTH. Items: 18.
AVAILABILITY. In Li, 1973 (Chinese version) and from NAPS-2
(English and Chinese versions).
ABSTRACTED BY: Anita K-F. Li.
REFERENCES.
     Li,A.K-F. A parental attitude scale in Chinese.
Psychologia, 1973, 16, 174-176.
     Li,A.K-F. Parental attitudes, test anxiety, and

achievement   motivation: a   Hong   Kong   study.   Journal of
Social Psychology, 1974, 93, 3-11.

LYLE,W.H.JR.   and   LEVITT,E.E.   Child's   Perception   of
Parental Punitiveness Sentence Completion Test

VARIABLE MEASURED.   Parental punitiveness.
TEST DESCRIPTION.   A series of incomplete sentences.   Judges
score responses as punitive or nonpunitive.
SAMPLE ITEM.   When I disobey my parents they...
LENGTH.   Items: 20.
AVAILABILITY.   From Lyle and Levitt.
REFERENCE.
      Lyle,W.H.Jr.   and   Levitt,E.E.   Punitiveness,
authoritarianism,   and   parental   discipline of grade school
children.   Journal of Abnormal Social Psychology, 1955,   51,
42-46.

McKINLEY,D.   Severity of Socialization Scale

VARIABLE MEASURED.   Severity   of   socialization   techniques
used by parents.
TEST DESCRIPTION.   The subject is asked to answer this   lead
statement   twice   (cnce   for   father   and   once for mother):
"Below is a list of things a father (mother) might do when a
boy   about   10 or 12 years old had done something the father
(mother) regarded as definitely   bad   or   wrong.   Read   the
list, and thinking about your punishment during that period,
decide which three things in the list describe best   what
your   father   (mother)   was   likely   to do when you had done
something he (she) regarded as   definitely   bad   or   wrong."
This   is   followed   by   a   list   of ten different methods of
punishment.   The subject is then asked to go back   and   rank
the   three   chosen   from the most commonly to the third most
commonly used.   To establish the scale of severity   of   each
technique,   two   psychiatrists,   one   psychologist,   two
anthropologists, one sociologist, and   two   nonprofessionals
rated   the   items.   A   composite of   their ratings and the
researcher's resulted   in   the   final   ranking.   The   total
severity of   socialization   score is determined as follows:
Rank   of   70   of   first-chosen   technique X   3;   Rank   of
second-chosen technique X 2;   Rank of third-chosen technique
X 1.   These are summed.   Scores range from 10 to 56.
SAMPLE ITEM.   Reason with you calmly.
LENGTH.   Items: 10.
AVAILABILITY.   In McKinley, 1964.
ABSTRACTED BY: Kersti Yllo
REFERENCE.
      McKinley,D.   Social Class and Family Life.   New   York:
The Free Press, 1964.

MOULTON,R.W. BURNSTEIN,E. LIBERTY,P.G.Jr. and ALTUCHER,N.
Measure of Parental Dominance in Discipline

VARIABLE MEASURED. Dominance of mother or father in
discipline.
TEST DESCRIPTION. This index is composed of five items
concerned   with   which   parent   practiced   particular
disciplinary actions.   Responses are Mother, Father,
Neither, or Both. If the number of items checked as Mother
exceeds the number of items checked as Father, the subject
is designated as mother dominated.   A greater number of
Father responses than mother responses classifies the
subject as father dominated. (In cases where the subject
answered all five items Both or Neither, Moulton et al.
eliminated the subject from the analysis.)
SAMPLE ITEM. "Who disciplined you if you did something
wrong that was serious?" Mother, Father, Neither, Both.
LENGTH. Items: 5.
AVAILABILITY. In Moulton et al., 1966.
ABSTRACTED BY: Blair Nelson
REFERENCES.
    Altucher,N. Conflict in sex identification in boys.
Ph.D. dissertation, University of Michigan, 1956.
    Moulton,R.W.   Burnstein,E.   Liberty,P.G.Jr.   and
Altucher,N.   Patterning   of   parental   affection   and
disciplinary dominance as a determinant of guilt and sex
typing. Journal of Personality and Social Psychology, 1966,
4, 356-363.

PAYNE,D.E. and MUSSEN,P.H. Incomplete Story Technique for
Measuring Parent-Son Relationships

VARIABLES MEASURED. (1) Father as source of reward (FR),
(2) Mother as source of reward (MR), (3) Parents
(undifferentiated) as source of reward (FamR), (4) Positive
father-son   relationship   (PRF), (5) Positive mother-son
relationship   (PRM),   (6)   Positive   parent-son
(undifferentiated) relationship (PRFam).
TEST DESCRIPTION. Five incomplete stories to be completed
by child (son), by answering specific questions. The score
for each variable is obtained by summing the number of
story-completions in which either the parent is seen as the
source of reward or in which there is evidence of a positive
parent-son relationship. The FamR and PRFam scores are the
sum of the stories falling into the FR and MR categories (or
PRF and PRM) plus those stories in which parents are
rewarding (or showing positive parent-son relations) without
being referred to separately.
SAMPLE ITEM. A boy wants to use the family car for a date
on Friday evening.   He knows that neither of his parents
plans to use the car...Which of his parents would he ask for
the car, and what would happen then?

LENGTH. Items: 5.
AVAILABILITY. Partly described in Payne and Mussen, 1956.
REFERENCE.
     Payne,D.E. and Mussen,P.H. Parent-child relations and
father identification among adolescent boys. Journal of
Abnormal Social Psycology 1956, 52, 358-362.

PIKAS,A. Rational and Inhibiting Parental Authority
Inventories

VARIABLES MEASURED. Child's positive or negative reaction
to (1) Rational parental authority, (2) Inhibiting parental
authority, (3) Parental restrictive norms, (4) Altruistic
versus task-centered motives, (5) Authoritarian motives.
TEST DESCRIPTION. Variables 1 and 2 are included in the A
Inventory, consisting of statements expressing rational or
inhibiting authority of both a concrete and an abstract
nature.   Each item has a corresponding sentence completion
projective item. The O Inventory covers variables 4 and 5,
and   involves   a forced choice between altruistic and
authoritarian alternatives.
SAMPLE ITEMS. (A Inventory:) Should children go to bed at a
set time? Yes, No. If his parents think he should go to
bed at a set time in order to get enough sleep, he thinks
that__If his parents think he should go to bed at a set time
in order that they can be left in peace, he thinks that__The
sentence completion items also occur in a personal referent
form; If my parents__I think__(O Inventory:) As a judge, he
feels most satisfied: (1) when he knows no criminal escapes
punishment, (2) when all verdicts are as just as possible.
     The items also have both an impersonal and a
self-referent projective form. A girl's version of the test
replaces the male occupational references with female ones
of like status and relevance. All implication items are
scored as positive or negative.
LENGTH. Time: 90 minutes. Items: 324.
AVAILABILITY. From NAPS.
REFERENCE.
     Pikas,A. Children's attitudes toward rational versus
inhibiting parental authority. Journal of Abnormal Social
Psychology, 1961, 62, 315-321.

PITFIELD,M. and OPPENHEIM,A.N. Maternal Attitude Inventory

VARIABLES MEASURED. Maternal attitudes toward children
categorized   into 10 areas: overprotection (dominant),
overprotection (submissive), democracy,   autocracy,
acceptance, rejection, strict infant training, strictness
concerning habits and manners, strictness about sex play,
objectivity.
TEST DESCRIPTION. The instructions ask mothers to orient
themselves toward "children in general, and not specifically
your own children." There are five items in each of the 20

areas. Possible responses: Strong agreement (5), Agreement (4), Uncertain (3), Disagreement (2), and Strong disagreement (1). Ss check the category most representative of their feelings. Factor analyses define two factors: I. a general strictness factor (including autocracy, infant training, habits and manners, and sex); and II. acceptance/rejection (on which acceptance, overprotection, and objectivity have significant loadings).
SAMPLE ITEM. It is difficult for a mother to feel at ease when she does not know exactly what her child is doing. (overprotection--dominant).
LENGTH. Items: 50.
AVAILABILITY. From Dr. A.N. Oppenheim, London School of Economics, Houghton Street, London, W.C. 2.
REFERENCE.
    Pitfield,M. and Oppenheim,A.N. Child-rearing attitudes of mcthers of psychotic children. Journal of Child Psychology and Psychiatry, 1964, 5, 51-57.

RADKE,M.J. Parent's Inventory

VARIABLES MEASURED. The nature of parental authority and discipline in several areas: philosophy of authority and discipline, strictness or laxness of disciplinary policies, severity or mildness of punishments, amount and areas of parental supervision, friction over discipline (mother-father, parent-child), mother's versus father's role in home discipline, parent's rapport with child, sibling differences related to discipline and intra-family rapport, techniques of discipline, and effectiveness of discipline.
TEST DESCRIPTION. A multiple-choice questionnaire. Six scales were derived by combining weighted answers to selected items from the questionnaire. In the first part of the questionnaire the parents respond to statements according to discipline factors in their own childhood. In the second part they respond to statements about their own practices.
SAMPLE ITEM. (First part:) My parents liked to have me bring playmates into our house to play--Very much, Somewhat, Very little. (Second part:) I play with my child--Very much, Somewhat, Very little.
LENGTH. Items: 127.
AVAILABILITY. In Radke, 1946.
REFERENCES.
    Radke,M.J. The relation of parental authority to children's behavior and attitudes. University of Minnesota Child Welfare Monographs, 1946, 22.
    Wyer,R.S.Jr. Effect of child-rearing attitudes and behavior on children's responses to hypothetical social situations. Journal of Personality and Social Psychology, 1965, 2, 480-486.

SCHECK,D.C.   EMERICK,R.   and EL-ASSAL,M.M.   (1) Inconsistent
Parental Discipline Scale and (2) Parental Disagreement on
Expectations of the Child Scale

VARIABLES MEASURED.   (1) Inconsistent maternal discipline,
(2) Inconsistent paternal discipline, (3) Mother's
disagreement with father, and (4) Father's disagreement with
mother.
TEST DESCRIPTION. The respondent is instructed to think
back to when he/she was about 12 years old and rate both
his/her mother's and father's behavior toward him/her in a
variety of circumstances on five-point Likert-type items.
The respondent indicates separately his/her perception of
each parent's disciplinary behavior, the extent to which
his/her mother agrees with his/her father on expectations of
him/her when he/she was a child, and the extent to which
father is perceived to agree with mother on expectations of
him/her.   Each item can receive a score ranging from 1 to 5.
The scores for each item of the scales are summed to provide
a total scale score for each respondent; the higher the
score, the greater the perceived inconsistency.   To prevent
subjects from ascertaining the purpose of the test, the
items are randomly interspersed with items measuring other
dimensions of parental behavior.
SAMPLE ITEM.   (1) Inconsistent Parental Discipline: My
mother (father) sometimes carried out threatened punishment
and sometimes did not.   (2) Parental Disagreement on
Expectations of the Child: My mother (father) was almost
never able to agree with my father (mother) on what I should
be punished and rewarded for.
LENGTH. Items: Measures 1 and 2: 7. Measures 3 and 4:
6.
AVAILABILITY. From NAPS-2.
ABSTRACTED BY; Dennis C. Scheck
REFERENCE.
        Scheck,D.C.   Emerick,R.   and   El-Assal,M.M.
Adolescents' perceptions of parent-child relations and the
development of internal-external control orientation.
Journal of Marriage and the Family, 1973, 35, 643-654.

SCHMITT,D.R.   and   MARWELL,G.   Child-Rearing   Technique
Measure

VARIABLES MEASURED.   The use of love-oriented or
punishment-oriented techniques in child-rearing.
TEST DESCRIPTION. A questionnaire in which the respondent
assumes he/she is trying to gain the compliance of his/her
child. A situation is presented and 16 choices of action
he/she might take are given.   The respondent rates each
action according to the likelihood that he/she would use it
as a response to the given situation. The actions are rated
on a six-point scale ranging from Definitely would use to
Definitely would not use. Scores can be computed for each
of the 16 types of action.   These can range from 0

(Definitely would not use the action for any of the four situations) to 20 (Definitely would use the action for all four situations).
SAMPLE ITEM. Situation: Your teen-age son, Dick, who is a high school student, has been getting poor grades. You want him to increase the amount of time he spends studying from 6 to 12 hours a week. Response sample: Promise--(If you comply, I will reward you) "You offer to increase Dick's allowance if he increases his studying."
LENGTH. Items: 4 situations; 16 items for each.
AVAILABILITY. The four situations are in Marwell and Schmitt (1967). The four sets of 16 actions in Marwell and Schmitt (1967). The four sets of 16 actions are in NAPS-2.
ABSTRACTED BY: Deborah S. McDonald (modified)
REFERENCES.
    Marwell,G. and Schmitt,D.R. Attitudes toward parental use of promised rewards to control adolescent behavior. Journal of Marriage and the Family, 1967, 293, 500-504.
    Marwell,G. and Schmitt,D.R. Child-rearing experience and attitudes toward the use of influence techniques. Journal of Marriage and the Family, 1969, 31, 779-782.

SHAPIRO,M.B. Parental Opinion Inventory

VARIABLES MEASURED. Parent role presciptions, primarily in relation to restrictiveness.
TEST DESCRIPTION. Eighteen items represent parental restrictiveness; 4 represent conformity to psychoanalytic precepts; 9 contain both previous elements and are labeled mixed; and 8 are neutral. No scoring system is suggested.
SAMPLE ITEM. I want my child always to be neat and clean. Strongly agree, Mildly agree, Uncertain, Mildly disagree, Strongly disagree.
LENGTH. Items: 40.
AVAILABILITY. In Shapiro, 1952.
REFERENCES.
    Eysenck,H.J. Sense and Nonsense in Psychology. Harmondsworth, Middlesex: Penguin Books, 1957.
    Shapiro,M.B. Some correlates of opinions on the upbringing of children. British Journal of Psychology, 1952, 43, 141-149.

SHOBEN,E.J.Jr. Parent Attitude Survey

VARIABLES MEASURED. Parental attitudes characteristic of parents of problem children. Four subscores: (1) dominant, (2) possessive, (3) ignoring, and (4) miscellaneous.
TEST DESCRIPTION. Parent and child role prescriptive statements, with intensity of agreement multiple-choice response categories.
    Garmezy (Garmezy, Clarke and Stockner, 1961; Cicchetti, 1967; Fontana, 1967; Farina and Holzberg, 1967; Becker and Siefkes, 1969) used items which were similar in

form and content to those originally devised by Shoben
(1949) and subsequently used by Mark (1953) and Harris
(1955). Fifty-three of the 75 items were those which Mark
found significantly differentiated mothers of schizophrenics
from normals. The remaining items were constructed by the
senior author. All items were rated by five senior
clinicians into dominance, overprotection and ignoring
subcategories on the basis of Shoben's original definitions.
SAMPLE ITEM. A child should be seen and not heard.
Strongly agree, Mildly agree, Mildly disagree, Strongly
disagree.
LENGTH. Items: 85.
AVAILABILITY. In Shoben, 1949.
REFERENCES.
    Abbe,A.E. Maternal attitudes towards children and
their relationship to the diagnostic category of the child.
Journal of Genetic Psychology 1958, 92, 167-173.
    Becker,J. and Siefkes,H. Parental dominance conflict
and disciplinary coerciveness in families of female
schizophrenics. Journal of Abnormal Psychology, 1969, 74,
193-198.
    Burchinal,L.G. Parents' attitudes and adjustment of
children. Journal of Genetic Psychology, 1958, 92, 69-79.
    Cicchetti,D.V. Reported family dynamics and
psychopathology: I. the reactions of schizophrenics and
normals to parental dialogue. Journal of Abnormal
Psychology, 1967, 72, 282-289.
    Dickens,S.L. and Hobart,C.W. Parental dominance and
offspring ethnocentrism. Journal of Social Psychology,
1959, 49, 297-303.
    Drews,E.J. and Teahan,J.E. Parental attitudes and
academic achievement. Journal of Clincial Psychology, 1957,
13, 328-332.
    Farina,A. and Holzberg,J.D. Attitudes and behaviors
of fathers and mothers of male schizophrenic patients.
Journal of Abnormal Psychology, 1967, 72, 381-387.
    Fontana,A.F. Klein,E.B. and Cicchetti,D.V. Censure
sensitivity in schizophrenia. Journal of Abnormal
Psychology, 1967, 72, 294-302.
    Freeman,R.V. and Grayson,H.M. Maternal attitudes in
schizophrenia. Journal of Abnormal Social Psychology, 1955,
50, 45-52.
    Garmezy,N. Clarke,A.R. and Stockner,C. Child-rearing
attitudes of mothers and fathers as reported by
schizophrenic and normal patients. Journal of Abnormal
Social Psychology, 1961, 63, 176-182.
    Gordon,J.E. The validity of Shoben's Parent Attitude
Survey. Journal of Clinical Psychology, 1957, 3, 154-158.
    Hobart,C.W. Attitudes toward parenthood among Canadian
young people. Journal of Marriage and the Family, 1973, 35,
71-82.
    Huff,P. Does family life education change attitudes
toward child-rearing? The Family Coordinator, 1968, 17,
185-187.
    Johnson,O.G. and Bommarito,J.W. Tests and

Measurements   in   Child   Development: Handbook   II.   San
Francisco: Jossey-Bass, Inc., 1971, 357.
    Kantor,M.B.   Glidewell,J.C.   Mensh,I.N.   Domke,H.R.
and   Gildea,M.C-L.   Socio-economic   level   and   maternal
attitudes   toward   parent-child   relations.   Human
Organization, 1958, 16, 44-48.
    Kates,S.L. and Diab,L.N. Authoritarian ideology .and
attitudes   on   parent-child   relationships.   Journal   of
Abnormal Social Psychology, 1955, 51, 13-16.
    Leton,D.A.   A   study   of   the   validity   of   parental
attitude measurement. Child Development, 1958, 29, 515-520.
    Mark,J.C.   The   attitudes   of   the   mothers   of   male
schizophrenics toward child behavior. Journal of Abnormal
Social Psychology, 1953, 48, 185-189.
    Mosher,D.L.   and Mosher,J.B.   Relationships between
authoritarian   attitudes   in   delinquent   girls   and   the
authoritarian attitudes and authoritarian rearing practices
of their mother. Psychological Reports, 1965, 16, 23-30.
    Rapp,D.W.   Child-rearing   attitudes   of   mothers   in
Germany and the United States. Child Development, 1961, 32,
669-678.
    Shoben,E.J.Jr. The assessment of parental attitudes in
relation   to   child   adjustment.   Genetic   Psychology
Monographs, 1949, 39, 101-148.
    Trapp,E.P.   and Kausler,D.H.   Dominance   attitudes   in
parents' and adults' avoidance behavior in young children.
Child Development, 1958, 29, 507-513.
    Utton,A.C.   Recalled   parent-child   relations   as
determinants of vocational choice. Journal of Counseling
Psychology, 1962, 9, 49-53.

SMITH,T.E.   Parental Power Indexes

VARIABLES MEASURED.   (1) Parental influence in respect to:
a.   educational decisions of the child, b.   heterosexual
relations decision.   (2) Parental power resources of four
types: a.   outcome-control,   b.   referent value,   c.
legitimacy, and d. expertise.
TEST   DESCRIPTION.   The   indexes   are   designed   to
operationalize the French and Raven taxonomy of power
resources (1959), and to measure the actual exercise of
parental power as indicated by the degree to which parents
influence the decisions of a child in respect to education
and relations with the opposite sex. The .instrument is in
the form of a questionnaire suitable for administration to
high school and college students. The Parental Influence
measures consist of four items for each area of influence.
The Parental Power Resources measures also consist of four
items each, except for the outcome-control measure which is
three items.   Each index is scored by adding together the
weighted score for the items making up that index. The item
weights are based on factor analysis.

SAMPLE ITEM. My father has definitely influenced me in deciding whether to go to college. Strongly agree, Strongly disagree.
LENGTH. Time: 30 minutes. Items: 62.
AVAILABILITY. From NAPS-2.
ABSTRACTED BY: Thomas E. Smith.
REFERENCES.
    French,R.P.Jr. and Raven,B.H. The bases of social power, pp. 150-165 in Cartwright D. (Ed.) Studies in Social Power. Ann Arbor: Research Center for Group Dynamics, Institute for Social Research, University of Michigan, 1959.
    Smith,T.E. Social class and attitudes toward fathers. Sociology and Social Research, 1969, 53, 217-224.
    Smith,T.E. Foundations of parental influence upon adolescents: an application of social power theory. American Sociological Review, 1970a, 35, 860-873.
    Smith,T.E. Some bases for parental influence upon adolescents: an application of a social power model. Adolescence, 1970b, 5, 323-338.
    Smith,T.E. Birth order, sibship size and social class as antecedents of adolescents' acceptance of parents' authority. Social Forces, 1971, 50, 223-232.

SPECTOR,S.I. Home Discipline Patterns

VARIABLES MEASURED. Firmness versus permissiveness of home discipline as observed by the children.
TEST DESCRIPTION. Ten questions on specific parental discipline behaviors to be answered yes or no by child.
SAMPLE ITEM. Do your parents check on the kinds of friends you have?
LENGTH. Items: 10.
AVAILABILITY. In Spector, 1962.
REFERENCE.
    Spector,S.I. A study of firm and permissive home discipline. Journal of Educational Sociology, 1962, 36, 115-123.

STOGDILL,R.M. Attitudes Toward Parental Control of Children

VARIABLE MEASURED. Parental approval of freedom for children.
TEST DESCRIPTION. Parent and child role prescription statements to be rated on a seven-point scale from extreme agreement through neutral to extreme disagreement. Each item in the scale is scored 0 to 6.
SAMPLE ITEM. Children should be allowed to do as they please. Very strongly agree, Strongly agree, Agree, Neutral or Undecided, Disagree, Strongly disagree, Very strongly disagree.

LENGTH. Time: 15 minutes. Items: 70 reported in Stogdill
(1936). Printed test form supplied by author contains 20
items.
AVAILABILITY. From NAPS.
REFERENCES.
    Buros,O.K.   (ed.) Personality Tests and Reviews.
Highland Park, N.J.: Gryphon Press, 1970.
    Stogdill,R.M.   The measurement of attitudes toward
children. Ph.D. dissertation, Ohio State University, 1934.
    Stogdill,R.M.   The measurement of attitudes toward
parental control and the social adjustments of children.
Journal of Applied Psychology, 1936, 20, 359-367.

STONE,C.L. and LANDIS,P.H. Family Authority Pattern Scale.

VARIABLES   MEASURED.   Democratic   versus   authoritarian
parental control of teen-age children.
TEST DESCRIPTION. Five-interval multiple-choice questions
concerning the child's perception of the kind of control
exercised by his/her parents. Responses are dichotomized to
form a Guttman scale. Families are classified as
democratic, intermediate, or authoritarian using arbitrary
cutting points (Stone and Landis, 1952; 1953), or
empirically by the fold-over technique (Guttman and Suchman,
1947), or by intensity analysis (Empy, 1957).
SAMPLE ITEM. With regard to evenings out, my parents allow
me: Every evening out if I wish, Some school nights, Only
weekend evenings out, Almost no evenings out.
LENGTH. Items: 6.
AVAILABILITY. In Stone and Landis, 1952; 1953; in Empy,
1957.
REFERENCES.
    Empy,L.T. An instrument for the measurement of family
authority patterns. Rural Sociology, 1957, 22, 73-77.
    Guttman,L. and Suchman,E.A.   Intensity and a zero
point for attitude analysis. American Sociological Review,
1947, 12, 57-67.
    Papanek,M.L. Authority and sex roles in the family,
Journal of Marriage and the Family, 1969, 31, 88-96.
    Stone,C.L.   and Landis,P.H.   The   Relationship   of
Parental Authority Patterns to Teenage Adjustments.
Pullman: Washington State University Agricultural
Experiment Station Bulletin, 1952, 538.
    Stone,C.L. and Landis,P.H. An approach to authority
pattern in parent-teenage relationships. Rural Sociology,
1953, 18, 233-242.

STOTT,L.H. Parental Control Attitude Scale

VARIABLES MEASURED. Attitudes (role prescriptions) toward
parental control of children's activities.

TEST DESCRIPTION. A series of statements to be rated from complete and thorough agreement to complete and thorough disagreement. Half the items express attitudes favoring exercise of strict parental authority and children's strict obedience to that authority. Each item is scored from 0 to 6 with 6 indicating belief in an adolescent's freedom to act on his/her own rather than "according to the dictation of his parents."
SAMPLE ITEM. Young people should be trained to recognize the authority of their parents.
LENGTH. Items: 30.
AVAILABILITY. In Shaw and Wright, 1967; Stott, 1940.
REFERENCES.
    Shaw,M.E. and Wright,J.M. Scales for the Measurement of Attitudes. New York: McGraw-Hill, 1967.
    Stott,L.H. The Relation of Certain Factors in Farm Family Life to Personality Development in Adolescents. Lincoln: University of Nebraska Agricultural Experiment Station Bulletin 106, 1938.
    Stott,L.H. Parental attitudes of farm, town and city parents in relation to certain personality adjustments of their children. Journal of Social Psychology, 1940, 11, 325-339.

STRYKER,S. Dependence Index

VARIABLE MEASURED. Superordinate-subordinate relationship between parent and married child.
TEST DESCRIPTION. A set of true-false items scored by subtracting the number of items indicating subordination from those indicating superordination. Scores range from -10 to 10.
SAMPLE ITEM. I win our arguments most of the time. True, False.
LENGTH. Items: 10.
AVAILABILITY. In Stryker, 1955.
REFERENCES.
    Stryker,S. Attitude ascription in adult married offspring-parent relationships: a study of implications of the social psychological theory of G.H. Mead. Ph.D. dissertation, University of Minnesota, 1955.
    Stryker,S. Relationships of married offspring and parent: a test of Mead's theory. American Journal of Sociology, 1956, 62, 308-319.

SWITZER,D.K. Parental Attitude Scale

VARIABLES MEASURED. Overdemanding and rejecting as perceived by the subject.
TEST DESCRIPTION. The instrument is composed of 50 statements. The original source of 19 of these is Shoben's Southern California Parent Attitude Scale, 4 from the Traditional Family Ideology Scale (Levinson and Huffman,

1958), and 17 by Switzer. Other statements which are neutral as far as the two major attitudes are concerned were interspersed among these to make a total of 50. Subjects are asked to rate their agreement or disagreement to each statement on a scale of 1 to 5 in terms of how their fathers would respond, how their mothers would respond, and how they themselves respond.

SAMPLE ITEM. Sarcasm is an effective weapon of discipline: Father = 1 2 3 4 5, Mother = 1 2 3 4 5, Self = 1 2 3 4 5. The response categories are 1 = Agree strongly, 2 = Agree, 3 = neutral, can't say, 4 = Disagree, 5 = Disagree strongly. LENGTH. Items: 50 for each parent and for self. AVAILABILITY. From NAPS-2. ABSTRACTED BY: David K. Switzer REFERENCES.

Levinson,D.J. and Huffman,P.E. Traditional family ideology and its relation to personality. In DeDulaney, R.I.D. Beardslee,D.C. and Winterbottom,M.R. (Eds.) Contributions to Modern Psychology. New York: Oxford University Press, 1958, 274-292.

Shoben,E.J.Jr. The assessment of parental attitudes in relation to child adjustment. Genetic Psychology Monograph, 1949, 39, 103-145.

Switzer,D.K. Grigg,A.E. Miller,J.S. and Young,R.K. Early experiences and occupational choice: a test of Roe's Hypothesis. Journal of Counseling Psychology, 1962, 9, 1.

TIFFANY,D.W. Picture Q. Technique (PQT)

VARIABLES MEASURED. Degree of experienced control in parent-child interaction with male or female adult figures. The extreme scores were termed control (C) and freedom from control (FC).

TEST DESCRIPTION. The PQT consists of 48 cartoons on 5 x 7 cards. They are drawn in India ink to meet such specific criteria as: the boy in each picture is to look like the same child, but he is to be engaged in a different adult-child interaction from picture to picture. The adult figures are to be silhouetted in the background. There are two pictures of each specific adult-child interaction. In one the adult is male and in the other female. The pictures range from those representing extreme permissiveness to those representing almost complete adult control of the child. There are 24 C pictures and 24 FC pictures, and both of these groups of pictures contain a set with 12 male adult (M) figures and a corresponding set with 12 female adult (F) figures.

The child is presented the 48 pictures, shuffled to obviate sequence effects, and requested to sort them into five different categories along a continuum from "most descriptive" to "least descriptive" according to some instructional set (e.g., "describe yourself as you are now"; "describe yourself as you would like to be"; "describe yourself as you were last year," etc.).

The child is instructed to sort the 48 pictures into a quasi-normal distribution: 3, 12, 18, 12, and 3. He can sort and re-sort the pictures until satisfied with their arrangement.

Each picture is given a weighted score determined by the category in which it was placed. a picture placed in the "Most descriptive" category receives a weight of 5;   a picture placed in the next category receives a weight of 4; and so on. Separate scores can be computed for the C-FC and M-F dimensions by summing the weightings assigned to appropriate pictures. This allows the response to be treated in terms of dimension scores as well as in terms of the individual weightings of the separate pictures.

SAMPLE ITEMS.

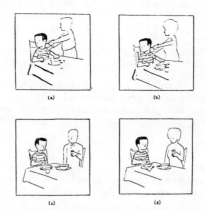

Fig. 1. Pictures depicting control (a and b), freedom from control (c and d), male adult (a and c), and female adult (b and d).

LENGTH. Time: 20 minutes. Items: 48 pictures.
AVAILABILITY. From American Documentation Institute. Order Document No. 7316 from ADI Auxilliary Publications Project, Photoduplication Service, Library of Congress, Washington 25, D.C.
ABSTRACTED BY: Donald W. Tiffany
REFERENCES.

Tiffany,D.W. and Shontz,F.C. The measurement of experienced control in preadolescents. Journal of Consulting Psychology, 1962, 26, 491-497.

Tiffany,D.W. and Shontz,F.C. Fantasized danger as a function of parent-child controlling practices. Journal of Consulting Psychology, 1963, 27, 278.

TROST,J.   Child-Rearing Scale

VARIABLES MEASURED.   Attitudes to punishment with or without physical violence and use of child-rearing theory.
TEST DESCRIPTION.   Subjects disagree or agree (five stages of disagreement-agreement) on attitude statements. A high score indicates a "democratic" attitude toward child rearing.
SAMPLE ITEM.   Children should not be punished but rather reasoned with.
LENGTH.   Items: 4.
AVAILABILITY.   In Trost, 1967 and with original Swedish items from NAPS-2.
ABSTRACTED BY: Jan Trost
REFERENCE.
    Trost,J.   Some data on mate selection: homogomy and perceived homogomy.   Journal of Marriage and the Family, 1967, 29, 739-755.

WATSON,G.   How I Am Bringing Up My Child Questionnaire

VARIABLES MEASURED.   Strictness-permissiveness in parental discipline.
TEST DESCRIPTION.   Questions asking for parental reaction to common situations such as children's eating, sleeping, and toilet training.   Three responses are possible: (1) Clearly permissive response (weight 5), (2) A middle of the road or sometimes this, somtimes that response (weight 3), (3) A reply characteristic of parents that set standards and enforce strict obedience (weight 1).   A score is derived by summing the weights.
SAMPLE ITEM.   NR.
LENGTH.   Items: 35.
AVAILABILILTY.   From author.
REFERENCE.
    Watson,G.   Some personality differences in children related to strict or permissive parental discipline. Journal of Psychology, 1957, 44, 227-249.

WILEY,J.H.   Child-Rearing Permissiveness Scale

VARIABLES MEASURED.   Strictness and permissiveness in the following areas: (1) General home standards;   (2) Verbal standards;   (3) Expression of hostility;   (4) Weaning, feeding, and thumbsucking;   (5) Toilet training;   (6) Sexual behavior;   (7) Boy-girl differences;   (8) Crying.
TEST DESCRIPTION.   Five-point intensity of agreement statements to be answered from Strongly agree to Strongly disagree.   Scoring weights 1-5 are given--the lowest score indicating permissiveness, the highest strictness, authoritarianism, and punitiveness.   The highest possible score is 490, the lowest 98.   Scores are also computed for the eight subscales.

SAMPLE ITEM. NR.
LENGTH. Items: 98 (Staples and Smith, 1954).
AVAILABILITY. In Wiley, 1950.
REFERENCES.
        Staples,R. Smith,J.W. Attitudes of grandmothers and
mothers toward child-rearing practices. Child Development,
1954, 25, 91-97.
        Wiley,J.H. A scale to measure parental attitudes
toward certain aspects of children's behavior. Ph.D.
dissertation, University of Southern California, 1950.

WILLIS,R.H. Authoritarian Upbringing Test (UPB)

VARIABLE MEASURED. Authoritarian upbringing.
TEST DESCRIPTION. Interview items dealing with subject's
recall of his/her upbringing. These deal with freedom of
activities (6 items) and the degree to which subject had a
voice in parent-child relations (6 items)--these might
conceivably be scored separately. E rates each response on
a   dichotomous   scale;   highest   possible   score is 24,
indicating high authoritarian upbringing.
SAMPLE ITEM. NR.
LENGTH. Items: 12.
AVAILABILITY. From ADI, Document Number 4838.
REFERENCE.
        Willis,R.H. Political and child-rearing attitudes in
Sweden. Journal of Abnormal Social Psychology, 1956, 53,
74-77.

WILLIS,R.H. Demands for Obedience Test (DFO)

VARIABLES   MEASURED.   Authoritarian   parent-role
prescriptions.
TEST DESCRIPTION. Interview items dealing with punishment
of children (7), obedience of children to parent decisions
(4), and items maintaining that parents know best (2). E
rates each response on a two- or three-point scale. Highest
possible score is 38.
SAMPLE ITEM. NR.
LENGTH. Items: 13.
AVAILABILITY. From ADI, Document Number 4838.
REFERENCE.
        Willis,R.H. Political and child-rearing attitudes in
Sweden. Journal cf Abnormal Social Psychology, 1956, 53,
74-77.

2. Control, Discipline, Power Combined With Affection,
Support, Love (See also Subject Index)

BACHMAN,J.G. MEDNICK,M.T. DAVIDSON,T.N. and JOHNSTON,L.D.
Composite Measure of Family Relations

VARIABLES MEASURED. Interpersonal relations with parents
including: Closeness to father, closeness to mother,
parental consultation with son and parental punitiveness.
TEST DESCRIPTION. Questionnaire composed of four
interrelated   scales   dealing   with   each   of   the   above
variables.   The items are scored on a five-point scale   with
4 or 5 indicating greater closeness or consultation or less
punishment. The total score on this scale consists of   the
mean of the item scores.
SAMPLE ITEM. Closeness to father: When you were growing
up, how did you feel about how much affection you got from
your father? Closeness to mother: How close do you feel to
your mother? Amount of reasoning with son: How much
influence do you feel you have in family decisions that
affect you?   Parental punitiveness: How often do your
parents completely ignore you after you've done something
wrong?
LENGTH. Items: 21.
AVAILABILITY. In Bachman, 1970.
ABSTRACTED BY: Thomas G. Sparhawk.
REFERENCES.
    Bachman,J.G. Youth in Transition, Volume II: The
Impact of Family Background and Intelligence on Tenth-Grade
Boys. Ann Arbor: Survey Research Center, Institute for
Social Research, 1970.
    Bachman,J.G.   Green,S.   and Wirtanen,I.   Youth   in
Transition, Volume III: Dropping Out: Problem or Symptom?
Ann Arbor: Survey Research Center, Institute for Social
Research, 1971.
    Bachman,J.G.   Kahn,R.L.   Mednick,M.T.   Davidson,T.N.
and Johnston,L.D.   Youth in Transition, Volume I: Blue
Print for a Longitudinal Study of Adolescent Boys.   Ann
Arbor: Survey   Research   Center Institute for Social
Research, 1967.
    Johnston,J. and Bachman,J.G.   Youth in Transition,
Volume IV: Young Men and Military Service. Ann Arbor:
Survey Research Center Institute for Social Research, 1972.

BRUNKAN,R.J. and CRITES,J.O.   Family Relations Inventory
(FRI)

VARIABLES MEASURED. (1) Parental acceptance, (2) Parental
avoidance, (3) Parental concentration.
TEST DESCRIPTION. The test is administered to children, who
evaluate the truthfulness of statements about their mother's
and father's behavior, attitudes, reactions to them, and

expectations for them during childhood and adolescence.
Parental acceptance is defined as parents regard the child
as a full-fledged member of the family, who needs a certain
degree of independence and who has the capacity to assume
responsibility; they encourage the child to fulfill his
potentialities as best he can. Parental avoidance is
defined as parents who either neglect or reject the
child--that is, they manifest no positive interest in the
child, at best merely tolerating him. Parental
concentration is defined as parents who devote a
disproportionate amount of time to the direction and control
of their children; they are overprotective or place
excessive demands for achievement on the child.
SAMPLE ITEM. Acceptance: "My mother gave me encouragement
when I needed it most." Avoidance: "If I kissed or hugged
my mother she seemed embarrassed." Concentration: "My
father often expected me to do more than I thought I could."
LENGTH. Items: 202.
AVAILABILITY. From Brunkan and Crites; and from NAPS.
REFERENCES.

        Brunkan,R.J. Perceived parental attitudes and parental
identification in relation to field of vocational choice.
Journal of Counseling Psychology, 1965, 12, 39-47.
        Brunkan,R.J. Perceived parental attitudes and parental
identification in relation to problems in vocational choice.
Journal of Counseling Psychology, 1966, 13, 394-402.
        Brunkan,R.J. and Crites,J.O. An inventory to measure
the parental attitude variable in Roe's theory cf vocational
choice. Journal of Counseling Psychology, 1964, 11, 3-11.
        Byers,A.P. Forrest,G.G. and Zaccaria,J.S. Recalled
early parent-child relations, adult needs, and occupational
choice. Journal of Counseling Psychology, 1968, 15,
324-328.
        Grigg,A.E. Childhood experiences with parental
attitudes: A test of Roe's hypothesis. Journal of
Counseling Psychology, 1959, 6, 153-155.
        Medvene,A.M. Occupational choice of graduate students
in psychology as a function of early parent-child
interactions. Jcurnal of Counseling Psychology, 1969, 16,
385-389.
        Medvene,A.M. Person-oriented and non-person-oriented
occupations in psychology. Journal of Counseling
Psychology, 1970, 17, 243-246.
        Medvene,A.M. Early parent-child interactions of
educational-vocational and emotional-social clients.
Journal of Counseling Psychology, 1973, 20, 94-96.
        Roe,A. Early determinants of vocational choice.
Journal of Counseling Psychology, 1957, 4, 212-217.
        Utton,A.C. Recalled parent-child relations as
determinants of vocational choice. Journal of Counseling
Psychology, 1962, 9, 49-53.

EMMERICH,W.A. (1) Child Nurturance-Control Scale and (2)
Parental Nurturance-Control Attitude Scale

VARIABLES MEASURED. (1) Children's identification with
parents. (2) Parent's nurturance-control attitudes.
TEST DESCRIPTION. The Nurturance-Control Scale is a
structured doll-play interview that is conducted
individually with children of preschool age who do not have
siblings. The objects used are dolls representing a mother,
a father, a baby, and the child itself. The purpose of the
scale is to obtain an identification index. In general, a
three-step procedure is followed in obtaining this index,
consisting of a two-part interview and a derived
identification index. The first part of the interview
assesses the child's expectations of parental attitudes with
eight standard situaticns. For example, the examiner says:
"The mother and the girl are in the store and the girl won't
leave. She sees a toy she wants. What does the mother do?"
    In the second part of the structured interview, the
same situations are represented, only with the child and
baby dolls as the essential characters. The scores for
responses range from +3 for strong nurturance (facilitation)
to -3 for strong control (interference). A zero score
applies either to two separate but diametrically opposed
responses for the same situation or to a remark by the child
that the doll does nothing. For example, any of the
responses below to the above toy episode in the parent-child
situations would be scored as +3 or strong nurturance
(Emmerich, 1959): Buys several toys; Reads for a long
time; Prepares special food; Plays with child.
    In the last step, two indices of identification are
developed. One refers to the absolute discrepancy in scale
values between six child-baby items and six part-child
items. Identification increases as the score approaches 0.
A second index is based simply on the direction of the
discrepancy between the above two sets of scores on the
nurturance-control dimension. A positive value here
indicates that the child is more nurturant in the same
situation than he/she perceives the parent to be; a
negative value suggests that he/she is more interfering than
he expects the parent to be. No attempt is made to
determine these values as quantitatively absolute.
    The Parental Nurturance-Control Attitude Scale is based
on a projective questionnaire consisting of eight
hypothetical situations in which the parents are asked how
they would deal with their child. The items contained in
the self-administering parental questionnaire resemble those
presented to the children in doll-play interview. For
example, item one is as follows: You and your child are in
the food store and she won't leave. She sees some candy she
wants. What do ycu do?
    The parents' responses are then rated on a
nurturance-control scale similar to the scales used to
evaluate the children's doll-play interview responses,
except that the specific examples of the major scale points

are expressed in more adult terms. The scale, then, rates
the parental responses with scores ranging from +3 (Strong
nurturance) to -3 (Strong control).
SAMPLE ITEM. See above.
LENGTH. Items: 8 for each scale.
AVAILABILITY. In Emmerich, 1959.
ABSTRACTED BY: Kersti Yllo based on Johnson and Bommarito,
1971, 257-258, 360.
REFERENCE.
    Emmerich,W.A. Parent identification in young children.
Genetic Psychology Monographs, 1959, 60, 257-308.

EMMERICH,W.A. Parent and Child Role Conception Pictures.

VARIABLES MEASURED. Child's perception of his/her own and
parental (1) Power (low or high) and (2) Function
(expressive or instrumental). The expressive function is
operationalized as goal agreement or facilitation; the
instrumental function as goal disagreement of interference.
TEST DESCRIPTION. Four cards on which stylized figures
represent four pairs of family members (mother-father,
mother-daughter, father-son, daughter-son) are presented to
the subject in random order 12 times. The experimenter asks
the subject, Who says? followed by a sentence indicative of
a family role classification. Each sentence is classified
as indicating low or high power and as facilitating or
interfering in function. Twelve questions are asked for
each of the four cards, making 48 presentations in all. The
test can be scored for Power or Function for any of the six
actors (father, mother, parents, son, daughter, children) by
counting the number of sentences assigned to each actor.
For example, the parental power score is the number of times
the subject assigns a high-power sentence to the parent plus
the number of times he assigns low power to the child. A
score of 6 means that the power assignments were random; a
score of 12 indicates that the subject in all cases assigns
high power to the parent and low power to the child.
SAMPLE ITEM. (High power, goal agreement:) Who says, You
can have it?
LENGTH. Time: Average testing, 11 minutes. Items: 48.
AVAILABILITY. In Emmerich, 1959a.
REFERENCES.
    Emmerich,W.A.   Parental   identification   in   young
children.   Genetic   Psychology   Monographs,   1959a,   60,
257-307.
    Emmerich,W.A.   Young   children's   discriminations   of
parent and child roles.   Child Development, 1959b, 30,
403-419.

EMMERICH,W.A. Parental Role Perceptions Questionnaire

VARIABLES MEASURED. (1) Nurturance-restriction, (2) Power.

TEST DESCRIPTION. A structured questionnaire asking parent
to indicate the frequency with which he or she responds to
each of several hypothetical child behaviors. There are
four sections: fcr father-son, father-daughter, mother-son,
mother-daughter, with eight questions each. The
nurturance-restriction scale is the sum of the nurturance
items minus the sum of the restriction items. The power
scale is the sum of the frequency with which the mother
responds to the child's actions on all eight items.
SAMPLE ITEM. Instructions: Mark 3 if you often act this
way toward your daughter; mark 2 if you sometimes act this
way toward your daughter; mark 1 if you seldom act this way
toward your daughter. (1) Giving her something at the time
she wants it. Example: You can have it now.
LENGTH. Items: 32.
AVAILABILITY. In Emmerich, 1962.
REFERENCE.
     Emmerich,W.A. Variations in the parent role as a
function of the parent's sex and the child's sex and age.
Merrill-Palmer Quarterly, 1962, 8, 3-11.

FUNKENSTEIN,D.H. KING,S.H. and DROLLETE,M.E. Measure of
Perception of Parental Roles

VARIABLES MEASURED. Relative importance of each parent in
terms of authority, identification (role model), and
affection.
TEST DESCRIPTION. A three-part questionnaire, including
five questions pertaining to authority; four on
identification; and three on affection. Subjects are asked
to rate each parent on all items. The rating of each
subject's perceptions of his/her parents in the three areas
follows steps: First, an inspection of answers for evidence
of clear-cut predisposition toward one parent or the other;
second, comparison of answers with those of the group as a
whole. The total rating combines the three parts into a
family pattern. For example, FFM signifies that the father
is the chief source of authority and the chief role model,
the mother is the chief source of affection.
SAMPLE ITEM. Authority: Which parent has the final word in
most family decisions? Identification: Which parent do you
admire the most? Affection: How close are you to your
mother? father?
LENGTH. Items: 12.
AVAILABILITY. In Funkenstein et al., 1957.
ABSTRACTED BY: Kersti Yllo
REFERENCE.
     Funkenstein,D.H. King,S.H. and Drolette,M.E. Mastery
of Stress. Cambridge, Mass.: Harvard University Press,
1957.

GLIDEWELL,J.C.   GILDEA,M.C-L.   KANTOR,M.B.   MENSH,I.N.
DOMKE,H.R.   and BUCHMUELLER,A.D.   Maternal Attitude Scale

VARIABLES MEASURED. (1) Certainty of opinion concerning
child-rearing practices, (2) Control of child's behavior,
(3) Parental protection of child.
TEST DESCRIPTION. The items were derived in part from a
group of items used by Shoben (1949) to differentiate a
group of mothers cf children with severe behavior problems
from a control group of mothers of normal children. Factor
analysis revealed three orthogonal factors. Factor I
includes six "hard to know" items. The items seem to
constitute a clear measure of the degree of certainty of
opinion concerning child-rearing doctrine and practices.
Factor II includes five items dealing with discipline,
conformity and rejection and seems to be a view of
controlling the behavior of the child. Factor III includes
three items dealing with parental protection of the child.
The responsibility items did not form a factor, nor did they
appear in the other factors. Items are equally weighted by
assigning a score to agreement or disagreement with each
item. Scores for the items comprising each factor are added
to obtain the factor score.
LENGTH. Items: 17.
AVAILABILITY. In Gildea, Glidewell and Kantor, 1961.
ABSTRACTED BY: Mildred Kantor Kaufman (modified).
REFERENCES.
      Gildea,M.C-L. Domke,H.R. Mensh,I.N. Buchmueller,A.D.
Glidewell,J.C.   and Kantor,M.B.   Community mental health
research: findings after three years. American Journal of
Psychiatry, 1958, 114, 970-976.
      Gildea,M.C-L.   Glidewell,J.C.   and Kantor,M.B.   Two
approaches to the study of maternal attitudes. Psychiatric
Research Reports   13.   American Psychiatric Association,
1960.
      Gildea,M.C-L.   Glidewell,J.C.   and   Kantor,M.B.
Maternal attitudes and general adjustment in school
children. In Glidewell,J.C.   (Ed.) Research on Parental
Attitudes and Child Behavior. Springfield: Charles C
Thomas, 1961, 42-89.
      Gildea,M.C-L.   Glidewell,J.C.   and Kantor,M.B.   St.
Louis County Mental Health Project: History and Evaluation.
In Cowen,E.L., Gardner,E.A., and Zax,M. (Eds.) Emergent
Approaches to Mental Health Problems. New York:
Appleton-Century Crofts, 1967, 290-306.
      Glidewell,J.C. Gildea,M.C-L.   and Kaufman,M.K.   The
preventive and therapeutic effects of two school mental
health programs. American Journal of Community Psychology,
1973, 1, 295-329.
      Irelan,L.M. Moles,O.C.   and O'Shea,R.M.   Ethnicity,
poverty and selected attitudes: a test of the Culture of
Poverty hypothesis. Sccial Forces, 1969, 47, 405-413.
      Kantor,M.B.   Gildea,M.C-L.   and   Glidewell,J.C.
Preventive and therapeutic effects of maternal attitude
change in the school setting. American Journal of Public

Health, 1969, 59, 490-502.
       Kantor,M.B.   Glidewell,J.C.   Mensh,I.N.   Domke,H.R.
and Gildea,M.C-L.   Socio-economic level and maternal
attitudes toward parent-child relationships.   Human
Organization, 1958, 16, 44-48.
       Shoben,E.J.Jr. The assessment of parental attitudes in
relation to child adjustment.   Genetic Psychology
Monographs, 1949, 39, 101-148.

HARRIS,D.B.   GOUGH,H.G.   and   MARTIN,W.E.   Parent
Questionnaire

VARIABLES MEASURED.   Parent role prescriptions and
performance in the following five areas: (1)
Authoritarianism, (2) Permissiveness, (3) Parent-child
integration, (4) Parental rigidity or "fussiness," (5) "Good
judgment." In addition, items from each of the scales which
differentiate significantly between mothers of high and low
prejudiced children "constitute an empirical scale,
[reflecting] child-rearing practices and opinions...held by
mothers of markedly prejudiced children."
TEST DESCRIPTION. The items and scales in this instrument
were selected on the basis of their theoretical relevance
for studying the child-rearing antecedents of ethnic
prejudice.   The number of items per scale ranges from 17
(permissiveness scale) to 65 ("good judgment" scale), with
some items appearing in more than one scale.
       There are three parts: (1) 36 "attitudes toward
children and child handling" items, answered on a true-false
basis; (2) 35 statements describing a child-handling
practice--parent indicates degree or frequency with which
he/she follows this practice by checking a three-interval
response category (either: Very much, Somewhat, Very
little; or Usually, Sometimes, Rarely); (3) 10 common
behavior problems, each described in a paragraph and
followed by five or six techniques parents might use in
handling the problem--the subject marks all those
alternatives which he/she would consider following and
rejects all those he/she would not consider.
SAMPLE ITEM. (Authoritarianism scale:) A child should learn
to keep quiet when there are adults around. True, False.
LENGTH. Items: 81.
AVAILABILITY.   All items except the behavior problem
descriptive paragraphs are given in Harris et al., 1950.
The Behavior Problem Descriptive paragraphs have been
deposited with the NAPS.
REFERENCES.
       Harris,D.B. Gough,H.G.   and Martin,W.E.   Children's
ethnic attitudes: II.   relationship to parental beliefs
concerning child training. Child Development, 1950, 21,
170-181.
       Mosher,D.L.   and Mosher,J.B.   Relationships between
authoritarian attitudes in delinquent girls and the
authoritarian attitudes and authoritarian rearing practices

of their mothers. Psychological Reports, 1965, 16, 23-30.

HETHERINGTON,E.M. Family Interaction Task

VARIABLES MEASURED. Parental warmth, hostility, conflict,
and dominance.
TEST DESCRIPTION. Parents, interviewed individually, are
given a set of seven hypothetical problem situations
involving child behavior, and asked how they would be
handled.   The parents are then brought together, and asked
to arrive at a compatible solution.   All sessions are
recorded.
      Scoring of parental dominance and conflict follows
Farina (1960). Warmth-hostility is measured on a six-point
scale, from 6, Marked hostility, to 1, Extremely warm.
Ratings are done on the basis of both sessions; a parent
scoring below the mean is classified as high in warmth,
above the mean is low in warmth.
SAMPLE ITEM. Your son/daughter loses his/her temper while
playing with a toy and intentionally breaks it.
LENGTH. Items: 7.
AVAILABILITY. In Hetherington and Frankie, 1967.
ABSTRACTED BY: Thomas G. Sparhawk.
REFERENCES.
      Farina,A. Patterns of role dominance and conflict in
parents of schizophrenic patients. Journal of Abnormal and
Social Psychology, 1960, 61, 31-38.
      Hetherington,E.M. A developmental study of the effects
of sex of the dominant parent on sex role preference,
identification and imitation in children.   Journal   of
Personality and Social Psychology, 1965, 2, 188-194.
      Hetherington,E.M. The effects of familial variables on
sex typing, on parent-child similarity, and on imitation in
children. Minnesota Symposia on Child Psychology, 1966, 1,
82-107.
      Hetherington,E.M. and Frankie,G. Effects of parental
dominance, warmth, and conflict on imitation in children.
Journal of Personality and Social Psychology, 1967, 6,
119-125.

ITKIN,W. Intra-Family Attitude Scales

VARIABLES MEASURED. Three groups of variables: (1)
Acceptance-rejection   of   children;   (2)
Dominance-submissiveness of parental control; and   (3)
Favorable attitude toward parents by child and toward child
by parents. The specific scales are: Parent Scale I and
Student   Scale   I: attitudes   toward   children:
acceptance-rejection. Parent Scale II and Student Scale II:
attitudes   toward   dominance-submissiveness   of control.
Parent Scale III: attitude toward the student S.   Student
Scale IV-F: attitude toward the father. Student Scale
IV-M: attitude toward the mother.   Student Scale V-F(1):

Father's dominance-submissiveness as judged by the S.
Student Scale V-M(1): mother's dominance-submissiveness as
judged by the S. Student Scale V-F(2): attitude toward
supervision exercised by father. Student Scale V-M(2):
attitude toward supervision exercised by the mother.
TEST DESCRIPTION. A questionnaire consisting of statements
to be answered using three- or five-interval response
categories, usually for intensity of agreement or
disagreement.
SAMPLE ITEM. None provided in Itkin, 1952. See Itkin,
1949.
LENGTH. Items: 30-37 per scale.
AVAILABILITY. In Itkin, 1949; Shaw and Wright, 1967.
REFERENCES.
        Itkin,W. Some relationships between intra-family
attitudes and pre-parental attitudes toward children. Ph.D.
dissertation, Northwestern University, 1949.
        Itkin,W. Some relationships between intra-family
attitudes and pre-marital attitudes toward children.
Journal of Genetic Psychology, 1952, 80, 221-252.
        Shaw,M.E. and Wright,J.M. Scales for the Measurement
of Attitudes. New York: McGraw-Hill, 1967.

KAGAN,J. Parent-Child Relations Picture Series

VARIABLES MEASURED. A variety of parent-child themes
including: (1) Dependency, (2) Nurturance, (3) Anger with a
parent, (4) Parental anger with a child, (5) Punishment.
TEST DESCRIPTION. Thirteen pictures, nine of which
illustrate either a man or woman interacting with a boy.
The other four pictures show two boys interacting. Subject
is asked to make up a story about each picture. Stories are
scored on a number of themes, presumably in a manner similar
to Murray's (1938) scoring method.
SAMPLE ITEM. A boy is sitting on a chair holding a broken
shoelace, and a woman is standing in the background.
LENGTH. Items: 9 out of 13 pictures.
AVAILABILITY. From author.
REFERENCES.
        Kagan,J. Socialization of aggression and the
perception of parents in fantasy. Child Development, 1958,
29, 311-320.
        Murray,H.A. Explorations in Personality. New York:
Oxford University Press, 1938.

MARK,J.C. Mark Attitude Survey

VARIABLES MEASURED. Parental role prescriptions for: (1)
Control, (2) Intellectual objectivity, and (3) Warmth of the
parent-child relationship.
TEST DESCRIPTION. Four-point intensity of agreement
statements to be administered to parents. Items are similar
to those used by Shoben (1949).

SAMPLE ITEM. A child should be seen and not heard. A
(strongly agree), a (mildly agree), d (mildly disagree), D
(strongly disagree).
LENGTH. Items: 139.
AVAILABILITY. The complete questionnaire and tables of
responses are deposited with ADI, Document Number 3672.
Microfilm $1.00, photocopies $1.50. The 67 differentiating
items are listed in Mark, 1953.
REFERENCES.
    Goldstein,A.P. and Carr,A.C. The attitudes of the
mothers of male catatonic and paranoid schizophrenics toward
child behavior. Journal of Consulting Psychology, 1956, 20,
190.
    Harris,J.G.Jr. Size estimation of pictures as a
function of thematic content for schizophrenic and normal
subjects. Journal of Personality, 1957, 25, 651-671.
    Mark,J.C. The attitudes of the mothers of male
schizophrenics toward child behavior. Journal of Abnormal
Social Psychology, 1953, 48, 185-189.
    Shoben,E.J.Jr. The assessment of parental attitudes in
relation to child adjustment. Genetic Psychology
Monographs, 1949, 39, 101-148.

OLSEN,N.J. Parental Socialization Scales

VARIABLES MEASURED. (1) Affection, (2) Direct punishment,
(3) Shame-oriented punishment, (4) Aggression control, (5)
Self-reliance values.
TEST DESCRIPTION. The items composing the above scales are
taken from a modification and expansion of the structured
interview schedule developed by the Six Cultures Project
(Whiting, Child, and Lambert, 1966) for cross-cultural use.
Items are included on a scale only if significantly
correlated with all other items on that scale. A parent's
response to any given item is scored from a low of 1 to a
high of 3, and the individual's score on each scale is the
sum of his/her scores on the component items.
SAMPLE ITEM. (Self-reliance values) In general, do you
think that a child ought to try to do things that are hard
for him, or do you think it is best to ask adults for help?
LENGTH. Items: 27 total for 5 scales.
AVAILABILITY. From NAPS-2.
ABSTRACTED BY: Nancy J. Olsen.
REFERENCES.
    Olsen,N.J. Family structure and socialization patterns
in Taiwan. American Journal of Sociology, 1974, 79,
1395-1417.
    Olsen,N.J. Social class and rural-urban patterning of
socialization in Taiwan. Journal of Asian Studies, 1975,
34, 659-674.
    Whiting,J.W.M. Child,I.L. and Lambert,W.W. Field
Guide for a Study of Socialization. New York: Wiley, 1966.

PETERSON,E.T.   Maternal Interest and Control Index

VARIABLE MEASURED. Daughter's perception of mother's
interest and control over her.
TEST DESCRIPTION. The interest scale consisted of six
questions. The subjects indicate the degree of interest
their mothers have in some of their activities and problems.
The control scale also consists of six questions. The Ss
indicate how strongly their mothers would disapprove if they
did various things.
SAMPLE ITEM. (Interest scale:) The clubs and organizations
to which you belonged. (Control scale:) If you started
coming home late without an acceptable reason.
LENGTH. Items: 12 for each scale.
AVAILABILITY. In Peterson, 1961.
REFERENCE.
     Peterson,E.T. The impact of maternal employment on the
mother-daughter relationship.   Marriage and Family Living,
1961, 23, 355-361.

PUMROY,D.K. Maryland Parent Attitude Survey (MPAS)

VARIABLES MEASURED. Disciplinarian, indulgent, protective
and rejecting attitudes toward child rearing.
TEST DESCRIPTION. The instrument is constructed so that
"social desirability" is controlled. It consists of 95
pairs of items. Each pair contains items representing two
different scales. The person responding to the instrument
is to select which of the pair most closely represents
his/her view. The score on each scale is the number of
items chosen which represent that scale.
SAMPLE ITEM. Pick one from the following pair: A. Parents
shouldn't let their children tie them down. B. Children
should depend on their parents.
LENGTH. Time: Approximately 30 minutes. Items: 95.
AVAILABILITY. From D.K. Pumroy, College of Education,
University of Maryland, College Park, Maryland 20742 and
from NAPS-2.
ABSTRACTED BY: Donald K. Pumroy (modified).
REFERENCES.
     Allan,T.K. and Hodgson,E.W. The use of personality
measurements as a determinant of patient cooperation in an
orthodontic practice. American Journal of Orthodontics,
1968, 54, 433-440.
     Brody,G.F.   A study of the relationship between
maternal attitudes and mother-child interaction.   Ph.D.
dissertation, American University, Washington, D.C., 1963.
     Brody,G.F. The relationship between maternal attitudes
and mother-child interaction. Paper read at Eastern
Psychological Association, Philadelphia, Pennsylvania, 1964.
     Brody,G.F. Relationship between maternal attitudes and
behavior. Journal of Personality and Social Psychology,
1965, 2, 317-323.
     Brody,G.F. Maternal child-rearing attitudes and child

behavior. Developmental Psychology, 1969, 1, 66.
    Buros,O.K.   (Ed.) Personality Tests and   Reviews.
Highland Park, N.J.: Gryphon Press, 1970.
    Davis,W.L. and Phares,E.J.   Parental antecedents of
internal-external control of reinforcement. Psychological
Reports, 1969, 24, 427-436.
    Gelso,C.J. The transmission of attitudes toward child
rearing: an   exploratory   study. Journal of Genetic
Psychology, 1974, 125, 285-293.
    Pumroy,D.K. A new approach to treating parent-child
problems.   Research   Grant   Report NIH (MH 10029-01),
University of Maryland, College Park, Maryland, 1964.
    Pumroy,D.K.   Maryland parent attitude   survey: a
research instrument with social desirability controlled.
Journal of Psychology, 1966, 64, 73-78.
    Schwitzgebel,R.K. and Baer,D.J. Intensive supervision
by parole officers as a factor in recidivism reduction of
male delinquents. Journal of Psychology, 1967, 67, 75-82.
    Tolor,A. An evaluation of the Maryland Parent Attitude
Survey. Journal of Psychology, 1967, 67, 69-74.
    Willerman,L. and Plomin,R. Activity level in children
and their parents. Child Development, 1973, 44, 854-858.

ROE,A.   and   SIEGELMAN,M.   Parent   Child   Relations
Questionnaire (PCR)

VARIABLES MEASURED. (1) Affectional behavior of parents:
loving, protecting, demanding, rejecting, neglecting or
casual. (2) Types cf reward and punishment: symbolic-love
reward, direct-object reward, symbolic-love punishment, and
direct-object punishment.
TEST DESCRIPTION. Two sets of items, cne referring to the
father's behavicr and the other to.the mother's behavior
during the period subject was growing up--especially before
age 12.   Responses are made on a graphic rating scale
ranging from Very true = 5 to Very untrue = 1. Each of the
four subscales referring to type of reward and punishment
contains ten items; each of the six subscales referring to
affectional behavior contains 15 items. A factor analysis
identified   three   factors: loving-rejecting   (LR),
casual-demanding (CD), and overt concern (O). The various
subscales are scored by summing the values checked for the
items composing each scale.
SAMPLE ITEM. My mother objected when I was late for meals.
LENGTH. Time: "The form for each parent is usually
completed in under 20 minutes." Items: 130 (10 subtests: 6
of 15 items each, 4 of 10 items each). LaVoie and Looft
(1973) adapted the loving scale from the PCR to measure
parental warmth.
AVAILABILITY. From NAPS.
REFERENCES.
    Bell,D.R. and McManus,D.L. Parental behavior ratings
by subjects classified as reward-seekers or punishment
avoiders. Psychclogical Reports, 1966, 19, 519-524.

Brigham,J.C.   Richketts,J.L.   and   Johnson,R.C.
Reported maternal and paternal behaviors of solitary and
social delinquents. Journal of Consulting Psychology, 1967,
31, 420-422.
    Brody,G.F. Relationship between maternal attitudes and
behavior.   Journal of Personality and Social Psychology,
1965, 2, 317-323.
    Brody,G.F.   Socioeconomic   differences   in   stated
maternal child-rearing practices and in observed maternal
behavior. Journal of Marriage and the Family, 1968, 30,
656-660.
    Cox,S.H. Intrafamily comparisons of loving-rejecting
child-rearing practices. Child Development, 1970, 41,
437-448.
    Cox,S.H. The association of peer acceptance-rejection
with children's perception of parental behaviors.
Psychology in the Schools, 1974, 11, 222-223.
    Datta,L.E.   and Parloff,M.B.   On the relevance of
autonomy: parent-child relationships and early scientific
creativity. Proceedings of the 75th Annual American
Psychological Association Convention, 1967, 149-150.
    Green,L.B. and Parker,H.J. Parental influence upon
adolescents' occupational choice: a test of an aspect of
Roe's theory. Journal of Counseling Psychology, 1965, 12,
379-383.
    Klein,E.B. Cicchetti,D.V. and Spohn,H. A test of the
censure-deficit model and its relation to premorbidity in
the performance of schizophrenics. Journal of Abnormal
Psychology, 1965a, 29, 150-154.
    Lasko,J.K. Parent behavior toward first and second
children. Genetic Psychology Monographs, 1954, 49, 97-137.
    LaVoie,J.C. and Looft,W.R. Parental antecedents of
resistance-to-temptation behavior in adolescent males.
Merrill-Palmer Quarterly, 1973, 19, 107-116.
    Medinnus,G.R.   Adolescents'   self-acceptance   and
perceptions of their parents. Journal of Consulting
Psychology, 1965a, 29, 150-154.
    Medinnus,G.R. Delinquents' perceptions of their
parents. Journal of Consulting Psychology, 1965b, 29,
592-593.
    Medvene,A.M. Occupational choice of graduate students
in psychology as a function of early parent-child
interactions. Journal of Counseling Psychology, 1969, 16,
385-389.
    Medvene,A.M. Early parent-child interactions of
educational-vocational and emotional-social clients.
Journal of Counseling Psychology, 1973, 20, 94-96.
    Moerk,E.L. Like father like son: imprisonment of
fathers and the psychological adjustment of sons. Journal
of Youth and Adolescence, 1973, 2, 303-312.
    Roe,A. and Siegelman,M. A parent-child relations
questionnaire. Child Development, 1963, 34, 355-369.
    Scheck,D.C.   Emerick,R.   and   El-Assal,M.M.
Adolescent's perceptions of parent-child relations and the
development of internal-external control orientation.

Journal of Marriage and the Family, 1973, 35, 643-654.
        Sears,R.R. Maccoby,E.E. and Levin,H. Patterns of
Child Rearing. Evanston, Illinois: Row, 1957.
        Siegelman,M. College student personality correlates of
early parent-child relationship. Journal of Consulting
Psychology, 1965, 29, 558-564.
        Stabler,J.R. and Goodrich,A.H. Personality and family
background correlates of students' response to physical
danger. Journal of Psychology, 1967, 67, 313-318.
        Wittmer,J. Perceived parent-child relationships: a
comparison between Amish and non-Amish young adults.
Journal of Cross-Cultural Psychology, 1971, 2, 87-94.
        Wittmer,J. Amish homogeneity of parental behavior
characteristics. Human Relations, 1973, 26, 143-154.

SALMON,P. Maternal Attitude Questionnaire

VARIABLES MEASURED. Mother's acceptance-rejection and
control-neglect of child.
        An abstract of this test is given in Johnson,O.G.
Tests and Measurements in Child Development: Handbook II.
San Francisco: Jossey-Bass, 1976, 809.

SCANZONI,J. Parental Nurture and Control Scales

VARIABLES MEASURED. "Nurture" is defined as degree of
warmth and supportiveness provided by parents to children as
perceived by latter; it is essentially expressive or
person-oriented behavior. "Control" is defined as
instrumental or task-oriented behavior, in which parents
place demands on children in an effort to train them for
achievement.
TEST DESCRIPTION. Data are obtained by questionnaire or by
face-to-face interview. The response categories are
Extremely, Quite, Slightly, or Not true. Responses are
weighted on the basis of a factor analysis and summed.
SAMPLE ITEM. Nurture: Took part in activities and projects
with me. Control: Reasoned with me when I misbehaved.
LENGTH. Time: 1 = 3 minutes. 2 = 3 minutes. Items:
Nurture = 13; Control = 14.
AVAILABILITY. In Scanzoni, 1967.
ABSTRACTED BY: John Scanzoni.
REFERENCE.
        Scanzoni,J. Socialization, N Achievement, and
Achievement Values. American Sociological Review, 1967, 32,
449-456.

SCHULMAN,R.E. SHOEMAKER,D.J. and MOELIS,I. Laboratory
Measurement of Parental Frustration and Model Behavior

VARIABLES MEASURED. A set of categories for rating parents
on: A. Extent and kind of parental control of child--(1)

parental domination, (2) parental rejection, (3) parent
takes over, (4) parent hostile to child, (5) parent gives
subtle direction. B. Extent and kind of model of
aggressive behavior the parents present to the child--(1)
parents argue, (2) dominance (of one parent over other), (3)
hostility between parents, (4) criticism (of each other).
TEST DESCRIPTION. Two observers rate the family interaction
in ten-second blocks of time for a total of 45 minutes while
the parents are keeping their child occupied with various
tasks--including free play with toys and the family
composing a story together. Type of interaction and
intensity (high-low) are recorded and scored as present.
Total scores by summation.
SAMPLE ITEM. Playroom task. Family makes up a story
beginning, "The family is in the house getting ready to go
on a picnic..."
LENGTH. Time: 45 minutes of observation.
AVAILABILITY. In Schulman et al., 1962. (Schulman suggests
that an interested researcher could develop "his own rating
sheets and technology" from the description of the scales
given in the article.)
REFERENCE.
      Schulman,R.E.   Shoemaker,D.J.   and   Moelis,I.
Laboratory measurement of parental behavior. Journal of
Consulting Psychology, 1962, 26, 109-114.

SLATER,P.E.   Parental Role Patterns

VARIABLES MEASURED. (1) Parent's emotional supportiveness
and warmth toward child (ESW); (2) Parent's inhibitory
demands and discipline of child (IDD); (3) Parental
involvement with child; (4) Parental tolerance.
TEST DESCRIPTION. Subjects are requested to recall the
extent to which 56 statements are characteristic of both
their mother and father. Each item can be answered with one
of the following categories: Strongly characteristic,
Characteristic, Slightly characteristic, No response,
Slightly uncharacteristic, Uncharacteristic, Strongly
uncharacteristic. Items are scaled from Strongly
uncharacteristic = 1 to Strongly characteristic = 7.
      Responses were intercorrelated and cluster analysis
yielded two separate scales: ESW and IDD for each parent,
with some items common to both. Items for the extreme ends
of the ESW and IDD scales were then factor analyzed to
provide additional scales of parental tolerance.
SAMPLE ITEM. Some parents are very effective in helping
their children through the various emotional crises usually
associated with growing up.
LENGTH. Items: 56.
AVAILABILITY. In Slater, 1955.
REFERENCES.
      Palmer,R.D. Birth order and identification. Journal
of Consulting Psychology, 1966, 30, 129-135.
      Palmer,R.D. Parental perception and perceived locus of

control in psychopathology. Journal of Personality, 1971, 39, 420-431.

Slater,P.E.   Psychological   factors   in   role specialization. Ph.D. dissertation, Harvard University, 1955.

Slater,P.E. Parental behavior and the personality of the child. Journal of Genetic Psychology, 1962, 101, 53-68.

WECHSLER,H. and FUNKENSTEIN,D.H.   Perceptions of Family Questionnaire

VARIABLES MEASURED. Perceptions of parental (1) Authority and (2) Affection.
TEST DESCRIPTION. A series of questions about the family to be answered on a four-point scale (Strongly agree, Agree, Disagree, Strongly disagree). The subject answers the questions three times--for himself/herself, his/her mother, and his/her father. Scoring includes (1) Role differentiation (perception of parents as sharing equally in authority, affection, etc.); (2) Differences between attitudes attributed to father and to mother; (3) Degree of perceived similarity of father and child; (4) Degree of perceived similarity of mother and child; (5) Degree to which mother was seen as the leading figure in terms of the variables of authority, affection, and role model.
SAMPLE ITEM. NR.
LENGTH. Time: 4 hours (includes several other measures).
AVAILABILITY. In Funkenstein et al., 1957.
REFERENCES.
Funkenstein,D.H. King,S.H. and Drolette,M.E. Mastery of Stress. Cambridge, Massachusetts: Harvard University Press, 1957.
Wechsler,H. and Funkenstein,D.H. The family as a determinant of conflict in self-perception. Psychological Reports, 1960, 7, 143-149.

WILLIAMS,W.C. Parental Authority-Love Statements (PALS Test and PEN PALS Test)

VARIABLES MEASURED. (1) Parental authority;   (2) Parental love; (3) Parental role type (based on classification of each parent in terms of authority and love)--(a) (high A, low L) authoritarian/exploitive, (b) (high A, high L) democratic/over-protective, (c) (low A, high L) permissive/overindulgent, (d) (low A, low L) ignoring/self-centered, (e) (intermediate scores on both variables) psychologically unknown/inconsistent.
TEST DESCRIPTION. PALS is a series of parent descriptive statements (set of 32 for each parent) which subject marks as like or not like his/her parent. PEN PALS consists of 16 cartoon fill-in items with multiple-choice response categories of parental actions. Each descriptive statement and each answer category is scored plus or minus for

Authority and Love. The PALS test produces a relatively
conscious evaluation, the PEN PALS a less conscious
evaluation. Scores are plotted on a profile grid to
determine the role type for each parent.
SAMPLE ITEM. (PALS:) My father asks other people what to do
about things. Like my father, Not like my father. (PEN
PALS:) Picture of father and child at dining table. But
Daddy, I don't like to eat that. Do I have to eat it? (1)
Of course not dear. You know you can eat anything you want.
(2) You need good food to grow. Maybe we can find something
else you do like instead. (3) You eat it. It is a sin to
waste good food. (4) If you don't want it I'll eat it. I'm
still hungry.
LENGTH. Time: 30 minutes. Items: 64, 16.
AVAILABILITY. From NAPS.
REFERENCES.
        Clarke,A.R.   Conformity behavior   of   schizophrenic
subjects with maternal figures. Journal of Abnormal and
Social Psychology, 1964, 68, 45-53.
        Crain,A.J. and Stamm,C.S.   Intermittent absence of
fathers and children's perception of parents. Journal of
Marriage and the Family, 1965, 27, 344-347.
        Johnson,O.G.   and   Bommarito,J.W.   Tests   and
Measurements   in   Child   Development: A   Handbook.   San
Francisco: Jossey-Bass, Inc., 1971, 265.
        Silver,A.W. and Derr,J. A comparison of selected
personality variables between parents of delinquent and
non-delinquent adolescents. Journal of Clinical Psychology,
1966, 22, 49-50.
        Williams,W.C.   The PALS tests: a   technique   for
children to evaluate both parents. Journal of Consulting
Psychology, 1958, 22, 487-495.

ZUK,G.H. MILLER,R.L. BARTRAN,J.B. and KLING,F.   Maternal
Acceptance of Retarded Children Questionnaire

VARIABLES MEASURED. Attitudes, feelings, and beliefs of
mothers   of   retarded   children--mother's   fulfillment,
overprotection, discipline, acceptance of diagnosis.
TEST DESCRIPTION. The questionnaire is composed of 50
intensity of agreement items reflecting Strongly agree,
Mildly agree, Mildly disagree,   or   Strongly   disagree
attitudes of mothers about their retarded children. A
number of the items are borrowed from the PARI, but revised
according to what are believed to be requirements of the
sample. The 50 items are classified into five subscales
listed under variables measured.
SAMPLE ITEM. I frequently ask, Why did my child have to be
slow?
LENGTH. Items: 50.
AVAILABILITY. From NAPS.
REFERENCE.
        Zuk,G.H.   Miller,R.L.   Bartran,J.B.   and   Kling,F.
Maternal acceptance of retarded children: a questionnaire

study of attitudes and religious background. Child
Development, 1961, 32, 525-540.

3. Activities, Tasks, Recreation (See also Subject Index)

DANZIGER,K.   Parental Expectations of Child's Task
Involvement.

VARIABLES MEASURED. Parental expectations for child to be
involved in necessary tasks.
TEST DESCRIPTION. A questionnaire for children in which,
"the subjects had to respond to each item on a five-point
scale separately for each parent, and item scores were
summed across the four items."
SAMPLE ITEM. Expects me to help around the house.
LENGTH. Items: 4.
AVAILABILITY. In Danziger, 1974.
ABSTRACTED BY: Thomas G. Sparhawk
REFERENCE.
    Danziger,K. The acculturation of Italian immigrant
girls in Canada. International Journal of Psychology, 1974,
9, 129-137.

DENTLER,R.A.   and MONROE,L.J.   Home Centered Activity Scale

VARIABLE MEASURED. Home centered activity.
TEST DESCRIPTION. A Guttman scale made up of items on
amount of time spent on dating, at hangouts, movie
attendance, household chores, and evenings spent at home.
Children assigned to the category of high home centered
activity are those who respond "favorably" (i.e. spend much
time at home) to all five items. The peer centered activity
class includes those who respond "unfavorably" (i.e. spend
much time with peers) to three, four, or five items. Those
responding "unfavorably" to one item are low home centered
and to two items, low peer centered.
SAMPLE ITEM. How frequently do you go out on dates?
(Answers of "weekly" or more are counted as "unfavorable.")
LENGTH. Items: 5.
AVAILABILITY. In Dentler and Monroe, 1961.
REFERENCE.
    Dentler,R.A. and Monroe,L.J. The family and early
adolescent conformity and deviance. Journal of Marriage and
the Family, 1961, 23, 241-247.

DINKEL,R.   Filial Responsibility of Aged Parents Index

VARIABLE MEASURED. Favorableness of children toward
providing financial support for aged parents.

TEST DESCRIPTION. The original version of this test (Dinkel, 1944) is based on 160 items, reduced through pre-testing to a questionnaire of 20 items of desired discriminative value. Wake and Sporakowski (1972) revised the test using 13 items from Dinkel plus an additional five items.
SAMPLE ITEM. (A) Dinkel: Aged parents should understand they have to stand on their own feet without help from children. Very favorable = +1 to Very unfavorable = -1; parents should be taken care of by their children unless the spouses of the children object. Strongly agree, Agree, Undecided, Disagree, and Strongly disagree.
LENGTH. (A) Dinkel: Items: 20. (B) Wake and Sporakowski: Items: 18.
AVAILABILITY. Thirteen of the 20 items are given in Dinkel, 1944. The five additional items are in Wake and Sporakowski, 1972.
REFERENCES.
    Dinkel,R. Attitudes of children toward supporting aged parents. American Sociological Review, 1944, 3, 370-379.
    Wake,S.D. and Sporakowski,M.J. An intergenerational comparison of attitudes toward supporting aged parents. Journal of Marriage and the Family, 1972, 34, 42-48.

FEINMAN,S. Measure of Disapproval of Cross-Sex Behavior

VARIABLES MEASURED. Attitude toward cross-sex role behavior of children.
    An abstract of this test is given in Johnson, O.G. Tests and Measurements in Child Development: Handbook II. San Francisco: Jossey-Bass, 1976, 817.

HARRIS,D.B. CLARK,K.E. ROSE,A.M. VALASEK,F. What Are My Jobs?

VARIABLES MEASURED. Frequency of performance and liking for specific home duties.
TEST DESCRIPTION. A list of 100 home duties, 17 of which would be appropriate only to children in rural communities. These are checked for frequency of performance and those which are performed sometimes or frequently are to be checked for liking or disliking.
SAMPLE ITEM. Keep your own room neat. (a) Frequently, Sometimes, Never. (b) Like, Dislike.
LENGTH. Items: 100.
AVAILABILITY. Twenty-four of the items of Group III (those which differentiated criterion groups) are listed in Harris et al., 1954; or from NAPS.
REFERENCE.
    Harris,D.B. Clark,K.E. Rose,A.M. and Valasek,F. The relationship of children's home duties to an attitude of responsibility. Child Development, 1954, 25, 29-33.

LANSKY,L. Sex-Role Attitude Test (SRAT)

VARIABLES MEASURED. Sex-role attitudes of parents.
TEST DESCRIPTION. The SRAT consists of two forms: "one for
preschool boys' parents, the other for preschool girls'
parents. Each form consists of 50 items and contains two
types of items." For one type, the subject judges a
preschool boy's (girl's) preference for one of two
sex-linked objects, games, or activities. For the second
type of items, subjects judge a parents' reaction to a boy's
(girl's) preference. In making these judgments, subjects
are asked to "think about an 'average' family with a
preschool boy (girl) about the age of your son (daughter)."
The scoring method is given in Lansky, 1967.
SAMPLE ITEM. "If a boy had a choice between playing with a
toy shaving kit and playing with a toy cosmetic kit, how
would his father feel if his son wanted to play with the toy
shaving kit (circle one)?" There are three possible answers,
each representing a set of feelings: Set 1: "Happy,
Pleased, Delighted, Content, Proud." Set 2: "Neutral or
between the feelings of Set 1 and Set 3, that is, "Neither
happy nor unhappy, Neither pleased nor angry, etc." Set 3:
"Angry, Unhappy, Sad, Discontent, Cross, Disappointed."
LENGTH. Time: 30 minutes. Items: 50.
AVAILABILITY. From NAPS-2.
ABSTRACTED BY: Kersti Yllo.
REFERENCE.
     Lansky,L. The family structure also affects the model:
sex-role attitudes in parents of preschool children.
Merrill-Palmer Quarterly, 1967, 13, 139-150.

RHEINGOLD,H.L. and COOK,K.V. Measuring the Contents of
Boys' and Girls' Rooms

VARIABLES MEASURED. Differences in parental behavior toward
male and female children.
     An abstract of this test is given in Johnson, O.G.
Tests and Measurements in Child Development: Handbook II.
San Francisco: Jossey-Bass, 1976, 818.

TULKIN,S.R. Family Participation Scale

VARIABLES MEASURED. (1) Time spent with parents and (2)
Verbal interaction between children and parents.
TEST DESCRIPTION. In section one, a point is given for each
activity of the child in which one or both parents
participate (Sunday activities, trips, etc.). In section
two, the child uses a scale from 0 to 3 to indicate how
often he/she talks with his/her parents about homework,
personal problems, newspapers, and what is going on in
school. Scores from sections one and two are summed.

SAMPLE ITEM. See above.
LENGTH. Time: 10 minutes. Items: 21.
AVAILABLITY. From NAPS-2.
ABSTRACTED BY: Thomas G. Sparhawk
REFERENCE.
       Tulkin,S.R.   Race,   class,   family   and   school
achievement.   Journal of Personality and Social Psychology,
1968, 9, 31-37.

WALTERS,J.   IRELAND,F.   STROMBERG,F.I.   and   LONIAN,G.
Children's Responsibility Inventory

VARIABLE MEASURED. Parental perceptions of children's
responsibility for behavior.
TEST DESCRIPTION. Parents are requested to indicate the
earliest age at which children could assume responsibility
for independence of behavior in 50 activities in the areas
of self-care and social skill. The scoring system followed
in the original design is to determine the median ages for
which children could assume responsibility for various acts
as indicated by responses of adults. These normative data
apply to separate sex groups. As an aid in developing norms
for evaluating the responses of the parents and students, 19
experts in child development were also asked to provide the
age level they considered most favorable for expecting
children to assume the responsibility depicted in each of
the 50 items.
SAMPLE ITEM. Examples of the responsibilities adults are
asked to rate follow: Washing hands before each meal
without being reminded; Wiping nose when needed without
being reminded; Polishing shoes without adult supervision;
Bathing with no adult help after reminded to do so.
LENGTH. Items: 50.
AVAILABILITY. In Walters, et al., 1957.
ABSTRACTED BY: Kersti Yllo based on Johnson and Bommarito,
1971, 339.
REFERENCES.
       Mitton,B.L.   and Harris,D.B.   The   development of
responsibility in children.   Elementary School Journal,
1954, 54, 268-277.
       Walters,J. Stromberg,F.I. and Lonian,G.   Perceptions
concerning development of responsibility in young children.
Elementary School Journal, 1957, 57, 209-216.

C. Interpersonal Competence

1. Adaptability, Parental Adequacy, Flexibility (See also
Subject Index)

BEHRENS,M.L. Maternal Character Rating Scales

VARIABLES MEASURED. (1) Integration of character traits to
meet maternal role requirements. (2) Maternal conduct, (3)
Mother's character structure (only this variable is
exclusively a "personality" rating).
TEST DESCRIPTION. Five-point rating scales to measure
components of each of the above variables. The number of
scales under each variable ranges from four (integration of
character traits) to nine (maternal conduct). Content of
the scales ranges from strictly individual personality
material, to overt maternal behavior, to intrafamilial
relations and influences. Indicators are provided for each
separate rating scale. All rating scale points are defined,
the low scores indicating "negative" ratings (e.g.,
inadequacy, coerciveness, rigidity). Definitions were
derived from a base definition of adequacy of adjustment
(character structure), ability to integrate into role
(integration of character traits), and quality of child care
(maternal conduct). Scores for the three main variables are
obtained by computing the mean of the ratings under the
particular variable. In addition, a Total Mother Person
score is the mean of the ratings on the three major
variables. Ratings are made on the basis of a large pool of
information about the mother -- interviews with all family
members by a psychiatric caseworker, psychological tests,
individual therapy interviews with all family members, group
therapy sessions, evaluations and observations of the
nursery school teacher, psychiatric staff analyses, and home
observations.
SAMPLE ITEM. Under maternal conduct (observed and overt
conduct in care of child), discipline of primary drives
(rearing practices): toilet training -- degree of rigidity
of routine, need to control child's body, use of coercion or
extreme permissiveness, consistency, appropriateness of
punishment-reward, ability to modify methods, adaptation to
child's maturational level. Rating: Coercion or no
training = 1; Inconsistent training, exaggerated concern
and discipline, very late training (after 24 months) = 2;
Self-trained (mother makes no attempt to train) = 3; Milder
forms of score value = 2; Mild concern or inconsistent but
gradual training = 4; Gradual training: bowel 1-2 years;
urine 1 1/2-2 1/2 years = 5.
LENGTH. Items: 20 rating scales.

AVAILABILITY. In Behrens, 1954. (Definitions are given
only for the child-rearing practice scales.)
REFERENCE.
        Behrens,M.L. Child rearing and the character structure
of the mother. Child Development, 1954, 25, 225-238.

BOLLES,M. METZGER,H.F. and PITTS,M.W.   Home Background
Scale

VARIABLE MEASURED. Favorableness of home background for
mental health.
TEST DESCRIPTION. A technique for classifying parent-child
relations and cther data about home background as: Very
unfavorable, Unfavorable, Slightly   unfavorable,   or
Favorable.   Specific   criteria   are provided for each
category.
SAMPLE ITEM. (Very unfavorable home) Evidence of factors
conducive to marked insecurity and instability.   Shows
definite positive evidence on one or more of the following
characteristics: No affection shown child by either parent.
LENGTH. Items: 18.
AVAILABILITY. In Bolles et al., 1941.
REFERENCE.
        Bolles,M. Metzger,H.F.   and   Pitts,M.W.   Early home
background and personality adjustment. American Journal of
Orthopsychiatry, 1941, 11, 530-534.

DALES,R.J. Developmental Tasks Scale For Sibling Relations

VARIABLE MEASURED. Ability to understand and deal with
siblings.
TEST DESCRIPTION. The test is given in the form of a
checklist.   Subject checks whether or not he/she considers
each area to be a problem for him/her and how important
he/she considers the problem to be. The scale dealing with
sibling relations contains five such problems.   For each
subject the following scores are obtained for each scale:
(1) Percentage of frequency, (2) Percentage of importance,
and (3) Mean scale score. Items were obtained by collecting
spontaneous statements of problems, organizing them into
tasks and subtasks or scales, pretesting a checklist of
these problems, reorganizing them, and using the most
promising items for the final test. This scale is one of 20
developmental task scales (21 for girls).
SAMPLE ITEM. Having arguments with brothers or sisters over
little things.
LENGTH. Time: 45 minutes. Items: 5 in the sibling scale
(out of 117).
AVAILABILITY From NAPS.
REFERENCE.
        Dales,R.J. A method for measuring developmental tasks:
scales for selected tasks at the beginning of adolescence.
Child Development, 1955, 26, 111-122.

DENTLER,R.A. and MONROE,L.J. Life Chance Scale

VARIABLE MEASURED. Life chance of a child, defined as the
combination of family circumstances which provide
competitive chances and a demanding reference group, in
varying degrees.
TEST DESCRIPTION. A Guttman scale of six items concerning
father's job status, parent subjects' education, family
intactness and family size.
     Individuals are categorized as follows: High Life
Chance includes children reporting "favorable" on all six
items. These are children whose families are intact, small
in size, whose parents are high school or college graduates,
and whose fathers hold high status jobs. Low Life Chance
includes children reporting "unfavorably" on four, five, or
six items. Intermediate categories are similarly assigned.
SAMPLE ITEM. Are both your parents alive? Yes, No.
LENGTH. Items: 6.
AVAILABILITY. In Dentler, and Monroe, 1961.
REFERENCE.
     Dentler,R.A. and Monroe,L.J. The family and early
adolescent conformity and deviance. Journal of Marriage and
the Family, 1961, 23, 241-247.

DUSEWICZ,R.A. Knowledge of Infant Development Scale

VARIABLES MEASURED. Knowledge of concepts and terminology
relating tc infant and child development.
     An abstract of this test is given in Johnson, O.G.
Tests and Measurements in Child Development: Handbook II.
San Francisco: Jossey-Bass, 1976, 803.

ELDER,G.H.JR. Index of Maternal Explanations

VARIABLE MEASURED. Frequency with which mother explains
events, personal feelings, and behavior limits which are not
understood by the child.
TEST DESCRIPTION. Children are asked to respond to three
questions concerning maternal explanations. Response
categories are Usually, Sometimes, and Never and are scored
2, 1, and 0 respectively. The total score is the sum of the
item scores with a high total score indicating a high
frequency of maternal explanations.
SAMPLE ITEM. When you don't know why your mother makes a
rule, will she explain the reason?
LENGTH. Items: 3.
AVAILABILITY. In Elder, 1971.
ABSTRACTED BY; Kersti Yllo
REFERENCE.
     Elder,G.H.Jr. Racial conflict and learning.
Sociometry, 1971, 34, 151-173.

GLUECK,S. and GLUECK,E.T.   Social Prediction Table

VARIABLE MEASURED.   Family characteristics predictive of
juvenile delinquency.
TEST DESCRIPTION. The "Social Prediction Table" is one of a
series of indexes designed to identify those who will commit
or repeat various crimes and those who will succeed or fail
in various treatment methods.   In common with most of the
other scales developed by the Gluecks, the Social Prediction
Table has five items with most items classified into a
trichotomy.   Scales are scored by linear summation.   The
scoring weight assigned to each category of the trichotomy
is the proportion of delinquents or failures, contained in
the Gluecks' Table IX-1, Identification of Potential
Juvenile Delinquents Based on Five Social Factors (1959, p.
233, reproduced here by permission of Harvard University
Press):

	Delinquency Scores
Predictive Factors	
Discipline of boy by father	
Firm but kindly	9.3
Lax	59.8
Overstrict or erratic	72.5
Supervision of boy by mother	
Suitable	9.9
Fair	57.5
Unsuitable	83.2
Affection of father for boy	
Warm (including overprotective)	33.8
Indifferent or hostile	75.9
Affection of mother for boy	
Warm (including overprotective)	43.1
Indifferent or hostile	86.2
Cohesiveness of family	
Marked	20.6
Some	61.3
None	96.9

General definitions are given for all subcategories of
each item--for example, those for family cohesiveness are:
"Good--strong we-feeling, as evidenced by cooperativeness,
group interest, pride in the home, affection for each other;
all for one and one for all. Poor--unintegrated; home is
just a place in which to 'hang your hat'; self interest of
the members exceeds group interest.   Fair--elements of
cohesiveness but some members of the family show evidence of
pulling away from the family group." (Glueck and Glueck,
1950, p. 68). Assignment into subcategories for each item
is based on a reading of the detailed case history collected
by personal interview.
SAMPLE ITEM.   See table in test description.

LENGTH. Time: 2-3 hour home interview. Items: 5.
AVAILABILITY. In Glueck and Glueck, 1950; 1959. The
material presented in these references consists of the items
to be scored and the definitions of the scoring criteria (as
in the case of family integration above). A specific
interview outline or form is not presented, since no
standardized forms were employed for gathering the data:
"Each home visitor was urged to use the method that was most
natural to him...as long as they succeeded in gaining the
confidence of their interviewees and the required data...we
did nct offer too many suggestions to them" (Glueck and
Glueck, 1950, p. 48).
REFERENCES.
        Glueck,E.T.   Toward   further   improving   the
identification of delinquents. Journal of Criminal Law,
Criminology and Police Science, 1963, 54, 178-180.
        Glueck,S.   Ten   years   of   unraveling   juvenile
delinquency: an examination and criticisms. Journal of
Criminal Law, Criminology, and Police Science, 1960, 51,
283.
        Glueck,S.   and   Glueck,E.T.   Unraveling   Juvenile
Delinquency. Cambridge,Mass.: Harvard University Press,
1950.
        Glueck,S.   and   Glueck,E.T.   Working   mothers   and
delinquency. Mental Hygiene, 1957, 41, 327-352.
        Glueck,S. and Glueck,E.T. Predicting Delinquency and
Crime. Cambridge, Mass.: Harvard University Press, 1959.
        Glueck,S.   and   Glueck,E.T.   Family   Environment and
Delinquency. Boston: Houghton Mifflin, 1962.
        Hirschi,T. and Selvin,H.C. Delinquency Research: An
Appraisal of Analytic Methods. New York: The Free press,
1967.
        Thompson,R.E.   A   validation   of   the   Glueck   Social
Prediction Scale fcr proneness to delinquency. Journal of
Criminal Law, Criminology, and Police Science, 1952, 43,
451-470.
        Thompson,R.E. Further validation of the Glueck Social
Prediction Table for identifying potential delinquents.
Journal of Criminal Law, Criminology, and Police Science,
1957, 48, 175-184.
        Voss,H.   The predictive efficiency of the Glueck Social
Prediction Table. Journal of Criminal Law, Criminology, and
Police Science, 1963, 54, 421-430.

JONES,P.A. Home Environment Measures

VARIABLES MEASURED. Aspects of the home environment, which
presumably influence child's cognitive development such as
academic and vocational aspirations, occupational status of
parents   and   provision of material and organizational
opportunities for the use and development of language.
TEST DESCRIPTION. Interview with mothers consisting of
questions taken from three scales developed by Mosychuk
(1969). These deal with (a) academic and socialization

aspirations and expectations of the parents;   (b) knowledge of and interest in the child's academic and intellectual develcpment   and   (c)   material   and   organizational opportunities for the use and development of language. Additional scales developed by Bernstein (1966) are also included in the interview: an avoidance index, a chatter index which with the avoidance index form an interaction index, and the mcther's view of the use of toys.   Weighting of the interaction index follows Brandis and Henderson (1970).   The other measures used are unweighted sums.
SAMPLE ITEM. Material and organizational opportunities for the use and development of language: Situations designed by the   parents   tc   encourage   vocalization   (mealtime conversation, family reading habits). The availability of verbal facilities (newspaper, word games, library use), as well as the conscious awareness in the home of the value of verbal facilities in the future.
LENGTH. Time: 70 minutes. Items: 25.
AVAILABILITY. From author.
ABSTRACTED BY: Thomas G. Sparhawk
REFERENCES.
      Bernstein,B. and Young,D.S.   Some aspects of the relationship   between   communication   and   performance interests. In Meade,J.E. and Parke,A.S.   (Eds.) Genetic and Environmental Factors in Human Abilities. New York: Plenum, 1966.
      Brandis,W. and Henderson,D.   Social   Class,   Language and Communication. Language, Primary Socialization, and Educaticn Monograph Series. London: Routledge and Kegan, Paul, 1970.
      Jones,P.A.   Home environment and the development of verbal ability. Child Development, 1972, 43, 1081-1086.
      Mosychuk,B.   Differential home environments and mental ability. Ph.D. dissertation, University of Alberta, 1969.

KLATSKIN,E.H. JACKSON,E.B.   and WILKIN,L.C.   Scales For Rating Flexibility cf Maternal and Child Behavior.

VARIABLE MEASURED. Degree of flexibility of maternal behavior   with   regard   to   feeding,   sleeping, toileting, affective aspects of socialization, and attitude toward maternal role.
TEST DESCRIPTION. A five-point rating scale for each variable, with points 1,3, and 5 verbally anchored by a precise description of the behavior under study. The scale is used to rate the behavior as recorded in rather extensive interview material. Ratings are made when the child is aged 1,2, and 3.
SAMPLE ITEM. Feeding, first year: 1(Mother feeds child on exact schedule, or attempts to achieve exact schedule; punishes for refusals and/or attempts to force feed; attempts to break child of bottle), 3 (Mother follows lenient feeding regime in early months; and works toward a three-meals-a-day schedule in second six months, does not

force feed or punish for refusals; may awaken child for
evening bottle), 5 (Mother makes no effort at guidance in
this area; during early months responds to every cry with
food;   permits child to choose own foods in kind as well as
amount).
LENGTH. Items: Five areas rated for child behavior and
five for mother behavior, at three age levels.
AVAILABILITY. In Klatskin and Jackson, 1955.
REFERENCES.
       Klatskin,E.H. and Jackson,E.B.   Methodology of the
Yale rooming-in project on parent-child relationship.
American Journal of Orthopsychiatry, 1955, 25, 81-108,
373-397.
       Klatskin,E.H.   Jackson,E.B.   and   Wilkin,L.C.   The
influence of degree of flexibility in maternal child care
practices on early child behavior. American Journal of
Orthopsychiatry, 1956, 26, 79-93.

LARSEN,V.L. et al. Perinatal Rigidity Scale

VARIABLES MEASURED. Rigidity of parent's attitudes toward
child rearing.
       An abstract of this test is given in Johnson,O.G.
Tests
and Measurements in Child Development: Handbook II.   San
Francisco: Jossey-Bass, 1976, 840.

POLANSKY,N.A. et al. Childhood Level of Living Scale (CLL)

VARIABLES MEASURED. Quality of home environment.
       An abstract of this test is given in Johnson, O.G.
Test and Measurements in Child Development: Handbook II.
San Francisco: Jossey-Bass, 1976, 754.

REMMERS,H.H. and STEDMAN,L.A. Bringing Up Children -- An
Inventory of Attitudes

VARIABLES MEASURED.   Knowledge of social and emotional
development of the young child.   Specific areas covered
include discipline, motivation, moral training, subjecst's
emotional   responses, family-child relations, and habit
formation.
TEST DESCRIPTION. Two equated forms, each printed in an
expendable, self-scoring booklet. Suggested uses include:
(1) Evaluation in elementary child-care courses,   (2)
Discussion aid for voluntary study groups, (3) Evaluation
and study guide in individual or group counseling with
parents and prospective parents, (4) Screening applicants
for positions concerned with child care, (5) Planning guide
for in-service training programs.

SAMPLE ITEM. A child pays little attention to whether his parents are or are not happy with each other. Yes, No.
LENGTH. Time: 36 minutes. Items: 45.
AVAILABILITY. In Stedman, 1966.
REFERENCE.
    Stedman,L.A.   An investigation of knowledge and attitudes toward child behavior. Purdue University, Division of Educational Reference, Studies in Higher Education No.62, Lafayette, Ind., March, 1966.

SIEGEL,I.E. Eight-Block Sorting Task

VARIABLES MEASURED. Parental teaching cognitive style.
    An abstract of this test is given in Johnson, O.G. Tests and Measurements in Child Development: Handbook II. San Francisco: Jossey-Bass, 1976, 767.

STROM,R.D. Parent as a Teacher Inventory (PAAT) and Parent as a Teacher Profile (PAT)

VARIABLES MEASURED. Child-rearing expectation in respect to: (1) Parental acceptance of creative functioning in their child and desire to encourage or suppress its development (creativity subset), (2) Parent child-rearing frustration and loci of the frustration (frustration subset), (3) Parent feelings about control and the extent to which parental control of child behavior is deemed necessary (control subset), (4) Parental understanding of play and its influence on child development (play subset), and (5) Parental perception of their ability to facilitate the teaching-learning process for their child (teaching-learning subset).
    An abstract of this test is given in Johnson, O.G. Tests and Measurements in Child Development: Handbook II. San Francisco: Jossey-Bass, 1976, 829.

STROUP,A.L. and ROBINS,L.N. 1) High Status Childhood Home Scale.   2)   Disorganized Family Life-Style Scale.   3) Conforming Family Life-Style Scale.

VARIABLES MEASURED.   (1) Status of a child's home environment.   (2) Disorganization and/or illegitimacy of a child's home environment. (3) Conformity and concern of a child's parents.
TEST DESCRIPTIONS. Subjects are given lists of criteria which may or may not have applied to their parents and childhood home life. They are asked to determine which of these criteria were met.
    High Status Childhood Homcale: This scale is made up of a list of seven criteria. The total score is the number of criteria which were met. The score range is 0 through 7.
    Disorganized Family Life-Style Scale: This scale is

composed of 12 criteria. The total score is the number of
criteria met, coded as follows: None = 0; One or two = 1;
Three or four = 2; Five or six = 3; Seven or eight = 4.
The score range is 0 to 4 (none to seven or eight criteria
met).
    Conforming Family Life-Style Scale: This scale
contains 10 criteria. The total score is the number of
criteria which were met, ranging from 0 to 10.
SAMPLE ITEM. High Status Childhood Home Scale: Parent or
guardian employed in a skilled job or better. Disorganized
Family Life-Style Scale: Respondent or his siblings
illegitimate. Conforming Family Life-Style Scale: No
desertions or illicit affairs mentioned.
LENGTH. Items: 7, 12, 10.
AVAILABILITY. In Stroup and Robins, 1972.
ABSTRACTED BY: Kersti Yllo
REFERENCE.
    Stroup,A.L. and Robins,L.N. Elementary school
predictors of high school dropout among black males.
Sociology of Education, 1972, 45, 212-222.

STRYKER,S. Role Ascription Scale

VARIABLE MEASURED. Role-taking ability with regard to adult
married offspring-parent relationships.
TEST DESCRIPTION. A self-administered schedule containing
questions on (1) Family ideology (autocratic-democratic),
(2) Dependency (subordinate-superordinate), and (3) Sympathy
(ego-involvement). Parents and their married children
respond for themselves and for each other. Index of
accuracy of role-taking consists of the number of correct
predictions A makes of B's responses expressed as a
percentage of total predictions of B's responses.
SAMPLE ITEM. Asks my advice more than I ask his. True,
False.
LENGTH. Items: 40.
AVAILABILITY. In Stryker, 1955.
REFERENCES.
    Stryker,S. Attitude ascription in adult married
offspring-parent relationships: a study of implications of
the social psychological theory of G.H.Mead. Ph.D.
dissertation, University of Minn., 1955.
    Stryker,S. Relationships of married offspring and
parent: a test of Mead's theory. American Journal of
Sociology, 1956, 62, 308-319.

TALLMAN,I. Parental Adaptability Instrument

VARIABLE MEASURED. Parental adaptability, including
motivation, affective involvement, empathy, and flexibility.
TEST DESCRIPTION. Open-ended interview in which the subject
is presented with 24 problematic parent-child situations.
Verbatim transcriptions are made from tape recordings.

Responses are grouped according to the question number and
component. Judges rate the responses on a six-point scale,
ordered a priori and based on the theoretical constructs
relevant to the particular component being measured.
SAMPLE ITEM. Flexibility question: How do you go about
training Johnny in table manners? Empathy question: Why do
you think Johnny behaves (as parent has previously stated)
at the dinner table? Motivation question: What would you
hope for (or like) in regard to Johnny's behavior at the
dinner table?
LENGTH. Items: 24 situations.
AVAILABILITY. From ADI, Doc. No. 6838.
REFERENCE.
    Tallman,I. Adaptability: A problem-solving approach
to assessing child-rearing practices. Child Development,
1961, 32, 651-668.
    Tallman,I. Spousal role differentiation and the
socialization of severely retarded children. Journal of
Marriage and the Family, 1965, 27, 37-42.

VEROFF,J. AND FELD,S. Parental Inadequacy Index (PII)

VARIABLES MEASURED. Parents' feelings of inadequacy in
three areas: (a) Tolerance (control of temper, impatience,
etc.), (b) Affiliation (not spending as much time with
children as desired), (c) All others.
TEST DESCRIPTION. The kinds of things which made subjects
feel inadequate are coded, and also their frequency using
five categories: Never = 1, Once or twice = 2, Once in a
while = 3, Often = 4, Lots of times = 5. The first type of
inadequacy mentioned is coded into one of the three areas
listed above. The two indices derived from this coding are
Tolerance Inadequacy and Affiliative Inadequacy. Each is a
two-point index scored: No mention = 1, or Mention of that
type of inadequacy = 2. Since only the first response is
considered in order to avoid compounding the number and type
of inadequacies, the two indices have a built-in, very high,
negative relationship, although a subject could be low on
both indices.
SAMPLE ITEM. Many men(women) feel they're not as good
fathers (mothers) as they would like to be. Have you ever
felt this way? (If yes) What kinds of things have made you
feel this way? Have you felt this way lots of times, or
only once in a while?
LENGTH. Two open-ended questions.
AVAILABILITY. In Veroff and Feld, 1970.
ABSTRACTED BY; Kersti Yllo.
REFERENCE.
    Veroff,J. and Feld,S. Marriage and Work in America.
New York: Von Nostrand Reinhold, Co., 1970, 141-142.

WAXLER,N.E. Artificial Family Technique

VARIABLES MEASURED. Information on whether family processes
cause or contribute to deviant behavior of a child (for
example, schizophrenia) or whether they are responses to the
deviant behavior.
TEST DESCRIPTION. Artifical families are constructed of
members of normal families and those with a deviant member,
in this example, a schizophrenic adolescent. Parent pairs
are teamed with adolescents with whom they are unacquainted.
Each group of three members participates in the following
tasks during an experimental session: Before: the
individual works alone to solve three trials of Mosher's 20
questions task; Group: three group members work together
to solve three trials of the 20 questions task and the group
members discuss together three items from the Revealed
Difference Questionnaire; After: the individual works
alone to solve three trials of the 20 questions task. The
scoring system is fully explained in Waxler, 1974.
LENGTH. NR.
AVAILABILITY. In Waxler,1974.
ABSTRACTED BY: Kersti Yllo.
REFERENCE.
     Waxler,N.E. Parent and child effects on cognitive
performance: an experimental approach to the etiological
and responsive theories of schizophrenia. Family Process,
1974, 13, 1-22.

ZIGLER,E. BUTTERFIELD,E. and GOFF,G. Social Deprivation
Scale

VARIABLES MEASURED. History of social deprivation of
institutionalized retarded individuals.
TEST DESCRIPTION. The social histories of institutionalized
children are rated. The scale begins with a single
subjective estimate of social deprivation which the rater
assesses before scoring the objective items. The 17
objective items are concerned with continuity of child's
residences, attitude of his/her parents toward
institutionalization, intellectual and economic richness of
his/her family and the marital harmony of his/her family.
Each item has a closed set of responses with a varying score
range for each. Item scores are summed to obtain a total
deprivation score. The higher the score, the greater the
deprivation.
SAMPLE ITEM. Marital relationship of parents: Score range
4 to 7 (7 = Parents divorced before child
institutionalized.)
LENGTH. Time: 15 minutes to 1 hour. Items: 18.
AVAILABILITY. From NAPS-2.
ABSTRACTED BY: Kersti Yllo
REFERENCE.
     Zigler,E. Butterfield,E. and Goff,G. A measure of
preinstitutionalized   social   deprivation   for

institutionalized retardates. American Journal of Mental
Deficiency, 1966, 70, 873-885.

2. Achievement Training (See also Subject Index)

AINSWORTH,M.D.S. and BELL,S.M.   Strange Situation Technique

VARIABLES MEASURED. The kind and degree of mother
attachment and stranger-fear manifested by the child in a
strange situation.
TEST DESCRIPTION. Children are observed in a toy-stocked
observation room to which they are brought by their mothers.
A standardized series of episodes occurs in which it is
possible to record how close to the mother the child remains
with or without the presence of a stranger; how much
"attention-seeking" the child does; how the child reacts to
being alone; whether the child accepts comfort from a
stranger; whether the child uses the mother as a "safe
retreat" when a stranger appears; and any changes in the
kind and amount of exploratory play that occurs with the
comings and goings of the mother and stranger.
SAMPLE ITEM. Sample episode: Mother has left child alone
in room.   Stranger enters, stands quietly at door for a
moment. Attempts to comfort child if distressed.   When
child is comfortable, stranger goes to chair and sits
quietly.
LENGTH. Time: Each episode separately timed.
AVAILABILITY. In Maccoby and Feldman, 1972.
ABSTRACTED BY: Kersti Yllo (This abstract is based on the
description in Maccoby and Feldman (1972) because we were
unable to obtain the necessary information from   Dr.
Ainsworth.)
REFERENCES.
        Ainsworth,M.D.S.   and   Bell,S.M.   Attachment,
exploration, and separation: illustrated by the behavior of
one-year-olds in a strange situation.   Child Development,
1970, 41, 49-67.
        Ainsworth,M.D.S.   Bell,S.M.   and   Stayton,D.J.
Individual differences in strange-situation behavior of
one-year-olds. In Schaeffer,H.R.   (Ed.) The Origins of
Human Social Relations.   New York: Academic Press, 1971,
17-52.
        Ainsworth,M.D.S.   Bell,S.M.   and   Stayton,D.J.
Individual differences in the development of some attachment
behaviors. Merrill-Palmer Quarterly, 1972, 18, 123-143.
        Maccoby,E.E. and Feldman,S.S.   Mother-attachment and
stranger-reactions in the third year of life. Society for
Research in Child Development Monographs, 1972, 37, 1-86.
        Stevens,A.G. Attachment behavior, separation anxiety,
and stranger anxiety in polymatrically reared infants. In
Schaeffer,H.R. (Ed.) The Origins of Human Social Relations.

New York: Academic Press, 1971, 137-144.

ALPERN,G.D. Parental Expectancy Scale

VARIABLES MEASURED. Beliefs about degree of child's
developmental handicap.
        An abstract of this test is given in Johnson,O.G.
Tests and Measurements in Child Development: Handbook II.
San Francisco: Jossey-Bass, 1976, 835.

BERG,I.   Self-Administered   Dependency   Questionnaire
(S.A.D.Q.)

VARIABLES MEASURED. Child dependence on mother for: (1)
Affection; (2) Ccmmunication; (3) Assistance; (4) Travel.
TEST DESCRIPTION. A questionnaire completed by mothers.
Each of the subscales is derived by summing the appropriate
question raw scores. The information applies to a typical
school week within the last three months.
SAMPLE ITEM. Did he/she come close to you for affectionate
contact?   (e.g.   sitting on knee or putting arm around, do
not include kissing). L = Less than once a week or not at
all;   O = As much as once a week; B = Between once a week
and once a day; E = As much as once a day; M = More than
once a day (several times a day).
LENGTH. Time: 20 minutes. Items: 21.
AVAILABILITY. In Berg, 1974a.
ABSTRACTED BY: Ian Berg
REFERENCES.
        Berg,I. A Self-Administered Dependency Questionnaire
(S.A.D.Q.) for use with the mothers of school children.
British Journal of Psychiatry, 1974a, 124, 1-9.
        Berg,I. and McGuire,R. Are mothers of school phobic
adolescents overprotective? British Journal of Psychiatry,
1974b, 123, 10-13.
        Berg,I.   McGuire,R.   and Whelan,E.   The   Highlands
Dependency Questionnaire (HDQ): an administered version to
use with mothers of school children. Journal of Child
Psychology and Psychiatry, 1973, 14, 107-121.

BOWERMAN,C.E. and KINCH,J.W. Family-Peer Group Orientation
Questionnaire

VARIABLES MEASURED. Family vs. peer group: (1)
Identification orientation, (2) Association orientation, (3)
Norm orientation.
TEST DESCRIPTION. A questionnaire used to classify subjects
on three orientations. For identification, subjects are
asked which group (family or friends) understands them
better and whether, when they grow up, they would rather be
the kind of person their parents are or the kind they think
their friends will be. For association, Ss are asked which

group they most enjoy doing things with, and with which they
would rather spend their evenings and weekends. The norm
questions ask whose ideas are most like theirs with respect
to decisions of right and wrong, things that are fun to do,
and the importance of school; subjects are asked what they
would do if one group wanted them to do something that the
other did not approve of. Each question or pair of
questions provides a choice of family, friends, or a neutral
response indicating that they feel the same about family and
friends or would choose neither.
SAMPLE ITEM. Identification orientation: Which group
(family or friends) understands you better?
LENGTH. NR.
AVAILABILITY. From NAPS.
REFERENCES.
     Ausubel,D.P. Theory and Problems of Adolescent
Development. New York: Grune and Stratton, 1954.
     Bowerman,C.E. and Kinch,J.W. Changes in family and
peer orientation of children between the fourth and tenth
grades. Social Forces, 1959, 37, 206-211.
     Curtis,R.L. Parents and peers: serendipity in a study
of shifting reference sources. Social Forces, 1974, 52,
368-375.

CALDWELL,B.M. Inventory of Home Stimulation I and II (STIM)

VARIABLES MEASURED. Quality of stimulation found in the
child's home environment.
     An abstract of this test is given in Johnson,O.G.
Tests and Measurements in Child Development: Handbook II.
San Francisco: Jossey-Bass, 1976, 796-799.

CROSS,H.J. Assessment of Parental Training Conditions
Interview

VARIABLES MEASURED. Unilaterality-interdependence of parent
behavior. Interdependence occurs when parents permit
maximum information feedback by the child and allow the
child to learn from the feedback. Unilaterality occurs when
parents force the child to fit a preconceived mold or to
attain a completely externally determined standard.
Variation on this dimension is assumed to influence the
"conceptual level" of the child's thinking (Harvey, Hunt,
Schroder, 1961).
TEST DESCRIPTION. Six interview questions asked of mothers
and fathers separately. The interviews are tape recorded.
Scores for each question range from a low of one ("Score one
if it is clear that parent is in complete control.
Standards come only from the parent and are imposed by the
parent who tolerates little or no deviation.") to a high of
five ("Score five if parent influences only through
dissemination of factual information. Child takes what
information is necessary and determines own standard.

Parent looks for information from the child. Parent permits
all feedback, even to the point where the child's welfare
may be in danger."). The seven items are scored
independently and then summed.
SAMPLE ITEM. What are your general ideas about disciplining
your child? Do you have any general guidelines or
underlying philoscphy?
LENGTH. Items: 6.
AVAILABILITY. In Cross, 1966.
ABSTRACTED BY: Thomas G. Sparhawk
REFERENCES.
        Cross,H.J.   The   relation   of   parental   training
conditions to conceptual level in adolescent boys. Journal
of Personality, 1966, 34, 348-365.
        Harvey,O.J. Hunt,D.E. and Schroder,H.M. Conceptual
Systems and Personality Organization. New York: Wiley,
1961.

CUNNINGHAM,J.L. and BOGER,R.P.   Parent-Child Interaction
Rating Procedure (P-CIRP)

VARIABLES MEASURED. Parent-child interaction, parental
teaching style.
        An abstract of this test is given in Johnson,O.G.
Tests and Measurements in Child Development: Handbook II.
San Francisco: Jossey-Bass, 1976, 822.

DANZIGER,K. Autonomy in Decision Making Index

VARIABLE MEASURED. Degree of autonomy child is granted over
decisions related to his/her own activities.
TEST DESCRIPTION. Questionnaire listing 12 decisions that
affect the subject, such as when to be home, when to go to
bed, what kind of shoes to buy, etc. The child indicates
who usually made the decision (the child, the mother, the
father, or some other person) and who ought to make the
decisions. The mean number of decisions for which the child
assigns responsibility for the decision to him or herself
rather than to someone else assesses the degree of autonomy
the child is granted.
SAMPLE ITEM. See above.
LENGTH. Items: 12.
AVAILABILITY. In Danziger, 1971.
ABSTRACTED BY. Thomas G. Sparhawk
REFERENCES.
        Danziger,K. The Socialization of Immigrant Children.
Toronto: York Institute of Behavioral Research, 1971.
        Danziger,K. The acculturation of Italian immigrant
girls in Canada. International Journal of Psychology, 1974,
9, 129-137.

DYK,R.B.   and   WITKIN,H.A.   Mother's   Differentiation
Fostering Behavior Index

VARIABLES   MEASURED.   Mother-child   interaction   which
interferes with or fosters the child's differentiation.
Differentiation is defined as "an articulated way of
experiencing the world;   a differentiated self, reflected
particularly in an articulated body concept and a developed
sense of separate identity;   and the use of structured,
specialized defenses."
TEST DESCRIPTION. Home interviews are conducted with the
mother at a time when the child is not at home. The
interviewer covers the following six areas: physical care,
child's   school   adaptation,   child's social relationships,
discipline, mother's attitudes toward child, information
about family members. A series of nine indicators are used
to classify mother-child interaction: (1) Self-assurance,
(2)   Self-realization,   (3) Impact on interviewer, (4)
Protectiveness toward child, (5) Acceptance of child's
masculine role, (6) Limitation of child's activities, (7)
Appropriateness of physical care, (8) Control as related to
child's maturity, (9) Conformity-inducing behavior. All
evidence in the interview record is rated for each of the
nine categories and a rating of + or - is given for each.
Then a final global rating of IID (mother's behavior
interferes with development of differentiation in child) or
IFD (mother's behavior fosters differentiation) is given.
SAMPLE ITEM. Indicator 1 - Mother in rearing child does not
have assurance in herself. Evidence on self-assurance was
sought in the nature of a mother's relations within the
family and in her general social relations, as well as in
the nature of her impact on the interviewer. We focused on
the way in which she seemed to experience a given situation
rather than on the facts she presented.
LENGTH. There are nine rating criteria applied to rating
the protocol of a long open-ended interview.
AVAILABILITY. In Dyk and Witkin, 1965.
REFERENCE.
     Dyk,R.B. and Witkin,H.A. Family experiences related
to the development of differentiation in children. Child
Development, 1965, 36, 21-55.

ELDER,G.H.Jr. Independence Training Index

VARIABLE MEASURED.   Independence   training: parental
preparation of offspring for responsible self-direction and
the provision of opportunities for such behavior.
TEST DESCRIPTION. A summated index constructed from five
dichotomized items which were designed for a survey of
adolescents (a separate index for each parent).   Two items
measure the structure of the parent-adolescent relationship
("In general, how are most decisions made between you and
your mother/father?") and perceived change in this structure
("Does your mother/father let you have more freedom to make

your own decisions and to do what you want than she/he did
two or three years ago?); and three items tap socialization
practices that bear on the preparation of adolescents for
self-direction--the explanation of rules and discipline, and
the use of reasoning.
SAMPLE ITEM.   See above.
LENGTH.   Time: 5 minutes. Items: 5.
AVAILABILITY.   From NAPS-2.
ABSTRACTED BY: Glen H. Elder, Jr.
REFERENCES.
        Elder,G.H.Jr.   Adolescent Achievement and   Mobility
Aspirations. Chapel Hill: Institute for Research in Social
Science, University of North Carolina, 1962.
        Evans,F.B.   and Anderson,J.G.   The   psychocultural
origins of achievement and achievement motivation: the
Mexican-American family.   Sociology of Education, 1973,   46,
396-416.

ERON,L.D.   WALDER,L.O.   AND   LEFKOWITZ,M.M.   Dependency
Conflict Scales (Parts A and B)

VARIABLES MEASURED. The Punishment for Dependency Scale
(Part A) measures "rewards and punishments of various
intensities administered by socializing agents when child
asks for help." The Dependency Avoidance Scale (Part B)
measures the "inability or unwillingness of the child to
accept help or rely on others."
TEST DESCRIPTION. Part A: Open-ended interview questions
asking parents how they respond to child's dependency.
Responses are coded by three judges on a scale from Giving
help = 1 to Punishing the child = 4. Item scores are
summed.
        Part B: Parents are asked how their child reacts to
his/her dependency. Response categories are structured and
are coded No = 0; Sometimes or Don't know = 1;   Yes = 2.
These scores are summed.
SAMPLE ITEM. Part A: "What do you usually do when NAME
asks for help?" Part B: "Does NAME try to hide his feelings
when he is upset?"
LENGTH. Items: Part A: 4; Part B: 6.
AVAILABILITY. In Eron,L.D. et al. 1971.
ABSTRACTED BY: Kersti Yllo
REFERENCE.
        Eron,L.D.   Walder,L.O.   and Lefkowitz,M.M.   Learning of
Aggression in Children.   Boston: Little, Brown, and Co.,
1971. 193-194, 207.

ERON,L.D.   WALDER,L.O.   AND   LEFKOWITZ,M.M.   Parental
Restrictiveness Scale

VARIABLE MEASURED. Extent to which the parent defines
proper behaviors for the child rather than permitting the
child to define behaviors which are proper for him/her to

perform.
TEST DESCRIPTION. Parents are asked eight questions
concerned with the behavior of their children. There are
three to five response categories per item which are coded
from 0 to 4. Zero points apply to the least restrictive
answer and 4 points to the most restrictive. A total score
is obtained by adding item scores.
SAMPLE ITEM. Do you make NAME finish up everything he is
served at mealtime? Yes = 2; Sometimes and Don't know = 1;
No = 0.
LENGTH. Items: 8.
AVAILABILITY. In Eron, et al., 1971.
ABSTRACTED BY: Kersti Yllo
REFERENCE.
      Eron,L.D. Walder,L.O. and Lefkowitz,M.M. Learning of
Aggression in Children. Boston: Little, Brown and Co.,
1971, 194, 202-203.

GOLIGHTLY,C.   NELSON,D.   and   JOHNSON,J.   Children's
Dependency Scale

VARIABLE MEASURED. Dependency in children.
TEST DESCRIPTION. The questionnaire is written in the form
of true-false statements and worded to be commensurate with
the vocabulary and attention spans of fourth-, fifth-, and
sixth-grade children. It has been used several times
successfully with first, second, and third grade children.
Items are representative of home, school, and play
situations. The score is the sum of items endorsing
dependency.
SAMPLE ITEM. My mother brings me to school. T F
LENGTH. Time: 15 to 20 minutes. Items: 65.
AVAILABILITY. From NAPS-2.
ABSTRACTED BY: Kersti Yllo
REFERENCE.
      Golightly,C. Nelson,D. and Johnson,J. Children's
dependency scale. Developmental Psychology, 1970, 3,
114-118.

GRAY,A.W.   and   KEITH,R.A.   Age   Independence   Scale,
Elementary Preschool Form and Adolescent Form

VARIABLES MEASURED. Attitude toward independence.
      An abstract of this test is given in Johnson,O.G.
Tests and Measurements in Child Development: Handbook II.
San Francisco: Jossey-Bass, 1976, 1051-1054.

GUINAGH,B.J. and JESTER,R.E. Parent as Reader Scale

VARIABLES MEASURED. Parent-child interaction as the parent
shows the child a story book.
      An abstract of this test is given in Johnson,O.G.

Tests and Measurements in Child Development: Handbook II.
San Francisco: Jossey-Bass, 1976, 828.

HARRIS,I.D.   AND HOWARD,K.I.   Child Responsibility and
Independence Indexes

VARIABLE MEASURED. "The age at which a child should begin
to have certain responsibilities and freedoms."
TEST   DESCRIPTION.   A   self-administered   questionnaire
containing six items concerned with the age at which "the
child ought to have certain responsibilities" and eight
items concerned with the age at which a child "should be
entitled to make certain decisions" and be involved in
certain activities.   For each question there are nine
response choices: Age period 4-5, 6-7, 8-9, 10-11, 12-13,
14-15, 16-17, 18 or more, and Never. The scores for each
item are added to obtain the total score except that the
Never category is treated as missing data and omitted from
analysis.
SAMPLE ITEM. Responsibility: At what age period should a
child begin to have lying and petty stealing firmly punished
by the parents? Independence: At what age period should a
child be to begin to be trusted to set his own time for
going to sleep?
LENGTH. Items: Responsibility = 6; Independence = 8.
AVAILABILITY. In Harris and Howard, 1968.
ABSTRACTED BY: Kersti Yllo.
REFERENCES.
     Harris,I.D.   and   Howard,K.I.   Birth   order   and
responsibility.   Journal of Marriage and the Family, 1968,
30, 427-432.
     Howard,K.I. and Forehand,G.A. A method for correcting
item total correlations for the effect of relevant item
inclusion. Educational Psychology Measurement, 1962, 22,
731-733.

KATKOVSKY,W.   PRESTON,A. and CRANDALL,V.J.   Parent Reaction
Questionnaire

VARIABLES MEASURED. Responses consist of parents' reports
concerning their reactions to their children's behavior in
achievement situations.   Positive, negative, and   total
reaction of parents to the child's behavior in   four
achievement areas (intellectual, mechanical, artistic, and
physical skills).
TEST DESCRIPTION. Parents respond to 12 items for each
achievement   area.   The items describe frequent   child
behaviors. Parents choose one or more responses that best
describe their reactions to their child. For each item
there is a positive, negative, and neutral alternative
presented.   The score is the total number of positive and
negative alternatives chosen for each area.

SAMPLE ITEM. Doing homework: Positive, "I told him/her I was pleased"; Negative, "I showed him/her some of his/her mistakes"; Neutral, "I was too busy to pay attention". Learning a new physical skill: Positve, "I praised him/her"; Negative, "I said he/she needs to improve"; Neutral, "I didn't say anything about it."
LENGTH. Time: No limit. Items: 48.
AVAILABILITY. From NAPS-2.
REFERENCES.
       Katkovsky,W. Crandall,V.J. and Good,S. Parental antecedents of children's beliefs in internal-external control of reinforcements in intellectual achievement situations. Child Development, 1967, 38, 766-776.
       Katkovsky,W. Preston,A. and Crandall,V.J. Parent's achievement attitudes and their behavior with their children in achievement situations. Journal of Genetic Psychology, 1964, 104, 105-121.
       Touliatos,J. and Lindholm,B.W. Influence of parental expectancies and responsiveness on achievement motivation of minimally brain-injured and normal children. Psychological Reports, 1974, 35, 394-400.

KOCH,H.L. DENTLER,M. DYSART,B. AND STREIT,H. Attitude Towards Children's Freedom Scale

VARIABLES MEASURED. Attitudes toward degree of freedom, independence, and self-management that children should be allowed.
TEST DESCRIPTION. A series of prescriptive statements to be answered Agree, Undecided, or Disagree. There are two equivalent scales, constructed by the Thurstone-Chave method.
SAMPLE ITEM. A young child must be disciplined until he has learned not to touch those objects in his environment which he cannot handle without damaging.
LENGTH. Items: 33 items per scale.
AVAILABILITY. In Koch et al., 1934; Shaw and Wright, 1967.
REFERENCES.
       Koch,H.L. Dentler,M. Dysart,B. and Streit,H. A scale for measuring attitude toward the question of children's freedom. Child Development, 1934, 5, 253-266.
       Shaw,M.E. and Wright,J.M. Scales for the Measurement of Attitudes. New York: McGraw-Hill, 1967.

LESLIE,G.R. AND JOHNSEN,K.P. Maternal Role Concept and Performance Scales

VARIABLES MEASURED. Prescription and performance in the maternal role for three areas of child-rearing: (1) Sex and modesty training, (2) Aggression toward the mother, and (3) Encouragement of self-direction.

TEST DESCRIPTION. I. Role concept scales, 15 relatively
general statements of what a mother should do. Statements
reflecting strict and permissive normative patterns are
equally distributed among the three areas (see variables
measured). There are five items in each group, forming a
scale with possible scores 0 to 15. The lower scores
indicate the more permissive positions. II. Role
performance scales. The mother is instructed to categorize
her "usual" action in response to two types of items: (1)
Nine hypothetical situations, each depicting a child engaged
in an overt expression of behavior typical of one of the
three areas. Response alternatives range from Unqualified
acceptance of the behavicr to Punishment for it. The more
permissive responses are scored lower. (2) Tolerance for
child behavior in each of the three areas, expressed by
responses to general descriptions of the behavior rather
than concrete situations. Six responses reflecting varying
tolerance of the behavior are provided for each item.
Complete acceptance = 0; Complete restriction = 5. The two
measures of tolerance yield six scales with scores from 0
(most permissive) to 15 (least permissive).
SAMPLE ITEM. A mother should teach her children that anger
should not be expressed toward their mother.
LENGTH. Items: 15 for the role concept scales, 18 for the
role performance scales.
AVAILABILITY. From NAPS.
REFERENCE.
      Leslie,G.R. and Johnsen,K.P. Changed perceptions of
the maternal role. American Sociological Review, 1963, 28,
919-928.

MARJORIBANKS,K. Marjoribanks Family Environment Schedule

VARIABLES MEASURED. Learning environment of the family.
      An abstract of this test is given in Johnson,O.G.
Tests and Measurements in Child Development: Handbook II.
San Francisco: Jossey-Bass, 1976, 805.

NAKAMURA,C.Y. AND ROGERS,M.M. Parents' Expectations
Inventory

VARIABLES MEASURED. Parents' expectations for the child's
practical autonomy and assertive autonomy.
TEST DESCRIPTION. The inventory items describe behavior in
a specific situaticn concerning a child. The Practical
Autonomy Scale measures parental expectations for the child
to attain responsibility that has practical or convenience
value to the parents. The Assertive Autonomy Scale measures
self-assertive and exploratory types of behavior that may or
may not have immediately recognizable practical value, and
may even have a degree of nuisance value. Parents rate each
item on a six-point scale ranging from Very common to Very
uncommon. "If the behavior was rated as very common, then

the parent would have relatively high expectations of its occurrence in his child."
SAMPLE ITEM. Practical: Ann is three. She can pour milk from a small pitcher into her cup without spilling. Assertive: Johnny is two. He refuses to eat at meal times unless he can feed himself.
LENGTH. Items: 20.
AVAILABILITY. From NAPS-2.
ABSTRACTED BY; Thomas G. Sparhawk
REFERENCE.
    Nakamura,C.Y. and Rogers,M.M. Parents' expectations of autonomous behavior and children's autonomy. Developmental Psychology, 1969, 1, 613-617.

OJEMANN,R.H. Self-Reliance Test

VARIABLE MEASURED. Self-reliance expectations of parents for children.
TEST DESCRIPTION. Each item asks for the age at which subject expects a child to be able to carry out the activity specified by the item. The test is scored by assigning a value from 1 to 11 to the ages listed. Scores of 11 are assigned when the age listed is extremely young, and scores of 1 are assigned when the age given in response to the item is relatively late. Ages corresponding to these 11 points on the scale are given for each item, and the total test score is the average of the item scores. There are three parallel tests, for preschool children (available in two alternate forms), for elementary school, and for high school age children.
SAMPLE ITEM. (Preschool test, form 1) I think a child should be able to cut his own meat (if reasonably tender) with a knife by the age of...
LENGTH. Items: Preschool form 1 - 51; Preschool form 2 - 52; Elementary school - 37; High school - 25.
AVAILABILITY. In Ojemann, 1934; Shaw and Wright, 1967.
REFERENCES.
    Ojemann,R.H. Measurement of self-reliance. University of Iowa Studies in Child Welfare, 1934, 10, 103-111.
    Shaw,M.E. and Wright,J.M. Scales for the Measurement of Attitudes. New York: McGraw-Hill, 1967, 48-60.

OLSEN,N.J. Independence Training Measure

VARIABLE MEASURED. Independence training of child by mother.
TEST DESCRIPTION. Interview items from Whiting, Child, and Lambert, are dichotomized and summed. The items cover: (1) Response tc dependency, (2) Age of independence training, (3) Age of playing away from home, and (4) Attitude towards independence.

SAMPLE ITEM. When did you feel that P was old enough for
you to start training him to take care of himself?
LENGTH. Items: 4.
AVAILABILITY. In Olsen, 1973.
ABSTRACTED BY: Thomas G. Sparhawk
REFERENCES.
      Olsen,N.J. Family structure and independence training
in a Taiwanese village. Journal of Marriage and the Family,
1973, 35, 512-519.
      Whiting,J.W.M. Child,I.L. Lambert,W.W.   Field Guide
for a Study of Socialization. New York: Wiley, 1966.

PEARLIN,L.I. Parental Aspirations

VARIABLES MEASURED. Parents' aspirations and expectations
for their children, assessed in two domains: (1) Education
and (2) Occupation.
TEST DESCRIPTION. Levels of educational aspiration are
distinguished by formal school that parents hoped their
children would attain. Other questions ask parents what
they hope their children would gain from their educations --
occupational skills, an appreciation of ideas, interest in
community and world affairs. They are further asked what
level of education they expect the child to reach and about
reasons for any discrepancies between aspiration and
expectation.
      Levels of occupational aspirations are determined by
asking which job they would eventually like their child to
enter. The jobs are then classified according to their
prestige on the North-Hatt scale.   In addition, parents
indicate what they feel their children should gain from
their work, and answers are classified by whether they
stress congeniality with personality and self-development or
economic advancement and security.
SAMPLE ITEM. What level of education would you like (name
of index child) to attain?
LENGTH. Items: Four questions on educational aspirations
and three dealing with occupation.
AVAILABILITY. In Pearlin, 1971.
REFERENCE.
      Pearlin,L.I.   Class Context and Family   Relations.
Boston: Little, Brown, 1971, 73-98 and 206-208.

PEARLIN,L.I. YARROW,M.R.   AND SCARR,H.A.   Parental Pressure
for Success Scale

VARIABLE MEASURED. The extent to which parents exert a
focused   pressure   for successful performance on their
children.
TEST DESCRIPTION. The scale is scored from parent-child
interactions while the child attempts to complete six
problem-solving tasks, three of them with the child and
his/her mother and three with the child and his/her father.

In presenting the task, the experimenter emphasizes the importance of doing well. Parents are forbidden to actually perform the task for their child but are encouraged to extend themselves otherwise. The degree of pressure for success imposed on children is determined through observation of three types of parental behavior. The first is the frequency of highly specific directives given to children such as, "Do this, now do that." Such directions border on violation of the instructions given. The second aspect of behavior reflecting pressure is the number of strategic suggestions parents make. Last, is the extent to which parents maintain a restrained unintrusive interest while their children are at work. These three types of behavior form a Guttman scale. A maximum pressure score of 3 is awarded a parent who gives nine or more specific directions, four or more strategic suggestions and is quietly attentive for less than eight intervals of sufficient duration to be recorded. "Lowest are highly attentive parents making few or no suggestions and giving few or no directions."
SAMPLE ITEM. See above.
LENGTH. Items: 6 tasks.
AVAILABILITY. In Pearlin, et al., 1967.
ABSTRACTED BY: Kersti Yllo
REFERENCES.
    Pearlin,L.I. Class Context and Family Relations: A Cross-National Study. Boston: Little, Brown and Co., 1970.
    Pearlin,L.I. Class Context and Family Relations. Boston: Little, Brown and Co., 1971. Chapter V.
    Pearlin,L.I. Yarrow,M.R. and Scarr,H.A. Unintended effects of parental aspirations: a case of children's cheating. American Journal of Sociology, 1967, 73, 73-83.

RADIN,N. and WEIKART,P. Cognitive Home Environment Scale

VARIABLES MEASURED. Five factors relevant to cognitively stimulating home conditions: (1) Educational materials in the home. (2) Grades expected. (3) Future expectations for the child. (4) Direct teaching activities. (5) Educational oriented activities.
TEST DESCRIPTION. The test is a semi-structured questionnaire designed to be administered to mothers of preschoolers by an interviewer. Each of 25 questions receives a score of 1 to 7. The scores of specific questions are averaged to obtain factor scores. Instructions for scoring individual questions and computing factor scores appear in the manual accompanying the test.
SAMPLE ITEM. What newspaper and/or magazines do you have in the home at present? Who reads them?
LENGTH. Items: 25.
AVAILABILITY. In Radin and Sonquist, 1968; from Norma Radin; and from NAPS-2.

ABSTRACTED BY: Norma Radin
REFERENCES.
      Radin,N. The impact of a kindergarten home counseling
program. Exceptional Children, 1969, 36, 251-256.
      Radin,N.   Maternal warmth, achievement motivation, and
cognitive functioning in lower-class preschool children.
Child Development, 1971, 42, 1560-1565.
      Radin,N. Father-child interaction and the intellectual
functioning   of   four-year-old   boys.   Developmental
Psychology, 1972a, 6, 353-361.
      Radin,N. Three degrees of maternal involvement in a
preschool program: impact on mothers and children.   Child
Development, 1972b, 43, 1355-1364.
      Radin,N. Observed paternal behaviors as antecedents of
intellectual   functioning in young boys.   Developmental
Psychology, 1973, 8, 369-376.
      Radin,N. Observed maternal behavior with four-year-old
boys and girls in lower-class families. Child Development,
1974, 45, 1126-1131.
      Radin,N. and Glasser,P.H. The utility of the parental
research instrument for intervention program with low-income
families. Journal of Marriage and the Family, 1972, 34,
448-458.
      Radin,N. and Sonquist,N. The Gale Preschool Program:
Final   Report.   Ypsilanti, Michigan: Ypsilanti Public
Schools, 1968.
      Wittes,G. and Radin,N. Two approaches to group work
with parents in a compensatory preschool program. Social
Work, 1971, 16, 42-50.

SANDLER,H.M. and BARBRACK,C.R.   Maternal Teaching Style
Instrument (MTSI)

VARIABLES MEASURED. Components of maternal teaching style.
      An abstract of this test is given in Johnson,O.G.
Tests and Measurements in Child Development: Handbook II.
San Francsco: Jossey-Bass, 1976, 815.

SCHVANEVELDT,J.D.   Mother-Child Interaction Test (MCIT)

VARIABLES MEASURED. Perceptions of maternal overprotection
of children aged preschool through adolescence.
      An abstract of this test is given in Johnson,O.G.
Tests and Measurements in Child Development: Handbook II.
San Francisco: Jossey-Bass, 1976, 619.

SCHWARTZ,A.J. Independence from Family Authority Scale

VARIABLES MEASURED.   Areas of behavior which children
believe are legitimate elements of parental authority.
Independence refers to the individual's orientation toward
decision-making, that is, whether he or she is both able and

favorably inclined to take action without the assistance or
approval of others.
TEST DESCRIPTION. A four-item Guttman scale based on
responses from two samples of 9th and 12th grade children.
SAMPLE ITEM. Children should obey all the rules their
parents make for them.
LENGTH. Time: A few minutes. Items: 4.
AVAILABILITY. In Schwartz, 1971.
ABSTRACTED BY: Audrey James Schwartz
REFERENCES.
       Schwartz,A.J. Affectivity orientation and academic
achievement of Mexican-American youth. Ph.D. dissertation,
University of California, Los Angeles, 1967. University
Microfilm 68-7483.
       Schwartz,A.J. Comparative values and achievement of
Mexican-American and Anglo pupils. Center for the Study of
Evaluation, Report 37. University of California, Los
Angeles. February, 1969.
       Schwartz,A.J. A comparative study of values and
achievement: Mexican-American and Anglo Youth. Sociology
of Education, 1971, 44, 438-462.

SHERMAN,A.W.JR. Sherman Emancipation Questionnaire

VARIABLES MEASURED. Social and emotional emancipation of
college students from their parents.
TEST DESCRIPTION. Statements of behavior or feelings
indicating emancipation from parents. Items are scored +1
or 0. Item analysis, comparing the upper quartile with the
lower quartile, showed that 59 of the 60 items
differentiated.
SAMPLE ITEM. I write to my mother for suggestions on the
clothing I should wear to a formal dance. Yes, No.
LENGTH. Items: 60.
AVAILABILITY. In Sherman, 1946.
REFERENCE.
       Sherman,A.W.Jr. Emancipation status of college
students. Journal of Genetic Psychology, 1946, 68, 171-180.

SMITH,H.T. Maternal Behavior Interview Rating Scales

VARIABLES MEASURED. Mother's handling of child's dependency
behavior: infant care and training, present demands made
upon the child, amount and kind of attention requested by
child at home, and ways in which mother responds to child's
dependent behavior.
TEST DESCRIPTION. A set of scales to be used in rating
material from an interview schedule of 36 open-ended
questions relating to above variables. Scales include
classifications of factual information (such as separation
from child, use of do and don't, offering of help);
information on feelings of mother for the child (such as
degree of warmth, nature of affectional relationship,

rejection   by   the   mother);   information   about   the
restrictions imposed upon the child (such as scheduling or
feeding,   restrictiveness   of   physical   mobility,   and
overprotectiveness).   The ratings are made along a
five-point scale.
SAMPLE ITEM. NR.
LENGTH. Items: 37 cpen-ended questions. Number of rating
scales finally used and their names are not indicated in
Smith (1958).
AVAIIABILITY. In Smith, 1953, or from ADI,Doc.No.5635.
$2.00 microfilm, $3.75 photocopies.
REFERENCES.
     Smith,H.T. A comparison of interview and observation
measures of mother behavior. Ph.D. dissertation, Radcliffe
College, 1953.
     Smith,H.T. A comparison of interview and observation
measures of mother behavior.   Journal of Abnormal Social
Psychology, 1958, 57, 278-282.

SMITH,H.T.   Observation Scales For Maternal And Child
Behavior

VARIABLES MEASURED. Child's dependency behavior, and
mother's handling of it: behavior of the child to evoke the
attention of the mother and ways the mother reacts --
teaching, structuring, and so forth.
TEST DESCRIPTION. A set of scales to be used in observing
behavior of mcther and child together in a playroom
situation, both when the mother is free and when she is
occupied with a task. A unit of behavior was defined as the
equivalent of a simple sentence, although an element might
be implied.   The sequence as well as the number and nature
of elements were recorded and scored.
SAMPLE ITEM. X behavior in which the child engages to evoke
the attention or affection of the mother (e.g., whining,
leaning against her).
LENGTH. Time: 45 minutes, treated as three 15-minute
intervals.   Items: Behavior was coded into 16 scoring
categories.
AVAILABILITY. In Smith, 1953, or from ADI,Doc. No. 5635.
REFERENCES.
     Smith,H.T. A comparison of interview and observation
measures of mother behavior. Ph.D. dissertation, Radcliffe
College, 1953.
     Smith,H.T. A ccmparison of interview and observation
measures of mother behavior.   Journal of Abnormal Social
Psychology, 1958, 57, 278-282.

STAFF CF JOHN TRACY CLINIC. John Tracy Clinic. Parents'
Attitude Scale

VARIABLES MEASURED. Parental attitudes toward child
rearing, especially restrictiveness-autonomy.

An abstract of this test is given in Johnson,O.G. Tests and Measurements in Child Development: Handbook II. San Francisco: Jossey-Bass, 1976, 799.

SUNDBERG,N. SHARMA,V. WODTLI,T. and ROHILA,P. Adolescent Autonomy Index.

VARIABLE MEASURED. Adolescents' autonomy or independence from their parents.
TEST DESCRIPTION. A two-part questionnaire. Section 1 is a list of 10 statements with Yes or No responses, taken from the Edwards Personal Preference Schedule. Section 2 is a list of 40 decisions concerning the subject's daily life and future plans; he is asked which of five people (mother, father, another family member, himself, or others) usually makes each decision. The autonomy score is the number of independence-oriented answers to the first section plus the number of times "self" was checked in Section 2. The number of times each response category is checked in Section 2 is also used for comparisons on the relative importance of different family members for adolescent decision-making.
SAMPLE ITEM. Section 1: I like to do things in my own way no matter what others may think about it: Yes, No. Section 2: The games or amusements you should take part in: M, F, OFM, S, O.
LENGTH. Items: 50.
AVAILABILITY. From NAPS-2.
REFERENCES.
      Sundberg,N. Sharma,V. Wodtli,T. and Rohila,P. Family cohesiveness and autonomy of adolescents in India and the United States. Journal of Marriage and the Family, 1969, 31, 403-407.

TEC,N. Parental Pressure for Educational Achievement Index

VARIABLE MEASURED. Parental pressure for educational achievement.
TEST DESCRIPTION. Parents are assigned to one of the following categories on the basis of the configuration of the child's responses to the three questions making up the test: Strong pressure, Pressure, Moderate pressure, No pressure.
SAMPLE ITEM. Do you feel that your parents ask the impossible as far as your school grades are concerned? (1) Yes, definitely; (2) Yes, sometimes; (3) No, they never demand too much; (4) No, they really don't care how I do in school.
LENGTH. Items: 3.
AVAILABILITY. In Tec, 1973.
ABSTRACTED BY: Susan Murray
REFERENCE.
      Tec,N. Parental educational pressure, adolescent educational conformity and marijuana use. Youth and

Society, 1973, 4, 291-312.

TORGOFF,I.   Parental Development Timetable

VARIABLES MEASURED.   Expectancies   toward   childrearing
control   functions: (1) Achievement inducing and (2)
Independence granting.
TEST DESCRIPTION.   Respondent indicates the age he/she
believes to be appropriate for a parent to initiate
activities intended to induce an average, normal child to
adopt   more   mature modes of behavior (achievement inducing)
or which   would   allow   a   child to engage in activities
requiring   autonomy and independence of judgment and action,
granting   freedom from parental supervision and control
(independence   granting).   Scoring   consists of summing the
ages for the 24 items, separately for each scale. The lower
the   score,   the   earlier   the   respondent believes it
appropriate to a parent to initiate achievement induction
or   independence granting. The intercorrelation between the
two scales is low (r = .3), but significant.
SAMPLE ITEM.   Achievement inducing--"I believe a parent
should begin to teach their child not to fight but to first
try   to   reason   with   other   children..."   Independence
granting--"I   believe   parents   should begin to allow their
child to take full responsiblity as a baby sitter, caring
for   a   younger   brother or sister, for an afternoon..." The
respondent is asked to write in the "most appropriate age"
separately for boys and girls.
LENGTH.   Items: 48.
AVAILABILITY.   From NAPS-2.
ABSTRACTED BY: Irving Torgoff
REFERENCES.
     Collard,E. Achievement motive in the four-year-old
child and its relationship to achievement expectancies of
the mother. Doctoral Dissertation, University of Michigan,
1964.
     Daugherty,M.   An investigation of the relationship
between   maternal   expectations   and classroom behavior of
preschool   children.   Doctoral   Dissertation, Wayne State
University, 1968.
     Dreyer,A.S. and Wells,M.B. Parental values, parental
control, and creativity in young children.   Journal of
Marriage and the Family, 1966, 28, 83-88.
     Farber,B. Kinship and Class. New York: Basic Books,
1971.
     Johnson,O.G.   and   Bommarito,J.W.   Tests   and
Measurements   in   Child Development: A Handbook.   San
Francisco: Jossey-Bass, Inc., 1971, 358.
     Jordan,B.E.   Radin,N.   and   Epstein,A.   Parental
behavior and intellectual functioning in preschool boys and
girls. Developmental Psychology, 1975, 11, 407-409.
     O'Leary,V.E.   and   Braun,J.S.   Antecedents   and
personality   correlates   of   academic   careerism in women.
Proceedings, 80th Annual Convention, American Psychological

Association, 1972, 277-278.

    Torgoff,I. Parental developmental timetable. Paper presented at the meeting of the American Psychological Association, Washington,D.C., 1958.

    Torgoff,I. Synergistic parental role components: application to expectancies and behavior: consequences for child's curiosity. Paper presented at the meeting of the American Psychological Association, Chicago, 1960.

    Torgoff,I. Parental developmental timetable: parental field effects on children's compliance. Paper presented at the meeting of the Society for Research in Child Development, State College, Pennsylvania, 1961.

    Torgoff,I. and Dreyer,A.S. Achievement inducing and independence granting--synergistic parental role components: relation to daughters' "parental" role orientation and level of aspiration. Paper presented at the meeting of the American Psychological Association, New York City, 1961.

    Torgoff,I. and Dreyer,A.S. Achievement-inducing and independence-granting parental role components: relation to daughters' parental role orientation and level of aspiration. American Psychologist, 1961, 16, 345.

    Torgoff,I. Freides,D. and Grisell,J. Parental control attitudes as a function of sex of parent, religion, and presence of a psychiatrically disturbed child in the family. Paper presented at the meeting of the Society for Research in Child Development, Berkeley, 1963.

    Touliatos,J. and Lindholm,B.W. Influence of parental expectancies and responsiveness on achievement motivation of minimally brain-injured and normal children. Psychological Reports, 1974, 35, 394-400.

TURNER,J.H. Familism-Individualism Scale

VARIABLE MEASURED. Family Autonomy: the extent to which individuals (particularly adolescents) feel that they must maintain strong affective and obligatory ties to their parents.
TEST DESCRIPTION. An adaptation of Likert-type questions from similar measures developed by Rosen(1956), Kahl(1965), and Strodtbeck (1958). The scale items are scored either 1 or 0 (Agree-Disagree) and then summed to produce an individualism or familism orientation.
SAMPLE ITEM. When looking for a job a person ought to find a position in a place near his parents, even if that means losing a good opportunity elsewhere.
LENGTH. Time: 1 minute. Items: 5.
AVAILABILITY. In Turner, 1972.
ABSTRACTED BY: Jonathan H. Turner
REFERENCES.
    Kahl,J. Some measures of achievement orientation. American Journal of Sociology, 1965, 70, 669-681.

    Rosen,B.C. The achievement syndrome: a psychocultural dimension of social stratification. American Sociological Review, 1956, 21, 203-211.

Strodtbeck,F.L.   Family,   interaction,   values,   and achievement.   In D.C.McClelland, (Ed.), Talent and Society. New York: Van Nostrand, 1958.

Turner,J.H.   Structural conditions of achievement in the rural South. Social Problems, 1972, 19, 496-508.

UTECH,D.A. and HOVING,K.L. Parent Conformity Measure

VARIABLE MEASURED. Conformity to advice of parents.
TEST DESCRIPTION. Questionnaires are given consisting of social situations, each of which presents a child who has to make a decision. The child in each situation is advised to take one course of action by the parents and another choice of action by friends. The respondents are asked to indicate in each case what choice the described child would actually pick if the child is just like the respondent or like one of the respondent's friends. After a period of 10 to 13 days the respondents are asked to answer the questionnaire again. Although the respondents are told that it is the same questionnaire, the parent/peer suggestions are reversed.   A frequency count is made of the number of times a respondent agrees to the advice of parents on both forms of the questionnaire, and the same for advice of friends. The score is the proportion of conformity to parents to the total number of items.
SAMPLE ITEM. Susan likes music and is trying to decide whether to join the band or the choir. Her mother and father think the band would be more fun because the band plays at all the basketball and football games. Susan's friends think she would have more fun in the choir because the choir goes tc many different tours to sing. What do you think Susan will decide to do? (1) Do as her parents say, and join the band. (2) Do as her friends say and join the choir.
LENGTH. Items: 10.
AVAILABILITY. From NAPS-2.
ABSTRACTED BY; Susan Murray
REFERENCE.

Utech,D.A. and Hoving,K.L.   Parents and peers as competing   influences   in   the decision of children of differing ages. Journal of Social Psychology, 1969, 78, 267-274.

WINTERBOTTOM,M.R.   Independence and Achievement Training Scales

VARIABLES MEASURED. (1) Parents' standards of training in independence and mastery (achievement), and in restrictions on independent activity;   (2)   Sanctions   (reward   and punishment) used to secure compliance with these standards.
TEST DESCRIPTION. (1) A list of 20 independence and mastery behaviors, and another list of 20 behaviors that a parent might wish tc discourage. The two lists are parallel -- for

example, the item "standing up for his own rights with other children" also appears as "not to fight with other children." The subject is asked to check each item considered to be a goal in his/her training of the child and to indicate the age by which the child is expected to have learned the behavior. The instrument is scored by counting the number of demands for independent accomplishments and the number of restrictive demands, or by counting the number of behaviors which the parent expects the child to accomplish before the median age (8 years). The average age at which the child is expected to accomplish each of these behaviors may also be computed. (2) The sanctions measure consists of a list of six items concerning the subject's response when the child fulfills his/her expectation and another six-item list concerning his response when the child does not fulfill parental demands. Each list is made up of three neutral items such as "don't show any feeling about it," and three reward or punishment items such as "kiss or hug him," "scold or spank him." This is scored for: number of rewards chosen, number of punishments chosen, and intensity of reward or punishment (based on summing the weights assigned to each item which are assumed to represent intensity of effective consequences).
SAMPLE ITEM. See test description.
LENGTH. See test description.
AVAILABILITY. In Winterbottom, 1958.
REFERENCES.

Bartlett,E.W. and Smith,C.P. Childrearing practices, birth order, and the development of achievement-related motives. Psychological Reports, 1966, 19, 1207-1216.

Chance,J.E. Independence training and first graders' achievement. Journal of Consulting Psychology, 1961, 25, 149-154.

Gordon,J.E. and Smith,E. Children's aggression, parental attitudes, and the effects of an affiliation-arousing story. Journal of Personality and Social Psychology, 1965, 1, 654-659.

Jacobs,S. Acquisition of achievement motive among mentally retarded boys. Sociology of Education, 1972, 45, 223-232.

McClelland,D.C. Rindlisbacher,A. and DeCharms,R. Religious and other sources of parental attitudes toward independence training. In McClelland,D.C. (Ed.), Studies in Motivations. New York: Appleton, 1955, 389-397.

Sampson,E.E. and Hancock,F.T. An examination of the relationship between ordinal position, personality, and conformity: an extension, replication, and partial verification. Journal of Personality and Social Psychology, 1967, 5, 398-407.

Teevan,R.C. and McGhee,P.E. Childhood development of fear of failure motivation. Journal of Personality and Social Psychology, 1972, 21, 345-348.

Winterbottom,M.R. The relation of need for achievement to learning experiences in independence and mastery. In Atkinson,G.W. (Ed.) Motives in Fantasy, Action, and

Society.   New York: Van Nostrand, 1958, 453-478.

3. Identification, Modeling, Parent-Child Similarity,
Empathy
(See also Subject Index)

BOWERMAN,C.E.   and BAHR,S.J.   Parental Identification Scale

VARIABLE MEASURED.   Adolescent identification with   parents,
defined as "the   value orientations that adolescents have
toward mother and father." Identification includes   feelings
of respect, admiration, affection, acceptance of parental
values and advice, and viewing the parent as   a   significant
other.
TEST DESCRIPTION.   The   scale consists of   eight   items
concerning the identification of an adolescent toward his or
her parents.   It includes items on how   much   one   respects,
depends on, and is influenced by his/her parents.
     Each of the items has   five   response   categories   from
Very   negative   to   Very   positive.   It   is   a Guttman-type
quasi-scale   that   was   constructed   by   combining
non-differentiating   responses.   Values   range from 0 to 14
and the reproducibility index   was   about   75   percent   with
simple scoring.
SAMPLE ITEM.   Would you like to be the kind of   person   your
mother (father) is? Responses were Yes, completely, In most
ways, In many ways, In just a few ways, and Not at all.
LENGTH.   Items: 8.
AVAILABILITY.   In Bowerman and Bahr, 1973.
ABSTRACTED BY: Stephen J.   Bahr
REFERENCE.
     Bowerman,C.E.   and   Bahr,S.J.   Conjugal   power   and
adolescent   identification   with parents.   Sociometry, 1973,
36, 366-377.

BRITTAIN,C.V.   Cross-Pressures Test (CPT)

VARIABLE MEASURED.   The   extent   to   which   adolescents   are
peer-conforming   or   parent-conforming   when   making choices
concerning certain dilemmas.
TEST DESCRIPTION.   Situations   involving   conflict   between
parent-peer expectations   are   described   to   the   subjects.
There are two choices,   one   of   which   is   favored   by   the
subject's friends.   There are two versions of the test which
are identical except that the parent-favored alternatives on
form   A are the peer-favored alternatives on form B.   Ss can
be administered fcrm A (or B) at a   first   testing   and   the
alternate form at a second testing one to two weeks later to
obtain a shift sccre.   Larson (1972) used four   hypothetical
situations   similar   but   not   identical   to   those   used by

Brittain. Two situations measure peer-parent pressures in situations that have current role implications. Two other situations are designed to measure future-oriented situations.
SAMPLE ITEM. Larson (1972): You have been invited to a party which you want very much to go to. Your best friends have decided to go and are urging you to go, too. They will be very unhappy if you don't go. Your parents, however, do not approve of the party and are urging you not to go. Your parents will be very unhappy if you do go. What would you do? 1. ( ) Go to the party. 2. ( ) Stay at home.
LENGTH. Items: 12.
AVAILABILITY. In Brittain, 1963 for 12-item form; in Larson, 1972 for 4-item form.
REFERENCES.
      Brittain,C.V.   Parents and peers as competing influences in adolescence. Ph.D. dissertation. University of Chicago, 1959.
      Brittain,C.V. Adolescent choices and parent-peer cross pressures. American Sociological Review, 1963, 28, 385-391.
      Brittain,C.V. Age and sex of siblings and conformity toward parents versus peers in adolescence. Child Development, 1966, 37, 709-714.
      Brittain,C.V. An exploration of the bases of peer-compliance in adolescence. Adolescence, 1967/68, 2, 445-458.
      Brittain,C.V. A comparison of rural and urban adolescents with respect to peer vs. parent compliance. Adolescence, 1969, 4, 59-68.
      Devereux,E.C.Jr. Socialization in cross-cultural perspective: a comparative study of England, Germany and the United States. Paper read at the Ninth International Seminar on Family Research, 1965.
      Larson,L.E. The influence of parents and peers during adolescence: the situation hypothesis revisited. Journal of Marriage and the Family, 1972, 34, 67-74.
      Thomas,D.L. and Weigert,A.J. Socialization and adolescent conformity to significant others: a cross-national analysis. American Sociological Review, 1971, 36, 835-847.

BRONFENBRENNER,U.   DEVEREUX,E.C.Jr.   SUCI,G.J.   and
RODGERS,R.R.   Moral Dilemma Experiment

VARIABLES MEASURED. Response to adult vs. peer pressure in moral conflict situations. Factor I. An overall measure of the child's degree of conformity to adult standards (30 items). Factor II. A measure of the child's willingness to inform on one's peers (6 items).
TEST DESCRIPTION. The questionnaire asks children to respond to a series of conflict situations under three different conditions: (a) Base Condition. The children are told that no one will see their responses except the investigators conducting the research. (b) Adult Condition.

They are informed that the responses of everyone in the
class will be posted on a chart and shown to parents and
teachers at a special meeting scheduled for the following
week; (c) Peer Condition. The children are notified that
the chart will be prepared and shown a week later to the
class itself. Each response is scored on a scale from -2.5
to +2.5, a negative value being assigned to the behavior
urged by age-mates. To control for a positional response
set, scale direction is reversed in half of the items. The
situations are divided into three alternate forms of 12
items each, with a different form used for each experimental
condition. Thus under any one condition a child can obtain
a conformity score ranging from -25 to +25, and an informing
score ranging from -5 to +5, with zero representing equal
division between behavior urged by peers and adults.
SAMPLE ITEM. The Lost Test: You and your friends
accidentally find a sheet of paper which the teacher must
have lost. On this sheet are the questions and answers for
a quiz that you are going to have tomorrow. Some of the
kids suggest that you not say anything to the teacher about
it, so that all of you can get better marks. What would you
really do?
REFUSE TO GO ALONG WITH MY FRIENDS: Absolutely certain,
Fairly certain, I guess so.
GO ALONG WITH MY FRIENDS: I guess so, Fairly certain,
Absolutely certain.
LENGTH. Items: 36.
AVAILABILITY. From NAPS-2.
ABSTRACTED BY: Urie Bronfenbrenner
REFERENCES.
      Beloff,H. and Patton,X. Bronfenbrenner's moral
dilemmas in Britain: children, their peers and their
parents. International Journal of Psychology, 1970, 1,
27-32.
      Bronfenbrenner,U. Response to pressure from peers
versus adults among Soviet and American school children.
International Journal of Psychology, 1967, 2, 199-207.
      Bronfenbrenner,U. Two Worls of Childhood. New York:
Russell Sage Foundation, 1970.
      Bronfenbrenner,U. Reactions to social pressure from
adults versus peers among Soviet day school and boarding
school pupils in the perspective of an American sample.
Journal of Personality and Social Psychology, 1970, 15,
179-189.
      Condry,J. and Siman,M.A. Characteristics of peer and
adult oriented children. Journal of Marriage and the
Family, 1974, 36, 543-556.
      Desai,K.G. Adaptation of Bronfenbrenner's moral
dilemma test--a cross-cultural study. Vidya, Journal of
Gujarat University, 1971, 14, No. 2.
      Devereux,E.C.Jr. The role of the peer-group experience
in moral development. In Hill,J.P. (Ed.) Minnesota
Symposia on Child Psychology, Vol. IV. Minneapolis:
University of Minnesota Press, 1970a, 94-104.
      Devereux,E.C.Jr. Socialization in cross-cultural

perspective: comparative study of England, Germany and the
United States.   In Hill,R. and Konig,R. (Eds.) Families in
East and West. Paris: Mouton and Co., 1970b.
        Devereux,E.C.Jr. Authority and moral development among
German   and American children: a cross-cultural pilot
experiment. The Journal of Comparative Family Studies,
1972, Vol. III. Spring 1972.
        Devereux,E.C.Jr. Some antecedents and correlates of
differential patterns of response to pressure from peers and
adults among Israeli kibbutz children.   Dittoed working
paper, February 1972.
        Devereux,E.C.Jr. Suci,G.J. and Rodgers,R.R.   Adults
and peers as sources of conformity and autonomy. Paper
presented at the Conference on Socialization for Competence,
sponsored by the Social Science Research Council, Puerto
Rico, April 1965.
        Garbarino,J. and Bronfenbrenner,U. The socialization
of moral judgment and behavior in cross-cultural
perspective. In Lickona,T. (Ed.) Morality: A Handbook of
Moral Development and Behavior. New York: Holt, Rinehart,
and Winston, 1976.
        Kav-Venaki,S. Eyal,N. Bronfenbrenner,U.   Kiely,E.
and   Caplan,D.   The   effect of Russian versus Hebrew
instructions on the reaction to social pressure of
Russian-born Israeli children. Journal of Experimental
Social Psychology, 1976, 12, 70-86.
        Luescher,K. Dreizehnjaehrige Schweizer zwischen Peers
und Erwachsenen im interkulturellen Vergleich. (13 year old
Swiss children between peers and adults in cross-cultural
comparison.) Schweizerische Zeitschrift fuer Psychologie und
Ihre Anwendungen, Revue Suisse de Psychologie Pure et
Appliquee, 1971, 3, 219-229 (Separatabzug aus 30).
        Mason,G.P. A note on Bronfenbrenner's moral dilemmas.
International Journal of Psychology, 1972, 7, 105-108.
        Rim,Y. and Seidoenross,H. Personality and response to
pressure from peers vs.   adults. Personality, 1971, 2,
35-43.
        Rodgers,R.R. Family authority structures and   the
disposition to inform on peers among urban children in West
Germany and Israel. Paper presented at the 80th Annual
Convention of the American Psychological Association,
Honolulu, Hawaii, September 1972.
        Shouval,R.   Bronfenbrenner,U.   Kav-Venaki,S.
Devereux,E.C.Jr.   Kiely,E. The anomalous reactions to
social pressure of Israeli and Soviet children raised in
family vs. collective settings. Journal of Personality and
Social Psychology, 1975, 32, 477-489.
        Siman,M.A. Peer group influence during adolescence: a
study of 41 naturally existing friendship groups. A thesis
presented to the Faculty of the Graduate School of Cornell
University for the degree of Doctor of Philosophy, January
1973.
        Smart,R. and Smart,M.S. New Zealand preadolescents'
parent-peer orientation: parent perceptions compared with
English and American. Journal of Marriage and the Family,

1973, 35, 142-149.

CALONICO,J.M. and THOMAS,D.L. Role-Taking Scale

VARIABLE MEASURED. Role-Taking: Defined as the degree to
which a child can predict a parent's response, or a parent
can predict a child's response to certain given situations.
TEST DESCRIPTION. Each of 10 items presents a hypothetical
situation in which an "abstract other," i.e., neither actor
nor the specific person whose role he/she is taking, is
placed in a behavioral dilemma. The abstract other is shown
as perceiving two possible responses to his/her dilemma.
The actor must indicate how he/she would advise the abstract
other to respond. He/she must then indicate how each of two
significant others, persons whose roles he/she is taking
would advise the abstract other to respond. Parents are
asked to take the role of each of the two participating
children and each child is asked to take the role of each
parent.
    A role-taking accuracy or difference score is computed
for each respondent by comparing the other's actual response
with the actor's prediction of that response. Thus the
range of absolute difference between any two subjects of any
item is from 0 to 3. Higher scores denote greater
role-taking inaccuracy.
SAMPLE ITEM. A young man about to graduate from college is
opposed to military service but is sure he will be drafted
shortly after he graduates. He is trying to decide whether
to allow himself to be drafted and serve in the armed forces
or to unlawfully resist the draft, thereby risking the
chance of arrest and imprisonment. (a) I would advise this
young man to allow himself to be drafted and serve in the
armed forces. No = 1; Probably no = 2; Probably yes = 3;
Yes = 4. (b) In my opinion, my father (older child) would
advise this young man to allow himself to be drafted and
serve in the armed forces. Yes = 4; Probably yes = 3;
Probably no = 2; No = 1. (c) In my opinion my mother
(younger child) would advise this young man to allow himself
to be drafted and serve in the armed forces. No = 1;
Probably no = 2; Probably yes = 3; Yes = 4.
LENGTH. Time: 20 to 30 minutes. Items: 10.
AVAILABILITY. From NAPS-2.
ABSTRACTED BY: J.M. Calonico
REFERENCE.
    Calonico,J.M. and Thomas,D.L. Role-taking as a
function of value similarity and affect in the nuclear
family. Journal of Marriage and the Family, 1973, 35,
655-665.

CASS,L.K. Parent-Child Relationship Questionnaire

VARIABLES MEASURED. (1) Awareness--the ability of the
mother to predict her child's response; (2)

Identification--the similarity of preferences, ambitions, and fears of the mother and her child; (3) Projection--mother's assignment to the child of preferences, ambitions, and fears that she professes but which are not claimed by the child.

TEST DESCRIPTION. A checklist questionnaire: "the meaning of the data was sought not in the responses themselves but in the degree of correspondence between responses on questionnaires answered by mothers and their adolescent sons and daughters." Questionnaires administered to the adolescents contain items in seven areas of personal preferences, one of vocational ambitions, one of fears, and one of descriptive adjectives. In each of nine sections, the subject chooses 3 of 20 items which he/she believes apply to himself/herself; in addition, in two sections pertaining to school subjects, he/she is asked to name a dislike. Each mother is given two identical questionnaires and instructed to answer one questionnaire for herself and the other for her child. Three scores are derived: (1) Awareness--the number of correspondences between items checked by the mother for her child and items checked by the child for himself/herself; (2) Identification--the number of correspondences between items checked by the mother for herself and by the child for himself/herself; (3) Projection--the number of items checked by the mother for herself and for her child but not checked by the child for himself/herself.

SAMPLE ITEM. NR

LENGTH. NR.

AVAILABILITY. In Cass, 1953; and from ADI, Doc. No. 3498. Microfilm, $2.30; photocopies, $22.65.

REFERENCES.

    Cass,L.K. Parent-child relationships and delinquency. Journal of Abnormal Social Psychology, 1952, 47, 101-104.

    Cass,L.K. An investigation of some important variables in the parent-child relationship. Ph.D. dissertation, Ohio State University 1953.

CHANG,J. and BLOCK,J.H. Parent Identification Adjective Checklist

VARIABLES MEASURED. (1) Conceptions of (a) ideal self, (b) mother, (c) father, (d) self; (2) Identification with each parent; (3) Self-acceptance.

TEST DESCRIPTION. Booklets containing a total of 79 adjectives selected to permit comprehensive personality description. The S, who can be anonymous, is asked to check 30 adjectives as characteristic and 30 as uncharacteristic of: (a) his/her ideal self, (b) his/her mother, (c) his/her father, and (d) himself/herself. Identification with each parent is scored by the number of correspondences between the ideal self and the parent in question, self-acceptance by correspondences of self with ideal self.

SAMPLE ITEM. Dependent, Determined, Personally charming, Tactful, and so forth.
LENGTH. Items: 79, 4 descriptions.
AVAILABILITY. From NAPS.
REFERENCE.
        Chang,J. and Block,J.H. A study of identification in male homosexuals. Journal of Consulting Psychology, 1960, 24, 307-310.

COUNT-VANMANEN,G. Intrafamily Identification Measures

VARIABLES MEASURED. Four methods of measuring similarity or "identification" between parents and children.
TEST DESCRIPTION.   (1) Assumed personality likeness. A "score derived from a comparison of the child's placement of himself/herself and each parent on a five-degree Likert-like scale on a list of 24 personality characteristics" such as "gets angry easily," "assumes responsibility willingly." The response categories are Very much so, Considerably, Somewhat, A little, and Not at all. The score is the sum of the absolute differences. (2) Real value difference. The "score is derived from comparing actual responses of each parent and of each child on the question 'Please check the five qualities (out of 18) which you think are the most important for your daughter' (asked of parents) or 'a daughter' (asked of daughters) to develop." The value items include such things as "good judgment," "affection for you," and "obedience." The score is the number of nonoverlapping items.   (3) Real value similarity. The child is given a list of issues such as "choice of friends," "outlook on life," and "chores," and is asked to indicate his or her degree of agreement with each parent on a six-point Likert-like scale.   (4) Global assumed similarity. The child responds to the question "I am like (unlike) my mother in personality and temperament," and again for the father, each time using a five-point Likert-like rating scale.
SAMPLE ITEM. See above.
LENGTH. See above.
AVAILABILITY. In Count-VanManen, 1973.
ABSTRACTED BY: Murray A. Straus
LENGTH. NR.
        Count-VanManen,G.   Father roles and adolescent socialization. Adolescence, 1968, 10, 139-152.
        Count-VanManen,G.   The validity of parent-child socialization measures: a comparison of the use of assumed and real parent-child similarity with criterion variables. Genetic Psychology Monographs, 1973, 88, 201-227.

DEVEREUX,E.C.JR. Actual Association Scale

VARIABLES MEASURED. Time spent with parents and siblings relative to time with peers.

TEST DESCRIPTION. Questionnaire that asks each child to
rank order from most to least, how much of his/her spare
time he/she spent with each of the following: Father,
Mother, Both parents together, Brothers and Sisters, A
single best friend, A group of friends, or Alone.
SAMPLE ITEM. See above.
LENGTH. Items: 7.
AVAILABILITY. In Devereux, 1970.
ABSTRACTED BY: Thomas G. Sparhawk
REFERENCES.
        Devereux,E.C.Jr. The Role of Peer Group Experience in
Moral Development.   In Hill,J.P. (Ed.) Minnesota Symposia
on Child Psychology, Vol. 4, Minneapolis: University of
Minnesota Press, 1970.
        Devereux,E.C.Jr.   Bronfenbrenner,U.   and   Suci,G.J.
Patterns of parent behavior in the United States of America
and in the Federal Republic of Germany: a cross-national
comparison. International Social Science Journal, 1962, 14,
488-506.

DEVEREUX,E.C.JR. Association Preference Scale

VARIABLES MEASURED. The extent to which a child prefers a
best friend versus a group of friends; parents versus
peers; and mother versus father.
TEST DESCRIPTION. The subject is asked to indicate with
whom he or she would prefer to do each of six activities.
Two of the activities require a choice between parents
versus peers, two between mother versus father, and two
between a best friend and a group of friends. Each item is
scored from one to four. Therefore, the Group preference,
Father preference, and Friends preference score can each
range from two to eight.
SAMPLE ITEM. It is a Saturday afternoon.   There is a
special movie in town that you've been wanting to see.
Somebody will take you and bring you back.   You have a
choice of going just with your best friend or a gang of
friends. Which would you rather do? Definitely go with a
gang of my friends. Probably go with a gang of my friends.
Probably go with just my best friend, but I'm not really
sure. Definitely go with just my best friend.
LENGTH. Items: 9.
AVAILABILITY. In Avishar, 1964.
ABSTRACTED BY: Thomas G. Sparhawk
REFERENCES.
        Avishar,R. Some correlates of association preference
of pre-adolescent children.   Unpublished Master's Thesis.
Cornell University, 1964.
        Devereux,E.C.Jr. The role of peer-group experience in
moral development.   In Hill,J.P. (Ed.) Minnesota Symposia
on Child Psychology, Vol. 4. Minneapolis: University of
Minnesota Press, 1970.

FLOYD,H.H.Jr.   AND SOUTH,D.R.   Parent-Peer Orientation Scale

VARIABLE MEASURED. Reference group orientation: the degree
to which youth are oriented toward their parents or peers as
a reference for behavior.
TEST DESCRIPTION. The scale is composed of 20 Likert-type
items. The items consist of statements concerning three
broad   categories   of   activity: dress   and   taste,
identification and decision making, and companionship.
SAMPLE ITEM. When there is a direct conflict between what
my parents say should or should not be done, as opposed to
what my friends say should or should not be done, I consider
more strongly the wishes of my friends.
LENGTH. Time: 15 minutes. Items: 20.
ABSTRACTED BY: H. Hugh Floyd, Jr.
AVAILABILITY. From NAPS-2.
REFERENCE.
     Floyd,H.H.Jr.   and South,D.R.   Dilemma of youth: the
choice of parents or peers as a frame of reference for
behavior. Journal of Marriage and the Family, 1972, 34,
627-634.

GRAY,S.W.   Parental Identification Index

VARIABLE MEASURED. Child's perceived similarity to each
parent.
TEST DESCRIPTION. Forty bipolar adjectives modeled after
Helper (1955) for which the child rates himself/herself and
both parents on a seven-point scale.   Two scores are
obtained: (1) Osgood and Suci's D statistic is used to
express the degree of agreement between the child's
self-ratings and his/her ratings of each parent;   (2)
"Direction of identification" is measured by the difference
between the D's for each parent.
SAMPLE ITEM. Brave 1 2 3 4 5 6 7 Timid
LENGTH. Items: 40.
AVAILABILITY. From author.
REFERENCES.
     Gray,S.W.   Perceived similarity to parents and
adjustment. Child Development, 1959, 30, 91-107.
     Gray,S.W.   and Klaus,R.   The assessment of parental
identification. Genetic Psychology Monographs, 1956, 54,
87-114.
     Helper,M.M. Learning theory and self-concept. Journal
of Abnormal Social Psychology, 1955, 51, 184-194.

GUERNEY,B.G.Jr.   STOVER,L.   and O'CONNELL,M.   Behavioral
Measure of Empathy

VARIABLES MEASURED. Empathy in adult-child interactions,
subdivided into: Communication of acceptance, Allowing the
child self-direction, and Involvement of the adult in the
interaction.

TEST DESCRIPTION. Adult-child interactions are rated over a
period of from 10 minutes to half an hour on each of the
three dimensions of empathy. Ratings are made once every
three minutes. The highest level of empathy is present when
(a) the adult is fully attending,(b) responds to the child
in a genuinely accepting manner, and (c) the child is
allowed to be self-directing in his/her activities. The
lowest level would be when the adult is (a) shutting
himself/herself off from the child, (b) rejects the child's
feelings, and (c) redirects the child's activities. Scores
are entered retrospectively for each three-minute period.
SAMPLE ITEM. The interactions are rated on five-point
scales for each of the dimensions. Lowest scores are taken
for the self-direction and involvement subscales. Highest
and lowest scores for the three-minute periods are averaged
for the communication of acceptance dimension.
LENGTH. Items: 3.
AVAILABILITY. In Stover, Guerney, and O'Connell, 1971.
ABSTRACTED BY: Ethan Levine
REFERENCES.
     Guerney,B.G.Jr. and Stover,L. Filial Therapy. Final
Report on MH 18264-01, December, 1971.
     Guerney,B.G.Jr. Stover,L. and DeMeritt,S. A measure
of empathy in parent child interaction. Journal of Genetic
Psychology, 1968, 112, 49-55.
     Stover,L. and Guerney,B.G.Jr. The efficacy of
training procedures for mothers in filial therapy.
Psychotherapy Theory Research and Practice, 1967, 4,
110-115.
     Stover,L. Guerney,B.G.Jr. and O'Connell,M.
Measurements of acceptance allowing self-direction,
involvement and empathy in adult-child interactions.
Journal of Psychology, 1971, 77, 261-269.

HALLER,A.O. and WOELFEL,J. with FINK,E.L. The Wisconsin
Significant Other Battery

VARIABLES MEASURED. The extent to which parents (or any
other category of person) is a (1) Significant Other for
educational and occupational attainment and (2) Significant
Other and educational and occupational expectations.
TEST DESCRIPTION. A questionnaire to permit (1)
identification of Significant Others in a given behavior
domain, by means of Significant Other elicitors; and (2)
measurement of variables by which Significant Others
influence individual educational and occupational goal
orientations by means of Significant Others expectation
elicitors. Elicitors use questionnaire data from the focal
individual to identify specific persons who have told
him/her his/her educational and occupational alternatives
(definers), or have exemplified (acted as models of) an
educational or occupational social role (or more generally
object) or his/her relation to it. A given Significant
Other can be a definer or a model or both. Four filter

categories (means) of educational and occupational roles are
employed: Intrinsic function, extrinsic function, intrinsic
nature, and extrinsic nature.

Significant Others are identified by determining a
person's definers and models for filter categories for
education and occupation. Expectations are elicited
directly from the Significant Others named by the focal
person. Significant Others may hold expectations for the
focal person's educational or occupational attainment (or
that of others like him/her) and for the degree of
importance he/she (or others like him/her) would attach to a
type of filter category for the object. From definer
Significant Others, expectations regarding the focal person
are elicited from model Significant Others who are not
definers, expectations regarding youth in general are
elicited. The test is scored in the following way: (1) The
Significant Other elicitors: (a) Significant Other model =
one point, (b) Significant Other definer = one point, (c)
Both = two points, (d) Significant Other for object = one
point, Significant Other for self = one point, (f) Both =
two points, (g) Maximum score = four points for either
education or occupation (eight points for both). (2) The
Significant Other expectations elicitors: These are scored
simply by summing the item scores.
SAMPLE ITEM. (1) Significant Other elicitor: Who have you
spoken with about the kind of work that is right for you?
(2) Significant Other expectation elicitor: Of the jobs
listed in this question, which is the best one you are
really sure he can get when his schooling is over?
1__Lawyer, 2__Welfare worker for city government, 3__United
States Representative in Congress, 4__Corporal in the Army,
5__United States Supreme Court Justice, 6__Night watchman,
7__Sociologist, 8__Policeman, 9__County agricultural agent,
10__Filling station attendant.
LENGTH. Items: (1) Significant Other elicitor, 16. (2)
Significant Other expectation elicitor, 8.
AVAILABILITY. Order ERIC Document No. ED 035 990.
ABSTRACTED BY: Mary Olson
REFERENCES.

Haller, A.O. and Woelfel, J. Significant Others and
their expectations, concepts and instruments to measure
interpersonal influence on status aspirations. Rural
Sociology, 1972, 37, 591-622.

Haller, A.O. and Woelfel, J. with Fink, E.L. The
Wisconsin Significant Other Battery, construction,
validation and reliability tests of questionnaire items to
identify Significant Others and measure their educational
and occupational expectations for high school youth.
Madison, University of Wisconsin: Final Report to U. S.
Office of Education, Project No. 51170 (mimeographed).

HARTUP, W.W. Parental Imitation Interview

VARIABLES MEASURED. Imitation of like-sex parent in choice

of goal, in value judgments, and in conflicting parental judgments.

TEST DESCRIPTION. Eighteen test situations in which the experimenter manipulates father and mother dolls and the subject manipulates a child doll. In six situations the subject chooses between two paths to the same goal--one that has been taken by the mother doll or a route of equal length taken by the father doll. In the final six situations the subject chooses between a "perceptual judgment" made by the mother doll and a conflicting judgment made by the father doll. The score is the number of times the subject used the child dcll to imitate the like-sex parent doll.

SAMPLE ITEM. Situation involving alternate routes to a goal. The people are all having their supper. Now they all want to watch TV. Mama gets up and goes this way (E moves the doll). Daddy gets up and goes this way (E moves the doll). Which way does the little boy (girl) go, the way daddy goes (E points) or the way mama goes (E points)?

LENGTH. Items: 18 situations.

AVAILABILITY. From ADI,Doc. No. 7745.

REFERENCES.

   Hartup,W.W. Some correlates of parental imitation in young children. Child Development, 1962, 33, 85-96.

   Hartup,W.W. Patterns of imitative behavior in young children. Child Development, 1964, 35, 183-191.

   Santrock,J.W. Parental absence, sex typing and identification. Developmental Psychology, 1970, 2, 264-272.

   Ward,W.D. Sex-role preference and parental imitation within groups of middle-class whites and lower-class blacks. Psychological Reports, 1972, 30, 651-654.

HEILBRUN,A.B.Jr. Parent-Child Identification Measures

VARIABLES MEASURED. Child's identification with parent in relation to: (1) Child's personality, (2) Assessment by child of parent's behavior, and (3) Sex-role appropriateness of child's identification.

TEST DESCRIPTION. A three-part instrument, the first part being the Gough and Heilbrun "Adjective Check List" (1965), used to determine the personality of the child. For 15 of the adjectives, the child indicates which parent they describe. For each item in which the child's self-description corresponds to an item checked for a parent, a plus is scored for identification with that parent. Finally, of the 15 items, 9 are sex-linked. These are used to score the sex-role appropriateness or inappropriateness of the parent model.

SAMPLE ITEM. Achievement: to strive to be outstanding in pursuit of socially recognized significance. Endurance: to persist in any task undertaken.

LENGTH. Items: 1 = 300, 2 = 15, 3 = 9.

AVAILABILITY: In Heilbrun, 1965.

ABSTRACTED BY: Thomas G. Sparhawk
REFERENCES.
     Gough,H.G. and Heilbrun,A.B.Jr. Joint manual for the
Adjective Check List and the Need Scales for the ACL. Palo
Alto, California: Consulting Psychologist Press, 1965.
     Heilbrun,A.B.Jr. The measurement of identification.
Child Development, 1965, 36, 111-127.
     Heilbrun,A.B.Jr. Parent identification and filial
sex-role behavior: the importance of biological context.
In Cole,J.K. and Dienstbier,R. (Eds.), Nebraska Symposium
on Motivation, Vol.21, Nebraska: University of Nebraska
Press, 1974.
     Heilbrun,A.B.Jr.   Kleemier,C.   and   Piccola,G.
Developmental and situational correlates of achievement
behavior in college females. Journal of Personality, 1974,
42, 420-436.
     Jchnson,R.W. Parental identification and vocational
interests of college women. Measurement and Evaluation in
Guidance, 1970, 3, 147-151.

HETHERINGTON,E.M.   and FRANKIE,G.   Parent-Imitation Task

VARIABLES MEASURED. (1) Which parent the child imitated
most closely. (2) Extent of imitation.
TEST DESCRIPTION. The child watches both of his parents
perform four trials in a free play situation. Parents are
given instructions which involve postural, verbal, and motor
responses that make their behaviors distinct from one
another.
     Following each pair of parent trials, the child is
given a period in the play room. Imitative responses are
checked on a response check list. "The imitation scores
were obtained by summing the frequency of responses the
child made which were similar to those of a given parent."
SAMPLE ITEM. In a dart game, one parent is instructed to
always shoot with two hands, sitting sideways on a chair.
LENGTH. Time: 5 minutes. Items: 4.
AVAILABILITY. The general description of the procedure is
given in Hetherington and Frankie, 1967.
ABSTRACTED BY: Thomas G. Sparhawk
REFERENCE.
     Hetherington,E.M. and Frankie,G. Effects of parental
dominance, warmth, and conflict on imitation in children.
Journal of Personality and Social Psychology, 1967, 6,
119-125.

JOHNSON,M.H.   and   MEADOW,A.   Measure   of   Parental
Identification

VARIABLE MEASURED. Identification with parents.
TEST DESCRIPTION. This measure is obtained in conjunction
with a 70-item Q-sort consisting of adjectives and short
phrases to be sorted into seven categories of 10 items each.

Five separate Q-sorts are performed by each subject: two self sorts, an idea-self sort, a father sort and a mother sort. The sorts are completed in counterbalanced order. The two self sorts are intended to establish the sorting reliability of each S, the first self sort being used in subsequent analyses. Four identification scores are derived for each S: mother, father, ideal mother, and ideal father. Parental identification measures for each S are derived from the Pearson product moment correlations between the self sort and each parent sort. Ideal-parental identification measures are derived from Pearson product moment correlations between the ideal-self sort and each parent sort.
SAMPLE ITEMS. Considerate, Cruel, Mean.
LENGTH. Items: 70.
AVAILABILITY. In Johnson and Meadow, 1966.
ABSTRACTED BY: Blair Nelson.
REFERENCE.
        Johnson,M.H. and Meadow,A. Parental identification among male schizophrenics. Journal of Personality, 1966, 34, 300-309.

KANDEL,D.B. and LESSER,G.S.   Index of Reliance

VARIABLE MEASURED. Who a child would rely on for advice and guidance.
TEST DESCRIPTION. A questionnaire presents 10 possible problem areas (school grades, career plans, college, personal problems with parents, personal problems not involving parents, morals and values, dating, what clothing to buy, choice of friends, and what books to read). For each area, seven choices of persons to be relied upon for advice or guidance are given (Friends, Father, Mother, Siblings, Teachers, Guidance Counselor, and Other). The score is the number of times a particular person (Father, Mother, Friend, etc.) is checked as someone to rely on.
SAMPLE ITEM. See above.
LENGTH. Items: 10.
AVAILABILITY. In Kandel and Lesser, 1972.
ABSTRACTED BY: Thomas G. Sparhawk
REFERENCES.
        Aldous,J. and Kamiko,T. A cross-national study of the effects of father absence: Japan and the U.S. In Sussman,M.B. and Cogswell,B.E. (Eds.) Cross-National Family Research (International Studies in Sociology and Sociology and Anthropology, Volume XII), Leiden, Netherlands: Brill,E.J., 1972, 86-101.
        Kandel,D.B. and Lesser,G.S. Youth in Two Worlds. San Francisco: Jossey-Bass, Inc., 1972.
        Sussman,M.B. and Cogswell,B.E. Cross-National Family Research. Leiden, Netherlands: E.J.Brill, 1972.

MILLER,E.E.   and   SCHVANEVELDT,J.D.   Parent-Affinity
Perception Scale

VARIABLES MEASURED. Perceived parent preference.
     An abstract of this test is given in Johnson, O.G.
Tests and Measurements in Child Development: Handbook II.
San Francisco: Jossey-Bass, 1976, 621.

OLINER,M. Measure of Parental Identification

VARIABLE MEASURED. Perceived similarity of self and
parents.
TEST DESCRIPTION. A questionnaire consisting of 44 items
dealing with a variety of interests and activity patterns is
administered to subjects.   They indicate their reaction on a
four-point scale ranging from "Very much like" to "Very much
dislike." These items are responded to initially by subjects
for themselves, after which instructions call for responding
as "Person I would like to be" and then as the items apply
to "Mother" and to "Father." Relative perceived similarity
of self to mother as opposed to father is scored by the
formula (Self-Father) minus (Self-Mother). A high score on
this variable indicates that subject reports the difference
between own interests and those of father to be greater than
the difference between own interests and those of mother. A
score based on the absolute difference between perceived
interests of fathers and mothers is also calculated.
SAMPLE ITEM. NR.
LENGTH. Time: 15 to 20 minutes. Items: 44.
AVAILABILITY. From NAPS-2.
ABSTRACTED BY: Kersti Yllo
REFERENCE.
     Singer,J.L. and Schonbar,R.A. Correlates of day
dreaming: a dimension of self-awareness. Journal of
Consulting Psychology, 1961, 25, 1-6.

STEIMEL,R.J.   and   SUZIEDELIS,A.   Perceived   Parental
Influence Scale

VARIABLES MEASURED. Perceived influence of the mother and
father when subject was a child. Scores derived give a
mother-father ratio.
TEST DESCRIPTION. This instrument is an adaptation of one
developed by Steimel in an earlier study (1960). The
subjects either agree or disagree with 10 statements
regarding their mother's influence when they were children
and 10 statements regarding their father's influence.   Only
positive responses are scored "since it was considered
incorrect to assume that nonacceptance of a statement
necessarily indicated the opposite." The score is the ratio
of mother's agree scores to father's.   Theoretically
possible scores range from 10 to 10 (Agree with all 10
statements concerning the mother and all 10 concerning the

father) to 0 to 0 (Disagree with all statements). For the
research reported in Steimel and Suziedelis (1963),
comparisons were made of "extreme father groups" and
"extreme mother groups." An individual was placed in an
extreme group if there was a difference of 4 or more in the
ratio (i.e., 4 to 0, 10 to 6, 6 to 2, etc.).
SAMPLE ITEMS. Mother: My mother was more a source of
encouragment to me in my childhood than my father. Father:
I was more attached to my father than to my mother.
LENGTH. Items: 20 (10 for mother, 10 for father).
AVAILABILITY. In Steimel and Suziedelis, 1963.
REFERENCES.
     Steimel,R.J.   Childhood   experiences   and
masculinity-femininity scores. Journal of Counseling and
Psychology, 1960, 7, 212-217.
     Steimel,R.J. and Suziedelis,A. Perceived parental
influence and inventoried interests. Journal of Counseling
and Psychology, 1963, 10, 289-295.

STEWART,L.H.   Q-Sort For Mother-Son Identification

VARIABLES MEASURED.   (1) Self-satisfaction, (2) Meeting
perceived mother ideal, (3) Accepting perceived mother ideal
as his own, (4) Mother's satisfaction with her son, (5)
Accepting mother's perception as own, (6) Accepting mother's
perception as his ideal, (7) Interpreting mother's
perception as her ideal, (8) Meeting mother's ideal, (9)
Accepting mother's ideal, (10) Awareness of mother's ideal.
These are all derived from combination and discrepancy of
five Q-sorts: the son's Q-sort of self, ideal self, and
what he thinks his mother would like him to be; and the
mother's Q-sort of her son as he is and as she would like
him to be.
TEST DESCRIPTION. Composed of 76 items, all positive in
affect, selected from sentence-completion statements of
students of comparable age, which were thought to be
adequately descriptive of personality and social
relationships. They are sorted on the standard forced
normal distribution (from Most like to Least like the person
or concept being measured), by the son and by the mother
with reference to her son.
SAMPLE ITEMS. Get along well with girls.   My parents are
satisfied with me.
LENGTH. Items: 76--ranked three times by boys, twice by
mothers.
AVAILABILITY. In Stewart, 1959.
REFERENCES.
     Stewart,L.H. Mother-son identification and vocational
interest. Genetic Psychology Monographs, 1959, 60, 31-63.
     Stewart,L.H. Relationship of two indices of interest
stability to self-satisfaction and to mother-son
identification. California Journal of Educational Research,
1962, 13, 51-56.

TEEVAN,J.J.Jr.   Parent Orientation Index

VARIABLE MEASURED. The extent to which parents serve as the
primary reference group for adolescents.
TEST DESCRIPTION. The subject is asked a set of questions
with reference to each parent. Scores are computed for
"difference from mother" (the number of No answers) and
"difference from father" separately. The two scores are
combined to form one index.
SAMPLE ITEM. Do your feel that your father (mother)
understands you as you really are?
LENGTH. Items: 3 for each parent.
AVAILABILITY. In Teevan, 1972.
REFERENCE.
    Teevan,J.J.Jr. Reference groups and premarital sexual
behavior. Journal of Marriage and the Family, 1972, 34,
283-291.

WOLFENSBERGER,W. and KURTZ,R.A. Parent Realism Assessment
Technique (PRAT), and Parental Expectations of Child
Development Technique (PECDT)

VARIABLES MEASURED. PRAT: Parental estimates of their
(possibly retarded) child's developmental level in seven
behavioral areas, plus the child's academic achievement
level, as follows: (1) Understanding of verbal
communication directed at the child (auditory decoding):
(2) Verbal and pre-verbal communication directed at the
child; (3) Gross motor development and coordination; (4)
Manual dexterity and eye-hand coordination; (5) Self-help
skills; (6) Play, occupation, and pre-vocational and
vocational development; (7) General intellectual
functioning; (8) Academic achievement level. PECDT:
Precisely the same areas covered in relation to the parent's
expectations regarding the child's eventual attainments as
an adult.
TEST DESCRIPTION. PRAT: Parents are given a test form on
which they are asked to fill in blanks which ask for an
estimate of the age level at which the child is functioning
in each of the eight behavioral areas. Each of these
parental estimates is then compared to estimates of the
child's behavior level which have been derived by testing
the child's level by applying standardized objective tests
for each area. The comparison between parental estimates
and standardized test estimates of the child's level leads
to an understanding of parental agreement with objective
tests; the closer the two, the more "realistic" the
parents.
    PECDT: Precisely the same procedure is followed as in
the PRAT, except in this case, the parents are asked to
estimate the child's developmental level when he or she will
be an adult. For the "objective" measure of future
development, the child's current behavior levels are
extrapolated to adulthood.

SAMPLE ITEM. PRAT: At what age level do you think your child is functioning in ability to understand what is said to him? PECDT: At what age level do you think your child will be functioning in ability to understand what is said to him or her when he or she is an adult?
LENGTH. Time: 20 minutes. Items: 8 and 8 respectively.
AVAILABILITY. Order Document Number 01183 from Microfiche Publications, 305 E. 46th Street, New York, NY 10017.
ABSTRACTED BY: Richard A. Kurtz and Wolf Wolfensberger
REFERENCE.
    Wolfensberger,W. and Kurtz,R.A.   Measurement   of parent's perception of their children's development. Genetic Psychology Monographs, 1971, 83, 3.

WON,G.Y.M. YAMAMURA,D.S. and IKEDA,K. Parental and Peer Guidance Index.

VARIABLE MEASURED. The relative frequencies with which adolescents turn to their parents and peers for advice on problems and issues significant to them.
TEST DESCRIPTION. A list of 17 issues and problems of concern to adolescents, developed from an open-end pre-test form. Respondents are asked to check the items that are of concern to them and indicate who they consult on each of the problems and issues they have checked. Respondents are allowed to add extra items which are significant to them. The levels of parental and peer guidance are determined by the number of issues on which the respondent seeks advice from each source.
SAMPLE ITEMS. (1) My future work. (2) My plans for going to school. (3) Money matters in the family.
LENGTH. Items: 17.
AVAILABILITY. In Won, Yamamura, and Ikeda, 1969.
REFERENCE.
    Won,G.Y.M. Yamamura,D.S. and Ikeda,K. The relation of communication with parents and peers to deviant behavior of youth. Journal of Marriage and the Family, 1969, 31, 43-47.

4. Communication (See also Subject Index)

ALKIRE,A.A. Parent-Child Communication Assessment

VARIABLE MEASURED. Accuracy of parent-child communication.
TEST DESCRIPTION. This task, originally designed by Krauss and Glucksberg (1965), was modified by Alkire. It requires family members' to communicate information to each other concerning graphic nonsense designs. Each family member serves as the "sender" while the others are "receivers" who must identify the designs being described. The task permits

comparison of individual family members' communication and
use of informaticn. Communication effectiveness is assessed
by the number of correct nonsense design choices made by
"receivers."
SAMPLE ITEM. See above.
LENGTH. Time: 90 seconds for transmission and selection of
each design. Items: 16 designs.
AVAILABILITY. From NAPS-2.
ABSTRACTED BY: Bruce Brown
REFERENCES.
        Alkire,A.A. Social power and communication within
families of disturbed and nondisturbed preadolescents.
Journal of Personality and Social Psychology, 1969, 13,
335-349.
        Goldstein,M.J. Judd,L.L. Rodnick,E.H. Alkire,A.A.
and Gould,E. A method for studying social influence and
coping patterns within families of disturbed adolescents.
Journal of Nervous and Mental Disease, 1968, 147, 233-251.
        Krauss,R.M. and Glucksberg,S. Some aspects of verbal
communication in children. American Psychologist, 1965, 20,
499.

ANANDAM,K. and HIGHBERGER,R. Communication Congruence
Measure

VARIABLE MEASURED. Congruence between verbal and nonverbal
communication.
TEST DESCRIPTION. A method for coding and classifying the
verbal and nonverbal mother-child communication observed
during a laboratory session in which the mother is
instructed to "encourage her son to play with certain
items...and also to play a brain teaser game on her own for
the last few minutes." All verbal and nonverbal
communications are coded into the following four categories:
EP--encouraging positive; EN--encouraging negative,
RP--restricting positive; RN--Restricting negative.
Positive congruity is the number of communications which are
both verbally and nonverbally positive. Negative congruity
is the number of communications which are both verbally and
nonverbally negative. Incongruity is when either verbal or
nonverbal communication is positive and the other is
negative.
SAMPLE ITEM. See above.
LENGTH. Time: two 30-minute sessions. Items: 8 (4
verbal, 4 nonverbal).
AVAILABILITY. In Anandam and Highberger, 1972.
ABSTRACTED BY: Gwen Pearson
REFERENCE.
        Anandam,K. and Highberger,R. Child compliance and
congruity between verbal and nonverbal maternal
communication--a methodological note. Family Process, 1972,
11, 219-226.

BIENVENU,M.J.Sr. Parent-Adolescent Communication Inventory

VARIABLE MEASURED.   Interpersonal communication between
parent   and   adolescent,   defined   as   the   process   of
transmitting feelings, attitudes, facts, beliefs and ideas
between two or more individuals. Includes verbal and nonverbal means such as listening, facial expressions,
silences, gestures, touch, hearing and vision.
TEST DESCRIPTION. The test items refer to various styles
and characteristics of parent-teenager communication such as
listening   habits,   self-expression,   understanding,
acceptance, criticism, sarcasm, and trust. The 40 items
were developed from a study of 376 high school students in
which a quartile comparison was made between the top scorers
and the bottom scorers. The inventory is also used in
teaching communication, in family life education, and as a
counseling tool.
     Matteson (1974) used a modification of Bienvenu's
technique, devising a "Mother-Adolescent Communication
Inventory, A   Father-Adolescent   Inventory   and   A
Parent-Adolescent Inventory."
SAMPLE ITEM. Do your parents respect your opinion even if
they don't agree with it? Yes, No, Sometimes.
LENGTH. Time: 17 minutes. Items: 40.
AVAILABILITY. Family Life Publications, Inc. Box 419,
Saluda, N.C.
ABSTRACTED BY: Millard J. Bienvenu, Sr.
REFERENCES.
     Bienvenu,M.J.Sr. Measurement of parent-adolescent
communication. The Family Coordinator, 1969, 18, 117-121.
     Bienvenu,M.J.Sr. A Counselor's Guide to Accompany a
Marital Communication Inventory. Family Life Publications,
Inc. Saluda, N.C. 1969.
     Buros,O.K. (Ed.) The Seventh Mental Measurements
Yearbook. Highland Park: New Jersey: The Gryphon Press,
1972.
     Matteson,R. Adolescent self-esteem, family
communication, and marital satisfaction. Journal of
Psychology, 1974, 86, 35-47.
     Murphy,D.C. and Mendelson,L.A. Communication and
adjustment in marriage: investigating the relationship.
Family Process, 1973, 12, 317-326.

GOOD,L.R. GOOD,K.C. and NELSON,D.A. Parent-Child
Communication and Similarity Measures

VARIABLES MEASURED. (1) Similarity of perceived and actual
opinions between child and parents. (2) Extent of perceived
communication and understanding between child and parents.
TEST DESCRIPTION. Similarity is measured by an 18-item
Survey of Attitudes (Byrne,1971) completed by both the child
and the parents, who rate their opinion on a six-point scale
for each issue. The subject then rates his/her mother and
father on the same item. Similarity of opinions is obtained

by comparing child and parent answers. Answers on the same
side of the mid-point of the six-point scale indicate child-
parent agreement.
    Perceived communication and understanding is measured
by eight questions, answered on a Very Much to Very Little
seven-space horizontal scale. Four questions each are
directed toward the mother and father. The communication
and understanding items are summed for each parent, forming
a 4- to 28-point index for each.
SAMPLE ITEM. Attitudes: Legalizing the use of marijuana.
Communication and Understanding: How much does your mother
(father) discuss with you things which are of concern to
herself (himself)?
LENGTH. Items: 62.
AVAILABILITY. Survey of Attitudes in Byrne, 1971.
Communication and understanding in Good, Good, and Nelson,
1973.
ABSTRACTED BY: Thomas G. Sparhawk
REFERENCES.
    Byrne,D. The Attraction Paradigm. New York: Academic
Press, 1971.
    Good,L.R. Good,K.C. and Nelson,D.A. Assumed attitude
similarity and perceived intrafamilial communication and
understanding. Psychological Reports, 1973, 32, 3-11.

GORDON,T. Listening for Feelings of Children

VARIABLE MEASURED. Recognition of "feelings" behind
children's messages to parents.
TEST DESCRIPTION. Test consists of a list of 20 "typical"
messages which children send. Respondents are instructed to
read each message separately and then record the feeling or
feelings behind the message. The test is scored by
comparing the respondent's answers with those on a scoring
key: items which closely match those on the scoring key get
four points, items which only partially match get two
points, items which do not match at all are scored 0.
SAMPLE ITEM. Oh boy, only ten more days until school's out.
Scoring key: Either "Glad" or "Relieved" gets four points.
LENGTH. Items: 20.
AVAILABILITY. In Gordon, 1970.
ABSTRACTED BY: Bruce Brown
REFERENCE.
    Gordon,T. Parent Effectiveness Training. New York:
Peter H. Wyden, 1970.

LaVOIE,J.C. Family Communication Patterns

VARIABLES MEASURED. Parent communicativeness.
    An abstract of this test is given in Johnson, O.G.
Tests and Measurements in Child Development: Handbook II.
San Francisco: Jossey-Bass, 1976, 774.

LOEFFLER,D.   BERDIE,R.   AND   ROTH,J.   Intergeneration
Communication Questionnaire

VARIABLES MEASURED.   Degree of congruity between
mother/daughter and father/son on a set of informational and
attitudinal variables.
TEST DESCRIPTION. The intergeneration communication
questionnaire was designed to identify topics of information
interchange between college freshmen and their same-sex
parents and to elicit from both students and parents their
evaluations of the nature and pattern of their communication
with each other.   The inventory has three parts: Part I
includes 50 questions about the lives of the parent and the
student. The questions are open-ended and include inquiries
regarding facts as well as preferences. The number of items
to which parent and student respond in agreement is designed
as the agreement score for Part I. Part II includes eight
statements of possible student problem areas and the student
and parent are asked to check the person or persons with
whom the student would discuss the situation with seven
possibilities listed for each problem.   Part II includes
seven open-ended statements designed to elicit the attitude
of students and parents about the content and nature of the
communication between them.
SAMPLE ITEM. Check the person or persons with whom you
would discuss the following situation: I can't seem to
study the right things for a test: Counselor, Teacher,
Mother, Father, Friend, No one, Other.
LENGTH. Time 30-40 minutes. Items: 65.
AVAILABILITY. From NAPS-2.
ABSTRACTED BY: Dorothy Loeffler
REFERENCES.
      Loeffler,D.   Counseling and the psychology of
communication. Personnel and Guidance Journal, 1970, 48,
629-636.
      Loeffler,D. Berdie,R. and Roth,J.   Content and
process of inter-generation communication, The Family
Coordinator, 1969, 18, 345-352.
      Watzlawick,P. Berlin,J. and Jackson,D.D.   Pragmatics
of Human Communication. New York: Norton, 1967

McLEOD,J.M. Family Communications Patterns

VARIABLES MEASURED. Socio-oriented family communication
defined as encouraging one's children to maintain harmonious
personal relationships with parents and others.
Concept-oriented family communication defined as encouraging
one's children to express their ideas and challenge other's
beliefs.
TEST DESCRIPTION. The wording of the items in the scales
differed between parents' and children's questionnaires.
The items were statements concerning positions on these
communication dimensions.   Four categories ranging from
"Often" to "Never" depending on the frequency with which the

parent emphasized the practice constituted the possible responses. Each response was assigned a numerical value, and the sum value of the responses checked provided an individual's score for each of the two scales. The two dimensions of communication were dichotomized, making a fourfold typology of parent-child communication patterns. The names and explanations of these types are as follows:

Laissez-faire families emphasize neither type of relation. Children are not prohibited from challenging parental views, but neither are they exposed to information relevant to expressing independent ideas.

Protective families stress socio-relations at the expense of concept relations. The child is encouraged to get along with others by steering clear of the controversial realm of ideas. Not only is he/she prohibited from expressing dissent, but he/she is given little chance to encounter information on which to base his/her own views.

Pluralistic families emphasize the development of strong and varied concept-relations in an environment comparatively free of social restraints. The child is encouraged to explore new ideas and is often exposed to controversial material; thus, he/she can make up his/her own mind without fear that reaching a different conclusion from his/her parents will endanger social relations in the family.

Consensual families stress both types of relations. Although the child is exposed to controversy, he/she is constrained to develop concepts that are consonant with the existing socio-relations--i.e., to learn his/her parents' ideas and to adopt their values.
SAMPLE ITEM. With your children how often do you emphasize the following: That they should not show anger in a group situation.
LENGTH. Items: 10.
AVAILABILITY. From NAPS-2.
ABSTRACTED BY: Bruce Brown
REFERENCE.
    Chaffee,S.H. McLeod,J.M. and Atkin,C.K. Parental influences on adolescent media use. American Behavioral Scientist, 1971, 14, 323-340.

D. Multi-Variable Measures of Parent-Child Relations

1. Observed or Reported Interaction (See also Subject Index)

ANTONOVSKY,H.F.   Mother-Child Interaction Rating Scales and
Observation Categories

VARIABLES MEASURED.   Mother   behavior   variables: (1)
Affectional contact, (2) Expectations, (3) Restrictiveness,
(4)   Punishment.   Child   behavior   variables: (1)
Dependency--help, affectional contact, non-interactive play;
(2)   Aggression-noncompliance/compliance;   (3)
Initiative--suggestions   by   child   to   mother   of play
activities, initiating new activities.
TEST DESCRIPTION. A set of seven-point rating scales for
maternal behavior, and a set of categories for recording
child's interaction with mother. The rating scales can be
used for both interview and observational protocols.   In the
observational session the room is supplied with   toys
designed   to   induce interaction.   Mother's and child's
behaviors are recorded separately in terms of the smallest
separable units of action. Child behavior scores, obtained
only from the observational session, are the number of units
in a behavior category over the total number of units
scored. The disobedience score is the ratio of noncompliant
to compliant responses to mother's requests or restrictions.
SAMPLE ITEM. See variables measured.
LENGTH.   Time: Structured   interview,   one   hour;
observation, 30 minutes; unstructured interview, one hour.
Items: mother behavior, four categories;   child behavior,
three major categories, six subcategories.
AVAILABILITY. From Helen F. Antonovsky.
REFERENCE.
     Antonovsky,H.F.   A contribution to research in the area
of the mother-child relationship. Child Development, 1959,
30, 37-51.

APPERSON,L.B.   Perception of Parent Behavior Scale

VARIABLES MEASURED.   Perceived attitudes of parents in
respect to seven aspects of child's behavior: (1) Concern,
(2) Restrictiveness, (3) Discouragement of   pride,   (4)
Cleanliness, (5) Giving to younger children, (6) Father's
possessions, and (7) Over-protection.
TEST DESCRIPTION. The test consists of 90 items, from which
the subjects are asked to select 30 situations which they
feel would have "bothered" (been of concern to)   their
parents while the subjects were growing up. Factor analysis
produced seven clusters of items, on which subjects can be
scored and groups compared. Forms are analyzed separately

for fathers and mothers. The score for each factor is
obtained by adding factor loadings and normalizing scores.
SAMPLE ITEMS. Failing to keep a promise to a friend,
Complaining of a headache, Seeming over-confident about your
ability.
LENGTH. Time: 20 minutes. Items: 90.
AVAILABILITY. From NAPS-2 or Louise B. Apperson.
ABSTRACTED BY: Louise B. Apperson.
REFERENCES.

Apperson,L.B. Childhood experiences of schizophrenics
and alcoholics. Journal of Genetic Psychology, 1965, 106,
301-313.

Apperson,L.B. and McAdoo,W.G. Paternal reactions in
childhood as described by schizophrenics and alcoholics.
Journal of Clinical Psychology, 1965, 21, 369-373.

Apperson,L.B. and McAdoo,W.G. Parental factors in the
childhood of homosexuals. Journal of Abnormal Psychology,
1968, 73, 201-206.

Apperson,L.B. and Stinnett,P.W. Parental factors as
reported by patient groups. Journal of Clinical Psychology,
1975, 31, 419-425.

BALDWIN,A.I. KALHORN,J.C. and BREESE,F.H. Fels Parent
Behavior Rating Scales

VARIABLES MEASURED. Thirty variables, 25 of which are
grouped into eight clusters: (1) Warmth--acceptance of
child, direction of criticism, affection, rapport,
childcenteredness, intensity of contact; (2)
Adjustment--Adjustment of home, discord, effectiveness of
policy, disciplinary friction; (3) Indulgence--babying,
protectiveness, solicitousness; (4) Democracy--Democracy of
policy, justification of policy; (5)
Intellectuality--readiness of explanation, accelerational
attempt, understanding; (6)
Restrictiveness--restrictiveness of regulations,
coerciveness of suggestions; (7) Clarity--Clarity of
policy, readiness of enforcement; (8)
Interference--quantity of suggestion, readiness of
criticism, severity of punishment. The remaining five
variables are activeness, coordination, sociability,
duration of contact, and emotionality.

Factor analysis of the original data indicates three
main factors: (1) warmth, (2) objectivity, and (3) type of
parental control. Additional factor analyses generally
confirming these results were done by Lorr and Jenkins
(1953) and Roff (1949).
TEST DESCRIPTION. The family is visited by the rater who
observes and rates the "impact of the parent's behavior on
the child." Scale positions are verbally defined. The
rating is determined by observation of actual parent-child
interaction as well as other sources of information. If one
family member is not present, the rater secures information
about him/her by interviewing another adult member and

estimates the effect of the missing person. A family is
rated on the 30 scales with respect to each child in the
family. Utton (1962) used an adaptation of these scales.
SAMPLE ITEM. Readiness of enforcement (Vigilant-Lax). Rate
the parent's tendency to enforce the standards of conduct
set up for the child. Does the parent follow up to see that
the child conforms, or sustains a penalty? Or are lapses in
compliance disregarded? This variable applies only to
situations where there is an opportunity for the parent to
enforce an accepted standard which has been, is being, or is
about to be violated by the child. Disregard the methods of
enforcement and the severity of enforcement. Disregard the
effectiveness of enforcement and clarity to the child of
standards involved. Do not confuse with the nonregulational
type of parental domination covered by the "suggestion"
scales. Check cne: (1) Eternally vigilant. Goes out of
way to discover and discipline misconduct. Often pounces
before lapse occurs. (2) Seldom lets child "get away with
anything." Enforces rules strictly wherever violations come
to attention, but seldom deliberately hunts for misbehavior.
(3) Moderately firm. Strict about important requirements
and prohibitions; but rather lax with minor violations,
especially when they are not an issue at the moment. (4)
Reluctant to enforce standards. Tends to overlook
violations unless they are flagrant, cumulative, or threaten
serious consequences. (5) Extremely lax. Disregards
obvious misbehavior. Enforces regulations only when pressed
by the strongest motives or the severest circumstances.
     Baumrind's (1971, 1972) Parent Behavior Rating Scales
come in part from the Fels Parent Behavior Rating Scale.
LENGTH. Time: 240 minutes (approximately). Items: 30.
AVAILABILITY. In Baldwin, et al., 1949.
REFERENCES.
     Baldwin,A.L. The appraisal of parent behavior.
Abstract. American Psychologist, 1946, 1, 251.
     Baldwin,A.L. Differences in parent behavior toward
three- and nine-year-old children. Journal of Personality,
1946, 15, 143-65. (PA 21:3296)
     Baldwin,A.L. Changes in parent behavior during
pregnancy: an experiment in longitudinal analysis. Child
Development, 1947, 18, 29-39.
     Baldwin,A.L. The effect of home environment on nursery
school behavior. Child Development, 1949, 20, 49-61.
     Baldwin,A.L. Kalhorn,J.C. and Breese,F.H. Patterns
of Parent Behavior. American Psychological Association,
Psychological Monographs. Washington, D.C.: The
Association, Inc., 1945, 58, Whole No. 268.
     Baldwin,A.L. Kalhorn,J.C. and Breese,F.H. The
Appraisal of Parent Behavior. American Psychological
Association, Psychological Monographs. Washington, D.C.:
The Association, Inc., 1949, 63, Whole No. 299.
     Baumrind,D. Current patterns of parental authority.
Developmental Psychology Monograph, 1971, 4, Part 2, 1-103.
     Baumrind,D. The development of instrumental competence
through socialization. Minnesota Symposium on Child

Psychology, Vol. 7. Minneapolis: University of Minnesota
Press, 1972, 3-46.

Becker,W.C. Peterson,D.R. Hellmer,L.A. Shoemaker,D.J.
and Quay,H.C. Factors in parental behavior and personality
as related to problem behavior in children. Journal of
Consulting Psychology, 23, 1959, 107-118.

Becker,W.C.   Peterson,D.R.   Luria,Z.   Shoemaker,D.J.
and Hellmer,L.A. Relations of factors derived from parental
interview ratings to behavior problems of five-year-olds.
Child Development, 1962, 33, 509-535.

Buros,O.K.   (Ed.) Personality Tests and Reviews.
Highland Park N.J.: Gryphon Press, 1970.

Champney,H. Measurement of parent behavior as part of
the child's environment. Ph.D. dissertation, Ohio State
University, 1939.

Champney,H. Some measurable aspects of the child's
home environment. Abstract. Psychological Bulletin, 1939,
36, 628-629.

Champney,H. The measurement of parent behavior. Child
Development, 1941, 12, 131-166.

Champney,H. The variables of parent behavior. Journal
of Abnormal Social Psychology, 1941, 36, 525-542.

Champney,H. and Marshall,H.R. Optimal refinement of
the rating scale. Journal of Applied Psychology, 1939, 23,
323-331.

Crandall,V.C. The antecedents and adult correlates of
academic and intellectual achievement effort. Minnesota
Symposium on Child Psychology, Vol. 4. Minneaplis:
University of Minnesota Press, 1969, 36-39.

Crandall,V.C.   Katkovsky,W.   and   Crandall,V.J.
Children's beliefs in their own control of reinforcements in
intellectual-academic achievement situations. Child
Development, 1965, 36, 91-109.

Crandall,V.J. and Preston,A. Patterns and levels of
maternal behavior. Child Development, 1955, 26, 267-277.

Crandall,V.J. and Preston,A. Verbally expressed needs
and overt maternal behaviors. Child Development, 1961, 32,
261-270.

Donnelly,E.M. The quantitative analysis of parent
behavior toward psychotic children and their siblings.
Genetic Psychological Monographs, 1960, 62, 331-376.

Eckhoff,E. Gauslaa,J. and Baldwin,A.L. Parental
behavior toward boys and girls of pre-school age. Acta
Psychologica, 1961, 18, 85-99.

Hartson,M.F. and Champney,H. Parent behavior as
related to child development: II. social maturity.
Abstract. Psychological Bulletin, 1940, 7, 583.

Kalhorn,J.C. The diagnosis of parent behavior.
Abstract. American Psychologist 1:251-2 July 1946. (PA
20:3742, title only).

Katkovsky,W. Crandall,V.C. and Good,S. Parental
antecedents of children's beliefs in internal-external
control of reinforcements in intellectual achievement
situations. Child Development, 1967, 38, 765-776.

Lorr,M. and Jenkins,R.L. Three factors in parent

behavior. Journal of Consulting Psychology, 1953, 17, 306-308.

Medinnus,G.R. The relation between several parent measures and the child's early adjustment to school. Journal of Educational Psychology, 1961, 52, 153-156.

Ray,M. Cameron,E.S. and Gilbert,C. The use of behavior rating scales in the analysis of clinical case records. Abstract. American Psychologist, 1948, 3, 364.

Roff,M. A factorial study of the Fels Parent Behavior Scales. Child Development, 1949, 20, 29-45.

Sanford,R.N. Adkins,M.M. Miller,R.B. and Cobb,E.A. Physique, personality and scholarship: a cooperative study of schoolchildren. Monographs of the Society for Research in Child Development, 1943, 8, No. 1 (Serial No. 34).

Scarr,S. The adjective check list as a personality assessment technique with children: validity of the scales. Journal of Consulting Psychology, 1966, 30, 122-128.

Schaefer,E.S. A circumplex mode 41 for maternal behavior. Journal of Abnormal and Social Psychology, 1959, 59, 226-235.

Utton,A.C. Recalled parent-child relations as determinants of vocational choice. Journal of Counseling Psychology, 1962, 9, 49-53.

Waters,E.C. and Crandall,V.J. Social class and observed maternal behavior from 1940 to 1960. Child Development, 1964, 35, 1021-2032.

BISHOP,B.M. Mother-Child Interaction Observation Categories

VARIABLES MEASURED. (1) Amount of interaction between mother and child. (2) Specificity of control over child's behavior by mother. (3) Degree and manner of facilitation and inhibition of child's ongoing behavior. (4) Descriptive categories for child's behavior.
TEST DESCRIPTION. A system of categories for recording parents' behavior in interaction with child in a laboratory setting (0 behind one-way mirror). The mother's behavior is recorded every five seconds. The revised system (Bishop, 1951) uses similar categories and recording system, but the number of categories is fewer, the categories allow for qualitative differentiations, and the child's behavior toward the adult is measured by 13 categories, 4 of which are different from those used in measuring adult patterns.
SAMPLE ITEM. (1) Mother is carrying on independent activity at the adult level--any act divorced from the expermental setup or the child, such as reading magazines, looking out the windows, busying herself with the contents of her pocketbook.
Brody used Bales' (1951) recording method with behavior categories developed by Barbara Merrill Bishop (1946, 1951) and Moustakas, Sigel and Schalock (1956) among others.
LENGTH. Experiment 1. Time: NR. Items: 22 categories. Experiment 2. Time: Two half-hour sessions with mother; two half-hour sessions with neutral adult. Items: child,

13 categories;   mother, 11 categories.
AVAILABILITY. In Bishop, 1951;   Merrill, 1946.
REFERENCES.
    Bishop,B.M. Mother-child interaction and the social
behavior of children. Psychological Monographs, 1951, 65,
No. 11 (Whole No. 328), 1-34.
    Brody,G.F. Relationship between maternal attitudes and
behavior.   Journal of Personality and Social Psychology,
1965, 2, 317-323.
    Merrill,B. A measurement of mother-child interaction.
Journal of Abnormal Social Psychology, 1946, 41, 37-49.

BRODY,G.F.   Maternal Behavior Observation Categories

VARIABLES MEASURED. Observed maternal behavior, divided
into fifteen categories: attentive observation, directing,
restriction, non-attention, forbidding, criticism, verbal
interaction, responsiveness to questions, interactive play,
helping,   praise-approval-affection,
teaching-explaining-demonstrating, explaining-demonstrating,
questioning, structurizing, and rate of compliance.
TEST DESCRIPTION. The criteria for the selection of
categories are that they lend themselves to clear
definition, that they be descriptive rather than
inferential, that they be easily recognized in the process
of social interaction, and that they be sufficiently
comprehensive to cover the behavior that would occur during
the play situation. The behavior categories, with their
descriptions, are contained in Table A3 and Table B3 (of ADI
document   8464).
    Recording is continuous, with each observed verbal or
nonverbal behavior on the part of the mother or child
tallied in the appropriate category. The verbal recording
unit is approximately equal to a simple sentence.
SAMPLE ITEM.   Category: Structurizing.   Description:
Mother facilitates or channels child's activity by offering
knowledge or guidance, or indicates limits, boundaries, and
roles, but leaves the responsibility of the decision to the
child. Example: You can make a nice house out of these
blocks.
LENGTH. Time: 30 minutes.
AVAILABILITY. From NAPS. Doc. No. 8464.
REFERENCES.
    Brody,G.F. Relationship between maternal attitudes and
behavior, Journal of Personality and Social Psychology,
1965, 2, 317-323.
    Brody,G.F. Socioeconomic differences in stated
maternal child-rearing practices and in observed maternal
behavior. Journal of Marriage and the Family, 1968, 30,
656-660.
    Pumroy,D.K.   Revised preliminary manual for the
Maryland Parent Attitude Survey. Unpublished manuscript,
University of Maryland, 1960.
    Roe,A. and Siegelman,M. A parent-child relations

questionnaire. Child Development, 1963, 34, 355-369.
    Schaefer,E.S. and Bell,R.Q. Development of a parental
attitude research instrument. Child Development, 1958, 29,
339-361.

BRONFENBRENNER,U. and DEVEREUX,E.C.Jr. Cornell Parent
Behavior Inventory

VARIABLES MEASURED. Parental role performance in relations
to an adolescent child. The variables are grouped into two
classes: I. Expressive functions: (1) Nurturance, (2)
Affection, (3) Protectiveness, (4) Affective punishment, (5)
Expressive rejection, (6) Indulgence, (7) Intercession, (8)
Affiliative companionship, (9) Affective reward, (10)
Parental presence; and II. Instrumental functions: (11)
Physical punishment and threats, (12) Deprivation of
privilege of property, (13) Material reward, (14) Power,
(15) Achievement demands, (16) Social isolation, (17)
Instrumental companionship, (18) Principled discipline, (19)
Neglect, (20) Parental absence.
    Factor analysis of the variables revealed two
substantially independent factors: support (or positive
interaction), which has heaviest loadings on affection,
nurturance, and companionship; and control (or pressure or
negative interaction), which has heavy loadings on physical
punishment, rejection, and deprivation of privileges.
    Factor analysis of an 11-item short form (called the
Cornell Socialization Inventory) reveals two main factors:
Support and Discipline.
TEST DESCRIPTION. The inventory is designed for
adolescents. The subject is asked to indicate the extent to
which each item "applies to each parent's treatment of you
as you were growing up." The response alternatives for most
items are: Never = 0; Seldom = 1; Sometimes = 2; In most
cases = 3; In every case = 4. Where the sense of the item
requires it, responses ranging from Never = 0 to Practically
every day = 4 are used. Each of the 20 variables is
represented by five items, and each is answered twice, once
for the father and once for the mother. A revision for a
study of German families (Devereux et al., 1962) used only
variables 1, 5, 11, 12, 14, 15, 17, 18, and prescriptions of
responsibility. Siegelman (1965) has performed a factor
analysis and other evaluations.
    An 11-item short form called the Cornell Socialization
Agent Inventory (CSAI) was developed by Devereux et al.
(1974). This version is modified so that it provides
descriptions for teachers and peers as well as for parents.
It therefore permits a comparison of the extent to which the
various types of socialization behaviors are practiced by
mother, father, teacher, peer group, cr other agents of
socialization.
SAMPLE ITEM. (Father, 0 1 2 3 4) (Mother, 0 1 2 3 4)
Punished me by sending me out of the room.

LENGTH. Items: 100.
AVAILABILITY. From NAPS. A short version based on factor
analysis is available in Devereux et al., 1962.
REFERENCES.
     Bronfenbrenner,U.   Some   familial   antecedents   of
responsibility   and   leadership   in   adolescents.   In
Petrullo,L.   and   Bass,B.L.   (Eds.)   Leadership   and
Interpersonal Behavior. New York: Holt, 1961a, 239-271.
     Bronfenbrenner,U. Toward a theoretical model for the
analysis of parent-child relationships in a social context.
In Glidewell,J.C.   (Ed.) Parental Attitudes and Child
Behavior. Springfield, Illinois: Charles C Thomas, 1961b.
     Devereux,E.C.Jr. Family authority and child behavior
in West Germany and the United States: some problems and
strategies   in   a   cross-national   validation   study.
Transactions of the Fifth World Congress of Sociology,
Washington,   D.C.,   1962,   4,   303-312.   International
Sociological Association, 1964.
     Devereux,E.C.Jr. Permissiveness vs. control: a false
dilemma.   Pre-Adolescents--Why   is   Each   One Different?
Ithaca, N.Y.: Cooperative Extension Service, Cornell
University, 1964, 7-17.
     Devereux,E.C.Jr. The role of peer group experience in
moral development. Minnesota Symposia on Child Psychology.
Vol. 4. Minneapolis: University of Minnesota Press, 1969,
94-140.
     Devereux,E.C.Jr.   Socialization   in   cross-cultural
perspective: comparative study of England, Germany, and the
United States. In Hill,R. and Konig,R. (Eds.) Families in
East and West. Paris: Mouton, 1970.
     Devereux,E.C.Jr. Bronfenbrenner,U.   and Rodgers,R.R.
Child-rearing in England and the United States: a
cross-national comparison, Journal of Marriage and the
Family, 1969, 257-270.
     Devereux,E.C.Jr.   Bronfenbrenner,U.   and Suci,G.J.
Patterns of parent behavior in the United States of America
and the Federal Republic of Germany: a cross-national
comparison. International Social Science Journal, 1962, 14,
488-506.
     Devereux,E.C.Jr. Shouval,R. Bronfenbrenner,U. Rodgers,R.
R. Kav-Venaki,S. Kiely,E. and Karson,E. Socialization
practices of parents, teachers, and peers in Israel: the
kibbutz versus the city. Child Development, 1974, 45,
269-281.
     Fodor,E.M.   Resistance   to   temptation,   moral
development, and perceptions of parental behavior among
adolescent boys. Journal of Social Psychology, 1972, 88,
155-156.
     Gecas,V.   Parental   behavior   and   dimensions   of
adolescent self-evaluation. Sociometry, 1971, 34, 466-482.
     Gecas,V. Parental behavior and contextural variations
in adolescent self-esteem. Sociometry, 1972, 35, 332-345.
     Gecas,V.   Thomas,D.L.   and Weigert,A.J.   Perceived
parent-child interaction and boys' self-esteem in two
cultural contexts. International Journal of Comparative

Sociology, 1970, 11, 317-324.

Levenson,H.   Perceived parental antecedents of
internal, powerful others, and chance locus of control
orientations. Developmental Psychology, 1973, 9, 260-265.

Rodgers,R.R.   Personal and dittoed correspondence.
Cornell University, 1968.

Rodgers,R.R. Changes in parental behavior reported by
children in West Germany and the United States. Human
Development, 1971, 14, 208-224.

Scanzoni,J.   Inconclusiveness in family sources of
achievement. Pacific Sociological Review, 1966, 9, 108-114.

Siegelman,M.   Evaluation   of   Bronfenbrenner's
questionnaire for children concerning parental behavior.
Child Development, 1965, 36, 163-174.

Siegelman,M. Loving and punishing parental behavior
and introversion tendencies in sons. Child Development,
1966, 37, 985-992.

Smith,T.E. Social class and attitudes toward fathers.
Sociology and Social Research, 1969, 53, 217-224.

Steinmetz,S.K. Occupation and physical punishment: a
response to Straus. Journal of Marriage and the Family,
1971, 33, 664-666.

Straus,M.A.   Some social antecedents of physical
punishment: a linkage theory interpretation. Journal of
Marriage and the Family, 1971, 33, 658-663.

Stuart,R.C.   and   Smart,M.S.   New   Zealand
preadolescents' parent-peer orientation and parent
perceptions compared with English and American. Journal of
Marriage and the Family, 1973, 35, 142-148.

Thomas,D.L.   Gecas,V.   Weigert,A.L.   and   Rooney,E.
Family Socialization and the Adolescent. Lexington,
Massachusetts: Lexington Books, 1974.

Thomas,D.L. and Weigert,A.J.   Socialization and
adolescent ccnformity to significant others: a
cross-national analysis. American Sociological Review,
1971, 36, 835-847.

CLARKE-STEWART,K.A. Mother-Child Interaction Scales

VARIABLES MEASURED. (1) Infant variables: "Measures of
competence in all areas of development-cognitive, language
and social..." (2) Maternal variables: One complex factor
subsuming all measures of "optimal" maternal care, including
expression of affection, social stimulation, acceptance of
child's behavior, etc.   (3) Mother-child relations: The
sequential relaticnships between the variables listed above.
TEST DESCRIPTION. The Interaction Scales method examines
relations between behavicrs of mothers and children. Over a
nine-month period repeated observations are made of mothers
and a firstborn child (9 to 18 months old) as they
interacted at home, spontaneously and in structured
situations.   Ratings,   frequencies,   and   measures   of
contingencies between sequential maternal and child
behaviors are based on these observations. The method of

observation, codes for observed behaviors and measurement of
other variables are given in Clarke-Stewart, 1973.
SAMPLE ITEM. See above.
LENGTH. NR.
AVAILABILITY. In Clarke-Stewart, 1973.
ABSTRACTED BY: Kersti Yllo
REFERENCE.
    Clarke-Stewart,K.A. Interactions between mothers and
their young children: characteristics and consequences.
Society for Research in Child Development Monographs, 1973,
38, 1-100.

COHEN,D.J. and DIBBLE,E. Parent's Report

VARIABLES MEASURED. The behavior of parents toward their
children on five dimensions: (1) Respect for autonomy; (2)
Control through guilt and anxiety; (3) Consistency; (4)
Child-centeredness; and (5) Parental temper and detachment.
TEST DESCRIPTION. The questionnaire is a self-rating scale
of parental behavior containing operationally defined,
behavioral items describing various types of parent-child
interactions, appropriate for use with children from ages 2
years through early adolescence. The parent rates
him/herself on a seven-point scale, from "Never" = 0 to
"Always" = 6. There are parallel columns for the parent to
rate actual behavior (the "real" scale) and for the parent
to rate how the ideal parent would behave with the child
(the "ideal" scale). It is possible to derive a real-ideal
disparity measure. A short form correlates highly with the
long form.
SAMPLE ITEM. I let him help me decide about things that
affect him.
LENGTH. Items: Long form, 48; short form, 20.
AVAILABILITY. In Dibble and Cohen, 1974.
ABSTRACTED BY: Donald Cohen
REFERENCES.
    Cohen,D.J. Dibble,E. and Grawe,J.M. Parental style:
mothers' and fathers' perceptions of their relations with
twin children. Archives of General Psychiatry. In press.
    Dibble,E. and Cohen,D.J. Companion instruments for
measuring children's competence and parental style.
Archives of General Psychiatry, 1974, 30, 805-815.

COX,F.N. and LEAPER,P.M. Parent Behavior Question Schedule

VARIABLES MEASURED. (1) Parental love, (2) Parental
restriction, (3) Household responsibilities, (4) Family
cohesion.
TEST DESCRIPTION. A questionnaire for 11- to 12-year-olds,
divided into two parts, "My Ordinary Day" and "My Usual
Weekend." Seventy-four items are arranged in a time sequence
in which there is a natural division of questions about
weekday and weekend activities. The items intended to

measure love and restriction consist of a related series of open-ended and closed questions. The family cohesion scale is the sum of weights for multiple-choice questions about joint recreational activities. There are also buffer questions asking the sociological characteristics of the families. Criteria for scoring of the items is derived from a priori definition of these variables.
SAMPLE ITEM. (Items to measure love:) If you do something especially good, does someone in your family praise you for doing it? Put a ring or circle around the person or people who praise you--Mother, Father, Older brother, Older sister, Younger brother, Younger sister, Others. How do these people praise you?
LENGTH. Time: two and a half hours. Items: 74.
AVAILABILITY. In Cox, 1963.
REFERENCES.
    Beswick,D.G. and Cox,F.N. Reputed aggression and dependence in children. Australian Journal of Psychology, 1958, 10, 144-150.
    Cox,F.N. A second study of four family variables. Child Development, 1963, 34, 619-630.
    Cox,F.N. and Leaper,P.M. Assessing some aspects of the parent-child relationship. Child Development, 1961, 32, 637-649.

CRANDALL,V.J. PRESTON,A. and RABSON,A. Rating Scales for Home Observations cf Mother-Child Interaction

VARIABLES MEASURED. Child variables: (1) Amount of achievement effort, (2) Approval-seeking, (3) Help-seeking, (4) Emotional support-seeking. Mother variables: (1-4) Extent to which the mother rewards each of the preceding child behaviors, (5) Amount of general affection expressed toward the child.
TEST DESCRIPTION. Rating scales for each of the mother and child variables. Ratings are based on observation of the mother and child together in the home.
SAMPLE ITEM. NR.
AVAILABILITY. Frcm Fels Research Institute, Yellow Springs, Ohio 45387.
REFERENCES.
    Crandall,V.J. and Preston,A. Verbally expressed needs and overt maternal behaviors. Child Development, 1961, 32, 261-270.
    Crandall,V.J. Preston,A. and Rabson,A. Maternal reactions and the development of independence and achievement behavior in young children. Child Development, 1960, 31, 243-251.

FARBER,B. and JENNE,W.C. Parent-Child Relationship Indexes

VARIABLES MEASURED. Effectiveness of (1) Parent-child communication; (2) Child's perception of parental

criticism;   (3) Parental dissatisfaction with child's
behavior and (4) Child's perception of that dissatisfaction.
TEST DESCRIPTION. Each index is based on answers by parents
and children to 50 questionnaire items. Each parent is
requested to check an answer--Much less, A little less, As
he does now, A little more, Much more, Does not apply--for
50 activities as follows (Farber and Jenne, 1963):   I wish
my son would do this activity: think about school work;
help around the house; listen to radio and TV programs;
play outdoor games such as baseball, tennis, etc.; visit
his friends. The child is also requested to check each
statement in the same manner but the prefatory statement
reads "My father (or mother) wishes that I would do this
activity." Each index is scored differently in order to
measure specific variables.
        (1) Effectiveness of parent-child communication: The
scoring for the measure consists of four elements: the
number of items on which the child accurately perceives
parental satisfaction (A);   the number of times the child
accurately perceives parental dissatisfaction (B);   the
number of items in which either parent or the child (or
both) does not respond or gives conflicting answers (G);
and the total number of items (N = 50). The index of
effectiveness of parent-child communication is, then, (A +
B)/(N - G). The index of effectiveness, then, is the ratio
of accurate perceptions by the child to the total number of
acceptable responses.   Theoretically, the numerical values
of scores can range from .00 to 1.00.
        (2) Overcritical perception by the child: This index
may be most easily derived as a two-part operation. First,
one obtains the difference between the number of items on
which the child perceives a parent as dissatisfied with
his/her behavior and the number of times the parent actually
indicates dissatisfaction.   The index then constitutes the
ratio between this difference to the total number of items
on the activities list.   Theoretically, the numerical value
of the ratio can range from +1.00 to -1.00, with a positive
score indicative of a child's tending to be overcritical;
that is, the child perceives the parent as dissatisfied more
often than is, in fact, the case.
        (3) Parents' dissatisfaction;   (4) Child's perception
of Parents' dissatisfaction with child's behavior: The
index of level of parents' dissatisfaction with the child's
behavior is the ratio of items on which the parent expresses
dissatisfaction to the total number of acceptable responses.
The index of the child's perception of parents'
dissatisfaction with child's behavior is calculated in a
similar fashion,   the score being the ratio of the items on
which the child perceives parental dissatisfaction to the
total number of acceptable responses. On these scales, the
total number of acceptable responses is equal to all of the
responses (N = 50) less the number of items in which either
the the parent or child does not respond or gives
conflicting responses.   In both indices, the values can
theoretically range from .00 to 1.00, with the higher value

being in the direction of dissatisfaction.
SAMPLE ITEM. See above.
LENGTH. Items: 50.
AVAILABILITY. In Farber and Jenne, 1963.
ABSTRACTED BY: Kersti Yllo based on Johnson and Bommarito,
1963, 261, 348, 474.
REFERENCE.
       Farber,B. and Jenne,W.C. Family organization and
parent-child communications. Monographs of the Society For
Research in Child Development, 1963, 28 (Whole Monograph,
No. 7).

FERDINAND,T.N. and LUCHTERHAND,E.G. Family Background
Scores

VARIABLES MEASURED. Estrangement from family, Parental
permissiveness, Seeking parental advice, and Family discord.
TEST DESCRIPTION. Subjects are asked questions or asked to
respond to statements which relate to each of the areas
listed above. The answers to each item are weighted and
total scores are calculated for each of the four areas.
SAMPLE ITEM. Parental permissiveness: How much freedom do
your parents give you on when to get home at night? (Factor
weighting .66)
LENGTH. Items: 16 (short form).
AVAILABILITY. In Ferdinand and Luchterhand, 1970, for the
short form containing only the four most heavily weighted
items for each area.
ABSTRACTED BY: Kersti Yllo
REFERENCE.
       Ferdinand,T.N. and Luchterhand,E.G. Inner-city youth,
the police, the juvenile court, and justice. Social
Problems, 17, 1969-1970, 510-527.

FINNEY,J.C. Maternal Behavior Rating Scales

VARIABLES MEASURED. Maternal: (1) Nurturance, (2)
Hostility, (3) Select time reinforcement of dependence, (4)
Failure to be firm, (5) Rigidity, (6) Achievement need, and
(7) Hysterical character.
TEST DESCRIPTION. Two sets of rating scales to be used in
conjunction with a standard interview. In first set, 5- or
7-point ratings are made on the scales: a rigidity scale,
six scales for selective reinforcement of dependency, 21
scales for nurturance, 4 for firmness, and 5 for hostility.
The second set consists of 7-point scales ranging from 3,
very true, to -3, completely false: 26 for nurturance, 6
for selective reward of dependency, 39 for firmness or lack
of it, 11 for rigidity, 25 for hostility, 4 for need
achievement, and 6 for repression or hysterical character.
Fifty items cover these qualities in general, and 87 as they
are related to the child. These scales, plus selected items
from the MMPI, are combined to give ratings for each mother.

These are values representing the number of SDs; the rating is from the mean of the clinicians' ratings of the mothers. Rating scores are then summed.

SAMPLE ITEMS. (Nurturance:) When he makes an appeal for help or attention, she responds readily, extending help to him sympathetically. (Hostility:) His angry or aggressive actions are often pleasing to her (though she might not admit it) because she feels resentment against some of the same, or similar people, herself.

LENGTH. Items: 154 ratings.

AVAILABILITY. In Finney, 1959.

REFERENCES.

Finney,J.C. Some maternal influences on children's personality and character. Ph.D. dissertation, Stanford University, 1959.

Finney,J.C. Some maternal influences on children's personality and character. Genetic Psychological Monographs, 1961, 63, 199-278.

Powell,L.F. The effect of extra stimulation and maternal involvement on the development of low-birth weight infants and on maternal behavior. Child Development, 1974, 45, 106-113.

HATTWICK,B.W. Home Factors Rating Scales

VARIABLES MEASURED. The following home factors: (1) Mother favors child, (2) Mother oversolicitous, (3) Mother babies child, (4) Household revolves around child, (5) Mother irresponsible, (6) Mother negligent, (7) House calm, (8) Mother cheerful, (9) Mother fatigued, (10) Mother ill, (11) Mother nervous, (12) Mother impatient, (13) Mother quarrelsome, (14) Child shares homework, (15) Child shares play with parents. An overattentiveness variable is obtained by combining the first four variables.

TEST DESCRIPTION. Three-point frequency of occurrence rating scales to be answered Never occurs, Sometimes occurs, or Usually occurs. Items are rated on the basis of home observations (Hattwick used nursery school teachers). All items are analyzed separately except that items 1-4 are combined to yield an overattentiveness score.

SAMPLE ITEM. See variables measured.

LENGTH. Items: 15.

AVAILABILITY. In Hattwick, 1936.

REFERENCE.

Hattwick,B.W. Interrelations between the preschool child's behavior and certain factors in the home. Child Development, 1936, 7, 200-226.

HELSON,R. Sibling Differences Questionnaire

VARIABLES MEASURED. Differences between siblings in family relationships in terms of: (1) Nonadaptive position in family; (2) Confidence, effort, and initiative; (3)

Symbolic facility and intuitiveness versus practicality;
(4) Indication of rewards for creative activity and, (5)
Parents treating siblings differently.
TEST DESCRIPTION. Each question is scored on a three-point
scale: for true-false questions, True = 3, False = 2, and
Other = 1; for relative to self scale, Stronger = 3, Weaker
= 2, or About the same = 1; for value questions, according
to stress placed by parents. Scores for each subscale are
summed; the higher the score, the greater the difference
between siblings in each category.
SAMPLE ITEM. Our parents treated us differently, with
different expectations. True = 3, False = 2, Other = 1.
LENGTH. Time: 15 minutes. Items: 60.
AVAILABILITY. From NAPS-2.
ABSTRACTED BY: Thomas G. Sparhawk
REFERENCE.
      Helson,R. Effects of sibling characteristics and
parental values on creative interest and achievement.
Journal of Personality, 1968, 36, 589-605.

HILTON,I.R.   Observation   Schedule   for   Mother-Child
Interaction

VARIABLES MEASURED. Dependence-independence of the child
and interference, inconsistency and overreactivity on the
part of the mother.
TEST DESCRIPTION. a two-part observations schedule: Part 1
is designed to systematically record the behavior of the
mother and child in a situation where the child is involved
in a task with the experimenter. The instrument categorizes
responses to positive, neutral and negative reinforcement
for the child's performance on the task (experimental
session schedule). Part 2 is designed to systematically
record and distinguish the behavior of the mother and child
when they are alone after an experimental session. It
records those behaviors that the mother and child might
inhibit in the presence of the experimenter.
SAMPLE ITEM. (Task-oriented suggestions) Code as
interfering: Try to concentrate, You should have put that
piece here. (Dependent-evaluation seeking): Did I do all
right? How should I do it?
LENGTH. Items: Part 1 = 7, Part 2 = 12.
AVAILABILITY. American Documentation Institute. Order
Document 9554 from ADI Auxiliary Publications Project,
Photoduplication Service, Library of Congress, Washington,
D.C. 20540.
ABSTRACTED BY: Irma Hilton
REFERENCE.
      Hilton,I.R. Differences in the behavior of mothers
towards first and later born children. Journal of
Personality and Social Psychology, 1967, 7, 282-290.

JURKOVIC,G.J.   and   PRENTICE,N.M.   Mother-Son Interaction
Ratings

VARIABLES MEASURED. Mother's interaction with her son, in
terms of (1) Conflict, (2) Maternal dominance, (3) Maternal
Hostility,   (4)   Maternal   complexity,   (5)   Maternal
encouragement, and (6) Maternal warmth.
TEST DESCRIPTION. Subjects are presented with three moral
dilemmas (Kohlberg, 1969) and asked to come to a joint
agreement. Conversations are recorded. Each of the
variables is measured by global ratings on a six-point scale
ranging frcm Not present at all in the interaction = 1 to
Strongly present in the interaction = 6.
SAMPLE ITEM. Conflict--The extent to which the mother and
son fail to interact and to resolve their disagreements in a
reciprocal and harmonious fashion, presence of open discord
and inability to reconcile differences.
LENGTH. Time: 15-20 minutes. Items: 6.
AVAILABILITY. In Jurkovic and Prentice, 1974.
ABSTRACTED BY: Thomas G. Sparhawk.
REFERENCES.
     Jurkovic,G.J. and Prentice,N.M. Dimensions of moral
interaction   and   moral   judgment   in   delinquent   and
nondelinquent families. Journal of Consulting and Clinical
Psychology, 1974, 42, 256-262.
        Kohlberg,L.   Stage   and   sequence: the
cognitive-developmental approach to socialization.   In
Goslin,D.A. (Ed.) Handbook of Socialization Theory and
Research. Chicago: Rand McNally, 1969.

KAFFMAN,M.   Parent-Child Relationship Categories (PARC)

VARIABLES MEASURED.   Parental   behavior   patterns   and
parent-child   interaction,   specifically: (1)
Love-acceptance-warmth versus Emotional coldness-rejection;
(2)   Encouragement   of   autonomy versus Restriction of
autonomy;   (3) Fostering adequate frustration tolerance
versus Fostering low-frustration tolerance; (4) Adequate
protection versus Underprotection versus Overprotection;
(5)   Consistency   vs.   Inconsistency;   (6)   Parental
assertiveness versus Parental perplexity;   (7) Adequate
stimulation versus Understimulation vs. Overstimulation.
TEST DESCRIPTION. A modified version of the Schaefer, Bell,
and Bayley (1959) "Maternal Behavior Research Instrument."
The original items of parental behavior have been adapted to
kibbutz-rearing practices for diagnostic and clinical use.
A four-point scale is used to assess each of the seven
parental attitudes included in the instrument. The data on
parent-child interaction are obtained from questionnaires
filled in separately by each one of the parents and the
educators, as well as from a   semi-structured   family
interview conducted by family therapists.

SAMPLE ITEM. I definitely agree, Agree, Have no opinion, Do not agree: A parent must immediately reprimand his own child if, during the time spent with his parents, he appears in dirty or untidy clothing.
LENGTH. Items: Seven polarized parent-child relationship categories.
AVAILABILITY. Kibbutz Child and Family Clinic, Seminar Hakibbutzim, Tel Aviv, Israel and NAPS-2.
ABSTRACTED BY: Mordecai Kaffman
REFERENCES.
    Kaffman,M. Family diagnosis and therapy in child emotional pathology. Family Process, 1965, 4, 241-258.
    Kaffman,M. Family conflict in the psychopathology of the kibbutz child. Family Process, 1972, 11, 171-188.
    Schaefer,E.S. Bell,R.Q. and Bayley,N. Development of a maternal behavior research instrument. Journal of Genetic Psychology, 1959, 95, 83-104.

KAGAN,J. and LEMKIN,J. Parental Attributes Technique

VARIABLES MEASURED. Parental nurturance, Punitiveness, Source of fear, and Competence as perceived by the child.
TEST DESCRIPTION. Three methods are used to get the subject's description of the attributes or characteristics of his own parents: (1) Indirect method. Subject is shown a drawing of a father, mother, boy, and girl; then asked to tell which has certain attributes. (2) Picture method. A set of pictures is presented showing subject a situation in which a parent is nearby. Subject is asked whether the parent is mother or father. (3) Direct method. A series of questions identical to those used in method 1 are asked of the subject in a different order. The subject answers about his/her parents rather than about parents in general.
SAMPLE ITEM. Method 1: Who gives (the boy) (the girl) the most presents? Method 2: Some hands are shown giving the child an ice cream cone. Method 3: Who gives you the most presents? Your mommy or your daddy?
LENGTH. Items: 13 (methods 1 and 3); 10 (method 2).
AVAILABILITY. In Kagan and Lemkin, 1960.
REFERENCE.
    Johnson,O.G. and Bommarito,J.W. Tests and Measurements in Child Development: A Handbook. San Francisco: Jossey-Bass,Inc., 1971, 268.
    Kagan,J. and Lemkin,J. The child's differential perception of parental attributes. Journal of Abnormal Social Psychology, 1960, 61, 440-447.

LEON,G.R. Parent-Child Interaction Scores

VARIABLES MEASURED. For child: (1) Physical aggression, (2) Restlessness, (3) Verbal aggression or commands, (4) Passive non-compliance, and (5) Complaints or helplessness. For mother: (1) Ignores negative or non-cooperative

behavior, (2) Contingencies, (3) Controlling or directing,
(4) Teaching or information, (5) Verbal criticism or
disapproval, (6) Refusal to interact, and (7) Positive
reinforcement.
TEST DESCRIPTION. A set of categories for observing and
recording parent-child behavior as directly observed or as
reflected in response to projective stimuli such as picture
cards. Subjects are observed and coders separately rate
mother's and child's responses per 10-second interval. Leon
(1971) used the following procedure to obtain behavior
samples: (1) A 10-minute free play period, followed by (2)
A child interest questionnaire, administered by the mother,
(3) A jigsaw puzzle, and (4) A wire-basket task requiring
close mother-child interaction.
SAMPLE ITEM. Physical aggression: Acts by the child
against the mother or objects in the room. Forcefully
kicking a chair, the child slamming his hand on the table
top, grabbing and tearing up the questionnaire...
LENGTH. Time: 55 minutes. Items: 5.
AVAILABILITY. From NAPS-2.
ABSTRACTED BY: Thomas G. Sparhawk.
REFERENCE.
Leon,G.R. Case Report: The use of a structured
mother-child interaction and projective material in studying
parent influence on child behavior problems. Journal of
Clinical Psychology, 1971, 27, 413-416.

LYTTON,H. (1) Mother (Father) Rating Scales; (2) Child
Rating Scales

VARIABLES MEASURED. Parental: (1) Use of induction, (2)
Warmth, (3) Psychological rewards, (4) Material rewards, (5)
Enforcement of compliance, (6) Restrictiveness, (7)
Verbal-psychological punishment, (8) Physical punishment,
(9) Amount of play with child, (10) Support of dependence
behavior, (11) Encouragement of mature action, (12)
Monitoring, (13) Social desirability. Child's (1)
Compliance, (2) Emotional dependence (attachment),
(3) Instrumental independence, (4) Internalized standards.
TEST DESCRIPTION. The data are obtained from an interview
with the mother, mother's 24-hour diary, and also direct
observation of the child. The interview is designed for 2-
to 3-year-olds and is partly based on Sears, Maccoby and
Levin (1957). These data provide the information needed to
use a series of five-step rating scales.
SAMPLE ITEM. (From interview): How do you react to X when
he jumps up and does what you have asked him to do? (Reward
system)
LENGTH. Items: 62 interview items.
AVAILABILITY. From NAPS-2.
ABSTRACTED BY: H. Lytton.
REFERENCES.
    Lytton,H. Three approaches to the study of
parent-child interaction: ethological, interview and

experimental. Journal of Child Psychology and Psychiatry, 1973, 14, 1-17.
Lytton, H. Comparative yield of three data sources in the study of parent-child interaction. Merrill-Palmer Quarterly, 1974, 20, 53-64.

MASH, E.J. TERDAL, L.G. AND ANDERSON, K.   Response-Class Matrix

VARIABLES MEASURED. Parent-child interaction. The parent categories are (1) Command, (2) Question-command, (3) Question, (4) Praise, (5) Negative, (6) Interaction, (7) No response. The child categories are (1) Compliance, (2) Independent, (3) Play, (4) Question, (5) Negative, (6) Interaction, (7) No response.
An abstract of this test is given in Johnson, O.G. Tests and Measurements in Child Development: Handbook II. San Francisco: Jossey-Bass, 1976, 843.

MEADOW, K.P. and SCHLESINGER, H.S. Interaction Rating Scale for Mothers and Deaf Children

VARIABLES MEASURED. Twenty-eight aspects of mother-child interaction, including: control, intrusiveness, creativity, anxiety, rigidity, enjoyment of other, irritability, mutual understanding.
TEST DESCRIPTION. Rating scales for evaluating video-taped semi-structured interaction of children and their mothers. The scales have been used with samples of deaf and normal children at three different ages: 2 1/2 to 4 years, 4 1/2 to 6, and 7 1/2 to 9. Ten scales describe the mother's behavior during a video-taped scenario: her approach to interaction with the deaf child, her response to the situation, her personal behavioral style. Fourteen scales describe the child's behavior during the scenario. Ten of these parallel the items describing the mother's behavior. Four additional scales describe the child's speech and response to auditory cues. Four scales describe the reciprocal interaction of mother and child.
SAMPLE ITEM. Controlling directs or initiates most activities, 1 2 3 4 5 6 7 8.
LENGTH. Items: 28 rating scales.
AVAILABILITY. In Schlesinger and Meadow, 1972 and from NAPS-2.
ABSTRACTED BY: K.P. Meadow
REFERENCE.
Schlesinger, H.S. and Meadow, K.P. Sound and Sign: Childhood Deafness and Mental Health. Berkeley: University of California Press, 1972.

MOUSTAKAS,C.E. SIGEL,I.E. and SCHALOCK,H.D. Adult-Child
Interaction Schedule

VARIABLES MEASURED. A predetermined set of general-purpose
observational categories that can be applied to different
types of adult-child interaction. Includes 89 adult and 82
child categories. A scale for recording intensity of
anxiety and hostility accompanies each of the interactive
categories.
TEST DESCRIPTION. Behavior of child (C) and adult (A) is
recorded individually for each five-second period.
Recordings are made in terms of category code letters and
entered on a prepared scoring sheet designed for 16 minutes
of continuous recording, each square representing five
seconds of time. A symbol denoting degree of anxiety or
hostility immediately follows each behavioral entry. The
schedule concentrates primarily on verbal behavior; such
nonverbal behaviors as tone of voice, gestures, and facial
expressions are omitted. Brody (1965) used Bales'
Interaction Process Analysis recording method with these
categories.
SAMPLE ITEM. Attention categories: Nonattention: A
directs his/her attention to something other than C, or C
directs his/her attention to something other than A.
LENGTH. Items: 171.
AVAILABILITY. In Moustakas et al., 1956.
REFERENCES.
      Brody,G.F. Relationship between maternal attitudes and
behavior. Journal of Personality and Social Psychology,
1965, 2, 317-323.
      Johnson,O.G. and Bommarito,J.W. Tests and
Measurements in Child Development: A Handbook. San
Francisco: Jossey-Bass, Inc., 1971, 478.
      Moustakas,C.E. Children in play therapy. New York:
McGraw Hill, 1953.
      Moustakas,C.E. The frequency and intensity of negative
attitudes expressed in play therapy: a comparison of
well-adjusted and disturbed young children. Journal of
Genetic Psychology, 1955, 86, 309-325.
      Moustakas,C.E. and Schalock,H.D. An analysis of
therapist-child interaction in play therapy. Child
Development, 1955, 26, 143-157.
      Moustakas,C.E. Sigel,I.E. and Schalock,H.D. An
objective method for the measurement and analysis of
child-adult interaction. Child Development, 1956, 27,
109-134.

MYERS,T.R. Intra-Family Relationships Questionnaire

VARIABLES MEASURED. (1) Parent-child relationships
(parental supervision, discipline, parental attitudes); (2)
Relations between children (dominance, conflict,
cooperation, jealousy); (3) Relationships between parents
(companionship, conflict, quarrels, dominance); (4)

Parental supervision; and (5) Discipline are reported on as separate parts of the questionnaire.
TEST DESCRIPTION. A questionnaire for children consisting of items answered in most cases by checking a category from Always to Never, Constantly to Never, and so on. The score for supervision is based on summing 23 items, for discipline on 27 items, for parent-child relationships on 30 items, for relations between children on 7 items, and for relations between parents on 17 items. The total score is obtained by adding the scores from each section. Some pupils had no siblings; thus a second total score is entered which disregards the 7 questions concerning sibling relations.

Both the original and revised scoring keys are printed in Myers (1935). The original key used scores based on judgments of the writer and five psychiatrists and social workers. The key was revised by internal consistency item analysis which resulted in the revision of scoring for 14 items. The correlation between scores using the original and revised keys was .994. Anderson (1940) used an adaptation of this instrument in his study.
SAMPLE ITEM. My mother: (1) Pays little attention to what I do, (2) Usually attends to the important things I do, (3) Directs everything I do.
LENGTH. Items: 113.
AVAILABILITY. In Myers, 1935.
REFERENCES.
    Anderson,J.P. A study of the relationship between certain aspects of parental behavior and attitudes and the behavior of junior high school pupils. Teachers College Contribution to Education, 1940, No. 809.
    Myers,T.R. Intra-family relationships and pupil adjustment. Teachers College Contribution to Education, 1935, No. 651.
    Symonds,P.M. Diagnosing Personality and Conduct. New York: Appleton, 1931.

NYE,F.I. Nye Family Relationships Scale

VARIABLES MEASURED. (1) Rejection of parents; (2) Rejection of child; (3) Favorable attitude toward parental discipline; (4) Perception of freedom; (5) Perception of family recreation; (6) Perception of parent disposition; (7) Value agreement with parents; (8) Perception of parental money management; (9) Family communication.
TEST DESCRIPTION. Multiple-choice items (5-11 per scale), usually with frequency of occurrence response categories. Designed for questionnaire administration. Parallel questions are asked for mother and father, making a total of 18 instruments.
SAMPLE ITEM. Do you enjoy letting your father in on your "big moments?" (1) Very much, (2) Somewhat, (3) Hardly at all, (4) Not at all.

LENGTH. Items: 5-11.
AVAILABILITY. In Nye, 1958.
REFERENCES.
    Fraser,G.S.   Parent-adolescent   relationships   and
delinquent   behavior: a   cross-national   comparison.
Sociological Quarterly, 1967, 8, 505-513.
    Nye,F.I. Family Relationships and Delinquent Behavior.
New York: Wiley, 1958.

OSOFSKY,J.D.   and   DANZGER,B.   Parent-Infant   Feeding
Observation Scale

VARIABLES MEASURED.   Parent and infant behaviors during
feeding.
    An abstract of this test is given in Johnson,O.G.
Tests and Measurements in Child Development: Handbook II.
San Francisco: Jossey-Bass, 1976, 824.

RHEINGOLD,H.L. Maternal Care Checklist

VARIABLES MEASURED. Operations mother performs in caring
for infant.
TEST DESCRIPTION. A technique for observing and recording
maternal care activities. Items on a checklist are marked
once every 15 seconds for the first 10 minutes of each
quarter hour from 9 a.m. to 1 p.m. of first day and from 1
p.m. to 5 p.m. of second. Of 42 items in the checklist,
16 are under the heading maternal care-taking. The score is
the frequency of occurrence of each item on the checklist
over the 8-hour period for each S.
SAMPLE ITEM. Looks at face, talks, pats, and so forth.
LENGTH. Items: 16.
AVAILABILITY. In Rheingold, 1960.
REFERENCES.
    Candill,W. and Weinstein,H. Maternal care and infant
behavior in Japanese and American urban middle class
families. In Hill,R. and Konig,R. (Eds.) Families in East
and West. Paris: Mouton, 1970.
    Johnson,O.G.   and   Bommarito,J.W.   Tests   and
Measurements in Child Development: A Handbook. San
Francisco: Jossey-Bass, Inc., 1971, 331.
    Rheingold,H.L. The measurement of maternal care.
Child Development, 1960, 31, 565-575.

RUBENSTEIN,J.L.   YARROW,L.J.   PEDERSON,F.A.   FIVEL,M.
DURFEE,J. and JANKOWSKI,J.J. Mother-Infant Observation

VARIABLES MEASURED. Mother-infant interaction.
    An abstract of this test is given in Johnson,O.G.
Tests and Measurements in Child Development: Handbook II.
San Francisco: Jossey-Bass, 1976, 819.

SCHAEFER,E.S. Children's Reports of Parental Behavior

VARIABLES MEASURED. Parental behaviors toward the child.
Molar dimensions and concepts (in parentheses) are:
autonomy (extreme autonomy, lax discipline); autonomy and
love (moderate autonomy, encouraging sociability,
encouraging independent thinking, equalitarian treatment);
love (positive evaluation, sharing, expression of affection,
emotional support); love and control (intellectual
stimulation, child-centeredness, possessiveness,
protectiveness); control (intrusiveness, suppression of
aggression, control through guilt, parental direction);
control and hostility (strictness, punishment, nagging);
hostility (irritability, negative evaluation, rejection);
hostility and autonomy (neglect, ignoring).
TEST DESCRIPTION. Scales for each concept are listed in the
parentheses above. Separate forms for mother and father are
given to children in contrabalanced order in a single
testing session. Each of the 26 scales contains 10 items to
which the subject responds in a Yes-No or True-False manner.
(Scores could be derived by summing Yes answers for each
scale or by some other method, although no summation
procedure is specified.) Schluderman and Schluderman (1970)
developed a shortened version (18 scales, 5 or 8 items per
scale) which consistently revealed three major factors:
acceptance, psychological control, and firm control. A
scoring procedure, emphasizing the three basic dimensions,
accompanies the shortened version. Raskin et al. (1971)
used a shortened, 90-item version of the CRPBI to measure
memories of parental behavior by normal and depressed,
hospitalized patients.
SAMPLE ITEM. (Extreme autonomy:) Allows me to go out as
often as I please. Lets me go any place I please without
asking.
LENGTH. Items: 260 (10 for each of the 26 scales) in
Schaefer's version. Time: 30-45 minutes. Items: 108 in
Schluderman and Schluderman's shortened version.
AVAILABILITY. Both original and revised versions from NAPS.
Schluderman and Schluderman's version from authors.
REFERENCES.
    Armentrout,J.A. Relationships among preadolescents'
reports of their parents' child-rearing behaviors.
Psychological Reports, 1970, 27, 695-700.
    Armentrout,J.A. Parental child-rearing attitudes and
preadolescents' problem behaviors. Journal of Consulting
and Clinical Psychology, 1971, 37, 278-285.
    Armentrout,J.A. Sociometric classroom popularity and
children's reports of parental child-rearing behaviors.
Psychological Reports, 1972, 30, 261-262.
    Armentrout,J.A. and Burger,G.K. Children's report of
parental child-rearing behavior at five grade levels.
Developmental Psychology, 1972, 7, 44-48.
    Biller,H.B. and Zung,B. Perceived maternal control,
anxiety, and opposite sex role preference among elementary
school girls. Journal of Psychology, 1972, 81, 85-88.

Bourdon,K.H.   and   Silber,D.E.   Perceived   parental
behavior among stutterers and non-stutterers. Journal of
Abnormal Psychology, 1970, 75, 93-97.
Burger,G.K.   and Armentrout,J.A. A factor analysis of
fifth and sixth graders' reports of parental childrearing
behavior. Developmental Psychology, 1971, 4, 483.
Carrow,R.A.   A comparative study of the family
relationships   of   immigrant   Chinese and Puerto Rican
children. Graduate Research in Education and Related
Disciplines, 1969, 4, 85-87.
Crandall,V.C. The antecedents and adult correlates of
academic and intellectual achievement effort. In Pick,A.D.
(Ed.) Minnesota Symposia on Child Psychology, Vol. 4.
Minneapolis: University of Minnesota Press, 1970.
Cross,H.J.   College students' memories of their
parents: a factor analysis of the CRPBI.   Journal of
Consulting and Clinical Psychology, 1969, 33, 275-278.
Cross,H.J. and Aron,R.D. Relationship of unobtrusive
measures of marital conflict to remembered differences
between parents. Reprinted from the Proceedings, 79th
Annual Convention, American Psychological Association, 1971,
365-366.
Datta,L.E.   and Parloff,M.B.   On the relevance of
autonomy: parent-child relationships and early scientific
creativity. Proceedings, 75th Annual Convention, American
Psychological Association, 1967, 149-150.
Davis,G.L. and Cross,H.J. College student drug users'
memories of their parents. Adolescence, 1973, 8, 475-480.
Davis,W.L.   and Phares,E.J.   Parental antecedents of
internal-external control of reinforcement. Psychological
Reports, 1969, 24, 427-536.
Doherty,A.   Influence of parental cotrol on the
development of feminine sex role and conscience.
Developmental Psychology, 1970, 2, 157-158.
Droppelman,L.F. and Schaefer,E.S. Boys' and girls'
reports of maternal and paternal behavior. Journal of
Abnormal Social Psychology, 1963, 67, 648-654.
Fish,K.D.   and   Biller,H.B.   Perceived   childhood
paternal relationships and college females' personal
adjustment. Adolescence, 1973, 8, 415-420.
Hicks,J.W. The father-son relationship as perceived by
low, average and high achieving ninth grade boys. Master's
Thesis. University of Wisconsin, Madison, Wisconsin, 1965.
Lauterbach,C.G. Schaefer,E.S. and Vogel,W. Reports
of parent behavior and the MMPIS of psychiatrically
disturbed soldiers. American Psychologist, 1964, 19, 486.
(Abstract)
Raskin,A. Bothe,H.H. Reatig,N.A. Schulterbrandt,J.G.
and Odle,D. Factor analyses of normal and depressed
patients' memories of parental behavior. Psychological
Reports, 1971, 29, 871-979.
Renson,G.J. Belgian children's perception of parent
behavior as measured by Schaefer's Technique. Master's
Thesis, George Washington University, Washington,D.C., 1965.
Renson,G.J.   Schaefer,E.S.   and   Levy,B.I.

Cross-national validity of a spherical conceptual model for parent behavior. Child Development, 1968, 39, 1229-1235.

Reuter,M.W. and Biller,H.B. Perceived paternal nurturance availability and personality adjustment among college males. Journal of Consulting and Clinical Psychology, 1973, 40, 339-342.

Rode, A. Perceptions of parental behavior among alienated adolescents. Adolescence, 1971, 6, 19-38.

Schaefer,E.S. A configurational analysis of children's reports of parent behavior. Journal of Consulting Psychology, 1965a, 29, 552-557.

Schaefer,E.S. Children's reports of parental behavior: an inventory. Child Development, 1965b, 36, 413-424.

Schaefer,E.S. and Bayley,N. Validity and consistency of mother-infant observations, adolescent maternal interviews, and adult retrospective reports of maternal behavior. Proceedings, 75th Annual Convention, American Psychological Association, 1967, 147-148.

Schaefer,E.S. and Lauterbach,C.G. Mapping the projections of child variables upon a spherical parent-behavior model and vice versa. American Psychologist, 1965b, 20, 502 (Abstract).

Schludermann,S. and Schludermann,E. Replicability of factors in children's report of parent behavior (CRPBI). Journal of Psychology, 1970, 76, 239-249.

Schludermann,S. and Schludermann,E. Adolescent perception of parent behavior (CRPBI) in Hutterite communal society. Journal of Psychology, 1971, 79, 29-39.

Vogel,W. and Lauterbach,C.G. Relationships between normal and disturbed sons' percepts of their parents' behavior and personality attributes of the parents and sons. Journal of Clinical Psychology, 1963, 19, 52-56.

Vogel,W. Lauterbach,C.G. Livingston,M. and Halloway,H. Relationship between memories of their parents' behavior and psychodiagnosis in psychiatrically disturbed soldiers. Journal of Consulting Psychology, 1964, 28, 126-132.

Woods,M.B. The unsupervised child of the working mother. Developmental Psychology, 1972, 6, 14-25.

SCHAEFER,E.S. BELL,R.Q. and BAYLEY,N. Maternal Behavior Research Instrument

VARIABLES MEASURED. Form I: Rating scales for quantifying observations on the following aspects of maternal behavior: ignoring, perceive child as burden, emotional involvement, use of fear tc control child, fostering dependency, intelligence, equalitarianism, anxiety, rejection of the homemaking role, expression of affection, irritability, positive evaluation, sociability, achievement demand, concern about health of child, autonomy of child, strictness, punitiveness, intrusiveness, excessive contact, financial stress, punishment, competitiveness, poor physical health of mother, overconscientiousness, mood swings, narcissism, self-abasement, negative emotional state, suppression of aggression, cooperativeness, dependency of mother. Form II: Rating scales for quantifying interview data on the first 19 maternal behavior variables listed above together with: marital happiness, positive emotional state, positive mother-child relationship, wish to control, communicativeness, social isolation, withdrawal. Variables on Form II with different names on Form I include cooperation, dependency cf mother.

TEST DESCRIPTION. Form I: Notes on observations of 56 mothers at the Institute of Child Welfare, University of California, were used to rate each trait from Not at all true = 1 through Average = 4 to Extremely = 7. These observations were taken during the first three years of the child's life at one-month intervals for the first 15 months, three-month intervals thereafter. Those traits on which judges showed little agreement were omitted. Each subject's total score on a concept is determined by adding the scores for the traits. Each judge's distribution of total scores was transformed into a standard score distribution equating means and variances.

Form II: The original concepts of Form I and the traits defining them were retained whenever possible. Some traits were added, however, and there are some differences in the titles of variables (see Variables Measured). The same procedures were used to rate, judge, and score the interview material as were used for the observation material except that no attempt was made to maximize interjudge reliabilities by eliminating traits.

SAMPLE ITEM. (Form I:) Does this mother ignore or reject her child? (1) Does she often comment on how much extra work or trouble the child is? (2) Does she tend to "leave the situation" during the examination as though she is glad the baby is in someone else's hands? (3) Would she be willing to have others assume most of the responsibility for care of the child? (4) Does the mother seem to know very little about the child? (5) Does she tend to overlook the needs of the child? (6) Does she give the impression that the child is not necessarily her principal interest? (7) Does she fail to show much beyond polite interest in the child during the examination? (The items on Form II are similar to those on Form I.)

LENGTH. Time: Majority cf mothers attended 10-20 sessions. Items: Form I, 165 specific items within 32 area questions; Form II, 156 specific items within 28 area questions.

AVAILABILITY. In Schaefer et al., 1959.

REFERENCES.

Bayley,N. Mental growth during the first three years: A developmental study of 61 children by repeated tests. Genetic Psychological Monographs, 1933, 14, 1-91.

Bayley,N. and Schaefer,E.S. Maternal behavior and personality development data from the Berkeley growth study. Psychiatric Research Report, 1960, 13, 155-173.

Bayley,N. and Schaefer,E.S. Relationships between socioeconomic variables and the behavior of mothers toward

young children. Journal of Genetic Psychology, 1960, 96, 61-77.
        Brody,G.F. Relationship between maternal attitudes and behavior. Journal of Personality and Social Psychology, 1965, 2, 317-323.
        Jones,H.E. and Bayley,N. The Berkeley growth study. Child Development, 1941, 12, 167-173.
        Kaffman,M. Family diagnosis and therapy in child emotional pathology. Family Process, 1965, 4, 241-258.
        Kaffman,M. Family conflict in the psychopathology of the kibbutz child. Family Process, 1972, 11, 171-188.
        Schaefer,E.S. A circumplex model for maternal behavior. Journal of Abnormal Social Psychology, 1959, 59, 226-235.
        Schaefer,E.S. Converging conceptual models for maternal behavior and for child behavior. In Glidewell,J.C. (Ed.) Parental Attitudes and Child Behavior. Springfield, Illinois: Charles C Thomas, 1961, 124-146.
        Schaefer,E.S. and Bayley,N. Consistency of maternal behavior from infancy to preadolescence. Journal of Abnormal Social Psychology, 1960, 61, 1-6.
        Schaefer,E.S. Bell,R.Q. and Bayley,N. Qualification of maternal behavior and consistency of mother-child interaction. American Psychologist, 1957, 12, 401.
        Schaefer,E.S. Bell,R.Q. and Bayley,N. Development of a maternal behavior research instrument. Journal of Genetic Psychology, 1959, 95, 83-104.

SCHAEFER,E.S. and FINKELSTEIN,N.W. Child Behavior Toward The Parent Inventory

VARIABLES MEASURED. Child behavior toward the parent.
        An abstract of this test is given in Johnson,O.G. Tests and Measurements in Child Development: Handbook II. San Francisco: Jossey-Bass, 1976, 747.

SEARS,R.R. MACCOBY,E.E. and LEVIN,H. Child-Rearing Practices Scales

VARIABLES MEASURED. Complete range of child-rearing practices, especially with reference to feeding, toilet training, dependency, sex, aggression, restrictions and demands, techniques of training, development of conscience, and so forth.
TEST DESCRIPTION. (1) A comprehensive interview schedule of 72 open-ended questions with follow-up probes for many of them, designed to elicit all of the child-rearing practices of mothers covering the first five years of a child's life, including the period of pregnancy. (2) A group of scales (N=143) used to quantify the interview material. The scales were developed according to the degrees of difference which could be distinguished by a panel of 10 graduate student judges and thus differ in number of degrees. For example,

the "rejection of child by father" scale is a Yes-or-No
(i.e., a two-point) scale, whereas the "extent of use of
physical punishment" scale has seven intervals.
   Lytton's (1973) parent-child interview was patterned on
that used by Sears, Maccoby and Levin (1957). Questions
were geared to slightly different issues, those being the
mother's perceptions of the child's characteristics and her
own habitual practices and attitudes to child-rearing.
   The "Child Rearing Practices Scale" has been the basis
for the adaptation of a child-parent interaction technique
(Baumrind, 1972).
SAMPLE ITEM. Mother's responsiveness to infant's crying.
Unresponsive = 1; Highly responsive = 9.
LENGTH. Items: 72 for interview schedule; 143 for rating
scales.
AVAILABILITY. In Sears et al., 1957.
REFERENCES.

   Baron,K. Dielman,T.E. and Cattell,R.B. Child-rearing
practices and achievement in school. Journal of Genetic
Psychology, 1974, 124, 155-164.
   Barsch,R.H. The Parent of the Handicapped Child,
Springfield, Illincis: Charles C Thomas Publishers, 1968.
   Baumrind,D. The development of instrumental competence
through socialization. Minnesota Symposia on Child
Psychology, Vol. 7. Minneapolis: University of Minnesota
Press, 1972, 3-46.
   Becker,W.C. Peterson,D.R. Luria,Z. Shoemaker,D.J.
and Hellmer,L.A. Relations of factors derived from
parent-interview ratings to behavior problems of
5-year-olds. Child Development, 1962, 33, 509-535.
   Blau,Z.S. Class structure, mobility and change in
child rearing. Socicmetry, 1965, 28, 210-219.
   Dielman,T.E. Barton,K. and Cattell,R.B.
Cross-validation evidence on the structure of parental
reports of child-rearing practices. Journal of Social
Psychology, 1973, 90, 243-250.
   Dielman,T.E. and Cattell,R.B. The prediction of
behavior problems in 6-to-8-year-old children from mothers'
reports of child-rearing practices. Journal of Clinical
Psychology, 1972, 28, 13-17.
   Dielman,T.E. Cattell,R.B. Lepper,C. and Rhoades,P.A.
A check on the structure of parental reports of
child-rearing practices. Child Development, 1971, 42,
893-903.
   Dielman,T.E. Cattell,R.B. and Rhoades,P.A.
Child-rearing antecedents of early school child personality
factors. Journal of Marriage and the Family, 1972, 34,
431-436.
   Lytton,H. Three approaches to the study of
parent-child interaction: ethological, interview and
experimental. Journal of Child Psychology and Psychiatry,
1973, 14, 1-17.
   Milton,G.A. A factor-analytic study of child-rearing
behavior. Child Development, 1958, 29, 381-392.
   Mussen,P.H. and Parker,A.L. Mother nurturance and

girls' incidental imitative learning. Journal of Personality and Social Psychology, 1965, 2, 94-97.

Osofsky,J.D. and O'Connell,E.J. Parent child interaction: daughters' effects upon mothers' and fathers' behaviors. Developmental Psychology, 1972, 7, 157-168.

Papanek,M.L. Authority and sex roles in the family. Journal of Marriage and the Family, 1969, 31, 88-96.

Peterson,D.R. and Migliorino,G. Pancultural factors of parental behavior in Sicily and the United States. Child Development, 1967, 38, 967-999.

Prothro,E.T. Socialization and social class in a transitional society. Child Development, 1966, 37, 219-228.

Sears,R.R. Comparison of interviews with questionnaires for measuring mother attitudes toward sex and aggression. Journal of Personality and Social Psychology, 1965, 2, 37-44.

Sears,R.R. Maccoby,E.E. and Levin,H. Patterns of child rearing. New York: Row, 1957.

Sollenberger,R.T. Chinese-American child-rearing practices and juvenile delinquency. Journal of Social Psychology, 1968, 74, 13-23.

SEARS,R.R. WHITING,J.W.M. NOWLIS,V. and SEARS,P.S. Child-Rearing Procedures Rating Scales

VARIABLES MEASURED. (1) Infancy frustration, (2) Current frustration, (3) Current nurturance, (4) Maternal punitiveness, (5) Maternal responsiveness.
TEST DESCRIPTION. A set of 10-point graphic rating scales, defined by a title and a descriptive phrase indicating the nature of the extreme points. The scales were developed for rating transcripts of intensive interviews focused on child-training practices. There are 12 basic scales, and six formed by combinations of the basic scales converted to standard scores: (M27) scheduling versus self-demand; (M28) severity of weaning; (M39) toilet-training frustration; (M147) total infancy frustration--sum of M27, M28, and M39; (M149) total nursing and weaning frustration--sum of M27 and M28; (M31) eating frustration; (M40) sickness and danger frustration; (M41) orderliness and cleanliness frustration; (M144) total current frustration--sum of M31, M40, and M41; (M146) total current and infancy frustration--sum of M144 and M147; (M32) nurturance at bedtime and at night; (M34) nurturance when mother is busy; (M36) apparent general nurturance of father; (M38) nurturance when child is sick, upset, or injured; (M142) total current nurturance--sum of M32, M34, M36, and M38; (M145) total current frustration and non-nurturance--sum of M144 and M142; (M57) punitiveness; (M59) responsiveness to aggression.
SAMPLE ITEM. (M27, scheduling versus self-demand:) (10) Complete self-demand nursing schedule; Always feeds child when he cries; Permits child to eat as much as he wants at each feeding; Permits child to nurse or retain bottle for

as many years as he wants; Continues night feeding as long
as the child awakes; and so forth. (1) Rigid feeding
schedule; Feeds child by the clock rather than by demand;
Weans early (e.g., 6 months or less); Doesn't feed child if
he wakes up at night.
LENGTH. Time (for interview coded by these scales): 2 1/2
to 4 hours. Items: 15 general topics covered in the
interview, each with many specific questions.
AVAILABILITY. Scales are given in Sears et al., 1953.
Interview outline (not the specific questions) is also given
in this reference.
REFERENCES.
      Campbell,D.T.   and   Fiske,D.W.   Convergent   and
discriminant   validation   by   the   multitrait-multimethod
matrix. Psychological Bulletin, 1959, 56, 81-105.
      DeLissovoy,V. High school marriages: a   longitudinal
study.   Journal   of   Marriage   and   the   Family,   1973, 35,
245-255.
      Lynn,R.   Personality   characteristics   of   mothers   of
aggressive   and   unaggressive   children.   Journal of Genetic
Psychology, 1961, 99, 159-164.
      Sears,R.R.   Whiting,J.W.M.   Nowlis,V.   and   Sears,P.S.
Some   child-rearing   antecedents of aggression and dependency
in young children. Genetic Psychology Monographs, 1953, 47,
135-236.

SINAY,R.D.   YSIN,A.   and NIHIRA,K.   Parental Attitude   Scale
(PAS)

VARIABLES MEASURED. Parent's report of   their   adolescent's
behavior   in   respect   to: (1) Positive   parent-child
communication,   (2) Depreciatory behaviors,   (3) Positive
affectional expression, (4) Negative affectional expression,
(5) Externally disciplined behaviors,   (6)   Self-disciplined
behaviors,   (7)   Prosocial   behaviors,   (8)   Antisocial
behaviors, and (9) Drug-taking behaviors.
      An abstract of this test is given in Johnson,O.G.
Tests   and   Measurements in Child Development: Handbook II.
San Francisco: Jossey-Bass, 1976, 1115.

STAYTON,D.J.   HOGAN,R.   and   AINSWORTH,M.D.S.   Maternal
Behavior Measures

VARIABLES MEASURED.   Degree   of   harmony   in   mother-infant
interaction: (1)   Sensitivity-insensitivity,   (2)
Acceptance-rejection, and (3) Cooperation-interference,   (4)
Frequency   of   verbal   commands,   (5) Frequency of physical
intervention, and (6) Extent of floor   freedom.   Also,   (7)
Compliance to commands and (8) Internalized controls.
TEST DESCRIPTION. A method for rating narrative reports of
home   observations   of mothers and their infants.   There are
three rating scales (1,2,3 above),   three   count   variables
(4,5,6 above),   and   two infant behavior variables (7 and 8

above).
SAMPLE ITEM. The acceptance-rejection scale focuses on the
balance between a mother's positive and negative feelings
about her baby and on the extent to which she has been able
to integrate and resolve these conflicting feelings.
       Floor freedom refers to the degree to which a baby was
permitted to be free on the floor or in a walker during
his/her waking hours. Internalized controls refers to
self-inhibiting, self-controlling behavior.
LENGTH. Time: Four one-hour sessions at three-week
intervals during the first year of life. Items: 8
observation categories.
AVAILABILITY. From NAPS. Order Document Number 01594.
ABSTRACTED BY: Thomas G. Sparhawk.
REFERENCES.
       Ainsworth,M.D.S.   Bell,S.M.   and   Stayton,D.J.
Individual differences in the development of some attachment
behaviors. Merrill-Palmer Quarterly, 1972, 18, 123-143.
       Stayton,D.J. Hogan,R. and Ainsworth,M.D.S. Infant
obedience and maternal behavior: the origins of
socialization reconsidered. Child Development, 1971, 42,
1057-1069.

STOLIAK,G.E. Sensitivity to Children Questionnaire

VARIABLES MEASURED. The following factors in adult
communications with children in problem situations: (1)
Lecturing-directing, (2) Power assertion-control, (3) Adult
expression of child's influence upon them, (4) Empathy, (5)
Ridicule-interrogation, (6) Instrumental control.
TEST DESCRIPTION. Subject is asked to respond to projective
items. Instructions are: "A series of situations will be
found on the following pages. You are to pretend or imagine
you are the parent (mother or father) of the child
described. All the children in the following situations are
to be considered six years old. Your task is to write down
exactly how you would respond to the child in each of the
situations, in a word, sentence or short paragraph. Write
down your exact words and/or actions, but please do not
explain why you said what you described. Again, write down
your exact words or actions as if you were writing a script
for a play or movie (e.g., do not write "I would reassure or
comfort him," instead, for example, write "I would smile at
him and in a quiet voice say, "Don't worry, Billy, Daddy and
I love you!")"
       Each item is scored for the variables listed above.
Category scores across items can be summed. Item scores as
well as factor scores are used in data analyses.
SAMPLE ITEM. Your son, Carl, comes running in the house
yelling, "I won! I won!" He bumps right into you and knocks
over a glass of water you had in your hand, the glass
falling to the floor and the water spilling over your
clothes.

LENGTH. Time: 15-30 minutes. Items: 8 or 16 (STC I and/or II)
AVAILABILITY. From G.E. Stollak or NAPS-2.
ABSTRACTED BY: Gary E. Stollak.
REFERENCES.
    Kallman,J.R. and Stollak,G.E. Maternal behavior toward children in need-arousing situations. Paper presented at the annual meeting of the Midwestern Psychological Association, Chicago, 1974.
    Stollak,G.E. An integrated graduate-undergraduate program in the assessment, treatment, and prevention of child psychopathology. Professional Psychology, 1973, 4, 158-169.
    Stollak,G.E.   Scholom,A.   Kallman,J.R.   and Saturansky,C. Insensitivity to children: responses of undergraduates to children in problem situations. Journal of Abnormal Child Psychology, 1973, 4, 158-169.
    Stollak,G.E. Scholom,A. Schreiber,J. Green,L. and Messe,L. The process and outcome of play encounters between undergraduates and clinic-referred children: preliminary findings. Psychotherapy: Theory, Research and Practice (in press).

TULKIN,S.R. and KAGAN,J. Maternal Behavior Measures

VARIABLES MEASURED. Nine aspects of mother's behavior in relation to her infant.
TEST DESCRIPTION. Observers code each of the following variables at five-second intervals: Location (distance of mother from infant), Physical contact, Prohibitions (mother interfered with child), or Maternal vocalization (mother says words to child), and Keeping infant busy (mother provides activity). Other variables measure the sequences of mother and infant behaviors: Positive response to nonverbal behavior, Percentage of reciprocal vocalization, Response to child's frets and, Interaction (both mother and child acting in response to each other).
SAMPLE ITEM. Location: distance of mother from infant, coded each time it changes. (a) Face to face, (b) Within two feet (within arm's distance), (c) More than two feet away.
LENGTH. Time: 2 hours on 2 days. Items: 9.
AVAILABILITY. Tulkin and Kagan, 1972.
ABSTRACTED BY: Thomas G. Sparhawk.
REFERENCES.
    Tulkin,S.R. and Cohler,B.J. Childrearing attitudes and mother-child interaction in the first year of life. Merrill-Palmer Quarterly, 1973, 19, 95-106.
    Tulkin,S.R. and Kagan,J. Mother-child interaction in the first year of life. Child Development, 1972, 43, 31-41.

TYLER,F.B.   TYLER,B.B.   and RAFFERTY,J.E.   Parent-Child Need
Assessment

VARIABLES MEASURED.   Five general need categories: (1)
Recognition-status,   (2)   Protection-dependency,   (3)
Dominance, (4) Independence, (5) Love and affection.   Need
potential of these needs is measured in terms of need value
and freedom of movement.
TEST DESCRIPTION.   Parent-interview and child-observation
protocols are scored on all variables except that parents
are not given scores for protection-dependency or
independence. Scoring rationale allows for consideration of
the situation or context of the need in assigning importance
to it.   "Need value scores were arrived at by assuming an
inverse relationship between the degree of situational
structure and the need importance required to elicit a
response." The freedom of movement (expectancy) variable is
measured by the "constructive-defensive quality of the
behavior...That is, direct friendly overtures or
unhesitating and enthusiastic affectional behaviors are
thought to indicate high expectancy;   tentative behaviors,
abortive attempts to initiate friendly interactions,
withdrawal, etc., are thought to indicate low expectancy or
freedom of movement." Scores are obtained by rating the
variables on seven-point scales.   Preliminary
scoring-by-example manuals were developed for ratings.
Tyler (1960) describes the scoring method for love and
affection need value.
SAMPLE ITEM. See Tyler, 1960, 812-813.
LENGTH. Items: 10 scored variables.
AVAILABILITY. From NAPS.
REFERENCES.
     Rafferty,J.E.   Tyler,B.B.   and Tyler,F.B.   Personality
assessment from free play observations. Child Development,
1960, 31, 691-702.
     Tyler,B.B.   Tyler,F.B.   and Rafferty,J.E.   A systematic
approach to interviewing as a method of personality
assessment.   Paper read at American Psychological
Association meeting, Cincinnati, September 1959.
     Tyler,B.B.   Tyler,F.B.   and Rafferty,J.E.   The
development of behavior patterns in children.   Genetic
Psychology Monographs, 1966, 74, 165-213.
     Tyler,F.B.   A conceptual model for assessing
parent-child motivations.   Child Development, 1960, 31,
807-815.
     Tyler,F.B.   Tyler,B.B.   and Rafferty,J.E.   Need value
and expectancy interrelations as assessed from motivational
patterns of parents and their children.   Journal   of
Consulting Psychology, 1961, 25, 304-311.
     Tyler,F.B.   Tyler,B.B.   and   Rafferty,J.E.
Relationships among motivation of parents and their
children. Journal of Genetic Psychology, 1962a, 101, 69-81.
     Tyler,F.B.   Tyler,B.B.   and Rafferty,J.E.   A threshold
conception of need value. Psychology Monographs, 1962b, 76,
No. 11.

WHITING,J.W.M.   CHILD,I.L.   and   LAMBERT,W.W.   Child
Socialization Techniques Scales

VARIABLES MEASURED. Twelve aspects of child socialization:
Warmth of mother, Hostility of mother, Positiveness versus
Negativeness of rules, Communication of rules, Consistency
of aggression rules, Amount of praise, Consistency of
mother's follow-through on routine responsibilities and
nonroutine demands for obedience, Frequency and intensity of
physical punishment, teasing, and ridicule, Contingency of
privilege and material gifts, and Referent of praise and
punishment.
TEST DESCRIPTION. Twelve rating scales (rated from 1 to 7)
concerning child socialization techniques used by mothers or
mother surrogates. These scales are scored based on casual
observation of mother-child interaction in the field
setting.
SAMPLE ITEM. Contingency of warmth of mother. Mother's
expression of warmth is largely independent of the child's
behavior: does not use warmth as a reward or punishment =
1; Mother's expression of warmth is entirely contingent:
manipulates her affection mainly to incite, reward, or
punish the child = 7.
LENGTH. Repeated observation of the family over an
unspecified time period.
AVAILABILITY. In Whiting, et al., 1966.
ABSTRACTED BY: Bruce Brown.
REFERENCE.
    Whiting,J.W.M.   Child,I.L.   and   Lambert,W.W.   Field
Guide for a Study of Socialization. New York: John Wiley
and Sons, Inc., 1966, 140-143.

WHITING,J.W.M.   CHILD,I.L.   and   LAMBERT,W.W.   Maternal
Behavior Factor Indexes

VARIABLES MEASURED. Seven aspects of maternal behavior
toward the child: Maternal warmth, Maternal instability,
Responsibility for baby care, Responsibility for child care,
Responsibility training, and Aggression training in relation
to child-to-mother and child-to-child aggression.
TEST DESCRIPTION. An interview schedule of approximately 84
open-ended questions designed to elicit the child-rearing
practices of mothers with children ranging from 3 to 10
years of age. These data are used to score 28 rating scales
such as "General hostility of mother" (rated from 1 to 7)
and "Degree to which mother is positive when child fights
with other children" (rated from 1 to 9). Factor analysis
of these 28 scales produce seven independent factor indexes.
SAMPLE ITEM. (Rating Scale): Degree to which mother is
positive when child fights with other children. Mother
physically punishes or deprives of privileges = 1; Mother
gives reward or gives active help = 9.

LENGTH. Items: approximately 84.
AVAILABILITY. In Whiting et al., 1966.
ABSTRACTED BY: Bruce Brown.
REFERENCES.
    Minturn,L. and Lambert,W.W. Mothers of Six Cultures.
New York: John Wiley and Sons, Inc., 1964.
    Whiting,J.W.M. Child,I.L. and Lambert,W.W. Field
Guide for Study of Socialization. New York: John Wiley and
Sons, Inc., 1966, 78-82.

WILLIAMS,J.R. and SCOTT,R.B. Child Care Rating Scales

VARIABLES MEASURED. (1) Duration of breast-feeding, (2)
Flexibility of feeding schedule, (3) Age of inception of
bottle-weaning, (4) Food forced against will, (5) Age of
inception of toilet training, (6) Flexibility of sleep
routine, (7) Restrictiveness of discipline, (8) Punitiveness
of attitudes toward nonapproved habits, (9) Area
restriction, (10) Mechanical restriction, (11) Freedom to
experiment, (12) Permission to reach out, (13) Bodily
contact permitted with others, (14) Time permitted with
others, (15) Motor development, (16) Global home atmosphere
(permissive-accepting or rigid-rejecting).
TEST DESCRIPTION. Rating scales to be applied to mother
interview and observation of mother-child interaction.
Ratings are dichotomous (rigid-flexible, yes-no, before 12
months-after 12 months, etc.), except for breast-feeding,
where 4 ratings are possible, depending on its duration.
The more rigid pattern is scored as positive, the flexible
or permissive one as negative.
SAMPLE ITEM. See test description.
LENGTH. Time: approximately 1-hour interview. Items: 15
ratings.
AVAILABILITY. In Williams and Scott, 1953.
REFERENCE.
    Williams,J.R. and Scott,R.B. Growth and development
of Negro infants. IV. motor development and its
relationship to child rearing practices in two groups of
Negro infants. Child Development, 1953, 24, 103-121.

WINDER,C.L. and RAU,L. Stanford Parent Questionnaire

VARIABLES MEASURED. Parental (1) Ambivalence, (2)
Strictness, (3) Aggression and punitiveness, (4) Adjustment,
(5) Models, (6) Mastery. There are subvariables for each
variable, a total of 27 for mothers and 28 for fathers.
TEST DESCRIPTION. Items are answered on a four-point scale
(Strongly agree, Agree, Disagree, Strongly disagree), and a
dichotomous method of scoring is based on the distribution
of answers to each item. Items are summed for each
variable, separate forms for mothers and fathers.
Vernacular phrasing is retained as far as possible. Duncan
(1975) revised the instrument from one appropriate for

preadolescent boys to one appropriate for adolescent girls.
This revision holds the flavor of Winder and Rau's original
SPQ, which uses the language of parents themselves. Eight
scales from the original were omitted as inappropriate or
not sufficiently reliable. The answers are framed in
check-form: Strongly agree, Agree, Disagree and Strongly
disagree for each of the 157 items.
SAMPLE ITEM. NR.
LENGTH. Time: 90 minutes. Items: 518 (fathers), 491
(mothers), 157 (Duncan revision).
AVAILABILITY. From ADI Doc. No. 7091. Duncan revision
from NAPS-2.
REFERENCES.
    Duncan,P. Parental attitudes and interactions in
delinquency. Child Development, 1971, 42, 1751-1765.
    Hetherington,E.M. and Stouwie,R.J. Patterns of family
interaction and child-rearing attitudes related to three
dimensions of juvenile delinquency. Journal of Abnormal
Psychology, 1971, 78, 160-176.
    Hetherington,E.M.   Stouwie,R.J.   and   Ridberg,E.H.
Patterns of family interaction and child-rearing attitudes
related to three dimensions of juvenile delinquency.
Journal of Abnormal Psychology, 1971, 78, 160-176.
    Winder,C.L. and Rau,L. Parental attitudes associated
with social deviance in preadolescent boys. Journal of
Abnormal Social Psychology, 1962, 64, 418-424.

YARROW,M.R.   CAMPBELL,J.D.   and   BURTON,R.V.   Child
Questionnaire   for   Early   Childhood   Behavior   and
Relationships, and Mother Interview of Child Behavior and
Relationships

VARIABLES MEASURED. Mother's and child's recollection of
child's (1) Infant characteristics, (2) Maternal care in
infancy, (3) Developmental process, (4) Familial environment
and child rearing of the first five years, and (5)
Personality characteristics of the child in the pre-school
period.
TEST DESCRIPTION. An interview with the mother and a
parallel questionnaire for the child, containing open-ended
questions (mother) and structured response alternatives
(child). Raters assign scores to the mother's answers to
each question, paralleling the structured responses allowed
the child. A variety of procedures are utilized, ranging
from Yes-No responses to a nine-point scale.
SAMPLE ITEM. Were you a quiet or a lively baby? (child)
Would you say X was a quiet or a lively baby? (mother)
LENGTH. Items: 50.
AVAILABILITY. In Yarrow, Campbell and Burton, 1970.
ABSTRACTED BY: Thomas G. Sparhawk
REFERENCES.
    Yarrow,M.R.   Campbell,J.D.   and   Burton,R.V.
Reliability of maternal retrospection: a preliminary
report. Family Process, 1964, 3, 207-218.

Yarrow,M.R.   Campbell,J.D.   and   Burton,R.V.
Recollection of childhood: a study of the retrospective
method. Monographs of the Society for Research in Child
Development, 1970, 35.

YOURGLICH,A. and SCHIESSL,D. Sibling Systems Scale

VARIABLE MEASURED. The network of actions and expectations
between siblings.
TEST DESCRIPTION. System is conceptualized as a network of
actions and expectations. It is then operationalized as the
frequency cf occurrence of actions and expectations for
actions of subjects with their siblings. It is assumed that
the more actions and expectations a subject has relative to
his/her siblings, the more systemic these relationships are.
A summated rating scale was developed on a sample of college
students. The scale consists of 62 items demonstrated to be
highly discriminatcry. It consists of 21 action statements,
11 general expectation statements, and 30 specific
expectation statements. The reliability coefficient for
this scale on this sample is .92.
SAMPLE ITEM. Action statements: When something very
important happens to you, do you tell your sibling(s) first,
before you tell anyone else? General expectation
statements: Do you enjoy doing things together with your
siblings? Specific expectation statement: When your
sibling makes a decision which involves some behavior of
yours, do you feel responsible for carrying out that
decision?
LENGTH. Time: 1/2 hour. Items: 62.
AVAILABILITY. From NAPS-2.
ABSTRACTED BY: Anita Yourglich
REFERENCES.
        Yourglich,A. Constructing a sibling systems
measurement device. Family Life Coordinator, 1966, 15,
107-111.
        Yourglich,A. A comparative analysis of two studies of
age-sex differentiations in sibling systems. Family Life
Coordinator, 1969, 16, 73-77.

ZUNICH,M. Mother-Child Interaction Test

VARIABLE MEASURED. Mothers' behavior toward children.
TEST DESCRIPTION. This is a frame of reference for use in
observing mother-child "interaction," although the 17
categories refer primarily to the behavior of the mother
toward the child, and involve little if any reciprocal
behavior on the part of the child. Each category has a
name, a short description of the kind of behavior to be
observed, and an example. Thus, the first category is
"Being Uncooperative--for example, Mother ignores the
child's stimulation. Example: Mother continues to read
magazine when child addresses her." Other categories are

"Giving Permission--for example, Mother consents to child's proposed activity. Example: 'Yes, you may use the towel.'" "Observing Attentively--for example, Mother noticeably directs her attention to the child or the child's activity by silently watching. Example: Mother watches child as the child plays with the stove." The total list of categories used is: being uncooperative, contacting, criticizing, directing, giving permission, giving praise or affection, helping, interfering, interfering by structurizing, lending cooperation, observing attentively, playing interactively, reassuring, remaining out of contact, restricting, structurizing, teaching.
SAMPLE ITEM. See above.
LENGTH. Items: 17.
AVAILABILITY. In Zunich, 1962.
ABSTRACTED BY: Kersti Yllo based on Johnson and Bommarito, 1971, 477.
REFERENCE.
     Zunich,M.   Relationship from maternal behavior and attitudes toward children. Journal of Genetic Psychology, 1962, 100, 155-165.

2. Attitudes, Values, Ideology Concerning Parent-Child Relations
(See also Subject Index)

AHSEN,A. Eidetic Parents Test

VARIABLES MEASURED. Images of parents in the mind, including difference between conscious memory, thought and opinion, and what is revealed in imagery and strength of emotions attached to them.
TEST DESCRIPTION. The 30 interview test items evoke painful, pleasurable or conflictual images connected with various parts of parents' bodies in relationship to each other as well as to the patient. Image situations involve house, open space, and interactions in a developmental context involving various parts of parents' figures, such as body movement, eyes and voice experience, images of touch, hand grasp, and brain, heart, intestines, and genital perceptions. The test can be induced in short or long form for inter-family diagnosis as well as for individual diagnosis and psychotherapy. The test provides procedures for developing therapeutic imagery measures out of basic test images.
SAMPLE ITEM. Item 3. As you see your parents standing in front of you, do they appear separated or united as a couple? Describe the character of the space each occupies. Do your spaces differ in temperature and illumination?

LENGTH. Time: 1 hour. Items: 30.
AVAILABILITY. Brandon House, 555 Riverdale Station, New
York, NY 10471.
ABSTRACTED BY: Akhter Ahsen
REFERENCES.
    Ahsen,A. Eidetic Psychotherapy: A Short Introduction.
New York: Brandon House, Inc., 1965.
    Ahsen,A. Basic Concepts in Eidetic Psychotherapy. New
York: Brandon House, 1968.
    Ahsen,A. Eidetic Parents Test and Analysis. New York:
Brandon House, Inc., 1972.
    Ahsen,A. Psycheye. New York: Brandon House, Inc.,
1976.

BELLAK,L. and BELLAK,S.S. Children's Apperception Test

VARIABLES MEASURED. Family roles and accompanying affect.
TEST DESCRIPTION. A projective test for ages 3-10. Subject
tells a story about pictures of anthropomorphized animals in
various situations. Responses are recorded verbatim and
analyzed according to test manual. One variable for which
the protocol is scored is called family roles.
SAMPLE ITEM. Picture 1. Chicks seated around a table on
which there is a large bowl of food. Off to one side is a
large chicken, dimly outlined.
LENGTH. Time: 15-50 minutes. Items: 10 cards.
AVAILABILITY. From CPS Co., P.O. Box 42, Gracie Station,
New York, New York 10028.
REFERENCES.
    Bellak,L. The Thematic Apperception Test and the
Children's Apperception Test in clinical use. New York:
Grune and Stratton, 1954.
    Bellak,L. and Bellak,S.S. Children's Apperception
Test: Manual and CAT recording and analysis blank. New
York: CPS, 1949.
    Bird,E. and Witherspoon,R.L. Responses of preschool
children to the Children's Apperception Test. Child
Development, 1954, 25, 35-44.

BLOCK,J.H. The Child-Rearing Practices Report (CRPR)

VARIABLES MEASURED. Parental child-rearing orientations and
values. Scales include Encouraging openness to experience,
Emphasis on achievement, Authoritarian control, Affective
quality of parent-child relationship, Encouraging
individuation, Suppression of aggression, Tolerance for
expression of affect, Control by anxiety induction, Control
by guilt induction, Emphasis on early training. In all, 21
scales have been developed using factor analytic methods.
TEST DESCRIPTION. The CRPR is composed of 91
socialization-relevant items to be Q-sorted by the
respondent according to detailed instructions into seven
categories with 13 items placed in each category. The items

tap a wide range of parenting orientations and are appropriate for administration to parents heterogeneous with respect to educational level, socioeconomic status, ethnic background, and age. The test is available in the First Person Form for administration to parents and the Third Person Form permitting older children to describe the child-rearing orientations of their mothers and/or fathers. The test has been translated into several languages (Norwegian, Swedish, Danish, Finnish, Croatian, Chinese, Arabic, Dutch) and has been successfully used in cross-cultural research.
SAMPLE ITEMS. First Person Form: I feel a child should have time to think, daydream, and even loaf sometimes. Third Person Form: My mother (father) felt I was a bit of a disappointment to her (him).
LENGTH. Time: 30-45 minutes. Items: 91.
AVAILABILITY. From NAPS-2 or J.H. Block, Institute of Human Development, Tolman Hall, University of California, Berkeley, California 94720.
ABSTRACTED BY: Jeanne Block.
REFERENCES.

Arnell,N. A study of factors which affect maternal teaching styles. Unpublished Masters Thesis, San Francisco State College, 1968.

Biller,H.B. and Bahm,R.M. Father absence, perceived maternal behavior, and masculinity of self-concept among junior high school boys. Developmental Psychology, 1971, 4, 178-181.

Block,J.H. The Q-sort Method in Personality Assessment and Psychiatric Research. Springfield, Illinois: Charles C Thomas, 1961.

Block,J.H. The Child-rearing Practices Report (CRPR): A set of Q items for the description of parental socialization attitudes and values. Berkeley, California: Institute of Human Development, University of California, 1965. In Mimeo.

Block,J.H. Generational continuity and discontinuity in the understanding of societal rejection. Journal of Personality and Social Psychology, 1972, 22, 333-345.

Block,J.H. Conceptions of sex-role: Some cross-cultural and longitudinal perspectives. American Psychologist, 1973, 28, 512-526.

Block,J.H. Another look at sex-differentiation in the socialization behaviors of mothers and fathers. In Denmark,F. and Sherman,J. (Eds.), Psychology of women: Future directions of research. New York: Psychological Dimensions, Inc, 1976.

Block,J. and Block,J.H. Ego development and the provenance of thought: A longitudinal study of ego and cognitive development in young children. Progress Report for National Institute of Mental Health, 1973. Department of Psychology, University of California, Berkeley, California. In Mimeo.

Block,J.H. and Christiansen, B. A test of Hendin's hypotheses relating suicide in Scandinavia to child-rearing orientations. Scandinavian Journal of Psychology, 1966, 7, 267-288.

Block,J.H. Haan,N. and Smith,M.B. Socialization correlates of student activism. Journal of Social Issues, 1969, 25, 143-177.

Block,J.H. Jennings,P.H. Harvey,E. and Simpson,E. Interaction between allergic potential and psychopathology in childhood asthma. Psychosomatic Medicine, 1964, 26, 307-320.

Durrett,M.E. O'Bryant,S. and Pennebaker,J.W. Child-rearing reports of White, Black, and Mexican-American families. Developmental Psychology, 1975, 11, 871.

Feshbach,N.D. Cross-cultural studies of teaching styles in four-year-olds and their mothers. In Pick,A.D. (Ed.) Minnesota Symposia on Child Psychology, Vol. 6. Minneapolis: University of Minnesota Press, 1973, 87-116.

Haan,N. Changes in young adults after Peace Corps experiences: Political-societal views, moral reasoning, and perceptions of self and parents. Journal of Youth and Adolescence, 1974, 3, 177-194.

Haan,N. Smith,M.B. and Block,J.H. The moral reasoning of young adults: Political-social behavior, family background, and personality correlates. Journal of Personality and Social Psychology, 1968, 10, 183-201.

Haley,M.E. Sex differences in internal and external adolescents' perceptions of their child rearing. M.A. Thesis, Purdue University, 1974.

Hesselbart,S.L. Self-concepts, achievement patterns, and perceived parental rearing practices in honors college women. Unpublished Honors Thesis, University of Michigan, 1968.

Mussen,P.H. Rutherford,E. Harris,S. and Keasey,C.B. Honesty and altruism among preadolescents. Developmental Psychology, 1970, 3, 169-194.

Smith,M.B. Haan,N. and Block,J.H. Social-psychological aspects of student activism. Youth and Society, 1970, 1, 261-288.

COBB,H.V. Sentence-Completion Wish Test

VARIABLES MEASURED. The child's wishes concerning a number of personal and inter-personal areas, including nine which deal with desired characteristics and behavior of parents and siblings.
TEST DESCRIPTION. Sentence completion items dealing with the S's wishes about specific and general things. Scoring may be done in various ways.
SAMPLE ITEM. I wish my folks were...
LENGTH. Items: 24.
AVAILABILITY. In Cobb, 1954.
REFERENCE.
Cobb,H.V. Role-wishes and general wishes of children and adolescents. Child Development, 1954, 25, 161-171.

COHLER,B.J.   WEISS,J.L.   and GRUNEBAUM,H.   Maternal Attitude
Scale-Form DD.

VARIABLES MEASURED.   (1) Appropriate control of the child's
aggressive impulses,   (2) Encouragement vs. discouragement
of reciprocity,   (3) Establishment of appropriate vs.
inappropriate closeness with the child, (4) Acceptance vs.
denial of emotional complexity in childrearing, (5) Comfort
vs. discomfort in perceiving and meeting the baby's needs.
TEST DESCRIPTION. The measure consists of 233 items written
to measure attitudes toward the resolution of the issues in
the relationship of mothers and their pre-school children as
described by Sander (1962).   The items use seven-point
Likert-type response categories and are scored into the
second order factor scales described above. Each of the
above factors refers to a particular issue in the early
mother-child relationship.
SAMPLE ITEM. Newborn babies are fragile and delicate and
must be handled extremely carefully (seven-point Likert-type
scales).
LENGTH. Time: 40 minutes. Items: 233.
AVAILABILITY. From NAPS Order Document Number 00963, or
from B.J.Cchler.
ABSTRACTED BY: Bertram J. Cohler.
REFERENCES.
     Cohler,B.J.   Gallant,D.   Grunebaum,H.   Weiss,J.L.   and
Gamer,E.   Child-care attitudes and the child's cognitive
development among hospitalized and nonhospitalized mothers
and their young children. Unpublished paper. Committee on
Human Development, University of Chicago, 1974.
     Cohler,B.J.   Gallant,D.   Grunebaum,H.   Weiss,J.L.   and
Gamer,E.   Child-care attitudes and attention dysfunction
among hospitalized and nonhospitalized mothers and their
young children. In Glidewell,J.C.   (Ed.) The Social Context
of Learning and Development. New York: Gardner-Wiley (in
press).
     Cohler,B.J.   Grunebaum,H.   Weiss,J.L.   Hartman,C.   and
Gallant,D.   Child-care attitudes and adaptation to the
maternal role amcng mentally ill and well mothers. American
Journal of Orthopsychiatry, 1976, 46, 123-134.
     Cohler,B.J.   Grunebaum,H.   Weiss,J.L.   and Moran,D.
The child-care attitudes of two generations of mothers.
Merrill-Palmer Quarterly, 1971, 17, 3-71.
     Cohler,B.J.   Weiss,J.L.   and Grunebaum,H.   Child-care
attitudes and emctional disturbance among mothers of young
children. Genetic Psychology Monographs, 1970, 82, 3-47.
     Cohler,B.J.   Woolsey,S.   Weiss,J.L.   and Grunebaum,H.
Childrearing attitudes among mothers volunteering and
revolunteering for a psychological study. Psychological
Reports, 1968, 23, 603-612.
     Sander,L. Issues in early mother-child interaction.
Journal of the Academy of Child Psychiatry, 1962, 2,
141-166.
     Tulkin,S.R.   and Cohler,B.J.   Childrearing attitudes
and mother-child interaction in the first year of life.

Merrill-Palmer Quarterly, 1973, 19, 95-106.

DUVALL,E.M. Family Ideology Technique

VARIABLES MEASURED. Role prescription for "a good mcther" and "a good child" (Duvall, 1946). Areas (work, school, siblings, etc.) toward which forces (parental pressures) on the child are directed (Middleton, 1954).
TEST DESCRIPTION. Two open-ended questions patterned after Bavelas's group ideology technique (1942). Answers are categorized as traditional or developmental using criteria presented in Duvall (1946). In the Middleton (1954) adaptation of the test, the child is asked what are good things he/she does at home, what are very good things, and best things, and similarly for bad things he/she does. Responses are classified by both positive and negative mention.
SAMPLE ITEM. (Duvall) What are five things a good mcther does? and What are five things a good child does?
LENGTH. Duvall: 2 items (5 answers for each). Middleton: NR.
AVAILABILITY. In Duvall, 1946; Middleton, 1954.
REFERENCES.
    Bavelas,A. A method of investigating individual and group ideologies. Sociometry, 1942, 5, 371-377.
    Duvall,E.M. Conceptions of parenthood. American Journal of Sociology, 1946, 52, 193-203.
    Middleton,M.R. The child in the family. Classification of "Bavelas" responses. In Oeser,O.A. and Hammond,S.B., Social structure and personality in a city. London: Routledge, 1954.
    Straus,M.A. Childhood experience and emotional security in the context of Sinhalese social organization. Social Forces, 1954, 33, 152-160.

EISERER,P.E. Projective Film Technique for Studying Adolescent-Parent Relationships.

VARIABLES MEASURED. Various aspects of adolescent-parent relations, including need-press, intraceptive language, and discomfort-relief.
TEST DESCRIPTION. Fifteen silhouette motion pictures, varying in projection time from 10 to 21 seconds, with (15) equivalent still pictures (slides) depicting varying combinations of man-woman-boy-girl situations are available. The stimulus is projected on screen, the subject tells a story which is tape recorded (or in group administration, stories are written).
    Responses scored by four quantitative systems: need-press, intraceptive language, disccmfort-relief words, rating scale of whole story from descriptive to projective. Other scoring systems are applicable. Mean reliabilities for scoring: need-press (.85), intraceptive language (.79),

discomfort-relief (.82).
SAMPLE ITEM. Woman-man-boy seated at dinner table.
LENGTH. Time: Depends upon the number of items used.
Average amount of response time was 10 minutes for 12
stimuli when responses are tape recorded.
AVAILABILITY. In Eiserer, 1949, complete description of
stimuli and production methods. Original film in possession
of investigator.
ABSTRACTED BY: Paul E. Eiserer
REFERENCE.
    Eiserer,P.E. The relative effectiveness of motion and
still pictures as stimuli for eliciting fantasy stories
about adolescent-parent relationships. Genetic Psychology
Monographs, 1949, 39, 205-278.
    Haworth,M.R. Repeat study with a projective film for
children. Journal of Consulting Psychology, 1961, 25,
78-83.

EMMERICH,W.A. Parental Role Questionnaire (PRQ)

VARIABLES MEASURED. Five components of the parental role
defined as follows: (1) Goal values--parental selection of
positive (valued) and negative (disvalued) behavioral
outcomes in the child. (2) Means-ends beliefs--parental
beliefs concerning the effectiveness of various
child-rearing methods for producing desirable outcomes and
for preventing undesirable outcomes in the child. (3)
Means-ends capacities--the parents' (perceived) capacities
for implementing the various Means-ends beliefs. (4) Goal
achievements--the extent to which the parent sees the child
as meeting the standards of performance implied by parental
goals.
TEST DESCRIPTION. A structured questionnaire is
administered to parents of children of a specified age
group. The test is composed of four parts, each designed to
assess one of the parental role components listed above.
SAMPLE ITEM. Could you bring yourself to act this way if
you felt it necessary: Express pleasure or approval when
child trusts others. Mark 4 if you would find it very easy
to act this way. No special effort would be required. Mark
3 if you would find it fairly easy to act this way. A
little effort would be required. Mark 2 if you would find
it somewhat difficult to act this way. It would require
real effort. Mark 1 if you would find it quite difficult to
act this way. It would require a good deal of effort, but
you could do it if you had to. Mark 0 if you would find it
extremely difficult to act this way. You probably could not
bring yourself to do it.
LENGTH. Items: 151.
AVAILABILITY. In Emmerich, 1969.
ABSTRACTED BY: Kersti Yllo.
REFERENCE.
    Emmerich,W.A. Variations in the parent role as a
function of the parent's sex and the child's sex and age.

Merrill-Palmer Quarterly, 1962, 8, 3-11.
    Emmerich,W.A. Continuity and stability in early social
development, II: teacher ratings. Child Development, 1966,
37, 17-27.
    Emmerich,W.A. A parental role and functional-cognitive
approach. Society for Research in Child Development
Monographs, 1969, 34, 1-71.
    Emmerich,W.A. and Smoller,F. The role patterning of
parental norms. Sociometry, 1964, 26, 382-390.

HAWORTH,M.R. Rock-A-Bye Baby (Projective Film for Children)

VARIABLES MEASURED.   (1) Identification,   (2)   Jealousy
(sibling rivalry), (3) Aggression toward parents, (4) Guilt
(masturbatory), (5) Anxiety (castration), and (6)   obsessive
trends.
TEST DESCRIPTION. A projective puppet film dealing with the
story of a little boy, Casper, and his baby sister. The
film is shown to small groups of subjects and stopped in the
middle, when each subject is asked to give his/her ending
for the story. After the film is finished, subjects are
asked a standard list of questions about what Casper
thought, how he felt, and so forth. Ss' responses are
scored in terms of presence or absence of deviant responses.
SAMPLE ITEM. NR.
LENGTH. NR.
AVAILABILITY. In Haworth and Woltmann, 1959.
REFERENCES.
    Haworth,M.R. The use of a filmed puppet show as a
group projective technique for children. Genetic Psychology
Monographs, 1957, 56, 257-296.
    Haworth,M.R. Repeat study with a projective film for
children. Journal of Consulting Psychology, 1961, 25,
78-83.
    Haworth,M.R. and Woltmann,A.G.   Rock-A-Bye Baby: A
group projective test for children.   University Park,
Pennsylvania: Psychological Cinema Register, 1959.   Manual
and film.

HEREFORD,C.F. Parental Attitude Survey Scales

VARIABLES MEASURED. Parents attitudes in relation to: (1)
Confidence in the parental role, (2) Causation of the
child's behavior, (3) Acceptance of the child's behavior and
feelings, (4) Mutual understanding, and (5) Mutual trust.
TEST DESCRIPTION. Questionnaires in which 15 items for each
variable are presented.   Items are scored on a five-point
scale: Strongly Agree, Agree, Undecided, Disagree   or
Strongly Disagree.   Each item is scored from -2 to +2 or
from +2 to -2, depending on whether agreement with the item
is to add to or subtract from the index score.
    Holtzman, et al. (1967), adapted this test to form a
68-item scale, focusing on familial intellectual stimulation

and press for achievement toward the child.
SAMPLE ITEM. (1) Confidence: I feel I am faced with more
problems than most parents. (2) Causation: Some children
are just naturally bad. (3) Acceptance: A child who
misbehaves should be made to feel guilty and ashamed of
himself. (4) Understanding: Children don't try to
understand their parents. (5) Trust: Children who are not
watched will get into trouble.
LENGTH. Time: 15 to 20 minutes. Items: 75.
AVAILABILITY. In Hereford, 1963.
ABSTRACTED BY: Thomas G. Sparhawk.
REFERENCES.
    Friedman,S.T. Relation of parental attitudes toward
child rearing and patterns of social behavior in middle
childhood. Psychological Reports, 1969, 24, 575-579.
    Hereford,C.F. Changing Parental Attitudes Through
Group Discussion. Austin: University of Texas Press, 1963.
    Holtzman,W.H. Diaz-Guerrero,R. Schuartz,J.D. and
Lara-Tapia,L. Cross cultural longitudinal research on child
development: studies of American and Mexican
schoolchildren. In Hill,J.P. (Ed.) Minnesota Symposia on
Child Psychology, Vol. 2. Minneapolis: The University of
Minnesota Press, 1967.

JACKSON,L. A Test of Family Attitudes

VARIABLES MEASURED. Dependency on mother, exclusicn from
intimacy between parents, jealousy of sibling, transgression
and ensuing guilt, fear of parental aggression, longing for
the forbidden, and threat of punishment.
TEST DESCRIPTION. A set of black and white line drawings
about which the subjects make up stories. Stories are taken
down verbatim. Inhibited Ss are prodded to talk. Responses
are scored according to a set of types.
SAMPLE ITEM. Drawing of a woman sitting by a child's
cradle.
LENGTH. Time: 30-40 minutes. Items: 6 cards.
AVAILABILITY. In Jackson, 1950; and from Methuen and
Company, Ltd., 32 Essex Street, Strand, London, W.C. 2,
England.
REFERENCES.
    Buros,O.K. (Ed.) Personality Tests and Reviews.
Highland Park, N.J.: Gryphon Press, 1970.
    Jackson,L. A study of sado-masochistic attitudes in a
group of delinquent girls by means of a specially designed
projection test. British Journal of Medical Psychology,
1949, 22, 53-65.
    Jackson,L. Emotional attitudes towards the family of
normal, neurotic, and delinquent children. British Journal
of Psychology, 1950, 41, 35-51.
    Jackson,L. Emotional attitudes towards the family of
normal, neurotic, and delinquent children, part II. British
Journal of Psychology, 1950, 41, 173-185.
    Jackson,L. Aggression and its interpretation. London:

Methuen and Co. Ltd., 1954, 237.
        Jackson,L. A study of 200 school children by means of
the test of family attitudes. British Journal of
Psychology, 1964, 55, 333-354.

KAGAN,J. HOSKEN,B. and WATSON,S.   Child's Symbolic
Conceptualization of Parents' Pictures

VARIABLES MEASURED. Child's conceptualization of father,
mother and self on 11 polar dimensions: stong-weak,
big-small, nurturant-nonnurturant, competent-incompetent,
punitive-nonpunitive, dangerous-harmless, dirty-clean,
dark-light, cold-warm, mean-nice, and angular-rounded.
TEST DESCRIPTION: An adaptation of the "semantic
differential" (Osgood et al., 1957) for preschool children.
Sixty-six pairs of pictures, paired to illustrate the polar
opposites of a descriptive dimension. Each of the 11
dimensions is presented 6 times with 6 different pairs of
relevant pictures. The pictures contain no illustrations of
men or women or any clue that the subject might interpret as
directly suggestive of a male or female. The presentation
of the 11 dimensicns is randomized, as is the position of
the pictures in each pair. After the experimenter's verbal
description of each stimulus, the subject points to the
picture that reminds him/her of his/her father, mother or
self. The test is given three times. The first time the
subject says which picture is most like his/her father in
each pair; the second time, his/her mother; the third
time, himself/herself.
SAMPLE ITEM. Here is a strong rabbit and here is a weak
rabbit. Which one reminds you of your (father, mother,
self)?
LENGTH. Items: 66.
AVAIIABILITY. In Kagan et al., 1961, except for the
pictures used.
REFERENCES.
        Kagan,J. Hosken,B. and Watson,S. Child's symbolic
conceptualization of parents. Child Development, 1961, 32,
625-636.
        Osgood,C.E. Suci,G.J. and Tannenbaum,P.H. The
measurement of meaning. Urbana: University of Illinois
Press, 1957.
        Patterson,G.R. Parents as dispensers of aversive
stimulation. Journal of Personality and Social Psychology,
1965, 2, 844-851.

KOHN,M.L. and SCHOOLER,C. Index of Parental Values

VARIABLES MEASURED. Parents' valuation of a number of
characteristics as more or less "desirable" for children of
the age and sex of one of their own children. The index
also measures parents' valuation of two main dimensions of
values: Self-directicn/conformity and Maturity/immaturity.

TEST DESCRIPTION. Each parent is asked to rank the
following list of 13 characteristics in terms of their
relative desirability for a child of the same age and sex as
a predesignated child of his or her own: Considerate of
others, Interested in how and why things happen,
Responsible, Self-control, Good manners, Neat and clean,
Good student, Honest, Obeys his parents well, Good sense and
sound judgment, Acts as a boy (girl) should, Tries hard to
succeed, Gets along well with other children. The ranking
is done by asking the parent to choose the three most
desirable characteristics in the list, the one that is most
desirable of all, the three least important (even if
desirable), and the one least important of all. This
provides a basis for classifying each parent's valuation of
each characteristic along a five-point scale, as follows: 5
= The most valued of all; 4 = One of the three most valued,
but not the most valued; 3 = Neither one of the three most
valued nor one of the three least valued; 2 = One of the
three least valued, but not the least valued; and 1 = The
least valued of all.

    The indices of Self-direction/conformity and
Maturity/immaturity are based on a factor analysis of the
ratings of the 13 individual characteristics (Kohn, 1969:
Table 4-3, p. 58).
SAMPLE ITEM. (See above).
LENGTH. Four questions asked, to rank the 13
characteristics. (Approximately 2-5 minutes.)
AVAILABILITY. In Kohn, 1969.
ABSTRACTED BY: Melvin L. Kohn.
REFERENCES.
    Kohn,M.L. Class and Conformity: A Study in Values.
Homewood, Illinois: Dorsey Press, 1969.
    Kohn,M.L. and Schooler,C. Class, occupation, and
orientation. American Sociological Review, 1969, 34,
659-678.
    Kohn,M.L. and Schooler,C. Occupational experience and
psychological functioning: an assessment of reciprocal
effects. American Sociological Review, 1973, 38, 97-118.

LETON,D.A. Parental Attitude Inventory (PAI)

VARIABLES MEASURED. Attitudes toward children.
TEST DESCRIPTION. One hundred eighteen items taken from the
Minnesota Teacher Attitude Inventory (MTAI). Leton felt
these items could "readily be identified as 'attitudes
toward children.'" Items are reworded to be appropriate for
parents and children. Items are keyed and scored in the
same manner as the MTAI.
SAMPLE ITEM. NR.
LENGTH. Items: 118.
AVAILABILITY. From NAPS-2 for revised 120 item version.
REFERENCE.
    Leton,D.A. A study of the validity of parent attitude
measurement. Child Development, 1958, 29, 515-520.

MEYER,M.M. and TOLMAN,R.S. Parent Image Checklist

VARIABLES MEASURED. Twelve parent-to-child attitudes: (1)
Comforting, giving affection; (2) Solicitous, concerned;
(3) Advice-giving; (4) Indifferent; (5) Excessively
attached; (6) Over-giving; (7) Dependent; (8)
Self-centered; (9) Demanding; (10) Dominating; (11)
Scolding; (12) Rejecting. Five parental images: (1)
Attractive, good, appetizing; (2) Competent, effective;
(3) Incompetent, ineffective; (4) Bad, evil, unattractive;
(5) Friction between parents.
TEST DESCRIPTION. A checklist for recording parental
attitudes and images in TAT stories or from child
interviews. Each TAT story is checked for the presence of
each variable. A total frequency score could be obtained
for each variable, although the authors do not do this.
Interview data are similarly scored.
SAMPLE ITEM. See variables measured.
LENGTH. Items: 12 attitudes, 5 images.
AVAILABILITY. In Meyer and Tolman, 1955.
REFERENCE.
     Meyer,M.M. and Tolman,R.S. Correspondence between
attitudes and images of parental figures in TAT stories and
in therapeutic interviews. Journal of Consulting
Psychology, 1955, 19, 79-82.

NEUGARTEN,B.L. and GUTMANN,D.L. Adult Family Scene (AFS)

VARIABLES MEASURED. Intergenerational relationships between
young adults and parents and age and sex role
characteristics.
TEST DESCRIPTION. A Thematic-Apperception picture showing
four people in a group arrangement: a young man, a young
woman, an older man, and an older woman. R is asked to tell
a story in response to the picture, to give a general
description of each figure, and to tell how each figure
relates to the others in the picture.
     The stories can be analyzed in various ways. Sets of
categories are described in the original publication,
whereby stories can be grouped according to
dominance-submission, extra- versus intra-familial
orientation, altruism, and affiliation attributed to each of
the four figures in the picture.
LENGTH. Time: 5 to 10 minutes.
AVAILABILITY. The picture can be obtained from the
Committee on Human Development, University of Chicago, 5730
S. Woodlawn Avenue, Chicago, Illinois 60637.
ABSTRACTED BY: Bernice L. Neugarten
REFERENCES.
     Friedman,C.J. and Friedman,A.S. Characteristics of
schizogenic families during a joint family story-telling
task. Family Process, 1970, 9, 333-354.
     Neugarten,B.L. and Gutmann,D.L. Age-sex roles and
personality in middle age: a thematic apperception study.

Psychological Monographs, 1958, 72, (Whole No. 470).

OPPENHEIM, A. N.   Parent Attitude Inventory

VARIABLES MEASURED. Attitudes about the following aspects
of   child raising: (1) Overprotection (dominant),   (2)
Overprotection (submissive), (3) Democracy, (4) Autocracy,
(5) Acceptance,   (6) Rejection, (7) Strict infant training,
(8) Strictness concerning habits and manners, (9) Strictness
about sex play, (10) Objectivity.
TEST DESCRIPTION.   The parent answers each item on a
five-point scale--Strongly disagree, Disagree, Uncertain,
Agree, Strongly agree. There are five items measuring each
of ten subscales, and two warm-up items at the beginning.
SAMPLE ITEMS. It is difficult for a mother to feel at ease
when she does not know exactly what her child is doing.
Looking after children really demands too much of me.
LENGTH. Items: 52.
AVAILABILITY. From Dr. A.N. Oppenheim, London School of
Economics. Houghton Street, London, W.C.2. or from NAPS-2.
ABSTRACTED BY: Kersti Yllo based on Johnson and Bommarito,
1971, 363.
REFERENCE.
     Pitfield, M.   and Oppenheim, A. N.   Child   rearing
attitudes of mothers of psychotic children. Journal of
Child Psychology and Psychiatry, 1964, 5, 51-57.

RADKE, M. J.   Doll Play

VARIABLES MEASURED. (1) Emotional tone of family situation
created with doll materials, (2) Child's attitude toward
mother doll, (3) Child's attitude toward father doll, (4)
Function of home, (5) Child's relations with siblings, (6)
Function of mother,   (7)   Function   of   father,   (8)
Mother-father relations, (9) Kinds of controls used by
parents, (10) Dominant themes
or interests, (11) Handling of play situation.
TEST DESCRIPTION. Subject is allowed to play with a set
dolls (mother, father, son, daughter) and some doll
furniture. The subject can do whatever he/she wants with
the materials. The experimenter observes without the
subject being aware of it. A running account of the
subject's actions is recorded. The doll play is scored by
judges who read the protocols and rate the subject's actions
according to a set of categories that describes the
variables measured.
SAMPLE ITEM. NA.
LENGTH. Time: 20 minutes. Items: NA.
AVAILABILITY. In Radke, 1946.
REFERENCE.
     Green, R. and Fuller, M. Family doll play and female
identity in preadolescent males. American Journal of
Orthopsychiatry, 1973, 43, 123-127.

Radke,M.J.   The relation of parental authority to
children's behavior and attitudes. University of Minnesota
Child Welfare Monographs, 1946, No. 22.

ROTHBART,M.K. and MACCOBY,E.E.   Parental Attitudes About
Sex Differences Questionnaire

VARIABLES MEASURED. Two aspects of parents' attitudes about
sex differences: (1) Opinions about differences they feel
actually existed between boys and girls.   (2) Differences
they feel should exist between boys and girls.
TEST DESCRIPTION. In Part 1 of the questionnaire parents
are asked to determine whether there is an actual difference
between boys and girls ccncerning a list of characteristics.
The measure of sex-role differentiation for this part of the
scale is the total number of X (no sex difference)
responses,   a   high   score   indicating   low   sex-role
differentiation. In Part 2, boys and girls are rated
separately on how important it is to the parent that his/her
child be described by each characteristic. The measure of
sex-role differentiation for this part is the absolute
difference between ratings of an item's importance for girls
and its importance for boys, summed. The higher this total
difference score, the higher the sex role diffentiation
indicated.
     The Perception questionnaire yields a single score,
computed by summing the number of X responses, called the X
score. The two expectancy questionnaires (one for boys, one
for girls) are compared for each item, and the difference
scored. Thus if boys and girls are checked at the same
point for how a child should behave with respect to the
item, the score for that item would be zero. If boys are
checked Very important to (score of 5) and girls checked
Very important not to (score of 1) the difference score for
the item would be 4. Difference scores are summed across
items to yield the D (Differentiation) score.
SAMFLE ITEM. Part 1. More likely to be obedient are:_G
(Girls) _B (Boys) _X (No sex difference).   Part 2:   Be
obedient: Very important not to, Fairly important   not to,
Unimportant to, Fairly important to, Very important to.
LENGTH. Items: Part 1 = 40. Part 2 = 80.
AVAILABILITY. From NAPS-2.
ABSTRACTED BY: Kersti Yllo
REFERENCE.
     Rothbart,M.K. and Maccoby,E.E.   Parents differential
reactions to sons and daughters. Journal of Personality and
Social Psychology, 1966, 4, 237-243.

SHAW,M.E. Parental Childrearing Attitude Measure

VARIABLES MEASURED.   (1) Child's self-perception and
self-acceptance. (2) Parents' perception and acceptance of
child.

TEST DESCRIPTION. Children and parents are each given a list of 24 adjectives selected from the Adjective Checklist (Gough, 1950; Sarbin and Rosenberg, 1955). Each is asked to estimate on a five-point scale ranging from "Seldom" to "Most of the time," the amount of times they feel each adjective is descriptive of the child. For each of these ratings, they are asked to assess on a five-point scale ranging from "Dislike very much" to "Like very much" their feelings about themselves (or their child in the parents' case) in that respect. A variety of scores including "Self-perception," "Self-acceptance," "Parental perception," "Parental-acceptance," "Parental discrepancy," and "Child-parent discrepancy" can be calculated.
SAMPLE ITEM. Acceptable, Stable, Worthy, etc.
LENGTH. Items: 24.
AVAILABILITY. In Wyer, 1965.
ABSTRACTED BY: Kersti Yllo
REFERENCE.
       Wyer,R.S.Jr. Self-acceptance, discrepancy between parents' perceptions of their children, and goal-seeking effectiveness. Journal of Personality and Social Psychology, 1965, 2, 311-316.

SYMONDS,P.M. Symonds Picture-Story Test

VARIABLES MEASURED. Hostility and aggression, love and eroticism, ambivalence, punishment, anxiety, defenses against anxiety, moral standards and conflicts, ambitions, conflicts, guilt, guilt reduction, depression, happiness, family relationships, and sublimation.
TEST DESCRIPTION. A projective technique for the study of the personality of adolescent boys and girls. Consists of 20 pictures (selected from among 42 prepared and tried out in preliminary experiments) of adolescents in various social relationships: alone; with peer-figures and with parent-figures of the same and opposite sex; in situations suggesting acceptance, rejection, competition, and contrast of characters. Two forms may be used--with 10 plates or with 20. The subjects are asked to tell stories about the figures in the pictures.
SAMPLE ITEM. Picture of an adolescent boy standing on a city street corner with a suitcase in his hand.
LENGTH. Time: 2 hours. Items: 20.
AVAILABILITY. From Columbia University Press, 2960 Broadway, New York, N.Y. 10027.
REFERENCES.
       Symonds,P.M. Adolescent fantasy: An investigation of the picture-story method of personality study. New York: Columbia University Press, 1949. Symonds,P.M. Symonds Picture-Story Test. New York: Columbia University Press, 1958.

THOMES,M.M. Children's Concept of Parental Characteristics

VARIABLE MEASURED. The child's perception of the number of
desirable and undesirable traits which are characteristic of
"most mothers" and "most fathers."
TEST DESCRIPTION. Children are asked to select from a list
of 32 items, which are characteristic of "most mothers" and
most fathers." The checklist of 32 personal qualities or
traits is composed of 17 items representing desirable
qualities and 15 items representing undesirable qualities.
Desirable and undesirable categories were based on sorting
by two small samples of judges. Scores are computed by
subtracting the number of undesirable qualities from the
number of desirable qualities checked. Scores may be
standardized for number of responses. This procedure is
followed first for the concept of "most fathers" and then
for the concept of "most mothers." Devised for 9-to-11
year-old children.
SAMPLE ITEM. Fun, lonely, afraid...
LENGTH. Items: 32.
AVAILABILITY. From NAPS-2.
ABSTRACTED BY: Bruce Brown
REFERENCE.
     Thomes,M.M. Children with absent fathers. Journal of
Marriage and the Family, 1968, 30, 89-96.

THOMES,M.M. Children's Concept of Parental Roles

VARIABLE MEASURED. Children's ideas of parental roles.
TEST DESCRIPTION. An interview in which children (age 9 to
11) answer questions focused on role activities such as
taking care of children, disciplining them, protecting them
and the like. The child is asked to choose whether father
or mother should do these things in a family with both
father and mother present. The score is the number of roles
a parent is expected to perform.
SAMPLE ITEM. Who would see that you do your homework?   (1)
Mother (2) Father.
LENGTH. Items: 15.
AVAILABILITY. From NAPS-2.
ABSTRACTED BY: Thomas G. Sparhawk
REFERENCE.
     Thomes,M.M. Children with absent fathers. Journal of
Marriage and the Family, 1968, 30, 89-96.

WITTENBORN,J.R. Social Reaction Interview

VARIABLES MEASURED. For younger child: (1) Dependence on
adults, (2) Aggression, (3) Socialized compliance, (4)
Taking an adult role, (5) Weakness-avoidance. For older
child: (1) Goody-goody, (2) Responsible attitude, (3)
Cooperation with authority. For mother's child-rearing
practices, younger child: (1) Compulsive, (2) Aggressive,

(3) Phobic, (4) Dependence, (5) Suppression of aggression.
For mother's child-rearing practices, older child: (1)
Aggressive, (2) Anxiety, (3) Dependence, (4) Spoiled child,
(5) Control.
TEST DESCRIPTION. The child is asked what he/she would do
if faced with a variety of situations. E records answer by
checking it as most like one of several likely answers, or
records it verbatim if it is not listed. The mother is
interviewed at length on child-rearing practices. Both
sources of data are scored to measure each of the variables
listed.
SAMPLE ITEMS. (Child, dependency:) Let's pretend you just
got up in the morning and want to get dressed. What do you
do? (Mother, aggression:) When he is angry at the mother,
what does he do? What does the mother do?
LENGTH. Items: 53 (for child).
AVAILABILITY. In Wittenborn, 1956, Appendix A.
REFERENCES.
        Wittenborn,J.R. A study of adoptive children. I.
Interviews as a source of scores for children and their
homes. Psychological Monographs, 1956, 70, No. 1.
        Wittenborn,J.R. A study of adoptive children. III.
Relationships between some aspects of development and some
aspects of environment for adoptive children. Psychological
Monographs, 1956, 70, No. 3.

                        E. Other

BRIM,O.G.JR. GLASS,D.C. and LAVIN,D.E.   Parental Concern
Test

VARIABLES MEASURED. Drive strength or affect in 10
child-rearing areas: (1) Obedience, (2) Sex behavior, (3)
Health habits, (4) Honesty, (5) General child-rearing, (6)
Peer group relations, (7) Religious behavior, (8) Work
habits, (9) Sibling relations, (10) economic behavior.
TEST DESCRIPTION. Each of the 10 subtests consists of five
items to be rated on a five-point scale from Strongly agree
to Strongly disagree. The assessment of motivational
strength or affect is based on the extremity of the
response, and not on its direction--Strongly agree and
Strongly disagree are scored 2; Agree or Disagree, 1; and
Uncertain or Not answered, 0.
SAMPLE ITEM. 1. It's bad for a 10-year-old boy to argue
with his parents about what TV programs to watch. SA, A, ?,
D, SD.
LENGTH. Items: 50.
AVAILABILITY. In Brim, Glass and Lavin, 1962.
REFERENCE.
        Brim,O.G.Jr. Glass,D.C. and Lavin,D.E.   Personality
and Decision Processes: Studies in the Social Psychology of

Thinking. Stanford, California: Stanford University Press, 1962.

EVANS,R.B.   Family Background Questionnaire

VARIABLES MEASURED. Childhood experiences related to later homosexuality of a son: (1) Childhood fears and activities, (2) Mother-son relationship, (3) Father-son relationship.
TEST DESCRIPTION.   Items concern subject's fears, activities, and especially family relationships as a child. One of four answers is to be selected for each item, and scored on a 0 to 3 scale. A total score can be obtained, plus subscores on the three variables above. The items were adapted from I. Bieber's work on parent-child relationships associated with homosexuality in males.
SAMPLE ITEM. Did your mother ally herself with you against your father? Often, Sometimes, Seldom, Never.
LENGTH. Time: About 10 minutes. Items: 27.
AVAILABILITY. From NAPS-2.
ABSTRACTED BY; Ray B. Evans
REFERENCES.

   Bieber,I.   Dain,H.J.   Dince,P.R.   Drellich,M.G. Grand,H.G.   Gundlach,R.H   Kremer,M.W.   Rifkin,A.H. Wilburn,C.B.   and   Bieber,T.B.   Homosexuality: A Psycholanalytic Study. New York: Basic Books, 1962.
   Evans,R.B.   Childhood parental relationships of homosexual men. Journal of Consulting and Clinical Psychology, 1969, 33, 129-135.
   Thompson,N.L.Jr.   McCandless,B.R.   and   Strickland,B.R. Personal adjustment of male and female homosexuals and heterosexuals. Journal of Abnormal Psychology, 1971, 78, 237-240.
   Thompson,N.L.Jr.   Schwartz,D.M.   McCandless,B.R.   and Edwards,D.A.   Parent-child relationships and sexual identity in male and female homosexuals and heterosexuals.   Journal of Consulting and Clinical Psychology, 1973, 41, 120-127.

HEATH,I.L.   ROPER,B.S.   and   KING,C.D.   Contribution   of Children to Marital Stability Index

VARIABLES MEASURED. Extent to which respondents see children as a factor in marital stability.
TEST DESCRIPTION. Subjects respond to the following statements on a four-point scale ranging from Strongly agree = 4 to Strongly disagree = 1: (1) Having children makes a marriage more successful. (2) Having a baby right away can cause a lot cf prcblems for a young couple. (3) When there are children, a marriage is more likely to last. (4) When there are children, couples appreciate each other more. (5) The feeling that my partner did not want very many children greatly influenced our family size. The scale is tabulated by totaling the numbers associated with each response. A high score indicates that the respondent views children as

an important aid to marital stability, and a low score
indicates the opposite.
SAMPLE ITEM. See above.
LENGTH. Items: 5.
AVAILABILITY. In Heath, Roper, and King, 1974.
ABSTRACTED BY: Brent S. Roper (modified)
REFERENCE.
       Heath,L.L. Roper,B.S. and King,C.D. A research note
on children viewed as contributors to marital stability:
the relationship to birth control use, ideal and expected
family size. Journal of Marriage and the Family, 1974, 36,
304-306.

HILL,R.L.   STYCOS,J.M.   and   BACK,K.W.   Parental
Traditionalism Index

VARIABLES MEASURED. Traditionalism-modernism in roles of
child and mother.
TEST DESCRIPTION. A response to an item that endorses
modernism is assigned a score of 1; a response that
endorses traditionalism, 0. The index is computed by
summing the scores--from 0 (low traditionalism) to 4 (high
traditionalism).
SAMPLE ITEM. Everybody wants their children to love and
respect them. However, if your child could not give you
both love and respect in general, which would you prefer,
love or respect? Respect = 1, Love = 0.
LENGTH. Items: 4.
AVAILABILITY. In Hill, Stycos, and Back, 1959.
REFERENCE.
       Hill,R.L. Stycos,J.M. and Back,K.W. The Family and
Population Control: A Puerto Rican Experiment in Social
Change. Chapel Hill: University of North Carolina Press,
1959.

LUCAS,C.M. and HORROCKS,J.E. Adolescent Needs Test

VARIABLES MEASURED. Twelve adolescent need categories: (1)
Acceptance, (2) Achievement, (3) Affection, (4) Approval,
(5) Belonging, (6) Conformity, (7) Dependence, (8)
Independence, (9) Dominance, (10) Recognition, (11)
Self-realization, and (12) To be understood. Each category
contains specific needs representing seven social settings,
one of which is the family. In addition, six items, for six
of the need categories, represent a nonsocial setting--the
self.
TEST DESCRIPTION. Statements about hypothetical boys and
girls behaving in certain social settings. Girls' names are
used with female subjects, boys' names with male. Subject
indicates whether or not he/she is like the hypothetical
person in the statement (self-perception) and whether he/she
would like to be like that person (perceived goals). The
item is scored as a need if there is a discrepancy between

the perception of self and the perceived goal for self.
SAMPLE ITEM. Charles can often make his parents change
their minds. Am I like Charles? Yes, No. Do I want to be
like him? Yes, No.
LENGTH. Time: about 1 hour. Items: 90 (100 for the
factor pilot test).
AVAILABILITY. Items with loadings greater than .50 on each
factor are given in Lucas and Horrocks, 1960.
REFERENCES.
       Lucas,C.M. An emergent category approach to the
analysis of adolescent needs. Ph.D. dissertation, Ohio
State University, 1951.
       Lucas,C.M. and Horrocks,J.E. An experimental approach
to the analysis of adolescent needs. Child Development,
1960, 31. 479-487.

MILLER,T.W. Parental Response Inventory

VARIABLES MEASURED. The extent to which a person is
descriptive or evaluative in verbal interaction.
       An abstract of this test is given in Johnson, O.G.
Tests and Measurements in Child Development: Handbook II.
San Francisco: Jossey-Bass, 1976, 837.

RUSSELL,C.S. Gratification Checklist

VARIABLE MEASURED. Gratification associated with the
first-time parent role.
TEST DESCRIPTION. Respondents rate items according to how
much they have enjoyed each: Not at all = 0, Somewhat = 1,
or Very much = 2, since becoming a parent. The score is a
product of the number of items checked times the degree of
enjoyment. Scores can range from 0 to 24.
SAMPLE ITEM. New appreciation of my own parents.
LENGTH. Items: 12.
AVAILABILITY. In Russell, 1974.
ABSTRACTED BY: Candyce S. Russell
REFERENCE.
       Russell,C.S. Transition to parenthood: problems and
gratifications. Journal of Marriage and the Family, 1974,
36, 294-302.

SEIDL,F.W. and PILLITTERI,A. Parent Participation Attitude
Scale

VARIABLES MEASURED. Attitudes of nursing personnel toward
parental involvement in hospital pediatric programs.
TEST DESCRIPTION. The test consists of 24 self-administered
Likert-type items which are summed to obtain the scale
scores.

SAMPLE ITEM. When parents stay beyond the scheduled
visiting hours, the normal hospital routine is upset.
Strongly agree, Mildy agree, Uncertain, Mildly disagree,
Strongly disagree.
LENGTH. Time: 10 to 15 minutes. Items: 24.
AVAILABILITY. Frcm author or NAPS-2. Scoring instructions
are in Seidl and Pillitteri, 1967.
ABSTRACTED BY: Frederick W. Seidl
REFERENCES.
     Seidl,F.W. Pediatric nursing personnel and parent
participation: a study in attitudes. Nursing Research,
1969, 18.
     Seidl,F.W. and Pillitteri,A. Development of an
attitude scale toward parent participation. Nursing
Research, 1967, 16.

VEROFF,J. and FELD,S. Parental Negative Orientation Index
(PNOI) Parental Restrictiveness Index (PRI)

VARIABLES MEASURED. (1) The PNOI measures subject's
perception of whether cr not the changes brought about by
parenthood are satisfying (positive) or frustrating
(negative). (2) The PRI measures the perceived restrictions
or burdens accompanying being a parent.
TEST DESCRIPTION. Subjects are asked "Thinking about a
man's (woman's) life, how is a man's (woman's) life changed
by having children?" For the PNOI the responses to this
question are coded to determine whether or not they indicate
that the changes brought about by parenthood were positive
or negative. In addition, a further coding judgment is made
of the affective tone of the entire reply; this is a
six-point rating scale: Very positive, Positive,
Ambivalent, Negative, Very negative and Neutral. These two
sets of ratings are then combined to yield the eight
categories of the PNOI, which accounts for both the
frequency of positive or negative responses and the overall
affective tone of the reply: (1) All positive responses and
rated very positive. (2) All positive responses and rated
positive or neutral. (3) Both positive and negative
responses and rated very positive or positive. (4) Both
positive and negative responses and rated ambivalent. (5)
Both positive and negative responses and rated ambivalent.
(6) Both positive and negative responses and rated negative
or very negative. (7) All neutral responses and rated
neutral. (8) All negative responses and rated neutral,
negative, or very negative.
     The PRI is derived from replies to the same question as
the PNOI Each reply to that question is also rated by a
coder for whether or not the parent mentioned any
restrictions or burdens accompanying being a parent. These
ratings of each response are summarized in a three-point
index: (1) No responses include anything about the
restrictions of being a parent, (2) some responses concern
restrictions and others do not, (3) all responses imply that

parenthood is restrictive to the person.
SAMPLE ITEM. See above.
LENGTH. NR.
AVAILABILITY. In Veroff and Feld, 1970.
ABSTRACTED BY: Kersti Yllo
REFERENCE.
    Veroff,J. and Feld,S. Marriage and Work in America.
New York: Van Nostrand Reinhold Company, 1970, 139-140.

Chapter IV

Measures Covering Both Husband-Wife and Parent-Child Variables

A. Conflict and Integration

1. Acceptance-Rejection, Adjustment, Cohesiveness,
Integration, Nuclear Familism, Satisfaction, Solidarity
(See also Subject Index)

BARDIS,P.D. Borromean Family Index

VARIABLES MEASURED. Forces attracting a person to or away
from his or her family of orientation (for unmarried
respondents) and to or away from his/her family of
procreation (for married respondents).
TEST DESCRIPTION. A Likert-type scale consisting of 18
items selected from many more initial statements. Of these,
9 represent internal, or pro-family, attractions, the
remaining 9 dealing with external, or anti-family, forces.
Since the subject responds to each item by means of a
five-point scale (Absent = 0 to Very strong = 4), the
theoretical range of scores is 0 (least pro-family or
internal attractions and most pro-family or external
attractions) to 36 (most pro-family or internal attractions
and least pro-family or external attractions). There are
two versions of the index: one for married respondents and
one for single respondents.

SAMPLE ITEMS. Internal: My family understands me.
External: Difference between my ideas and those of my
family.
LENGTH. Time: 12 minutes. Items: 18.
AVAILABILITY. From NAPS-2.
ABSTRACTED BY: Panos D. Bardis
REFERENCE.
    Bardis,P.D. The Borromean family. Social Science,
1975, 3, 144-158.

BARNETT,L.D. General Familism Index and Religious Familism
Index

VARIABLES MEASURED. The two scales measure the degree to
which the individual feels the family should be a cohesive
unit and its members should participate together in
activities.
TEST DESCRIPTION. Two Guttman scales with coefficients of
reproducibility of .958 for the General Familism Index and
.975 for the Religious Familism Index. Each scale
apparently measures a different attiltude; the correlation
coefficient between the two scales was .27.
SAMPLE ITEM. It is not important for parents to show an
active interest in their children's activities outside the
home. Strongly agree, Agree, Don't know, Disagree, Strongly
disagree.
LENGTH. Time: 5 minutes. Items: General Familism: 5;
Religicus Familism: 3.
AVAILABILITY. In Barnett, 1969.
ABSTRACTED BY: Larry D. Barnett
REFERENCE.
    Barnett,L.D. Women's attitudes toward family life and
U.S. population growth. Pacific Sociological Review, 1969,
12, 95-100.

BELL,H.M. Bell Adjustment Inventory

VARIABLES MEASURED. Personal and social adjustment,
including a subscore for home adjustments.
TEST DESCRIPTION. A multiple-choice personality inventory.
There are three forms: for adults, for high school and
college students, and for measuring high school students'
adjustment and attitude toward school. There is no family
score on the third form of the test.
SAMPLE ITEM. Adult form: Has there ever been a divorce
among the members of your immediate family? Yes, No. High
school and college: Did you ever have a strong desire to
run away from home? Yes, No, ?.
LENGTH. Time: 20-30 minutes. Items: 60 on adult form;
140 on high schocl-college form.
AVAILABILITY. From Consulting Psychologists Press, Inc.,
577 College Avenue, Palo Alto, California 94306.

REFERENCES.
Aarons,W.B. A study of intra-family personality similarities and differences as measured by test performance on the Bell Adjustment Inventory. M.A. Thesis, Temple University, Philadelphia, 1942.

Bell,H.M. The Adjustment Inventory. Palo Alto: Consulting Psychologists Press. Adult form (1938), Student Form (1934), Manual.

Buros,O.K. (Ed.) Personality Tests and Reviews. Highland Park, N.J.: Gryphon Press, 1970.

Dean,D.G. Romanticism and emotional maturity: a preliminary study. Marriage and Family Living, 1961, 23, 44-45.

Duncan,M.H. Home adjustment of stutterers versus nonstutterers. Journal of Speech and Hearing Disorders, 1949, 14, 255-259.

Granlund,E. and Knowles,L. Child-parent identification and academic underachievement. Journal of Consulting and Clinical Psychology, 1969, 33, 495-496.

Husain,M.Q. and Ray-Chowdhury,K. Epigenetic factor like birth-order influencing adjustment patterns of criminals and normals during adolescence. Indian Psychology Bulletin, 1961, 6, 53-57.

Jessen,M.S. Factors in parent's prediction of adolescent responses to selected items on the Bell Adjustment Inventory. American Psychologist, 1955, 10, 365.

Lindgren,H.C. and Mello,M.J. Emotional problems of over- and underachieving children in a Brazilian elementary school. Journal of Genetic Psychology, 1965, 106, 59-65.

Long,H.H. Tested personality adjustment in Jewish and non-Jewish groups. Journal of Negro Education, 1944, 13, 64-69.

Majumdar,A.K. Adjustment pattern of adopters and non-adopters. Indian Journal of Applied Psychology, 1966, 3, 103.

McAllister,R.J. The relationship of Bell Adjustment Scores to family constellation. Master's Thesis, Catholic University of America, 1949.

Nimkoff,M.F. and Wood,A.L. Courtship and personality. American Journal of Sociology, 1948, 53, 263-269.

Peters,C.C. The validity of personality inventories studied by a "guess who" technique. Psychological Bulletin, 1940, 37, 453.

Vail,J.P. and Staudt,V.M. Attitudes of college students toward marriage and related problems: I. Dating and mate selection. Journal of Psychology, 1950, 30, 171-182.

Wittman,M.P. and Huffman,A.V. A comparative study of developmental, adjustment, and personality characteristics of psychotic, psychoneurotic, delinquent, and normally adjusted teen-aged youths. Journal of Genetic Psychology, 1945, 66, 167-182.

Woodruff,L. and Mull,H.K. The relation of home adjustment to social adjustment in northern and in southern college students. American Journal of Psychology, 1944, 57,

86.
     Woolf,M.D.   a study of some relationships between home
adjustment and the behavior of junior college students.
Journal of Social Psychology, 1943, 7, 275-286.

BERDIE,R.F.   and LAYTON,W.L.   Minnesota Counseling Inventory

VARIABLES MEASURED.   Family relationships.
TEST DESCRIPTION.   A personality test in which the subject
indicates whether a statement does or does not apply to
him/her. The score refers to the relationships between the
subject and his/her family. Subjects with "low scores are
most likely to have friendly and healthy relationships with
parents and with brothers and sister. They probably receive
much affection in the home and feel much affection toward
members of their families.   Such persons usually regard
their parents as making reasonable demands on them and
granting them a reasonable amount of independence. They
spend much time at home and participate in activities with
their families" (Berdie and Layton, 1957).
SAMPLE ITEM. My home is a very pleasant place.   True,
False.
LENGTH. Time: 50 minutes. Items: 36.
AVAILABILITY. From Psychological Corporation, 304 East 45th
Street, New York, N.Y.   10017.
REFERENCES.
     Berdie,R.F.   and Hood,A.B.   Personal values and
attitudes as determinants of post-high school plans.
Personnel and Guidance Journal, 1964, 42, 754-759.
     Berdie,R.F.   and Layton,W.L.   Minnesota Counseling
Inventory. New York: Psychological Corporation, 1955.
     Berdie,R.F.   and Layton,W.L.   Manual for the Minnesota
Counseling Inventory, New York: Psychological Corporation,
1957.
     Buros,O.K.   (Ed.) Personality Tests and Reviews.
Highland Park, N.J.: Gryphon Press, 1970.
     Crabtree,B.D. Predicting and determining effectiveness
of homemaking teachers. Ph.D. dissertation, Iowa State
University, 1965.
     Jones,E.G. An analytical study of the relationship
between the expression of familial conflict and the presence
of potential counseling problems in male adolescents. Ph.D.
dissertation, University of Minnesota, 1958.
     Loeffler,D.   Berdie,R.F.   and Roth,J.   Content and
process of inter-generation communications. The Family
Coordinator, 1969, 18, 345-352.
     Stein,J.B. The relation of two personality traits to
some measures of socio-economic level and student plans
after high school. Masters Thesis, University of Minnesota,
1966.
     Surette,R.F.   The relationship of personal and
work-value orientations to career versus homemaking
preference among twelfth grade girls. Ph.D. dissertation,
Catholic University of America, 1965.

Walster,E. Aronson,V. Abrahams,D. and Rottman,L. Importance of physical attractiveness in dating behaviour. Journal of Personality and Social Psychology, 1966, 4, 508-516.

BOWERMAN,C.E. and KINCH,J.W. Family Adjustment Index

VARIABLE MEASURED. Adjustment to the family.
TEST DESCRIPTION. A four-item questionnaire with four- or five-interval response categories summed to obtain scores of 0 to 14.
SAMPLE ITEM. (1) How well do you get along with the members of your family? (2) Does your family give you the attention you think they should? (3) Do you talk over your personal problems with your family? (4) Does your family treat you the way you think you should be treated?
LENGTH. Items: 4.
AVAILABILITY. In Bowerman and Kinch, 1959.
REFERENCE.
Bowerman,C.E. and Kinch,J.W. Changes in family and peer orientation of children between the fourth and tenth grades. Social Forces, 1959, 37, 206-211.

COUGHENOUR,M.C. Family Functions of Activities in Food Consumption

VARIABLES MEASURED. (1) Adaptivity: defined as the functional aspect of family food consumption activities in which food interests of individual family members and family resources are combined to obtain food items for attaining family food consumption goals. (2) Integrativeness: defined as the functional aspect of family food consumption activities whereby family organization is maintained for attainment of food consumption or reinforced as a result of goal attainment. (3) Goal attainment and gratification: defined as the felt satisfaction with activities connected with the family food consumption process.
TEST DESCRIPTION. Respondents indicate on a five-category scale--Almost never, Seldom, Sometimes (about one-half), Often, Almost always--the perceived frequency with which they perform various activities or feel dissatisfied with their activity. The interview or questionnaire items refer to common activities of the homemaker or person principally involved in food acquisition, meal planning, and preparation. The instrument contains 16 items: 5 adaptive, 5 integrative and 6 goal attainment satisfaction items. The satisfaction items ask for the perceived frequency with which the respondent is displeased or unhappy with the activity and are reverse scored to obtain a measure of satisfaction with goal attainment activity. An index is constructed by summing the item response weights and then normalizing the total, with a mean of 50 and standard deviation of 10.

SAMPLE ITEMS. (1) Adaptivity: When shopping for food, how often do you take advantage of specials? Almost never, Seldom, Sometimes, Often, Almost always. (2) Integrativeness: How often do you prepare foods to celebrate special occasions? Almost never, Seldom, Sometimes, Often, Almost always. (3) Goal-attainment satisfaction: How often are you displeased or unhappy with the amount of time your family spends eating together? Almost never, Often, Sometimes, Seldom, Almost always. (Response categories are reverse scored to obtain a homemaker satisfaction score.)
LENGTH. Items: 16.
AVAILABILITY. In Keefe, Badenhop, and Bargmann, 1970 or from NAPS-2.
ABSTRACTED BY: C. Milton Coughenour.
REFERENCES.
    Coughenour,C.M. Functional aspects of food consumption activity and family life cycle stages. Journal of Marriage and the Family. 1972, 34, 656-664.
    Keefe,D.R. Badenhop,S.B. Bargmann,R.E. The measurement of structure and process in family food buying behavior. (abridged) Working Paper Number Three, Southern Regional Food Marketing Project SM-35, Consumer Buying Behavior and Decisions about Foods with Cooperating Agricultural Experiment Stations in Alabama, Georgia, Kentucky, Mississippi, South Carolina, Texas and Virginia, 1970.

CRAWFORD,C.O. Attachment to Family of Orientation Index

VARIABLES MEASURED. Willingness and frequency of family members sharing activities.
TEST DESCRIPTION. Attachment to the family of orientation is measured by means of four items dealing with the respondents' willingness and frequency of sharing activities with other family members. Responses to the four items are trichotomized, each item being scored according to a scale ranging from 0 to 2. The total score ranges from 0 to 8.
SAMPLE ITEM. Frequency of eating the daily meal together.
LENGTH. Items: 4.
AVAILABILITY. In Crawford, 1966.
ABSTRACTED BY: Eruce Brown.
REFERENCE.
    Crawford,C.O. Family attachment, family support for migration and migration plans of young people. Rural Sociology, 1966, 31, 293-300.

DAGER,E.Z. and BREWER,O.L. Family Integration Index

VARIABLE MEASURED. Family integration or joint activity.
TEST DESCRIPTION. Six items concerning family's shared activities and decision-making. Scored by linear summation of arbitrary weights.

SAMPLE ITEM. What kinds of things did you and your family
do together in the last week?   If nothing, what do you
usually do together? Responses are counted and weighted: 3
or more activities = 3, 2 activities = 2, 0-1 activities =
0.
LENGTH. Items: 6.
AVAILABILITY. In Dager and Brewer, 1958.
REFERENCE.
        Dager,E.Z. and Brewer,O.L. Proceedings of the Purdue
Farm Cardiac Seminar. Lafayette, Indiana: Purdue
University Agricultural Experiment Station, 1958, 62-64.

FERREIRA,A.J. Color Flag Test

VARIABLES MEASURED. (1) Overt or explicit rejection of
another family member, (2) Expectation of rejection by
another family member, (3) Interpersonal perceptivity
(accuracy of expectation of rejection).
TEST DESCRIPTION. Each family member is asked to color a
number of flags drawn on pieces of cardboard, and each is
provided with a standard box of eight crayons and a set of
11 2 X 3 cards bearing a stamped drawing of a tri-striped
flag. The subjects are instructed to try to color each flag
differently, but always strive toward "the most pleasing
color combinations." During this task, family members are
isolated from each other. When the coloring is concluded,
the subjects are instructed to place the flags in an
envelope and write their first names on the outside.
        The testing itself consists of two successive steps,
resulting in two scores.   In the first step, the flags
colored by one family member are presented to another member
with the statement: "These are the flags painted by your
(mother, or son, or husband, etc.)...Go through them one by
one, and throw away those you do not like for whatever
reason." Meanwhile, the envelope containing the flags and
bearing the visible signature of the family member in
question is placed on the table, face up, together with a
box bearing a conspicuous sign reading, "Bad. Throw away."
The subject is instructed that this box is to function
symbolically as a wastebasket into which the rejected flags
are to be thrown. Thus each family member is invited to
throw away, that is, to reject, the productions of the other
family members; the number of flags thrown away, from zero
to eleven, constitutes the score R, which is assumed to
measure the overt or explicit nonacceptance, that is,
rejection, of the other family member. In a second step,
aimed at determining the "expectancy of rejection," each
family member is asked to make a guess, based on his or her
knowledge of the other family member, as to how many of the
flags he or she has colored were being thrown away by the
other family member. The number of flags the subject
expected another family member to reject constituted the E
score, which is assumed to measure the "expectancy of
rejection" for the particular relationship with that family

member. It is apparent that the correspondence between, say, a father's expectancy of his son's rejection (score E) and the son's actual rejection of his father (score R) can be assessed only in a gross and general way. Accordingly, the guesses are categorized simply as "good" or "bad." A guess is considered good whenever the E score of a given subject coincides with the R score, plus or minus one, of the family member whose rejecting behavior he/she is trying to guess; in other words, when the difference between the expectancy of rejection and the actual rejection is 0 $\pm$ 1, the guess was considered a good one, as opposed to a bad guess which, by definition, misses the target by two or more flags.
SAMPLE ITEM. See above.
LENGTH. See above.
AVAILABILITY. Described in Ferreira, 1964.
ABSTRACTED BY: Bruce Brown
REFERENCE.
     Ferreira,A.J. Interpersonal perceptivity among family members. American Journal of Orthopsychiatry, 1964, 34, 64-70.

GERBER,G.L. and KASWAN,J.W. Family Distance Doll Placement Technique

VARIABLES MEASURED. Psychological distance in the family; defined as the degree to which family members feel close and related to one another and at the same time maintain their own boundaries as separate and distinct individuals.
TEST DESCRIPTION. In the family doll placement technique, the subject tells stories and places a family of four dolls to represent two positive and three negative story themes. Psychological distance within the family as a whole is determined by the types of groupings or subgroupings into which the dolls are arranged. This is done by categorizing the doll arrangements into eight "family grouping schemata" categories.   Psychological   distance   between dyads is determined in two ways: (1) the physical distance between members of the dyad and (2) the way each member of the dyad is oriented in relation to the other, as measured by four "focus categories."
     The technique can be administered to an individual child or adult, and to the entire family group.
SAMPLE ITEM. "Think of a story about a happy family, place the dolls on the board to show what is happening in your story, and then tell me the story you have made up."
LENGTH. Time: 15 to 30 minutes. Number of story themes: 5.
AVAILABILITY. In Gerber and Kaswan, 1971.
ABSTRACTED BY: Gwendolyn L. Gerber
REFERENCES.
     Gerber,G.L. Psychological closeness expressed through spatial relationships by families of normal and disturbed children. Doctoral Dissertation, University of California,

1967.
Gerber,G.L. Psychological distance in the family as schematized by families of normal, disturbed, and learning-problem children. Journal of Consulting and Clinical Psychology, 1973, 40, 139-147.
Gerber,G.L. Family schemata in families of symptomatic and normal children. Journal of Clinical Psychology, in press.
Gerber,G.L. and Kaswan,J.W. Expression of emotion through family grouping schemata, distance, and interpersonal focus. Journal of Consulting and Clinical Psychology, 1971, 36, 370-377.

GUERNEY,B.G.Jr. The Family Life Questionnaire

VARIABLES MEASURED. Harmony and satisfaction in family life.
TEST DESCRIPTION. The test items seek to ascertain current feelings about living within the family such as amount of fighting, family happiness, concern for one another, understanding, and communication. It is completed by all literate members of the family, thereby providing comparable assessments from all family members on a single measure. There are forms appropriate for three specific dyadic relationships: married couples, fathers and sons, and mothers and daughters. Respondents rate how they currently feel about each of the items. The choices are: Yes, strongly agree; Yes, mildly agree; Yes, but not so sure; No, mildly disagree, No, not so sure; and No, strongly disagree. Items are arranged to avoid direction of wording effects. Scores range from 24 to 96; higher scores indicate more harmony in the relationship.
SAMPLE ITEM. One of us is always criticizing one another.
LENGTH. Items: 24.
AVAILABILITY. In Guerney, 1977.
ABSTRACTED BY: Carole Hatch
REFERENCES.
Ely,A.L. Guerney,B.G.Jr. and Stover,L. Efficacy of the training phase of conjugal therapy. Psychotherapy: Theory, Research, and Practice, 1973, 10, 201-208.
Guerney,B.G.Jr. Filial therapy: description and rationale. Journal of Consulting Psychology, 1964, 28, 304-310.
Guerney,B.G.Jr. Psychotherapeutic Agents: New Roles for Nonprofessionals, Parents and Teachers. New York: Holt, Rinehart and Winston, 1969.
Guerney,B.G.Jr. Relationship Enhancement Skill Training Programs for Therapy, Prevention, and Enrichment. San Francisco: Jossey-Bass, 1977.
Guerney,B.G.Jr. Guerney,L. and Andronico,M.P. Filial Therapy. Yale Scientific Magazine, 1966, 40, 6-14.
Guerney,B.G.Jr. Stollak,G.E. and Guerney,L. A format for a new mode of psychological practice: or how to escape a zombie. The Counseling Psychologist, 1970, 2, 97-104.

Guerney,B.G.Jr. Stollak,G.E. and Guerney,L. The practicing psychologist as educator--an alternative to the medical practitioner model. Professional Psychology, 1971a, 3, 276-282.

Guerney,B.G.Jr. Stollak,G.E. and Guerney,L. The potential advantages of changing from a medical to an educational model in practicing psychology. Interpersonal Development, 1971b, 4, 238-246.

Stover,L. and Guerney,B.G.Jr. Efficacy of training procedures for mothers in filial therapy. Psychotherapy: Theory, Research and Practice, 1967, 4, 110-115.

HELLER,P.L. Nuclear Familism Attitude Scale

VARIABLES MEASURED. Attitudes toward familism, which here refers to two generations of a nuclear family rather than to the extended family. Five aspects of familism are used: (1) Feeling that one belongs primarily to the family group and that other persons are outsiders, (2) Integration of individual activities for the achievement of family objectives, (3) Feeling that material goods are family property and one is obligated to give assistance when an individual needs it, (4) Concern for perpetuation of the family as indicated by helping an adult child begin economic and household activities, and (5) Mutual aid and friendly exchange.
TEST DESCRIPTION. A Likert-type scale with response choices ranging from Strongly agree (scored 5) to Strongly disagree (scored 1). The raw scores for the sum of these items are then grouped into a standard scale (sten scores) which ranges from 0 to 9 (high score) and forces the final scores into a normal curve. "Trace line analysis" (Copp, 1960) was applied to a 37-item questionnaire. Fifteen items (three representing each of the above aspects of familism) were chosen to form the final familism scale.
SAMPLE ITEM. (Mutual aid): Married children should live close to their parents so that mutual aid and cooperation might better be carried on.
LENGTH. Items: 15.
AVAILABILITY. In Heller, 1970.
REFERENCES.
Copp,J.H. Trace line analysis. Unpublished paper presented at the 1960 meeting of the Rural Sociological Society.
Heller,P.L. Familism scale: a measure of family solidarity. Journal of Marriage and the Family, 1970, 32, 73-80.

HILL,R.L. Adjustment to Reunion Score

VARIABLES MEASURED. Adjustment to reunion. The items cover the areas of husband-wife relations, division of labor within the home, relocation of roles, father-child

relations, and areas of conflict likely to occur in a
reunion.
TEST DESCRIPTION. Subject (husband or wife) checks
statements which apply. The responses are weighted on a
five-point scale (Excellent adjustment = 5; Satisfactory
adjustment = 4; Average or fair adjustment = 3; Poor
adjustment = 2; Broken up = 1). A score is derived by
summing the weights and dividing by the number of items
checked. Part B of the test calls for information about the
feelings of belongingness and tenderness toward husband and
wife during recent events, the reunion, and afterward.
SAMPLE ITEM. I feel at home with husband/wife again as if
we were old companions. (weight, 5).
LENGTH. Items: 20.
AVAILABILITY. In Hill, 1949.
REFERENCE.
     Hill,R.L. Families under Stress: Adjustment to the
Crises of War Separation and Reunion. New York: Harper,
1949.

HILL,R.L. Family Integration Scale

VARIABLES MEASURED. Affection, joint activity, willingness
to sacrifice for family objectives, pride in family
tradition (esprit de corps), solidarity.
TEST DESCRIPTION. The test consists of five items. The E
classifies the family on each variable by asking the
question and then assigning the family to the appropriate
weighted category on each item. Each item has a five-point
rating scale.
SAMPLE ITEM. How frequently did you get out as a family to
social activities? Do everything together = 5; Do most
things together = 4; Enough things done as a family to
maintain unity = 3; Few family activities, many individual
activities = 2; Almost none, most activities individual =
1.
LENGTH. Items: 5.
AVAILABILITY. In Hill, 1949.
REFERENCE.
     Hill,R.L. Families under Stress: Adjustment to the
Crises of War Separation and Reunion. New York: Harper,
1949.

KASWAN,J.W. and LOVE,L.R. Family Adjective Rating Scale

VARIABLES MEASURED. Interpersonal assessment of family
members, especially negative and positive social impact.
     An abstract of this test is given in Johnson, O.G.
Tests and Measurements in Child Development: Handbook II.
San Francisco: Jossey-Bass, 1976, 773.

KLAPP,O.E. Family Solidarity Index

VARIABLE MEASURED. Degree of solidarity in family.
TEST DESCRIPTION. A three-part questionnaire. In Part 1,
the S indicates whether the statement applies All, Most,
Some, Little, or None of the time.   In Part 2, the subject
indicates whether the statement applies to his/her group
Very much, Much, Some, Little, or Not at all.   In Part 3,
the subject indicates whether the statement applies to
himself/herself Very much, Much, Some, A little, or Not at
all.   There are different statements for each part. Items
from all three parts are summed (using the response weights
in Klapp, 1959) to obtain the family solidarity score.
SAMPLE ITEM. Part 1: When the family gets together I am
there.   Part 2:   I feel a part of this group. Part 3: I
sometimes feel I am not a part of this group.
LENGTH. Items: 21.
AVAILABILITY. In Klapp, 1959.
REFERENCE.
     Klapp,O.E.   Ritual and family solidarity.   Social
Forces, 1959, 37, 212-214.

MOXLEY,R.L. Family Solidarity Scale

VARIABLE MEASURED. Organizational solidarity: defined as
"the degree to which a social unit attempts to generate,
maintain and project a unified image or definition of the
situation.
TEST DESCRIPTION. "Organizational solidarity" is used to
emphasize the distinction from psychological measures. Each
of the eleven items reflects an aspect of solidarity which
has figured in previous writing on family solidarity. Items
refer to such factors as the treatment of house guests,
involvement of parents in school activities, and the
spending of family income. An interview schedule is used to
collect data on family group characteristics of both a
symbolic and behavioral nature.   These indicators are
combined using Guttman scaling.
SAMPLE ITEM. The whole family eats meals together.   Yes,
No.
LENGTH. Items: 11.
AVAILABILITY. In Moxley, 1973.
ABSTRACTED BY: Robert L. Moxley
REFERENCE.
     Moxley,R.L.   Family solidarity and quality of life in
an agriculture Peruvian community. Journal of Marriage and
the Family, 1973, 35, 497-504.

PLESS,I.B. and SATTERWHITE,B.B. Family Functioning Index

VARIABLE MEASURED. "Functioning," defined as the strength
of relationships and life style of the family as a whole.

TEST DESCRIPTION. The index includes 16 questions dealing
with   intra-family   communication,   cohesiveness,
decision-making,   marital   satisfaction,   frequency   of
disagreements, communications, weekends together, problem
solving, and a general assessment of the level of happiness
and closeness of the family unit. Each response is assigned
a score: 0 being the lowest and 2 the highest.   The total
index score is obtained by the addition of scores for each
question.
SAMPLE ITEM. Would you say, all in all, that your family is
Happier than most others you know, About the same, or Less?
(Scale: Happier, Same, Less)
LENGTH. Time: 10 minutes. Items: 16.
AVAILABILITY. From NAPS-2.
ABSTRACTED BY; I.B. Pless
REFERENCES.
      Pless,I.B. and Satterwhite,B.B.   A measure of family
functioning and   its application.   Social Science and
Medicine, 1973, 7, 613-621.
      Satterwhite,B.B.   The Family Functioning Index--Five
Year Test-Retest Reliability, 1976. Dept. of Pediatrics,
University of Rochester Medical Center, 601 Elmwood Avenue,
Rochester, NY 14642.
      Satterwhite,B.B. Zweig,S.R. Iker,H.P. and Pless,I.B.
The   Family   Functioning   Index-five   year   test-retest
reliability   and   implications   for   use.   Journal   of
Comparative Family Studies, 1976, 7, 111-116.

SEBALD,H. and ANDREWS,W.H. Family Integration Index

VARIABLE MEASURED.   Family integration, operationally
defined as the extent of common nuclear family activities.
TEST DESCRIPTION. Eight items consisting of questions on
the amount of family participation in common. There are
four responses possible on each question: Often, Sometimes,
Seldom, Never.
SAMPLE ITEM. How often do you help your children with their
schoolwork and problems?
LENGTH. Items: 8.
AVAILABILITY. In Sebald and Andrews, 1962.
REFERENCES.
      Rogers,E.M.   and   Sebald,H.   Familism,   family
integration and kinship orientation. Marriage and Family
Living, 1962, 24, 25-30.
      Sebald,H. and Andrews,W.H.   Family integration and
related factors in a rural fringe population. Marriage and
Family Living, 1962, 24, 347-351.

STRODTBECK,F.L.   HUTCHINSON,J.G.   and   RAY,M.P.   Family
Consensus Score (FCS) and Adolescent Autonomy Scale (AAS)

VARIABLES MEASURED. The FCS measures value consensus among
family members. The Autonomy Scale is a subscale which taps

family consensus with regard to various situations and problems involving parents and an adolescent offspring.
TEST DESCRIPTION. A questionnaire containing 76 items is administered to family members. All items must be answered "Yes" or "No". The score is derived by counting the number of items on which all members of a family participating in the study gave the same answer. The score can also be used for subfamily group such as Mother-Father, Father-Son, Mother-Son, Mother-Daughter, etc. The 22 of the 76 items which deal with parent-adolescent situations comprise the "Adolescent Autonomy Scale."
SAMPLE ITEM. A parent has a right to read a high school student's letter without first asking permission. Agree, Disagree.
LENGTH. Items: 76.
AVAILABILITY. Adolescent Autonomy Scale from NAPS-2. For Family Consensus Scale see Revealed Difference Technique (Strodtbeck).
ABSTRACTED BY: Kersti Yllo
REFERENCES.
    Dentler,R.A. and Hutchinson,J.G. Socioeconomic versus family membership status as sources of family attitude consensus. Child Development, 1961, 32, 249-254.
    Hutchinson,J.G. Family interaction patterns and the emotionally disturbed child. In Winter,W. and Ferreira,A.J. (Eds.) Family Interactions. Palo Alto, Calif.: Science and Behavior Books, Inc., 1969.
    Strodtbeck,F.L. Family interaction, values and achievement. In McClelland,D.C. (Ed.) Talent and Society. Princeton,N.J.: Van Nostrand, 1958.

SUNDBERG,N. SHARMA,V. WODTLI,T. and ROHILA,P. Family Cohesiveness Score

VARIABLE MEASURED. Adolescents' reports of family cohesiveness, as indicated by the number of, and a positive attitude toward, joint family activities.
TEST DESCRIPTION. A 25-item questionnaire for which some of the items were taken from Bell's Adjustment Inventory. Subjects check Yes or No for each question; the score is based on the total number of items checked "showing acceptance of family togetherness and positive interaction."
SAMPLE ITEM. Do you and your brothers and sisters share your personal belongings (for instance, clothes, books, toys) with each other? Yes, No.
LENGTH. Items: 25.
AVAILABILITY. From NAPS-2.
REFERENCE.
    Sundberg,N. Sharma,V. Wodtli,T. and Rohila,P. Family cohesiveness and autonomy of adolescents in India and the United States. Journal of Marriage and the Family, 1969, 31, 403-407.

2. Love, Support, Involvement (See also Subject Index)

ALEXANDER,J.F. Defensive and Supportive Communication
Interaction Manual

VARIABLES MEASURED. Two types of verbal and molar
non-verbal marital communication; (1) System disintegrating
defensive (judgmental dogmatism, control and strategy,
indifference, superiority) communication, (2) System
integrating supportive (genuine information seeking and
giving, spontaneous problem solving, empathic understanding,
equality) communications.
TEST DESCRIPTION. Raters observe live or videotaped
marriage and family interaction situations in which verbal
behaviors predominate. Although global ratings may be used,
usually a time-sampling procedure is followed in which
raters indicate the presence/absence of a defensive or
supportive communication during a specified interval (e.g.,
10 seconds) for each member present. Summed frequencies
provide measures of the relative density of each type of
communication, and may be used for intrafamily and
interfamily comparison.
SAMPLE ITEM. Judgmental-dogmatism: "Anybody knows that;"
"Just how do you propose to do that;" "What is that supposed
to mean;" "You're so smart;" "How do you ever expect...;"
"You know-it-all."
LENGTH. Time: A function of the duration of rated
interaction.
AVAILABILITY. From NAPS-2.
ABSTRACTED BY: James F. Alexander
REFERENCES.
     Alexander,J.F. Defensive and supportive communications
in normal and deviant families. Journal of Consulting and
Clinical Psychology, 1973, 40, 223-231.

ANTHONY,E.J. AND BENE,E. The Family Relations Test

VARIABLE MEASURED. Number and intensity of positve and
negative feelings toward each member of the family. These
scores can be used in various combinations--for example, to
estimate reciprocal regard.
TEST DESCRIPTION. Twenty figures of persons of all ages and
sexes, each mounted on a small box, and a series of
emotionally toned statements about family relations printed
on small cards. The S is asked to select a figure to
represent each member of his/her family, including one for
himself/herself. After he/she has set up his/her family
circle, the E adds a figure for Nobody. E then shows the
item cards, and explains that each little card contains a
message and should be put into the box of that person the
message fits best. If the message does not fit anybody, the
card should be put in Nobody's box. The E proceeds by

reading the cards and handing them to the subject one by
one. If an item is supposed to fit several people, the E
makes a note of it. Scores consist of the number of items
of each kind of feeling that the subject assigns to each
member of the family. Bene(1965) devised an adult version
of the test.
SAMPLE ITEM. This person in the family is very
kind-hearted.
LENGTH. Time: 25 minutes. Items: 86 (preschool version
with 40 items also available).
AVAILABILITY. From National Foundation for Educational
Research, The Mere, Upton Park, Slough, Bucks, England.
REFERENCES.
      Anthony,E.J. and Bene,E. A technique for the
objective assessment of the child's family relationships.
Journal of Mental Science, 1957, 103, 541-555.
      Barton,K. Dielman,T.E. and Cattell,R.B. An item
factor analysis of intrafamilial attitudes of parents.
Journal of Social Psychology, 1973, 90, 67-72.
      Bene,E. The family relations test. Rorsch Newsletter,
1957, 2, 5-6.
      Bene,E. The objective assessment of the emotional
atmosphere in which children live in their homes. Abstract.
Acta Psychologica, 1959, 15, 495-496.
      Bene,E. Family relations as experienced by
psychologically disturbed children. British Journal of
Medical Psychology, 1959, 32, 226-231.
      Bene,E. On the genesis of male homosexuality: an
attempt at clarifying the role of parents. British Journal
of Psychiatry, 1965, 111, 803-813.
      Bene,E. Reply to Kauffman and Ball's note regarding
the family relations test. Journal of Personality
Assessment, 1973, 37, 464-466.
      Bene,E. and Anthony,E.J. Manual for the Family
Relations Test. London: The authors, 1957.
      Buros,O.K. (Ed.) Personality Tests and Reviews.
Highland Park, N.J.: Gryphon Press, 1970.
      Frankel,J.J. The relation of a specific family
constellation and some personality characteristics of
children. Ph.D. dissertation, George Peabody College for
Teachers, 1965.
      Frost,B.P. Family relations test; a normative study.
Journal of Projective Techniques and Personality Assessment,
1969, 33, 409-413.
      Frost,B.P. Studies of family relations test patterns:
I: Test inhibition. Journal of Personality Assessment,
1973, 37, 544-550.
      Gratton,L. and Murray,J.D. An experimental approach
to the study of family dynamics. Proceedings of the Annual
Conference of Air Force Behavioral Scientists, 1966, 13,
124-141.
      Gross,S.Z. Critique: children who break down in
foster homes: a psychological study of patterns of
personality growth in grossly deprived children. Journal of
Child Psychology and Psychiatry, 1963, 4, 61-66.

Kauffman,J.M.   Validity of the family relations test: a review of research. Journal of Projective Techniques and Personality Assessment, 1970, 34, 186-189.

Kauffman,J.M.   Family relations test responses of disturbed and normal boys; additional comparative data. Journal of Personality Assessment, 1971, 35, 128-138.

Kauffman,J.M. and Ball,D.W. A note on item analysis of family relations test data. Journal of Personality Assessment, 1973, 37, 248.

Kauffman,J.M.   Weaver,S.J.   and   Weaver,A.   Family relations test responses of retarded readers: reliability and comparative data. Journal of Personality Assessment, 1972, 36, 353-360.

Lingren,R.H. Child-parent attitudes: a comparison of the family relations test and perceptions on Rorschach Cards III, IV, and VII. Psychology in the Schools, 1968, 5, 81-84.

Linton,H. Berle,B.B. Grossi,M. and Jackson,B. Reactions of children within family groups as measured by the Bene-Anthony tests. Journal of Mental Science, 1961, 107, 308-325.

Lockwood,B.   and   Frost,B.P.   Studies   of   family relations test patterns: II. Most-mentioned family members and   intersibling   involvement.   Social   Behavior   and Personality, 1973, 2, 137-143.

Meyer,H. The investigation of the adopted child by means of the Bene-Anthony Test compared with the Lowenfeld World Technique. Rorsch Newsletter, 1961, 6, 20-31.

Meyer,M.M. Family relations test. Journal of Projective Techniques and Personality Assessment, 1963, 27, 309-314.

Morrow,W.R.   and   Wilson,R.C.   Family relations of bright high-achieving and under-achieving high school boys. Child Development, 1961, 32, 501-510.

Rakoff,V. and Rose,A.M. Patterns of response to out-of-focus slides of families with an emotionally disturbed member. Family Process, 1972, 11, 339-346.

Roche,D. The Bene-Anthony Family Relations Test: variations and reliability of administration procedure. Papers in Psychology, 1970, 4, 12-15.

Sutton-Smith,B.   and Rosenberg,B.G.   Modeling   and reactive components of sibling interaction. Minnesota Symposia on Child Psychology, Vol. 3, 1969, 131-152.

Swanson,B.M. and Parker,H.J. Parent-child relations: a child's acceptance by others, of others, and of self. Child Psychiatry and Human Development, 1971, 1, 243-254.

Thomes,M.M. Children with absent fathers. Journal of Marriage and the Family, 1968, 30, 89-96.

VanSlyke,V. and Leton,D.A. Children's perception of family relationships and their school adjustment. Journal of School Psychology, 1965, 4, 19-28.

Williams,J.M. Children who break down in foster homes: a psychological study of patterns of personality growth in grossly deprived children. Journal of Child Psychology and Psychiatry, 1961, 2, 5-20.

BALSWICK,J. Expression of Emotion Scale

VARIABLE MEASURED. Expression of love, hate, happiness, and
sadness.
TEST DESCRIPTION. The subject gives one of four forced
answer responses to each item. Factor analysis reveals that
the scale contains four distinct factors. Four items load
on each of the four factors in the scale, thus yielding four
subscales: (1) Expression of Love, (2) Expression of Hate,
(3) Expression of Happiness, and (4) Expression of Sadness
Scale. The scale has been given to over 1200 high school
students over 500 college students. For the Expression of
Emotion Scale, the Love Factor accounts for 17% of the
variance, the Hate Factor accounts for 13% of the variance,
the Happiness Factor accounts for 16.2% of the variance, the
Sadness Factor accounts for 12.9% of the variance, and all
four factors together account for 59.6% of the variance in
the scale.
SAMPLE ITEM. When I do feel love toward people I tell them:
Never; Seldom; Often; Very often.
LENGTH. Time: 3-5 minutes. Items: 16.
AVAILABILITY. Jack Balswick, Sociology, University of
Georgia, Athens, Georgia 30602.
ABSTRACTED BY: Jack Balswick.
REFERENCES.
    Balswick,J. The development of an emotion scale and an
expression of emotion scale. Paper reread at the annual
meeting of the American Sociological Association, San
Francisco, 1975.
    Balswick,J. Male inexpressiveness. Journal of Social
Issues, forthcoming.
    Balswick,J. and Averett,C. Sex differences in
expressiveness: gender, interpersonal orientation, and
perceived parental expressiveness as contributing factors.
Journal of Marriage and the Family, 1977, 39, 121-127.

BROWN,A.W. MORRISON,J. and COUCH,G.B. Affectional Family
Relationships Questionnaire

VARIABLES MEASURED. Affectional family relationships which
"contribute to healthy character development." Ten
subscores: (1) Common participation in work and play, (2)
Degree of approval-disapproval, (3) Regularity in the home,
(4) Confidence shared, (5) Sharing in family decisions, (6)
Child's acceptance of the standards of the home, (7) Trust
and faith in child by parents, (8) Parental attitude toward
peer activities, (9) Interparental relations, (10) Signs of
personal tension.
TEST DESCRIPTION. Questionnaire designed for grades 4-12.
Multiple-choice answers are weighted by a panel of experts
according to their "contribution to healthy character
development" (see Sample Item). Morrow and Wilson (1961)
used a revised questionnaire and added some items.

SAMPLE ITEM.   Do you talk to your parents about your
problems and worries?   Very often = 4; Fairly often = 5;
Occasionally = 3; Very seldom = 2; Almost never = 1.
LENGTH. NR.
AVAILABILITY. In Havighurst and Taba, 1949.
REFERENCES.
  Brown,A.W. Morrison,J. and Couch,G.B.   Influence of
affectional family relationships on character development.
Journal of Abnormal Social Psychology, 1947, 42, 422-429.
  Brown,A.W. Morrison,J. and Duddman,J.M.   Methods of
studying   affectional   family   relationships.   In
Havighurst,R.J. and Taba,H. (Eds.) Adolescent Characters
and Personality. New York: Wiley, 1949, 233-242.
  Morrow,W.R.   and Wilson,R.C.   Family relations of
bright high-achieving and under-achieving high school boys.
Child Development, 1961, 32, 501-510.

ROSENBERG,S.   Stein Family Attitudes Sentence Completion
Test

VARIABLE MEASURED.   Positive affect toward parent and
family.
TEST DESCRIPTION. Sentence-completion test of 100 items
referring to either parent. Scored as positive, negative,
or evasive, the percentages of each in each category are the
total score.
SAMPLE ITEMS. His father is... His mother tries...
LENGTH. Items: 100 (nct reported how many specifically
referred to parents).
AVAILABILITY. In Stein, 1947.
REFERENCES.
  Rosenberg,S.   Some relationships between attitudes
expressed toward the parent in a sentence completion test
and case history data. Journal of Project Technique, 1950,
14, 188-193.
  Stein,M.I. The use of a sentence completion for the
diagnosis of personality. Journal of Clinical Psychology,
1947, 3, 47-56.

SWENSEN,C.H.   Scale of Feelings and Behavior of Love

VARIABLES MEASURED. The things subjects did, said, or felt
toward people they love.
TEST DESCRIPTION. Subjects are given a list of 120 ways (or
items) of expressing love. They are asked to answer the
items for their relationship with five people: mother,
father, closest sibling, closest friend of the same sex and
closest friend of the opposite sex (or spouse).   The scale
is made up of six subscales: (1) Verbal expression; (2)
Self-disclosure;   (3)   Toleration;   (4)   Non-material
evidence, (5) Feelings non-verbally expressed, (6) Material
evidence. "The scale is scored by simply adding up the
numbers of the choices made by the subjects to each item in

a subscale. The lowest score possible for each item is 1
and the highest possible for an item is 3." Thus for a
subscale containing 20 items, the score range is 20 to 60.
SAMPLE ITEM. The loved one tells you that he(she) feels you
get along well together. a. He(she) never tells you this =
1; b. He(she) occasionally tells you this = 2; and c.
He(she) frequently tells you this = 3.
LENGTH. Items: 120.
AVAILABILITY. In Swensen, 1973.
ABSTRACTED BY: Kersti Yllo
REFERENCE.
       Swensen,C.H.   Scale of feelings and behavior of love.
In   Annual   Handbook   for   Group   Facilitators.   La
Jolla,California: University Associates Publishers, 1973.

3. Aggression, Conflict, Disapproval, Discrepancy, Pathology
Rejection, Violence (See also Subject Index)

BARDIS,P.D.   Family Violence Scale

VARIABLES MEASURED. Physical and verbal violence in family
interaction during subject's childhood.
TEST DESCRIPTION. A Likert-type scale consisting of 25
differentiating items, selected from hundreds of initial
statements and covering various dimensions or areas of
violence within the family. Since each item is responded to
by means of a five-point frequency scale (Never = 0 to Very
often = 4), the theoretical range of scores on the entire
scale is 0 (Ideal-typical nonviolence) to 100 (Highest
degree of violence).
SAMPLE ITEM. Did your father threaten physical violence
against you?
LENGTH. Time: 10 minutes. Items: 25.
AVAILABILITY. In Bardis, 1973; from Panos D. Bardis, The
University of Toledo, Toledo, Ohio; or from NAPS-2.
ABSTRACTED BY: Panos D. Bardis.
REFERENCE.
       Bardis,P.D.   Violence: theory and   quantification.
Journal of Political and Military Sociology, 1973, 1,
121-146.

BEIER,E.G.   YOUNG,D.M.   KORNER,K.M.   and   IZATT,G.
Aggression Game Measure: Pillow Clubs

VARIABLE MEASURED. Aggression.
TEST DESCRIPTION. The pillow clubs are electronically wired
to measure interpersonal game-aggression defined as
frequency and intensity of pillow-club blows exchanged
between subjects during game-aggression bouts. Simultaneous
blows can also be measured. The pillow clubs (cloth-covered

foam bats) consist of two modified "Bataca" clubs each of
which is emplanted with a piezoelectric transducer sensing
device which relays both frequency and intensity information
to a two channel audio tape recorder. A slight impact on
the club surface results in a voltage pulse with an
amplitude proportional to the strength of impact. Clubs are
standardized by a fall-drop test. Following data
collection, the tape deck is real-time interfaced through
the analogue inputs of a PDP-12 computer (Digital Equipment
Corporation) for data analysis. Programming was designed to
permit subtotaling at operator supplied intervals.
SAMPLE ITEM. See above.
LENGTH. NR.
AVAILABILITY. Described more fully in the references cited
below. For design and computer program information, write
Mr. Kim M. Korner, Dept. of Psychology, University of
Utah, Salt Lake City, Utah.
ABSTRACTED BY: David M. Young
REFERENCES.

      Korner,K.M. Young,D.M. and Beier,E.G. Description of
an instrument for the measurement of game aggression. Paper
presented at the meeting of the Western Psychological
Association, Sacramento, California, April, 1975.
      Young,D.M. Beier,E.G. Beier,P. and Barton,C. Is
chivalry dead? Journal cf Communication, 1975, 25, 57-64.
      Young,D.M. Korner,K.M. Gill,J.D. and Beier,E.G.
Relationship of game aggression to quality of marriage.
Paper presented at the meeting of the Western Psychological
Association, Sacramento, California, April, 1975.
      Young,D.M. Korner,K.M. Gill,J.D. and Beier,E.G.
Aggression as communication in marital interaction. Journal
of Communication, in press.

BLOCH,D.A. and BEHRENS,M.L. Multiproblem Family Index

VARIABLE MEASURED. Family pathology.
TEST DESCRIPTION. In an interview with a child's social
worker who is thoroughly familiar with his/her case history,
the incidence of the following areas of family pathology are
computed: (1) marriage (parents' marriage broken other than
by death); (2) parent-child relationship (child abuse or
overdisciplining of child); (3) social pathology (a family
member is an alcoholic, drug addict or convicted criminal);
(4) physical illness (of either parent); (5) mental illness
(of any family member); (6) financial support (family
partially or wholly dependent on public assistance funds).
A family pathology score is computed by summing the
incidence of any of the above problems in the child's
family.
SAMPLE ITEM. See above.
LENGTH. Items: 6.
AVAILABILITY. In Wagner, 1960.

ABSTRACTED BY: Kersti Yllo
REFERENCES.
    Bloch,D.A. Behrens,M.L. Gullenberg,H. King,F.G. and
Tendler,D. A study of children referred for residential
treatment in New York State. Albany: New York State
Interdepartmental Health Resources Board, 1959.
    Wagner,N. Developmental aspects of impulse control.
Journal of Consulting Psychology, 1960, 24, 537-540.

BROWN,G.W.   and RUTTER,M.   Interview Measure of Family
Activities and Relationships

VARIABLES MEASURED. (1) Critical comments about the spouse
and individual children, (2) Dissatisfaction with the
marriage, (3) Hostility toward the spouse, (4) Warmth toward
spouse and individual children, and (5) Positive remarks
about the spouse.
TEST DESCRIPTION. The data are obtained by interview.   (1)
Critical comments are measured by tone of voice, and whom
directed toward, (2) Dissatisfaction is a summary score,
based on 8 ratings, 5 dealing with involvement with various
tasks, and 3 with aspects of leisure, sexual activity, and
finance and employment, (3) Hostility is measured as either
present or absent, (4) Warmth is measured mainly by tone of
voice, and is also a summary measure, (5) Positive remarks
are also summed.
SAMPLE ITEM. See above.
LENGTH. NR
AVAILABILITY. General description in Brown and Rutter,
1966.
ABSTRACTED BY: Thomas G. Sparhawk.
REFERENCE.
    Brown,G.W. Birley,J.L. and Wing,J.K. Influence of
family life on the course of schizophrenic disorders: a
replication. British Journal of Psychiatry, 1972, 121,
241-258.
    Brown,G.W. and Rutter,M. The measurement of family
activities and relationships. Human relations, 1966, 19,
241-264.
    Quinton,J.D. and Rutter,M. An evaluation of an
interview assessment of marriage. Psychological Medicine,
1976, 6, 577-586.
    Vaughn,C. and Leff,J. The influence of family and
social factors on the course of psychiatric illness: a
comparison of schizophrenic and depressed neurotic patients.
British Journal of Psychiatry, 1976a, 129, 125.
    Vaughn,C. and Leff,J. The measurement of expressed
emotion in the families of psychiatric patients. British
Journal of Social and Clinical Psychology, 1976b, 15,
157-165.

FERREIRA,A.J. Interpersonal Perceptivity: Rejection

VARIABLES MEASURED. Perception of rejection by another
family member: Three scores are obtained (1) R, the
rejection score; (2) E, the expectancy of rejection score;
and (3) An empathy index, the difference between E and R.
TEST DESCRIPTION. Father, mother, and child each colors 11
flags drawn on 2-by-2-inch pieces of cardboard bearing a
stamped tri-striped flag. Each subject is provided with
eight crayons. The subjects are asked to try to color each
flag differently and to strive toward "the most pleasing
color combinations." Each subject then receives the flags
colored by the other two members, and is instructed to throw
away any that he/she dislikes for any reason. The subject
is told who drew the flags, and the envelope with the
drawer's name is placed on the table so it is visible. The
subject throws the flags into a box labeled "Bad-Throw
Away."

     Three scores are derived: (1) The R Score, the number
of flags of each family member thrown away; (2) The E
Score, how many flags each family member says he/she thinks
the other two will throw away; (3) The empathy index, the
difference between the guess (E) and the fact (R).   There
are six scores for each family member: two E scores, two R
scores, and the empathy indexes for them. The E scores were
categorized simply as good or bad: a guess was considered
good if the difference between the E and R score was less
than $\pm$ 1.
SAMPLE ITEM. See test description.
LENGTH. Items: 11 flags to color for each S.
AVAILABILITY. Fully described in Ferreira, 1964.
REFERENCE.
     Ferreira,A.J. Interpersonal perceptivity among family
members. American Journal of Orthopsychiatry, 1964, 34,
64-70.

GALLAGHER,B.J.III Generationalism Scale

VARIABLES MEASURED. Intergenerational differences in
attitudes of family members.
TEST DESCRIPTION. The test items measure degree of
conservatism and/or liberalism in five areas of life:
sexual freedom, political activism, importance of
traditional religion, child-rearing ideology and the social
role of women. All items are worded in a way that a strong
disagreement response manifests extreme liberalism using a
five-point scale response.
SAMPLE ITEM. For the most part, do you think a woman's
place is in the home? Definitely yes = 1 (conservative);
Yes = 2; Not certain = 3; No = 4; Definitely no = 5
(liberal).
LENGTH. Time: approximately 10 minutes. Items: 16
(originally more with the inclusion of other attitudinal
areas).

AVAILABILITY. From NAPS-2.
ABSTRACTED BY: Bernard J. Gallagher, III.
REFERENCES.
    Gallagher,B.J.III An empirical study   of   attitude
differences   between   three   kin-related   generations.
Dissertation Abstracts International, 1973, 33, No.   7,
Order No. 73-1390.
    Gallagher,B.J.III An empirical analysis of attitude
differences between three kin-related generations. Youth
and Society, 1974, 5, 327-349.
    Gallagher,B.J.III Ascribed and self-reported attitude
differences   between   generations.   Pacific Sociological
Review, 1976, 19, 317-333.
    Gallagher,B.J.III Attitude differences across three
generations: class and sex components. Adolescence, 1977.

GREENBERG,I.M.   Family Interaction Questionnaire

VARIABLES MEASURED. Intactness of family both physically
and emotionally. Degree of illness in family both medically
and psychiatrically.   Social embedment of family.   The
overall   rating   measures   the   degree   of   combined
intra-familial and social-familial function.
TEST DESCRIPTION. The interviewer takes a family history
dealing with psychiatric and medical illness, broken home,
parental aggression, social embedment of family, emotional
distance between parents, degree of income, breadwinners'
work performance, clinical disruption of home, parental
acceptance of patient and level of social aspiration.
    The   questionnaire   was   originally   designed   for
adolescents and young adults.   However, it is easily
adjusted to older, married persons with the word spouse
substituted for "father" or "mother" in the questionnaire.
    The family is considered to be "asocial" if all the
following criteria are met: (1) there is serious
psychiatric or medical illness in family before patient's
13th birthday;   (2) there is social isolation of family;
(3) one of the following is present: severe chronic
disease, severe emotional distance between parents, or
broken home.
SAMPLE ITEM. Social embededness of family: 1 = No visiting
to and from members of the extended family, or friends. No
participation in community activities or social organization
other than work and/or routine church attendance. 2 =
Minimal involvement in activities as described in (1). 3 =
Some relationship to one or few friends, and/or occasional
visits with extended family; or a small amount of social
and community participation.   4 = A moderate amount of
ordinary social activity, by the above standards;   either
community or extended family activity is sufficient. 5 = A
slightly higher than average amount of social activity, as
in (4). 6 = A family with full active participation in all
aspects of community participation. 7 = An extremely active
family, which is not active socially at the expense of its

members' relationships with each other.
LENGTH. Time: 2 hours. Items: 13.
AVAILABILITY. Educational Testing Service, Princeton, New
Jersey.
ABSTRACTED BY: Irwin M. Greenberg
REFERENCES.
        Greenberg,I.M. Developmental and clinical correlates
of cerebral dysrythmia. Archives of General Psychiatry,
1969, 21, 595-601.
        Greenberg,I.M. Clinical correlates of 14 and 60/sec.
Positive EEG spiking and family pathology. Journal of
Abnormal Psychology, 1970, 76, 403-413.
        Greenberg,I.M. and Rosenberg,G. Familial correlates
of the 14 and 6 CPS positive spike pattern. American
Psychiatric Association Psychiatric Research Report, 1966,
20, 121-130.

HAYWARD,R.S. Family Inventory

VARIABLES MEASURED.   Family maladjustment and eight
subscores to indicate extent of (1) Personal adjustment of
parents, (2) Attitude toward child adjustment, (3)
Husband-wife personal incompatibility, and (4) Family
incompatibility.
TEST DESCRIPTION. Questionnaire for children aged 9 and
over requiring Yes, No, or ? answers. Parallel questions
referring to mother and father under each of the four
variables; two forms: 319 items in long, 80 in short.
Internal consistency item analysis was used to select
questions scored.
SAMPLE ITEM. Will your father always let you do things when
your mother won't?
LENGTH. Items: 319 or 80.
AVAILABILITY. In Hayward, 1935.
REFERENCE.
        Hayward,R.S. The child's report of psychological
factors in the family. Archives of Psychology, New York,
1935, 189, 75.

HOBART,C.W. Marital Role Inventory

VARIABLES MEASURED. (1) Disagreement, (2) Offspring lack of
insight score, (3) Parent lack of insight, (4) Offspring
disagreement estimate, (5) Parent disagreement estimate.
TEST DESCRIPTION. A 70-item inventory with five responses
for each item: Strongly agree, Agree, No opinion, Disagree,
or Strongly disagree. Each subject responds to the
inventory twice--first he/she predicts the responses of
his/her same sex parent or of his/her offspring if he is a
parent, and second, he/she responds in terms of his/her own
opinions. Offspring also predict their marriage partner's
response. The responses are weighted 1 to 5. The five
scores are obtained as follows: (1) Disagreement score is

obtained by comparing, for example, a father's own responses
with his son's own responses to each of the 70 role items.
(2) The offspring lack of insight score is obtained by
comparing a son's predictions of his father's responses with
the father's own responses. (3) The parent lack of insight
score is obtained by comparing the father's predictions of
the son's responses with the son's own responses. (4) The
offspring disagreement estimate score is obtained by
comparing a son's predictions of his father's responses with
the son's own responses for each of the 70 role items, and
summing the individual item disagreement score. (5) The
parent disagreement estimate score is obtained in the same
way as the offspring disagreement estimate score.
SAMPLE ITEM. I would prefer in marriage to have only one
child, if having more meant a sacrificing of companionship
with my mate.
LENGTH. Items: 70.
AVAILABILITY. From author.
REFERENCES.
    Hobart,C.W. Some changes in parent-offspring
interaction during courtship and marriage. Pacific
Sociological Review, 1962, 5, 54-59.
    Hobart,C.W. Attitudes toward parenthood among Canadian
young people. Journal of Marriage and the Family, 1973, 35,
71-82.

MARTIN,B. Three-Way Family Interaction Task

VARIABLES MEASURED. Family interaction patterns focusing on
interaction involving blaming.
TEST DESCRIPTION. Three family members sit in chairs facing
each other around a coffee table. Interaction between
members is structured through the use of small movable
panels which allow communication between only two of the
three at any one time. The main point of this procedure is
to insure that each person directs all of his/her
expressions to one other person at a time. The verbal
interaction is recorded from microphones in the panels. A
second channel of the tape recorder records a signal that
indicates to whom each expression is directed. "Family
members are first asked to talk among themselves and decide
upon some recent incident involving disagreement or where
one or more family members were upset, disappointed, hurt or
angry; and then second, describe what happened, who did
what, who said what; and third, to tell each other what
their own feelings were in the situation." This sequence is
repeated for three different incidents. Raters rate each
unit of speech with respect to the following categories:
Indirect blaming = 1, Direct blaming = 2, Self blaming = 3,
Non-blaming description of a situation = 4; Non-blaming
description of own feelings = 5, Further explanation is
available in Martin, 1967.

SAMPLE ITEM.   See above.
LENGTH.   NR.
AVAILABILITY.   In Martin, 1967.
ABSTRACTED BY: Kersti Yllo
REFERENCE.
      Martin, B.   Family   interaction   associated   with   child
disturbance: assessment   and modification.   Psychotherapy:
Theory, Research and Practice, 1967, 4, 30-35.

SEVERY, L.J.   Exposure to Family Deviance Measure

VARIABLE MEASURED.   Family exposure to crime.
TEST DESCRIPTION.   To construct the index, offense rates   of
other   family members, seriousness of the offenses committed
by the other family members, and the depth of involvement in
the   formal   legal   structure   are   standardized.   The three
scores are added together into a single measure.
SAMPLE ITEM.   NR.
LENGTH.   Items: 3.
AVAILABILITY.   General description in Severy, 1973.
ABSTRACTED BY: Susan Murray
REFERENCE.
      Severy, L.J.   Exposure to deviance committed   by   valued
peer   group   and   family   measures.   Journal of Research in
Crime and Delinquency, 1973, 10, 35-46.

SPREITZER, E.A.   and   RILEY, L.E.   Family   of   Orientation
Pathology Index

VARIABLE MEASURED.   Family of orientation pathology.
TEST DESCRIPTION.   Data   are   obtained   by   extensive   life
history   interview.   The   index   summarizes   information
concerning the person's childhood family   experiences   along
several dimensions: stability of the family of orientation,
reasons for its disruption, the age of   departure   from   the
family   and   reasons   for this departure, and quality of the
respondent's   childhood   relationships   with   parents   and
siblings.   The family pathology index assigns weights to the
negative   features   of   these   dimensions   with   the   scores
ranging frcm 0 to 14.   Persons receiving scores of 0 to 3, 4
to 6, and 7 or more were classified as having low, moderate,
or high "childhocd family pathology," respectively.
SAMPLE ITEM.   If the individual left his   or   her   parents'
home   before   15   years   of   age   because   of   interpersonal
difficulties   with   the   parents,   a   weight   of   three   was
assigned.
LENGTH.   Items: 3 rating scales.
AVAILABILITY.   From NAPS-2.
ABSTRACTED BY: Lawrence E.   Riley
REFERENCES.
      Riley, L.E.   and   Spreitzer, E.A.   A   model   for   the
analysis of lifetime marriage patterns.   Journal of Marriage
and the Family, 1974, 36, 64-70.

Spreitzer,E.A. and Riley,L.E. Factors associated with singlehood. Journal of Marriage and the Family, 1974, 36, 533-542.

STRAUS,M.A. Conflict Tactics (CT) Scales

VARIABLES MEASURED. Three modes of dealing with intrafamily conflict: (1) Reasoning, (2) Verbal aggression, (3) Violence (physical aggression).
TEST DESCRIPTION. The CTS consists of a list of actions which a family member might take in relation to a conflict with another member. The items start with those low in coerciveness (such as discussing the issue with the other) and become gradually more coercive and aggressive towards the end of the list (such as slapping and hitting). The response categories ask for the number of times each action occurred during the past year, ranging from Never to More than 20 times. In the original version of the CTS (Straus, 1974) items A through D are summed to obtain the Reasoning score, items E through I the Verbal Aggression score, and items J through O the Violence score.
    The CTS items are presented with pairs of response categories, one pair for each family "role relationship" to be measured. Thus, if the husband-wife relationship is the focus, respondents are asked to indicate how often they did each act in relation to their spouse in the past year, and how often the spouse carried out each action. Similar pairs can be presented for the parent-child and the sibling-sibling roles. Thus, for each of the three conflict tactics, there can be at least seven individual actor scores: husband, wife, father, mother, child A (or all children), sibling A, and sibling B. The scores for the two partners in a role relationship can be combined into three role scores: spousal, parent-child, and sibling. A total family score can also be obtained for each conflict tactic.
    A revised version of the CTS (Straus, 1979) modified the original for use in a face to face interview rather than a self-administered questionnaire, and with a greater focus on Verbal Aggression and Violence. The changes consist of (1) Dropping one item and adding two Verbal Aggression and three Violence items. (2) Increasing the response category range from 0 to 5 to 0 to 6, and presenting them as a "response card." (3) Changes in some items. (4) Adding a place to record if the action "ever" happened.
SAMPLE ITEM. (revised version) Discussed the issue calmly. Never, Once, Twice, 3 to 5 times, 6 to 11 times, More than 20 times in the past year.
LENGTH. Time: 10 minutes for each role pair. Items: 14 (original); 18 (revised).
AVAILABILITY. In Straus, 1974; revised version in Straus 1979 or from NAPS-2.

REFERENCES.

Allen,C.M. and Straus,M.A. Resources, power, and husband-wife violence. In M.A.Straus and G.T.Hotaling (eds.) The Social Causes of Husband-Wife Violence. Publication now being arranged, 1978.

Bulcroft,R.A. and Straus,M.A. Validity of husband, wife, and child reports of conjugal violence and power. Mimeographed paper, 1975.

Steinmetz,S.K. The use of force for resolving family conflict: the training grcund for abuse. The Family Coordinator, 1977, 26, 19-26.

Steinmetz,S.K. The Cycle of Violence: Assertive, Aggressive, and Abusive Family Interaction. New York: Prager, 1977.

Straus,M.A. A general systems theory approach to a theory of violence between family members. Social Science Information, 1973, 105-125.

Straus,M.A. Leveling, civility, and violence in the family. Journal of Marriage and the Family, 1974a, 36, 13-29, plus addendum in August, 1974 issue.

Straus,M.A. Wife-beating: how common and why? Victimology, 1977-78, 2, 443-458.

Straus,M.A. Measuring intrafamily conflict and violence: The Conflict Tactics (CT) scales. Journal of Marriage and the Family, 1979, 41.

Straus,M.A. Gelles,R.J. and Steinmetz,S.K. Violence in the American Family. New York: Anchor/Doubleday, 1978.

VAN-DER-VEEN,F. HUEBNER,B.F.   JORGENS,B.   AND NEJA,P.Jr.
Family Concept Test

VARIABLES MEASURED. Feelings and attitudes concerning (1) Ideal family. (2) Real family. (3) The extent to which these coincide with expert opinion (family adjustment score), and (4) With spouse's view (mother-father agreement score).
TEST DESCRIPTION. Eighty cards, each containing a statement describing the family, are presented to subject in random order and placed by him/her in 9 piles ranging from Least like my family (pile 1) to Most like my family (pile 9). Subject is instructed to place only a certain number of cards in each pile: 3 on pile 1, 6 on pile 2, 9 on pile 3, 13 on pile 4, 18 on pile 5 (piles 6, 7, 8, and 9 correspond in decreasing order to the first half of the progression).

The technique can be used not only to describe the person's real family concept but also to describe his/her ideal family concept, the S's family of orientation, the typical family, and so forth. There are four basic measures derived from the Q-sort: (1) The description of the family concept (real or ideal)--items are scored by assigning the

numerical value cf the piles in which they are placed;   (2)
the family adjustment score--a simple arithmetic addition of
the number of 47 items subject placed on the same side of
the Q-sort as did a group of professional judges (the 10
judges were professional clinicians who placed the items in
terms of their evaluation of the ideal family concept; the
47 items are those items upon which the judges substantially
agreed);   (3) The real-ideal agreement score--correlation
between a parent's real and ideal family concepts;   (4) The
father-mother   agreement   sccre--correlation between   the
family concepts of the father and of the mother.
     A factor analysis by Van-der-Veen, Howard, and
O'Mahoney (1971) revealed the following eight factors:
Consider action versus conflict, Venture some enjoyment
versus Concern with problems, Open personal communication,
Extrafamilial   sociability,   Family   ambition,
Acceptance-rejecticn of responsibility, Togetherness versus
separateness, and Importance of family. The score for each
of these factors is the mean of the raw scores for those
items that had high loadings on that factor, but did not
load highly on any other factor. In addition, the ninth
score (Affectionate trust versus alienation) is computed
from three items not included in one of the factor scores
because of being loaded cn two or more factors.
SAMPLE ITEM. We just cannot tell each other our real
feelings.
LENGTH. Time: 30 to 45 minutes. Items: 80.
AVAILABILITY. From NAPS.
REFERENCES.
     Berkowitz,N.   Perceived family relationships in
families differing in adjustment level. M.A. Thesis,
University of Wisconsin, 1963.
     Hurley,J.R. and Palonen,D.P. Marital satisfaction and
child density among university student parents. Journal of
Marriage and Family, 1967, 29, 483-484.
     Melnick,B. and Hurley,J.R. Distinctive personality
attributes of child-abusing mothers. Journal of Consulting
and Clinical Psychology, 1969, 33, 746-749.
     Novak,A.L. and Van-der-Veen,F. Family concepts and
emotional   disturbance   in   the   families of disturbed
adolescents with normal siblings. Family Process, 1970, 9,
157-171.
     Van-der-Veen,F.   The   Family   Concept   Q-sort.
Unpublished paper, Dane County Guidance Center, Madison,
Wisconsin, 1960.
     Van-der-Veen,F. The parent's concept of the family
unit and child adjustment. Journal of Counseling
Psychology, 1965, 12, 196-200.
     Van-der-Veen,F. Family Unit Inventory Family Research
Institute. Chicagc,Ill.: Institute for Juvenile Research,
1969.
     Van-der-Veen,F. Dimensions of the family concept and
their relation to gender, generation, and disturbances.
Mimeographed. Chicago: Institute for Juvenile Research,
1975.

        Van-der-Veen,F.   Howard,K.I.   and   Austria,A.M.
Stability and equivalence of scores based on three different
response formats. Proceedings of the seventy-eighth annual
meeting,   American   Psychological   Association,
Washington,D.C., 1970.
        Van-der-Veen,F.   Howard,K.I.   and   O'Mahoney,M.T.
Dimensions of the family concept in relation to emotional
disorder and family position. Proceedings, 79th Annual
Convention, APA, 1971, 451-452.
        Van-der-Veen,F.   Huebner,B.F.   Jorgens,B.   and
Neja,P.Jr. Relationships between the parent's concept of
the family and family adjustment. American Journal of
Orthopsychiatry, 1964, 34, 45-55.
        Van-der-Veen,F. and Novak,A.L. Perceived parental
attitudes and family concepts of disturbed adolescents,
normal siblings and normal controls. Family Process, 1971,
10, 327-343.
        Van-der-Veen,F. and Novak,A.L. The family concept of
the disturbed child: a replication study. American Journal
of Orthopsychiatry, 1974, 44, 763-772.

WATZLAWICK,P.   BEAVIN,J.   SIKORSKI,L.   and   MECIA,B.
Structured Family Interview

VARIABLES MEASURED. (1) Scapegoating: tendency of family
to blame family member for things he/she is not guilty of;
(2) Protection: tendency of family to protect family member
from possible blame.
TEST DESCRIPTION. "Family is seated around the table with
the father to the left of the interviewer, the mother to the
father's left, followed by the children in clockwise
direction from the oldest to the youngest. Each family
member is asked to write down the main fault of the person
sitting on his left. The family members are assured that
the interviewer will not reveal the author of any statement.
In addition, they are told that the interviewer will himself
add two statements to the ones written by them. (These
statements are always 'too good' and 'too weak'. They are
added to increase the degree of freedom available to the
family and are hopefully ambiguous enough to be applicable
to anyone.) ...After writing his statements, the interviewer
shuffles the cards and begins to read them out, one after
the other, to the family. After reading each card he asks
all family members in turn, beginning with the father and
finishing with the youngest child: "to whom do you think
this applies?" However, although he shuffles the cards in
plain sight of the family, the interviewer always starts
with his own two statements ('too good' and 'too weak'). If
necessary the interviewer will insist on a forced choice and
will not accept responses like 'This applies to both our
children' or 'This does not apply to anybody in our family'.
Each family member is thus forced to blame somebody, and by
doing so implies automatically that in his opinion this
criticism was levelled by the person sitting on the right of

the victim."
From the data generated by this method, a number of
scores can be created for each family member. These scores
can be compared to overall family mean to see if the score
of any one family member is particularly high or low. The
scores are: (a) Receiving item actually written about
oneself, i.e. how accurately is one perceived. (b)
Receiving items not actully written about oneself, i.e., a
scapegoating score. (c) The combined accuracy of the two
previous scores. (d) Total family attributions received.
(e) Total extrafamilial items received ("too good" and "too
weak," experimenter introduced items). (f) Total criticisms
received. (g) Correct attributions of fault statements
written by others. (h) Written by self and correctly
assigned, i.e. how honest was person about fault statement
he wrote. (i) Overall accuracy of attribution.
SAMPLE ITEM. See above.
LENGTH. NR.
AVAILABILITY. In Watzlawick,et al., 1970.
ABSTRACTED BY: David Finkelhor
REFERENCE.
Watzlawick,P. Beavin,J. Sikorski,L. and Mecia,B.
Protection and scapegoating in pathological families.
Family Process, 1970, 9, 27-39.

WELLS,C.F. and RABINER,E.L. Family Index of Tension (FIT)

VARIABLES MEASURED. Three factor analysis derived scores:
(1) Incongruence of identified patient-family expectations.
(2) Frustration of identified patients basic needs by
family. (3) Family disagreement regarding problem
definition and approach to the problem.
TEST DESCRIPTION. The FIT is a rating form to be used to
score the protocols from the "Conjoint Family Diagnostic
Interview" (CFDI). Each factor consists of a subset of the
15 rating scales. The CDFI is a problem-focused conjoint
interview. The interview covers the presenting complaints,
an inventory of family operations, the kinds of
disagreements the family members have, typical transactions
in relation to these disagreements, to how well each member
of the family sees himself/herself and the others as
fulfilling their role responsibilities in the family.
Finally, mannerisms and behaviors which each member finds
provocative in the cthers are covered.
SAMPLE ITEM. NR.
LENGTH. Time: 90 minutes for CFDI, 20 minutes for FIT.
Items: 15 rating scales.
AVAILABILITY. From NAPS-2.
REFERENCE.
Wells,C.F. and Rabiner,E.L. The Conjoint Family
Diagnostic Interview and the Family Index of Tension.
Family Process, 1973, 12, 127-144.

4. Extended Familism, Interaction With Kin (See also Subject Index)

ABRAHAMSON,M. Pervasiveness of Kinship Organization Index

VARIABLE MEASURED. The degree to which residential patterns, work activities, and patterns of interaction generally, are regulated by kinship criteria.
TEST DESCRIPTION. The index contains four societal characteristics taken from Murdock (1967) and Swanson (1960). Guttman scale reproducibility of the four items is .95. Societal Scores on this index vary from 0 to 22.8.
SAMPLE ITEM. Present, Absent: Large extended families involving at least two families of procreation in at least two adjacent generations.
LENGTH. Items: 4.
AVAILABILITY. In Abrahamson, 1969.
ABSTRACTED BY: Mark Abrahamson
REFERENCES.
    Abrahamson,M. Correlates of political complexity. American Sociological Review, 1969, 34, 690-701.
    Murdock,G.P. Ethnographic Atlas. Pittsburg: University of Pittsburg Press, 1967.
    Swanson,G.E. Birth of the Gods. Ann Arbor: University of Michigan Press, 1960.

ALDOUS,J. Intergenerational Continuity Index

VARIABLES MEASURED. Continuity over generations in religious affiliation, educational achievement, marital role task specializaticn and marital role task conventionality.
TEST DESCRIPTION. The index is the sum of the scores of each descent group on the religious, educational and two marital task variables. Scores are assigned as follows: a 2 for each variable where continuity is shown over three generations, a 1 for the variables which have only parent-child continuity, and a 0 where there is discontinuity between the youngest and previous generation.
    To measure marital role specialization and conventionality the wives report the degree to which they and their husbands separately perform household tasks as contrasted with doing them together. From their answers, the degree to which marital partners perform only those tasks conventionally assigned to their sex is determined.
SAMPLE ITEM. See Test Description.
LENGTH. NR.
AVAILABILITY. In Aldous, 1965.
REFERENCES.
    Aldous,J. Family continuity patterns over three generations: content, degree of transmission and consequences. Ph.D. dissertation, University of Minnesota,

1963.
      Aldous,J. The consequences of intergenerational
continuity. Journal of Marriage and the Family, 1965, 27,
462-468.

BARDIS,P.D. Familism Scale

VARIABLES MEASURED. Familistic role prescriptions.
TEST DESCRIPTION. Sixteen intensity of agreement attitude
questions, scored by linear summation. Of 17 items selected
by a panel of judges, the 16 included are the ones which
item analysis (top and bottom 10 percent) showed to be
significant for a sample of 100 Albion College students.
SAMPLE ITEM. (1) A person should always support his uncles
or aunts if they are in need. Strongly disagree =
0...Strongly agree = 4.
LENGTH. Items: 16.
AVAILABILITY. In Bardis, 1959c; Shaw and Wright, 1967.
REFERENCES.
      Bardis,P.D. Attitudes toward the family among college
students and their parents. Sociology and Social Research,
1959a, 43, 352-358.
      Bardis,P.D. A comparative study of familism. Rural
Sociology, 1959b, 24, 362-371.
      Bardis,P.D. A familism scale. Marriage and Family
Living, 1959c, 21, 340-341.
      Bardis,P.D. Influence of a functional marriage course
on attitudes toward familism. Journal of Educational
Sociology, 1959d, 32, 232-239.
      Blair,M.J. An evaluation of the Bardis Familism Scale.
Journal of Marriage and the Family, 1972, 34, 265-268.
      Geersten,H.R. and Gray,R.M. Familistic orientation
and inclination toward adopting the sick role. Journal of
Marriage and the Family, 1970, 32, 638-646.
      Kassees,A.S. Cross-cultural comparative familism of a
Christian Arab people. Journal of Marriage and the Family,
1972, 34, 538-544.
      Larsen,K.S. Premarital sex attitudes--a scale and some
validity findings. Journal of Social Psychology, 1973, 20,
339-340.
      Shaw,M.E. and Wright,J.M. Scales for the Measurement
of Attitudes. New York: McGraw-Hill, 1967.

BERARDO,F.M. Kinship Interaction

VARIABLE MEASURED. Frequency of visiting relatives living
outside of the immediate household.
TEST DESCRIPTION. Data on visiting kin are gathered for
relatives who lived in and outside of the state and
specifically included parents, brothers, sisters, first
cousins, uncles, aunts, and grandparents and in-laws.
      Frequency of visiting each relative is recorded
separately. Respondents are asked, How often, on the

average, do you see your (relative) who lives in (outside) this state? (1) Do not have any, (2) Every day, (3) Once a week or more, (4) Once a month or more, (5) More than once a year, (6) About once a year, (7) Every two or three years, (8) Less often than every three years. Responses were converted to a yearly base and summed. Responses are then collapsed into low, medium, and high interaction.
SAMPLE ITEM. See above.
LENGTH. Time: 15 minutes. Items: The eight response categories indicated above.
AVAILABILITY. In Appendix A of Berardo, 1965 and from NAPS-2.
ABSTRACTED BY: Felix M. Berardo.
REFERENCES.
    Berardo,F.M. Internal migrants and extended family relations. Ph.D. dissertation. Florida State University, 1965.
    Berardo,F.M. Kinship interaction and migrant adaptation in an aerospace-related community. Journal of Marriage and the Family, 1966, 28, 296-304.
    Berardo,F.M. Kinship interaction and communications among space-age migrants. Journal of Marriage and the Family, 1967, 29, 541-554.

BULTENA,G.L. Familial Interaction Index

VARIABLE MEASURED. Frequency of face-to-face familial interaction.
TEST DESCRIPTION. An index score is obtained that measures the frequency with which elderly persons interact with their adult children and siblings. Predetermined interaction categories are used in the response format. Twenty-five points are assigned for each child or sibling seen daily; 19 for those seen several times a week; 16 if seen once a week; 9 if seen several times a month; 7 if seen once a month; 4 if several times a year; 2 if once a year; and 1 if less than once a year. Greater relative weight is given to weekly and monthly contacts than to daily contacts.
SAMPLE ITEM. See above.
LENGTH. Items: As many as there are adult children and siblings.
AVAILABILITY. In Bultena, 1969.
ABSTRACTED BY: Gordon L. Bultena
REFERENCE.
    Bultena,G.L. Rural-urban differences in the familial interaction of the aged. Rural Sociology, 1969, 34, 5-15.

CLELAND,C.B. Familism Scales

VARIABLES MEASURED. Five aspects of familism: (1) Family integration (shared activity), (2) Kinship contacts, (3) Family continuity on the land, (4) Father-centered decision-making, (5) Father-centered income allocation, and

(6) Division of labor by age and sex.
TEST DESCRIPTION. Each scale is composed of 4 to 10 items
scored 0 or 1. Some items are applicable only to farm
families. Information obtained by interview. Score on the
scale is the percentage of possible positive answers.
Intercorrelations of scale scores show that scales 1, 2, and
3 form one cluster; 4 and 5 another cluster; 6 is
independent of all the others.
SAMPLE ITEM. Does the whole family go into town as a group?
Yes, No.
LENGTH. Items: 38.
AVAILABILITY. In Saskatchewan Report, 1956, and summarized
in Cleland, 1955.
REFERENCES.
     Cleland,C.B. Familism in rural Saskatchewan. Rural
Sociology, 1955, 20, 249-257.
     Province of Saskatchewan, Royal Commission on
Agriculture and Rural Life. Report No. 10: The Home and
Family in Rural Saskatchewan. Regina: The Queen's Printer,
1956, 60-88, 154-189.

KEY,W.H. Family Participation Scale

VARIABLES MEASURED. (1) Participation in the extended
family; (2) Participation in the immediate family.
TEST DESCRIPTION. An 11-item questionnaire with two to four
weighted responses (weights 0 to 3). The questionnaire has
five items for measuring the first variable, six items for
the second. The responses from each subject for each
variable are totaled to give the score.
SAMPLE ITEM. How often do you visit in the homes of
relatives whether here or elsewhere? At least once a month
= 2; At least once a year but less than once a month = 1;
Less often than once a year = 0.
LENGTH. Items: 11.
AVAILABILITY. In Key, 1961.
REFERENCE.
     Key,W.H. Rural-urban differences and the family.
Sociological Quarterly, 1961, 2, 49-56.

KHATRI,A.A. Family Jcintness Scale

VARIABLE MEASURED. Extent to which respondent's family
approaches complete jointness.
TEST DESCRIPTION. A scale for use in India to measure
jointness of families consists of four sections: (1)
residence, (2) pooling of income and financial help, (3)
property and (4) decision making. There are in all 10 items
in the scale. Section on residence has three items which
deal with the number of persons staying with the respondent,
and the members of "ideal joint family" who do not stay with
the respondent (staying separately i.e. "nonresidential")
and number of kitchens in the residence. Section 2 on

pooling of income and financial help taps other information like number of earning members, who keeps the income of the family, and nature of financial help to one another or from nonresidential units. Section 3 on property has two items, one for residentially nuclear family and the other for residentially joint family which taps whether the property is common or divided. The last section on decision making has two items which tap how major decisions are taken in the family and role of family head on such occasions. Scores from the four sections are totaled. The higher the score, the more completely joint the family.
SAMPLE ITEM. Do the family members who are not living with you contribute to your family expenses. Yes--total expenses = 20, Part of the expenses = 10, No = 0.
LENGTH. Time: 10 minutes. Items: 10.
AVAILABILITY. From NAPS-2.
ABSTRACTED BY: Bruce Brown
REFERENCE.
        Khatri,A.A. Manual of the scale to measure jointness of families in India. Amedabad, India: Rajratan Press.

LITWAK,E. Extended Family Orientation Scale

VARIABLE MEASURED. Extended family cohesion.
TEST DESCRIPTION. A series of intensity of agreement interview questions to determine degree of liking and interaction with kin.
SAMPLE ITEM. Generally I like the whole family to spend evenings together.
LENGTH. Items: 4.
AVAILABILITY. In Litwak, 1960b.
REFERENCES.
        Dyer,E.D. Upward social mobility and extended family cohesion as perceived by the wife in Swedish urban families. Journal of Marriage and the Family, 1972, 34, 713-724.
        Litwak,E. Primary group instruments for social control in industrial society: the extended family and the neighborhood. Ph.D. dissertation, Columbia University, 1958.
        Litwak,E. Geographical mobility and extended family cohesion. American Sociological Review, 1960a, 25, 385-394.
        Litwak,E. Occupational mobility and extended family cohesion. American Sociological Review, 1960b, 25, 9-21.

MAPSTONE,J.R. Familism Index

VARIABLE MEASURED. Individuals' commitment to familistic behavior patterns.
TEST DESCRIPTION. Eleven attitude and behavior questions reflecting Burgess's description of familism. These include parental supervision of children's earnings, the parental role in mate selection, and interest in occupational and ethnic continuity. Responses which appear to contribute to

the creation, continuity and maintenance of an integrated and solid family system are regarded as familistic ones. To provide a gross assessment of these responses, each answer which appears to be familistic is given a value of 1; non-familistic responses receive a value of 0. Scores are totalled and divided at the median.
SAMPLE ITEM. Do you think that children should seek the approval of their parents before they promise to marry someone?
LENGTH. Items: 11.
AVAILABILITY. In Mapstone, 1970.
ABSTRACTED BY: James R. Mapstone
REFERENCE.
    Mapstone,J.R. Familistic determinants of property acquisition. Journal of Marriage and the Family, 1970, 32, 143-150.

ROGERS,E.M. SEBALD,H. and ANDREWS,W.H. Family Integration and Kinship Orientation Scales

VARIABLES MEASURED. (1) Family integration; (2) Kinship orientation.
TEST DESCRIPTION. Three sets of interview or questionnaire items summed to measure solidarity within the nuclear and extended Family: (1) Family integration (Iowa)--12 items, both attitudinal and behavioral, to be answered by farm husbands and wives; (2) family integration (Ohio)--8 items asking how often the family participates in certain activities, answered: Often, Sometimes, Seldom, Never; and (3) Kinship orientation (Iowa)--7 items to measure the degree to which the individual fulfills the role expectations of the extended kinship reference group.
SAMPLE ITEMS. Attend community events with immediate family rather than with others (Iowa). How often do you help your children with their schoolwork and problems? (Ohio)
LENGTH. Items: 1 = 12, 2 = 8, 3 = 7.
AVAILABILITY. In Rogers and Sebald, 1962.
REFERENCES.
    Havens,A.E. Alienation and community integration in a suburban community. M.A. Thesis, Ohio State University, 1960.
    Rogers,E.M. A conceptual variables analysis of technological change. Ph.D. dissertation, Iowa State University, 1957.
    Rogers,E.M. and Sebald,H. Familism, family integration and kinship orientation. Marriage and Family Living, 1962, 24, 25-30.
    Sebald,H. Family integration in a rural fringe population. M.A. Thesis, Ohio State University, 1959.
    Sebald,H. and Andrews,W.H. Family integration and related factors in a rural fringe population. Marriage and Family Living, 1962, 24, 347-351.

ROHWER,R.   Familism in Farming Index

VARIABLE MEASURED. Familism in farming, defined as mutual
assistance and the subordinating of individual interests to
those of the family group.
TEST DESCRIPTION. A technique for classifying farm operator
families according to the following five aspects of familism
in farming and for combining the classifications into a
familism index: (1) Operators starting farming through
family arrangements, (2) Working together of the family in
regular farming activities, (3) Siblings' choice of the
occupation of farming, (4) Continuity of the family on a
home   farm,   and   (5) Family policy favoring business
arrangements and cooperation within the family. Each of the
factors is thought of as a continuum, but, for purposes of
scoring the index, each is dichotomized as representing
either familism or individualism. The subject's family is
rated as familistic or individualistic on each of the five
factors.   The index score consists of the number of aspects
of familism on which the subject's family is classified as
familistic. Data is obtained by interview.
SAMPLE ITEM.   Operators starting farming through family
arrangements: Operators who received their start through
arrangements that involved family members   more   than
nonrelatives (score value 1). Operators who obtained less
help from their families than from nonrelatives (score value
0).
LENGTH. Items: 5.
AVAILABILITY. In Rohwer, 1950.
REFERENCE.
    Rohwer,R.   Family Factors   in   Tenure   Experience:
Hamilton County, Iowa, 1946. Ames: Iowa State College
Agricultural Experiment Station Bulletin 375, 1950.

ROSEN,B.C.   Familistic-Individualistic Value Orientation

VARIABLE MEASURED. Degree to which subject is oriented
toward his/her family or toward an individualistic pattern.
TEST DESCRIPTION. Subscale of a test designed to measure
values functional for achievement motivation. Total scale
contains 14 statements (reduced to 8 on the basis of factor
analysis by Strodtbeck, 1958) which attempt to measure an
active-passive orientation, a present-future orientation,
and   familistic-individualistic   orientation.   Subject
indicates Agree, Disagree, or Undecided for each statement
(sometimes a five-point scale, from Strongly Agree to
Strongly disagree, is used). In the 14-item scale, 7 items
relate to the family.
SAMPLE ITEM. Nothing in life is worth the sacrifice of
moving away from your parents.
LENGTH. Items: 9.
AVAILABILITY. In Rosen, 1956.

REFERENCES.
    Rosen,B.C. The achievement syndrome: a psychocultural
dimension of social stratification. American Sociological
Review, 1956, 21, 203-211.
    Strodtbeck,F.L.   Family   interaction,   values   and
achievement.   In   McClelland,D.C.   Baldwin,A.L.
Bronfenbrenner,U. and Strodtbeck,F.L. (Eds.) Talent and
Society. New York: Van Nostrand, 1958.

SCHNAIBERG,A.   Extended Family Ties Index

VARIABLE MEASURED. Extended family ties.
TEST DESCRIPTION. The index covers items relating to adult
respondents' relationships to their own parents and adult
kin, as well as to their expectations from their own
children.   These include co-residence with parents or
in-laws, attachment to kin rather than to non-kin as
friends, arranged marriage and marriage to a relative, and
obligations of their children to them (both generally and in
old   age).   The items were selected on an a priori
theoretical basis, with no statistical screening criteria
used.
    Because of the indeterminacy of some items owing to
extraneous factors (such as the death of all parents and
in-laws, making impossible co-residence), two forms of the
scale were coded: a "voluntaristic" one, in which
respondents would have to choose a nonextended response, and
a "life-style" one, in which de facto arrangements were
coded, regardless of implied choice.   Little difference
appeared in the covariation patterns of these two forms of
coding.
SAMPLE ITEM. Feels closer to friends than relatives, or
closer to neither versus feels closer to relatives.
LENGTH. Items: 7.
AVAILABILITY. In Schnaiberg, 1970a, 1970b, 1971.
ABSTRACTED BY: Allan Schnaiberg.
REFERENCES.
    Schnaiberg,A. Rural-urban residence and modernism: a
study of Ankara province, Turkey. Demography, 1970a, 7,
71-85.
    Schnaiberg,A. Measuring modernism: theoretical and
empirical explorations. American Journal of Sociology,
1970b, 76, 399-425.
    Schnaiberg,A. The modernizing impact of urbanization:
a causal analysis. Economic Development and Cultural
Change, 1971, 20, 80-104.

SCHWARZWELLER,H.K.   Kinship Involvement Measures

VARIABLE MEASURED. Degree of interaction with nearby kin.
In   the   case   of   a   migrant   the variable refers to
"branch-family ties" in the area of destination.

TEST DESCRIPTION. Through interview or questionnaire, subjects are asked to list all their close kin living elsewhere, inclusive of parents, parents-in-law, siblings, siblings-in-law, and adult children. Infcrmation is then obtained on the frequency of visiting exchanges and the residential locaticn of each family unit. The "effective kinship group" is defined as kin families within a 50-mile radius of subject's place of residence. Frequency of visiting is converted to a yearly basis. The sum total of kin visiting divided by the total number of close kin families in the area yields an average visiting frequency. For migrants, this kinship involvement measure is interpreted as an indicator of the degree of interaction maintained with kinsfolk in the area of destination and, indirectly, of the strength of familial bonds within the kinship circle. A ccmparable measurement strategy is employed to ascertain "stem-family ties" of migrants in the area of origin.
SAMPLE ITEM. Are any members of your parental family--your brothers, sisters, parents or guardians--living elsewhere at present (not this household)? How often do you see them?
LENGTH. Time: about 5 minutes. Items: Depends on the number of kin.
AVAILABILITY. In Schwarzweller, Brown, and Mangalam, 1971.
ABSTRACTED BY: Harry K. Schwarzweller.
REFERENCES.
    Schwarzweller,H.K.   Brown,J.S.   and   Mangalam,J.J. Mountain Families in Transition. University Park, Pennsylvania: The Pennsylvania State University Press, 1971.
    Schwarzweller,H.K.   and   Seggar,J.F.   Kinship involvement: a factor in the adjustment of rural migrants. Journal of Marriage and the Family, 1967, 29, 662-671.

STRAUS,M.A. Kinship Integration and Network Connectedness Indexes

VARIABLES MEASURED. (1) Kinship integration is measured by the proportion of one's social life which involves relatives. (2) Network Connectedness is measured by the extent to which cne's friends are friends of each other.
TEST DESCRIPTION. Respondents are asked to give the first names of the eight people "you most often visit socially," and whether each of these people is a relative of themselves or their spouse. Respondents are then asked to indicate for each person on the list how many of the other seven that person visits socially. The Kinship Integration Index (Straus, 1969) is the number (ranging from 0 to 8) of those who are relatives. Separate scores can be computed for consanguinal and affinal kin integration. The Network Connectedness Index (Aldous and Straus, 1966) is the sum of the number of others cn the list which each respondent visits, divided by seven.

SAMPLE ITEM. See above.
LENGTH. Items: Two for each of the eight persons named.
AVAILABILITY. From NAPS-2.
REFERENCES.
     Aldous,J.   and   Straus,M.A.   Social   networks   and
conjugal roles: a test of Bott's Hypothesis.   Social
Forces, 1966, 44, 576-580.
     Straus,M.A. Social class and farm-city differences in
interaction with kin in relation to societal modernization.
Rural Sociology, 1969, 34, 476-495.

STRAUS,M.A. Kinship Solidarity Indexes

VARIABLE MEASURED. Integration into a patrilineal and/or
matrilineal kin group.
TEST DESCRIPTION. Respondents list their own brothers and
sisters and those of their father and mother. For each of
these listed plus the parents and grandparents,   the
respondent indicates how often they have been visited during
a specified referent time period (for example, during the
last year), and how much they like each of these persons.
The indexes are computed by multiplying the sum of the
visiting scores by the sum of the liking scores on the
assumption that "integration" or "solidarity" implies that
there is interaction and that this interaction has positive
value for the persons involved.   Separate scores can be
computed   for   integration   into   the patrilineage and
matrilineage, as well as the overall score combining these
two.
SAMPLE ITEM. Visiting: How often did you see this
(brother, sister, uncle, etc.)? Never = 0, Less than once
in 3 years = 1, Every 2 or 3 years = 2, About once a year =
3, 2 to 4 times a year = 4, 4 to 8 times a year = 5, Once or
twice a month = 6, 3 or more times a month = 7.
     Liking: How much do you like this (brother, sister,
uncle, etc.)?   Dislike a great deal = 0, Dislike
considerably = 1, Dislike somewhat = 2, Dislike a little =
3, Like a little = 4, Like somewhat = 5, Like considerably =
6, Like extremely well = 7.
LENGTH. Items: 2 questions for each person in the kin
network.
AVAILABILITY. See test description and from NAPS-2.
REFERENCES.
     Hutter,M. Transformation of identity, social mobility,
and kinship solidarity. Journal of Marriage and the Family,
1970, 32, 133-137.
     Straus,M.A. Laboratory Problems in Comparative Family
Organization.   Minneapolis.   Privately   Printed.   Also
available from NAPS-2.

SUSSMAN,M.B.   Intergenerational Family Continuity Rating
Scale

VARIABLES MEASURED.   (1) Feeling about children's marriage,
(2) Feeling about child-in-law, (3) Closeness of family now,
(4) Children come for advice and take advice now, (5) Family
celebrations now, (6) Visits between parents and children
now, (7) Communication between parents and children now, (8)
Help given to children now.
TEST DESCRIPTION.   Interview schedule, including both
open-ended and structured questions.   Each part of the
interview is rated on a three-point scale.   Scores are
assigned to one of four levels of family continuity: High,
Good, Fair, or Poor (a fifth possibility, "No family
continuity," did not occur in this sample).
SAMPLE ITEM.   NR.
LENGTH. Time: 1 1/2 to 4 hours for interview.
AVAILABILITY. From author.
REFERENCE.
     Sussman,M.B.   Intergenerational family relationships
and social role changes in middle age. Journal of
Gerontology, 1960, 15, 71-75.

SWEETSER,D.A. Communication Scale

VARIABLE MEASURED. Frequency of interaction (between adult
siblings).
TEST DESCRIPTION. The scale consists of the number of
positive replies to the following three items: whether the
person being interviewed said that he/she and the sibling
visited each other without special invitation, whether they
had seen and talked with each other in the last month, and
whether they had talked on the telephone in the last month.
A positive answer = 1; a negative answer = 0.
     The items were selected for the scale because they had
a strong unidimensional component underlying them, and
because they pertained to an aspect of interaction which is
not a priori a sex-specialized task, as are such things as
baby-sitting. The scale is a good indicator of interaction
in general.
SAMPLE ITEM.   Do you visit each other without special
invitation?
LENGTH. Time: 5 minutes. Items: 3.
AVAILABILITY. In Sweetser, 1970.
ABSTRACTED BY: Dorrian Apple Sweetser.
REFERENCE.
     Sweetser,D.A. The structure of sibling relationships.
The American Journal of Sociology. 1970, 76, 47-58.

UDRY,J.R.   and HALL,M.   Interconnectedness   of   Social
Networks Index

VARIABLE MEASURED. Interconnectedness of social networks.

TEST DESCRIPTION. The four persons named by each spouse as having had the most frequent social contact with him/her during the past year are interviewed. Each respondent is asked if he/she knows each of the other three persons named by that spouse, and if so, whether well or slightly. The interconnectedness index for each spouse is derived by scoring two points for each "Know well" response, one point for each "Know slightly" response, and no points for "Don't know."
SAMPLE ITEM. See test description.
LENGTH. Items: 3.
AVAILABILITY. In Udry and Hall, 1965.
REFERENCES.
     Bott,E. Family and Social Network. London: Tavistock Publications, 1957.
     Udry,J.R. and Hall,M. Marital role segregation and social networks in middle-class middle-aged couples. Journal of Marriage and the Family, 1965, 27, 392-395.

VENEZIA,P.S. Family Information Test (FIT)

VARIABLE MEASURED. Factual knowledge about family members, taken as indicative of integration into the family.
TEST DESCRIPTION. The Family Information Test (FIT) consists of 32 factual questions about family members, and is comprised of four sections: questions concerning siblings, parents, father, and mother. The test is given as an interview. In addition to the response the interviewer indicates for each question if it was answered with certainty (fact), the answer was not known (D.K.), or the respondent was not sure of the answer and guessing (guess). Each D.K. or guess response is scored as a failure, as is any multipart answer which gives definite responses to less than half the parts. The final score for each test is simply the total number of questions wrong.
SAMPLE ITEM. What is your mother's first, middle, and maiden name.
LENGTH. Items: 32.
AVAILABILITY. In Venezia, 1968.
ABSTRACTED BY: Susan Murray.
REFERENCE.
     Venezia,P.S. Delinquency as a function of intrafamily relations. Journal of Research in Crime and Delinquency, 1968, 5, 148-173.

WILKENING,E.A. Familism Index

VARIABLE MEASURED. Degree of dependence upon obligation to kin.
TEST DESCRIPTION. The index is composed of items of four types: (1) Influence of parents in occupational choice of children, (2) Nature of expectations pertaining to transfer of farm to children and to support of parents in old age,

(3) Extent to which parents are the source of knowledge
about farming and homemaking, and (4) The extent of social
contact and mutual aid among relatives as compared with
nonrelatives. Information needed to score the items is
obtained by interview.
SAMPLE ITEM. Have you thought that one of the children
should take over the farm?
LENGTH. Items: 15.
AVAILABILITY. In Wilkening, 1953, Appendix Table 7; see
also Wilkening, 1954.
REFERENCES.
    Wilkening,E.A. Adoption of Improved Farm Practices as
Related to Family Factors. Madison: University of
Wisconsin Agricultural Experiment Station Bulletin 183,
1953.
    Wilkening,E.A. Change in farm technology as related to
familism, family decision making, and family integration.
American Sociological Review, 1954, 19, 29-36.

WINCH,R.F. and GREER,S.A. Extended Familism Scale

VARIABLES MEASURED. Four aspects of extended familism: (1)
Extensity, (2) Intensity, (3) Interaction, and (4)
Functionality.
TEST DESCRIPTION. Information is obtained by interview.
(1) Extensity is defined as the number of households of kin
of both spouses in the community: None = 0, Some = 1-8,
High = 9 and above. (2) Intensity is defined as the degree
of kin of both spouses in the community: High = both
spouses have "nuclear" kin (parents, siblings, and
offspring) and also other households of kin in the
community; Some = presence of households of kin, but not
enough to qualify as High; None = no households of kin in
the community. (3) Interaction is defined as the number of
households of kin with which some member of the respondent's
household has contact at least monthly; None = 0, Some =
1-3, High = 4-6. (4) Functionality is defined as the number
of categories of service given to and/or received from some
kinsman: None = 0, Some = 1-2, High = 3 and above.
SAMPLE ITEM. (Extensity) How many households of kin do you
and your spouse have in this community?
LENGTH. NR.
AVAILABILITY. From NAPS-2.
REFERENCES.
    Winch,R.F. and Greer,S.A. Urbanism, ethnicity, and
extended familism. Journal of Marriage and the Family,
1968, 30, 40-45.
    Winch,R.F. Greer,S.A. and Blumberg,R.L. Ethnicity
and extended familism in an upper-middle-class suburb.
American Sociological Review, 1967, 32, 265-272.

B. Role Differentiation and Performance

1. Authority, Control, Power, Dominance (See also Subject Index)

ALKIRE,A.A. GOLDSTEIN,M.J. AND WEST,K.L. UCLA Family Project Social Influence and Counterinfluence Coding System

VARIABLES MEASURED. Verbal styles with which family members attempt to influence one another and the counterinfluence strategies used tc ward off such social pressures.
TEST DESCRIPTION. A coding system to identify a number of verbal styles through which social influence is exerted in interpersonal relationships observed in experimental interactions between parents and an adolescent child. A simulated interaction task is set up where each interviewee is instructed to react to a hypothetical social influence situation as though the cther person was present (called cue statements); then to predict the response of the other person (expectancy statement). The other family members, in separate rooms, respond to the taped cue statements after hearing the hypcthetical situation. They then respond to the same cue statements after hearing the taped expectancy statements. The social influence coding system is applied to the transcript tc measure expectation of others' responses, actual responses, and shifts in responses following awareness of expectations.
SAMPLE ITEM. Social influence coding categories: (a) legitimate influence, (b) expert influence, (c) referent influence, (d) infcrmation giving (e) information seeking, (f) yielding.
LENGTH. NR.
AVAILABILITY. A descriptive listing of the codes and examples of experimental interactions to which the codes have been applied, and a three-page set of notes on theory and rules of precedence compiled by Dr. Alkire is available upon request from UCLA Family Project, Franz Hall, UCLA, Los Angeles, Ca. 90024 and from NAPS-2.
ABSTRACTED BY: Kathryn L. West
REFERENCES.
    Alkire,A.A. Goldstein,M.J. Rodnick,E.H. and Judd,L.L. Social influence and counterinfluence within families of four types of disturbed adolescents. Journal of Abnormal Psychology, 1971, 77, 32-41.
    Goldstein,M.J. A follow-up study of disturbed adolescents. Paper presented at the American Psychological Association Convention, September, 1971.
    Goldstein,M.J. Judd,L.L. Rodnick,E.H. Alkire,A.A. and Gould,E. A method for studying social influence and coping patterns within families of disturbed adolescents. Journal of Nervous and Mental Disease, 1968, 147, 233-251.

ASTON,P.J. and DOBSON,G. (1) Family Participation Score
(2) Family Pairing Score

VARIABLES MEASURED. (1) Participation score: the
percentage of the total number of verbal participations
occurring during a triadic family discussion made by Father,
Mother and Child respectively. (2) Pairing score: amount
of pairing shown by a particular family member with one of
the other two members as compared with the amount shown to
the third member, expressed as a percentage.
TEST DESCRIPTION. The family, consisting of father, mother
and child, are set a discussion task (for example,
discussion on a series of ambiguous pictures) which is
recorded and transcribed verbatim.
(1) Participation score: working from the transcript, one
point is given for each participation regardless of length
or number of themes introduced. If the speaker is
interrupted and later continues what he/she was saying, this
counts as one and the same participation even if fresh
themes are added. Participation scores for each family
member are calculated as a percentage of the total number of
family participations.
(2) Pairing score: pairing behavior is scored when: (a) a
remark is clearly addressed to one other person only; (b) a
remark takes up something said by another unless it clearly
is not addressed to that person; (c) a question is directed
toward one other person. If it is unclear to whom the
question is addressed, the person answering it is assumed to
be the recipient. If a participation contains a remark
directed at each of the other two family members in turn, a
point is scored for each recipient. In no case is more than
one pairing point given per participation per recipient.
The amount of pairing shown by any one member with any other
member is then expressed as a percentage of the amount of
pairing he or she shows with both other members combined.
(A father addressing 70 participations to his wife and 50 to
his child, would, for example, obtain a 58% pairing score in
relation to his wife, and a 42% child-pairing score.)
SAMPLE ITEM. See above.
LENGTH. NR.
AVAILABILITY. From authors.
ABSTRACTED BY: P. Jean Aston
REFERENCES
    Aston,P.J. and Dobson,G. Family interaction and
social adjustment in a sample of normal school children.
Journal of Child Psychology and Psychiatry, 1972, 13, 77-89.

DYER,E.D. Democratic Companionship Conception of the Family

VARIABLES MEASURED. Conception of integration of an ideal
family, in terms of companionship and shared decision
making.

TEST DESCRIPTION. A series of multiple-choice interview
questions, each with five response categories, ranging from
Very necessary or desirable for a happy home to Decidedly
not desirable or necessary.
SAMPLE ITEM. How important is it for the ideal home or
family life that family members should decide together what
self-improvement activities (as music lessons, Scouts, etc.)
children must undertake?
LENGTH. Items: 6.
AVAILABILITY. In Dyer, 1970.
ABSTRACTED BY: Thomas G. Sparhawk.
REFERENCE.
     Dyer,E.D. Upward Social Mobility and Nuclear Family
Integration as Perceived by the Wife in Swedish Urban
Families. Journal of Marriage and the Family, 1970, 32,
341-350.

FARINA,A. Structured/Family Interaction Test (SFIT)

VARIABLES MEASURED. Dominance and conflict behaviors in
interaction between family members.
TEST DESCRIPTION. There are two versions: parents-only (12
situations) and parents plus a child (6 situations). Each
of the 12 open-ended hypothetical situations involves
difficulties or misbehaviors of a son (adapted from Jackson,
1956). In the first session, parents are asked separately
to indicate how he or she would handle the specific
situation. Following Strodtbeck (1955), the couple is asked
in a joint session to decide how they would handle the
situation. The E implies that modification of the
individual solutions is possible. From taped protocols of
all sessions, a series of measures is obtained "suggestive
of dominance behavior and extent of conflict between the
parents."
     All dominance and conflict scores except for yielding
measures are taken only from the joint parent interview.
The dominance indexes are: (1) Speaks first, (2) Speaks
last, (3) Total first and last, (4) Passive acceptance of
solution, (5) Total time spoken, (6) Yielding-maximum, and
(7) Yielding-minimum. The last two yielding scores are
obtained by comparing the solution arrived at during the
joint session with the solutions given individually; if the
joint score is closer to that originally proposed by the
father, then the mother is considered to have yielded to the
father. These yielding scores are based on Jackson's
scoring system of severity of solution. Minimum and maximum
scores are computed to allow for the fact that more than one
solution may be offered (e.g., yielding-minimum is derived
from the least severe solution offered).
     All dominance indexes result in one score for both
parents, since the score for the mother is subtracted from
the score for the father (e.g., if the father speaks first 8
times and the mother speaks first four times, the
speaks-first score is 4). Therefore, a positive score

indicates father dominance, a negative score mother dominance. For total time spoken, a score more than 1 indicates father dominance, a score less than 1 indicates mother dominance. The conflict indexes are: (1) Frequency of simultaneous speech, (2) Duration of simultaneous speech, (3) Interruptions by mother, (4) Interruptions by father, (5) Interruptions-total, (6) Disagreements and Aggressions by mother, (7) Disagreements and Aggressions by father, (8) Total Disagreements and Aggressions, (9) Failure to agree, (10) Verbal activity. A measure of parental dominance was adapted from a procedure using the SFIT (Hetherington, 1966). She modified Farina's problem situations to make them more suitable for all age levels in her study. Hetherington and Frankie (1967) adapted Farina's instrument to measure parental dominance, warmth, hostility and conflict.

SAMPLE ITEM. Your husband (wife) has punished your 10-year-old son for something he did. As he walks by now you hear him mumble a nasty description about his father (mother).

LENGTH. Items: 12 hypothetical situations, 17 dominance and conflict indexes.

AVAILABILITY. Three problem situations are given and all dominance and conflict measures are reported in Farina, 1960. Other problem situations are reported in Farina, 1958; also see Garmezy et al., 1960.

REFERENCES.

Becker,J. and Iwakami,E. Conflict and dominance with families of disturbed children. Journal of Abnormal Psychology, 1969, 74, 330-335.

Biller,H.B. Father dominance and sex-role development in kindergarten-age boys. Developmental Psychology, 1969, 1, 87-94.

Cicchetti,D.V. Reported family dynamics and psychopathology: I: the reaction of schizophrenics and normals to parental dialogues. Journal of Abnormal Psychology, 1967, 72, 282-289.

Cicchetti,D.V. and Farina,A. Relationship between reported and observed dominance and conflict among parents of schizophrenics. Journal of Consulting Psychology, 1967, 31, 223.

Cicchetti,D.V. and Ornston,P.S. Reported family dynamics and psychopathology: II: the reactions of mental patients to a disturbed family in psychotherapy. Journal of Abnormal Psychology, 1968, 73, 156-161.

Farina,A. Patterns of role dominance and conflict in the interaction of parents of schizophrenic patients. Ph.D. dissertation, Duke University, 1958.

Farina,A. Patterns of role dominance and conflict in parents of schizophrenic patients. Journal of Abnormal and Social Psychology, 1960, 61, 31-38.

Farina,A. and Holzberg,J.D. Attitudes and behaviors of fathers and mothers of male schizophrenic patients. Journal of Abnormal Psychology, 1967, 72, 381-387.

Farina,A. and Holzberg,J.D. Interaction patterns of

parents and hospitalized sons diagnosed as schizophrenic or nonschizophrenic. Journal of Abnormal Psychology, 1968, 73, 114-118.
    Farina,A. Holzberg,J.D. and Dies,R.R. Influence of the parents and verbal reinforcement on the performance of schizophrenic patients. Journal of Abnormal Psychology, 1969, 74, 9-15.
    Farina,A. Stoors,C. and Dunham,R. Measurement of family relationships and their effects. Archives of General Psychiatry, 1963, 9, 64-73.
    Garmezy,N. Farina,A. and Rodnick,E.H. Direct study of child-parent interactions: The structured situational test. A method for studying family interaction in schizophrenia. American Journal of Orthopsychiatry, 1960, 30, 445-452.
    Gassner,S. and Murray,E.J. Dominance and conflict in the interactions between parents of normal and neurotic children. Journal of Abnormal Psychology, 1969, 74, 33-41.
    Hetherington,E.M. A developmental study of the effects of sex of the dominant parent on sex-role preference, identification and imitation in children. Journal of Personality and Social Psychology, 1965, 2, 188-194.
    Hetherington,E.M. The effects of familial variables on sex typing, on parent-child similarity, and on imitation in children. Minnesota Symposia on Child Psychology, Vol. 1, 1967, 82-107.
    Hetherington,E.M. and Frankie,G. Effects of parental dominance, warmth and conflict on imitation in children. Journal of Personality and Social Psychology, 1967, 6, 119-125.
    Hetherington,E.M. Stouwie,R.J. and Ridberg,E.H. Patterns of family interaction and child-rearing attitudes related to three dimensions of juvenile delinquency. Journal of Abnormal Psychology, 1971, 78, 160-176.
    Jackson,P.W. Verbal solutions to parent-child problems. Child Development, 1956, 27, 339-349.
    LaVoie,J.C. and Looft,W.R. Parental antecedents of resistance-to-temptation behavior in adolescent males. Merrill-Palmer Quarterly, 1973, 19, 107-116.
    Phillips,L. Case history data and prognosis in schizophrenia. Journal of Nervous and Mental Disease, 1953, 117, 515-525.
    Strodtbeck,F.L. Husband-wife interaction over revealed differences. In Hare, P., Borgatta,E.F., and Bales,R.F. eds. Small groups. New York: Knopf, 1955.
    Turk,J.L. and Bell,N.W. Measuring power in families. Journal of Marriage and the Family, 1972, 34, 215-222.

HALEY,J. Family Coalition Experiment

VARIABLES MEASURED. Ability to form and maintain coalitions among family members.

TEST DESCRIPTION. Father, mother, and child are placed at a
round table with high partitions so that they cannot see
each other. In front of each person is a counter which
accumulates a score and two buttons labeled for the persons
on the left and right. Besides these two "coalition
buttons" there are two "signal buttons." By pushing either
of the signal buttons, for example, mother can signal father
or child. The counters begin to add up a score whenever two
people choose each other by pressing each other's coalition
button. Each person can gain a score only if he/she joins
another person, and then he/she and that person gain exactly
the same amount of score. Each person can signal another
with the signal button to invite a coalition. The family is
placed at the table and told this is a game they are to
play. They should try to win by getting the highest score.
They may push buttons one at a time, two at a time, or not
at all. The game consists of four rounds of two minutes
each. To win, each person must shift coalitions and gain
scores from both of the other two players. Talking is not
permitted but there are no restrictions on combinations of
signaling and coalition button pressing. For the fourth
game, however, they are asked to talk together and decide
who is to win and who is to lose and to see if they can make
the score come out as they planned.
SAMPLE ITEM. See test description.
LENGTH. Time: 8 minutes or more. Items: four two-minute
games plus instruction time and discussion time before the
fourth game.
AVAILABILITY. In Haley, 1962.
REFERENCE.
      Haley,J. Family experiments: A new type of
experimentation. Family Process, 1962, 1, 265-293.

STRODTBECK,F.L. Revealed Difference Technique

VARIABLES MEASURED. Any variable which it is possible to
score from observation of family members attempting to
resolve a difference of opinion. See the scores developed
for the Bales Interaction Process Analysis (p. 24). In
addition to these, Strodtbeck has developed a decision power
score and an index of supportiveness.
TEST DESCRIPTION. A questionnaire requiring agreement or
disagreement with a series of opinion and role prescriptive
statements is administered separately to each member of the
family. Items on which there is disagreement are then
selected, and the family is asked to "talk this over and see
if it's possible to agree on one of the choices." The
principal purpose of the revealed difference technique is to
counter the tendency for family members to avoid public
discussion of differences and present a united front to the
E, as tends to happen when a problem is simply presented to
the entire family for discussion and a decision (Vidich,
1956). The interaction which occurs in attempting to
resolve this "revealed difference" is recorded for later

scoring by the Bales Interaction Process Analysis or other
suitable scoring system. If the family group contains
children, differences in responses can be selected to
represent each of the possible types of coalitions.
   The decision power score is the percentage of decisions
reached which are resolved in favor of each family member,
converted to angular readings by the arcsine transformation
(Strodtbeck, 1958). The index of supportiveness is the sum
of the negative acts (using Bales's categories) from person
1 to person 2, subtracted from the sum of the positive acts,
and the total divided by the number of acts from person 2 to
person 1 (Strodtbeck, 1958). The decision power index can
also be scored without recording any of the interaction
except the person in whose favor the decision was resolved,
as in the case of Middleton and Putney's Family Decision
Dominance Index (Middleton and Putney, 1960; Putney and
Middleton, 1960).
   A Revealed-Difference questionnaire was developed by
Mishler and Waxler (1968) by combining items previously used
by Strodtbeck with new items. Some of the original items
which were considered threatening to family members and
difficult for them to discuss were omitted or less
controversial items were substituted.
   Liu, Hutchinson and Hong (1972) presented couples with
a series of short story stimuli which terminate in a
problematic dilemma.
   In Ferreira and Winter's variation (see abstract),
after family members separately answer the questionnaire
their differences are not made available to them and they
jointly answer the questionnaire as a family. They are
encouraged to discuss their choices and this verbal
interaction is recorded for later coding.
SAMPLE ITEM. Two fathers were discussing their sons, one a
brilliant student and the other a promising athlete. Some
people believe that one father was more fortunate than the
other. Do you think the father with the more athletic son
or the father with the studious son was more fortunate?
Athletic son's father, Studious son's father.
LENGTH. Time: about 2 1/2 hours to administer the Revealed
Difference Technique and record interaction (three-person
families) over nine revealed differences. Items: 47.
(This entry refers to the Revealed Difference Technique as
administered by Strodtbeck. It should be noted, however,
that questions referring to any set of shared experiences
can be used as the basis for determining differences to be
presented for discussion.)
AVAILABILITY. The questionnaire used to determine revealed
differences by Strodtbeck is available from ADI, Doc. No.
5501. Photocopies $2.50, microfilm $1.75.
REFERENCES.
   Alexander,J.F. Defensive and supportive communications
in family systems. Journal of Marriage and the Family,
1973, 35, 613-617.
   Bauman,G. and Roman,M. Interaction testing in the
study of marital dominance. Family Process, 1966, 5,

230-242.

Garmezy,N. Farina,A. and Rodnick,E.H.   Direct study of   child-parent   interactions.   I.   The   structured situational test. A method for studying family interaction in schizophrenia.   American Journal of Orthopsychiatry, 1960, 30, 445-452.

Hutchinson,I.W.   The   functional   significance   of conjugal communication in a transitional society. Journal of Marriage and the Family, 1974, 36, 580-587.

Hutchinson,J.G. Family interaction patterns and the emotionally   disturbed   child.   In   Winter,W.   and Ferreira,A.J.   (Eds.) Research in Family Interaction. Science and Behavior Books, Inc., Palo Alto, California, 1969, 187-191.

Karlsson,G.   A   reliability   test   of   the   Foote observational technique for studying interaction in the family. Gottingen: Vandenboech and Ruprecht, 1958.

Liu,W.T. Family interactions among local and refugee Chinese families in Hong Kong. Journal of Marriage and the Family, 1966, 28, 314-323.

Liu,W.T.   Hutchinson,I.W.   and   Hong,L.K.   The structural significance of conjugal power measure.   In Sussman,M.B.   and Cogswell,B.E.   (Eds.) Cross National Family Research.   Leiden, Netherlands: E.J. Brill, 1972, 161-177.

Liu,W.T.   Hutchinson,I.W.   and Hong,L.K.   Conjugal power and decision-making: A methodological note on cross-cultural study of the family. American Journal of Sociology, 1973, 79, 84-98.

March,J.G.   Husband-wife interaction over political issues. Public Opinion Quarterly, 1953, 54, 17, 461-470.

Middleton,R. and Putney,S. Dominance in decisions in the   family: Race   and   class differences. American Sociological Review, 1960, 65, 605-609.

Miller,A.G.   The   relationship   between   family interaction and sexual behavior in adolescence. Journal of Community Psychology, 1974, 2, 285-288.

Mishler,E.G. and Waxler,N.E. Interaction in Families. New York: John Wiley and Sons, Inc., 1968, 24, 307-313.

O'Connor,W.A.   and   Stachowiak,J.G.   Patterns   of interaction in families with low adjusted, high adjusted, and mentally retarded members. Family Process, 1971, 10, 229-241.

Olson,D.H.L.   The measurement of family power   by self-report and behavioral methods. Journal of Marriage and the Family, 1969, 31, 545-550.

Olson,D.H.L.   and Rabunsky,C.   Validity of   four measures of family power. Journal of Marriage and the Family, 1972, 34, 224-234.

O'Neill,M.S. and Alexander,J.F.   Family interaction patterns as a function of task characteristics. Journal of Applied Social Psychology, 1971, 1, 163-172.

Putney,S. and Middleton,R.   Effect of husband-wife interaction on the strictness of attitudes toward child rearing. Marriage and Family Living, 1960, 22, 171-173.

Schuham,A.I. Power Relations in emotionally disturbed
and normal family triads. Journal of Abnormal Psychology,
1970, 75, 30-37.
Schuham,A.I. Activity, talking time, and spontaneous
agreement in disturbed and normal family interaction.
Journal of Abnormal Psychology, 1972, 79, 68-75.
Strodtbeck,F.L. Husband-wife interaction over revealed
differences.   American   Sociological   Review,   1951,   16,
468-473.
Strodtbeck,F.L. The family as a three-person group.
American Sociological Review, 1954, 19, 23-29.
Strodtbeck,F.L.   Family   interaction,   values,   and
achievement.   In   McClelland,D.C.   Baldwin,A.L.
Bronfenbrenner,U. and Strodtbeck,F.L. Talent and Society.
New York: Van Nostrand, 1958, 135-194.
Strodtbeck,F.L. A Summary of Current Works on Family
Interaction Studies Using Revealed Differences. Chicago:
University of Chicago, Social Psychology Laboratory Working
Paper 31, offset print, 1964a.
Strodtbeck,F.L. Considerations of meta-method in cross
cultural   studies.   American Anthropologist, 1964b, 66,
223-229.
Titchener,J.L. D'Zmura,T. Golden,M. and Emerson,R.
Family transaction and derivation of individuality. Family
Process, 1963, 2, 95-120.
Turk,J.L. and Bell,N.W. Measuring power in families.
Journal of Marriage and the Family, 1972, 34, 215-222.
Vidich,A.J. Methodological problems in the observation
of husband-wife interaction. Marriage and Family Living,
1956, 18, 234-239.

2. Authority, Control, Discipline, Power with Affection,
Support, Love (See also Subject Index)

LEVINGER,G. and GUNNER,J. Interpersonal Grid

VARIABLES MEASURED. Family relationships in terms of two
orthogonial axes, love-hate and dominance-submission.
TEST DESCRIPTION. The test provides a way of describing
relationships along the two axes, adapting a figure
placement technique introduced by Kuethe (1962) for the
measurement of "social schemata." The S is asked to place
pairs of silhouette figures (human or rectangle) onto a
large neutral background "...in any manner you wish."
Closeness on the horizontal dimension indicates love-hate,
distance above or below another figure indicates
dominance-submission. In an unpublished report (Levinger,
1967, deposited with NAPS-2) Levinger used the Interpersonal
Grid to compare married with unmarried subjects in terms of
the degree of intimacy.

SAMPLE ITEM. On the first page, imagine that the standing figure is your father. Then pull off a female figure from the beige backing strip, and imagine that this is your mother. Place her in a relation to your father that you would consider ideal.
LENGTH, Items: 10 trials.
AVAILABILITY. In Levinger and Gunner, 1967.
ABSTRACTED BY: Bruce Brown.
REFERENCES.

Bhalla,S. and Turner,C. Cross-Cultural Comparisons of Interpersonal Schemas. Proceedings, 79th Annual Convention, American Psychological Association, 1971, 355-356.

Kuethe,J.L. Social Schemas. Journal of Abnormal Social Psychology, 1962, 64, 31-38.

Levinger,G. Developing a Comparative Measure of Family Interactions: A Pilot Project. Mimeographed paper, 1967.

Levinger,G. and Gunner,J. The Interpersonal Grid: 1. Felt and tape techniques for the measurement of social relationships. Psychonomic Science, 1967, 8, 4, 173-174.

Levinger,G. and Moreland,J. Approach-avoidance as a function of imagined shock threat and self-other similarity. Journal of Personality and Social Psychology, 1969, 12, 3, 245-251.

SCHUTZ,W.C. Fundamental Interpersonal Relations Orientation (FIRO) Scales

VARIABLES MEASURED. Interpersonal needs for inclusion, control and affection. These are measured in behavior or feeling, or both, and also with respect to desired feelings and expressed feelings.
TEST DESCRIPTION. FIRO-E. Contains six scales measuring characteristic behavior toward other people in the areas of inclusion, control, and affection.

FIRO-F. Identical to the FIRO-B except that questions assess the feeling level rather than the behavior level.

FIRO-BC. Developed with the assistance of Marilyn Wood, to measure characteristic behavior of children in the three interpersonal areas. For upper elementary and junior high children.

MATE (Marital Attitude Evaluation). These inventories are designed to explore the relationship between husband and wife or other closely related persons. On separate forms, respondents indicate the kinds of inclusion, control, and affection they desire from their partner and their understanding of his or her desires.

LIPHE (Life InterPersonal History Enquiry). Developed to assess the respondent's account of his or her relationships with parents before the age of six. Scales for relationships with each parent and for respondent's perception of the relationship between the parents.
SAMPLE ITEM. LIPHE: When I was a child, I wanted my mother to allow me more freedom. MATE: I want you (Mate) to spend more time with me. 1 = Strongly disagree....6 = Strongly

agree.
LENGTH. (MATE) Time: 10 minutes. Items: 45. (LIPHE)
Time: 20 minutes. Items: 108.
AVAILABILITY. Consulting Psychologists Press, 577 College
Avenue, Palo Alto, California 94306.
ABSTRACTED BY: William C. Schutz
REFERENCES.

Buros,O.K. (Ed.) Personality Tests and Reviews.
Highland Park, N.J.: Gryphon Press, 1970.

Hooper,D. and Sheldon,A. Evaluating newly married
couples. British Journal of Social and Clinical Psychology,
1969, 8, 169-182.

Kerckhoff,A.C. and Bean,F.D. Role-related factors in
person perception among engaged couples. Sociometry, 1967,
30, 176-186.

Levinger,G. Cenn,D.J. and Jorgensen,B.W. Progress
toward permanence in courtship: a test of the
Kerckhoff-Davis hypotheses. Sociometry, 1970, 427-443.

Ryan,L.F. Clinical Interpretation of the FIRO-B. Palo
Alto, Ca: Consulting Psychologists Press.

Schutz,W.C. The Interpersonal Underworld (FIRO). Palo
Alto, Ca: Consulting Psychologists Press, 1967.

Schutz,W.C. A Three-Dimensional Theory of
Interpersonal Behavior. New York: Rinehart, 1968.

SLOCUM,W.L. and STONE,C.L. Family Image Scales

VARIABLES MEASURED. (1) Family affection, (2) Family
cooperation, (3) Family democracy, (4) Disciplinary
fairness.
TEST DESCRIPTION. A questionnaire designed for teen-age Ss.
Each variable is indexed by combining four to six questions
into Guttman scales.
SAMPLE ITEM. Is your family like this? Parents dislike
children: 1 = Yes, 2 = No, 3 = Partly.
LENGTH. Items: 21.
AVAILABILITY. In Slocum and Stone, 1959.
REFERENCES.

Nye,F.I. and Short,J.F.Jr. Scaling delinquent
behavior. American Sociological Review, 1957, 22, 326-331.

Rallings,E.M. Family situations of married and
never-married males. Journal of Marriage and the Family,
1966, 28, 485-490.

Slocum,W.L. The influence of community variations in
family culture on Guttman-type scales. Rural Sociology,
1963, 8, 408-413.

Slocum,W.L. and Stone,C.L. A method for measuring
family images held by teen-agers. Marriage and Family
Living, 1959, 21, 245-250.

Snow,C. Differential marriage and family perceptions
and attitudes cf adolescents living in child care
institutions and adolescents living in intact families.
Adolescence, 1973, 8, 373-378.

Templeton, J.A. The influence of family size on

aspects of teen-agers' attitudes, behavior, and perception
of home life. Family Life Coordinator, 1957, 11, 51-57.

STRAUS,M.A. and CYTRYNBAUM,S.   Family Power and Support
Score System

VARIABLES MEASURED. (1) Affective or personal support, (2)
Power of family members.   Separate scores on these two
variables are provided for each of the possible role systems
of the nuclear family (father-son, husband-wife, etc.).
TEST DESCRIPTION. A scoring system designed for use with
TAT protocols.   The procedures can also be applied to other
written materials--for example, to determine historical
trends in family power structure by scoring representative
fiction, newspaper reports, or magazine editorials.   The
scores are designed to measure the interactional aspects of
power and support rather than motivational aspects.
Protocols are scored literally and nonevaluatively. A unit
is scored each time the protocol depicts a family member
attempting to influence or to provide or seek affective
support from another member of the same nuclear family.   A
protocol may yield a single or numerous units. Each unit is
classified in terms of the originating act and/or the
recipient actor (husband, wife, son, daughter). In the case
of power interactions, the units are further classified
according to: (1) Control initiating role, (2) Control
sanctions, (3) Authority recognition, and (4) Compliance or
power.   In the case of support, each unit is classified
according to: (1) Direction of support, (2) Intended
support role, (3) Instrumental modality of support, (4)
Acceptance of support, and (5) Reciprocity of support.   In
addition to these descriptive categories, three quantitative
scores expressing the amount of power or support which a
family member holds or provides in relation to the others
are obtained: (1) Saliency: the number of units of the
protocol which are scored for power and for support; (2)
Impact: the sum of the compliance scores or the sum of
acceptance of support scores;   (3) Effectiveness: the
percentage derived from dividing the impact score by the
theoretical maximum impact score for the number of units in
a protocol.
SAMPLE ITEM. See test description.
LENGTH. Depends on source of data.
AVAILABILITY. From NAPS-2.
REFERENCES.
      Straus,M.A. and Cytrynbaum,S. A scoring manual for
intra-familial   power   affective   support.   Minneapolis:
Minnesota Family Study Center, 1961.
      Straus,M.A.   and Cytrynbaum,S.   Support and power
structure in Sinhalese, Tamil, and Burgher student families.
International Journal of Comparative Sociology, 1962, 3,
138-153.

3. Activities, Tasks, Recreation, Role Differentiation, Sex
Roles (See also Subject Index)

ALDOUS,J. Household Task Performance Index

VARIABLE MEASURED. Extent to which husband and wife engage
in household and child care tasks.
TEST DESCRIPTION. Long, semi-structured interviews produce
the men's reports as to who did the following tasks: shops
for groceries, takes dirty clothes to the coin laundry,
takes out garbage, prepares supper, borrows money,
disciplines children, pays bills, talks with the landlord or
deals with the mortgage company, does laundry at home, and
gets up with the children at night. The Index is the summed
weights for the number of tasks the respondent reports he
and/or his wife performs divided by the numbers of tasks
done.
SAMPLE ITEM. Shops for groceries: 0 = Wife all the time;
1 = Both perform the task, but the wife more than the
husband; 2 = Both perform the task; 3 = Both perform the
task, but the husband more than the wife; and 4 = The
husband all the time.
LENGTH. Items: 10.
AVAILABILITY. See Aldous, 1969.
REFERENCE.
        Aldous,J. Wives' employment status and lower-class men
as husband-fathers: support for the Moynihan thesis.
Journal of Marriage and the Family, 1969, 31, 469-476.

BEERS,H.W. Shared Activities Index

VARIABLES MEASURED. Activities a family shares, or lack of
role differentiation.
TEST DESCRIPTION. Families are rated on whether they carry
out certain activities together. Each shared activity is
given a weight of 1. The weights are summed, and this score
is divided by the total number of items that could have been
shared to yield the index of shared activities.
SAMPLE ITEM. Husband and children help in the home.
LENGTH. Items: 20.
AVAILABILITY. In Beers, 1935.
REFERENCE.
        Beers,H.W. Measurements of Family Relationships in
Farm Families of Central New York. Ithaca, N.Y.: State
Agricultural Experiment Station Bulletin 183, December 1935.

BLOOD,R.O.JR.   Traditional-Developmental   Family   Role
Concepts Scale

VARIABLES MEASURED. Traditional and developmental
conceptions of a good mother, a good father, and a good

child.
TEST DESCRIPTION.   Three lists of 10 items each--first list consists of "things a good child does"; second, "things a good mother does"; and third, "things a good father does." Each list contains five items representing "traditional" family roles, and five "developmental" roles.   The subject chooses the five most important items from each list.   Score is the number of developmental items chosen as most important.
SAMPLE ITEM.   Obeys and respects adults.
LENGTH.   Items: 30.
AVAILABILITY.   From NAPS and in Connor, Green, and Walters, 1958.
REFERENCES.
    Blood,R.O.Jr.   Developmental   and   traditional child-rearing philosophies and their family situational consequences.   Ph.D.   dissertation, University of North Carolina, 1952.
    Blood,R.O.Jr.   A situational approach to the study of permissiveness in child rearing.   American Sociological Review, 1953, 18, 84-87.
    Connor,R.   Greene,H.   and Walters,J.   Agreement of family member conceptions of "good" parent and child roles. Social Forces, 1958, 36, 354-358.
    Connor,R.   Johannis,T.B.Jr.   and   Walters,J. Parent-adolescent relationships. Journal of Home Economics, 1954, 46, 183-191.
    Connor,R.   Johannis,T.B.Jr.   and Walters,J.   Family recreation in relation to role conceptions of family members.   Marriage and Family Living, 1955, 17, 306-309.
    Duvall,E.M.   Conceptions   of   parenthood.   American Journal of Sociology, 1946, 52, 193-303.
    Hill,R.   Family Development in Three   Generations. Cambridge, Mass: Schenkman Publishing Co., Inc., 1970.

COUCH,C.J.   Family Role Specialization Questionnaire

VARIABLE MEASURED.   Role specialization within the family.
TEST DESCRIPTION.   A 17-item questionnaire.   Each item is answered: 4 = Usually, 3 = Sometimes, 2 = Seldom, or 1 = Never for mother, father, female teenager, and   male teenager.   The role-specialization score is computed for "father-mother" and for "male-female teenager." The score is the difference between the subject's indicated response for the father and the mother and the difference between indicated responses for the male and female teenagers.
SAMPLE ITEM.   In the spaces provided below write in one of the following words: Usually, Sometimes, Seldom, or Never.

	Mother	Father	Female Teenager	Male Teenager
Shops for groceries......	____	____	____	____
Earns money for family...	____	____	____	____

LENGTH. Items: 17.
AVAILABILITY. From NAPS.
REFERENCE.
    Couch,C.J.   Family   role   specialization   and
self-attitudes in children. Sociological Quarterly, 1962,
3, 115-121.

DANZIGER,K. Household Sex Role Specialization Index

VARIABLE MEASURED. Sex-role specialization in regard to
household tasks.
TEST DESCRIPTION. A list of household activities. The
respondent indicates how often father, mother, and child do
each, using response categories: Often, Sometimes, and
Never. The results are dichotomized, Often and Sometimes
indicating involvement, Never indicating noninvolvement.
    A high degree of sex role specialization is indicated
by a high incidence of nonmatches (Child and parent differ
in relation to a task.) with the opposite sex parent and a
low incidence of nonmatches with the same sex parent. The
index of sex role specialization is obtained by subtracting
the number of nonmatches for the same sex parent from the
number of nonmatches with the opposite sex parent.
SAMPLE ITEM. Fix things around the house.
LENGTH. Items: 6.
AVAILABILITY. In Danziger, 1974.
ABSTRACTED BY: Thomas G. Sparhawk.
REFERENCE.
    Danziger,K. The acculturation of Italian immigrant
girls in Canada. International Journal of Psychology, 1974,
9, 129-137.

DYER,E.D. Leisure Time Index

VARIABLE MEASURED.   Amount   of   shared   leisure   time
activities.
TEST DESCRIPTION. Respondent lists all things generally
done with leisure time, and then is asked "which of these
things do you do with immediate family members (husband
and/or children), and about how often." Each item is scored
from Generally = 5 to Infrequently = 1.
SAMPLE ITEM. See test description.
LENGTH. Items: variable.
AVAILABILITY. In Dyer, 1970.
ABSTRACTED BY: Thomas G. Sparhawk.
REFERENCE.
    Dyer,E.D. Upward social mobility and nuclear family
integration as perceived by the wife in Swedish urban
families. Journal of Marriage and the Family, 1970, 32,
341-350.

OLSEN,M.E. Household Division of Labor Schedule

VARIABLE MEASURED. Division of labor in the family.
TEST DESCRIPTION. Subject is asked which member of the
family usually performs each of 100 household duties.
Possible responses: Wife always or almost always, Wife
sometimes and husband sometimes, Husband always or almost
always, Not done in the family, Child or children usually do
it, Someone outside the family paid to do it. Scores for
each family are the percentages of total responses to the
schedule for the wife, for the husband, for the children,
and for outsiders.
SAMPLE ITEM. Mop, vacuum, wax, and dust house.
LENGTH. Items: 100; 26 (two different forms).
AVAILABILITY. The 26-item version is in Olsen, 1960.
REFERENCE.
     Olsen,M.E. Distribution of family responsibilities and
social stratification. Marriage and Family Living, 1960,
22, 60-65.

WALTERS,J. and OJEMANN,R.H.   Adolescent   Attitudes
Concerning the Role of Women

VARIABLES MEASURED. (1) Generalized role prescription ("the
interiorized norm") and (2) Self-role prescription ("the
behavioral disposition") concerning the role of women on a
superordinate-partnership-subordinate continuum.
TEST DESCRIPTION. A brother-sister test and a husband-wife
relationships test, each containing 36 situations. The
brother-sister situations are from the areas of work, play,
and education; the husband-wife situations are from work,
play, and child-rearing activities. A third of each of the
situations presents the woman as superordinate, a third as
equal, and a third as subordinate. For the behavioral
disposition score, the subject is asked whether he/she would
do what the situation suggests. For the interiorized norm
score, the subject is asked if he/she thinks he/she should
do the same.
SAMPLE ITEM. Barbara and James's parents had enough money
to send only one of the children to college, and since they
think that a man needs an education more than a woman, they
gave the money to James.
LENGTH. Time: 2 hours. Items: 72.
AVAILABILITY. From NAPS.
REFERENCE.
     Walters,J. and Ojemann,R.H. A study of the components
of adolescent attitudes concerning the role of women.
Journal of Social Psychology, 1952, 35, 101-110.

C.   Interpersonal Competence

1. Adaptability, Creativity, Family Adequacy, Flexibility, Parental Adequacy, Problem Solving Ability (See also Subject Index)

BLECHMAN,E.L. Family Contract Game, Family Problem Solving Behavior Coding System, and Problem Solving Efficiency Scale

VARIABLES MEASURED. Problem solving efficiency of the family group and behaviors which facilitate or inhibit resolving family conflicts.
TEST DESCRIPTION. The Family Contract Game is a tool to facilitate resolution of family conflicts and to train families in enduring problem solving skills. "Family members can, in 15 minutes, write a contract that identifies a displeasing problem behavior, describe a pleasing replacement behavicr, and arrange contingent reinforcement and recording of pleasing behavior." The game is played on a board with 14 squares representing four basic components of problem solving. Each square instructs one player to perform an action (e.g. draw a problem card), make a statement (e.g. "Red, tell Blue what to do more of and when."), cr ask a question (e.g. "Blue, ask Red if he agrees to the reward you chose."). The players alternate who is the one to raise a problem. Players are supplied with contract forms, bonus and risk cards, blank problem and reward cards, play money, and tracking coupons.
     The Family Problem Solving Behavior Coding System and the Problem Solving Efficiency Scale are used by observers to record the behaviors which occur during the course of the game.   The Family Problem Solving Behavior Coding System is a modification of the Patterson et al. Marital Interaction Coding System (MICS) described elsewhere in this book, in which certain MICS codes are combined or modified, two new codes added, and the style of coding changed from continuous to interval coding.
SAMPLE ITEM. See above.
LENGTH. Time: 15 minutes.
AVAILABILITY. The game is described in Blechman, 1974a,b. The Family Problem Solving Behavior Coding System and Family Problem Solving Efficiency Scale are in Nickerson, Light, Blechman, and Gandelman, 1976. A game kit can be obtained by sending $40 (Ccnn. residents add sales tax) to ASIP, Inc. Box 389, Madison, Conn 06443.
ABSTRACTED BY: Elaine A. Blechman
REFERENCES.
     Blechman,E.A. The family contract game: a tool to teach interpersonal problem solving. Family Coordinator, 1974a, 269-281.
     Blechman,E.A. A new way to teach contracting: the

family contract game. Psychotherapy, 1974b, 11, 194.

Blechman,E.A.   A problem-solving training   package   for
the   single   parent   family.   Unpublished   manuscript, Yale
University, 1975. Submitted for publication.

Blechman,E.A.   and Olson,D.H.L.   The effects of a
contracting   game   on   parent-child   problem-solving
interactions. Mimeographed paper, Yale University, 1973.

Blechman,E.A.   and Olson,D.H.L.   The family contract
game: description   and   effectiveness.   In Olson,D.H.L.
(Ed.) Treating Relationships. Iowa: Graphic, 1975.

Blechman,E.A.   Olson,D.H.L.   Schornagel,C.Y.
Halsdorf,M.J.   and   Turner,A.J.   The family contract game:
technique   and   case   study.   Journal   of   Consulting   and
Clinical Psychology, 1976, 44, 449-455.

Nickerson,M. Light,R. Blechman,E.A. and Gandelman,B.
Three measures of problem solving behavior: a procedural
manual. JSAS Catalog of Selected Documents in Psychology,
1976, Winter Issue.

Turner,A.J.   and Blechman,E.A.   All Together Now:
Exercises in Family Living. Unpublished manuscript, Yale
University, 1975./

GEISMAR,L.L.   LASORTE,M.A.   and AYRES,B.   St.   Paul Scale of
Family Functioning

VARIABLES MEASURED. Family functioning in nine categories
(and 26 subcategories) of social functioning: (1) Family
relations and family unity, (2) Individual behavior and
adjustment, (3) Care and training of children, (4) Social
activities, (5) Economic practices, (6) Household practices,
(7) Health conditions and practices, (8) Relation with
social worker, (9) Use of community resources.
TEST DESCRIPTION. Judges (caseworkers, some familiar, some
unfamiliar with the cases) complete a rating scale on the
basis of written case records of multi-problem or
disorganized families.   There are seven categories for each
scale, ranging from (1) Inadequate (community has a right to
intervene), (4) Marginal (behavior not sufficiently harmful
to justify intervention), (7) Adequate (behavior is in line
with community expectations). Ratings for each of the nine
categories are dichotomized and ranked as in a Guttman
scale.
SAMPLE ITEM. Family relations and family unity--marital
relationship: (1) Inadequate. Separated partner does not
support when so ordered, or is   extremely   disturbing
influence on family. (4) Marginal. Separated partner does
not support adequately or regularly or is a disturbing
influence on family. (7) Adequate. Couple lives together.
LENGTH. Items: 9 categories, 26 subcategories.
AVAILABILITY. In Geismar, 1960, 1971.
REFERENCES.
Brown,G. The Multi-Problem Dilemma.   Metuchen, N.J.:
The Scarecrow Press, 1968.
Geismar,L.L. Measuring Family Functionings: A Manual

on a Method for Evaluating the Social Functioning of
Disorganized Families. St. Paul, Minnesota: Family
Centered Project, Greater St. Paul Community Chest and
Councils, Inc., 1960.
    Geismar,L.L. Family functioning as an index of need
for welfare services. Family Process, 1964, 2, 99-113.
    Geismar,L.L. The results of social work intervention:
a positive case. American Journal of Orthopsychiatry, 1968,
38, 444-456.
    Geismar,L.L. Family and Community Functioning: A
Manual of Measurement for Social Work Practice and Policy.
Metuchen, N.J.: The Scarecrow Press, Inc., 1971.
    Geismar,L.L. 555 Families. New Brunswick, N.J.:
Transaction Books, 1973.
    Geismar,L.L. and Ayres,B. A method for evaluating the
social functioning of families under treatment. Social
Work, 1959, 4, 102-106.
    Geismar,L.L. and Gerhart,U.C. Social class,
ethnicity, and family functioning: exploring some issues
raised by the Moynihan report. Journal of Marriage and the
Family, 1968, 30, 480-487.
    Geismar,L.L. and Krisberg,J. The Forgotten
Neighborhood. Metuchen, New Jersey: Scarecrow Press, 1967.
    Geismar,L.L. and Lagay,B. et. al. Early Supports
for Family Life. Metuchen, N.J.: The Scarecrow Press,
1972.
    Geismar,L.L. and LaSorte,M. Factors associated with
family disorganization. Marriage and Family Living, 1963,
25, 479-481.
    Geismar,L.L. LaSorte,M.A. and Ayres,B. Measuring
family disorganization. Marriage and Family Living, 1962,
24, 51-56.
    McIntire,W.G. and Payne,D.C. The relationship of
family functioning to school achievement. The Family
Coordinator, 1971, 20, 265-268.
    Tierney,L. Measuring family functioning: the
contribution of Ludwig Geismar. Australian Journal of
Social Work, 1968, 21, 1-9.
    Weller,L. and Luchterhand,E.G. Comparing interviews
and observations on family functioning. Journal of Marriage
and the Family, 1969, 31, 115-122.

HILL,R.L. Adjustment of Family to Separation Scale

VARIABLE MEASURED. Family adjustment to separation from the
father.
TEST DESCRIPTION. A list of one-sentence statements. S
checks all that apply to her. The responses are weighted on
a five-point scale according to the degree of adjustment
they represent (5 = Excellent adjustment; 4 = Satisfactory
adjustment; 3 = Average or fair adjustment; 2 = Poor
adjustment; 1 = Broken up). A score is derived by summing
the weights and dividing by the number of items checked.
Good adjustment is defined as "closing of ranks, shifting of

responsibilities and activities of father to other members,
continuing   the   necessary family routines, maintaining
husband-wife   and   father-child   relationships   by
correspondence   and visits, utilizing the resources of
friends, relatives and neighbors, and carrying on plans for
the reunion."
SAMPLE ITEM.   Husband-wife relationships often take   a
beating in the face of prolonged separation. Which of the
following statements appear to describe the situation in
your case?   From my husband's letters and furloughs I have
been able to understand all the changes the service has made
in him. (weight, 5)
LENGTH. Items: 48.
AVAILABILITY. In Hill, 1949.
REFERENCE.
       Hill,R.L. Families under Stress: Adjustment to the
Crises of War Separation and Reunion. New York: Harper,
1949.

HOLROYD,J.   Questionnaire on Resources and Stress (QRS)

VARIABLES MEASURED.   Fifteen aspects of response to a
physically or mentally handicapped family member: (1) Poor
health/mood, (2) Excess time demands, (3) Negative attitude
toward index case, (4) Overprotection/dependency, (5) Lack
of social support,   (6) Overcommitment (martyrdom),   (7)
Pessimism, (8) Lack of family integration, (9) Limits on
family opportunity, (10) Financial problems, (11) Physical
incapacitation, (12) Lack of activities for index case, (13)
Occupational limitations for index case,   (14)   Social
obtrusiveness, (15) Difficult personality characteristics.
TEST DESCRIPTION.   The   test   consists   of   True-False
questions, which are grouped into the 15 variables listed
above, each measuring a variable pertinent to caring for a
chronically ill or handicapped family member.
SAMPLE ITEM.   Demands that others do things for him/her more
than is necessary: True, False.
LENGTH. Items: 285.
AVAILABILITY. From NAPS-2.
ABSTRACTED BY: Thomas G. Sparhawk
REFERENCES.
       Holroyd,J.   The questionnaire on resources and stress:
an instrument to measure family response to a handicapped
family member. Journal of Community Psychiatry, 1974, 2,
92-94.
       Holroyd,J.   Brown,N.   Wikler,L.   and   Simmons,J.Q.
Stress   in   families   of   institutionalized   and
noninstitutionalized autistic children.   Journal   of
Community Psychology, 1975, 3, 26-31.
       Holroyd,J. and McArthur,D.   Mental retardation and
stress on the parents: a contrast between Down's Syndrome
and childhood autism.   American Journal of   Mental
Deficiency, 1976, 80, 431-436.

HUDSON,W.W. Family Functioning Instrument (FFI)

VARIABLES MEASURED. Adequacy of social and familial
functioning.
    An abstract of this test is given in Johnson, O.G.
Tests and Measurements in Child Development: Handbook II.
San Francisco: Jossey-Bass, 1976, 778.

PRATT,L. The "Energized Family" Model of Family Structure

VARIABLES MEASURED. The Energized Family is a proposed
model for an effectively functioning family unit, one that
has the capability of serving its members' needs
effectively. Dimensions of the family structure model are
interaction pattern, freedom-constraint, coping effort,
family effort, family links to the community, and role
structure.
TEST DESCRIPTION. Data are obtained through personal
interviews with husband/father, wife/mother, and child
members of families, using a precoded interview guide with
fixed-alternative answer categories.
SAMPLE ITEM. (Husband-Wife Interaction) Which of the
following do you do with your (husband) (wife) Often,
Occasionally, or Never? Go to parties, Attend church...
LENGTH. Approximately 30 minutes per interview. Each
dimension of family structure is represented by one or more
indexes, and each index is based on several interview
questions.
AVAILABILITY. In Pratt, 1976.
ABSTRACTED BY: Lois Pratt
REFERENCE.
    Pratt,L. Family Structure and Effective Health
Behavior: The Energized Family. Boston: Houghton Mifflin
Company, 1976.

REISS,D. Hypothesis Testing Task

VARIABLES MEASURED. Family styles in exploring and
investigating pattern and structure in the environment;
specifically, the following aspects of the family's
information-search strategies: (1) Riskiness or
conservativeness, (2) The degree to which members utilize
each others' approaches and ideas, (3) The degree of
inter-member imitation, and (4) The dependence of the
strategies on continuous, outside feedback. A
computer-automated version of this procedure is designed to
measure the effect, on these problem-solving processes, of
progressively isolating members of the family from one
another.
TEST DESCRIPTION. Four teletypes are arranged in a row,
with movable screens separating one from the other. A fifth
teletype is used to control the procedure. All five
teletypes are connected to a LINC computer.

The procedure is designed to model two naturally occurring processes: (1) The interaction of the family group with its environment; and (2) Variations in intimacy or relatedness among family members as they explore that environment.

The family-environment interaction is modelled by a pattern recognition task. Each member is given a sequence of letters (e.g. CSTTTTTTTS) and asked to recognize the sequential pattern of the letters. He/she can discover the pattern by typing any sequence he/she wishes--these sequences are called hypotheses--on his/her teletype. The teletype prints a plus if the sequence exemplifies the pattern; a minus if it does not. Each member goes in turn until satisfied he/she recognizes the pattern; he/she indicates he/she is finished by pressing a special key. The task is over when all members have pushed their keys.   In each of the three puzzles the parents receive an example constructed by one pattern, and the children an example constructed by another. Plusses, however, are typed when either parent or child types a sequence according to either pattern; this situation provides the opportunity--not always taken--for intergenerational learning in the family. There are three puzzles of this kind. Before and after each one, each member is asked to select, from a set of 20 sequences, those sequences he/she believes would get a plus. This is called a private inventory; no other family members ever see it.

Variations in intimacy within the family are modelled by operating the puzzle in three distribution modes. In the public mode, each time a member types a sequence it is immediately distributed to everyone else in the family along with an identification of which member constructed it.   In the anonymous mode the same sequence is distributed, somewhat later in the task, by a randomization procedure that effectively conceals its author. In the standard mode, family-authored sequences are never distributed;   the computer constructs a sequence--similar in information content to ones produced by the family.   In this way the family works at three levels of intimacy: immediate contact, concealed and ambiguous contact, and in isolation with only the computer as companion. Computer-automation permits almost identical problem-solving information in all three modes; this control of information input, across the three modes, is the unique advantage of computer automation.

Scores for assessing the organization of information and effectiveness of problem-solving are derived by canonical formulae from the responses on the private inventories. Scores assessing information search strategies are developed from the corpus of hypotheses produced by the family in the course of the three tasks.

An earlier version of the procedure is operated manually and uses only the public mode (Reiss, 1967).

SAMPLE ITEMS. If the parents are given the example sequence VDMDMDMDMDMDMDMV, and the children are given the example VMMMMMMMVV, then the following sequences would, if

constructed by any member, receive a plus: VDMDMV, VMVV,
VDMDMDMDMV, VMMMMVV.
LENGTH. Time: About 2 hours, including instructions for
computer-automated procedure;   the earlier   version takes
about 45 minutes, including instructions.
AVAILABILITY. The earlier version is in Reiss, 1967;   the
computer-automated   version   is described   in Reiss and
Sheriff, 1970.
ABSTRACTED BY: David Reiss.
REFERENCES.
        Reiss,D. Individual thinking and family interaction.
II. A study of pattern recognition and hypothesis testing
in   families   of   normals,   character   disorders   and
schizophrenics.   Journal of Psychiatric Research, 1967, 5,
193-211.
        Reiss,D. Individual thinking and family interaction.
III. An experimental study of categorization performance in
families of normals, character disorders and schizophrenics.
Journal of Nervous and Mental Disease, 1968, 146, 384-403.
        Reiss,D. Individual thinking and family interaction.
IV. A study of information exchange in families of normals,
those with character disorders and schizophrenics.   Journal
of Nervous and Mental Disease, 1969, 149, 473-490.
        Reiss,D. Individual thinking and family interaction.
V.   Proposals for the contrasting character of experiential
sensitivity and expressive form in families.   Journal of
Nervous and Mental Disease, 1970, 151, 187-202.
        Reiss,D. Intimacy and problem solving: an automated
procedure for testing a theory of consensual experience in
families.   Archives of General Psychiatry,   1971,   25,
442-455.
        Reiss,D.   and Sheriff,W.H.Jr.   A computer-automated
procedure for testing some experience of family membership.
Behavioral Science, 1970, 15, 431-443.

REISS,D. Pattern Recognition Card Sort for Families

VARIABLES   MEASURED.   (1)   Family   problem-solving
effectiveness,   (2) Coordination, and (3) Penchant for
closure. The procedure provides several variables for
assessing the family's position on each dimension. Using
all three dimensions, the family can be classified into one
of eight types.   The typology is based on the family's
dominant orientation to its immediate social and physical
environment.   The three most carefully studied types are:
(a)   Environment-sensitive;   (b)   Inter-personal
distance-sensitive;   and   (c)   Consensus-sensitive.   In
addition, the procedure permits the measurement of many
facets of verbal interaction using scales such as those
developed by Bales (1950) and Mishler and Waxler (1968) as
well as nonlexical characteristics of speech such as length,
duration and interruption patterns (Haley, 1964; Matarazzo,
1968; Reiss and Salzman, 1972; Reiss, 1972).

TEST DESCRIPTION. Three members of the family are tested simultaneously. Each member sits at a small ledge facing the observation window and is separated from the other members by a semi-soundproof partition. Verbal communication among members, and between members and the experimenter, is entirely by means of an earphone-microphone arrangement. In front of each subject, on his/her ledge, is a sorting surface with seven ruled columns and a signal box by which E signals the start of a trial and by which each member signals completion of a trial. Signals by both E and the subjects are recorded on an event recorder. All vocalizations of the subjects are recorded on tape and on a low-capacitance pclygraph to produce a visible record of the occurrence, duration and amplitude of family speech.

The family is instructed to work on three pattern recognition tasks; in the initial and final task the members work silently and on their own. In the second task, the family is encouraged to discuss the puzzle among themselves. Each task presents the family with a deck of 15 cards. Each card contains a sequence of nonsense syllables (initial and final task) or letters (family task). The letters or syllables on each card are arranged in a sequential pattern using simple finite-state grammars (Miller, 1967). It is possible for a subject to recognize in each task that he/she can group the cards into three piles of equal size with the cards in each pile having the symbols arranged in the same sequential pattern. This is called the "pattern sort." Most subjects who do not use this scheme for sorting use a length system; they put all the cards with three symbols in one pile, those with four in a second, etc. In the initial and final task the subjects sort the entire deck in one trial. In the family task they start with the first two cards in the deck; when subjects decide for themselves the best arrangement they press a button on their signal box. When all subjects are done, E signals the family to pick up the next card; the procedure is repeated for 14 trials. The instructions purposely omit any mention that the family must agree on their sorts or on the time for signaling they are through with a trial. They are told to use the seven-columned sorting surface for grouping their cards, one group in each column; hence, a maximum of seven groups in each sort is permissible. The sort for each subject is recorded after each trial.

A single scoring concept is used to develop three different sets of scores. A formula adapted from Shipstone (1960) is used to ccmpare subject's score to a fully worked out pattern or length sort; if subject uses either system effectively he/she gets a maximum score. This procedure can yield a variety of individual and family problem-solving scores that assess family problem-solving effectiveness. The same formula is somewhat altered to provide a score expressing the similarity of sorts between members of the same family. These sort similarity scores are among those that assess coordination. The formula is also used to measure how much subject changes his/her sorting system as

he/she considers additional cards in the family task. Low
scores (no change) indicate a penchant for closure. In
addition, scores are derived from the event recorder's
record of trial times. The simultaneity of trial-ending in
the family tasks reflects both coordination and closure.
The actual duration of trials reflects closure.

A procedure using numbers instead of syllables and
letters has been developed to permit re-testing with minimal
proactive facilitation from test to re-test (Reiss and
Salzman, 1972; Reiss, 1972). An earlier version of the
task lacked the initial and final sorts and had only one
trial in the family task during which members sorted all 15
cards; their speech was scored according to several of the
Mishler and Waxler (1968) scales as well as a Level of
Abstraction scale developed especially for the procedure
(Reiss, 1968).

SAMPLE ITEMS. See above.
LENGTH. Time: About 40 minutes including instructions.
AVAILABILITY. Procedure outlined in Reiss (1968, 1971c).
Details in NAPS-2.
ABSTRACTED BY: David Reiss.

REFERENCES.

Bales,R.F. Interaction Process Analysis: A Method for
the Study of Small Groups. Cambridge, Massachusetts:
Addison-Wesley, 1950.

Haley,J. Research on family patterns: an instrument
measurement. Family Process, 1964, 3, 41-65.

Matarazzo,J.D.   Wiens,A.N.   Matarazzo,R.G.   and
Saslow,G.J. Speech and Silence Behavior in Clinical
Psychotherapy and Its Laboratory Correlates, in John M.
Shlien (Ed.) Research in Psychotherapy, Vol. III,
Washington, D.C.: American Psychological Association, 1968,
347-394.

Miller,G.A. Project Grammarama. The Psychology of
Communication, New York: Basic Books, 1967, 125-187.

Mishler,E.G. and Waxler,N.E. Interaction in Families:
An Experimental Study of Family Processes and Schizophrenia.
New York: Wiley, 1968.

Reiss,D. Individual thinking and family interaction.
III. An experimental study of categorization performance in
families of normals, those with character disorders and
schizophrenics. Journal of Nervous and Mental Disease,
1968, 146, 384-403.

Reiss,D. Varieties of consensual experience I. A
theory for relating family interaction to individual
thinking. Family Process, 1971a, 10, 1-28.

Reiss,D. Varieties of consensual experience II.
Dimensions of a family's experience of its environment.
Family Process, 1971b, 10, 28-35.

Reiss,D. Varieties of consensual experience III.
Contrast between families of normals, delinquents and
schizophrenics. Journal of Nervous and Mental Disease,
1971c, 152, 73-95.

Reiss,D. Intimacy and problem solving: An automated
procedure for testing a theory of consensual experience in

families.   Archives of General Psychiatry, 1971d,   25,
442-455.
       Reiss,D. Drug impact and family integrity, II: Drug
Action, 1972. (Mimeographed)
       Reiss,D.   and Salzman,C. Drug Impact and Family
Integrity, I: Theory, Methods and Major Findings, 1972.
(Mimeographed)
       Shipstone,E.I.   Some   variables   affecting   pattern
conception. Psychological Monographs, 1960, 74: No. 17.

2. Empathy, Similarity (See also Subject Index)

HOBART,C.W.   and FAHLBERG,N.   Empathy Ratio Score (ERS)

VARIABLE MEASURED.   Empathy in the sense of taking the role
of another.
TEST DESCRIPTION. This index is designed to measure empathy
while controlling for projection.   Two respondents, a judge
(J) and an other (O), are asked to respond to questions with
their cwn response, and then predict the response of the
other. Two raw scores are formed. The dissimilarity score
is the number of items to which the pair gave nonidentical
own responses. The raw empathy score is the number of items
to which the pair gave nonidentical own responses and the J
correctly predicted the O's own response. The raw empathy
score is divided by the dissimilarity score to form the
Empathy Ratio Score. RES/DS = ERS.
SAMPLE ITEM.   Not applicable.   The   above   measurement
procedure can be used with a wide variety of instruments.
See, for example, Leary's InterpersoNA.l Check List.
LENGTH. NA.
AVAILABILITY. Hobart, Charles W. and Nancy Fahlberg, 1965.
ABSTRACTED BY: Susan Murray.
REFERENCES.
       Bronfenbrenner,U.   Harding,J.   and Gallwey,M.   The
Measurement   of   Skill   in   Social   Perception,   in
McClelland,D.C.   et al.   (eds.) Talent and Society.
Princeton, N.J.: D. VanNostrand Co., 1958.
       Hobart,C.W.   and Fahlberg,N. The measure of empathy,
American Journal of Sociology, 1965, 70, 595-603.

LAFORGE,R. and SUCZEK,R.F.   The Interpersonal Check List

VARIABLES MEASURED. Similarity of husband and wife (or
parent and child) in respect to: (1) Managerial-autocratic,
(2) Competitive-narcissistic, (3) Aggressive-sadistic, (4)
Rebellious-distrustful, (5) Self-effacing-masochistic, (6)
Docile-dependent, (7) Cooperative-overconventional, and (8)
Responsible-hypernormal.   The test can also be used to
measure family rcle prescriptions and empathy (in the sense

of ability to estimate the responses to the test of another member).

TEST DESCRIPTION. "The data of interpersonal behavior from each of [five] levels of personality are ordered in terms of a classificatory system made up of 16 basic interpersonal variables..."

The 144 words which comprised form IIIb are rated on a four-point scale measuring degree of intensity, ranging from 1, a mild or necessary amount of a trait to 4, an extreme or highly inappropriate amount. The words are arranged in 16 clusters in a circular schema according to their interpersonal score or meaning.

Adjacent sixteenths are combined into octants representing the eight variables listed above. The scores may also be summarized in terms of two major axes: dominance-submission and love-hate.

The subject may be asked to use the ICL to describe himself/herself, his/her mother, father, spouse and ideal self. It has been used to measure role perceptions of wives of alcoholics (Kogan and Jackson, 1961, 1965). In Kogan and Jackson (1965), six sets of instructions for using the ICL were given. "One series of three instructions referred to concepts of the wife's role: 'Ideal Wife,' 'When my husband is sober I am' and 'When my husband is drunk I am.' A parallel series cf three instructions dealt with the role of the husband: 'Most husbands,' 'When my husband is sober he is' and 'When my husband is drunk he is.' Comparison subjects substituted 'When things are going smoothly in our family' and 'When things are not going smoothly in our family' and for the husband-sober or husband-drunk situations." A 128-item version of the ICL was administered to wives of alcoholics in the study reported in Kogan and Jackson, 1961. See also the abstract of T. Leary.

SAMPLE ITEM. Able to give orders.

LENGTH. Time: 15-45 minutes. Items: 144.

AVAILABILITY. In LaForge and Suczek, 1955.

ABSTRACTED BY: Blair Nelson.

REFERENCES.

Buros,O.K. (Ed.) Personality Tests and Reviews. Highland Park, N.J.: Gryphon Press, 1970.

Franzini,B.S. A Multilevel Assessment of Personality and Interpersonal Behavior of Mothers of Asthmatic Children as Compared With Mcthers of Non-Asthmatic Children. Ph.D. dissertation, New York University, 1965. (DA 29:366B)

Gough,H.G. The Adjective Checklist as a personality assessment research technique. Psychological Reports, 1960, 6, 107-122.

Kogan,K.L. and Jackson,J.K. Some role perceptions of wives of alcoholics. Psychological Reports, 1961, 9, 119-124.

Kogan,K.L. and Jackson,J.K. Alcoholism: the fable of the noxious wife. Mental Hygiene, 1965, 49, 428-437.

LaForge,R. and Suczek,R.F. The interpersonal dimension of personality: III. An interpersonal checklist. Journal of Personality, 1955, 24, 94-112.

McDonald,R.L. Fantasy and the outcome of pregnancy.
Archives of General Psychiatry, 1965, 12, 602-606.
Mitchell,H.E. Application of the Kaiser Method to
marital pairs. Family Process, 1963, 2, 265-279.
Romano,R.L. The use of the interpersonal system of
diagnosis in marital counseling. Comment by T.Leary.
Journal of Counseling Psychology, 1960, 7, 10-19.

LEARY,T.F. Leary Interpersonal Check List

VARIABLES MEASURED. Similarity of husband and wife (or
parent and child) in respect to Dominance-submission,
Affection-hostility, and the eight dimensions formed by
combinations of these two aspects of personality
(managerial-autocratic,   responsible-hypernormal,
cooperative-overconventional,   docile-dependent,
selfeffacing-masochistic,   rebellious-distrustful,
aggressive-sadistic, and competitive-narcissistic). The
test can also be used to measure empathy, in the sense of
ability to estimate how another family member will answer
the test.
TEST DESCRIPTION. Each member of the family or couple is
given a checklist of 64 items. These items can also be used
by observers to describe the behavior and personality of the
family members. Subjects are asked to check those items
which describe themselves and then go back and check those
which describe their spouse. "Each respondent's eight-scale
score is divided by his/her total score to remove the effect
of response style (i.e. the tendency to check more or fewer
items than others)." The level of agreement between the
self-reported scores for each spouse can be used as a
measure of couple similarity or identification. The level
of agreement between the scores obtained when a subject
checks items to describe his or her spouse with the scores
obtained from that spouse can be considered a measure of
couple empathy. (Bronfenbrenner et al., 1958). See also
the abstract for LaForge and Suczek.
Jacobs's "Parent-Child Questionnaire," consisting of 60
adjectives under the categories: benevolent, domineering,
over-protective, ineffective, cold and harsh, which are
rated on a continuum of 0 to 3 (from Not at all like a
child's parent to Exactly like his/her parent) is derived
from Leary's ICL.
SAMPLE ITEM. Forceful, good leader, likes responsibility.
LENGTH. Fifteen to 45 minutes depending on the number of
persons rated. Items: 64.
AVAILABILITY. In Leary, 1957.
ABSTRACTED BY: Kersti Yllo.
REFERENCES.
Bronfenbrenner,U. Harding,J. and Gallwey,M. The
measurement of skill in social perception. In
McClelland,D.C. Baldwin,A.L. Bronfenbrenner,U. and
Strodtbeck,F.L. (Eds.). Talent and Society. Princeton,
N.J.: D. VanNostrand Co., Inc., 1958, 29-111.

Brooks,M.   and   Hillman,C.H.   Parent-daughter
relationships as factors in nonmarriage studied in identical
twins. Journal of Marriage and the Family, 1965, 27,
383-385.

Buros,O.K.   (Ed.) Personality Tests and Reviews.
Highland Park, N.J.: Gryphon Press, 1970.

Cairns,R.B.   and Lewis,M.   Dependency   and   the
reinforcement value of a verbal stimulus.   Journal of
Consulting Psychology, 1962, 26, 1-8.

Cone,J.D. Social desirability, marital satisfaction,
and   concomitant   perceptions   of   self   and   spouse.
Psychological Reports, 1971, 28, 173-174.

Cooper,B.   Parents of Schizophrenic Children Compared
With the Parents of Non-Psychotic Emotionally Disturbed and
Well Children: A Discriminant Function Analysis.   Ph.D.
dissertation,   Temple   University   (Philadelphia,
Pennsylvania), 1963. (DA 24:1694)

Gartner,D.   and Goldstein,H.S.   Leary's "Interpersonal
Diagnosis"   in   mothers   of   severely   disturbed   children
attending a therapeutic nursery.   Psychological Reports,
1973, 32, 693-694.

Graff,R.L.   Identification as Related to Perceived
Parental Attitudes and Powerlessness in Delinquents and
Normals.   Ph.D.   dissertation, Claremont Graduate School and
University Center (Claremont, California), 1967.   (DA
29:369B)

Gravatt,A.E.   Perception as a Factor in Mate Selection.
Ph.D.   dissertation, Oregon State University (Corvallis,
Oregon), 1964. (DA 25:684)

Guerney,B.G.Jr.   Meininger,S.   and Stover,L.   Normative
and validation studies of the interpersonal check list for
young children as seen by their mothers.   Journal of
Clinical Psychology, 1973, 29, 219-225.

Jacobs,M.A.   Spilken,A.A.   Norman,M.M.   Anderson,L.
and   Rosenheim,E.   Perceptions   of   faulty   parent-child
relationships and illness behavior. Journal of Consulting
and Clinical Psychology, 1972, 39, 49-55.

Kerckhoff,A.C.   and Bean,F.D.   Social   status   and
interpersonal   patterns   among   married   couples.   Social
Forces, 1970, 49, 264-271.

King,E.V.   Personality   Characteristics--Ideal   and
Perceived   in   Relation   to   Mate   Selection.   Ph.D.
dissertation,   University   of   Southern   California   (Los
Angeles, California), 1961. (DA 21:3882)

Kogan,K.L.   and Jackson,J.K.   Conventional sex role
stereotypes and actual perceptions. Psychological Reports,
1963, 13, 27-30.

Kogan,K.L.   and Jackson,J.K.   Perceptions of self and
spouse: some contaminating factors. Journal of Marriage
and the Family, 1964, 26, 60-64.

Kogan,W.S.   Boe,E.E.   and   Gocka,E.F.   Personality
changes in unwed mothers following parturition. Journal of
Clinical Psychology, 1968, 24, 3-11.

Kotlar,S.L.   Middle-class marital role perceptions and
marital adjustment.   Sociology and Social Research, 1965,

49, 283-293.

Kotlar,S.L.   Role   theory   in   marriage   counseling.
Sociology and Social Research, 1967, 52, 50-62.

Leary,T.F.   Multi-level   measurement   of   interpersonal
behavior.   Berkeley: Psychological   Consultation   Service,
1956.

Leary,T.F.   Interpersonal   Diagnosis   of   Personality.
The Ronald Press Co.:   New York, 1957, 135, 455-463.

Luckey,E.B.   An Investigation of the Concepts of the
Self,   Mate,   Parents,   and   Ideal   in Relation to Degree of
Marital Satisfaction.   Ph.D.   dissertation,   University   of
Minnesota (Minneapolis, Minnesota),   1959.   (DA 20:396)

Luckey,E.B.   Implications for   marriage   counseling   of
self   perceptions   and   spouse   perceptions.   Journal   of
Counseling Psychology, 1960, 7, 3-9.

Luckey,E.B.   Marital   satisfaction   and   congruent
self-spouse   concepts.   Abstract.   Social   Forces,   1960,   39,
153-157.

Luckey,E.B.   Marital satisfaction and   its   association
with   congruence of perception.   Marriage and Family Living,
1960, 22, 49-54.

Luckey,E.B.   Marital satisfaction and parent   concepts.
Journal of Consulting Psychology, 1960, 24, 195-204.

Luckey,E.B.   Marital satisfaction and   its   concomitant
perceptions   of   self   and   spouse.   Journal   of Counseling
Psychology, 1964, 11, 136-145.

Luckey,E.B.   Marital   satisfaction   and   personality
correlates   of   spouse.   Journal of Marriage and the Family,
1964, 26, 217-220.

Luckey,E.B.   Number of   years   married   as   related   to
personality perception and marital satisfaction.   Journal of
Marriage and the Family, 1966, 28, 44-48.

McDonald,R.L.   Intrafamilial   conflict   and   emotional
disturbance.   Journal   of   Genetic   Psychology,   1962,   101,
201-208.

McDonald,R.L.   Effects of sex, race, and class on self,
ideal-self,   and   parental   ratings   in southern adolescents.
Perception and Motor Skills, 1968, 27, 15-25.

McDonald,R.L.   and Gynther,M.D.   Relations between self
and   parental   perceptions   of   unwed   mothers and obstetric
complications.   Psychosomatic Medicine, 1965, 27, 31-38.

McDonald,R.L.   and Gynther,M.D.   Relationship   of   self
and   ideal-self   descriptions   with   sex, race, and class in
southern adolescents.   Journal   of   Personality   and   Social
Psychology, 1965, 1, 85-88.

Murstein,B.I.   and   Glaudin,V.   The   relationship   of
marital adjustment to personality: a factor analysis of the
inter-personal check list.   Journal   of   Marriage   and   the
Family, 1966, 28, 37-43.

O'Neill,M.S.   and   Alexander,J.F.   Family   interacting
patterns   as a function of task characteristics.   Journal of
Applied Social Psychology, 1971, 1, 163-172.

Smith,D.C.   Personal and Social   Adjustment   of   Gifted
Adolescents.   CEC   Research   Monograph,   Series   A,   No.   4.
Washington, D.C.:   Council for Exceptional   Children,   1962,

iv, 65.
     Strahl,G.T.   The   Relationship   of   Centrality   of
Occupational   Choice   to   Sex,   Parental Identification, and
Socioeconomic Level in University Undergraduate Students.
Ph.D.   dissertation,   Michigan   State   University   (East
Lansing, Michigan), 1967, (DA 28:4917A)
     Taylor,A.B.   Role   Perception,   Empathy,   and   Marital
Adjustment.   Ph.D.   dissertation,   University of Southern
California (Los Angeles, California), 1965, (DA 26:3527)
     Taylor,A.B.   Role   perception,   empathy,   and   marriage
adjustment. Sociology and Social Research, 1967, 52, 22-34.
     Terrill,J.M.   and Terrill,R.E.   A method   for   studying
family communication. Family Process, 1965, 4, 259-290.
     Zuckerman,M.   Levitt,E.E.   and Lubin,B.   Concurrent and
construct   validity   of   direct   and   indirect   measures   of
dependency. Journal of Consulting Psychology, 1961, 25,
16-23.

SCOTT,R.D. and ASHWORTH,P.L. Family Relationship Test

VARIABLES MEASURED. Interpersonal perceptions within the
family.   Relationships between perceptions are considered
interactions, and used   to obtain measures of perceptual
accuracy and family alliances.
TEST DESCRIPTION. The test is a self-rating adjective check
list of 47 terms selected from those used by the families of
schizophrenics to attribute identity to themselves and each
other.   It is an interpersonal perception test in which the
family members score how they see themselves, each other,
and how they think they are seen by each of the others, and
they do so at one conjoint session. It is intended to catch
general   cultural   issues,   especially the Cultural Image of
Mental Illness and the use made of it by a family, i.e.,   it
is nomothetic but it has ideographic implications useful for
therapy. The Agreement Score measures the Tenability of
family relationships by measuring critical distances which
determine tenability.   The cutting points distinguishing
tenable from untenable relationships have proved reliable
over three replications involving samples of 17, 17, 40, 18
families.   A California trial shows it as functioning
reasonably well but it may need recalibrating for different
cultures.   It has been found that the tenability of the
patient's home situation has considerable implications for
social and work cutcomes.
SAMPLE ITEM. Below is a list of descriptive terms.   Tick
off those you think apply: (1) Demanding, (2) Popular, (3)
Respectful, (4) Anxious, etc.
LENGTH. Time: 40-45 minutes for a triad, 20 minutes for a
dyad.
AVAILABILITY. Mainly in Scott, Ashworth and Casson, 1970.
The Cutting Scores and the method of computing the Agreement
Score can be obtained from the NAPS-2.

ABSTRACTED BY: R.D. Scott and Kersti Yllo.

REFERENCES.
    Alperson,B.L.   A Boolean Analysis of interpersonal
perception. Accepted for publication in Human Relations,
Vol. 28, 1975.
    Alperson,B.L.   In search of Buber's ghosts: a calculus
for interpersonal phenomenology. Behavioural Science, 1975,
20, 3, 179-190.
    Scott,R.D.   The treatment barrier: Part 2.   The
patient as an unrecognised agent.   British Journal of
Medical Psychology, 1973, 46, 57-67.
    Scott,R.D.   Cultural frontiers in the mental health
service. Schizophrenia Bulletin, 1974, 10, 58-73.
    Scott,R.D.   Family   patterns   and   outcome   in
schizophrenia.   Indications for and against the use of
family therapy.   In New Perspectives in Schizophrenia.
Forrest,A.   and   Affleck,J.   (Eds.) London: Churchill
Livingstone, 1975, 156-180.
    Scott,R.D. and Ashworth,P.L. The 'Axis Value' and the
transfer of psychosis. A scored analysis of the interaction
in the families of schizophrenic patients. British Journal
of Medical Psychology, 1965, 38, 97-116.
    Scott,R.D. Ashworth,P.L. and Casson,P.D.   Violation
of parental role structure and outcome in schizophrenia. A
scored analysis of features in the parent-patient
relationship. Social Science and Medicine, 1970, 4, 41-64.
    Scott,R.D. and Montanez,A. The nature of tenable and
untenable patient-parent relationships and their connection
with hospital outcome. In Rubinstein,D.   and Alanen,Y.O.
(Eds.), Proceedings of the Fourth International Symposium on
Psychotherapy of   Schizophrenia.   Amsterdam: Excerpta
Medica, 1972.

3. Communication (See also Subject Index)

BUGENTAL,D.B.   Measure of Conflicting Communication

VARIABLE MEASURED. Evaluative inconsistency between verbal
content and vocal intonation.
TEST DESCRIPTION. The measure of conflicting communication
is obtained by use of evaluative ratings made for a
speaker's verbal content and vocal intonation in the same
message. Independent ratings are made on an evaluative
scale from +6 to -6 with a neutral 0 point between.   The
dimension is defined for the judges by polar examples and
verbal description.   Any given message is defined   as
inconsistent if it receives a rating +1.00 or higher in one
channel, -1.00 or less in the other channel.
SAMPLE ITEM.   Unfriendly, disapproving or inconsiderate
-6//////////////+6 Friendly, approving or considerate.

LENGTH. Items: The same ratings are obtained on as many
distinguishable messages as are desired.
AVAILABILITY. In Bugental, Love, and Kaswan, 1971.
ABSTRACTED BY: Daphne Blunt Bugental.
REFERENCE.
     Bugental, D.B.   Love, L.R.   and   Kaswan, J.W.
Verbal-nonverbal conflict in parental messages to normal and
disturbed children. Journal of Abnormal Psychology, 1971,
77, 6-10.

HALEY, J. Restricted Family Communication Task

VARIABLE MEASURED. Family interaction in a restricted
communication setting.
TEST DESCRIPTION. Family members are placed in separate
rooms   at   the   laboratory   and asked to fill out a
questionnaire concerned with various activities (the
Ferreira-Winter Questionnaire). After completing the
questionnaire individually, family members are asked to fill
it out again, but this time as a family. They are asked to
come to an agreement on various items. The discussion
occurs in a restricted setting. Each person is in a
different room talking over an intercommunications system.
They cannot see each other or talk simultaneously. Only two
persons are able to talk at once and when they are
communicating, other members cannot hear them or be heard
themselves. Each person has an intercom box which has a
microphone, a headset and two buttons, each marked with the
name of another family member. The conversation consists of
switching dyads, since all must reach agreement but only two
can talk to each other at the same time. All interaction is
recorded.
LENGTH. NR.
AVAILABILITY. In Haley, 1967.
ABSTRACTED BY: Kersti Yllo
REFERENCE.
     Haley, J. Experiment with abnormal families: testing
done in a restricted communication setting. Archives of
General Psychiatry, 1967, 17, 53-63.

JOURARD, S.M. and LASAKOW, P. Self-Disclosure Questionnaire

VARIABLES MEASURED. Degree of self-disclosure to specified
others in areas of: (1) Attitudes and opinions, (2) Tastes
and interests, (3) Work (or studies), (4) Money, (5)
Personality, (6) Body.
TEST DESCRIPTION. This 60-item questionnaire contains six
categories of 10 items each, for which the subject is rated
on extent of self-disclosure to Mother, Father, Male Friend,
Female Friend, and Spouse. The subject is asked to use the
following rating scale in response to each item: Have told
the other person nothing about this aspect of me = 0, Have
talked in general terms about this item. The other person

has only a general idea about this aspect of me = 1, Have talked in full and complete detail about this item to the other person. He knows me fully in this respect, and could describe me accurately = 2, Have lied or misrepresented myself to the other person so that he has a false picture of me = X (counts as zero). Numerical entries are summed to obtain the self-disclosure scores. The questionnaire was adopted with minor modifications by Komarovsky (1974). In this modification, respondents rate on a scale of 0-3 extent of openness on each item to each of six others: mother, father, closest brother, closest sister, closest male friend, and closest female friend.

SAMPLE ITEM. Attitudes and Opinions: What I think and feel about religion; my personal religious views.

LENGTH. Items: 60.

AVAILABILITY. In Jourard, 1964; Jourard and Lasakow, 1958.

ABSTRACTED BY: Blair Nelson.

REFERENCES.

Dimond,R.E. and Munz,D.C. Ordinal position at birth and self-disclosure in high school students. Psychological Reports, 1967, 21, 829-833.

Doster,J.A. and Strickland,B.R. Perceived child-rearing practices and self-disclosure patterns. Journal of Consulting and Clinical Psychology, 1969, 33, 382.

Jourard,S.M. Personal Adjustment: An Approach Through the Study of Healthy Personality. 2nd Edition. New York: Macmillan Co., 1963.

Jourard,S.M. Disclosing Man to Himself. Princeton, New Jersey: Van Nostrand Co., 1968.

Jourard,S.M. Self Disclosure: an Experimental Analysis of the Transparent Self. New York: Wiley-Interscience, 1971a.

Jourard,S.M. The Transparent Self. Revised Edition. Princeton, New Jersey: Van Nostrand Reinholt Co., 1971b.

Jourard,S.M. and Lasakow,P. Some factors in self-disclosure. Journal of Abnormal and Social Psychology, 1958, 56, 91-98.

Komarovsky,M. Patterns of self-disclosure of male undergraduates. Journal of Marriage and the Family, 1974, 36, 671-686.

Shapiro,A. and Swenson,C. Patterns of self-disclosure among married couples, Journal of Counseling Psychology, 1969, 16, 179-180.

Wiebe,B. and Williams,J.D. Self-disclosure to parents by high school seniors. Psychological Reports, 1972, 690.

REISS,D. Lattice Language Communication Task

VARIABLES MEASURED. (1) Communication efficiency. (2) The strategies by which family members exchange information among themselves.

TEST DESCRIPTION. All information relevant to the experiment is in the possession of at least one family member; therefore, the family's performance does not depend, in any way, on obtaining information from their environment. The core of the procedure is an artificial language. Its designatum is a lattice which can vary in size and shape. The lattice consists of an array of circles, each filled with a letter. For visual display, each circle is joined to the one above, below, to the right and to the left, by a line. Messages in the artificial language describe the lattice. Each message must consist of any two letters that are immediately adjacent to each other in the lattice. A subject sends a message by selecting any two adjoining letters in the lattice and writing them down on an especially printed slip of paper that shows whether the adjacent letters bear a right-left or above-below relationship in the sender's lattice. For any given task, each member of the family has the same lattice as other members; the lattices have the same letters in the same relationship to each other. However, each member has three lattice circles empty; moreover, the three circles that are empty are different for each member. In this sense, each member lacks a certain amount of information, the missing letter, which is in the possession of the other three members of his family. The objective of the task is for everyone in the family to fill in their empty circles. This places the burden on each member of finding out what letters others have in the circles, that, in his/her lattice, are empty. Each member must develop a strategy for indicating to others where his/her empty circles are. Almost all subjects recognize this, and to varying extents can repeat, sequence and order their messages in a way that indicates where their empty circles are. For example, some subjects send messages that point to the empty circles, i.e. messages that are immediately adjacent to their empties. In this way they endow the basic message, "letter X is next to letter Y," with a second level of meaning, "letter X and Y are next to my empty circle"; "what do you have in that circle?" In this way families elaborate a metacommunicative level of exchange as a way of making the primary level of information exchange more efficient.

The procedure tests four members simultaneously. Each is in a booth arranged in such a way that the member can pass a slip of paper to any other member in the family. The members go in turn and the task is complete when everyone has signaled to the experimenter (and to others in the family) that they have filled in their lattices. An example puzzle is used to illustrate the procedure during the instructions. There are two experimental puzzles; the first with a square 16-circle lattice, the second with a cruciform 21-circle lattice. A number of scores are derived from the families' performance: the number of turns required to complete the task (communication efficiency); the extent to which metacommunicative strategies were employed and which type predominated; and the readiness to

use available information to fill in the lattice circles
(information utilization).
SAMPLE ITEMS. See above.
LENGTH. Time: About 90 minutes including instructions.
AVAILABILITY. In Reiss (1969).
ABSTRACTED BY: David Reiss.
REFERENCES.
    Mishler,E.G. and Waxler,N.E. Interaction in Families.
An Experimental Study of Family Processes and Schizophrenia.
New York: Wiley, 1968.
    Reiss,D. Individual thinking and family interaction.
IV. A study of information exchange in families of normals,
those with character disorders and schizophrenics. Journal
of Nervous and Mental Disease, 1969, 149, 473-490.
    Reiss,D. Individual thinking and family interaction.
V. Proposals for the contrasting character or experiential
sensitivity and expressive form in families. Journal of
Nervous and Mental Disease, 1970, 151, 187-202.

THOMAS,E.J. WALTER,C.L. and O'FLAHERTY,K. The Verbal
Problem Checklist

VARIABLE MEASURED. Nine categories of verbal response that
may be problematic for marital partners or family members
are rated, grouped into six types: (1) Vocal
characteristics (e.g., overtalk), (2) Referent
representation (e.g., overgeneralization), (3) Information
given (e.g., redundancy), (4) Content (e.g., negative talk),
(5) Content handling (e.g., content avoidance), (6)
Conversational control (e.g., obtrusions).
TEST DESCRIPTION. Each family member is rated on each of
the 49 categories cf verbal response for amount from Not at
all = 1 to A large amount = 4. The VPC is completed
immediately after the rater listens to a live or
tape-recorded discussion of family members on an assigned
topic (e.g., problems and strengths of your marriage).
SAMPLE ITEM. Overtalk
LENGTH. Time: 6-10 minutes. Items: 49.
AVAILABILITY. In Thomas, Walter and O'Flaherty, 1974.
ABSTRACTED BY: Edwin J. Thomas.
REFERENCES.
    Thomas,E.J. Marital Communication and Decision Making:
Analysis, Assessment and Change. New York: The Free Press,
1976.
    Thomas,E.J. Walter,C.L. and O'Flaherty,K. A verbal
problem checklist for use in assessing family verbal
behavior. Behavior Therapy, 1974, 5, 235-246.

D. Multi-Variable Measures

1. Observed or Reported Interaction (See also Subject Index)

ADAMS,W.J. Family Life Information Inventory

VARIABLES MEASURED. The FLII attempts to measure knowledge
in eight content areas, they are: (1) Family crises, (2)
Masculine and feminine roles, (3) Sex adjustment in
marriage, (4) Early marital adjustment and conflict, (5)
Premarital sex behavior,(6) Dating, courtship and engagement
period, (7) Love, and (8) Difference between men and women.
TEST DESCRIPTION. The FLII serves two purposes. The first
purpose is to measure several different areas of family life
knowledge for students enrolled in a functional marriage
course.   The second purpose is to provide statements taken
from the FLII for class discussion.
      There are 79 statements which comprise the FLII. These
statements come from a pool of 300 items contained in a
study guide developed by Kirkendall (1965). A panel of 14
family life experts scattered through the U.S. provide
content validation by a simple majority agreement on a given
item.   A score based on summing total correct items serves
as an indicator of student's overall knowledge.   Also,
scores from each of eight subscales, as mentioned above, may
serve as an additional index of specific knowledge, or lack
thereof, in family life content.
SAMPLE ITEM. Agree/Disagree. Practically all college
students who engage in premarital intercourse use some
method of contraception.
LENGTH. Time: 20 Minutes. Items: 79.
ABSTRACTED BY: Wesley J. Adams
REFERENCES.
      Adams,W.J. Family life information. The Family
Coordinator, 1971, 20, 55-62.
      Kirkendall,L.A. A Reading and Study Guide for Students
in Marriage and Family Relations. 3rd. Edition. Dubuque,
Iowa: W.C.Brown, 1965, 149.

BALES,R.F. Interaction Process Analysis

VARIABLES MEASURED: A set of 12 categories for recording or
coding interaction of small groups including families.
Combinations of these categories provide scores for six
"functional problems of group interaction." Other
combinations provide scores for Social-Emotional and Task
areas of interaction. (See accompanying figure for list of
categories and basic combination variables.) Other
combination and ratio scores include: degree of control,
direct and indirect access to resources, communication

difficulty,   control   difficulty,   control directiveness,
evaluation difficulty,   expressive-malintegrative behavior,
generalized   status,   interindividual   solidarity,   role
differentiation (Bales, 1950); and the following measures
reported by Strodtbeck (1954):   supportiveness index and
four support   types   (solidary,   contending,   dominant,
conflicting).
TEST DESCRIPTION. Categories are exhaustive of all possible
interactions in small groups. The observer classifies the
behavior in terms of its significance for the recipient of
the act. The unit of recording is a single interaction
capable of classification--typically, a sentence.   Each
minute, 10-20 scores are recorded in most groups session;
nonverbal behavior is also scored at one-minute intervals.
Os consider   only   the   immediately preceding act in
classifying an interaction.   A recording chronograph has
been designed (Bales and Gerbrands, 1948). The categories
can also be used to score a written or tape-recorded

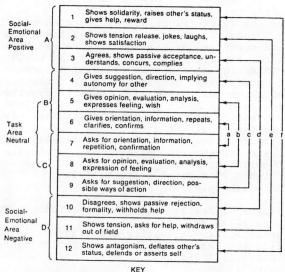

KEY

a Problems of Communication   A Positive Reactions
b Problems of Evaluation   B Attempted Answers
c Problems of Control   C Questions
d Problems of Decision   D Negative Reactions
e Problems of Tension Reduction
f Problems of Reintegration

Interaction Process Analysis. After Robert F. Bales, *Interaction Process Analysis: A Method for the Study of Small Groups* (Reading,
Mass.: Addison-Wesley, 1950). Used by permission of Robert F. Bales.

interaction protocol (Strodtbeck, 1951; 1954). Levinger
(1959) has developed a set of 10 decision problems
(requiring a total of 30-45 minutes of observation time) for
use as standard stimuli in observing family interaction.
Rosen and D'Andrade (1959) have modified the categories for
use in a study of parent-child interaction. Borgatta and
Crowther (1965) have revised and amended Bales's categories
and developed a new interaction observation system--the
Behaviorial Scores System--using Bales's types but "focusing
on definitions that would maximize content areas
corresponding to peer assessments."
SAMPLE ITEM. Interaction category 1. Shows Solidarity:
raises other's status, gives help or reward. (Detailed
definitions and examples are given in Bales, 1950.)
LENGTH. Items: 12 scoring categories.
AVAILABILITY. In Bales, 1950.
REFERENCES.
       Bales,R.F. Interaction Process Analysis: A Method for
the Study of Small Groups. Cambridge, Mass.:
Addison-Wesley, 1950.
       Bales,R.F. A set of categories for the analysis of
small group interaction. American Sociological Review,
1950, 15, 275-363.
       Bales,R.F. Some statistical problems in small group
research. Journal cf American Statistics Association, 1951,
46, 311-322.
       Bales,R.F. The equilibrium problem in small groups.
In Parsons,T. Bales,R.F. and Shils,E.A. Working papers in
the theory of action. Glencoe, Ill.: Free Press, 1953,
111-161.
       Bales,R.F.   and Gerbrands,H.   The   "interaction
recorder": an apparatus and check list for sequential
content analysis cf social interaction. Human Relations,
1948, 1, 456-463.
       Bales,R.F.   and Slater,P.   Role differentiation in
small, decision-making groups. In Parsons,T. and
Bales,R.F. Family, Socialization, and Interaction Process.
Glencoe, Ill.: Free Press, 1955, 259-306.
       Bales,R.F. and Strodtbeck,F.L. Phases in group
problem solving. Journal of Abnormal Social Psychology,
1951, 46, 485-495.
       Borgatta,E.F.   and Bales,R.F. The consistency of
subject behavior and the reliability of scoring in
interaction process analysis. American Sociological Review,
1953, 18, 566-569.
       Borgatta,E.F. and Crowther,B. A Workbook for the
Study of Social Interaction Processes. Chicago: Rand
McNally, 1965.
       Brody,G.F. Relationship between maternal attitudes and
behavior. Journal of Personality and Social Psychology,
1965, 2, 317-323.
       Buros,O.K. (Ed.) Personality Tests and Reviews.
Highland Park, N.J.: Gryphon Press, 1970.
       Cheek,F.E. A serendipitous finding: sex roles and
schizophrenia. Journal of Abnormal and Social Psychology,

1964, 69, 392-400.

Cheek,F.E. Family socialization techniques and deviant behavior. Family Process, 1966, 4, 199-217.

Cheek,F.E. Parental social control mechanisms in the family of the schizophrenic--a new look at the family environment of schizophrenia. Journal of Schizophrenia, 1967, 1, 18-53.

Kenkel,W.F. Influence differentiation in family decision making. Sociology and Social Research, 1957, 42, 18-25.

Kenkel,W.F. Traditional family ideology and spousal roles in decision making. Marriage and Family Living, 1959, 21, 334-339.

Kenkel,W.F. and Hoffman,D.K. Real and conceived role in family decision making. Marriage and Family Living, 1956, 18, 311-316.

Levinger,G. The assessment of family relationships. Bryn Mawr, Penn.: Dept. of Social Work and Social Research. Mimeographed progress report on National Institute of Mental Health Project No. M-2617, 1959.

March,J.G. Husband-and-wife interaction over political issues. Public Opinion Quarterly, 1953-1954, 17, 461-470.

Miller,A.G. The relationship between family interaction and sexual behavior in adolescence. Journal of Community Psychology, 1974, 2, 285-288.

Mishler,E.G. and Waxler,N.E. Interaction in Families. New York: John Wiley and Sons, Inc., 1968.

O'Rourke,J.F. Field and lab: the decision-making behavior of family groups in two experimental conditions. Sociometry, 1963, 26, 422-435.

Rosen,B.C. and D'Andrade,N. The psychological origins of achievement motivation. Sociometry, 1959, 22, 185-218.

Scott,F.G. Family group structure and patterns of social interaction. American Journal of Sociology, 1962, 68, 214-228.

Sharan,S. Family interaction with schizophrenics and their siblings. Journal of Abnormal Psychology, 1970, 75, 30-37.

Schuham,A.I. Bales IPA profiles of disturbed and normal family interaction. Proceedings of the Annual Convention of the American Psychological Association, 1970, 5, 437-438.

Schuham,A.I. Power relations in emotionally disturbed and normal family triads. Journal of Abnormal Psychology, 1970, 75, 30-37.

Schuham,A.I. Activity, talking time and spontaneous agreement in disturbed and normal family interaction. Journal of Abnormal Psychology, 1972, 79, 68-75.

Strodtbeck,F.L. Husband-wife interaction over revealed differences. American Sociological Review, 1951, 16, 468-473.

Strodtbeck,F.L. The family as a three-person group. American Sociological Review, 1954, 19, 23-29.

Turk,J.L. and Bell,N.W. Measuring power in families. Journal of Marriage and Family, 1972, 34, 215-222.

Vidich,A.J.   Methodological problems in the observation of husband-wife interaction. Marriage and Family Living, 1956, 18, 234-239.

Williams,J.A.Jr.   and   Stockton,R.   Black   family structures and functions: an empirical examination of some suggestions made by Billingsley. Journal of Marriage and the Family, 1973, 35, 39-49.

Winter,W.D.   and   Ferreira,A.J.   Interaction   process analysis of family decision-making. Family Process, 1967, 6, 155-172.

BECKER,W.C.   Parent Behavior Rating Scale.

VARIABLES   MEASURED.   Parent-child   and   inter-spouse relations.   Seventy-three   different   variables are combined into   scores   for   (1)   Hostile-withdrawal, (2) Dominance-strictness,   (3)   Nervousness,   (4) Immature emotionally,   (5)   Commonness,   (6)   Solicitousness,   (7) Nonprotectiveness,   (8)   Harmony,   (9) Social effectiveness, and (10) Playfulness.
TEST   DESCRIPTION.   The   rating   schedule   consists of 73 bipolar seven-point rating scales with antonym pairs of adjectives defining the extremes. For each scale, parents are   asked   to   rate   the following concepts: (1) Myself in relation to my child;   (2) Myself in relation to my husband (wife):   (3)   My husband (wife) in relation to me;   (4) The person I should like to be in relation to my child;   (5) The person I should like to be in relation to my husband (wife). The grouping of scales into the   10 variables listed   was determined by factor analysis.
SAMPLE ITEM.   Loving-unloving.
LENGTH.   Time: 40-60   minutes.   Items: 73,   rated   five times.
AVAILABILITY.   A modified version is in Patterson et al., 1975.
REFERENCES.
Becker,W.C.   The relationship of   factors   in   parental ratings   of   self   and   each   other   to   the   behavior of kindergarten children as rated by mothers, fathers, and teachers.   Journal   of   Consulting   Psychology, 1960, 24, 507-527.
Becker,J.   and Iwakami,E.   Conflict and dominance with families   of   disturbed   children.   Journal   of   Abnormal Psychology, 1969, 74, 330-335.
Patterson,G.R.   and   Togot,B.J.   Selective responsiveness in social reinforcers and deviant behavior in children.   The Psychological Record, 1967, 17, 369-378.

BEHRENS,M.L.   MEYERS,D.I.   GOLDFARB,W.   GOLDFARB,N.   and FIELDSTEEL,N.D.   Henry   Ittleson   Center Family Interaction Scales.

VARIABLES MEASURED.   Seven   aspects   of   family   life: (1)

Family investment of selves in home, (2) Family group patterns of interaction, (3) Interaction of husband and wife as marital partners, (4) Interaction of husband and wife as parents, (5) Parent-child interaction, (6) Child-parent interaction, (7) Child-child interaction.

TEST DESCRIPTION. "The scales are used for the appraisal of the functioning of family groups. Data are obtained by participant observation of the family in its real life setting, a three-hour home visit at mealtime, which focuses on the family as a dynamic unit and on the interactions among family members. Each scale contains four anchoring, descriptions of behavior for scores 1,3,5,7, respectively." These descriptions serve only as guidelines in making judgements. Scales are additive.

SAMPLE ITEM. Division of Labor in Care of Children (part of variable 6):
1. There is an absence of division of labor in care of children. One partner assumes the entire burden of care of children with no help from the other partner. Or both parents participate minimally in care of children.
2.
3. There is occasional sharing of care of children. Or care is carried out more as individuals in an isolated way rather than as a parental pair; there is isolated attention by a parent to children without reference to the other parent. Or any sharing with grudging or minimal compliance by the other.
4.
5. Parents share in care of children, although one bears a disproportionate burden. Or the sharing is frequently on the basis of demands one parent makes on the other.
6.
7. The parents divide and share and share care of children in ways that are in accord with their specific culture.
LENGTH. Items: 2,9,8,5,15,3,2, respectively.
AVAILABILITY. In Behrens,M.L., et.al., 1969.
ABSTRACTED BY: Bruce W. Brown.
REFERENCES.
    Behrens,M.L. Meyers,D.I. Goldfarb,W. Goldfarb,N. and Fieldsteel,N.D. The Henry Ittleson Center family interaction scales. Genetic Psychology Monographs, 1969, 80, 203-295.
    Stollak,G.E. An integrated graduate-undergraduate program in the assessment, treatment, and prevention of child psychopathology. Professional Psychology, 1973, 4, 158-169.

BORKE,H.   A   Method   for   Systematically   Observing   Family
Interaction

VARIABLE MEASURED.   Family   interaction: defined   as   any
verbalization which represents one family member's intent to
communicate with another family member.
TEST DESCRIPTION.   A   method   for   categorizing   a   taped
transcription   of a family interacting according to Horney's
broad categorization of all interpersonal behavior   as   (1)
Going   toward,   (2) Going against, or (3) Going away from the
other.   The actual   categories   used   for   anlayzing   family
interaction are:
      (1) Goes toward other.   Contributes-intent: to initate
or   participate   in   social   interaction;   e.g.,   seeks
information,   gives   information,   entertains,   etc.
Supports-intent: to uphold or further the interests of the
other;   e.g., promotes other's cause, expresses concern   for
other.   Petitions-intent: to ask   for something from the
other;   e.g.,   seeks   support,   seeks   attention,   etc.
Directs-intent: to   guide   the   other;   e.g.,   suggests,
instructs, etc. Accepts from   Others-intent: to   take   or
receive   something   from   the   other;   e.g.,   thanks other,
agrees   with   other.   (2)   Going   against   other.
Resists-intent: to go counter to the other; e.g., ignores,
opposes.   Attacks-intent: to begin a controversy with   the
other;   e.g.,   teases,   criticizes,   belittles,   challenges.
(3) Goes away from other.   Retreats-intent: to withdraw or
pull   back   from   social   interaction;   e.g.,   responds
evasively, leaves situation.
SAMPLE ITEM.   See above.
LENGTH.   Items: 8 primary categories and 20 subcategories.
AVAILABILITY.   In Borke, 1967.
REFERENCES.
      Borke,H.   The communication of intent: a   systematic
approach   to   the   observation of family interaction.   Human
Relations, 1967, 20, 13-28.
      Borke,H.   The   communication of intent: a   revised
procedure for analyzing family interaction from video tapes.
Journal of Marriage and the Family, 1969, 31, 541-544.

BORKE,H.   A Procedure for Analyzing Family Interaction   from
Video Tapes

VARIABLE MEASURED.   Family   interaction: defined   as   any
verbal   or   nonverbal   behavior   representing   one   family
member's intent to communicate with another family member.
TEST DESCRIPTION.   A set of 12 categories used   to describe
the   probable   intent of family members as they communicated
with one another.   The categories are as follows: (1) Seeks
information--used   infrequently.   Score   only when no other
intent.   (2)   Seeks   guidance--e.g.,   seeks   direction,
permission,   confirmation.   (3)   Seeks   emotional
support--e.g.,   seeks reassurance, acceptance, affection.
(4)   Gives   information--used infrequently.   Score only when

no other intent.   (5) Gives   guidance--e.g.,   directs,
instructs.   (6) Gives emotional support--e.g., shows
affection, concern, approval.   (7) Accepts opinion--e.g.,
agrees with other.   (8) Focuses attention--e.g., pays
attention to other.   (9) Affiliates--e.g.,   cooperates,
shares with other.   (10) Asserts self--e.g., tries to get in
limelight, bids for attention,   promotes own views.   (11)
Encourages   independence--e.g.,   delegates responsibility to
other.   (12) Opposes--e.g., refuses to cooperate, competes,
teases, disagrees, criticizes, etc.
SAMPLE ITEM.   See above.
LENGTH.   Items: 12 categories.
AVAILABILITY.   In Borke, 1969.
REFERENCES.
        Borke,H.   The communication of intent: a revised
procedure for analyzing family interaction from video tapes.
Journal of Marriage and the Family, 1969, 31, 541-544.
        Borke,H.   The communication of intent: a systematic
approach to the observation of family interaction.   Human
Relations, 1967, 20, 13-28.

CALDWELL,B.M. and HONIG,A.S. Approach: A Procedure for
Patterning the Response of Adults and Children.

VARIABLES MEASURED.   Approach records   and   codes   all
behavioral   transactions--cognitive,   locomotive,
socio-emotional, caregiving,   etc.--that   occur   between
children and adults and their environment.   Approach code
designations may be modified to refer to other variables or
molar behaviors of interest to the investigator.
TEST DESCRIPTION.   Approach (applicable across all age
ranges of childhccd) is a technique for coding observations
and behavior sequences and of the settings in which they are
emitted.   The ccde is applied to a behavior record obtained
by stationing an observer near the subject to be observed
and having the cbserver whisper into a tape recorder every
change of behavior noted in the subject and every response
directed toward the subject or emitted within his social
range.   Coding is at present being done as efficiently
directly from the tape as it was from a typescript of the
behavior record earlier in our program.   Ongoing behaviors
are recorded every five seconds.   Simultaneous or complex
behaviors are recorded consecutively or by means of a
modifying clause--for example: "Mother shows Jim the
picture book while smiling at him."
        Emitted behaviors are coded by breaking up   the
narrative description into behavioral clauses, each of which
contains four basic components: The subject of the clause
.(who or what does something), the predicate (what is done),
the object (toward whcm or what the action is directed), and
some qualifier (adverbial descriptions of the action).   Each
of those four components is then translated into a numerical
code and grouped into a five-digit statement (two digits
being required for the predicates) which summarizes the

subject-predicate-object-adverb involved in a single behavior unit. The complete chain of numerical statements is then key-punched for computer analysis. Behavior settings are also converted to numerical statements describing the type of activity taking place in the observation environment, the geographic region in which the behavior occurs, and the dramatis personae of the total social scene.

This type of code permits a running sequential picture of actions emitted by the child or the adult who is the central figure of the observation and of behaviors received by him or her. In general the resulting description is a very fine-grained one containing much that might be considered irrelevant for some types of behavior analysis but at the same time rich in the sort of sequential data essential for true ecological analyses.

SAMPLE ITEMS. Johnny has his mother around her leg. This behavioral clause translates numerically to: 04422.

Jenny stared as Mr. Jones asked Tina how much the toy cost. Numerical translation: 81631, 00189.

AVAILABILITY. The Approach manual is available for purchase for $7.00 through the Journal Supplement Abstract Service (of the American Psychological Association, 1200 Seventeenth St. N.W., Washington, D.C. 20036) as JSAS Manuscript Number 2.

ABSTRACTED BY: Alice Sterling Honig.

LENGTH. Time: As many minutes of observation time as the investigator requires. Five minutes of detailed behavioral sequences can provide a fine-grained picture of personal interactions and transactions. Items: The present five-digit code can provide for 10 subject and object codes, 99 behavioral predicates, and 10 behavioral modifiers. Increasing Approach to a seven-digit code flexibly increases the potential number of subject-object codes (see Brogden reference). Increasing Approach to a six-digit code flexibly increases the potential number of adverbial predicate modifiers to 99 (see Wright et al. reference).

REFERENCES.

Brogden,N.J. A study of the social interactions of three and four-year-old children and the adults in their day care environment. Ph.D. dissertation, Syracuse University, 1973.

Caldwell,B.M. A new "approach" to behavioral ecology. In Hill,J.P. (Ed.) Minnesota Symposium on Child Psychology. Vol. 2. Minneapolis, University of Minnesota Press, 1969.

Caldwell,B.M. and Honig,A.S. Approach--A Procedure for Patterning the Responses of Adults and Children: A demonstration training film in color, Syracuse University Children's Center, 1968.

Caldwell,B.M. and Honig,A.S. Approach--A Procedure for Patterning Responses of Adults and Children. Washington, D.C.: American Psychological Association Journal Supplement Abstract Service. Abstracted in: Catalog of Selected Documents in Psychology, 1971, 1, 1-2, Manuscript No.2. Price $7.00.

Caldwell,B.M.   and Tannenbaum,J.A.   A new approach in naturalistic observations.   Paper presented at the conference of the American Educational Research Association, Chicago, Illinois, February 1968.

Honig,A.S.   Caldwell,B.M.   and   Tannenbaum,J.A. Patterns of infcrmation processing used by and with young children in a nursery school setting.   Child Development, 1970, 41, 1045-1065.

Honig,A.S.   and   Mercurio,R.M.   Mother-infant interactions in structured teaching situations.   Unpublished mansucript. Syracuse University, 1975.

Honig,A.S.   Tannenbaum,J.A.   and   Caldwell,B.M. Maternal behavior in verbal report and in laboratory observation: A methodological study.   Child Psychology and Human Development, 1973, 3, 216-230.

Lytton,H.   Three   approaches   to   the   study   of parent-child   interaction: ethological,   interview and experimental.   Jcurnal of Child Psychology and Psychiatry, 1973, 14, 1-17.

Mercurio,R.M.   A study of maternal teaching style as an aspect of   mother-child   interaction.   Ph.D.   dissertation. Wayne State University, 1972.

Schilling,L.S.   An observational study of reciprocity in infant-mother interaction during the feeding situation and its relationship to selected infant and maternal variables.   Ph.D.   dissertation, Syracuse University, 1976.

Tse,M.   Maternal teaching styles and strategies as a function of five years of intervention: a videotape study. Ph.D.   dissertation, Syracuse University, 1977.

Wright,C.   Honig,A.S.   Lally,J.R.   and   Tse,M.   A videotape in-home study of the social and educational teaching styles of mothers and their five-year-olds. Abstracted in Research in Education, Dec.   1975, ERIC, Doc. No.   Ed.   110 163.

CAVAN,R.   Rating Scales   for   Family   Integration   and Adaptability.

VARIABLES   MEASURED.   Degree   of   affection,   mutual cooperation,   joint activities, esprit de corps, absence of tension,   economic   interdependence,   nonmaterialistic philosophy,   lack of traditionalism, adaptability of roles, responsibility, previous experiences in crises.
TEST DESCRIPTION.   Rating   scale   to   be   applied   to   case reports.   The ratings are combined in a weighted sum to arrive at   scores.   Hill   (1949)   used   a   modification   of Cavan's   scale tc form scales for adaptability, integration, and dynamic stability in his study of the effects of war separation and reunion on families.
SAMPLE ITEM.   Degree of affection--father and mother: 5 = Deeply and romantically in   love;   4 = In love more than average;   3 = Average,   congenial,   loyal;   2 =   Minor disagreements   or   impersonal;   1 =   Estranged   or   very detached.

LENGTH. Items: 17 rating scales.
AVAILABILITY. In Burgess and Locke, 1945.
REFERENCES.
      Burgess,E.W. and Locke,H.J. The Family.   New York:
American Book, 1945, 781-784.
      Cavan,R. and Ranck,K. The Family and the Depression.
Chicago: University of Chicago Press, 1938.
      Hill,R.L. Families under Stress: Adjustment to the
Crises of War Separation and Reunion. New York: Harper,
1949.

CHANCE,E. Family Interaction Scoring System.

VARIABLES MEASURED.   (1) Interpersonal relations among
family members on two dimensions: (a) positive-negative (or
love versus hate), and (b) active-passive (or control versus
submit) role, (2) Conflict in relation to these roles, (3)
Defense mechanisms in relation to these roles.
TEST DESCRIPTION. A set of 20 categories for scoring
interview   protocols   on   the   positive-negative   and
active-passive variables, and a parallel set of Q-sort cards
for the same variables. The 20 categories are divided into
four groups of five categories each.   Each group of
categories represents one of the four quadrants formed by
the dichotomizing of these two variables, and corresponds to
a "type of interpersonal relations." The four types and the
categories comprising each are: (1) Positive-active (lead,
teach,   give,   support,   love);   (2)   Positive-passive
(appreciate, cooperate, trust, admire,   conform);   (3)
Negative-active (boss, rebel, compete, punish, hate); and
(4) Negative-passive (resent, complain, distrust, retreat,
submit).   Interview protocols are scored by assigning an
intensity weight of 1, 2, or 3 to each statement which
reflects one category, and summing the resulting scores for
each group of five categories.   To control for protocol
length, scores are ranked for each subject separately, and
the rank constitutes the subject's score on each variable.
      The Q-sort deck consists of three statements reflecting
each of the 20 categories, and can be administered for
self-description or to describe other family members.   The
Q-sort items, however, are worded as personality dimensions,
rather than intra-family role specific (e.g., "He conforms"
rather than "He conforms to the family's way of doing
things").
      Conflict is scored from the interview protocols using
four indicators: (1) and (2) Self or other descriptions
which are judged to indicate culturally inappropriate roles;
(3) The proportion of coded items which are judged to imply
self-rejection;   (4)   Inconsistent   or   contradictory
statements about own role.
      Defense mechanisms are indicated by discrepancy between
interview obtained scores and Q-sort derived scores, and by
discrepancy or excessive agreement between self-description
of other family members.

SAMPLE ITEM. See the set of categories and the sample
Q-sort item in test description.
LENGTH. Items: 60-card Q-sort.
AVAILABILITY. In Chance, 1955.
REFERENCE.
    Chance, E. Measuring the potential interplay of forces
within the family during treatment. Child Development,
1955, 26, 241-265.

CHAPPLE, E.D.   Interaction Chronograph.

VARIABLES MEASURED. (1) Tempo, how often a person starts to
talk;   (2) Activity or energy, how much longer he/she talks
or responds than is silent and unresponsive;   (3)
Adjustment, length of interruptions compared to failures to
respond; (4) Initiative, frequency of; (5) Dominance,
frequency with which one subject outtalks or outacts the
other when there has been an interruption;   (6)
Synchronization, frequency of interruption or failure to
respond;   (7) Flexibility;   (8) Ability to listen.
Additional variables have been developed and may be used to
give an interactional pattern of personality (Chapple,
1962).
TEST DESCRIPTION. An observational technique for recording
interactions of two subjects based on the assumption that
objective events such as the amount and duration of
interaction between two individuals reflect group structure
and emotional relations among people and their attitudes
toward one another. The observer uses an Interaction
Chronograph, which continuously records and integrates the
time of the ways one subject adjusts to the other. The
observer records when an action begins, how long it
continues, and such physical acts as gestures and nods. A
unit of observation is a unit of action. Content is not
recorded, so the record is made up of the characteristics of
interaction such as interruptions, delays in response, and
so forth. The eight variables are conceptualizations of
these interactions. Current versions of the Interaction
Chronograph are for recording the interaction of only two
subjects at a time.
SAMPLE ITEM. See above.
LENGTH. Determined by the events being observed.
AVAILABILITY. Price information and sales arrangements for
renting the Interaction Chronograph available from E.D.
Chapple Co., Inc., Noroton, Conn.   06820.
REFERENCES.
    Chapple, E.D.   The interaction chronograph: its
evolution and present application. Personnel, 1949, 25,
295-307.
    Chapple, E.D.   Quantitative analysis of complex
organizational systems. Human Organization, 1962, 21,
67-87.
    Chapple, E.D.   and Arensberg, C.M.   Measuring human
relations: an introduction to the study of the interaction

of individuals. Genetic Psychology Monograph, 1940, Whole
No. 22.
        Chapple,E.D. and Lindeman,E. Clinical implications of
measurements of interaction rates in psychiatric interviews.
Applied Anthroplogy, 1942, 1, 1-11.
        Matarazzo,R.G.   Matarazzo,J.D.   Saslow,G.J.   and
Phillips,J.S. Psychological test and organismic correlates
of interview interaction patterns. Journal of Abnormal
Social Psychology, 1958, 56, 329-338.
        Matarazzo,J.D. Saslow,G.J. and Matarazzo,R.G. The
interaction chronograph as an instrument for objective
measurement of interaction patterns during interviews.
Journal of Psychology, 1956, 41, 347-367.
        Phillips,J.S. Matarazzo,J.D.   Matarazzo,R.G.   and
Saslow,G. Observer reliability of interaction patterns
during interviews. Journal of Consulting Psychology, 1957,
21, 269-275.
        Saslow,G.J.   Matarazzo,J.D.   Phillips,J.S.   and
Matarazzo,R.G. Test-restest stability of interaction
patterns during interviews conducted one week apart.
Journal of Abnormal Social Psychology, 1957, 54, 295-302.

DANZIGER,K. and GREENGLASS,E.R.   Verbal Exchange Analysis

VARIABLES MEASURED. Utterances that serve four functions:
to convey information, to please (evaluations), to move
others to action (demands), and to defend oneself
(justifications).
TEST DESCRIPTION. When the subclassification of the four
major functional categories is made on the basis of the
dimensions described above, 29 coding categories are
generated. The coding of a given verbal unit involves the
matching of that unit with a set of category definitions.
The coder scans these category definitions and then decides
on the appropriate classification. The order in which
categories are scanned is predetermined by the procedure
outlined in the coding manual. First, the coder must decide
which of the four major functional categories best describes
the verbal unit in question. Having selected one of these
categories, the remainder of the coding process is reduced
to a series of clearly identifiable binary decisions between
subcategories describing the various dimensions of the four
major functional categories.
SAMPLE ITEM. Demands: Imperatives and requests; for
orientation and confirmation.
LENGTH. Items: 29 coding categories.
AVAILABILITY. From NAPS-2.
ABSTRACTED BY: E.R.Greenglass
REFERENCES.
        Greenglass,E.R. Some processes of child-rearing--with
particular reference to the Italian family. Journal:
Ontario Association of Children's Aid Societies, 1971a, 1-5.
        Greenglass,E. A cross-cultural comparison of the
child's communication with his mother. Developmental

Psychology, 1971b, 5, 494-499.
   Greenglass,E. A cross-cultural comparison of maternal
communication. Child Development, 1971c, 42, 685-692.
   Greenglass,E.   A   cross-cultural study of   the
relationship between resistance to temptation and maternal
communication. Genetic Psychology Monographs, 1972a, 86,
119-139.
   Greenglass,E. A comparison of maternal communication
style   between   immigrant Italian and second-generation
Italian women living in Canada. Journal of Cross-Cultural
Psychology, 1972b, 3, 185-192.

FERREIRA,A.J.   and WINTER,W.D.   Unrevealed Differences
Technique.

VARIABLES MEASURED.   (1) Spontaneous agreement, (2)
Decision-time,   (3)   Choice-fulfillment: the   sum of
individual choices which became family choices, (4) Index of
normality choices (NN).
TEST DESCRIPTION.   The technique starts with a
self-administered questionnaire, designed to examine
intrafamily exchange of self-revealing information when the
opinion of other family members is not known. There are
seven "situations" with 10 alternatives or choices each.
For every situation, family members indicate the three
choices they like most and the three choices they like least
or at all.   Subjects are first asked to fill out the
questionnaire individually, and then together with responses
representing a family decision.   (1) Spontaneous Agreement
(SA) indicates the number of agreements among family members
before any family discussion. This SA score (agreement of
both positive and negative choices) has a theoretical range
of 0 to 42 for any dyad.   The score for the family is
obtained by summing the scores for all dyads.   (2)
Decision-Time (DT) is defined as the time in minutes spent
by the family to complete the joint questionnaire.   It is
regarded as a measure of the efficiency of family
functioning.   (3) Choice-Fulfillment (CF) reflects the
extent to which the family choices fulfill the individuals'
choices. An individual's CF score is defined as the number
of instances where the individual's choices became the
family's choices.   (4) Index of Normality is a global
measure of the balance and quality of family functioning.
It is the sum of the SA scores, plus 2 times the PP score,
minus 1.33 times the DT score. (The PP score is the number
of instances in which a positive individual choice agreed
with the family choice.)
SAMPLE ITEM. You are going to choose the color of your next
car. Below is a list of choices you might have: (a) maroon
and white, (b) black and gold, (c) white and blue, etc.
LENGTH. Time: Variable. Items: 7.
AVAILABILILTY. From NAPS-2.

ABSTRACTED BY: Blair Nelson

REFERENCES.
        Byassee,J.E. and Murrell,S.A.A.   Interaction patterns
in families of autistic, disturbed, and normal children.
American Journal of Orthopsychiatry, 1975, 45, 473-478.
        Ferreira,A.J.   Value consensus and partner satisfaction
among dating couples. Journal of Marriage and the Family,
1966, 28, 166-173.
        Ferreira,A.J.   and Winter,W.D.   Family interaction and
decision-making.   Archives of General Psychiatry, 1965, 13,
214-223.
        Ferreira,A.J.   and   Winter,W.D.   Stability   of
interactional variables in family decision-making. Archives
of General Psychiatry, 1966, 14, 352-355.
        Ferreira,A.J.   and   Winter,W.D.   Decision-making   in
normal and abnormal two-child families. Family Process,
1968, 7, 17-36.
        Haley,J.   Experiment with abnormal families: testing
done in a restricted communication setting. Archives of
General Psychiatry, 1967, 17, 53-63.
        Haley,J.   Speech sequences of normal and abnormal
families with two children present. Family Process, 1967,
6, 81-97.
        Mead,D.E.   and Campbell,S.S.   Decision-making   and
interaction by families with and without a drug-abusing
child. Family Process, 1972, 11, 487-498.
        Murrell,S.A.   Family   interaction   variables   and
adjustment of nonclinic boys. Child Development, 1971, 42,
1485-1494.
        Schuham,A.I. Activity, talking time and spontaneous
agreement in disturbed and normal family interaction.
Journal of Abnormal Psychology, 1972, 79, 68-75.
        Winter,W.D.   and Ferreira,A.J.   Research in Family
Interaction.   Palo Alto, California: Science and Behavior
Books, 1969.
        Winter,W.D.   Ferreira,A.J.   and   Bowers,N.
Decision-making in married and unrelated couples. Family
Process, 1973, 12, 83-94.

GERARD,D.L. and SIEGEL,J. Family Background Interview and
Rating Scales.

VARIABLES   MEASURED.   (1)   Hostililty-warmth of   the
relationship between parents, (2) Strength of mother-child
relationship,   (3) Mother dominance,   (4)   Strength of
father-child relationship, (5) Attitude toward childhood
illness,   (6)   Parental   overprotection,   (7)   Sibling
favoritism,   (8) Parental indulgence, (9) Prohibition of
social experiences, (10) Sociological disparities within
family or between family and community, (11) Parental
personality maladjustment, (12) Child's position of
importance in family, (13) Breast-feeding, (14) Toilet
training, (15) Rejective attitudes toward pregnancy, (16)
Feeding problems of infancy and childhood, (17) Conventional

behavior problems, (18) Broken home, and (19) Punitive
treatment.
TEST DESCRIPTION The parents are interviewed intensively by
an unstructured method which attempts to get a maximum of
information with a minimum of direct questioning. The
information from the prototcols is subsequently transferred
to a questionnaire from which the ratings are made. Most of
the ratings are made on three-point scales, ranging from 0
to 1. Definiticns and sample protocol. materials are
provided for each of the scales. The more pathological end
of the scale is given the highest score. Pathology is
defined in terms of theory about the psychological etiology
of schizophrenia. Scores for various scales may be added
for pathological background score.
SAMPLE ITEM. Strength of the mother-child relationship:
Markedly heightened relationship with mother = 1;
Moderately heightened relationship with mother = 1/2;
Normal, interested relationship with mother = 0;
Diminished, disinterested, rejective relationship = 0; Data
insufficient to make a judgement = ?.
LENGTH. Time: Average length of interviews, 3 hours.
Items: 19 rating scales.
AVAILABILITY. In Gerard and Siegel, 1950.
REFERENCE.
     Gerard,D.L. and Siegel,J. The family background of
schizophrenia. Psychiatric Quarterly, 1950, 24, 47-73.

GUTTMAN,H.A. Time Unit Method of Coding Intrafamilial
Interaction.

VARIABLES MEASURED. Interaction of mother, father and
child.
TEST DESCRIPTION. Tape recordings are made of the
discussion among the three family members who are requested
to make choices from a series of lists (the Ferreira and
Winter Questionnaire). The discussions are coded directly
from the audio tape. Intrafamilial interaction (including
silences) are coded in five-second units. "Unitizing
directly from the audiotape produces results which are
highly ccmparable to those obtained from unitizing a
transcript. Tedious transcribing is completely eliminated"
with this method.
SAMPLE ITEM. See Ferreira and Winter abstract.
LENGTH. NR.
AVAILABILITY. In Guttman, 1972a, b.
ABSTRACTED BY: Kersti Yllo.
REFERENCES.
     Guttman,H.A. A time-unit method of coding
intrafamilial interaction from the audiotape.
Psychotherapy: Theory, Research and Practice, 1972a, 9,
267-268.
     Guttman,H.A. Time unit coding from the audiotaped
interview: a simple method of coding therapist behavior.
Journal of Clinical Psychology, 1972b, 28, 112-114.

Guttman,H.A.   Sigal,J.J.   and Chagoya,L.   Time-unit
coding from the audiotaped interview: a simple method of
coding therapist behavior. Journal of Clinical Psychology,
1972, 28, 112-114.
Guttman,H.A.   Spector,R.M.   Sigal,J.J.   Epstein,N.B.
and Rakoff,V.   Coding of affective expression in conjoint
family therapy. American Journal of Psychotherapy, 1972,
26, 185-194.
Guttman,H.A.   Spector,R.M.   Sigal,J.J.   Rakoff,V.   and
Epstein,N.B.   Reliability of coding affective communication
in family therapy sessicns: problems of measurement and
interpretation.   Journal of Consulting and Clinical
Psychology, 1971, 37, 397-402.

HERBST,P.G.   Herbst Family Relationships Questionnaire.

VARIABLES MEASURED.   (1) Family activity region (household
duties, child care, social, economic) in which husband and
wife participate and decide;   (2) Tension index
(disagreement concerning decisions);   (3) Family interaction
pattern (husband dominance, wife dominance, autonomic,
syncratic);   (4) Family structure pattern (autocratic,
autonomic, average, syncratic) assigned on the basis of the
relative frequency of the family interaction patterns using
the classification in Table 7 (Herbst, 1952) or Table 52
(Herbst, 1954).
TEST DESCRIPTIONS. Subject is asked which family member
does each of 33 tasks and activities, who decides about
them, and how often there is disagreement about the
activity.   The activities cover four regions: household
duties, child ccntrol and care, social activities, and
economic activities.   All are things both spouses could do.
The questionnaire was presented to schoolchildren under the
name "The Day at Home." Part I contains the activity
questions, and Part II the decision and disagreement
questions referring to these activities. (Note: siblings
and others are listed as response categories but not
scored.)
SAMPLE ITEM.   (1) Who gets Dad's breakfast? Mother, Father.
(2) Who decides what Dad has for breakfeast? Mother,
Father. (3) Does he like what he gets for breakfast?
Often, Sometimes, Never.
LENGTH. Items: 97.
AVAILABILITY. Herbst, 1952; 1954.
REFERENCES.
Adler,D.L.   The contemporary Australian family.   Human
Relations, 1966, 19, 265-282.
Brown,L.B.   The day at home in Wellington, New Zealand.
Journal cf Social Psychology, 1959, 50, 189-206.
Coe,W.C.   Curry,A.E.   and Kessler,D.R.   Family
interactions of psychiatric inpatients.   Family Process,
1969, 8, 119-130.
Herbst,P.G.   The measurement of family relationships.
Human Relations, 1952, 5, 3-35.

Herbst,P.G.   Family living--patterns of interaction. In Oeser,O.A. and Hammond,S.B.   (Eds.) Social Structure and Personality in a City. London: Routledge, 1954, Chapter 12.

Hooper,D.   and Sheldon,A.   Evaluating newly-married couples. British Journal of Social and Clinical Psychology, 1969, 8, 169-182.

King,K.   Adolescent perception of power structure in the Negro Family. Journal of Marriage and the Family, 1969, 31, 751-755.

Larson,L. and Johannis,T.B.Jr. Religious perspective and the authcrity structure of the family. Pacific Sociological Review, 1967, 10, 13-24.

Maxwell,J.W.   Rural negro-father participation in family activities. Rural Sociology, 1968, 33, 80-83.

Oeser,O.A.   and Emery,F.E.   Social Structure and Personality in a Rural Ccmmunity. London: Routledge, 1954, Chapter 7.

Papanek,M.L.   Authority and sex roles in the family. Journal of Marriage and the Family, 1969, 31, 88-96.

Stone,A.R.   Inter-parental concordance and severity of children's psychiatric conditions. Journal of Marriage and the Family, 1966, 28, 491-494.

Taft,R.   Some subcultural variables in family structure in Australia.   Australian Journal of Psychology, 1957, 9, 69-90.

Yamamura,D.S.   and Zald,N.M.   A note on the usefulness and validity of the Herbst family questionnaire. Human Relations, 1956, 9, 217-221.

KOGAN,K.L. and STAFF OF THE PARENTING CLINIC, UNIVERSITY OF WASHINGTON.   Interpersonal Behavior Constructs (Formerly Status-Affection-Involvement Ratings).

VARIABLES MEASURED. Verbal and nonverbal social interaction representing various degrees and combinations of high or low: (1) Relative status, defined as the relative position one person maintains with reference to the other person. (2) Affection, "the giving and seeking or receiving of warmth, love, etc." (3) Involvement, "the extent to which one person's attention is directed to or focused on the other."

TEST DESCRIPTION. Videotaped interactions are assessed in 40-second units for the presence or absence of seven "duration behaviors" (behavior occurs during at least 70% of the 40-second unit) and 16 "frequency behaviors" (momentary occurrences with no defined duration). Absolute frequencies of behaviors for each participant and contingencies between participants are calculated. Tentative norms are available for 20 children, 2-1/2 to 10 years of age, and their mothers.

SAMPLE ITEM.   (1) Watches.   Definition: visual attention primarily on other or other's acitivity.

LENGTH. Time: Two half-hour sessions, each yielding 45 40-second time units.
AVAILABILITY. In Kogan et al., 1975a; available from Kogan and NAPS-2.
ABSTRACTED BY: Kate L. Kogan.
REFERENCES.

Carey,K. and Kogan,K.L. A pilot study of mother-child interactions in children with brochial asthma. Journal of Asthma Research, 1974, 11, 169-179.

Gordon,B.N. and Kogan,K.L. A mother-instruction program: behavior changes with and without therapeutic intervention. Child Psychiatry and Human Development, 1975, 6, 89-106.

Gordon,B.N. and Kogan,K.L. A mother-instruction program: analysis of intervention procedures. Family Process, 1975, 14, 205-221.

Kogan,K.L. Specificity and stability of mother-child interaction styles. Child Psychiatry and Human Development, 1972, 2, 160-168.

Kogan,K.L. Carey,K. Jarvis,M.A. Layden,T.A. Turner,P.A. and Vann,D.M. Interpersonal behavior constructs: a means for analyzing videotaped dyadic interaction. Mimecgraphed Laboratory Manual, 1975a.

Kogan,K.L. and Gordon,B.N. Interpersonal behavior constructs: a revised approach to defining dyadic interaction styles. Psychological Reports, 1975b, 36, 835-846. Also available from senior author at University of Washington Parenting Clinic, Seattle, Washington 98195, the Laboratory Manual for Interpersonal Behavior Constructs: a Means for Analyzing Videotaped Dyadic Interaction.

Kogan,K.L. and Tyler,N. Mother-child interaction in young physically handicapped children. American Journal of Mental Deficiency, 1973, 77, 492-497.

Kogan,K.L. Tyler,N. and Turner,P.A. The process of interpersonal adaptation between mothers and their cerebral palsied children. Developmental Medicine and Child Neurology, 1974, 16, 518-527.

Kogan,K.L. and Wimberger,H.C. An approach to defining mother-child interaction styles. Perceptual and Motor Skills, 1966, 23, 1171-1177.

Kogan,K.L. and Wimberger,H.C. Analysis of mother-child interaction in young mental retardates. Child Development, 1969, 40, 799-812.

Kogan,K.L. and Wimberger,H.C. Interaction patterns in disadvantaged families. Journal of Clinical Psychology, 1969, 25, 347-352.

Kogan,K.L. and Wimberger,H.C. Behavior transactions between disturbed children and their mothers. Psychological Reports, 1971, 28, 395-404.

Kogan,K.L. and Wimberger,H.C. Status behaviors in mother-child dyads in normal and clinic samples. Psychological Reports, 1972, 31, 87-92.

Taylor,M.K. and Kogan,K.L. Effects of birth of sibling on mother-child interaction. Child Psychiatry and Human Development, 1973, 4, 53-58.

Tyler,N. and Kogan,K.L.   The social by-products of
therapy with young children. Physical Therapy, 1972, 52,
508-513.
        Wimberger,H.C. and Kogan,K.L.   Interpersonal behavior
ratings. Journal of Nervous and Mental Disorder, 1968, 147,
260-271.

LAWLIS,G.F.   Four Relationship Factor (4FR) Questionnaire.

VARIABLES MEASURED.   Four factors   interpreted as positive
ingredients in the development of specific interpersonal
relationships: (1) Parental/respect, (2) Identification,
(3) Problem-solving, (4) Sexual/affection.
TEST DESCRIPTION.   A self-administering questionnaire to
measure the above dimensions of intimate relationships based
on perceptions of past behaviors.   The scales are derived
from a factor analysis. Self scoring dimension items are
summed for normative comparison in standard scores (STENS).
SAMPLE ITEM.   Identification scale: We think a lot alike.
Always true, Sometimes true, Sometimes false, Always false.
LENGTH.   Time: 10 minutes. Items: 44.
AVAILABILITY.   Test Systems, Inc.: Wichita, Kansas.
ABSTRACTED BY: G. Frank Lawlis.
REFERENCES.
        Kluge,C.A.   An investigation of personality variables
and helping styles of nonprofessional volunteers in a
telephone crisis center. Ph.D. dissertation, Texas Tech.
University, 1974.   Dissertation Abstracts International,
1975, 36, 913B.
        Lawlis,G.F.   The Four Relationship Factors and Their
Measurement. Wichita, Kansas: Test Systems, Inc. 1973.
        McGahee,B.M.   A psychosocial reinforcement model of
alcoholism.   Ph.D.   dissertation, Texas Tech. University,
1974. Dissertation Abstracts International, 1975, 35, 465B.
        Norman,W.B.   Relationship factors in the counseling
dyad Ph.D. dissertation, Texas Tech. University, 1976.
        Randolph,K.D.   Dialectical correlates of juvenile
delinquency.   Ph.D. dissertation, Texas Tech. University,
1973.   Dissertation Abstracts International, 1974,   35,
1926B.
        Spears,B. and Lawlis,G.F.   Relationship factors of
alcoholics. Psychological Reports, 1974, 34, 946.
        Tan,G.   and   Lawlis,G.F.   Correlates   of   school
achievement and parental relationship.   Psychological
Reports, 1975.
        Waters,E.C.   Functioning and non-functioning marriages:
a study of personalities, roles, and relationships. Ph.D.
dissertation, Texas Tech. University, 1974.   Dissertation
Abstracts International, 1975, 36.

MacFARLANE,J.W.   Scales for Rating Family Situations.

VARIABLES MEASURED.   Numerous aspects of family life

including   use of leisure time, marital adjustment of
parents, parental similarities and dissimilarities in
background and personality, cooperation of parents, and
status of the child in the family.
TEST DESCRIPTION. Rating scales based on structured,
quasi-conversational interviews. There are two sets of
five-point rating scales: (1) the Scale for Rating Family
Background Data, which is used to categorize the interview
protocol; (2) the Code Sheet on the Family Situation, which
is completed by the E immediately after his interview with
the family.
SAMPLE ITEM. (Family Background Scale:) Relatives: No data
for rating = 0; Great companionability, happy relationship,
no conflict = 1; Enjoys relatives, contributes to happiness
= 2; Smooth exterior, occasional annoyance at minor details
= 3; Considerable stress and strain chronically present =
4;   Serious conflict or strain, open hostility = 5. (Code
on Family Situation:) Status of child in family--father,
mother, others: 1.   Acutely resented to the point of
mistreatment; 2. Not overly mistreated... 3. Treated as
sibs save for occasional disciplinary episodes; 4. Favored
but not overtly so; 5. Openly favored, indulged.
LENGTH. Time: The minimum time for the family background
interview was three hours, and the interview frequently ran
into several sessions. Items: 41 (family background);   39
(family situation).
AVAILABILITY. In MacFarlane, 1938.
REFERENCES.
    MacFarlane,J.W.   Studies in   child   guidance: I.
methodology of data collection and organization. Monographs
of the Society for Research in Child Development, 1938, 3
Serial No. 6, Ch. V and Appendix D.
    Weinstock,A.R. Family environment and the development
of defense and coping mechanism. Journal of Personality and
Social Psychology, 1967, 5, 67-75.

MISHLER,E.G.   and   WAXLER,N.E.   Mishler   and   Waxler
Interaction Codes.

VARIABLES MEASURED. Specific aspects of family interaction,
each of which is measured by an independent code. The
interaction codes are: (1) Acknowledgement Stimulus and
Acknowledgment Response.   "These are two independent codes
that together measure the degree to which the intent and
content of a particular statement are acknowledged, or taken
into account, by the following speaker." (2) Affect.   "The
affect code classifies each act according to the affective
quality of the words used, from the point of view of their
meaning in common culture." (3) Focus.   The focus code
refers "to aspects of the immediate situation mentioned by
family members." (4) Fragments. "These are five independent
codes, each of which refers to one kind of deviation from a
smooth and continuous flow of speech." (5) Interaction
Process Analysis. This code is a slightly modified version

of Bales IPA.   (6) Interruptions.   This code includes both
successful and unsuccessful interruptions.   (7) Pause.
"Measured the occurrence of silences in the family
interaction." (8) Statement Length.   "Used to measure
average length of statements." (9) To Whom. "This code is
applied to each act on the basis of who is the target of
that act."
TEST DESCRIPTION. The experimental procedure which makes
use of the Interaction Codes draws upon the
Revealed-Difference Questionnaire to generate discussions
among the three family members present at each session.   The
tape recordings of the family's interaction in a small
groups laboratory room provide the basic data source.   The
experiment uses ongoing observation of the interaction by a
coder behind a one-way mirror as a source of only one
variable, "who speaks to whom." Other interaction codes are
applied to typescripts made from tape recordings.   A
complete discussion of how the experiment is conducted and
how the interaction is broken down into units and coded is
available in Mishler and Waxler, 1968.
SAMPLE ITEM. For sample code see Variables Measured, for
sample discussion item see Revealed-Difference Questionnaire
sample item.
LENGTH. Items: 9 codes.
AVAILABILITY. In Mishler and Waxler, 1968.
ABSTRACTED BY: Kersti Yllo.
REFERENCE.
     Mishler,E.G. and Waxler,N.E.   Interaction in Families.
New York: John Wiley and Sons, 1968.

MITCHELL,R.E.   Mitchell Family Relationship Indexes.

VARIABLES MEASURED. (1) Extent of openness and frequency of
husband-wife communications, (2) Amount of open conflict in
a husband-wife relationship, (3) Degree to which spouses
influence various family decisions, (4) Number of complaints
and expressions of dissatisfaction with one's spouse, (5)
Frequency with which children talk with parents over various
issues, (6) Degree to which parents have close visible
control over their children, (7) Degree to which married
adults have in the past, are now, or might in the future
rely on others for assistance in solving their personal and
family problems.
TEST DESCRIPTION. A set of additive indexes.   Each index
score is obtained by adding the weighted response categories
to pre-coded interview questions.
     (1) Husband-wife Communication Index: Each of the five
questions asks frequency with which a topic is discussed.
There are four answer categories for each question: Many
times and Sometimes = 2, Seldom = 1, Never = 0. Example:
Some couples discuss more things than other couples.   In
general, how often do you and your (spouse) discuss the
following topics... Amusing or interesting incidents that
happen to you?

(2) Tension in Marital Relations Index: Each question asks the frequency with which spouses quarrel over topics. Often and sometimes = 2, Hardly ever = 1, Never = 0. Example: Could you tell me how often you and your spouse argue or disagree about how the family's money should be used?

(3) Authority Indexes: Separate additive indices constructed for outright husband dominance, outright wife dominance, and shared influence. Each index can range from 0 to 4. Example: Who usually makes most of the decisions about each of the following: Do you make more than your spouse, does your spouse make more than you, do you two make about equal number of decisions, or does someone else in the family make these decisions...How the family's money should be used?

(4) Dissatisfaction with Spouse Index: Four separately worded questions. Complaints = 1; No complaint = 0. Example: Do you wish that your husband/wife had more affection for you and the family, or do you feel that he/she has enough affection for you and the family as it is now?

(5) Parent-Child Communications: Four questions administered only to those respondents with children. Example: How often do your children do the following: Do they do it: Many times, Sometimes, Hardly ever, or Never...Tell you their worries and problems?

(6) Looseness of Control over Children: Two questions administered only to those respondents with children. Example: How often do you do the following to or with your children: Do you do it: Many times, Sometimes, Hardly ever, or Never?...You leave the youngest child at home all by him/herself because you could not find anyone to look after him/her?

(7) Dependency on Non-Family People: Six precoded questions. Do not seek advice or assistance = 1. Example: Here are some problems that many people in Hong Kong have. If you or someone in your family has these problems, whom would you go to for advice and assistance: Would you go to a relative, a social welfare or government agency, or wouldn't you ask anyone for advice and assistance?...One of your children became unruly and no one in the family could control him?

(8) Withdrawal from Family Role Responsibilities: Four precoded questions. Those answering Many times or Sometimes = 1, Others = 0. Example: Can you tell me how often these things happen to you while you are at home: Do they happen Many times, Sometimes, Hardly ever, or Never?...You go to bed early because you are so tired.

SAMPLE ITEM. See above.
LENGTH: See above.
AVAILABILITY. From Mitchell, 1972
ABSTRACTED BY: R.E. Mitchell (modified).
REFERENCES.
Mitchell,R.E. Some social implications of high density housing. American Sociological Review, 1971, 36, 18-29.
Mitchell,R.E. Levels of emotional strain in Southeast

Asian cities, Volumes I and II. Tapei: The Orient Cultural
Service, Asian Folklore and Social Life Monographs, 1972a,
Volumes 27 and 28.
        Mitchell,R.E.   Husband-wife   relations   and
family-planning practices in Urban Hong Kong. Journal of
Marriage and the Family, 1972b, 34, 139-146.
        Mitchell,R.E. Family life in Urban Hong Kong, Volumes
I and II. Taipei: The Orient Cultural Service, Asian
Folklore and Social Life Monographs, 1972c, Volumes 24 and
25.
        Mitchell,R.E. Pupil, parent, and school: a Hong Kong
study. Taipei: The Orient Cultural Service, Asian Folklore
and Social Life Monographs, 1972d, Volume 26.
        Mitchell,R.E.   Housing, urban growth, and economic
development.   Taipei: The Orient Cultural Service, Asian
Folklore and Social Life Monographs, 1972e, Volume 31.

MOOS,R.H.   Family Environment Scale (FES).

VARIABLES MEASURES.   The FES has three subscales which
assess how family members relate to each other (Cohesion,
Expressiveness, Conflict); five subscales which assess the
emphasis   within   the   family   on important developmental
processes which may be fostered by the family (Independence,
Achievement orientation, Intellectual-cultural orientation,
Active recreational orientation, More religious emphasis)
and two subscales which obtain information about the
structure or organization within the family (Organization,
Control).
TEST DESCRIPTION. The Family Environment Scale assesses the
social climates of all types of families. It focuses on the
measurement   and   description   of   the   interpersonal
relationships among family members, on the directions of
personal growth which are emphasized in the family, and on
the basic organizational structure of the family. The Scale
can be used to describe family environments as seen by
family members themselves, or as seen by "observers" such as
psychotherapists, marriage counselors, and so on. The Scale
can also be used to compare and contrast the social climates
of different families, or different types of families, to
study families over time, to evaluate changes in family
social environments related to intervention programs such as
counseling or psychotherapy, and to enhance the richness of
clinical case descriptions.
SAMPLE ITEM. Family members often keep their feelings to
themselves.
LENGTH. Time: 10-15 minutes. Items: There are 90 items
in the regular Form R and 40 items in the Short Form S.
AVAILABILITY. The manual, scale, answer sheets, scoring
stencils, and profile sheets can be obtained from Consulting
Psychologists Press, 577 College Avenue, Palo Alto,
California 94306.

REFERENCES.
    Bromet,E. and Moos,R.H. Environmental resources and
the   pcsttreatment   functioning   of alcoholic patients.
Unpublished manuscript (available from   Social   Ecology
Laboratory, Department of Psychiatry, Stanford University,
Stanford, California 94305).
    Moos,R.H.   The Family Environment Scale Preliminary
Manual.   Consulting   Psychologists   Press,   Palo   Alto,
California, 1974.
    Moos,R.H.   The Social Climate Scales: An Overview.
Consulting Psycholcgists Press, Palo Alto, California, 1974.
    Moos,R.H. and Moos,B.   Families, Chapter 11 in R.
Moos.   Evaluating Correctional and Community Settings. New
York: Wiley Interscience, 1975.
    Moos,R.H. and Moos,B.   Toward a typology of family
social environments. Family Process, forthcoming, 1977.
    Rosenthal,M. Effects of parent training groups on
behavior   change   in   target children: durability,
generalization, and patterns of family interaction.   Ph.D.
dissertation, University of Cincinnati, 1975.
    Scoreby,A.   and   Christensen,B.   Differences   in
interaction and environmental conditions of clinic and
non-clinic families: implications for counselors.   Journal
of Marriage and Family Counseling, 1976, 2, 63-71.

MURRELL,S.A. and STACHOWIAK,J.G. Family Interaction Tasks.

VARIABLES MEASURED.   (1) Stability of intra-family patterns,
(2)   Intermember   interaction   distribution,   (3) Power
patterns, (4) Family productiveness,   (5)   Spontaneous
agreement, (6) Choice fulfillment, (7) Decision making time,
(8) Index of normality.
TEST DESCRIPTION.   Family (mother, father and   child)
interaction on three tasks is observed. The first task
requires the family to write answers to questions about the
family.   The second asks them to list adjectives about their
family in a given time period.   The third is a
situation-choice questionnaire developed by Ferreira and
Winter (1968). All members must agree on the final answers.
    Stability of intrafamily patterns: "The rank order of
the six possible pairs of the family, on the number of
statements the two people had made to each other, is
compared across the three rating segments using Kendall's
Coefficient of Concordance."
    Intermember Interaction Distribution: A measure of how
evenly members of a family distribute their statements to
one another. The total number of statements sent by any one
member is divided by three;   this average score is then
subtracted from the actual number of statements he/she sent
to each of the three members, which yield three deviation
scores. These scores are then squared, the three squared
scores are totaled, and a square root is taken of this
total.   The lower the score, the more even the distribution.
    Power Patterns: Total number of statements received by

a member divided by the total number of statements received
by all members.
Family Productiveness: Total number of words written
while preforming the tasks plus two times the number of
items completed.
See Winter and Ferreira Situation-Choice Questionnaire
abstract for variables 5, 6, and 7.
SAMPLE ITEMS. Who is the boss in the family? What sort of
things does the family argue about?
LENGTH. Time: first two tasks = 10 minutes, third =
unlimited.   Items: first = 11, second = unlimited, third =
8.
AVAILABILITY. In Murrell and Stachowiak, 1967 and Ferreira
and Winter, 1968.
ABSTRACTED BY: Thomas G. Sparhawk.
REFERENCES.
    Ferreira,A.J.   and Winter,W.D.   Decision making in
normal and abnormal two child families. Family Process,
1968, 7, 17-36.
    Murrell,S.A.   Family   interaction   variables   and
adjustment of nonclinic boys. Child Development, 1971, 42,
1485-1494.
    Murrell,S.A.   and   Stachowiak,J.G.   Consistency,
rigidity, and power in the interaction patterns of clinic
and nonclinic families. Journal of Abnormal Psychology,
1967, 72, 265-272.

PATTERSON,G.R.   JONES,R.R. and REID,J.B. Behavioral Coding
System (BCS)

VARIABLES MEASURED. Verbal and nonverbal behaviors,
especially aspects of behavior which are relevant for
assessment and intervention in respect to family conflict
and   aggression: approval, attention, command, command
(negative), compliance,   cry,   disapproval,   dependency,
destructiveness,   high   rate, humiliate, ignore, laugh,
noncompliance, negatives, normative, no response, play,
negative physical contact, positive physical contact,
receive, self-stimulation, talk, tease, touching and
handling, whine, work, yell.
TEST DESCRIPTION. A system for observing and coding the
interaction of family members, especially for use in natural
settings. The categories are descriptions of behavior which
require little if any inference by observers to code the
events. For example, rather than coding "aggression," the
BCS codes specific behaviors such as hitting, teasing and
destructiveness. Observers record the interaction sequences
for 10 consecutive 30-second intervals, each of which is
subdivided into 6-second units, using a recording form
divided into 10 rows, each with five columns. This
procedure permits the codes to be converted to rates per
minute. Codes may be combined to obtain rates for a class
of behavior such as Deviant Behavior (combines the 14
aversive, hostile, irritating behavior categories) and Total

Targeted Behaviors (combines all behaviors which are being treated in a clinical intervention).

Patterson and Dawes (1975) applied Guttman scaling to seven of the categories dealing with coercive acts by a sample of aggressive boys and a control sample. In both samples, the analysis revealed a unidimensional progression in the performance of these acts (coefficient of reproducibility = .92).

SAMPLE ITEM. Command (CM): Used when an immediate and clearly stated request or command is made to another person.

LENGTH. Time: Six to ten observation sessions over a two-week period. Since each family member is observed for five minutes, the time for an observation session depends on the size of the family group. Items: 28 categories.

AVAILABILITY. In Jones, Reid and Patterson, 1974; further details in Patterson, Ray, Shaw and Cobb, 1969.

REFERENCES.

Ferber,H. Keeley,S.M. and Shemberg,K.M. Training parents in behavior modification: outcome of and problems encountered in a program after Patterson's work. Behavior Therapy, 1974, 5, 415-419.

Jones,R.R. Behavioral observation frequency data: problems in scoring, analysis, and interpretation. In Hamerlynch,L.A. Handy,L.C. and Mash,E.J. (Eds.) Behavior Change: Methodology Concepts and Practice. Champaign, Illinois: Research Press, 1973, 119-145.

Jones,R.R. Reid,J.B. and Patterson,G.R. Naturalistic observation in clinical assessment. In McReynolds,P. (Ed.) Advances in Psychological Assessment, Vol. 3. San Francisco, California: Jossey Basss, 1974.

Patterson,G.R. An application of conditioning techniques to the control of a hyperactive child. In Ullman,L.P. and Krasner,L. (Eds.) Case Studies in Behavior Modification. New York: Holt, Rinehart and Winston, 1965, 370-375.

Patterson,G.R. Follow-up evaluations of a program for parents' retraining their aggressive boys. In Lowey,F. (Ed.) Symposium on the seriously disturbed preschool child. Canadian Psychiatric Association Journal, 1974a.

Patterson,G.R. Multiple evaluations of a parent training program. In Thompson,T. (Ed.) Proceedings of the First International Symposium on Behavior Modification. New York: Appleton-Century-Crofts, 1974b.

Patterson,G.R. and Cobb,J.A. A dyadic analysis of "aggressive" behaviors. In Hill,J.P. (Ed.) Minnesota Symposia on Child Psychology. Vol. 5. Minneapolis: University of Minnesota Press, 1971, 72-129.

Patterson,G.R. Cobb,J.A. and Ray,R.S. A social engineering technology for retraining the families of aggressive boys. In Adams,H. and Unikel,I.P. (Eds.) Issues and Trends in Behavior Therapy. Springfield, Illinois: Charles C Thomas, 1973, 139-224.

Patterson,G.R. and Dawes,R.M. A Guttman scale of children's coercive behavior. Journal of Clinical and Consulting Psychology, 1975, 43, 594.

        Patterson,G.R.   and   Fagot,B.I.   Selective
responsiveness to social reinforcers and deviant behavior in
children. The Psychological Record, 1967, 17, 369-378.
        Patterson,G.R.   and   Harris,A.   Some   methodological
considerations for observations procedures. Paper presented
at the meeting of the American Psychological Association,
San Francisco, September 1968.
        Patterson,G.R. Ray,R.S. Shaw,D.A. and Cobb,J.A.   A
manual for coding of family interations, 1969 revision.
Available as Document *01234, 33 pages of materials.   Order
from ASIS/NAPS, c/o Microfiche Publications, 305 E.   46th
Street, New York, NY 10017.   Remit in advance $5.45 for
photocopies or $1.50 for microfiche. Make checks payable to
Microfiche Publications.
        Patterson,G.R.   and   Reid,J.B.   Reciprocity   and
coercion: two facets of social systems. In Neuringer,C.
and Michael,J.L.   (Eds.) Behavior Modification in Clinical
Psychology.   New   York: Appleton-Century-Crofts, 1970,
133-177.
        Patterson,G.R.   and   Reid,J.B.   Intervention   for
families of aggressive boys: a replication study. Behavior
Research and Therapy, 1973, 11, 383-394.
        Reid,J.B. Reliability assessment of observation data:
a possible methodological problem. Child Development, 1970,
41, 1143-1150.
        Reid,J.B.   and DeMaster,B.   The efficacy   of   the
spot-check procedure in maintaining the reliability of data
collected by observers in quasi-natural settings: two pilot
studies. Oregon Research Institute Research Bulletin, 1972,
12.
        Reid,J.B.   and   Hendriks,A.F.C.J.   A   preliminary
analysis of the effectiveness of direct home intervention
for treatment of predelinquent boys who   steal.   In
Hamerlynch,L.A.   Handy,L.C. and Mash,E.J. (Eds.) Behavior
Change: Methodology Concepts and Practice.   Champaign,
Illinois: Research Press, 1973, 209-219.
        Taplin,P.S. and Reid,J.B.   Effects of instructional
set and experimenter influence on observer reliability.
Child Development, 1973, 44, 547-554.
        Wahl,G. Johnson,S.M. Johansson,S. And Martin,S.   An
operant analysis of child-family interaction.   Behavior
Therapy, 1974, 5, 64-78.

RISKIN,J. Family Interaction Scales.

VARIABLES MEASURED. Characteristics of interaction as
evidenced in both verbal and nonverbal aspects of
communication.   Specific   variables: clarity,   topic
(sameness of subject's and companion's verbal content),
appropriateness (of a change in content), commitment,
agreement, intensity (emphasis and force of speech),
relationship (acceptance or rejection of companion).   The
rater also characterizes the role subject takes as speaker:
dominant accepting, dominant rejecting, submissive

accepting, or submissive rejecting.
TEST DESCRIPTION. The family discusses an item such as "I
would like you to plan something you could do together as a
family." The interviews are taped and transcribed. The
scoring or coding of these typed transcripts is done on the
first 76 speeches and also on a second block of 76 speeches
starting at about minute four. Each group of 76 speeches
usually takes a family two-three minutes. Two Es listen
jointly to the tape and determine who speaks and to whom
without discussion of intuitive impressions. Their versions
of the transcript and judgments are then checked by Os of
the original interview.
      The clarity scale is scored clear or unclear. If
unclear, the reason is categorized as incongruent, vague, or
a linear disqualification (a self-contradiction); the topic
scale is scored same or different topic (if rated different,
then appropriateness of the change is marked as appropriate
or inappropriate); commitment is scored as made, not made
when requested, or not applicable; agreement is scored as
explicit agreement or diasgreement or not applicable.
(There is also a NS--nonscorable--category for each of the
above.) Intensity is scored as increased, normal tone, or
decreased; relaticnship is scored as friendly, neutral, or
attacking. In addition to these scale categories, there are
three categories not on the scale: (1) who speaks, (2) to
whom, and (3) interrupted speeches. Each speech is rated in
each of the categories; thus, at least eight statements can
be made about any speech. Statistical analysis of the data
includes percentages (e.g., of unclear speeches in the block
of 76), ratios (such as the number of commitments to
agreements), and simple rank orders (e.g., the percentage of
unclear speeches in one family compared with the sample).
SAMPLE ITEM. See TEST DESCRIPTION.
LENGTH. Time: 10 minutes of discussion. Items: One topic
to be discussed.
AVAILABILITY. In Riskin, 1964.
REFERENCES.
      Faunce,E.E. and Riskin,J. Family interaction scales:
II. Data analysis and findings. Archives of General
Psychiatry, 1970, 22, 513-526.
      Haley,J. Research on family patterns: instrument
measurement. Family Process, 1964, 3, 41-65.
      Jackson,D.D. Riskin,J. and Satir,V. Method of
analysis of family interaction. Archives of General
Psychiatry, 1961, 5, 321-339.
      Riskin,J. Methodology for studying family interaction.
Archives of General Psychiatry, 1963, 8, 343-348.
      Riskin,J. Family interaction scales. Archives of
General Psychiatry, 1964, 11, 484-494.
      Riskin,J. and Faunce,E.E. Family Interaction Scales
and Scoring Manual. Published privately, 1968.
      Riskin,J. and Faunce,E.E. Family interaction scales:
I. Theoretical framework and method. Archives of General
Psychiatry, 1970, 22, 503-512.
      Riskin,J. and Faunce,E.E. Family interaction scales:

III.   Discussion of methodology and substantive findings.
Archives of General Psychiatry, 1970, 22, 527-537.
     Riskin,J. and Faunce,E.E.   An evaluative review of
family interaction research. Family Process, 1972, 11,
365-455.
     Titchener,J.L. Vanderheide,G. and Woods,E. Profiles
of family interaction systems. Journal of Nervous and
Mental Disease, 1966, 143, 473-480.

ROSEN,B.C.   Family Interaction Observation System.

VARIABLES MEASURED. (1) Level of communication, (2) Degree
of   reciprocity,   (3) Flow of affect, (4) Power, (5)
Achievement behavior, (6) Aspiration level.
TEST DESCRIPTION.   A quasi-structured, experimental test
situation   in   which   father-mother-son   (10-12 years)
interaction is observed. Family members (primarily son) are
involved in tasks and games under conditions set by the
experimenter.   Interaction is scored by an   observer
according to category system specifically devised to assess
variables listed above.   Observation occurs in subject's
home.   Tasks are (1) block stacking, (2) tinker toy
construction, (3) pick up sticks.
SAMPLE ITEM. Father to son controlling action (C).
LENGTH.   Time: 1 1/2 hrs.   Items: Six   category
observational scoring system, three experimental tasks.
AVAILABILITY. In Rosen, 1973.
ABSTRACTED BY: B.C. Rosen.
REFERENCE.
     Rosen,B.C.   Social change, migration and family
interaction in Brazil. American Sociological Review, 1973,
38, 198-212. of Michigan, 1959, 99-117.

SCHULTZ,K.V.   Image Inventory

VARIABLES MEASURED. There are eight forms of which the
following deal with the family: Form II, Match Mate; Form
III, Courtship, Pre-Marriage; Form IV, Marriage; Form VII,
Parents;   Form VIII, Sex and Intimacy. Some of the forms
measure the subject's view of his/her present situation, the
ideal situation, discrepancy between the actual and the
ideal, and the subject's satisfaction with the present
situation.   Form IV (Marriage) measures the subject's view
of the marriage, the subject's perception of his/her mate's
view of the marriage, discrepancy between the two views, and
the subject's perception of the effect of these items on the
marriage.
TEST DESCRIPTION. The Image Inventory Series uses a common
theoretical, item structuring and scoring model but with
different content appropriate to the particular social
relationship being explored. Each inventory has 10 items.
Each item is made up of two bi-polar items described by
pairs of statements.   The subject responds in three ways:

(1) How things are now (three-point scale);   (2) How she/he
would like them to (three-point scale);   and (3) How
satisfied she/he is with the state of affairs.
SAMPLE ITEM. Lets life go by--waits for things to happen
versus Alive, interesting person, helps make things happen.
Effect on marriage: Negative, Neutral, Positive.
LENGTH. Time: 15 minutes per form. Items: 10 per form.
AVAILABILITY. Psychological Services Press, 111 Fairmount
Ave., Oakland, CA 94611 or from NAPS-2 (Forms IV and V).
ABSTRACTED BY: Karl V. Schultz.
REFERENCE.   Buros,O.K.   The   Sixth   Mental   Measurement
Yearbook (Vol. 2). Highland Park, New Jersey: Gryphon
Press, 1972.
        Schultz,K.V. Marriage-Personality Inventory. Oakland,
California: Psychological Services Press, 1969.
        Schultz,K.V. Life space images: a research model and
counseling aid. Jcurnal of Pastoral Care, 1977, in press.

SPEER,D.C.   Prisoner's Dilemma Game as a Measure of Marital
Interaction

VARIABLES MEASURED.   The following aspects of   marital
interaction: trustworthiness;   forgiveness or martyrdom;
repentance or responsiveness; trust;   seduction, set up;
retaliation;   exploitation, expectation of revenge; and
distrust, playing safe.
TEST DESCRIPTION. The Prisoner's Dilemma is a generic term
for a number of specific situations similar in the sense
that the subject must always choose between different
responses that carry different implications.   Luce and
Raiffa (1957:95) describe the nature of the Prisoner's
Dilemma situation as follows: "Two subjects are taken into
custody and separated. The district attorney is certain
they are guilty cf a specific crime, but he does not have
adequate evidence to convict them at a trial. He points out
to each prisoner that each has two alternatives: to confess
to the crime the police are sure they have done or not to
confess.   If they both do not confess then the district
attorney states that he will book them on some very minor,
trumped-up charge...;   if they both confess, they will be
prosecuted, (and) he will recommend (a rather severe)
sentence; but if one confesses and the other does not, then
the confessor will receive rather lenient treatment for
turning state's evidence whereas the latter will get the
"book" slapped at him." The essential nature of the game
involves the dilemma that the choice that leads to the most
individual gain is, in the long run, self-defeating.
Speer's (1972) version of the Prisoner's Dilemma Games used
with marital partners involved the usual "cooperation": and
"defections" responses, and added a "punish" response and a
"withdrawal" response. The subjects are informed that they
were being asked to perform an experimental two-person task,
the utility of which is being investigated as a means of
studying family interaction.   The subjects play only with

their own spouse. The subjects are seated back to back in
such a position as to allow E to be able to see the matrix
game boards held by each S. Neutral instructions are read
to the subjects explaining the payoffs and how they can
infer their partner's choice on the basis of the payoff
points awarded. Each game consists of 75 iterative and
simultaneous choices by each pair of Ss. After E records
each S's response, he announces within hearing of both, the
number of points gained cr lost by each. Payoffs consisted
only of points received. When subjects inquire about the
objectives of the game or the "right way" to play the game,
they are told that they can play "any way they wish." The
frequency of different responses is tabulated.

Santa-Barbara and Epstein (1974) and Epstein and
Santa-Barbara (1975) use another version of the game with
200 trials to classify the response patterns into four
types: (1) Doves = a cooperative solution, (2) Hawks =
continue to impose losses on the partner, (3)
Dominant-Submissive = allowing one to dominate at the
other's expense, (4) Mugwumps = couples who fail to
stabilize any of the above four patterns.
SAMPLE ITEM. See above.
LENGTH. See above.
AVAILABILITY. Described in Speer, 1972, Santa-Barbara and
Epstein, 1974.
ABSTRACTED BY: Bruce Brown.
REFERENCES.

Epstein,N.B. and Santa-Barbara,J.   Conflict behavior
in clinical couples: interpersonal perceptions and stable
outcomes. Family Process, 1975, 14, 51-66.

Luce,R.D. and Raiffe,H.H. Games and Decisions:
Introduction and Critical Survey. New York: Wiley, 1957.

Santa-Barbara,J. and Epstein,N.B.   Conflict behavior
in clinical families: preasymptotic interactions and stable
outcomes. Behavioral Science, 1974, 19, 100-110.

Speer,D.C. Variations of prisoner's dilemma game as
measures of marital interaction: sequential dyadic
measures. Journal of Abnormal Psychology, 1972a, 80,
287-293.

Speer,D.C. Marital dysfunctionality and two-person
non-zero game behavior: cumulative monadic measures.
Journal of Personality and Social Psychology, 1972b, 21,
18-24.

STRAUS,M.A. Family Interaction Schedule (FIS)

VARIABLES MEASURED. (1) Communication: (a) communication
affect, (b) dominance, (c) constraints, amount of (d) verbal
and (e) nonverbal communication.   (2) Support: (a)
affecticn, (b) ccmpanionship, (c) help, (d) praise,
and (e) nurturance. (3) Task roles: (a) task performance
(b) task role differentiation. (4) Decision roles: (a)
decision activity, (b) decision role differentiation.   (5)
Power: (a) immediate power, (b) final say power, (c) power

types.   (6) Conflict. For each of these variables, there
are separate scores for each "role-relationship" in the
family, e.g.   husband-wife, wife-husband,   father-child,
child-father, mother-child, etc.
TEST DESCRIPTION. A self-report inventory in which the
subject describes the frequency of occurrence of each of the
items used to measure the above variables.   The items are
designed to index the social structure of the family rather
than the personality structure of the respondent.   Further,
all items refer to role performance rather than to
"attitudes," or normative prescriptions. The version of the
FIS deposited with the National Auxiliary Publications
Service is structured for use by children to describe their
family of orientation. Parallel versions can be constructed
for use by husbands or wives to describe their family of
procreation.   The measures of task roles and the power
measures are based on instruments developed by Blood and
Wolfe (1960), Wolfe (1959), and Herbst (1954). With the
exception of the power types, all scores are obtained by
summing the response categories.
SAMPLE ITEM. (1) Verbal communication: Talks about his or
her job with me. Never = 0, Sometimes = 1, Half the time =
2, Usually = 3, Always = 4. (2) Support: Says nice things
about me. Same response categories. (3) Task roles: Fixes
breakfast on weekdays.   Same response categories.   (4)
Decision Roles: Who decides what to have for breakfast on
weekdays? Same response categories, repeated for respondent
and other family members. (5) Final Say Power: Who has the
final say about where to go on vacation? Mother always = 1,
Mother more than father = 2, Father and mother exactly the
same = 3, Father more than mother = 4, Father always = 5.
(6) Conflict: How often do you (or they) agree on where to
go for a vacation? Never = 0 to Always = 4.
LENGTH. Items: Communication 23, Support 10, Task roles
12, Decision roles 15, Final say power 10, Conflict 10.
Each of these sets of items must be repeated for each
role-relationship (e.g.   husband-to-wife, wife-to-husband,
father-to-child, child-to-father, mother-to-child,   etc.)
which is to be measured.
AVAILABILITY. From NAPS-2 or from Educational Testing
Service, Test Library, Princeton, New Jersey.
REFERENCES.
     Blood,R.O.Jr. and Wolfe,D.M. Husbands and Wives: The
Dynamics of Married Living.   Glencoe, Ill.: Free Press,
1960.
     Herbst,P.G. The measurement of family relationships.
Human Relations, 1952, 5, 3-35.
     Herbst,P.G. Family relationships questionnaire.   In
Oeser,O.A.   and Hammond,S.B.   (Eds.) Social Structure and
Personality in a City. London: Routledge, 1954, 316-321.
     Straus,M.A. Power and support structure of the family
in relation to socialization. Journal of Marriage and the
Family, 1964, 25, 318-326.
     Straus,M.A. The family interaction schedule. Test and
Manual. Minneapolis: Minnesota Family Study Center, 1965

(slightly revised, 1976). Available from NAPS-2 or ETS (see above.

> Straus,M.A.   Measuring families.   Chapter   10   in Christensen,H.T.   (Ed.) Handbook of Marriage and the Family. Chicago: Rand McNally, 1964.
> Straus,M.A.   Some social class differences in family patterns in Bombay.   In Kurian,G.D.   (Ed.) The Family in India: A Modern Regional View.   The Hague and Paris: Mouton, 1974.
> Straus,M.A.   Exchange and power in marriage in cultural context: a multimethod and multivariate analysis of Bombay and Minneapolis families.   Paper read at the 1977 meeting of the Association for Asian Studies, New York.
> Wolfe,D.M.   Power and authority in the family.   Chapter 7 in Cartwright,D.   (Ed.) Studies in Social Power.   Ann Arbor: University of Michigan, 1959, 99-107.

STRAUS,M.A.   and   TALLMAN,I.   Simulated Family   Activity Measurement (SIMFAM).

VARIABLES MEASURED.   (1) Power   exercised by   each family member,   (2) Support extended and received by each family member, (3) Communication frequency, channels, and ability, (4) Creativity,   (5)   Problem/solving ability of the family group and each member.
TEST DESCRIPTION.   A set of experimental tasks   designed   to elicit   a   sample   of   family   interaction, and a set of observational categories and other procedures necessary for measuring the variables listed above.   The tasks also provide a framework for experimentally varying such factors as   frustration, volume and channels of communication, and problem-solving ability of each family member.

One task makes use of colored balls and pushers and is restricted to specially equipped rooms, whereas the other task, using bean bags thrown onto a target on the floor, may be given in the home.   In both the ball-and-pusher task and the bean-bag task, the family members, as a group, are instructed to determine the rules of the game by inferring the correct actions from green lights flashed for correct responses and red lights for incorrect responses.   These lights are also connected to electrical counters which provide the   score for problem-solving ability (usually the percentage of green lights).

The other variables are measured by direct observation or by coding from a tape recording of the experimental session.   Each of these scores (except the creativity scores) are recorded in terms of the initiating and the recipient actor.   For power, each directive act is recorded as either +, -, or 0 to indicate whether the recipient complied, rejected, or ignored the power assertion.   For example, if the husband (H) tells the child (C) "push the ball now," and the child does so, this is scored HC+. Similarly, each supportive act is classified + or - on the basis of its assumed positive or negative contribution to group solidarity or integration. Acts scored + include praise, help, cooperation, terms of endearment, expressions of liking, physical expression of affection, encouragement, and nurturance, whereas the opposite of these are scored as minus. Scores for communication frequency and channels are obtained by combining the power and support scores, disregarding sign. Communication quality is scored from tape recordings, including abstractness of vocabulary, complexity of verbalization, length of statement, and so forth. Creativity is scored from a listing of each idea put forward to solve the task or each new solution actually tried. Following Guilford (1956) and Torrance (1962) these are scored for ideational fluency (the number of different solutions suggested) and also for flexibility (the number of different principles or approaches used in these proposed solutions).

SAMPLE ITEM. See TEST DESCRIPTION.

LENGTH. Time: about 30 minutes for tasks (plus about 30 minutes per family for introductions, explanations, and post-session interview and explanation).

AVAILABILITY. In Straus and Tallman, 1971.

REFERENCES.

Bahr,S.J. SIMFAM as a measure of conjugal power, 1970. (mimeographed).

Bahr,S.J. and Rollins,B.C. Crisis and conjugal power. Journal of Marriage and the Family, 1971, 33, 360-367.

Cromwell,R.E.   Klein,D.M.   and Wieting,S.G.   Family power: a multitrait-multimethod analysis. In Cromwell,R.E. and Olson,D.H.L. (Eds.)Power in Families. New York: John Wiley and Sons, 1975.

Foss,D.C.   and Straus,M.A.   Culture,   crisis,   and creativity of families in Bombay, San Juan, and Minneapolis. In Lenero-Otero,L.(Ed.) Beyond the nuclear family model: contemporary family sociology in cross-cultural perspective. London: Sage   Publications/International   Sociological Association, 1977.

Guilford,J.P. Structure of intellect. Psychological Bulletin, 1956, 53, 267-293.

Kolb,T.M. and Straus,M.A. Marital power and marital happiness in relaticn to problem-solving ability. Journal of Marriage and the Family, 1974, 36, 756-766.

O'Dowd,M.M. Family supportiveness related to illicit drug use immunity. Ph.D. dissertation, University of Maryland, 1973.

Olson,D.H.L. and Straus,M.A. A diagnostic tool for marital and family therapy: the SIMFAM technique. The Family Coordinator, 1972, 21, 251-258.

Rollins,B.C. The integration of laboratory and field methods in study of marital interaction: introduction. A paper presented at the Annual Meeting of the National Council on Family Relations, Washington, D.C., October 1969.

Russell,C.S. Model of family functioning: research evaluation. Paper presented at Annual Conference of the National Council on Family Relations, Salt Lake City, Utah, August 1975.

Sprenkle,D.H.   A behavioral assessment of flexibility, support, and power in clinic and non-clinic married couples. Paper presented at the Annual Meeting of the National Council on Family Relations, Salt Lake City, Utah, August 1975.

Straus,J.H. and Straus,M.A.   Family roles and sex differences in creativity of children in Bombay and Minneapolis. Journal of Marriage and the Family, 1968, 30, 46-53.

Straus,M.A.   The influence of sex of child and social class on instrumental and expressive family roles in a laboratory setting. Sociology and Social Research, 1967, 52, 7-21.

Straus,M.A.   Communication, creativity, and problem solving ability of middle and working class families in three societies. American Journal of Sociology, 1968, 73, 417-420.   Also reprinted in Sussman,M.B. (Ed.) Sourcebook in Marriage and the Family, 3rd Edition. Boston: Houghton, 1968, 15-27.

Straus,M.A.   Methodology of a laboratory experimental study of families in three societies. In Hill,R. and Koenig,R. (Eds.) Families East and West.   Netherlands: Mouton and Co, 1970, 522-577.

Straus,M.A.   Social class and sex differences in socialization for problem solving in Bombay, San Juan, and Minneapolis. In Aldous,J. et al., Family Problem Solving. Hinsdale, Ill.: The Dryden Press, 1971, 282-301.

Straus,M.A.   Husband-wife interaction in nuclear and joint households.   In Narain,D. (Ed.) Explorations in the Family and Other Essays: Prof. K.M. Kapadia Commemoration Volume, Bombay: Thacker and Co., 1975, 134-150.

Straus,M.A.   Exchange and power in marriage in cultural context: a multimethod and multivariate analysis of Bombay and Minneapolis families. Paper read at the meeting of the Association for Asian Studies, New York, 1977.

Straus,M.A. and Tallman,I. SIMFAM: a technique for observational measurement and experimental study of families. In Aldous,J. et al. (Eds.) Family Problem Solving. Hinsdale, Ill.: Dryden Press, 1971, 381-439.

Tallman,I. and Miller,G.A.   Class differences in family problem solving: the effects of verbal ability, hierarchical structure, and role expectations.   Sociometry, 1974, 37, 13-37.

Torrance,E.P.   Guiding Creative Talent.   Englewood Cliffs, N.J.: Prentice-Hall, 1962.

STUART,R.B. and STUART,F. Family Pretreatment Inventory.

VARIABLES MEASURED.   (1) Contact with other family members. (2) Perceived family strength and targets for change.   (3) Satisfaction with family interaction.
TEST DESCRIPTION. This inventory is intended for use in research and treatment with families. It is designed to offer a cross-sectional analysis of basic intrafamilial

processes in a manner which would facilitate intervention.
A "family locator" section identifies the times when family
members are in contact with one another. An inventory of
perceived strengths and targets for change indicates
therapeutically useful resources and goals. A nine-item
screening inventcry identifies satisfaction with decision
making, communication and attitudinal consensus. Each of
these areas is covered in an individual, multiscaled
supplement.   Separate forms are addressed to fathers,
mothers, and adolescents. All are asked to complete the
initital section, with supplements completed if indicated by
answers to the first series of questions.
SAMPLE ITEMS. The inventory is comprised of items with a
variety of formats.   Open-ended items are written in a
manner intended to maintain a narrative interest in the
questions. For example: "If you were applying for a job as
a member in your own family, how would you describe your
best assets for the position to the interviewer?" Other
items are presented in a Likert-type format.   For example:
"I feel free to tell all of the others in my family about
the things which have made me happy. Does not fit us at
all...Is usually true for us." And still other items are
patterned after the Strodtbeck Unrevealed Differences Test.
They contain story vignettes posing problems and sample
solutions. These items are intended to identify important
underlying social attitudes.
LENGTH. A five-page initial segment, two two- and one five-
page supplements.
AVAILABILITY. From Research Press, 2612 N. Mattis Avenue,
Champaign, Illincis, 61820.
ABSTRACTED BY: Richard B. Stuart (modified).
REFERENCE.
     Stuart, R.B.   and   Stuart, F.   Family   Pretreatment
Inventory. Champaign, Ill.: Research Press, 1975.

TALLMAN, I. MAROTZ-BADEN, R.   STRAUS, M.A.   and WILSON, L.R.
Simulated Career Choice Game (SIMCAR)

VARIABLES MEASURED. (1) Life styles and strategies for
obtaining them measured by typical educational,
occupational, marital, religious, consumption and leisure
time decisions made by and for late adolescents and young
adults.   (2) Power, support, and other aspects of
interaction between parents and their 12-14 year old son or
daughter as they make career decisions over the course of
the game. (3) Family response to the adolescent's economic
success vs. failure. (4) Adolescent's response to changes
in occupational cpportunities.
TEST DESCRIPTION. A greatly modifed version of the
teaching-game "Career" (Boocock, 1972). The game is played
on a board containing scales depicting the above listed
activities and the money and time requirements for each.
The game starts with the child assumed to be age 16 in the
first round. Each round represents two years in the child's

life. If six rounds are played, the game covers career
decisions for the ages 16 to 27. In the first round of the
game the child starts out with $20 and 60 hours of time
available. For each decision to engage in an activity, the
player places the indicated amount of play money and time
chips on the tile. In respect to occupation, five
alternative routes are presented. Two of these are more
common for men, two are more common for women, while one is
common to both. Each route is divided into four
hierarchical levels, each level requiring progressively more
education and work experience. Money earned in each round
is available for further education, marriage, consumption,
etc., and is proportional to the occupational level achieved
and time allocated to working. Points are awarded at the
end of each round proportional to the time and money
invested. The total game score (points summed across
rounds) indicates the extent to which an economic
maximization model was successfully followed, reflecting the
extent of a deferred gratification and occupational career
orientation. However, the game is often played with
different strategies in mind. Some of these strategies
include: (1) maximizing pleasure and recreation with the
least amount of work time or money investment possible; (2)
maximizing consumption of goods and services; (3)
maximizing familistic values like marriage and children and
visiting relatives; (4) maximizing occupational mobility;
that is, seeking the most prestigious and highest paid job
available; (5) acquiring the most "points" possible.

SIMCAR can be played by a single family member or a
family group. In the latter case, the interaction of family
members during the process of deciding on the various
alternatives can be scored using observational coding
systems described elsewhere in this book (such as those of
Bales, Patterson, or Straus and Tallman), or codes developed
to measure the substantive considerations in making each
decision. Families are not told to play the game as if it
represented the career of their own child. Almost
universally, however, they play with their own child as the
point of reference.

SIMCAR also provides for experimentally simulating
economic-occupational success or failure and social change.
This is done by means of "unplanned event" cards which the
family must pick at the beginning of each round. In the
success condition, a general aura of positiveness is created
by cards stating, for example, that the child was elected
president of his or her class or got a job promotion. To
simulate social change, the unplanned event cards indicate
that top positions are no longer avilable to people who
decide to enter a certain type of occupation.
SAMPLE ITEM. See above.
LENGTH. Time: 15-20 minutes for the first round, a
learning round, and 8-10 minutes for each subsequent round
when played by a three-person group.

AVAILABILITY.   The game is described in Tallman, Wilson   and
Straus, 1974.   Pictures of the game board, scoring forms and
other game materials are available from NAPS-2.
REFERENCES.
        Boocock,S.S.   "The life career   game."   Chapter   11   in
Inbar,M.   and   Stcll,C.S.   Simulation and Gaming in Social
Science.   New York, N.Y.:   The Free Press, 1972, 173-188.
        Cromwell,R.F.   Corrales,R.   and   Torsiello,P.M.
Normative   patterns   of   marital   decision making, power and
influence in Mexico and the United States: a   partial   test
of   resource   and   ideology   theory.   Journal of Comparative
Family Studies, 1973, 4, 177-196.
        Marotz,R.   Gender differentiation   and   inequality: a
U.S.-Mexican comparison.   Paper presented at the meetings of
the Society for the Study of Social   Problems,   New   Orleans
1972.
        Marotz,R.   Simulation gaming   as   a   technique   in   the
cross-cultural   analysis   of   sex roles.   Paper presented at
the   International   Sociological   Association   meetings,
Toronto, Canada, 1974.
        Marotz,R.   Sex   differentiation   and   inequality: a
Mexican-United States comparison of parental aspirations for
daughters.   Journal of Comparative Family Studies, 1976, 6,
41-55.
        Marotz,R.   and Tallman,I.   A comparison of U.S.   and
Mexican   parental aspirations for sons and daughters.   Paper
presented at the NCFR Meetings, Toronto, 1976.
        Tallman,I.   Social   structure   and   socialization   for
change.   Paper   presented   at   National   Council   on Family
Relations meeting, Portland, Oregon, 1974.
        Tallman,I.   and   Miller,G.   Social   structure   and
individual   problem   solving: a   theory   of social change.
Unpublished manuscript, University of Minnesota, 1976.
        Tallman,I.   and   Wilson,L.R.   Simulating   social
structures: the use of a simulation game in cross-national
research.   Simulation and Games, 1974, 5, 147-167.
        Tallman,I.   Wilson,L.R.   and   Straus,M.A.   SIMCAR: a
game   simulation   method for cross-cultural family research.
Social Science Information, 1974, 13, 121-144.

TERRILL,J.M.   and TERRILL,R.E.   Family Communication   Method
(Interpersonal System)

VARIABLES MEASURED.   Interpersonal aspects of   communication
within   the   family in terms of the eight variables isolated
by Timothy Leary (See section C.2 of this chapter).
TEST DESCRIPTION.   A   family   is   asked   to   plan   something
together,   "something   you   can do as a family."   For five to
eight minutes   the   family   discusses   the   problem   without
interruption.   The   complete   discussion   is   taped   and
transcribed.   The   discussion   is   then   coded   and   rated
according   to the Leary Interpersonal Check List categories.
To do this the definitions   of   the   eight   categories   were
modified.   An   explanation   of   the   rating   procedure   is

available in Terrill and Terrill (1965).
SAMPLE ITEM. Son to all: "Well, do I start off?" This
comment is rated as falling into the Leary
"docile-dependent" category.
LENGTH. NR.
AVAILABILITY. In Terrill and Terrill, 1965.
ABSTRACTED BY: Kersti Yllo
REFERENCES.
    Terrill,J.M. and Terrill,R.E. A method for studying
family communication. Family Process, 1965, 4, 259-290.

USANDIVARAS,R.   GRIMSON,W.   HAMMOND,H.   ISSAHAROFF,E.   AND
ROMANOS,D.   The Marbles Test

VARIABLES MEASURED. Various aspects of family interaction
such as rule making, cooperation, interference.
TEST DESCRIPTION. The test begins with the family members
standing around a table on which there are opaque bags, each
containing 20 marbles of one color. No two bags contain the
same color, and there are just enough bags for each family
member to choose one." A square board with an arbitrary
number of holes in which to place marbles is also on the
table (the number of holes varies with family size). "The
participants are asked only to put the marbles in the holes
to make something, working together with the others. These
vague instructions permit myriad possibilities of forming
different patterns, either all together (simultaneously) or
with some variation of turns." Besides providing information
on family interaction on the basis of marble distribution,
observations may be made regarding family communication and
rule-making. The test is given in three successive trials
per family to provide a basis for sequential comparisons and
description of changes.
SAMPLE ITEM. See above.
LENGTH. See above.
AVAILABILITY. In Usandivaras et al., 1967.
ABSTRACTED BY: Kersti Yllo.
REFERENCES.
    Bodin,A.M. Conjoint family assessment: an evolving
field. In McReynolds,P. (Ed.) Advances in Psychological
Assessment. Volume 1. Palo Alto, California: Science and
Behavior Books, 1968, 223-243.
    Usandivaras,R. Grimson,W. Hammond,H. Issaharoff,E.
and Romanos,D. The Marbles Test. Archives of General
Psychiatry, 1967, 17, 111-118.

WEINSTEIN,E.A. and GEISEL,P.N. Home Environment Rating
Scales.

VARIABLES MEASURED. A large number of variables dealing
with physical and psychological aspects of the home,
including the following family relations variables: (1)
Frequency of discipline, (2) Frequency of pleasurable

activity with mother, (3) Frequency of pleasurable activity
with father, (4) Social work rating cf home quality, (5)
Social work rating of marital relations, (6) Parents'
difficulty in supervising child, (7) Physical punishment
employed.
TEST DESCRIPTION. Ratings are made by a social worker on
the basis of an intensive interview with the mother. No
other information given.
SAMPLE ITEMS. Happy with other, mutually supported; both
husband and wife have status in family role and respect each
other's performance; many interests in common.
LENGTH. Items: total number of scales NR--12 listed in the
article.
AVAILABILITY. In Witmer, et al., 1963.
REFERENCES.
      Weinstein,E.A. and Geisel,P.N.   An analysis of sex
differences in adjustment.   Child Development, 1960, 31,
721-728.
      Witmer,H.L.   Herzog,E.   Weinstein,E.A.   and
Sullivan,M.E.   Independent Adoptions. New York: Russell
Sage Foundation, 1963, Appendix A.

WHITING,J.W.M.   CHILD,I.L.   and   LAMBERT,W.W.   Family
Structure Scales.

VARIABLES MEASURED. Five aspects of family organization:
Mother's responsibility for child training policy,
proportion of caretaking done by mother, amount of authority
mother has in family affairs, father's esteem of mother, and
mother's esteem of father.
TEST DESCRIPTION. Five rating scales (rated from 1 to 7)
concerning family structure variables. These scales are
scored based on informed observation of family interaction
in the field setting.
SAMPLE ITEM.   Mother's responsibility for child-training
policy.   Mother has no responsibility = 1; Mother has sole
responsibility = 7.
LENGTH. Repeated observation of the family over an
unspecified time period.
AVAILABILITY. In Whiting, et al., 1966.
ABSTRACTED BY: Bruce Brown.
REFERENCES.
      Minturn,L. and Lambert,W.W. Mothers of Six Cultures.
New York: Wiley, 1964.
      Olsen,N.J. Family structure and independence training
in a Taiwanese Village. Journal of Marriage and the Family,
1973, 35, 512-519.
      Whiting,J.W.M.   Child,I.L.   and   Lambert,W.W.   Field
Guide for a Study of Socialization. New York: John Wiley
and Sons, Inc., 1966, 138.

2. Attitudes, Values, Ideology, Projection, Role
Prescriptions (See also Subject Index)

ALEXANDER,T. Adult-Child Interaction Test (ACI Test)

VARIABLES MEASURED. Adults' perception of children and
children's perception of adults, analyzed by the following
categories: (1) Apperception and reasoning: (a) perceptual
approaches (total card; details); (b) reasoning processes
(variety of associations; appropriate organization of
content, logic, and originality); (c) response to internal
and external stimuli; (d) problem-solving approaches
(external and internal control; direct solutions versus
indirect and avoiding behavior); (2) Motivation and
emotion: (a) drive strength and channeling; (b) emotion
(intensity and range; appropriateness; acceptance of
emotion; thematic content; types of conflict; emotion
attached to external forces); (3) Acceptance
ratings--protocols of adult subjects are rated (three-point
scale) for degree to which subjects accept each of the
following seven variables indicating emotionality,
immaturity, or deviance in children's behavior: pleasure,
aggression, dependency, nonachievement, disorder, sexuality,
affection.
TEST DESCRIPTION. Projective technique, consisting of eight
cards picturing children and adults. Subjects are asked to
tell stories, including: (1) What is going on in the
picture; (2) What brought the situation about; (3) What
the outcome will be. The test must be given individually to
young children, with their responses recorded by the E. The
pictures can be presented to groups cf older children or
adults by using slides or booklets; the subjects write down
their stories.
SAMPLE ITEM. Card 1: A middle-aged man is seated holding a
skull in his hands. Two small boys are standing nearby
looking at the skull.
LENGTH. Time: 40 minutes. Items: 8.
AVAILABILITY. In Alexander, 1952.
REFERENCES.
     Alexander,T. The prediction of teacher-pupil
interaction with a projective test. Journal of Clinical
Psychology, 1950, 3, 273-276.
     Alexander,T. Certain characteristics of the self as
related to affection. Child Development, 1951, 22, 285-290.
     Alexander,T. The adult-child interaction test: a
projective test for use in research. Monographs of the
Society for Research in Child Development, 1952, 17, No. 2
(Serial No. 55).
     Alexander,T. and Alexander,M.B. A study of
personality and social status. Child Development, 1952, 23,
207-213.

BACH,G.R.   Father-Fantasy Categories for Doll-Play Scoring

VARIABLES MEASURED. The following doll-play scoring
categories for father-relevant behavior: (1) Stereotype
family life, (2) Aggression received by father, (3)
Aggression from father, (4) Affection received by father,
(5) Affection given by father, (6) Directions by father, (7)
Directions received by father, (8) Escape from father, (9)
Father in depressed mood, (10) Father in elated mood, (11)
Unclassified, individual. The following are included in the
above but are also computed separately: (12) Social
recreations, (13) Father's aggression against children, (14)
Mother's aggression against father, (15) All fantasy
aggresssions involving father, (16) Father's affection for
children.
TEST DESCRIPTION. Categories used in recording doll-play
sessions. A unit of behavior is defined as one thematic
action taking place for a doll character during a 15-second
interval. The score is the number of behavior units in each
category.
SAMPLE ITEM. Aggression: The subject made the doll act or
describes the doll as acting or intending to act
injuricusly, punishingly, disparagingly, or depreciatively
toward another doll, or the S describes the dcll character
as being in an aggressive attitude, nature, manner, or mood.
LENGTH. Time: Three 20-minute sessions. Items: 16
scoring categories.
AVAILABILITY.   In Bach, 1946.
REFERENCE.
      Bach,G.R.   Father-fantasies and father-typing in
father-separated children.   Child Development, 1946, 17,
63-79.

BLUM,G.S.   The Blacky Pictures

VARIABLES MEASURED. Psychosexual aspects of personality in
accordance with psychoanalytic hypotheses of development of
personality: Oral eroticism, Oral sadism, Anal
expulsiveness and retentiveness, Oedipal intensity,
Masturbation guilt, and so forth.
TEST DESCRIPTION. Cartocn pictures showing scenes in the
life of a dog name Blacky, about which subject tells a
story. Some set probes are asked. Responses are analyzed
by comparison with a list of standard responses for each of
the above variables.
SAMPLE ITEM. Oral sadism--a picture of Blacky energetically
biting a dcg collar marked Mama.
LENGTH. Time: 35-50 minutes. Items: 10 pictures.
AVAILABILITY. From Psychological Corporation, 304 East 45th
Street, New York, N.Y.   10017.
REFERENCES.
      Blum,G.S. A study of the psychoanalytic theory of
psychosexual development.   Genetic Psychology Monographs,
1949, 39, 3-99.

Blum,G.S. The Blacky Pictures, Test Record Blanks, Manual. New York: Psychological Corporation, 1950.
Charen,S. Reliability of the Blacky test. Journal of Consulting Psychology, 1956, 20, 16.
Granwick,S. and Scheflen,N.A. Approaches to reliability of projective tests with special reference to the Blacky pictures test. Journal of Consulting Psychology, 1958, 22, 137-141.
Leichty,M.M. The effect of father-absence during early childhood upon the oedipal situation as reflected in young adults. Merrill-Palmer Quarterly, 1960, 6, 212-217.
Reed,W.W. Parent-child relationships reflected by the Blacky pictures test. Ph.D. dissertation, University of Nebraska, 1955.
Smock,C.D. and Thompson,G.F. An inferred relationship between early childhood conflicts and anxiety responses in adult life. Journal of Personality, 1954, 23, 88-98.

BURNS,R.C. and KAUFMAN,S.H. Kinetic Family Drawing (K-F-D)

VARIABLES MEASURED. Actions, styles, and symbols of various family members and within the total family. Spatial relationships including ascendance of various members by age or sex.
TEST DESCRIPTION. Subject is asked to "Draw a picture of everyone in your family, including you, DOING something. Try to draw whole people, not cartoons or stick people. Remember, make everyone DOING something--some kind of action." The examiner then leaves the room and checks back periodically. The testing is terminated when the child indicates verbally or by gesture that he/she is finished. No time limit is given. Average test completion time is five minutes.
SAMPLE ITEM. See above.
LENGTH. Time: 5 minutes.
AVAILABILITY. In Burns and Kaufman, 1970.
ABSTRACTED BY: Louise Bates Ames
REFERENCES.
Burns,R.C. and Kaufman,S.H. Kinetic Family Drawings (K-F-D): An Introduction to Understanding Children through Kinetic Drawings. New York: Brunner/Mazel, 1970.
Burns,R.C. and Kaufman,S.H. Actions, Styles and Symbols in Kinetic Family Drawings (K-F-D). New York: Brunner/Mazel, 1972.
O'Brien,R.P. and Patton,W.F. Development of an objective scoring method for the Kinetic Family Drawing. Journal of Personality Assessment, 1974, 38, 156-164.
Sims,C.A. Kinetic Family Drawings and the Family Relations Indicator. Journal of Clinical Psychology, 1974, 80, 87-88.

CATTELL,R.B. and CABOT,P.S.   Family Attitude Scales

VARIABLES MEASURED. Emotional relations among family
members. Scales are presented for (1) Parent to child:
affection, hostility, domination, and overprotection;   (2)
Child tc parent: affection and dependence;   (3)
Inter-sibling: affection and jealousy;   and   (4)
Inter-spouse: affection and hostility.
TEST DESCRIPTION. For each of the available scales, 24
symptomatic acts are listed. These are the items of
behavior which a social worker looks for in judging the
strength of the attitude in question.
SAMPLE ITEM. Parent-to-child affection: Parent rarely
speaks to child without smiling.
LENGTH. Time: 55-65 minutes. Items: 10 scales of 24
items.
AVAILABILITY. In Cattell, 1948.
REFERENCES.
     Buros,O.K.   (Ed.) Personality Tests and Reviews.
Highland Park, N.J.: Gryphon Press, 1970.
     Cattell,R.B. A guide to mental testing.   London:
University of London Press, 1948, 302-325.

DELHEES,K.H.   CATTELL,R.B.   and   SWENEY,A.B.   Family
Motivation Test (FAMT)

VARIABLES MEASURED. Intrafamilial sentiments of: (1)
Assertion, (2) Fear, (3) Pugnacity-Aggression, (4)
Protectiveness, (5) Sensuality-Sex, (6) Gregariousness, (7)
Spouse sentiment, and (8) Child sentiment.
TEST DESCRIPTION The FAMT measures the variables listed
above by "objective indirect methods" rather than
self-reported attitudes. It is a modification of the
Motivational Analysis Test (MAT) developed by Cattell, Horn,
Sweney, and Radcliffe (Cattell, Horn, and Butcher, 1962;
Cattell, Horn, Sweney, and Radcliffe, 1963; Cattell,
Radcliffe, and Sweney, 1963). The following techniques are
used to measure each attitude for the husband-wife,
wife-husband, and parent-child "ties," making a total of 24
scores.
     (1) Autism Test. Multiple choice questions asking the
subject to estimate the extent or frequency of some
phenomenon related to a particular intrafamily attitude.
("What percentage of children sometimes tease their younger
brother?" (95%, 75%, 55%, 35%, 25%). The percentage chosen
is regarded as indicative of the subject's interest in
performing the action.
     (2) Paired Words. The subject is given a stimulus word
followed by two association words, each regarded as
representative of a different interpersonal attitude.   The
word chosen is regarded as indicative of the subject's
attitude.
     (3) Learning Language. The subject learns to associate
phrases describing interpersonal attitudes with nonsense

syllables. It is assumed that subjects will more readily learn associates for attitudes reflecting their involvement or interest.

(4) Memory. The subject is asked to memorize a list of phrases relevant to the interpersonal attitudes. Subjects are later given a larger list from which to indicate words from the first list. It is assumed that the words identified reflect attitudes of higher interest.

"The raw scores for Information and Word Association [are] added to yield integrated scores. The Autism and Memory raw scores [are] added to yield unintegrated scores." (Delhees, Cattell and Sweney, 1970). Results of factor analysis of the component items are described in a later article (Barton, Dielman and Cattell, 1973) in which the test is renamed as the Family Attitude Test (FAM). The factors identified in this analysis "are more complex than originally postulated by Delhees, Cattell and Sweney."
SAMPLE ITEM. See above.
LENGTH. NR.
AVAILABILITY. A general description of the tasks and other procedures is given in Barton, Dielman, and Cattell, 1973; Delhees, Cattell, and Sweney, 1970. Other relevant information is given in Cattell and Warburton, 1967. More specific information can be obtained from the Institute of Personality and Ability Testing, 1602 Coronado Drive, Champaign, Illinois, 61820.
ABSTRACTED BY: Blair Nelson
REFERENCES.

Barton,K. Dielman,T.E. and Cattell,R.B. An item factor analysis of intrafamilial attitudes of parents. Journal of Social Psychology, 1973, 90, 67-72.

Cattell,R.B. Horn,J. and Butcher,H.J. The dynamic structure of attitudes in adults: a description of some established factors and of their measurement by the motivational analysis test. British Journal of Psychology, 1962, 53, 57-69.

Cattell,R.B. Horn,J. Radcliffe,J.A. and Sweney,A.B. The nature and measurement of components of motivation. Genetic Psychology Monographs, 1963, 68, 49-211.

Cattell,R.B. and Warburton,F.W. Objective Personality and Motivation Tests: A Theoretical Introduction and Practical Compendium. Chicago: University of Illinois Press, 1967.

Delhees,K.H. Cattell,R.B. and Sweney,A.B. The structure of parent's intrafamilial attitudes and sentiments measured by objective tests and vector model. Journal of Social Psychology, 1970, 82, 231-252.

Delhees,K.H. Cattell,R.B. and Sweney,A.B. The objective measurement of children's intrafamilial attitude and sentiment structure and the investment subsidiation model. Journal of Genetic Psychology, 1971, 118, 87-113.

ELBERT,S.   ROSMAN,B.S.   MINUCHIN,S.M.   and   GUERNEY,B.G.Jr.
The Family Interaction Apperception Test (FIAT)

VARIABLES MEASURED.   Perceptions of self and others   in   the
family,   needs   and   defense   systems,   and degree   of
psychological adjustment and disturbance.
TEST DESCRIPTION.   A TAT-style test consisting of   10
pictures showing family members in different activities.
The test is administered separately to all family members
over 8 with instructions similar to those of the TAT.   This
test differs from the TAT in that all the scenes have to do
with families; also, the drawings are designed so that
racial   characteristics   are   ambiguous   "permitting
identification with the figures in the scene by any ethnic
group." The authors state that the pictures show scenes
which   are   "universally [i.e.,   cross-culturally   or
cross-subculturally]   recognizable,   familiar   and
interesting." Also "all the FIAT's show the father as a
shadowy figure..."
      The authors note that "in pooling the tests of all
family members, constellations of congruent and dissonant
perception of each other can be examined, as well as mutual
satisfaction and frustration of needs and interlocking
defensive systems." The authors are developing quantitative
methods of analysis for the objective testing of clinical
hypotheses for both this test and the Family Task--tests
which were originally designed as complementary. They state
that this test can be administered to children as well as
adults since the situations are concrete and do not require
great imagination or verbal ability. Also, "the suitability
of this test with different ethnic groups and across age
levels was determined after pilot testing with many
families." (Elbert et al., 1964.)
SAMPLE ITEM.   Pictures similar to those of the TAT (none are
reproduced in Elbert et al., 1964).
LENGTH.   Items: 10 pictures.
AVAILABILITY.   From authors.
REFERENCE.
      Elbert,S.   Rosman,B.S.   Minuchin,S.M.   and
Guerney,B.G.Jr.   A method for the clinical study of family
interaction. American Journal of Orthopsychiatry, 1964, 34,
885-894.
      Minuchin,S.M.   Montalvo,B.   Guerney,B.G.Jr.
Rosman,B.L.   and   Schumer,F.   Families of the Slums. New
York: Basic Books 1967.

ELIAS,G.   Family Adjustment Test

VARIABLES MEASURED.   Intra-family   homeyness-homelessness
(acceptance-rejection),   and 10 subscores: (1) Attitude
toward mother, (2) Attitude toward father, (3) Father-mother
attitude   quotient,   (4)   Oedipal,   (5)   Struggle   for
independence,   (6)   Parent-child   friction-harmony,   (7)
Interparental   friction-harmony,   (8)   Family

inferiority-superiority, (9) Rejection of child, (10)
Parental qualities.
TEST DESCRIPTION. A "disguised-structured-projective" test
of the "public opinion estimate" type (see Campbell, 1950;
Straus, 1964) which requires responses in terms of "what
people think about families in general," using frequency of
occurrence response categories.
SAMPLE ITEM. Parents are happy when they are together.
Always, Often, Sometimes, Rarely, Never.
LENGTH. Time: 35 minutes. Items: 114.
AVAILABILITY. From Psychometric Affiliates, Box 1625,
Chicago, Illinois 60690.
REFERENCES.

Blackshire,R.E. and Diles,D. Student cheating, M.S.
Thesis, University of Arkansas, 1950.

Buros,O.K. (Ed.) Personality Tests and Reviews.
Highland Park, N.J.: Gryphon Press, 1970.

Campbell,D.T. The indirect assessment of social
attitudes. Psychological Bulletin, 1950, 47, 15-38.

Crosby,J.F. The effect of family life education on the
values and attitudes of adolescents. The Family
Coordinator, 1971, 20, 137-140.

Elias,G. Construction of a test of non-homeyness and
related variables. Ph.D. dissertation, Purdue University,
1949.

Elias,G. The concept and an objective measure of
homelessness. Purdue University Studies in Higher
Education, 1951, 77, 49-74.

Elias,G. Self-evaluative questionnaires as projective
measures of personality. Journal of Consulting Psychology,
1951, 15, 496-500.

Elias,G. A measure of homelessness. Journal of
Abnormal Social Psychology, 1952, 47, 62-66.

Elias,G. The Family Adjustment Test, Manual of
Instructions. Chicago: Psychometric Affiliates, 1954.

Gardner,R. The relationship between Elias family
opinion survey scores and selected indices of undesirable
behavior. M.S. Thesis, University of Arkansas, 1951.

Lane,R.C. and Singer,J.L. Familial attitudes in
paranoid schizophrenics and normals from two socio-economic
classes. Journal of Abnormal Social Psychology, 1959, 59,
328-339.

McNeil,E.B. and Cohler,R.J.Jr. The effect of personal
needs on counselors' perception and behavior. Papers of the
Michigan Academy of Science, Arts and Letters, 1957, 42, pt.
2, 281-288.

Richmond,E. Relationship between selected variables
and homelessness test scores, and suggested varying
standardizations, M.S. Thesis, University of Arkansas,
1950.

Stevenson,F. A study of objective measurement of
family feelings among a high school population. Master's
Thesis, Alabama Polytechnic Institute, 1953.

Straus,M.A. Measuring families. In Christensen,H.T.
(Ed.) Handbook of Marriage and the Family. Chicago: Rand

McNally, 1964, 335-400.

HOWELLS,J.G.   and LICKORISH,J.R.   Family Relations Indicator
(FRI)

VARIABLE MEASURED.   Respondent's perception of family.
TEST DESCRIPTION.   Subjects are shown cards depicting
appropriate family members.   The respondents are asked to
tell what they think is going on in the picture.   Responses
to the pictures are recorded.   Responses that are
personality descriptions or a "directed component" are
analyzed.   (A directed component is an interaction between
two people and may be (1) verbal, such as "He grumbled at
the boy," (2) physical, such as "Mother hit the girl," or
(3) attitudinal, such as "Father hates the girl.")
Each directed component and each personality description is
entered on a rectangular relationships grid, divided into
rows and columns, one for each member of the family.   The
column represents doer of action, rows, the subject.
Personality descriptions are entered in the diagonal cells.
Directed components are entered in the remaining cells to
show direction of the action.
SAMPLE ITEM.   See above.
LENGTH.   Time: 60 minutes in two sessions.   Items: 24
cards.
AVAILABILITY.   In Howells and Lickorish, 1967.
ABSTRACTED BY: Susan Murray.
REFERENCES.
     Buros,O.K.   (Ed.) The Sixth Mental Measurements Year
Book.   New Brunswick, N.J.: Gryphon Press, 1965.
     Buros,O.K.   (Ed.) Personality Tests and Reviews.
Highland Park, N.J.: Gryphon Press, 1970.
     Howells,J.G.   and Lickorish,J.R.   The Family Relations
Indicator.   Edinburgh: Oliver and Boyd, 1967.
     Howells,J.G.   and Lickorish,J.R.   A projective
technique for assessing family relationships. Journal of
Clinical Psychology, 1969, 25, 304-307.
     Katkovsky,W.   The Family Relations Indicator.   In
Buros,O.K.   (Ed.) The Sixth Mental Measurements Year Book.
New Brunswick, N.J.: Gryphon Press, 1965.
     Lickorish,J.R.   Evaluating the child's view of his
parents.   Journal of Projective Techniques and Personality
Assessment, 1966, 30, 68-76.
     Lickorish,J.R.   The psychometric assessment of the
family.   In Howells,J.G.   (Ed.) The Theory and Practice of
Family Psychiatry.   Edinburgh: Oliver and Boyd, 1968.
     Sims,C.A.   Kinetic Family Drawings and the Family
Relations Indicator. Journal of Clinical Psychology, 1974,
30, 87-88.

LANE,R.C. and SINGER,J.L. Family Attitude Scale (FAS)

VARIABLES MEASURED. Parental: (1) Ambition, (2) Control,
(3) Dependence, (4) Hostility, (5) Idealization pattern, (6)
Independence, (7) Interparental friction, (8) Oedipal
relationships, (9) Overprotection, (10) Rejection.
TEST DESCRIPTION. Eleven line drawings of family scenes
(e.g., young boy watching his father shave; father, mother,
and boy at breakfast table; mother combing child's hair).
A total of 202 statements, about 18 per picture (selected on
the basis of pricr independent evaluation by judges for
relevance to theoretical dimensions and appropriateness to
specific drawing). The subject inspects each picture, and
then reads statements, which are presented on cards, one at
a time, and makes a judgment about each statement of how the
child in the picture really feels: Definitely possible,
Possible, Undecided, Not possible, Definitely not possible.
Scored by summation of the answers weighted 1 to 5
(Definitely possible).
SAMPLE ITEMS. For picture of family at breakfast: The boy
has pretty definite likes and dislikes about food and lets
his parents know. The boy accidentally spills his soup on
his father's newspaper. His mother nags his father all the
time. His father is quick to use his hands on the boy. The
boy wishes his father would go away so that he can take care
of his mother.
LENGTH. Items: 11 pictures, 202 statements.
AVAILABILITY. In Lane, 1955.
REFERENCES.
     Lane,R.C. Familial attitudes of paranoid schizophrenic
and normal individuals of different socio-economic levels.
Ph.D. dissertation, New York University, 1955.
     Lane,R.C. and Singer,J.L. Familial attitudes   in
paranoid schizophrenics and normals from two socioeconomic
classes. Journal of Abnormal Social Psychology, 1959, 59,
328-339.

LECOMTE,W.F. and LECOMTE,G.K. Family Traditionalism Scales

VARIABLES MEASURED. Approval of traditional standards in
relation to: (1) Choice of career, (2) Dating, (3)
Religion, (4) Woman's role, (5) Father's authority, (6)
Respect for elders, and (7) Marriage.
TEST DESCRIPTION. A questionnaire with five items for each
of the seven areas listed above. Responses are given on a
seven-pcint approval/disapproval scale. "The ratings were
scored by assigning standard positive or negative weights to
each statement, multiplying the ratings by the appropriate
weight and algebraically summing the results across the five
statements for each issue."
     LeComte and LeComte (1973) had respondents indicate
their own self-ratings, and then rated the questions on how
their fathers would approve or disapprove of their stated
ratings.

SAMPLE ITEM. Choice of Career: Choose my own career regardless of parents' feelings or opinions.
LENGTH. Items: 35.
AVAILABILITY. In LeComte and LeComte, 1973.
ABSTRACTED BY: Thomas G. Sparhawk.
REFERENCE.

LeComte,W.F.   and   LeComte,G.K.   Generational attribution in Turkish and American youth. Journal of Cross-Cultural Psychology, 1973, 4, 175-186.

LEVINSON,D.J. and HUFFMAN,P.E. Traditional Family Ideology Scale (TFI)

VARIABLES MEASURED. Traditionalism in family ideology as reflected in: (1) Parent-child relationships and child-rearing techniques, (2) Husband-wife roles and relationships, (3) General male-female relationships and concepts of masculinity and femininity, (4) General values and aims for the family. The same items are also classified according to aspects of authoritarian personality which they represent: (1)   Conventionalism, (2)   Authoritarian submission, (3) Exaggerated masculinity-femininity, (4) Extreme emphasis on discipline, (5) Moralistic rejection of impulse life. Item analysis of the 40 items showed that 35 adequately differentiated the extreme high and low quarters of the initial sample.
TEST   DESCRIPTION.   subjects   indicate   agreement   or disagreement with each item on a scale ranging from +3 (Strong agreement) to -3 (Strong disagreement). Linear combination scoring. There are no subscale scores, since items are not intended to represent any single component variable. A 12-item short form is suggested.
SAMPLE ITEM. A man who does not provide well for his family ought to consider himself pretty much a failure as husband and father.
LENGTH. Items: 40.
AVAILABILITY. In Levinson and Huffman, 1955; Shaw and Wright, 1967.
REFERENCES.

Becker,J. Spielberger,C.D. and Parker,J.B. Value achievement and authoritarian attitudes in psychiatric patients. Journal of Clinical Psychology, 1963, 19, 57-61.

Byrne,D. Parental antecedents of authoritarianism. Journal of Personality and Social Psychology, 1965, 1, 369-373.

Dreyer,A.S. and Rigler,D. Cognitive performance in Montessori and nursery school children. Journal of Educational Research, 1969, 62, 411-416.

Johnson,R.C. Occupational types and traditional family ideology. Child Development, 1963, 34, 509-512.

Kenkel,W.F. Real and conceived roles in family decision making. Marriage and Family Living, 1956, 18, 311-316.

Levin,J. and Spates,J.L. Closed systems of behavior

and traditional family ideology.   Psychological Reports,
1968, 23, 978.
       Levinger,G.   and Breedlove,J.   Interpersonal attraction
and agreement: a study of marriage partners.   Journal of
Personality and Social Psychology, 1966, 3, 367-372.
       Levinson,D.J.   and Huffman,P.E.   Traditional family
ideology and its relation to personality.   Journal of
Personality, 1955, 23, 251-273.
       Shaw,M.E.   and Wright,J.M.   Scales for the Measurement
of Attitudes. New York: McGraw-Hill, 1967.

LEWIN,M.   Family Relations Scales

VARIABLES MEASURED.   (1) Marital authority structure;   (2)
Parental preference for children's sex role differentiation;
(3) Parental   control;   (4)   Parental   achievement
expectations;   (5)   Parental   tolerance   of children's
aggression;   (6) Satisfaction with marital decision-making;
and   (7)   Children's   parental   choice   for expressive
interaction.
TEST DESCRIPTION.   Questionnaire items to measure the above
aspects of family relationships. Several of the scales are
available in husband/wife as well as adolescent response
forms (marital authority structure and parental control).
The scales are suitable for group or individual
administration.   Scoring procedures for the "marital
authority structure" scale are described in Papanek, 1969.
Scoring procedures for the remaining scales are described in
Papanek, 1957.
SAMPLE ITEM.   Marital Authority Scale: The Johnsons were
wondering whether Mrs. Johnson should take a part-time job
she knew about, or not. If this happened in your family,
how would you   decide?   (1) It would depend on how my wife
felt.   (2) It would mostly depend on how my wife felt.   (3)
It would depend equally on how my wife felt and how I felt.
(4) It would mostly depend on how I felt.   (5) It would
depend on how I felt.
LENGTH.   Items: 28, 7, 8, 6, 8, 5, and 6, respectively.
AVAILABILITY.   From NAPS-2.
ABSTRACTED BY: Miriam Lewin (modified).
REFERENCES.
       Papanek,M.L.   Authority and interpersonal relations in
the family.   Ph.D.   dissertation, Harvard University, or
University of Michigan microfilms, 1957.
       Papanek,M.L.   Authority and sex roles in the family.
Journal of Marriage and the Family, 1969, 31, 88-96.
Reprinted in Scarr-Salapatek,S.   and Salapatek,P.   (Eds.)
Socialization.   Columbus, Ohio: Merrill Publishing, 1973,
and in Xerox Psychological reprints.

MURRAY,H.A.   Thematic Apperception Test (TAT)

VARIABLES MEASURED.   A projective test which can be scored

to measure many family and family-related personality
variables.
TEST DESCRIPTION. A series of pictures which are presented
one at a time to the individual or group. The subject tells
or writes a story about what the figures in the picture are
doing, how they feel, what will happen next, and so forth.
There are many variations of presentation, including that of
having a family tell the story jointly (Hess and Handel,
1959). It is common to use only a portion of the 20
pictures, and frequently 10 or fewer cards are used. The
stories can be scored in terms of underlying personality
needs or in terms of manifest content. A variety of scoring
techniques have been developed.
     Minuchin et al. (1967) developed a TAT-type instrument
called the Wiltwyck Family Interaction Apperception
Technique (FIAT), designed specifically to assess the
following variables: Nurturance, Behavior control,
Guidance, Aggression, Cooperation, Affection, Family harmony
and Acceptance cf responsibility. The 10 pictures focus
generally on family situations.
     Murstein (1976) developed a 13-picture version of the
TAT called the Marriage Apperceptive Thematic Examination,
expressly focused cn heterosexual situations.
     Kadushin, Waxenberg and Sager (1971) developed a
slightly modified version of the TAT, called the Family
Story Technique (FST). The technique includes 10 of the
original TAT cards which were deemed most likely to elicit
stories of family functioning. An additional picture,
showing a family seated around a table for a birthday party,
one of a series used by Minuchin, et al. (1967) in the
Wiltwyck Family Interaction Apperception Technique is also
used.
SAMPLE ITEM. Card 1. A young boy is contemplating a violin
which rests on a table in front of him.
LENGTH. Time: Depends cn number of cards used. Items: 20
pictures.
AVAILABILITY. From Psychological Corporation, 304 East 45th
Street, New York, N.Y. 10017.
REFERENCES.
     Abt,L.E. and Bellak,L. (Eds.) Projective Psychology.
New York: Knopf, 1950.
     Alkire,A.A. Brunse,A.J. and Houlihan,J.P. Avoidance
of nuclear family relationships in schizophrenia. Journal
of Clinical Psychology, 1974, 30, 398-400.
     Alper,T.G. and Greenberger,E. Relationship of picture
structure to achievement motivation in college women.
Journal of Personality and Social Psychology, 1967, 7,
362-371.
     Anderson,H.A. and Anderson,G.L. Introduction to
Projective Techniques. New York: Prentice-Hall, 1951.
     Aron,B. A Manual for the Analysis of the Thematic
Apperception Test: A Method and Technique for Personality
Research. Berkeley, California: Willis E. Berg, 1949
(lithotyped).
     Auld,F. Eron,L.D. and Laffal,J. Application of

Guttman's scaling method to the TAT. Educational and Psychological Measurement, 1955, 15, 422-435.

Ausubel,D.P. Relationships between shame and guilt in the socializing process. Psychological Review, 1955, 62, 378-390.

Bieri,J. Lobeck,R. and Galinsky,M.D. A comparison of direct, indirect, and fantasy measures of identification. Journal of Abnormal and Social Psychology, 1959, 58, 253-258.

Bock,C. The attitudes of delinquent and non-delinquent boys to their parents as indicated by the Thematic Apperception Test. Master's Thesis, University of Toronto, 1949, 44.

Buros,O.K. (Ed.) Personality Tests and Reviews. Highland Park, N.J.: Gryphon Press, 1970.

Butler,O.P. Parent figures in Thematic Apperception Test stories of children in disparate family situations. Ph.D. dissertation, University of Pittsburgh, 1948. (Abstracts of Doctoral Dissertations...1948, 1949, 220-6.)

Carr,A.C. (Ed.) Symposium on the Prediction of Overt Behavior through the Use of Projective Techniques. Springfield, Illinois: Charles C Thomas, 1960.

Carrigan,W.C. and Julian,J.W. Sex and birth-order differences in conformity as a function of need affiliation arousal. Journal of Personality and Social Psychology, 1966, 3, 479-483.

Cox,F.N. An assessment of children's attitudes towards parent figures. Child Development, 1962, 33, 821-830.

Dana,R.H. Clinical diagnosis and objective TAT scoring. Journal of Abnormal Social Psychology, 1955, 50, 19-24.

DeVos,G. The relation of guilt toward parents to achievement and arranged marriage among the Japanese. Psychiatry, 1960, 23, 287-301.

Dyk,R.B. and Witkin,H.A. Family experiences related to the development of differentiation in children. Child Development, 1965, 36, 21-55.

Eron,L.D. The normative study of the Thematic Apperception Test. Psychological Monographs, 1950, 64, No. 9 (Whole No. 315).

Eron,L.D. Terry,D. and Callahan,R. The use of rating scales for emotional tone of TAT stories. Journal of Consulting Psychology, 1950, 14, 473-478.

Ferreira,A.J. and Winter,W.D. Information exchange and silence in normal and abnormal families. Family Process, 1968, 7, 251-276.

Ferreira,A.J. Winter,W.D. and Poindexter,E.J. Some interactional variables in normal and abnormal families. Family Process, 1966, 5, 60-75.

Fine,R. A scoring scheme for the TAT and other verbal projective techniques. Journal of Projective Techniques, 1955, 19, 306-309.

Fisher,S.K. Boyd,I. Walker,D. and Sheer,D. Parents of schizophrenics, neurotics, and normals. A.M.A. Archives of General Psychiatry, 1959, 1, 149-166.

Fisher,S.K. and Mendell,D. The communication of neurotic patterns over two and three generations. Psychiatry, 1956, 19, 41-46.

Friedman,I. Objectifying the subjective--a methodological approach to the TAT. Journal of Projective Techniques, 1957, 21, 243-247.

Goldstein,H.S. Internal controls in aggressive children from father-present and father-absent families. Journal of Consulting and Clinical Psychology, 1972, 39, 512.

Goldstein,M.J. Gould,E. Alkire,A.A. Rodnick,E.H. and Judd,L.L. Interpersonal themes in the thematic apperception test: stories of families of disturbed adolescents. Journal of Nervous and Mental Disease, 1970, 150, 354-365.

Greenstein,J.M. Father characteristics and sex typing. Journal of Personality and Social Psychology, 1966, 3, 271-277.

Haley,J. Speech sequences of normal and abnormal families with two children present. Family Process, 1967, 6, 81-97.

Hamilton,V. Maternal rejection and conservation: an analysis of sub-optimal cognition. Journal of Child Psychology and Psychiatry, 1972, 13, 147-166.

Haworth,M.R. Parental loss in children as reflected in projective responses. Journal of Projective Techniques and Personality Assessment, 1964, 26, 31-45.

Helson,R. Personality of women with imaginative and artistic interests: the role of masculinity, originality and the characteristics in their creativity. Journal of Personality, 1966, 34, 1-25.

Henry,W.E. The analysis of fantasy: the thematic apperception technique in the study of personality. New York: Wiley, 1956.

Hess,R.D. and Handel,G. Family Worlds: A Psychosocial Approach to Family Life. Chicago: University of Chicago Press, 1959.

Hokanson,J.E. and Gordon,J.E. The expression and inhibition of hostility in imaginative and overt behavior. Journal of Abnormal Social Psychology, 1958, 57, 327-333.

Howell,M.C. Some effects of chronic illness on children and their mothers. Ph.D. dissertation, University of Minnesota, 1962.

Ilan,L. and Resurreccion-Ventura,E. Response of pre-school children to the Philippine Children's Apperception Test (PCAT): a preliminary study. Philippine Journal of Psychology, 1971, 4, 44-52.

Jacob,T. and Davis,J. Family interaction as a function of experimental task. Family Process, 1973, 12, 415-427.

Jacobs,S. Acquisition of achievement motive among mentally retarded boys. Sociology of Education, 1972, 45, 223-232.

Kadushin,P. Toward a family diagnostic system. Family Coordinator, 1971, 20, 279-289.

Kadushin,P. Cutler,C. Waxenberg,S. and Sager,C. The family story technique and intrafamily analysis. Journal of Projective Techniques and Personality Assessment, 1969, 33, 438-450.

Kadushin,P. Waxenberg,S. and Sager,C. Family story technique changes in interaction and affects during family therapy. Journal of Personality Assessment, 1971, 35, 62-71.

Kagan,J. The measurement of overt aggression from fantasy. Journal of Abnormal Social Psychology, 1956, 52, 390-393.

Kagan,J. Socialization of aggression and the perception of parents in fantasy. Child Development, 1958, 29, 311-320.

Lakin,M. Assessment of significant role attitudes in primiparous mothers by means of a modification of the TAT. Psychosomatic Medicine, 1957, 19, 50-60.

Leary,T.F. The Administration, Scoring and Validation of the Level III--TAT. Interpersonal Diagnosis of Personality. New York: Ronald Press, 1957, 464-479.

Leichty,M.M. The absence of the father during early childhood and its effect upon the Oedipal situation as reflected in young adults. Ph.D. dissertation, Michigan State University, 1958.

Liccione,J.V. The changing family relationships of adolescent girls. Journal of Abnormal Social Psychology, 1955, 51, 421-426.

Lindsey,G. Projective techniques and cross-cultural research. New York: Appleton, 1951.

Maes,J.L. Identification of male college students with their fathers and some related indices of affect expressions and psychosexual adjustment. Ph.D. dissertation, Michigan State University, 1963.

Meadow,L. A study of dyadic relationships in the French family. Journal of Projective Techniques, 1956, 20, 196-206.

Melnick,B. and Hurley,J.R. Distinctive personality attributes of child-abusing mothers. Journal of Consulting and Clinical Psychology, 1969, 33, 746-749.

Meyer,M.M. and Tolman,R.S. Correspondence between attitudes and images of parental figures in TAT stories and in therapeutic interviews. Journal of Consulting Psychology, 1955, 19, 79-82.

Meyer,M.M. and Tolman,R.S. Parental figures in sentence completion test, in TAT, and in therapeutic interviews. Journal of Consulting Psychology, 1955, 19, 170.

Meyer,R.G. and Karon,B.P. The schizophrenogenic mother concept and the TAT. Psychiatry, 1967, 30, 173-179.

Minuchin,S.M. Montalvo,B. Guerney,B.G.Jr. Rosman,B.S. and Schumer,F. Families of the Slums. New York: Basic Books, 1967.

Mitchell,H.E. Social class and race as factors affecting the role of the family in Thematic Apperception Test stories. Abstract. American Psychologist, 1950, 5,

299-300.

Mitchell,H.E. Social class and race as factors affecting the role of the family in Thematic Apperception Test stories of males. Ph.D. dissertation, University of Pennsylvania, 1951. Abstract: Microfilm Abstracts, 1951, 11, 428-429, No. 2.

Mitchell,K.M. An analysis of the schizophrenogenic mother concept by means of the Thematic Apperception Test. Journal of Abnormal Psychology, 1968, 73, 571-574.

Mitchell,K.M. An analysis of the schizophrenogenic mother concept by means of the TAT. Proceedings of the Annual Convention of the American Psychological Association, 1968, 76, 461-462.

Mitchell,K.M. Concept of "Pathogenesis" in parents of schizophrenic and normal children. Journal of Abnormal Psychology, 1969, 74, 423-424.

Moss,H.A. and Kagan,J. Stability of achievement and recognition seeking behaviors from early childhood through adulthood. Journal of Abnormal and Social Psychology, 1961, 62, 504-513.

Murray,H.A. Thematic Apperception Test manual. Cambridge, Massachusetts: Harvard University Printing Office, 1943.

Murstein,B.I. The effect of long-term illness of children on the emotional adjustment of parents. Child Development, 1960, 31, 157-171.

Murstein,B.I. Interview behavior, projective techniques, and questionnaires in the clinical assessment of marital choice. Journal of Personality Assessment, 1972, 36, 462-467.

Murstein,B.I. A thematic test and Rorschach in predicting marital choice. Journal of Personality Assessment, 1972, 36, 213-217.

Murstein,B.I. Who Will Marry Whom? New York: Springer Publishing Company, Inc., 1976.

Mussen,P.H. and Kagan,J. Group conformity and perception of parents. Child Development, 1958, 29, 57-60.

Needelman,S.D. Ideational concepts of parental figures in paranoid schizophrenia: an investigation into the relationship between level of adjustment and an area of interpersonal relationships, as measured by four techniques. Ph.D. dissertation, New York University, 1951. Abstract: Microfilm Abstracts, 1951, 11, 1116-1117, No. 4.

Powell,K.S. Maternal employment in relation to family life. Marriage and Family Living, 1961, 23, 350-355.

Purcell,K. Some shortcomings in projective test validation. Journal of Abnormal Social Psychology, 1958, 57, 115-118.

Rabin,A.I. Growing up in the kibbutz: comparison of the personality of children brought up in the kibbutz and of family-reared Children. New York: Springer Publishing Co., Inc., 1965, 10, 230.

Rabin,A.I. and Haworth,M.R. Projective techniques with children. New York: Grune and Stratton, 1960.

Romano,R.L. The use of the interpersonal system of

diagnosis in marital counseling. Journal of Counseling
Psychology, 1960, 7, 10-18.
     Rosenzweig,S. and Isham,A.C. Complementary Thematic
Apperception Test patterns in close kin. American Journal
of Orthopsychiatry, 1947, 17, 129-142.
     Sahler,D.T. Halzberg,J.D. Fleck,S. Cornelison,A.R.
Kay,E. and Lidz,T. The prediction of family interaction
from a battery of projective techniques. Journal of
Projective Techniques, 1957, 21, 199-208.
     Saltzman,E.S. A comparison of patterns of
identification as shown by family members of three religious
denominations in Houston, Texas. Ph.D. dissertation,
University of Houston, 1965.
     Scarr,S. The Adjective Check List as a personality
assessment technique with children. Journal of Consulting
Psychology, 1966, 30, 122-128.
     Schludermann,S. and Schludermann,E. A methodological
note on conceptual frames of parental attitudes of fathers
(PARI). Journal of Psychology, 1970, 76, 145-148.
     Schorr,J.E. A proposed system for scoring the TAT.
Journal of Clinical Psychology, 1948, 4, 189-194.
     Schwartz,M. The relationship between projective test
scoring categories and activity preferences. Genetic
Psychology Monographs, 1952, 46, 133-188.
     Segal,A.S.B. The prediction of expressed attitudes
toward the mother. Ph.D. dissertation, University of
Michigan, 1954.
     Sigel,I.E. and Hoffman,M.L. The predictive potential
of projective tests for nonclinical populations. Symposium
on the use of projective techniques as research tools in
studies of normal personality development. Journal of
Projective Techniques, 1956, 20, 261-264.
     Silverman,B. Intra-family fantasy in terms of sexual
identification. Ph.D. dissertation, Yeshiva University,
1962.
     Singer,J.L. Projected familial attitudes as a function
of socioeconomic status and psychopathology. Journal of
Consulting Psychology, 1954, 18, 99-104.
     Singer,M.T. and Wynne,L.C. Differentiating
characteristics of parents of childhood schizophrenics,
childhood neurotics, and young adult schizophrenics.
American Journal of Psychiatry, 1963, 120, 234-243.
     Sohler,D.T. Holzberg,J.D. Fleck,S. Cornelison,A.R.
Kay,E. and Lidz,T. The prediction of family interaction
from a battery of projective techniques. Journal of
Projective Techniques, 1957, 21, 199-208.
     Sontag,L.W. Crandall,V. and Lacey,J. Dynamics of
personality: resolution of infantile dependent need.
Discussion by Harold H. Anderson. American Journal of
Orthopsychiatry, 1952, 22, 534-541.
     Stabenau,J.R. Tupin,J. Werner,M. and Pollin,W. A
comparative study of families of schizophrenics, delinquents
and normals. Psychiatry, 1965, 28, 45-59.
     Staples,F.R. and Walters,R.H. Anxiety, birth order,
and susceptibility to social influence. Journal of Abnormal

and Social Psychology, 1961, 62, 716-719.

Stein,M.I.   Thematic   Apperception   Test: An
Introductory Manual for Its Clinical Use with Adults, 2nd
Edition. Cambridge, Massachusetts: Addison-Wesley, 1955.

Stolz,L.M., et al. Father relations of war-born
children. Stanford, California: Stanford University Press,
1954.

Stone,G.B. II. A study of parent-child relationships
in patients with peptic ulcer and bronchial asthma, as
revealed by projective techniques. Ph.D. dissertation,
University of Southern California, 1950. (Abstracts of
Dissertations...1950, 1951, 188-191.)

Straus,M.A. and Cytrynbaum,S. A Scoring Manual for
Intrafamilial Power and Affective Support. Minneapolis:
Minnesota Family Study Center, 1961 (ditto).

Straus,M.A. and Cytrynbaum,S. Support and power
structure in Sinhalese, Tamil, and Burgher student families.
International Journal of Comparative Sociology, 1962, 3,
138-153.

Terry,D. The use of a rating scale of level of
response in TAT stories. Journal of Abnormal Social
Psychology, 1952, 47, 507-511.

Tompkins,S.S. The Thematic Apperception Test: The
Theory and Technique of Interpretation. New York: Grune
and Stratton, 1947.

Tsuiji,S. and Kato,N. Some investigations of parental
preference in early childhood: an attempt to obtain a
correspondence of verbally expressed preference with
projectively expressed preference. Japanese Psychological
Research, 1966, 8, 10-17.

Vassiliou,G. and Vassiliou,V. Transactional story
sequence analysis, a new procedure on family diagnosis.
International Congress on Rorschach and Projective Methods,
1967, 6, 99-107.

Veroff,J. and Feld,S. Marriage and Work in America.
New York: Van Nostrand Reinhold, Co., 1970.

Weatherly,D. Maternal permissiveness toward aggression
and subsequent TAT aggression. Journal of Abnormal and
Social Psychology, 1962, 65, 1-5.

Webster,H. Rac's multiple discriminant technique
applied to three TAT variables. Journal of Abnormal and
Social Psychology, 1952, 47, 641-648.

Werner,M.   Stabenau,J.R. and Pollin,W.   Thematic
Apperception Test method for the differentiation of families
of schizophrenics, delinquents, and "normals." Journal of
Abnormal Psychology, 1970, 75, 139-145.

Wilson,D.M. A study of the personalities of stuttering
children and their parents as revealed through projection
tests. Ph.D. dissertation, University of Southern
California, 1950.

Winter,S.K. Characteristics of fantasy while nursing.
Journal of Personality, 1969, 37, 58-72.

Winter,W.D. Hostility themes in the family TAT.
Journal of Projective Techniques, 1966, 30, 270-274.

Winter,W.D. and Ferreira,A.J. Interaction process

analysis of family decision-making. Family Process, 1967, 6, 155-172.

Winter,W.D. and Ferreira,A.J. Talking time as an index of intrafamilial similarity in normal and abnormal families. Journal of Abnormal Psychology, 1969, 74, 574-575.

Winter,W.D. and Ferreira,A.J. A factor analysis of family interaction measures. Journal of Projective Techniques and Personality Assessment, 1970, 34, 55-63.

Winter,W.D. Ferreira,A.J. and Olson,J.L. Story sequence analysis of family TAT's. Journal of Projective Techniques and Personality Assessment, 1965, 29, 392-397.

Winter,W.D. Ferreira,A.J. and Olson,J.L. Hostility themes in the family TAT. Journal of Projective Techniques and Personality Assessment, 1966, 30, 270-274.

OSGOOD,C.E.   SUCI,G.J.   and   TANNENBAUM,P.   Semantic Differential

VARIABLES MEASURED. The semantic differential is a "generalizable technique" for measuring the meaning of selected "concepts" to an individual. The concepts chosen for measurement depend upon the research problem at hand. For example, the semantic differential has been used to measure the meaning of the following family concepts: Children's affect for parents (South and Floyd, 1971); Actual and ideal spouse (Hooper and Sheldon, 1969); Marital communication and understanding (Hickman and Baldwin, 1971); Parental role concepts (McIntire, Nass and Dreyer, 1974); Parent image (McGinn, Harburg and Julius, 1965); Sexual behavior (Gerson, 1974); Perceived similarity to parents (Constantinople, 1974); and Parent-child interaction (Ginsburg, McGinn, and Harburg, 1970).

In Van der Veen's "Family Semantic Differential," five concepts related to the family are rated on 13 bipolar scales: my family, my ideal family, my parents' families, my child (or children), and family conversation. The 13 bipolar scales are: Evaluative: sociable-unsociable, interesting-boring, harmonious-harsh, clean-dirty; Potency: strong-weak, masculine-feminine, severe-lenient, stubborn-yielding; Activity: active-passive, excitable-calm; Stability: stable-changeable; Closeness: accepting-rejecting, near-far. Each scale has the two opposing terms at opposite ends of the scale, separated by seven spaces. The closeness in meaning of a concept to the adjectives is indicated by a check in the appropriate space. Scores on each of the concepts can be obtained for each factor by summing the ratings on each of the scales (e.g., a rating on the evaluative scale "My Family" is obtained by summing the ratings of the four evaluative scales).

In Katz' "Semantic Differential as applied to marital adjustment" discrepant affect states of the husband and wife are measured concerning connotative or emotive meaning of the following aspects of the marriage: compatibility,

sexual relations, understanding, love, companionship,
loyalty, husband, adaptability, wife, and responsibility.
For each of the 10 concepts, four polar adjective scales are
employed to represent each of three semantic factors. The
evaluative scales are: good-bad, pleasant-unpleasant,
clean-dirty, fair-unfair, the potency scales are:
strong-weak, hard-soft, deep-shallow, wide-narrow; the
activity scales are: fast-slow, active-passive, sharp-dull,
hot-cold. Scale ratings are scored by attributing integer
values 1 to 7 for the seven scale positions, correcting for
the reversals in polarity.
TEST DESCRIPTION. Respondents rate concepts in terms of
seven-point bipolar scales such as good-bad, active-passive.
SAMPLE ITEM. My family.
    Accepting . . . . Rejecting
                1 2 3 4 5 6 7
LENGTH. NR.
AVAILABILITY. Osgood et al., 1957.
ABSTRACTED BY: Bruce Brown
REFERENCES.
    Barclay,A. and Cusumanio,D.R. Father absence,
cross-sex identity, and field-dependent behavior in male
adolescents. Child Development, 1967, 38, 243-250.
    Bieri,J. and Lobeck,R. Self-concept differences in
relation to identification, religion, and social class.
Journal of Abnormal and Social Psychology, 1961, 62, 94-98.
    Bieri,J. Lobeck,R. and Galinsky,M.D. A comparison of
direct, indirect and fantasy measures of identification.
Journal of Abnormal and Social Psychology, 1959, 58,
253-258.
    Brunkan,R.J. Perceived parental attitudes and parental
identification in relation to field of vocational choice.
Journal of Counseling Psychology, 1965, 12, 39-47.
    Brunkan,R.J. Perceived parental attitudes and parental
identification in relation to problems in vocational choice.
Journal of Counseling Psychology, 1966, 13, 394-402.
    Constantinople,A. Analytical ability and perceived
similarity to parents. Psychological Reports, 1974, 35,
1335-1345.
    Dien,D.S. and Vinacke,W.E. Self-concept and parental
identification of young adults with mixed Caucasian-Japanese
parentage. Journal of Abnormal and Social Psychology, 1964,
69, 463-466.
    Dignan,M.H. Ego identity and maternal identification.
Journal of Personality and Social Psychology, 1965, 1,
476-483.
    Feshbach,N.D. and Beigel,A. A note on the use of the
semantic differential in measuring teacher personality and
values. Educational and Psychological Measurements, 1968,
28, 923-929.
    Gerson,A. Promiscuity as a function of the
father-daughter relationship. Psychological Reports, 1974,
34, 1013-1014.
    Ginsburg,G.P. McGinn,N.F. and Harburg,E. Recalled
parent-child interaction of Mexican and United States males.

Journal of Cross-Cultural Psychology, 1970, 1, 139-152.

Harburg,E. Covert hostility: its social origins and relationship with overt compliance. Ph.D. dissertation. University of Michigan, 1962.

Helper,M.M. and Garfield,S.L. Use of the semantic differential to study acculturation in American Indian adolescents. Journal of Personality and Social Psychology, 1965, 2, 844-851.

Hickman,M.E. and Baldwin,B.A. Use of programmed instruction to improve communication in marriage. The Family Coordinator, 1971, 20, 121-125.

Hooper,D. and Sheldon,A. Evaluating newly-married couples. British Journal of Social and Clinical Psychology, 1969, 8, 169-182.

Katz,M. Agreement on connotative meaning in marriage. Family Process, 1965, 4, 64-74.

McGinn,N.F. Ginsburg,G.P. and Harburg,E. Dependency relations with parents and affiliative responses in Michigan and Guadalajara. Sociometry, 1965, 28, 305-321.

McGinn,N.F. Harburg,E. and Julius,S. Blood pressure reactivity and recall of treatment by parents. Journal of Personality and Social Psychology, 1965, 1, 147-153.

McIntire,W.G. Nass,G.D. and Dreyer,A.S. Parental role perceptions of Ghanian and American adolescents. Journal of Marriage and the Family, 1974, 36, 185-189.

Medinnus,G.R. Adolescents' self-acceptance and perceptions of their parents. Journal of Consulting Psychology, 1965, 29, 150-154.

Nathanson,I.A. Semantic differential analysis of parent-son relationships in schizophrenia. Journal of Abnormal Psychology, 1967, 72, 277-281.

Osgood,C.E. Suci,G.J. and Tannenbaum,P. The Measurement of Meaning. Urbana: University of Illinois Press, 1957.

Schludermann,S. and Schludermann,E. Developmental study of social role perception among Hutterite adolescents. Journal of Psychology, 1969a, 72, 243-246.

Schludermann,S. and Schludermann,E. Scale checking style as a function of age and sex in Indian and Hutterite children. Journal of Psychology, 1969b, 72, 253-261.

Schludermann,S. and Schludermann,E. Social role perceptions of children in Hutterite communal society. Journal of Psychology, 1969c, 72, 183-188.

Secord,P.F. and Jourard,S.M. Mother concepts and judgments of young women's faces. Journal of Abnormal and Social Psychology, 1956, 52, 246-250.

South,D.R. and Floyd,H.H.Jr. Parental or peer orientation? Options and implications for youth and parents. Southern Quarterly, 1971, 10, 49-62.

Stedman,J.M. and McKenzie,R.E. Family factors related to competence in young disadvantaged Mexican American children. Child Development, 1971, 42, 1602-1607.

Thomas,D.L. Gecas,V. Weigert,A. and Rooney,E. Family Socialization and the Adolescent. Lexington, Massachusetts: Lexington Books, 1974.

Thompson,N.L.Jr. Schwartz,D.M. McCandless,B.R. and
Edwards,D.A. Parent-child relationships and sexual identity
in male and female homosexuals and heterosexuals. Journal
of Consulting and Clinical Psychology, 1973, 41, 120-127.
    Van-der-Veen,F.   Huebner,B.F.   Jorgens,B.   and
Neja,P.Jr. Relationships between parent's concept of the
family and family adjustment. American Journal of
Orthopsychiatry, 1964, 34, 45-55.
    Wallace,K. Construction and validation of mutual
adjustment and prediction scales. Ph.D. dissertation,
University of Southern California, 1947.

PETRICH,B.A. Traditional--Emerging Beliefs about Families

VARIABLES MEASURED. Traditional versus Emerging family
beliefs: (1) Importance of the family, (2) Parent-child
interaction, and (3) Family unity.
TEST DESCRIPTION. The test items are descriptive of
Traditional or Emerging family characteristics. Items are
arranged on an even-odd number basis to facilitate scoring
and there are an equal number of Traditional and Emerging
items. The items have no connotation of "good" or "bad" and
have been found acceptable by adults, adolescents, and
children. The three parts were determined by factor
analysis.
SAMPLE ITEM. The mother's opinion should be as important as
father's in money matters: Strongly agree, Agree,
Undecided, Disagree, Strongly Disagree.
LENGTH. Items: 54. Time: 20-30 minutes.
AVAILABILITY. From NAPS-2 or from author.
ABSTRACTED BY: Beatrice Petrich.
REFERENCES.
    Luett,C.E. Relationship of Family Concepts Held by
Home Economics Teachers and Pupils. Unpublished Master's
Thesis, Northern Illinois University.
    Petrich,B.A. Traditional--Emerging Family Beliefs, Ten
Years Later. In progress.
    Petrich,B.A. and Chadderdon,H. Family beliefs of
junior high school pupils. The Family Coordinator, 1969,
18, 374-378.

SCHAEFER,E.S. and BELL,R.Q. Parental Attitude Research
Instrument (PARI)

VARIABLES MEASURED. Attitudes toward 23 areas of family
life: (1) encouraging verbalization, (2) fostering
dependency, (3) seclusion of the mother. (4) breaking the
will, (5) martyrdom, (6) fear of harming the baby, (7)
marital conflict, (8) strictness, (9) irritability, (10)
excluding outside influences, (11) deification, (12)
suppression of aggression, (13) rejection of the homemaking
role, (14) equalitarianism, (15) approval of activity, (16)
avoidance of communication, (17) inconsiderateness of the

husband, (18) suppression of sexuality, (19) ascendancy of the mother, (20) intrusiveness, (21) comradeship and sharing, (22) acceleration of development, (23) dependency of the mother. Factor analysis by Schaefer and Bell (1957) indicates five factors: (1) harsh punitive-control, (2) suppression and interpersonal distance, (3) overpossessiveness, (4) excessive demand for striving, and (5) hostility-rejection. Factor analysis by Zuckerman, Ribback, Monashkin, and Norton (1958) indicates two factors: (1) authoritarian control and (2) hostility-rejection. Zuckerman and Norton (1961) also developed scores for the response sets: (1) acquiescence, (2) opposition, and (3) extremes.

TEST DESCRIPTION. Multiple-choice intensity of agreement-disagreement items. Zuckerman (1959) prepared a parallel form with items reversed in meaning. Davids et al. (1963) constructed a short form of the test consisting of 30 items indicative of maternal attitudes regarding family relations and child-rearing practices. See Glasser and Radin abstract for a short-form version of this test. Schludermann and Schludermann revised the test to select items with the lowest response set bias. A factor analysis of the mother's form (1974) revealed two factors: (1) authoritarianism and (2) family disharmony, while the revised father's form (1971) revealed these two factors: (1) paternal dominance and (2) male autonomy.

SAMPLE ITEM. Children should be allowed to disagree with their parents if they feel their own ideas are better. A = Strongly agree; a = Mildly agree; d = Mildly disagree; D = Strongly disagree.

LENGTH. Items: 115 (Schaefer and Bell version); 115 (Schludermann and Schludermann revised mother's form); 100 (Schludermann and Schludermann revised father's form).

AVAILABILITY. In Schaefer and Bell, 1958. A list of additional references from the first edition of Family Measurement Techniques (1969) has been deposited with the NAPS. Schludermann and Schludermann's revised forms are available from the authors.

REFERENCES.

Abel,H. and Singles,R. Development of scales to measure parental attitudes and behavior: a progress report. Family Life Coordinator, 1966, 15, 127-131.

Andrew,G. Determinants of Negro family decisions in management of retardation. Journal of Marriage and the Family 1968, 30, 613-617.

Barsch,R.H. The Parent of the Handicapped Child. Springfield, Illinois: Charles C Thomas, 1968.

Becker,W.C. The relationship of factors in parental ratings of self and each other to the behavior of kindergarten children as rated by mothers, fathers and teachers. Journal of Consulting Psychology, 1960, 24, 507-527.

Becker,W.C. and Krug,R.S. A circumplex model for social behavior in children. Child Development, 1964, 35, 371-396.

Becker,W.C.   and   Krug,R.S.   The   Parent   Attitude
Research Instrument--a research review. Child Development,
1965, 36, 329-365.
    Beckwith,L.   Relationships   between   attributes   of
mothers and their infants' IQ scores. Child Development,
1971, 42, 1083-1097.
    Beckwith,L.   Relationships   between   infants'
vocalizations and their mothers' behaviors. Merrill-Palmer
Quarterly, 1971, 17, 211-226.
    Beckwith,L.   Relationships between infants' social
behavior and their mothers' behavior. Child Development,
1972, 43, 397-411.
    Bell,R.Q.   List of current or planned studies of
parental attitudes using questionnaires. Mimeographed
compilaticn prepared at Child Development Section, National
Institute of Health, Bethesda, Md., August 1959.
    Bell,R.Q.   Isolation of elevation and scatter
components in personality and attitude questionnaires.
Educational Psychology Measurement, 1962, 22, 699-713.
    Bell,R.Q. Hartup,W.W. and Crowell,D.H. Mailed versus
supervised administration of a projective questionnaire.
Journal of Consulting Psychology, 1962, 26, 290.
    Brody,G.F. Relationship between maternal attitudes and
behavior.   Journal of Personality and Social Psychology,
1965, 2, 317-323.
    Brody,G.F. Maternal child-rearing attitudes and child
behavior. Developmental Psychology, 1969, 1, 66.
    Broussard,E.R. and Hartner,M.S.S. Maternal perception
of the neonate as related to development. Child Psychiatry
and Human Development, 1970, 1, 16-25.
    Bruni,P.   Analisi fatoriale 3 contributo alla
validazione esterna del Parental Attitude Research
Instrument (PARI) Bollettino di Psicologia Applicata, 1968,
No. 88-90, 77-86.
    Busse,T.V.   Child-rearing antecedents of flexible
thinking. Develcpmental Psychology, 1969, 1, 585-591.
    Chorost,S.B.   Parental child-rearing attitudes and
their correlates in adolescent hostility.   Genetic
Psychological Monographs, 1962, 66, 49-90.
    Cicchetti,D.V.   and Ornston,P.S.   Reported family
dynamics and psychopathology: II. the reactions of mental
patients to a disturbed family in psychotherapy. Journal of
Abnormal Psychology, 1968, 73, 156-161.
    Cline,V.B.   Richards,J.M.Jr.   and   Needham,W.E.   A
factor analytic study of the father form of the Parental
Attitude Research Instrument. Psychological Records, 1963,
13, 65-72.
    Costin,F.   Measuring attitudinal outcomes of child
psychology with the Parental Attitude Research Instrument.
Journal of Educational Research, 1960, 53, 289-294.
    Costin,F. Attitudinal outcomes of child psychology
courses having different orientations.   Journal of
Psychology, 1961, 51, 113-119.
    Crain,A.J. Sussman,M.B. and Weil,W.B.Jr. Effects of
a diabetic child cn marital integration and related measures

of family functioning. Journal of Health and Human Behavior, 1966, 7, 122-127.

Cross,H.J. The relation of parental training conditions to conceptual level in adolescent boys. Journal of Personality, 1966, 34, 348-365.

Cross,H.J. and Kawash,G.F. A short form of PARI to assess authoritarian attitudes toward child rearing. Psychological Reports, 1968, 23, 91-98.

Datta,L. Parloff,E. and Parloff,M.B. On the relevance of authonomy: parent-child relationships and early scientific creativity. Proceedings of the 75th Annual APA Convention, 1967, 149-150.

Davids,A. A research design for studying maternal emotionality before childbirth and after social interaction with the child. Merrill-Palmer Quarterly, 1968, 14, 345-354.

Davids,A. Personality and attitudes of child care workers, psychotherapist, and parents of children in residential treatment. Child Psychiatry and Human Development, 1970, 1, 41-49.

Davids,A. and Hainsworth,P.K. Maternal attitudes about family life and child-rearing as avowed by mothers and perceived by their under-achieving and high-achieving sons. Journal of Consulting Psychology, 1967, 31, 29-37.

Davids,A. and Holden,R.H. Consistency of maternal attitudes and personality from pregnancy to eight months following childbirth. Developmental Psychology, 1970, 2, 364-366.

Davids,A. Holden,R.H. and Gray,G.B. Maternal anxiety during pregnancy and adequacy of mother and child adjustment eight months following childbirth. Child Development, 1963, 34, 993-1002.

Dewing,K. and Taft,R. Some characteristics of the parents of creative twelve-year-olds. Journal of Personality, 1973, 41, 71-85.

Diener,E. Maternal child-rearing attitudes as antecedents of self-actualization. Psychological Reports, 1972, 694.

Emmerich,W. The parental role: a functional cognitive approach. Monographs of the Society for Research in Child Development, 1969, 34. Serial No. 132.

Eufemio,F. Foster mothers: their responses on the parent attitude research instrument (PARI) in relation to their role performance. Philippine Sociological Review, 1967, 15, 94-104.

Fanshel,D. Specializations within the foster parent role: a research report. Child Welfare, 1961, 40, 17-21.

Farina,A. Patterns of role dominance and conflict in parents of schizophrenic patients. Journal of Abnormal Social Psychology, 1960, 61, 31-38.

Ferreira,A.H. The pregnant woman's emotional attitude and its reflection on the newborn. American Journal of Orthopsychiatry, 1960, 30, 553-561.

Freedheim,D.K. and Reichenberg-Hackett,W. An experimental investigation of parent-child attitudes with the PARI scales. Child Development, 1959, 30, 353-362.

Garfield,S.L. and Helper,M.M. Parental attitudes and socio-economic status. Journal of Clinical Psychology, 1962, 28, 171-175.

Garmezy,N. Clarke,A.R. and Stockner,C. Child-rearing attitudes of mothers and fathers as reported by schizophrenic and normal patients. Journal of Abnormal Social Psychology, 1961, 63, 176-182.

Gerhart,U.C. and Geismar,L.L. The PARI as a predictor of parental behavior. Child Welfare, 1969, 48, 502-505.

Guertin,W.H. Are differences in schizophrenic symptoms related to the mother's avowed attitudes toward child rearing? Journal of Abnormal Social Psychology, 1961, 63, 440-442.

Guthrie,G.M. Structure of maternal attitudes in two cultures. Journal of Psychology, 1966, 62, 155-165.

Hall,C.L.Jr. Maternal control as related to schizoid behaviors in grossly normal males. Journal of Personality, 1965, 33, 613-621.

Hamilton,V. Maternal rejection and conservation: an analysis of sub-optimal cognition. Journal of Child Psychology and Psychiatry, 1972, 13, 147-166.

Hamilton's questionnaire contains 14 subscales of the PARI as well as the MMPI and MPI "Lie Scale" and acceptance-rejection items from the "U.S.C. Acceptance-Rejection Scale."

Hartup,W.W. Some correlates of parental imitation in young children. Child Development, 1962, 33, 85-96.

Heilbrun,A.B.Jr. Perception of maternal child-rearing attitudes in schizophrenics. Journal of Consulting Psychology, 1960a, 24, 169-173.

Heilbrun,A.B.Jr. Perceptual distortion and schizophrenia. American Journal of Orthopsychiatry, 1960b, 30, 412-418.

Heilbrun,A.B.Jr. Perceived maternal childrearing patterns and subsequent deviance in adolescence. Adolescence, 1966, 1, 152.

Heilbrun,A.B.Jr. Cognitive sensitivity to aversive maternal stimulation in late adolescent males. Journal of Consulting and Clinical Psychology, 1968, 32, 326-332.

Heilbrun,A.B.Jr. Perceived maternal child rearing and effects of delayed reinforcement upon constant acquisition. Developmental Psychology, 1969, 1, 605-612.

Heilbrun,A.B.Jr. Perceived maternal child-rearing experience and the effects of vicarious and direct reinforcement on males. Child Development, 1970, 41, 253-262.

Heilbrun,A.B.Jr. Style of adaptation to perceived aversive maternal control and internal scanning behavior. Journal of Consulting and Clinical Psychology, 1972, 39, 15-21.

Heilbrun,A.B.Jr. Gillard,B.J. and Harrell,S.N. Perceived maternal rejection and cognitive interference. Journal of Child Psychology and Psychiatry, 1965, 6, 233-242.

Heilbrun,A.B.Jr. and Harrell,S.N. Perceived maternal child-rearing pattern and the effects of social nonreactions upon achievement motivation. Child Development, 1967, 38, 267-281.

Heilbrun,A.B.Jr. and McKinley,R. Perception of maternal child-rearing attitudes, personality of the perceiver, and incipient psychopathology. Child Development, 1962, 33, 73-83.

Heilbrun,A.B.Jr.   and   Norbert,N.A.   Maternal child-rearing   experience   and   self-reinforcement effectiveness. Developmental Psychology, 1970, 3, 81-87.

Heilbrun,A.B.Jr. and Orr,H.K. Maternal childrearing control, history and subsequent cognitive and personality functioning of the offspring. Psychological reports, 1965, 17, 259-272.

Heilbrun,A.B.Jr. and Waters,D.B. Underachievement as related to perceived maternal child rearing and academic conditions of reinforcement. Child Development, 1969, 39, 913-921.

Hoffman,B.A. The effects of the behavior problems and physical handicaps of children on the child-rearing attitudes of mothers and fathers. Dissertation Abstracts, 1960, 21, 239.

Horowitz,F.D. and Lovell,L.L. Attitudes of mothers of female schizophrenics. Child Development, 1960, 31, 299-305.

Huff,P. Does family life education change attitudes toward child-rearing? The Family Coordinator, 1968, 17, 185-187.

Hurley,J.R.   Parental   acceptance-rejection   and children's intelligence. Merrill-Palmer Quarterly, 1965, 11, 19-31.

Irelan,L.M. Moles,O.C. and O'Sher,R.M. Ethnicity, poverty, and selected attitudes: a test of the 'culture of poverty' hypothesis. Social Forces, 1969, 47, 405-413.

Kamali,M.R. Effectiveness of counseling in a community parent-teacher education center. The Family Coordinator, 1969, 18, 401-402.

Kitano,H.H.L.   Differential child-rearing attitudes between first and second generation Japanese in the United States. Journal of Social Psychology, 1961, 53, 13-19.

Kitano,H.H.L. Inter- and intragenerational differences in maternal attitudes towards child rearing. Journal of Social Psychology, 1964, 63, 215-220.

Klebanoff,L.B. Parental attitudes of mothers of schizophrenics, brain-injured and retarded, and normal children. American Journal of Orthopsychiatry, 1959, 29, 445-454.

Loevinger,J. Measuring personality patterns of women. Genetic Psychology Monographs, 1962, 65, 53-136.

Madoff,J.M. The attitudes of mothers of juvenile delinquents toward child rearing. Journal of Consulting Psychology, 1959, 23, 518-520.

Mannino,F.V.   Kisielewski,J.   Kimbro,E.L.Jr.   and Morgenstern,B. Relationships between parental attitudes and behavior. The Family Coordinator, 1968, 17, 237-240.

Marschak,M. Imitation and participation in normal and disturbed young boys in interaction with their parents. Journal of Clinical Psychology, 1967, 23, 421-427.

Marshall,H.R. Relations between home experience and children's use of language in play interactions with peers. Psychological Monographs, 1961, 75, No. 509.

Maw,W.H and Maw,E.W. Children's curiosity and parental attitudes. Journal of Marriage and the Family, 1966, 28, 343-345.

McDavid,J.W. Imitative behavior in preschool children. Psychological Monographs, 1959, 73, No. 16.

Medinnus,G.R. The relation between several parent measures and the child's early adjustment to school. Journal of Educational Psychology, 1961, 52, 153-156.

Medinnus,G.R. The relations between inter-parent agreement and several child measures. Journal of Genetic Psychology, 1963, 102, 139-144.

Medinnus,G.R. and Mead,D.E. Comparison of a projective and a non-projective assessment of parent attitudes. Journal of General Psychology, 1965, 107, 253-160.

Nichols,R.C. A factor analysis of parental attitudes of fathers. Child Development, 1963, 33, 791-802.

Nichols,R.C. Parental attitudes of mothers of intelligent adolescents and creativity of their children. Child Development, 1964, 35, 1041-1049.

Paulson,M.J. Grossman,S. and Shapiro,G. Child-rearing attitude of foster home mothers. Journal of Community Psychology, 1974, 2, 11-14.

Paulson,M.J. Tien-Teh,L. and Hanssen,C. Family harmony: an etiologic factor in alienation. Child Development, 1972, 43, 591-603.

Platt,H. Jurgensen,G. and Chorost,S.B. Comparison of child-rearing attitudes of mothers and fathers of emotionally disturbed adolescents. Child Development, 1962, 33, 117-122.

Purcell,K. A method to assess aspects of parent-child relationships. Child Development, 1962, 33, 537-553.

Purcell,K. Distinctions between subgroups of asthmatic children: parental reactions to experimental separation. Journal of Abnormal Child Psychology, 1973, 1, 2-15.

Radin,N. Three degrees of maternal involvement in a preschool program: impact on mothers and children. Child Development, 1972, 43, 1355-1364.

Radin,N. and Glasser,P. The use of parental attitude questionnaire with culturally disadvantaged families. Journal of Marriage and the Family, 1965, 27, 373-382.

Radin,N. and Glasser,P. The utility of the parental attitude research instrument for intervention programs with low-income families. Journal of Marriage and the Family, 1972, 34, 448-458.

Reed,M.K. The intelligence, social maturity, personal adjustment, physical development, and parent-child relationships of children with congenital heart disease.

Dissertation Abstracts, 1959, 20, 385.

Schaefer,E.S. Organization of maternal behavior and attitudes within a two-dimensional space: an application of Guttman's radex theory. Paper presented at the American Psychological Association meeting, 1957.

Schaefer,E.S.   Converging conceptual models for maternal behavior and for child behavior. In Glidewell,J.C. (Ed.)   Parental   Attitudes   and   Child   Behavior. Springfield,Ill.: Thomas, 1961.

Schaefer,E.S.   and   Bell,R.Q.   Patterns of attitudes toward child rearing and the family. Journal of Abnormal Social Psychology, 1957, 54, 391-395.

Schaefer,E.S.   and Bell,R.Q.   Development of a parental attitude research instrument. Child Development, 1958,29, 339-361.

Schludermann,S. and Schludermann,E. A methodological note on conceptual frames of parental attitudes of fathers (PARI). Journal of Psychology, 1970a, 76, 245-248.

Schludermann,S. and Schludermann,E. Conceptual frames of parental attitudes of fathers. Journal of Psychology, 1970b, 75, 193-204.

Schludermann,S. and Schludermann,E. Conceptualization of maternal behavior. Journal of Psychology, 1970c, 75, 205-215.

Schludermann,S. and Schludermann,E. Maternal rearing attitudes in Hutterite communal society. Journal of Psychology, 1971a, 79, 169-177.

Schludermann,S.   and   Schludermann,E.   Paternal attitudes in Hutterite communal society. Journal of Psychology, 1971b, 79, 41-48.

Schludermann,S. and Schludermann,E. Response set analysis of a paternal attitude research instrument (PARI). Journal of Psychology, 1971c, 79, 213-220.

Schludermann,S.   and   Schludermann,E.   Response   set analysis of mother's form of Parental Attitude Research Instrument (PARI). Journal of Psychology, 1974, 36, 327-334.

Shaw,M.C. and Dutton,B.E.   The use of the Parent Attitude Research Inventory with the parents of bright academic underachievers. Journal of Educational Psychology, 1962, 53, 203-208.

Stollak,G.E.   An   integrated   graduate-undergraduate program in the assessment, treatment, and prevention of child psychopathclogy. Professional Psychology, 1973, 4, 158-169.

Thomas,D.L.   Gecas,V.   Weigert,A.   and Rooney,E. Family Socialization and the Adolescent. Lexington, Massachusetts: Lexington Books, 1974.

Tolor,A. and Jalowiec,J.E.   Body boundary, parental attitudes and internal-external expectancy. Journal of Counseling and Clinical Psychology, 1968, 32, 206-209.

Tolor,A. and Rafferty,W. The attitudes of mothers of hospitalized patients. Journal of Nervous and Mental Disorders, 1963, 136, 76-81.

Vogel,W. and Lauterbach,C.G.   Relationships between

normal and disturbed sons' percepts of their parents' behavior and personality attributes of parents and sons. Journal of Clinical Psychology, 1963, 19, 52-56.

Walsh,R.P. Parental rejecting attitudes and control in children.   Journal   of   Clinical   Psychology,   1968,   24, 185-186.

Wyer,R.S.Jr.   Effect   of   child-rearing   attitudes   and behavior   on   children's   responses   to   hypothetical social situations.   Journal of Personality   and   Social   Psychology, 1965, 2, 480-486.

Yater,A.   Oliver,K.   and   Barclay,A.   Factor   analysis study   of   PARI responses of mothers of head start children. Psychological Reports, 1968, 22, 383-388.

Zolik,E.S.   and   Welsand,E.   Changes   in   parental attitudes   as   a   function   of anxiety and authoritarianism. Journal of Social Psychology, 1963,60, 293-300.

Zuckerman,M.   Norton,J.A.Jr.   and   Sprague,D.S. Acquiescence   and   extreme   sets   and their role in tests of authoritarianism   and   parental   attitudes.   Psychiatric Research Reports, 1958, 10, 28-45.

Zuckerman,M.   Reversed scales to control   acquiescence response   set   in the Parental Attitude Research Instrument. Child Development, 1959, 30, 523-532.

Zuckerman,M.   Barrett,B.H.   and   Bragiel,R.M.   The parental   attitudes   of   parents   of   child   guidance cases. Child Development, 1960, 31, 401-417.

Zuckerman,M. Monashkin,I. and Oltean,M. Research on parental   attitudes,   I.   Mimeographed   report   of research activities.   Obtained from Dr.   M.   Zuckerman, Institute   of Psychiatric   Research,   Indiana   University   Medical Center, 1957.

Zuckerman,M.   and   Norton,J.A.Jr.   Response   set   and content   factors   in the California F Scale and the Parental Attitude Research Instrument.   Journal of Social Psychology, 1961, 53, 199-210.

Zuckerman,M.   and Oltean,M.   Some relationships between maternal   attitude factors and authoritarianism, personality needs,   psychopathology,   and   self-acceptance.   Child Development, 1959, 30, 27-36.

Zuckerman,M.   Oltean,M.   and Monashkin,I.   The parental attitudes   of   mothers   of   schizophrenics.   Journal   of Consulting Psychology, 1958, 22, 307-310.

Zuckerman,M.   Ribback,B.B.   Monashkin,I.   and Norton,J.A.Jr.   Normative   data   and factor analysis on the Parental   Attitude   Research   Instrument.   Journal   of Consulting Psychology, 1958, 22, 165-171.

Zuk,G.H.   Miller,R.L.   Bartram,J.B.   and   Kling,F. Maternal   acceptance   of retarded children: a questionnaire study   of   attitudes   and   religious   background.   Child Development, 1961, 32, 525-540.

Zunich,M. The relation between junior high school students'   problems   and   parental   attitude   toward   child rearing and family life. Journal of Educational Research, 1962a, 56, 134-138.

Zunich,M.   Relationship between maternal   behavior   and

attitudes toward children. Journal of Genetic Psychology,
1962b, 100, 155-165.
    Zunich,M.   The relation between parental attitudes
toward   child rearing and child behavior.   Journal of
Consulting Psychology, 1962c, 26, 197.
    Zunich,M. Attitudes of lower-class families.   Journal
of Social Psychology, 1964, 63, 367-371.
    Zunich,M.   Child behavior and parental attitudes.
Journal of Psychology, 1966, 62, 41-46.
    Zunich,M. Lower-class mothers' behavior and attitudes
toward child rearing.   Psychological Reports, 1971, 29,
1051-1058.

SZYRYNSKI,V.   Two Houses Technique (2HT)

VARIABLES MEASURED. Various aspects of "family dynamics"
such as parent versus child domination of the family, family
cohesiveness, child's insecurity within the family, and
amount of hostility in the family.
TEST DESCRIPTION. The child is invited to participate in a
"game" played by the examiner in the child's presence. The
technique consists of the examiner, with the child on
his/her lefthand side, drawing on a piece of paper of
standard size sketchy pictures of the members of the child's
family in the order given by the patient; then the two
houses are drawn and the child is asked to place all the
members of his/her family in one or the other house,
according to his/her free preference. After the family is
so divided it is suggested to the child to invite the
members placed in the other house from the one in which
he/she placed himself/herself, one after another to "his"
house. And finally, he/she is asked to send away those
people whom he/she placed primarily in his/her own house to
the opposite one. The results obtained are additionally
verified by some "built in" special technique and eventually
interpreted in the light of dynamic psychiatry with special
attention paid to the feelings of hostility, insecurity,
identification, rejection, withdrawal from social contact,
isolation, introjection, etc.
SAMPLE ITEM.   See above.
LENGTH.   NR.
AVAILABILITY.   From NAPS-2.
ABSTRACTED BY: Gwen Pearson
REFERENCES.
    Frank,I. The usefulness of the Two Houses Test in
general practice with reference to psychosomatic disorders
among adolescents. Presented before the Annual Meeting of
the Academy of Psychosomatic Medicine in New York, October
1964.
    Frank,I. Teenagers' psychosomatic disorders traced by
Two Houses Test. Hospital Topics, 1965a, 91-94.
    Frank,I. (Technique Report): Two Houses Technique
reveals family relationships. Frontiers of Psychiatry in
Clinical Medicine, 1965b, 2, 5-6.

Frank,I. A study of some differences in family relationship between achieving and under-achieving eighth-graders. Ed.D. Dissertation, Northern Illinois University, 1966.

Frank,I. and Powell,M. Psychosomatic Ailments in Childhood and Adolescence. Springfield, Illinois: Charles C Thomas, 1967.

Grygier,T. Some methods and techniques of planning in the social defence field. International Review of Criminal Policy, published by the United Nations Organization, 1967, 25, 61-66.

Grygier,T. et al. Social interaction in small units; new method of treatment and its evaluation. The Canadian Journal of Corrections, 1968, 10, 252-260.

Howells,J.G. Theory and Practice of Family Psychiatry. Edinburgh and London: Oliver and Boyd, 1968, 564, 585.

Lefebvre,R. Mode d'application de la technique des deux maisons (2ht). Universite de Toulouse-Le Mirail, 31076 Toulouse Cedex, France.

Lefebvre,R. La technique des deux maisons (2HT). Bulletin de la societe de Psychologie Midi-Pyrenees, Juillet 1973 Universite de Toulouse,-Le Mirail, 31076 Toulouse, Cedex, France.

Mutimer,D. Brief review of the Two Houses Technique. Child Psychiatry, Sandorama 1966, Basil, Switzerland.

Mutimer,D. Some differences in the family relationships of achieving and under-achieving readers. The Journal of Genetic Psychology, 1966, 109, 67-74.

Rydzynski,Z. and Stein,W. O Tescie Dwoch Domkow Szyrynskiego. Neurologia, Neurochirurgia i Psychiatria Polska, 1965,15, 933-936.

Rydzynski,Z. and Stein,W. Wstepne Radania Testem Dwoch Domkow. Neurologia, Neurochirurgia i Psychiatria Polska, 1966, 16, 125-129.

Semeonoff,B. Projective Techniques. England: John Wiley and Sons, 1976.

Sypniewska,J. Technika (Test) Dwoch Domkow W. Szyrynskiego (The Two Houses Technique--2HT). Zdrowie Psychiczne (Mental Health), 1973, 14, 101-121.

Szyrynski,V. Investigation of Family Dynamics with the Two Houses Technique. Psychosomatics, 1963a, 4, 68-72.

Szyrynski,V. A new technique to investigate family dynamics in child Psychiatry. Canadian Psychiatric Association Journal, 1963b, 8, 94-103.

Szyrynski,V. Pattern analysis of the Two Houses Technique in child psychiatry. II Congresso Europeo di Pedopsychiatria, Reports and Contributing Papers, 300, Roma, 1963c.

Szyrynski,V. Pattern analysis of the Two Houses Technique in Chile Psychiatry. Atti II Congresso Europeo de Pedopsichiatria, 1963d, 2, 1082-1093.

Szyrynski,V. The Two Houses Technique (2HT). Child Psychiatry. Grand Forks, North Dakota: University of North Dakota, 1964.

Szyrynski,V. A historical note on the 2HT. de

l'Universite d'Ottawa, 1966a, 36, 613-622.
    Szyrynski,V. The value of 2HT (The 2 Houses Technique)
in prognosis of psychiatric disorders in childhood and
adolescence. Proceedings of IVth World Congress of
Psychiatry, Madrid, Spain, September 1966b.
    Szyrynski,V. La technica delle due case. Panorama
Medico 1967, 1, 18-19.
    Szyrynski,V. A new technique for the exploration of
family dynamics in: Rorschach Proceedings, VIIth
International Congress of Rorschach and Other Projective
Techniques, London, August 1968, 951-959. Bern: Hans
Huber, 1970a.
    Szyrynski,V. Brief review of the Two Houses
Techniques. Skolepsykology, 1970b, 7, 113-120.
    Szyrynski,V. The international use of the 2HT in the
decade 1962-1972. Presented before The Athenian Institute
of Anthropos, Athens, Greece, June 1972.

        E. VALUES AND IDEOLOGY (See also Subject Index)

ADAMEK,R.J. and YOST,E.D. Conventionality Index

VARIABLE MEASURED. The conventionality of a person's
attitude toward the familial institution. This variable is
measured by ascertaining attitudes toward seven aspects of
the present familial institution: living in a commune,
group marriage, legal marriage vs. living together,
husband-wife roles, premarital sexual relations, abortion,
and homosexuality.
TEST DESCRIPTION. This index may be administered by
interview or questionnaire. It was developed as a secondary
analysis of items originally utilized by Aron (1969). The
"commune" and "group marriage" subvariables are each
measured by three items, while the other five subvariables
are each measured by one item. However, the index is
summated and scored so that each subvariable can
theoretically contribute the same score range (1-5) to the
total score.
SAMPLE ITEM. If you were planning a relationship with a
person of the opposite sex, including a commitment to have
children, would you envision a relationship: (a) with legal
ties (marriage), (b) without legal ties.
LENGTH. Time: 3 minutes. Items: 11.
AVAILABILITY. In Yost, 1972 and from NAPS-2.
ABSTRACTED BY: Raymond J. Adamek
REFERENCES.
    Aron,W.S. The culture and ideology of youth.
Mimeographed questionnaire, Community and Family Study
Center, The University of Chicago, 1969.
    Yost,E.D. Factors related to the conventionality of
students' attitudes toward the familial institution.

Master's Thesis, Kent State University, 1972.
    Yost,E.D. and Adamek,R.J.   Parent-child interaction
and   changing   family values: a   multivariate analysis.
Journal of Marriage and the Family, 1974, 36, 115-121.

CURCIONE,N.R. Family Religiosity Index

VARIABLE MEASURED.   Parents' involvement with the local
church.
TEST DESCRIPTION. A religiosity index was constructed from
items measuring the perceived frequency with which parents
attended church and received communion, the number of parish
organizations the   parents belonged to, and the frequency
with which their homes were visited by local clergy.   The
four items measuring the perceived frequency of parental
church attendance and reception of communion were assigned
ranks of 5 through 1 in order of decreasing involvement.
The number of parish organizations parents belonged to were
assigned ranks of 3 through 1, and the dichotomous responses
indicating whether or not clergy frequently visited the home
were ranked as 2 and 1, respectively.   High family
religiosity was defined as an index score of 17 or more;
low religiosity as a score of 16 or less.
SAMPLE ITEM. See above.
LENGTH. Items: 6.
AVAILABILITY. In Curcione, 1973.
REFERENCE.
    Curcione,N.R. Family influence on commitment to the
priesthood: a study of altar boys. Sociological Analysis,
1973, 34, 265-280.

INKELES,A. and MILLER,K.A. Comparative Family Modernism-1
Scale

VARIABLES MEASURED.   Modern versus traditional attitudes
toward various realms of family life.
TEST DESCRIPTION. The test is a result of an attempt to
build a scale of family modernism which consists of items
which are theoretically relevant, empirically coherent, and
strictly comparable across diverse cultures at different
levels of development. The comparative Family Modernism-1
Scale meets these criteria most successfully as compared to
similar family modernism scales reported in Inkeles and
Miller (1974).   The items in the scale measure opinions
toward family size limitation, autonomy from family elders,
the equal rights of women within the family and on the job,
and the family as a source of prestige in society. The mean
of these dichotomized items is obtained as the scale score.
SAMPLE ITEM. If a man must choose between a job which he
likes or a job which his parents prefer for him, which
should he choose? The job his parents prefer/The job he
prefers.

LENGTH. Items: 8.
AVAILABILITY. In Inkeles and Miller, 1974.
ABSTRACTED BY: Karen A. Miller
REFERENCE.
    Inkeles,A. and Miller,K.A.   Construction and
validation of a cross-national scale of family modernism.
International Journal of Sociology of the Family, 1974, 4.

MIDDENDORP,C.P.   BRINKMAN,W.   and   KOOMEN,W.   Family
Liberalism-Conservatism Attitude Index.

VARIABLE MEASURED. Approval of unconventional behavior with
respect to marriage and family norms.
TEST DESCRIPTION.   A six-item scale in which subject
indicates approval or disapproval of unconventional marriage
and family behavior.   Items were chosen from a 30-item
questionnaire in which response categories form trichotomies
(or dichotomies if less than 10% of the responses fell in
one category). Six items intercorrelated at the .001 level
and were included in the final measure. Scores vary from 0
to 12, with a high score indicating conservatism.
SAMPLE ITEM. Do you think it normal that parents of a
daughter who is 20 years of age tell her what time at night
she has to be home, or do you think it is better when they
leave this to their daughter?   Leave it to daughter or
discuss it with daughter. Parents must determine the time.
LENGTH. Items: 6.
AVAILABILITY. In Middendorp, et al., 1970.
REFERENCES.
    Middendorp,C.P.   Brinkman,W.   and   Koomen,W.
Determinants of premarital sexual permissiveness: a
secondary analysis. Journal of Marriage and the Family,
1970, 32, 369-379.
    Reiss,I.L. The Social Context of Premarital Sexual
Permissiveness.   New York: Holt,   Rinehart and Winston,
1967.

RAMIREZ,M.III. Mexican-American Family Attitude Scale

VARIABLE MEASURED. Traditional Mexican-American attitudes
and family values.
TEST DESCRIPTION. The scale consists of items designed to
differentiate between traditional Mexican-Americans and
non-Mexican-Americans. The pool of items from which the
final set was selected was drawn from a scale of Mexican
family values developed by Diaz-Guerrero (1955), the
Traditional Family Ideology Scale (Levinson and Huffman,
1962) and items developed by the author. The items include
factors of traditional Mexican-American family values and
attitudes such as separation of sex roles, strictness of
child rearing, importance of extended family, father's
authority, and self-abnegation of the mother.

SAMPLE ITEM. It helps a child in the long run if he is made
to conform to his parents' ideas. I agree very much; I
agree on the whole; I agree a little; I disagree a little;
I disagree on the whole; I disagree very much.
LENGTH. Time: 15-20 minutes. Items: 29.
AVAILABILITY. From NAPS-2.
ABSTRACTED BY. Manuel Ramirez, III.
REFERENCES.
      Kaplan,R.M. and Goldman,R.D Interracial perception
among black, white, and Mexican-American high school
students. Journal of Personality and Social Psychology,
1973, 28, 383-389.
      Ramirez,M.III.   Identification with Mexican-American
values and psychological adjustment in Mexican-American
adolescents. International Journal of Social Psychiatry,
1961, 15, 151-156.
      Ramirez,M.III.   Identification with Mexican   family
values and authoritarianism in Mexican-Americans. Journal
of Social Psychology, 1967, 73, 3-11.
      Ramirez,M.III.   Potential contributions by   the
behavioral sciences to effective preparation programs for
teachers of Mexican-American children.   New Mexico State
University, Las Cruces: Clearing House for Rural Education
and Small Schools, 1969.

                            F. Other

BOSSARD,J.H. Spatial Index for Family Interaction

VARIABLE MEASURED. Relation between spatial setting and the
number in the family.
TEST DESCRIPTION. A formula for computing a quantitative
expression of the above variable. The formula is based on
the theory that as the number of persons in the family
increases, "the number of personal interrelationships within
the group increases in order of triangular numbers." The
formula for this increase is: $X = (Y2 - Y)/2$, where X = the
number of personal interrelationships and Y = the number of
persons, and $Y2$ is Y squared. The index is computed by
dividing the number of square feet in the family home by the
number of interactions computed from the above formula.
SAMPLE ITEM. See above.
LENGTH. NR.
AVAILABILITY. In Bossard, 1951.
REFERENCES.
      Beaglehold,E. A critique of "the measurement of family
interaction." American Journal of Sociology, 1945, 51, 145,
147.
      Bossard,J.H. The law of family interaction.   American
Journal of Sociology, 1945, 50, 292-294.
      Bossard,J.H. A spatial index for family interaction.

American Sociological Review, 1951, 16, 243-246.

ELBERT,S.   ROSMAN,B.S.   MINUCHIN,S.M.   and   GUERNEY,B.G.Jr.
The Family Task

VARIABLE MEASURED. Family interaction.
TEST DESCRIPTION. A series of six questions presented for
family discussion.   The questions are prerecorded, and the
family, seated in an interview room furnished like a living
room, operate the tape recorder to hear each question. The
family's discussion is tape-recorded. An observer dictates
a continuous report on nonverbal behavior seen through a
one-way mirror. Three of the questions require the family
to agree on a group answer: planning a menu, spending $10,
and assigning labels to specific family members ("bossiest,"
"biggest cry-baby," etc.). A fourth question asks each to
describe likes and dislikes concerning all the other family
members.   A fifth task is to describe a family fight. The
sixth requires the family to copy a constructed wooden
model. The test was constructed as an aid in family therapy
and was designed to complement the Family Interaction
Apperception Test.   The authors note that they are
developing quantitative methods of analysis for the
objective testing of clinical hypotheses.
SAMPLE ITEM. See test description.
LENGTH. Items: 6 tasks.
AVAILABILITY. Tasks are almost fully described above;
information on interpretation is given in Elbert et al.,
1964; otherwise frcm authors.
REFERENCE.
        Elbert,S.   Rosman,B.S.   Minuchin,S.M.   and
Guerney,B.G.Jr.   A method for the clinical study of family
interaction. American Journal of Orthopsychiatry, 1964, 34,
885-894.

FERGUSON,L.W. Family Life Cycle Index

VARIABLE MEASURED. A quantitative score that indicates an
individual's position in the family life cycle.
TEST DESCRIPTION. The index combines age, marital status,
and   number   of dependents into a single score.   The
population for
which index scores are to be computed is divided into
married and single persons.   Within each marital status
group, each person's age and number of dependents is
transformed to "Stanine" scores. The two Stanine scores are
added to obtain the index.
SAMPLE ITEM. NA.
LENGTH. Items: 3.
AVAILABILITY. In Ferguson, 1967.
REFERENCE.
        Ferguson,L.W.   Quantifying the family life   cycle.
Psychological Record, 1967, 17, 219-227.

GIBSON,G. and LUDWIG,E.G. Family Composition Taxonomy

VARIABLE MEASURED. Family composition, based on marital
status, "children-ness," and the presence and relationship
of other household members.
TEST DESCRIPTION. A typology of family composition based on
all the possible ccmbinations of categories within the three
dimensions above. Marital status contains four categories:
(1) No spouse (single persons), (2) Spouse present (married
persons), (3) Common law unions, and (4) Spouse missing
(widowed, divorced, and separated persons); the last
category may be differentiated into three categories if
necessary. "Children-ness" contains five categories: (1)
No children, (2) Dependent children in the household, (3)
Both dependent and adult children in the household, (4)
Adult children only in the home, (5) Children have left the
household. The presence and relationship of other members
of the household includes four categories: (1) No other
members, (2) Lateral relatives, (3) Generational relatives
(other than direct off-spring), and (4) Non-relatives. The
member of the family used as the referent may be varied.
Eighty possible types of family composition may be generated
within the typology. The 20 types found useful in this
study are indicated in table 1 of Gibson and Ludwig, 1968.
SAMPLE ITEMS. Nuclear Family Type 1: Husband, wife, and
minor children. Nuclear Family Type II: Husband, wife,
minor, and adult children.
LENGTH. NR.
AVAILABILITY. In Gibson and Ludwig, 1968.
REFERENCE.
      Gibson,G. and Ludwig,E.G.   Family structure in a
disabled population. Journal of Marriage and the Family
1968, 30, 54-63.

HALEY,J. Family Interaction Patterns

VARIABLE MEASURED. "Organization" or patterning in family
interaction patterns.
TEST DESCRIPTION. Family triads are observed during
discussion of a family-decision on items of a questionnaire
and during the telling of a story based upon TAT cards.
Each member has a microphone connected to a machine (the
Family Interaction Analyzer, specially built by the Alto
Scientific Co., Palo Alto, California) which tallies
discussion sequences--FC, FM, MC, MF, CM, or CF. Each
sequence is assumed to have a probability of 1/6 if
interaction were random. The deviations from the zero point
of 16.66 are summed (ignoring sign) to give the R-deviation
index for the family. The extent to which the distribution
is skewed provides a measure of "organization" or patterning
in the family's interaction sequences (i.e., nonrandomness).
Less normal families are assumed to have more skewed
distributions owing to more rigid interaction patterns.

SMPLE ITEM. For questionnaire, NR. TAT items are used.
LENGTH. NR.
AVAILABILITY. Frcm Haley, 1964.
REFERENCE.
    Haley,J. Research on family patterns: an instrument
measurement. Family Process, 1964, 3, 41-65.

KAGAN,J. and MOSS,H.A.   Passive and Dependent Behavior
Rating Scales

VARIABLES MEASURED. Six adult behavior variables, two of
which deal directly with intrafamily behavior: (1) Degree
of dependent behavior toward a love object and (2) Degree of
dependent behavior with parents. Four childhood variables,
three of which deal with the subject's dependent behavior
toward his mother and/or other female adults: (1) General
dependence (age 3-6), (2) Emotional dependence (age 6-10),
(3) Instrumental dependence (age 6-10).
TEST DESCRIPTION.   Seven-point rating scales which the
authors apply tc interview data in the case of adults; and
to mother-interview, child-interview, and child-observation
data in the case cf children. Shortened definitions of the
variables are given in the article.
SAMPLE ITEM. NR.
LENGTH. Items: Six adult and four childhood rating scales.
AVAILABILITY. Frcm Kagan and Moss.
REFERENCE.
    Kagan,J. and Moss,H.A. The stability of passive and
dependent behavicr from childhood through adulthood. Child
Development, 1960, 31, 577-591.

KLAPP,O.E. Family Ritual Index

VARIABLE MEASURED. Ritual behavior, defined as "symbolic
behavior that develops in groups and is repeated 'for its
own sake' because of the meaning and satisfaction that
participants get out of it."
TEST DESCRIPTION. A list of rituals practiced in some
families, for which the subject indicates whether the ritual
occurs in his/her family and how important it is to his/her
family.
SAMPLE ITEM. Christmas dinner together. Much importance =
3; Some importance = 2; Little importance = 1; No
importance, undecided = 0.
LENGTH. Items: 26.
AVAILABILITY. In Klapp, 1959.
REFERENCE.
    Klapp,O.E.   Ritual and family solidarity.   Social
Forces, 1959, 37, 212-214.

LOVELAND,N.T.   WYNNE,L.C.   SINGER,M.T.   LEVY,J.   and
EPSTEIN,N.B. The Family Rorschach

VARIABLE MEASURED. Family interaction.
TEST DESCRIPTION. The Rorschach cards are used to elicit a
sample of family interaction, which may be scored by a
variety of techniques (unspecified).   Two approaches have
been used by Loveland et al.: In the first procedure, the
Rorschach is first administered in the traditional
individual fashion.   After this, all members of the family
are brought together into an observation room.   The family
is told by the E to discuss the Rorschach cards jointly and
determine how many resemblances they can find in each card
upon which they all agree. The E hands each member of the
family Card I and leaves the room.   The family is given five
minutes per card. After they signal that they are finished
with a card, the E returns and has them write down,
individually, each item they agree upon.   After all 10 cards
have been completed, the E returns with a Rorschach location
chart and has each independently locate the areas where
he/she felt agreement had been reached.   Clarification of
any ambiguities also takes place at this time.   The
discussions are observed and recorded from the observation
booth.
     In the second procedure, all family members come to the
examining room and are told about the test.   Then each is
escorted to a separate room where he/she writes down
responses to the test.   After all members have completed
their solo Rorschachs, they are gathered together again and
the Family Rorschach is administered as above.   The only
added feature is that after all individuals have completed
the Family Rorschach location chart, their solo Rorschach
responses are returned to them, and they locate (with a
different colored pencil) all their responses included on
the Family Rorschach.
     In the Levy and Epstein (1964) procedure, the
individual Rorschachs are completed separately by the family
members a week or more before the Family Rorschach.   Levy
and Epstein's application of the Family Rorschach is similar
to Loveland's except that the E remains in the room with the
family.
SAMPLE ITEM. Rorschach cards.
LENGTH. Time: for the Family Rorschach, 1-2 hours; for
the solo Rorschach, 1/2 to 3/4 hour.
AVAILABILITY. See Loveland et al., 1963.
REFERENCES.
     Levy,J. and Epstein,N.B.   An application of the
Rorschach test in family investigation. Family Process,
1964, 3, 344-376.
     Loveland,N.T. Wynne,L.C. and Singer,M.T. The Family
Rorschach: a new method for studying family interaction.
Family Process, 1963, 2, 187-215.
     Murstein,B.I. A thematic test and the Rorschach in
predicting marital choice.   Journal of Personality
Assessment, 36, 1972a, 213-217.

Murstein,B.I.   Interview   behavior,   projective
techniques, and questionnaires in the clinical assessment of
marital choice. Journal of Personality Assessment, 1972b,
36, 462-467.
     Odman,L. Seeman,J. and Newburgh,J.R. A study of
family communication patterns and personality integration in
children. Child Psychiatry and Human Development, 1971, 1,
275-285.
     Rorschach,H. Psychodiagnostic Plates. Berne: Huber,
1937. (Available from Psychological Corp. 304 E. 45th St.
New York, N.Y. 10017.)
     Willi,J.   Joint   Rorschach   testing   of   partner
relationships. Family Process, 1969, 8, 64-78.

NIEMI,R.   Bias in Perception of Family Relations Measure

VARIABLE MEASURED. Degree to which one member of a family
accurately   reports   the   activities and opinions of another
member..
TEST DESCRIPTION.   Children and parents are interviewed
separately, but asked the same questions with only the
references changed. Responses are generally made on a
three-point scale, ranging from 3 for Very close, to a 1 for
Not very close, but in some questions the score assignments,
while maintaining a three-point scale, are different.
SAMPLE ITEM. Do you usally watch/listen (radio, TV, etc.)
with other members of your family, or mostly by yourself?
LENGTH. Items: 10.
AVAILABILITY. In Niemi, 1974.
ABSTRACTED BY: Thomas G. Sparhawk
REFERENCE.
     Niemi,R. How Family Members Perceive Each Other.   New
Haven: Yale University Press, 1974.

PODELL,L. Familial-Occupational Exclusion-Inclusion Scale

VARIABLE MEASURED. Attitude concerning the direct inclusion
of family in occupational life.
TEST DESCRIPTION. A four-item Guttman scale.
SAMPLE ITEM. Top men in almost every field have wives who
made important contacts for them. Agree or Disagree.
LENGTH. Items: 4.
AVAILABILITY. In Podell, 1966.
REFERENCES.
     Podell,L. Sex and role conflict. Journal of Marriage
and the Family, 1966, 28, 163-165.
     Podell,L. Occupational and familial role-expectations.
Journal of Marriage and the Family, 1967, 29, 492-493.

SIGAL,J.J.   RAKOFF,V. and EPSTEIN,N.B.   Family Interaction
Score

VARIABLE MEASURED. Family's participation in therapeutic
work as described by therapist.
TEST DESCRIPTION. Therapists are asked to respond to the
following   statement: The family cooperates with the
therapist. Describe briefly the patterns of collaboration.
Each report of a person's interaction with any cther person,
including the therapist, is coded on a scale that ranges
from Resistant family unit = 0 to Active engagement = 5.
The family interaction score is obtained by taking the sum
of the individual interaction scores, dividing by N squared
(where N equals the number of people in the therapy session)
and multiplying by 10. Rank order Rho's of .449 (N = 18),
.906 (N = 15), .827 (N = 12), .863 (N = 8) and .980 (N = 6)
were obtained between the authors' scores and those of an
independent judge for therapist's report on a numbers of
families (the numbers of families rated are given in
parentheses after the correlations) at five different points
in the course of therapy.
SAMPLE ITEM. See above.
LENGTH. NA.
AVAILABILITY. In Sigal et al., 1967.
ABSTRACTED BY: John J. Sigal
REFERENCES.
      Guttman,H.A.   Spector,R.M.   Sigal,J.J.   Epstein,N.B.
and Rakoff,V. Coding of affective expression in family
therapy. American Journal of Psychotherapy, 1972, 26,
185-194.
      Guttman,H.A.   Spector,R.M.   Sigal,J.J.   Rakoff,V.   and
Epstein,N.B.   Reliability of coding affective communication
in family therapy sessions: problems of measurement and
interpretation.   Journal of Consulting and Clinical
Psychology, 1971, 37, 397-402.
      Sigal,J.J. Rakoff,V. and Epstein,N.B. Indicators of
therapeutic outcome in conjoint family therapy. Family
Process, 1967, 6, 215-226.

Chapter V

Sex and Premarital Relationships

A. Sex and Sex Education (See also Subject Index)

BARDIS,P.D. Coitometer

VARIABLE MEASURED. Knowledge of the physical aspects of
human coitus.
TEST DESCRIPTION. Fifty items selected from many more
initial statements and dealing with various anatomical and
physiological aspects of human heterosexual coitus. Since a
correct answer to each of the 50 true-false items represents
two points, the theoretical range of scores on the entire
Coitometer is 0-100.
SAMPLE ITEM. In humans, each act of coitus usually lasts
for a much shorter time than among other mammals.
LENGTH. Items: Fifty. Time: 15 minutes.
AVAILABILITY. In Bardis, 1975; from Panos D. Bardis,
University of Toledo, Toledo, Ohio; or from NAPS-2.
ABSTRACTED BY: Panos D. Bardis.
REFERENCE.
　　　Bardis,P.D. The Coitometer, 1975.

BARDIS,P.D.   Sexometer

VARIABLE MEASURED. Knowledge of physical aspects of sex.
TEST DESCRIPTION. Fifty questions, selected from an initial
500, of which questions 1-10 are on male anatomy and
physiology; 11-20 on female anatomy and physiology; 21-30
on sex diseases; 31-40 on reproduction and birth control;
and 41-50 on sex behavior. Since each correct answer gives
the respondent two points, the theoretical range of scores
is 0-100.
SAMPLE ITEM. Why is the scrotum outside the body cavity?
LENGTH. Items: 50. Time: 15 minutes.
AVAILABILITY. In Bardis, 1973 and 1974; copies of two
forms from Panos D. Bardis, University of Toledo, Toledo,
Ohio; or from NAPS-2.
ABSTRACTED BY: Panos D. Bardis
REFERENCES.
       Bardis,P.D. The Sexometer: a research note.   Journal
of Marriage and the Family, 1973, 35, 70.
       Bardis,P.D. Physical and nonphysical aspects of sex.
The Family Life Educator, 1974a, 6, 2-8.
       Bardis,P.D.   Research instrument for population
studies. Society and Culture, 1974b, 5, 177-191.

CHRISTENSEN,H.T. and CARPENTER,G.R. Sexual Permissiveness
Scale

VARIABLE MEASURED. Permissiveness toward premarital sexual
intimacy.
TEST DESCRIPTION. A Guttman scale in which the S checks
each item with which he/she agrees. The score consists of
the number of items checked.
SAMPLE ITEM. I would prefer marrying a non-virgin.
LENGTH. Items: 10.
AVAILABILITY. In Christensen and Carpenter, 1962; Shaw and
Wright, 1967.
REFERENCES.
       Christensen,H.T.   and Carpenter,G.R.   Value-behavior
discrepancies regarding premarital coitus in three western
cultures. American Sociological Review, 1962, 27, 66-74.
       Hampe,G.D.   and Ruppel,H.J.Jr.   The measurement of
premarital sexual permissiveness: a comparison of two
Guttman scales. Journal of Marriage and the Family, 1974,
36, 451-463.
       Shaw,M.E. and Wright,J.M. Scales For the Measurement
of Attitudes. New York: McGraw-Hill, 1967, 103-104.

DeLAMATER,J. Current Sexual Behavior

VARIABLES MEASURED. Whether or not the person has engaged
in each of nine sexual behaviors with his/her current
partner; a summary measure can be obtained by creating a
Guttman scale using the Cornell Ranking Technique.

TEST DESCRIPTION. The sequence of questions begins by asking whether the respondent has dated ("gone out with") a male/female in the past year. If so, she/he is asked how many times they have been together. She/he is then asked whether they have engaged in each of nine behaviors: necking--kissing and hugging: french or deep kissing; breast fondling; male fondling female genitals; female fondling male genitals; genital apposition (genital contact without penetration); intercourse; male oral contact with female genitals; and female oral contact with male genitals.

Guttman scaling techniques applied to the responses of 1642 single young people yielded a scale which ordered the behaviors as listed above. The coefficients of reproducibility were .97 and the minimum marginal reproducibilities were .64 to .66. Additional data on the reliability of the scale within the interview is included in DeLamater and MacCorquodale (1975).

SAMPLE ITEM. Have you and your partner ever engaged in heterosexual intercouse?

LENGTH. Time: 2 minutes. Items: 9.

AVAILABILITY. From NAPS.

ABSTRACTED BY: John DeLamater

REFERENCES.

DeLamater,J. Methodological issues in the study of premarital sexuality. Sociological Methods and Research, 1974, 3, 30-61. (Includes an earlier version of the scale and rationale)

DeLamater,J. and MacCorquodale,P. The effects of interview schedule variations on reported sexual behavior. Sociological Methods and Research, 1975a, 4, 215-236.

DeLamater,J. and MacCorquodale,P. Premarital sexuality: ideology, interaction and behavior. Unpublished manuscript, 1975b.

Johnson,W.B. and DeLamater,J. Response effects in sex surveys. Public Opinion Quarterly, 1976, 40, 165-181.

DeLAMATER,J. Lifetime Sexual Behavior Scale

VARIABLES MEASURED. Whether or not the person has ever engaged in each of nine sexual behaviors; a summary measure can be obtained by creating a Guttman Scale, using the Cornell Ranking Technique.

TEST DESCRIPTION. Separate questions inquire about participation in nine behaviors: necking--kissing and hugging; french or deep kissing; breast fondling; male fondling female genitals; female fondling male genitals; genital apposition (genital contact without penetration); intercourse; male oral contact with female genitals; and female oral contact with male genitals. In addition to Yes/No responses, the question format provides data on the age of first experience with each behavior.

Guttman scaling techniques applied to the responses of 1642 single young people yielded a scale which ordered the

behaviors as listed above. The coefficients of reproducibility were .98 and the minimum marginal reproducibilities were .77 to .84. Additional data on the scale and on reliability within the interview are included in DeLamater and MacCorquodale (1975).
SAMPLE ITEM. How old were you when you first engaged in heterosexual intercourse?
LENGTH. Time: 2 to 3 minutes. Items: 9.
ABSTRACTED BY: John DeLamater
REFERENCES.
   DeLamater,J. Methodological issues in the study of premarital sexuality. Sociological Methods and Research, 1974, 3, 30-61. (Includes an earlier version of the scale and rationale.)
   DeLamater,J. and MacCorquodale,P. The effects of interview schedule variations on reported sexual behavior. Sociological Methods and Research, 1975a, 4, 215-236.
   DeLamater,J. and MacCorquodale,P. Premarital sexuality: ideology, interaction, and behavior. Unpublished manuscript, 1975b.
   Johnson,W.B. and DeLamater,J. Response effects in sex surveys. Public Opinion Quarterly, 1976, 40, 165-181.

DeLAMATER,J. Premarital Sexual Ideology Scale

VARIABLES MEASURED. The extent to which three heterosexual behaviors are acceptable before marriage. Combining responses to the items via Guttman scaling techniques produces a summary scale comparable to Reiss's measure of Premarital Sexual Permissiveness.
TEST DESCRIPTION. The respondent is handed an index card which lists five categories of heterosexual relationships: Not before marriage; If engaged; If in love but not engaged; If feel affection but no love; and If both want it. She/he is then asked when in a relationship she/he feels that each of three behaviors is acceptable: breast fondling, genital fondling, and intercourse. She/he is instructed to answer in terms of one of the categories on the card. The set of three questions is asked twice, first in terms of the acceptability of each behavior for males, and second in terms of acceptability for females.
   Using data from 1642 single young people, Guttman scales were constructed via the Cornell Ranking Technique; employing responses to the three items for a given sex, a score was assigned based on the person's most "permissive" response (see DeLamater, 1974, for format). This yields two scores for each respondent, his/her ideology for males and for females. The resulting scales had coefficients of reproducibility of .90 to .93, and minimum marginal reproducibilities of .37 to .51.
   The referent of the item may be easily varied. Thus, the respondent can be asked about his/her current partner's, best friend's (friends'), and mother's and father's attitudes regarding these behaviors. (See DeLamater and

MacCorquodale, 1975.)
SAMPLE ITEM. At what point in a relationship do you feel
that genital fondling is acceptable for males?
LENGTH. Time: 1-2 minutes. Items: 6.
AVAILABILITY. From NAPS.
ABSTRACTED BY: John DeLamater
REFERENCES.
     DeLamater,J. Methodological issues in the study of
premarital sexuality. Sociological Methods and Research,
1974, 3, 30-61. (Includes the rationale and pretest data on
scale characteristics.)
     DeLamater,J. and MacCorquodale,P. The effects of
interview schedule variations on reported sexual behavior.
Sociological Methods and Research, 1975, 4, 215-236.
     DeLamater,J. and MacCorquodale,P. Premarital
sexuality: ideolcgy, interaction and behavior. Unpublished
manscript, 1975.
     Johnson,W.B. and DeLamater,J. Response effects in sex
surveys. Public Opinion Quarterly, 1976, 40, 165-181.

DRUCKER,A.J.   CHRISTENSEN,H.T.   and   REMMERS,H.H.
Sociosexual Modernism Scale

VARIABLE MEASURED. Degree of modernism in sociosexual
opinions.
TEST DESCRIPTION. A set of nine questions on various
aspects of sex and premarital behavior, answered Yes, No, or
Undecided.
SAMPLE ITEM. Do you believe that it would be a good thing
if girls could be as free as boys in asking for dates? Yes,
No, Undecided.
LENGTH. Items: 9.
AVAILABILITY. In Drucker et al., 1952.
REFERENCE.
     Drucker,A.J. Christensen,H.T. and Remmers,H.H. Some
background factors in sociosexual modernism. Marriage and
Family Living, 1952, 14, 334-337.

KILPATRICK,D.G. and SMITH,A.D. Sexual Attitude and
Behavior Survey (SABS)

VARIABLES MEASURED. Liberality of sexual attitudes and
behavior: (1) Male behavior, (2) Male fantasy, (3) Female
behavior, (4) Female fantasy, (5) Personal behavior, (6)
Personal fantasy, (7) Actual behavior score.
TEST DESCRIPTION. It consists of an Attitude Section and a
Behavior Section. In the Attitude Section, subjects are
asked to indicate under which circumstances a series of
sexual activities are permissible. The activities include
kissing, petting, heavy petting, sexual intercourse, anal
intercourse, oral-genital relations, group sexual
activities, and hcmosexual activity. Each subject is also
asked to select the circumstances under which it is

permissible to think about indulging in the above mentioned
activities. Each thought and activity item is responded to
in three ways: (1) permissible for males, (2) permissible
for females, and (3) permissible personally.
     On the basis of these responses, six attitude scores
are constructed: (1) Male behavior score (MBS), (2) Male
fantasy score (MFS) (2), Male fantasy score (MFS), (3)
Female behavior score (FBS), (4) Female fantasy score (FFS),
(5) Personal behavior score (PBS), and (6) Personal fantasy
score (PFS). Scores on each scale may range from 0 to 23
with a high score reflecting more permissive attitudes. In
the Behavior Section of the SABS, subjects are asked to
indicate the frequency with which they have: (1) Thought
about indulging in each sexual activity, and (2) Actually
indulged in the activity.
     A Double Standard score can be derived by subtracting
the Female Behavior Score from the Male Behavior Score.
     Twenty-one demographic items request pertinent data on
age, birth order, first sexual intercourse, dating
frequency, marital status, sex education, parents' education
and occupation.
SAMPLE ITEM. Kissing a woman is permissible: (a) Only if
partners are married, (b) Only if there is strong affection
between partners, (c) If the only emotional relationship
between partners is sexual attraction, (d) Never.
LENGTH. Time: 20 minutes. Items: 93 and 21 demographic
questions.
AVAILABILITY. From Dean G. Kilpatrick, Psychology
Services, VA Hospital, Bee Street, Charleston, S.C. 19402
or from NAPS-2.
ABSTRACTED BY: Alma Dell Smith
REFERENCES.
     Best,C.G. and Kilpatrick,D.G. Psychological profiles
of rape crisis counselors. Presented in a symposium
entitled, Perspectives of Rape. Southeastern Psychological
Association, New Orleans, Louisiana, March 1976.
     Marcotte,D.B. Geyer,P.R. Kilpatrick,D.G. and
Smith,A.D. The effect of a spaced sex education course on
medical students' sexual knowledge and attitudes. British
Journal of Medical Education, 1976, 10, 117-121.
     Smith,A.D. Kilpatrick,D.G. Sutker,P.B. and
Marcotte,D.B. Male student professionals: their attitudes
towards women, sex, and change. Psychological Reports,
1976, 39, 143-148.

LIBBY,R.W. Sex Education Content Scale (SECS)

VARIABLES MEASURED. Attitudes toward topics covered in high
school sex education.
TEST DESCRIPTION. The items refer to specific topics such
as venereal diseases, homosexuality, masturbation,
contraception, male and female sex roles, premarital sexual
intercourse, pornography and erotic literature, teenage
sexual slang, sexual deviations and perversions,

oral-genital sexual contacts, and sexual techniques, etc.
SAMPLE ITEM. Note the degree of your agreement or
disagreement as to whether each of the following should be
discussed in a high school sex education program if brought
up in any way by teacher or students: Menopause. Strongly
agree to Strongly disagree on a five-point Likert scale.
LENGTH. Time: 6-7 minutes. Items: 22.
AVAILABILITY. In Libby, 1971, and from NAPS-2.
ABSTRACTED BY: Roger W. Libby
REFERENCE.
    Libby,R.W. Parental attitudes toward content in high
school sex education programs: liberalism-traditionalism
and demographic correlates. Family Coordinator, 1971, 20,
127-136.

LIBBY,R.W. Sex Education Liberalism Scale (SELS)

VARIABLE MEASURED. Attitudinal liberalism toward high
school sex education.
TEST DESCRIPTION. The items deal with the relative roles of
the high school, home (parents) in sex education, and the
degree of moralizing considered appropriate in sex education
instruction. The sexual values desired in a sex education
program are included in the items, along with the degree of
parental control over sex education desired in high schools.
Reverse scoring is used so that "liberal" responses are
scored high and "conservative" responses low using the
Likert method. The original scale was composed of eight
items, but the final scale is a nine-item scale.
SAMPLE ITEM. The public high schools should assume more
responsibility for sex instruction. Strongly agree to
Strongly disagree (five-point scale).
LENGTH. Time: 4-5 minutes. Items: 9.
AVAILABILITY. In Libby, 1970 and from NAPS-2.
ABSTRACTED BY: Roger W. Libby
REFERENCES.
    Humphrey,F. Libby,R.W. and Nass,G. Attitude change
among professionals toward sex education for adolescents.
Family Coordinator, 1969.
    Libby,R.W. Parental attitudes toward high school sex
education programs: liberalism-traditionalism and
demographic correlates. Family Coordinator, 1971, 20,
127-136.

LIEF,H.I. and REED,D. Sex Knowledge and Attitude Test
(SKAT)

VARIABLES MEASURED. (1) Sexual attitudes. (a)
Masturbation, (b) Heterosexual Relations, (c) Sexual myths,
(d) Abortion. (2) Sexual Knowledge
TEST DESCRIPTION. The Attitude section of the SKAT consists
of 35 questions to which subjects respond on a five-point
scale (Strongly agree = A, Agree = B, Uncertain = C,

Disagree = D, Strongly disagree = E.) Each attitude item belongs to one of the four attitude subscales. Items are scored 1 to 5 according to which alternative (A to E) is given with higher numbers being given to endorsement of more liberal attitudes. For example, strongly agreeing (A) with a liberal sexual attitude statement is scored 5, and strongly disagreeing (E) with a conservative sexual attitude statement is also scored 5. A total raw score for each attitude subscale is obtained by summing the scores of each item in the subscale. Conversion tables allow for converting raw scores to T-scores with a mean of 50 and a standard deviation of 10 (U.S. medical students were used as the standardization sample). The Knowledge section of the SKAT consists of 71 True-False questions. Items are either "Test" items or "Lecture" items. Responses to the Test items are scored 1 if correct and 0 if incorrect, and the total raw Knowledge score is the sum of these item scores. Again, raw scores can be converted to T-scores with a mean of 50 and a standard deviation of 10. Lecture items are not scored. These are included to serve as the focal point for a lecture or group discussion. The SKAT also includes 12 questions about demographic information and 27 items dealing with personal sexual experience. The demographic and sexual experience items are not scored.
SAMPLE ITEM: (ATTITUDE) The spread of sex education is causing a rise in premarital intercourse: A. Strongly agree, B. Agree, C. Uncertain, D. Disagree, E. Strongly disagree. (KNOWLEDGE) Pregnancy can occur during natural menopause (gradual cessation of menstruation): True, False.
LENGTH. Items: 145.
AVAILABILITY. Center for the Study of Sex Education in Medicine, 4025 Chestnut Street (Second Floor) Philadelphia, Pa. 19104
ABSTRACTED BY: William R. Miller, Ph.D.
REFERENCES.
  Lief,H.I. Sexual knowledge, attitudes and behavior of medical students: Implications for medical practice. In Abse,D.W. Nash,E.M. and Louden,L.M.R. (Eds.) Marital and Sexual Counseling in Medical Practice. Hagerstown, Maryland: Harper and Row, 1974.
  Lief,H.I. and Payne,T. Sexuality -- knowledge and attitudes. American Journal of Nursing, 1975, 75, 2026-2029.
  Miller,W.R. and Lief,H.I. Masturbatory attitudes, knowledge, and experience: data from the Sex Knowledge and Attitude Test (SKAT). Archives of Sexual Behavior, 1976, 5, 447-467.

McHUGH,G. Sex Knowledge Inventory

VARIABLE MEASURED. Knowledge of sexual anatomy, sex technique, and contraception.

TEST DESCRIPTION. There are two forms. Form X consists of 80 multiple-choice questions. Form Y, emphasizing vocabulary and anatomy, consists of three parts: part 1 requires correctly naming the male and female genital organs shown in a diagram; part 2 requires identifying the functions of each organ; part 3 consists of 40 terms to be matched with definitions.
SAMPLE ITEM. (Form X:) What is the relation between sex attraction and love? Sex satisfies a physical need only; Love always plays a part in sex attraction; Sex attraction is more important than love; Sex attraction is a normal part of love; Sex attraction ends when there is no more love.
LENGTH. Items: Form X, 80; Form Y, 92.
AVAILABILITY. From Family Life Publications, Inc., Box 6725, College Station, Durham, N.C. 27708.
REFERENCES.
    Abramowitz,N.R. Human sexuality in the social work curriculum. The Family Coordinator, 1971, 20, 349-354.
    Bardis,P.D. Influence of family life education on sex knowledge. Marriage and Family Living, 1963, 25, 85-88.
    McHugh,G. Sex Knowledge Inventory, Forms X and Y. Durham, N.C.: Family Life Publications, 1952. Revised edition of Form X, 1967.
    McHugh,G. Marriage Counselors' Manual for the Sex Knowledge Inventory Form X. Durham, N.C.: Family Life Publications, 1967.
    Parmer,C.H. The relations between scores on the McHugh Inventory and self-rating marital satisfaction, Ph.D. dissertation, Pennsylvania State University, 1953.

MIDDENDORP,C.P. BRINKMAN,W. and KOOMEN,W. Premarital Sexual Permissiveness

VARIABLE MEASURED. Extent to which respondents agree with premarital sexual permissiveness.
TEST DESCRIPTION. The test is composed of three items and scored as follows: (1) A girl should remain a virgin until marriage. (Response categories: Don't agree at all; Don't really agree: Mainly agree; Agree completely), (2) Do you think that sexual intercourse between people willing to marry each other is in every way inadmissible? Do you object but do you think it understandable under certain circumstances, or do you have no fundamental objections? (Response categories: No fundamental objections; Objections, but under certain circumstances understandable; In every way inadmissible), (3) Do you have any objections against a boy and a girl having holidays together? (Response categories: No; It depends; Yes). The scores vary from 0 to 6. The higher the score the more the respondent disagrees with premarital sex.
SAMPLE ITEM. A girl should remain a virgin until marriage.

LENGTH. Items: 3.
AVAILABILITY. In Middendorp, et al., 1970.
ABSTRACTED BY: Bruce Brown
REFERENCE.
      Middendorp,C.P.   Brinkman,W.   and   Koomen,W.
Determinants of premarital sexual permissiveness: a
secondary analysis. Journal of Marriage and the Family,
1970, 32, 369-379.

REISS,I.L. Premarital Sexual Permissiveness Scales

VARIABLES MEASURED.   Sexual permissiveness;   sexual
equalitarianism.
TEST DESCRIPTION. Items describe the extent to which the S
finds kissing, petting or coitus acceptable under conditions
of no affection, strong affection, love, and engaged.   Each
item is answered as either Agree (Strong, Medium, Slight) or
Disagree (Strong, Medium, or Slight).   There are 12
questions referring to behavior for men and 12 parallel
questions referring to behavior for women.   The
equalitarianism index is the difference between the male and
female scores. On the basis of these responses the subject
is placed in a "sexual standards" category.   These
standards, along with several subgroups are:
      (1) Abstinence: a. petting without affection, b.
petting with affection, c. kissing without affection, d.
kissing with affection. (2) Double standard: a. orthodox,
b. transitional. (3) Permissiveness without affection: a.
orgiastic, b.   sophisticated.   (4) Permissiveness with
affection: a. love, b. strong affection. For example, if
the S agreed only with the first three "kissing" statements
on both the male and female scales, he/she is classified
under the "abstinence" standard as a kissing-with-affection
subtype. If the S also agreed to the fourth "kissing"
statement on both scales he/she would be a
kissing-without-affection subtype.
      Reiss has developed a short version of the scale,
combining questions 5 and 6 into one question which simply
asks acceptance of petting if in love or engaged;   question
7 which asks about the acceptance of petting if there is
strong affection; questions 9 and 10 which ask about the
acceptance of intercourse--if there is love and engagement;
question 11 which asks about the acceptance of intercourse
if there is strong affection; question 12 which asks about
the acceptance of intercourse even if there is no strong
affection. These five new items make a scale that has
universally scaled in the same manner in every sample that
it has been tried upon. If one has a very high permissive
group, one can make an even shorter scale and just use the
combined question of 9 and 10 and question 11 and question
12. It would seem that the kissing question would have to
be used predominantly when one is dealing with perhaps a
junior high school group or else a very conservative
subculture.

SAMPLE ITEM. I believe that kissing is acceptable for the male before marriage when he is engaged to be married. Agree: Strong = 1, Medium = 2, Slight = 3. Disagree: Strong = 1, Medium = 2, Slight = 3.
LENGTH. Items: 24.
AVAILABILITY. In Reiss, 1964a.
REFERENCES.

Bauman,K.E.   Volunteer bias in a study of sexual knowledge, attitudes and behavior. Journal of Marriage and the Family, 1973, 35, 27-31.

Cardwell,J.D.   The relationship between religious commitment and premarital sexual permissiveness: a five dimensional analysis. Sociological Analysis, 1969, 30, 72-80.

Clayton,R.R.   Religiosity and premarital sexual permissivness: elaboration of the relationship and debate. Sociological Analysis, 1971, 32, 81-96.

Clayton,R.R.   Premarital sexual intercourse: a substantive test of the contingent consistency model. Journal of Marriage and the Family, 1972, 34, 273-281.

Hampe,G.D.   Interfaith dating: religion, social class and premarital sexual attitudes.   Sociological Analysis, 1971, 32, 97-106.

Hampe,G.D.   and Ruppel,H.J.Jr.   The measurement of premarital sexual permissiveness: a comparison of two Guttman Scales. Journal of Marriage and the Family, 1974, 36, 470-473.

Harrison,D.E.   Bennett,W.H. and Globetti,G. Attitudes of rural youth toward premarital sexual permissiveness. Journal of Marriage and the Family, 1969, 31, 783-787.

Heltsley,M.E.   and Broderick,C.B.   Religiosity and premarital sexual permissiveness: a reexamination of Reiss's traditionalism proposition. Journal of Marriage and the Family, 1969, 31, 441-443.

Hobart,C.W.   Sexual permissiveness in young English and French Canadians. Journal of Marriage and the Family, 1972, 34, 292-303.

Kaats,G.R. and Davis,K.E.   The dynamics of sexual behavior of college students. Journal of Marriage and the Family, 1970, 32, 390-399.

Maranell,G.M.   Dodder,R.A. and Mitchell,D.F.   Social class and premarital sexual permissiveness: a subsequent test.   Journal of Marriage and the Family, 1970, 32, 85-88.

Mirande,A.M.   and   Hammer,E.L.   Premarital sexual permissiveness: a research note. Journal of Marriage and the Family, 1974a, 36, 356-357.

Mirande,A.M.   and   Hammer,E.L.   Premarital sexual permissiveness and abortion. Pacific Sociological Review, 1974b, 17, 485-488.

Perlman,D.   Self-esteem and sexual permissiveness. Journal of Marriage and the Family, 1974, 36, 470-473.

Reiss,I.L. Premarital Sexual Standards in America. Glencoe: Free Press, 1960.

Reiss,I.L. Sociological studies of sexual standards. In Winokur,G. (Ed.) Determinants of Human Sexual Behavior.

Springfield, Ill.: Charles C Thomas, 1963.
     Reiss,I.L.   The   scaling   of   premarital   sexual
permissiveness.   Marriage and Family Living, 1964a, 26,
188-198.
     Reiss,I.L.   Premarital sexual permissiveness   among
Negroes and whites.   American Sociological Review, 1964b,
29, 688-698.
     Reiss,I.L.   Social   class   and   premarital   sexual
permissiveness: a re-examination.   American Sociological
Review, 1965, 30, 747-756.
     Reiss,I.L.   Social Context of Premarital Sexual
Permissiveness.   New York: Holt, Rinehart, and Winston,
1967.
     Reiss,I.L. Response to the Heltsley and Broderick
retest of Reiss's proposition one. Journal of Marriage and
the Family, 1969, 31, 444-445.
     Rubin,A.M.   and Adams,J.R.   Sex attitudes of   sex
educators. The Family Coordinator, 1972, 21, 177-182.
     Ruppel,H.J.Jr.   Religiosity and premarital sexual
permissiveness: a   methodological   note.   Sociological
Analysis, 1969, 30, 176-188.
     Ruppel,H.J.Jr.   Religiosity and premarital sexual
permissiveness: a response to the Reiss-Heltsley and
Broderick debate. Journal of Marriage and the Family, 1970,
32, 647-655.
     Stratton,J.R. and Spitzer,S.P. Sexual permissiveness
and self-evaluation: a question of substance and a question
of method. Journal of Marriage and the Family, 1967, 29,
434-441.

SOARES,A.T.   AND SOARES,L.M.   Sex-Attitude   Scale   and
Role-Taking Sex-Attitude Scale.

VARIABLES MEASURED.   Sex attitudes and perceptions   of
others' sex attitudes.
     An abstract of this test is given in Johnson,O.G.
Tests and Measurements in Child Development: Handbook II.
San Francisco: Jossey-Bass, 1976, 630.

STUART,F. STUART,R.B. MAURICE,W.L. and SZASZ,G.   Sexual
Adjustment Inventory

VARIABLES MEASURED. General mood and self concept, aspects
of the social context of sexual interaction, communication
and decision making about sex, various attitudes toward sex
such as conventionalism, and descriptive information about
sexual interaction.
TEST DESCRIPTION. This inventory is intended for use in the
assessment of sexual functioning when sex is considered to
be an expression of important dimensions of the social
interaction   between   partners.   Variables such as
communication style and the manifestation of power in
decision making about such issues as birth control methods

(and by implication, family size) and the frequency and
character of sexual experiences are stressed. In addition,
questions concerning present and preferred modes of sexual
experience shed light on the partners' agreement and
understanding of one another's wishes.
SAMPLE ITEMS. Some items are Likert-type scales such as:
"Couples should be able to have good sex even though they
usally do not get along well together in other ways.
Strongly agree (1)...Strongly disagree (5)." Other items
call for open-ended responses such as: "Please list three
things which you would like your partner to do more often
during your sexual activity". These items are scored by
categorizing the responses and comparing the codes for both
partners.
LENGTH. Eight scales, 12 pages.
AVAILABILITY. Research Press, 2612 N. Mattis Avenue,
Champaign, Illincis 61820.
ABSTRACTED BY: Richard B. Stuart
REFERENCE.
        Stuart,F. Stuart,R.B. Maurice,W.L. and Szasz,G.
Sexual Adjustment Inventory and Guide. Champaign, Illinois,
Research Press, 1975.

VENER,A.M. and STEWART,C.S. Index of Heterosexual Activity

VARIABLE MEASURED. Heterosexual activity.
TEST DESCRIPTION. A series of five-choice questions
designed to elicit responses reflecting increasing levels of
sexuality. The respondents indicate their degree of
experience at each of eight levels of heterosexual activity
(Vener and Stewart, 1974). The score is the total or summed
value of the responses. The questions are asked in
ascending order of involvement.
        To gain acceptance in the communities sampled, items
tapping more explicit information (e.g., petting the breast
from outside the clothing or horizontal embrace with some
petting, but not undressed) were purposely avoided. Some
terms for coitus had to be rejected on the basis of
propriety, because of their provinciality, or because
younger children would be unable to understand them.
Regardless of age, sex and class differences, all
respondents in the pretest group had a common understanding
of the phrase "going all the way," despite the fact that
many thought it to be somewhat archaic.
SAMPLE ITEM. How often have you gone all the way with
someone of the opposite sex? (1) Never, (2) Once, (3) 2 to
5 times, (4) 6 to 12 times and (5) 13 or more times.
LENGTH. Items: 8.
AVAILABILITY. In Vener and Stewart, 1974.
ABSTRACTED BY: Cyrus S. Stewart
REFERENCES.
        Vener,A.M. and Stewart,C.S. Adolescent sexual
behavior in Middle America revisited: 1970-1973. Journal
of Marriage and the Family 1974, 34, 728-735.

Vener,A.M. Stewart,C.S. and Hager,D.L. The sexual behavior of adolescents in Middle America: generational and American-British comparisons. Journal of Marriage and the Family, 1972, 32, 696-705.

B. Romantic Love (See also Subject Index)

DEAN,D.G. Romanticism Scale

VARIABLE   MEASURED.   Romanticism   in   heterosexual relationships.
TEST DESCRIPTION. The definition of romanticism is Winch's: "A relationship between the sexes in which the affective component (emphasis on response) is regarded as primary, and all other considerations... are excluded from conscious reflection." Romanticism and companionship love (a relationship cf gradual development, more mature, responsible, and other-person centered) are conceived as polar types. Of the 32 items on the questionnaire, 27 are considered to be in the romantic dimension. No answering or scoring procedure given.
SAMPLE ITEM. One can't help falling in love if she meets the right person.
LENGTH. Items: 32.
AVAILABILITY. From NAPS.
REFERENCES.
     Dean,D.G. Romanticism and emotional maturity: A preliminary study. Marriage and Family Living, 1961, 23, 44-45.
     Spanier,G.B. Romanticism and marital adjustment. Journal of Marriage and the Family, 1972, 34, 481-487.

GROSS,L. Romanticism Scale

VARIABLE   MEASURED.   Romantic   heterosexual   role prescriptions.
TEST DESCRIPTION. Subjects respond to 80 statements on each of two forms by checking those with which they agree. Each romantic statement is followed by a realist one. The score is the number of romantic statements checked minus the number of realist statements checked.
     Hobart (1958a; 1958b; 1958c) modified the scale by selecting 12 items and changing the scoring procedure. Items are scored by counting the number of romantic responses, whether in agreement or disagreement with the statements. The romantic response is Disagree to six items and Agree to six.
SAMPLE ITEM. As long as they at least love each other, two people should have no trouble getting along with each other.

LENGTH. Items: 80 on each of two forms (Gross);   12
(Hobart).
AVAILABILITY. In Gross, 1939; Hobart, 1958b.
REFERENCES.
     Gross,L. Construction of a belief pattern scale for
measuring   attitudes   toward   romanticism.   Ph.D.
dissertation, University of Minnesota, 1939.
     Gross,L.   A belief pattern   scale   for   measuring
attitudes toward romanticism. American Sociological Review,
1944, 9, 463-472.
     Hobart,C.W. Emancipation from parents and courtship in
adolescents. Pacific Sociological Review, 1958a, 6, 25-29.
     Hobart,C.W.   The incidence of   romanticism   during
courtship. Social Forces, 1958b, 36, 362-367.
     Hobart,C.W.   Some effects of   romanticism   during
courtship on marriage role opinions. Sociology and Social
Research, 1958c, 42, 336-343.

POLLIS,C.A.   Idealization Score

VARIABLE MEASURED.   Idealization of dating partner.
TEST DESCRIPTION. Subjects representing different stages of
dating involvement with partners rate their partners, using
a five-point scale, on 17 characteristics drawn   from
previous   studies   of   traits desired in dating/marriage
partners. Two of each subject's best friends who know
his/her partner also rate that partner using the same scale.
The idealization score is derived from computing   the
direction and numerical discrepancy between the subject's
ratings compared separately with those of each friend.
SAMPLE ITEM. Characteristics: Considerate, Ambitious,
Honest.   Scale   points: Always,   Very often,   Often,
Occasionally, Rarely.
AVAILABILITY. From NAPS-2.
ABSTRACTED BY: Carol A. Pollis.
REFERENCE.
     Pollis,C.A.   Dating involvement and   patterns   of
idealization: A test cf Waller's hypothesis. Journal of
Marriage and the Family, 1969, 31, 765-771.

SCHULMAN,M.L.   Empathy Test for Idealization in Engaged
Couples

VARIABLES MEASURED. (1) Number of disagreements: Total
number of items on which one partner checks True and the
other partner checks False,   or   the   reverse.   (2)
Disagreement estimate: Total number of items on which one
partner predicts that the other partner will answer False.
(The disagreement estimate for the couple equals half the
female disagreement estimate plus the male disagreement
estimate.) (3) Accuracy estimate: Number of disagreements
minus the disagreement estimate. (a) Idealists: accuracy
estimate of +3.0 or more. (b) Realists: accuracy estimate

between -1.0 and +2.5.   (c) Pessimists: accuracy   estimate
of -1.5 or less.
TEST DESCRIPTION. The instrument is a true-false
questionnaire covering religion, sexual relations, role
relations, economic matters, parents and in-laws, and
political position. However, the validity of the instrument
does not reside in the answers to the questions per se, but
in the description of the individual or couple obtained from
the scoring. Each couple member completes the questionnaire
three   times: (1) Giving his or her own views, (2)
Predicting partner's views, and (3) Predicting partner's
predictions. (The third time may be omitted.) Operational
definitions of Idealistic, Realistic, and Pessimistic
couples are obtained by subtracting the number of times
couples think they disagree (disagreement estimate) from the
number of times they actually disagree. For example,
Idealists are couples who think they disagree less than they
actually disagree; i.e. number of disagreements exceeds
disagreement estimate by +3.0 or more. Realists are couples
who think they disagree at about the same rate that they
actually do; and Pessimists think they disagree more than
they actually do.
SAMPLE ITEM. I want to have friends of my own even if my
husband/wife doesn't like them.
LENGTH. Time: 20 minutes. Items: 37.
AVAILABILITY. In Schulman, 1971. A scoring manual and
score sheet, along with a test copy may be obtained from
NAPS-2.
ABSTRACTED BY: Marion L. Schulman.
REFERENCES.
        Schulman,M.L. Communication between engaged couples.
Ph.D. dissertation, University of Southern California,
1971.
        Schulman,M.L.   Idealization in engaged couples.
Journal of Marriage and the Family, 1974, 36, 139-147.

SPAULDING,C.B. The Romantic Love Complex

VARIABLE MEASURED. A form of idealized love deeply imbedded
in American culture.
TEST DESCRIPTION. The respondent indicates whether he/she
Strongly agrees = 5, Agrees = 4, is Neutral = 3, Disagrees =
2, or Strongly Disagrees = 1. Numbers are added to obtain
score. "The scales were created by a modified Leikert
technique in which items were selected [from an initial set
of 50] which correlated positively with the sum of all
proposed scale items and did not correlate negatively with
any other item in the scale."
SAMPLE ITEM. As long as they at least love each other, two
people should have no trouble getting along together in
marriage.
LENGTH. Items: 11.

AVAILABILITY. Items appear in footnote 36 of Spaulding,
1970. In the original research the items were scattered
through a long questionnaire. (Note: The cited source
contained a misprint. In item 11 "unknown" should be
"known.")
ABSTRACTED BY: Charles B. Spaulding.
REFERENCE.
       Spaulding,C.B. The Romantic Love Complex in American
Culture. Sociology and Social Research, 1970, 55, 82-100.

THEODORSON,G.A. Romanticism Index

VARIABLE MEASURED. Romantic orientation toward marriage in
contrast to a contractual arrangement.
TEST DESCRIPTION. Five indicators are used to measure a
distinction between a romantic as compared to a contractual
orientation toward marriage. Responses are made in terms of
five-point Likert scale categories. The article on which
this abstract is based obtains an overall romanticism index
only for data in the aggregate. However, such an index can
be computed for each respondent by a number of techniques
such as linear summation.
SAMPLE ITEM. The person I marry must be sexually
stimulating. Strongly agree, Agree, Uncertain, Disagree,
Strongly disagree.
LENGTH. Items: 5.
AVAILABILITY. In Theodorson, 1965.
ABSTRACTED BY: Bruce Brown.
REFERENCE.
       Theodorson,G.A. Romanticism and motivation to marry in
the U.S., Singapore, Burma, and India. Social Forces, 1965,
44, 17-27.

                 C. Dating (See also Subject Index)

BARDIS,P.D. Dating Liberalism Schedule

VARIABLE MEASURED. Liberalism in dating behavior.
TEST DESCRIPTION. Linear summation of frequency of
performance items.
SAMPLE ITEM. Kissing on the first date. (1) Never, (2)
Very seldom, (3) Seldom, (4) Frequently, (5) Very
frequently.
LENGTH. Items: 15.
AVAILABILITY. From NAPS.
REFERENCE.
       Bardis,P.D. Attitudes toward dating among foreign
students in America. Marriage and Family Living, 1956, 18,
339-344.

BARDIS,P.D. Dating Scale

VARIABLE MEASURED. Liberalism in dating attitudes.
TEST DESCRIPTION. A Likert-type attitude scale consisting
of items which are summed to obtain the liberalism score.
Items were selected by item analysis from a pool of 180.
All items have a discriminatory index of over 3.0.
SAMPLE ITEM. Girls should be allowed to ask boys for dates.
(0) Strongly disagree, (1) Disagree, (2) Undecided, (3)
Agree, (4) Strongly agree.
LENGTH. Items: 25.
AVAILABILITY. In Bardis, 1962; Shaw and Wright, 1967.
REFERENCES.
     Bardis,P.D. Attitudes toward dating among the students
of a Michigan high school. Sociology and Social Research,
1958, 42, 274-277.
     Bardis,P.D. A dating scale: a technique for the
quantitative measurement of liberalism concerning selected
aspects of dating. Social Science, 1962, 37, 44-47.
     Shaw,M.E. and Wright,J.M. Scales for the Measurement
of Attitude. New York: McGraw-Hill, 1967.

BLOOD,R.O.JR. and NICHOLSON,S.O. International Dating
Prejudice Score

VARIABLE MEASURED. Prejudice against dating foreign
students.
TEST DESCRIPTION. Seven multiple-choice questionnaire
items, summed to obtain a total score.
SAMPLE ITEM. Do you feel that dating foreign students would
lessen a girl's (your) chances of dating Americans? Yes;
Probably; Probably not; No.
LENGTH. NR.
AVAILABILITY. From NAPS; Blood and Nicholson, 1962.
REFERENCE.
     Blood,R.O.Jr. and Nicholson,S.O. The attitudes of
American men and women students toward international dating.
Marriage and Family Living, 1962, 24, 35-41.

McDANIEL,C.O.Jr. Dating-Courtship Questionnaire for Females

VARIABLES MEASURED. The following aspects of
dating-courtship relationships: (1) Assertiveness, (2)
Receptivity, (3) Assertive-receptive behavior, (4) Peer
group orientation, (5) Personal Orientation, (6) Original
family orientation, (7) Complementarity of traits, (8)
Dissatisfaction-satisfaction, (9) Commitment to dating
partner, (10) Anticipatory socialization for marriage, (11)
Mate selection, and (12) Recreation.
TEST DESCRIPTION. A series of Guttman scales to measure the
above variables: (1) Assertive Role Behavior: normative
statements concerning achievement orientation, autonomy,
dominance, hostility to males, and status aspiration and

status striving. (2) Receptive Role Behavior: Normative statements concerning abasement, deference, succorance, vicariousness, approach, and anxiety. (3) Assertive-Receptive Role Behavior: Combines scales (1) and (2). (4) Peer Group Orientation: Responses to hypothetical statements concerning whether specific acts in dating would be satisfying to the female only if they were appraised and sanctioned by her age-sex-association group. (5) Personal Orientation: Responses to hypothetical statements concerning whether specific acts in dating would be satisfying to the female only if they meet with her own approval. (6) Original Family Orientation: Hypothetical statements concerning whether specific acts in dating would be satisfying to the female only if they are appraised and sanctioned by her parents and siblings. (7) Complementarity of Traits: Statements concerning specific personality and behavioral traits in terms of whether or not the female desires them in a marriage mate and whether or not her dating partner possesses them. (8) Dissatisfaction-Satisfaction: Questions on whether the female is contented with her own dating behavior. (9) Commitment to Dating Partner(s): Hypothetical statements designed to elicit the extent to which the female would be willing to gratify certain wishes of the male when these wishes make progressively more demands on her. (10) Anticipatory Socialization for Marriage: Normative statements designed to elicit whether the female thinks dating activities should serve primarily as training or practice for her being a good wife when she eventually marries. (11) Mate Selection: Normative statements designed to elicit whether the female thinks dating activities should serve primarily as a mode of selecting the best marriage partner. (12) Recreation: Normative statements designed to elicit whether the female thinks dating activities should be primarily oriented toward fun and enjoyment.
SAMPLE ITEM. Anticipatory Socialization: The only good reason why a girl should date is to learn what behavior is necessary for her to be a good wife. Strongly agree = 1, Agree = 2, Slightly agree = 3, Slightly disagree = 4, Disagree = 5, Strongly disagree = 6.
LENGTH. Items: 9, 9, 18, 9, 8, 9, 10, 5, 11, 9, 10, 9 respectively.
AVAILABILITY. From NAPS-2.
ABSTRACTED BY: Bruce Brown
REFERENCE.
    McDaniel,C.O.Jr. Dating roles and reasons for dating. Journal of Marriage and the Family, 1969, 31, 97-107.

McHUGH,G. A Dating Problems Checklist

VARIABLES MEASURED. Problems encountered in dating, including dating conditions; home, parents, and family; personality and emotional self; sex attitudes; social

poise, physical self, dating, and definite commitments.
TEST DESCRIPTION. A teaching and counseling aid for high
school and college students, who read a list of dating
problems and check their own. They then go over the list
again and place an X by the problems that concern them most.
SAMPLE ITEM. There are too few places to go on dates.
LENGTH. Items: 128.
AVAILABILITY. From Family Life Publications, Inc., Box
6725, College Station, Durham, N.C. 27708. Specimen set,
.35.
REFERENCES.
          McHugh,G. A Dating Problems Checklist. Durham, N.C.:
Family Life Publications, 1961a.
          McHugh,G. Counselors' and teachers' guide to accompany
a Dating Problems Checklist. Durham, N.C.: Family Life
Publications, 1961b.

OLSON,D.H.L.   Premarital Attitude Scale

VARIABLES MEASURED. Attitudes toward the following topics:
(1) Dating and courtship, (2) Mate selection, (3) Early
marital adjustment, (4) Marital role expectations, (5) Sex
information, (6) Resolution of conflict, (7) When
relationships fail, (8) Self and course evaluation.
TEST DESCRIPTION. The test consists of three positive and
three negative items for each of eight categories relating
to topics generally presented in functional marriage and
family courses on the college level. Respondents are asked
to rate each item on a seven-point scale ranging from
Strongly disagree to Strongly agree. This is accomplished
in one of two methodologies; the Q-Sort method (Olson and
Gravatt, 1968), or the questionnaire method (Roberts, 1969).
Regardless of method, scores are interpreted in three main
ways: (1) Individual items compared to one of five
available norms, (2) items summed within categories yielding
eight separate attitude indices, (3) Summing the total score
for all items.
          This scale provides an estimation of current attitudes
toward aspects of marital behavior (Olson and Gravatt, 1968)
and in evaluating attitude change in marriage and family
courses (Olson and Gravatt, 1968; Roberts, 1969). Norms
are available for college students (N = 332), students with
marriage and family coursework (N = 97), professionals in
the marriage and family field (N = 10) (Olson, 1967); high
school students (N = 231) (Roberts, 1969); and, junior high
school students (N = 215) (Martin, 1973).
SAMPLE ITEM. The patterns of behavior I establish during my
serious dating with a person will be carried over into our
engagement.
AVAILABILITY. In Olson and Gravatt, 1968.
LENGTH. Time: Q-Sort 30 minutes; Questionnaire 20
minutes. Items: 48.

ABSTRACTED BY: David H. Olson

REFERENCES.
    Martin,K.S.   Premarital   attitudes   and   marriage
readiness of junior high school students.   Unpublished
Masters Thesis, University of Maryland, 1973.
    Olson,D.H.L.   Student   attitudes   toward   marriage.
College Student Survey, 1967, 1, 71-78.
    Olson,D.H.L. and Gravatt,A.E. Attitude change in a
functional marriage course. The Family Coordinator, 1968a,
17, 99-104.
    Olson,D.H.L.   and Gravatt,A.E.   The Q-Sort as an
attitude measure. College Student Survey, 1968b, 2, 13-22.
    Roberts,M.R. Attitude changes in a family relations
course in high school. Unpublished Masters Thesis, Texas
Tech University, 1969.

POWERS,E.C. Least Interest Scale for Dating Behavior

VARIABLE MEASURED. A person's willingness to modify his/her
own behavior on the basis of his/her relationship with a
current dating partner.
TEST DESCRIPTION. An interview is conducted in which 14
Likert-type items are asked.   Response categories are 1
through 5, the higher scores indicating greater involvement
and interest, the lower scores less interest.
SAMPLE ITEM.   I believe you should live up to the
expectations of your partner.
LENGTH. Items: 14.
AVAILABILITY. Powers, 1964; Eslinger, Clarke, and Dynes,
1972.
ABSTRACTED BY: Thomas G. Sparhawk

REFERENCES.
    Eslinger,K.N.   Clarke,A.C.   and Dynes,R.R.   The
principle of least interest, dating behavior, and family
integration settings. Journal of Marriage and the Family,
1972, 34, 269-272.
    Powers,E.C. An attempt to develop a scale to measure
the principle cf least interest. Unpublished manuscript.
Department of Sociology, Ohio State University, 1964.

REHM,L.F. and MARTSON,A.R. Dating Anxiety Index

VARIABLE MEASURED. Extent of discomfort or anxiety when
interacting with persons of the opposite sex.
TEST DESCRIPTION. Test consists of 30 interpersonal
situations which respondents rate according to the amount of
anxiety which each situation illicits. Ratings are made on
a seven-point scale ranging from (1) No anxiety to (7)
Extreme anxiety. The mean of the score for the 30 items
comprises the index of dating anxiety.
SAMPLE ITEM. Calling up a member of the opposite sex just
to talk.

LENGTH. Items: 30.
AVAILABILITY.   From NAPS-2.
ABSTRACTED BY: Bruce W.   Brown
REFERENCES.
        Curran,J.P.   An evaluation of a skills training program
and a systematic desensitization program in reducing dating
anxiety.   Reprints available from J.P.   Curran, Department
of Psychological   Sciences,   Purdue   University,   West
Lafayette, Indiana 47907.
        Curran,J.P.   and Gilbert,F.S.   A test of   the relative
effectiveness of a systematic desensitization program and an
interpersonal skills training program with date anxious
subjects.   Reprints available from J.P.   Curran, Department
of Psychological   Sciences,   Purdue   University,   West
Lafayette, Indiana 47907.
        Rehm,L.P.   and Martson,A.R.   Reduction of social
anxiety through modification of self-reinforcement: an
instigation therapy technique.   Journal of Consulting and
Clinical Psychology, 1968, 32, 5, 565-574.

VERNON,G.M. and STEWART,R.L.   Dating Empathy Score

VARIABLES MEASURED.   (1) Subject's satisfaction in each of
14 dating areas, (2) Empathy in dating: subject's guess of
the satisfaction felt by his/her partner in each area.
TEST DESCRIPTION.   A 14-item questionnaire with   five
response categories: (1) I was very satisfied, (2) I was
satisfied, (3) I was neutral, (4) I was unsatisfied, (5)   I
was very unsatisfied.   Dating areas included feelings about:
(1) Going with the person dated when the arrangements for
the date were made, (2) Time set for the beginning of the
date, (3) Kind of date, (4) Amount of money spent, (5) Means
of transportation used, (6) Individuals's own dating manners
while on the date, (7) Partner's dating manners while on the
date, (8) Decisions made while on the date, (9) Physical
intimacies which occurred on the date, (10) Extent of
physical intimacies while on the date, (11) Amount of time
spent on the date, (12) Going on another date with the
individual, and (13) Overall satisfaction with the date.
The measure of empathy is derived by determining how closely
the subject's guess of his or her partner's satisfaction
coincides with the satisfaction actually reported by the
partner.   Any deviation of the guessed satisfaction from the
stated satisfaction is determined and stated   as   the
deviation score.   Empathy is measured in terms of the size
of the deviation scores--the higher the deviation, the lower
the empathy.
SAMPLE ITEM.   Check one of the following statements which
best describes how you felt about the means of the
transportation used on the date.   (Response categories given
in test description.)
LENGTH. Items: 14.

AVAILABILITY. From NAPS
REFERENCE.
    Stewart,R.L.   and   Vernon,G.M.   Four   correlates   of
empathy in the dating situation. Sociology and Social
Research, 1959, 43, 279-285.
    Vernon,G.M. and Stewart,R.L. Empathy as a process in
the dating situation. American Sociological Review, 1957,
22, 48-52.

D. Premarital Counseling and Marriage Orientation (See also
Subject Index)

ADAMS,C.R.   Marriage Adjustment Prediction Index (MAP)

VARIABLES MEASURED. Variables that are thought to predict
successful   marital   adjustment   including   personality,
opinions   about   husband-wife   relationships,   family
background, educational level, and sexual attitudes and
experience.
TEST DESCRIPTION. This test is designed to be given to
unmarried people.   Items are derived from 4 tests: (1)
Terman's Prediction Scale for Happiness consisting of 143
items about interests and attitudes, general likes and
preferences, views about an ideal marriage, parents and
childhood;   (2)   the Adams-Lepley Personal Audit consisting
of nine tests each made up of 50 items which measure
seriousness,   firmness,   frankness,   stability,   tolerance,
steadiness,   persistence,   and   contentment;   (3)   the
Guilford-Martin   Personnel   Inventory   consisting of 150
questions that measure Objectivity (O), Agreeableness (Ag),
and Cooperativeness (Co); (4) the Burgess-Cottrell Marriage
Prediction Schedule.
SAMPLE ITEM. See tests cited in description.
LENGTH. Items: 743.
AVAILABILITY. In Adams, 1960.
REFERENCES.
    Adams,C.R. The prediction of adjustment in marriage.
Educational and Psychological Measurement, 1946, 6, 186-193.
    Adams,C.R. Evaluating personality tests. Marriage and
Family Living, 1950, 12, 55-58.
    Adams,C.R.   Marital happiness prediction inventory.
University Park, Pennsylvania: Division of Marriage and
Family Service, Pennsylvania State University, 1960.
    Reevy,W.R.   Premarital sexual behavior and marital
happiness prediction. Marriage and Family Living, 1959, 21,
349-355.
    Shope,D.F.   and Broderick,C.B.   Level   of   sexual
experience and predicted adjustment in marriage. Journal of
Marriage and the Family, 1967, 29, 424-427.

ALBERT,G.   The Albert Mate Selection Checklist

VARIABLE MEASURED.   Probability of success of a   prospective
marriage.
TEST DESCRIPTION.   This inventory   contains   73   descriptive
statements based on the findings from major marriage success
studies.   The items cover childhood happiness;   parent-child
relationships;   childhood   sex   information;   sexual
interests;   family   oriented   values   and   interests;
marriage-related   personality   traits.   Upper,   lower   and
inter-quartile ratings are   given,   based   on   a   sample   of
married and unmarried university students.
SAMPLE ITEM.   (The prospective marriage partner) does things
or believes in things that you find strongly disturbing.
LENGTH.   Items: 49 "favorable," 24 "unfavorable."
AVAILABILITY.   Personal Growth Press, P.O.   Box   M,   Berea,
Ohio 44017
ABSTRACTED BY: Gerald Albert
REFERENCE.
     Albert,G.   The Albert Mate Selection Checklist.   Berea,
Ohio: Personal Growth Press, 1971.

BRODERICK,C.B.   Adolescent Social Heterosexuality Score

VARIABLES MEASURED.   Social   heterosexuality   as   manifested
by: positive   attitude   toward   the   general   subject   of
romantic interaction with   the   opposite   sex,   emotional
attachment   to   some   particular member of the opposite sex,
absence of social prejudice toward the   opposite   sex   as   a
class, actual social interaction on a romantic pair basis.
TEST DESCRIPTION.   A self-administered questionnaire with   a
large   number   of   items.   Nine of these items are used for
this score.   One   point   is   assigned   for   each   response
indicating   heterosexuality.   Scores can range from 0 to 9.
The items were selected from the larger   pool   to   represent
each   of the above listed components of heterosexuality, and
because "each item differentiated between the sexes or among
ages or communities in a meaningful way."
SAMPLE ITEM.   Would you like to get married   someday?   Yes,
No, Don't know.
LENGTH.   Items: 9.
AVAILABILITY.   In Broderick, 1965.
REFERENCE.
     Broderick,C.B.   Social   heterosexual   development   among
urban Negroes and   whites.   Journal   of   Marriage and the
Family, 1965, 27, 200-203.

BRODERICK,C.B.   and   ROWE,G.P.   Preadolescent   Heterosexual
Development Scale

VARIABLE MEASURED.   Steps   in   the   process   of   heterosexual
development.

TEST DESCRIPTION. A five-item Guttman scale covering the following: desirability of eventual marriage, having a current girl- or boy-friend, having been in love, preference for a companion of the opposite sex when attending the movies, and beginning to date.
SAMPLE ITEM. Would you like to get married some day? Yes (scored positively); No or Don't Know (scored negatively).
LENGTH. Items: 5.
AVAILABILITY. In Broderick, 1968.
REFERENCES.
    Broderick,C.B. Socio-sexual development in a suburban community. Journal of Sex Research, 1966, 2, 1-24.
    Broderick,C.B. and Rowe,G.P. A scale of preadolescent heterosexual development. Journal of Marriage and the Family, 1968, 30, 97-101.
    Rowe,G.P. Patterns of interpersonal relationships among youth nine to thirteen years of age. Ph.D. dissertation, The Florida State University, 1966.

BURGESS,E.W. and COTTRELL,L.S. Burgess-Cottrell Marriage Prediction Schedule

VARIABLES MEASURED. Premarital social position, experience, interactions, and plans of husband and wife associated with successful marriage. Factor analysis of husband items shows 5 factors: (1) Psychogenic, (2) Cultural impress, (3) SES, (4) Economic role, (5) Affectional or response patterns.
TEST DESCRIPTION. Multiple-choice questions in five groups: (1) Social position and experiences in subject's family of orientation, (2) Personality traits of subject and prospective spouse, (3) Social relations and relations with prospective spouse's kin, (4) Relations with prospective spouse (joint activities, affection, confiding, arguments, etc.), (5) Marital plans (for children, residence, etc.). Score derived by adding weights for each response.
SAMPLE ITEM. What is your present state of health: Chronic ill health = 4, Temporary ill health = 5, Average health = 6, Healthy = 7, Very healthy = 8.
LENGTH. Time: 30-50 minutes. Items: 84.
AVAILABILITY. In Burgess and Cottrell, 1939; Burgess and Wallin, 1953; and from Family Life Publications, Inc., Box 6725 College Station, Durham, N.C. 27708.
REFERENCES.
    Burgess,E.W. and Cottrell,L.S. Predicting success or failure in marriage. New York: Prentice-Hall, 1939.
    Burgess,E.W. and Wallin,P. Engagement and marriage. New York: Lippincott, 1953, 507-557.
    Buros,O.K. (Ed.) Personality Tests and Reviews. Highland Park, N.J.: Gryphon Press, 1970.
    Dentler,R.A. and Hutchinson,J.G. Socioeconomic versus family membership status as sources of family attitude consensus. Child Development, 1961, 32, 249-254.
    Frumkin,R.M. The Kirkpatrick Scale of Family Interests as an Instrument for the indirect assessment of marital

adjustment. Marriage and Family Living, 1953, 15, 35-37.
     Frumkin,R.M.   Measurement of Marriage Adjustment.
Washington, D.C.: Public Affairs Press, 1954, II, 13.
Paper.
     King,C.E. Factors making for success or failure in
marriage among 466 Negro couples in a Southern city. Ph.D.
dissertation, University of Chicago (Chicago, Illinois),
1951.
     King,C.E. The Burgess-Cottrell method of measuring
marital adjustment applied to a non-White southern urban
population. Marriage and Family Living, 1952, 14, 280-285.
     McHugh,G. Counselor's Guide to Administration, Scoring
and Interpretation of Scores for Use with a Marriage
Prediction Schedule and a Marital Adjustment Form.   Durham,
N.C.: Family Life Publications, n.d.
     Skidmore,R.A. and McPhee,W.M. The comparative use of
the   California   Test   of   Personality   and   the
Burgess-Cottrell-Wallin Schedule in predicting marital
adjustment. Marriage and Family Living, 1951, 13, 121-126.
     Stroup,A.L. A Study of the Burgess-Cottrell System of
Predicting Marital Success or Failure. Ph.D. dissertation,
Ohio State University (Columbus, Ohio), 1950.
     Terman,L.M. and Wallin,P. The validity of marriage
prediction and adjustment tests. American Sociological
Review, 1949, 14, 497-504.

BURGESS,E.W. and WALLIN,P. Engagement Success Inventory

VARIABLE MEASURED. The prospects for success of an
engagement.
TEST DESCRIPTION. A 25-item questionnaire is administered
to engaged couples.   Each member of the couple answers
questions concerning the following areas: Areas of
agreement and disagreement, degree of satisfaction each of
the couple feels in matters such as demonstration of
affection, confiding, and common interests, complaints about
the prospective spouse and the engagement itself and whether
the relationship is more satisfactory to one of the couple
than to the other.
SAMPLE ITEM. Do you confide in your fiance(e)?   About
everything;   About most things;   About some things; All
other replies.
LENGTH. Items: 25.
AVAILABILITY. In Burgess, Wallin, and Schultz, 1954;   from
Family Life Publications, 219 Henderson Street, P.O. Box
427, Saluda, NC 28773.
ABSTRACTED BY: Kersti Yllo
REFERENCE.
     Burgess,E.W. Wallin,P. and Shultz,G.D. Courtship,
Engagement and Marriage.   Philadelphia: Lippincott Co.,
1954, 236-241 and 429-430.
     Schulman,M.L.   Idealization   in   engaged   couples.
Journal of Marriage and the Family, 1974, 36, 139-147.

CAVAN,R.S. A Dating-Marriage Scale of Religious Social
Distance

VARIABLE MEASURED. Horizontal social distance between major
religious groups in the United States: Catholic, Jewish,
Protestant.
TEST DESCRIPTION. A scale, based on work by Prince (1956)
ranges from complete rejection of other religions for
marriage (would neither date nor marry) through various
conditions making marriage acceptable, to assimilation
through conversion into another religion to make marriage
possible. The scale was embodied in a questionnaire
administered to university and college students. The scale
was partially validated by comparison of attitudes of
students with their dating practices.
SAMPLE ITEM. I would neither date nor marry a (name of
religious faith); I would date but not marry; marry if
mate convert to my religion; mate not to convert but rear
children in my faith; require neither of above; I would
convert to make marriage possible.
LENGTH. Time: 30 minutes. Items: 6 in scale for each
religion.
AVAILABILITY. In Cavan, 1971.
ABSTRACTED BY: Ruth Shonle Cavan
REFERENCE.
      Cavan,R.S. A dating-marriage scale of religious social
distance. Journal for the Scientific Study of Religion,
1971, 10, 93-100.
      Prince, A. Attitudes of college students toward
interfaith marriage. Family Life Coordinator, 1956, 6,
11-23.

HEISS,J.S. Courtship Progress Index

VARIABLE MEASURED. Courtship progress.
TEST DESCRIPTION. Subjects are asked if they have ever gone
steady. If they have, they are asked seven questions
designed to reveal the extent of their courtship progress.
These seven questions form a Guttman scale.
SAMPLE ITEM. Were you in love with any of your steadies?
Have you ever had a private agreement with any of your
steadies that you would someday get married?
LENGTH. Items: 8.
AVAILABILITY. In Heiss, 1960.
REFERENCE.
      Heiss,J.S. Variations in courtship progress among high
school students. Marriage and Family Living, 1960, 22,
165-170.

KEELER,R. Marriage Readiness Rating Scale (MRRS)

VARIABLES MEASURED. (1) Physical, social, and emotional
maturity; (2) Skills and abilities in getting along with

people; (3) Homemaking skills and abilities.
TEST DESCRIPTION. Three descriptive statements under a
seven-point graphic rating scale are used for each of the 41
items. Scores can be summed. This scale is designed to be
used cooperatively by the teacher and high school girl in
individual conferences, to attempt to estimate the student's
degree of readiness for marriage.
SAMPLE ITEM. Ability to see other people's point of view.
7 (readily see other people's points of view and respect
their right to their view), 6, 5, 4 (some ability of seeing
points of view other than your own), 3, 2 (lack of ability
to see other people's points of view), 1.
LENGTH. NR.
AVAILABILITY. From Department of Information, University of
Nebraska, Lincoln, Nebraska 68508. $.25 for copy for
teacher's use with suggestions and directions. Also in
Keeler, 1962a.
REFERENCES.
    Keeler,R. The development of a marriage readiness
rating scale. Lincoln: University of Nebraska Agricultural
Experiment Station Bulletin No. 204, 1962a.
    Keeler,R. A marriage readiness rating scale. Journal
of Home Economics, 1962b, 53, 217-218.

LEWIS,R.A. A Cross-Cultural Technique for Measuring Dyadic
Formation

VARIABLES MEASURED. (1) Pair similarity: "the extent to
which two persons' self reports on a personality assessment
scale concur;" (2) Perceived pair similarity: "the extent
to which a subject's self report concurs with his/her
perceptions of the partner's self view;" (3)
Self-disclosure: "the extent to which a subject's self
report concurs with his/her prediction of the partner's view
of the subject;" (4) Validation of the self: "the extent to
which a subject's view of his/her partner concurs with the
partner's prediction of how the subject views him/her;" (5)
Role-taking accuracy: "the extent to which subjects'
predictions of their partner's self report actually concur
with the partner's self report."
TEST DESCRIPTION. A personality test, such as the
Interpersonal Check List (Leary, 1957) is administered three
times: Each partner completes one form of the test in terms
of how they perceive themselves, a second in terms of how
they perceive their partners, and a third, in terms of how
they predict their partners perceive them. Various
comparisons of these six forms provide some relatively
"culture-free" assessments of dyadic formation, since the
procedures are intracultural, that is, each cultural group
determines its own scales.
SAMPLE ITEM. In most situations I see myself as "well
thought of". True, False.

LENGTH. See TEST DESCRIPTION.
AVAILABILITY. See TEST DESCRIPTION. The version used by
Lewis is given in NAPS-2.
ABSTRACTED BY: Robert A. Lewis.
REFERENCES.
        Leary,T.   Interpersonal Diagnosis   of   Personality.
N.Y.:   The Ronald Press Co., 1957.
        Lewis,R.A.   A   technique   for   the   cross-cultural
measurement of dyadic formation. International Journal of
Sociology of the Family, 1973, 3, 137-144.

LEWIS,R.A.   The Dyadic Formation Inventory

VARIABLES MEASURED.   (1) Dyadic crystallization: "the
degree to which two interacting personalities have formed a
discernible pair system;" (2) Dyadic inclusiveness: "the
extent to which pair members prefer each other to parents,
siblings and   friends   of   both   sexes;"   (3)   Dyadic
exclusiveness: "the extent to which pair members exclude
third persons from their two-person relationship;" (4) Pair
commitment: "the degree to which two persons determine to
continue their relationship;" (5) Couple identity: "the
extent to which a couple has achieved a sense of 'we-ness;'"
(6) Identification as a pair: "the degree to which the
couples' significant others identify the couple as a viable
pair;" and (7) Dyadic interaction: "the degree to which two
persons   interact   or   function   together   rather   than
autonomously."
TEST DESCRIPTION.   The Dyadic Formation Inventory is a
questionnaire made up of 74 items. Most of the individual
indices are formed by summing an individual's responses on
each of the items, multiplied by their factor loadings. The
final form of the Dyadic Formation Inventory has been
cross-validated   three   times   on   different groups of
college-age respondents. Longitudinal tests for assessing
the indices' predictive validity are reported in Lewis
(1973c).
SAMPLE ITEM. How often are you given an invitation to a
social function by friends who just assume that you would
bring along the other person?   Never, Seldom, Sometimes,
Fairly often, and Very often.
LENGTH. Items per scale: 25, 6, 9, 13, 6, 6, and 12.
AVAILABILITY. From NAPS-2.
ABSTRACTED BY: Robert A. Lewis.
REFERENCES.
        Lewis,R.A.   A developmental framework for the analysis
of premarital dyadic formation. Family Process, 1972, 11,
17-48.
        Lewis,R.A.   A longitudinal test of a developmental
framework for premarital dyadic formation. Journal of
Marriage and the Family, 1973a, 35, 16-25.
        Lewis,R.A.   The Dyadic Formation Inventory: an
instrument for measuring heterosexual couple development.
The International Journal of Sociology of the Family, 1973b,

3, 207-216.
    Lewis,R.A. Social reaction and the formation of dyads: an interactionist approach to mate selection. Sociometry, 1973c, 36, 409-418.

LOCKE,H.J. and WALLACE,K.M. Short Marital Prediction Test

VARIABLES MEASURED. Premarital background, experience, status, and personality characteristics conducive to marital success.
TEST DESCRIPTION. A questionnaire consisting of 35 multiple-choice items selected from previous studies as those having the highest level of discrimination. Weighted linear combination.
SAMPLE ITEM. Circle the number which represents the highest grade of schooling which you had completed at the time of your marriage.
LENGTH. Items: 35.
AVAILABILITY. In Locke and Wallace, 1959.
REFERENCES.
    Aller,F.D. Role of the self-concept in student marital adjustment. Family Life Coordinator, 1962, 11, 43-45.
    Locke,H.J. and Wallace,K.M. Short marital adjustment and prediction tests: their reliability and validity. Marriage and Family Living, 1959, 21, 251-255.
    Wallace,K.M. Construction and validation of marital adjustment and prediction scales. Ph.D. dissertation, University of Southern California, 1947.

MANSON,M.P. California Marriage Readiness Evaluation

VARIABLES MEASURED. Strength and weakness in three major aspects of marriage readiness: personality, preparation for marriage, and interpersonal compatibility.
TEST DESCRIPTION. A brief, true and false questionnaire for measuring marriage readiness. Provides scores indicating strengths and weaknesses in eight important areas of marriage readiness: Personality: (1) Character structure, (2) Emotional maturity, (3) Marriage readiness; Preparation for Marriage: (4) Family experiences, (5) Dealing with money, (6) Planning ability; Interpersonal Compatibility: (7) Marriage motivation, (8) Compatibility. In addition to the scores for each of the eight areas measured, a total score indicates overall readiness for marriage. The greater the number of items which are true about the respondent the higher his/her "marriage readiness."
SAMPLE ITEM. I often buy things I do not need. True, False.
LENGTH. Time: 10-15 minutes. Items: 115.
AVAILABILITY. From Western Psychological Services, 12031 Wilshire Bldg., Los Angeles, CA 90025.

ABSTRACTED BY: Ira R. Manson
REFERENCE.
     Manson,M.P. Manual for California Marriage Readiness
Evaluation.   Beverly   Hills,   California: Western
Psychological Services, 1965.

MCHUGH,G. A Courtship Analysis

VARIABLES MEASURED. Behaviors of the courting partner, and
conditions of courtship that are sources of concern to a
couple considering marriage: habits, religion, health,
common interests, sex attitudes, adaptability, background,
sense of humour, ambition, money, relationships, and
marriage.
TEST DESCRIPTION. A counseling and interviewing aid that is
filled out independently by the couple. After completion,
responses are compared and gone over with a marriage
counselor. The courtship analysis focuses attention on
possible problem areas.
SAMPLE ITEM. My courtship partner: has good taste in
choice of clothes: This makes me happy; Sometimes I worry
about this; This bothers me a lot; I don't know about
this.
LENGTH. Items: 127.
AVAILABILITY. From Family Life Publications, Inc., Box
6725, College Station, Durham, N.C. 27708. Specimen set,
$.35.
REFERENCES.
     McHugh,G. A Courtship Analysis. Durham, N.C.: Family
Life Publications, 1961a.
     McHugh,G. Counselors' and Teachers' Guide to Accompany
a Courtship Analysis. Durham, N.C.: Family Life
Publications, 1961b.

MURSTEIN,B.I. Expediency Scale (Scale E)

VARIABLE MEASURED. Desire to marry.
TEST DESCRIPTION. A structured questionnaire composed of 22
items is administered to subjects. Eighteen of the
questions require a Yes or No response. The remaining four
call for numerical responses (such as age or number of
people you have wanted to marry).
SAMPLE ITEM. Would you like to be married right now? Yes,
No.
LENGTH. Items: 22.
AVAILABILITY. In Murstein, 1976.
ABSTRACTED BY: Kersti Yllo.
REFERENCE.
     Murstein,B.I. Who Will Marry Whom? New York:
Springer Publishing Co., 1976.

MURSTEIN,B.I.   Marital Expectation Test

VARIABLES MEASURED. Expectations regarding characteristics
desired or perceived in partners contemplating marriage.
TEST DESCRIPTION. Contains items relating to appearance,
values, attitudes, personality, temperament, and roles
desired in partners and self from various perceptual "sets".
These include eight "sets"--Self, Ideal-Self, Partner,
Ideal-Spouse; How "A" perceives Self, Ideal-Self, Partner,
Ideal-Spouse. A test form contains 135 items for men, 130
for women, of which the first 76 are identical for each sex.
A factor analysis of the items resulted in nine primary
factors for men and for women. Subscales corresponding to
the items loading highly on each factor may be readily
selected for use. Tests are administered as a questionnaire
and answered on a five-point scale from Very true = 5 to
Very untrue = 1.
    The test is used by selecting any two perceptual sets
and computing the sum of the absolute discrepancy between
each item across all items. Comparison across all items of
the test can be made when the two tests compared deal with
one sex exclusively [(e.g. How Boyfriend sees his Self (by
woman) with Self (by boyfriend)]. When the target of the
test is different in each test [e.g. Self (by boyfriend)
compared with Self (by girlfriend)], only the first 76
items, which are identical, can be compared.
SAMPLE ITEM. (Men's form) I am admired by my girlfriend.
LENGTH. Time: Approximately 30 minutes. Items: 130 or
135.
AVAILABILITY. In Murstein, 1976.
ABSTRACTED BY: Bernard I. Murstein
REFERENCES.
    Murstein,B.I.   Stimulus-value-role. A theory of
marital choice. Journal of Marriage and the Family, 1970,
32, 465-481.
    Murstein,B.I. Self-ideal-self discrepancy and the
choice of marital partner. Journal of Consulting and
Clinical Psychology, 1971, 37, 47-52.
    Murstein,B.I.   Interview behavior,   projective
techniques, and questionnaires in the clinical assessment of
marital choice. Journal of Personality Assessment, 1972,
36, 462-467.
    Murstein,B.I. Person perception and courtship progress
among premarital couples. Journal of Marriage and the
Family, 1972, 34, 621-627.
    Murstein,B.I. Who Will Marry Whom? Theories and
Research in Marital Choice. New York: Springer Publishing
Co., 1976.
    Murstein,B.I. Qualities of desired spouse: a
cross-cultural comparison between French and American
college students. (In press).

NAVRAN,L.   Marital Diagnostic Inventory

VARIABLES MEASURED.   Provides information relevant to
counseling effort in three areas: Motivations for marrying
present spouse, specific marital problems and the
motivations for seeking counseling.
TEST DESCRIPTION. Structured, self-administered inventory
completed separately by each spouse seeking marriage
counseling, at intake. It requires client to check all
relevant items in motivations area and designate the three
most important ones. All current problems are checked,
responsiblity is allocated, and the three most important
problems are indicated. Client indicates, via checklist,
how counseling came to be sought, goals in mind, relative
desire for help and probable prognosis. It provides
counselor with an immediate grasp of the problems and
motivations of each spouse, and also gives the clients a
brief, therapeutic and meaningful opportunity to become
involved in the counseling process by giving their views a
full, unchallenged airing before the onset of the counseling
process.
SAMPLE ITEM. Check if applicable.   (Motivations   for
Marriage) __Love.
LENGTH. Time: 30 minutes. Items: 4-page inventory.
AVAILABILITY. From Western Psychological Services, 12031
Wilshire Blvd., Los Angeles, CA 90025.
ABSTRACTED BY: Leslie Navran
REFERENCE.
     Navran,L. Marital Diagnostic Inventory. Los Angeles:
Western Psychological Services, 1974.

ORLOFSKY,J.L.   and LESSER,I.M.   Intimacy Interview and
Intimacy Status Rating Manual

VARIABLES MEASURED. Intimacy status, or five styles of
coping with close interpersonal relationships during young
adulthood ranging from intimacy to isolation.
TEST DESCRIPTION. A semistructured interview concerning S's
close relationships with same and opposite sex peers and an
intimacy status rating manual for assigning subjects to one
of the five statuses based on the following three variables:
(1) the presence or absence of peer friendships, (2)
presence   or   absence   of   a   current (or recent)
enduring--committed--heterosexual love relationship and (3)
"depth"   versus   "superficiality"   of relationships.
Assessment of this third criterion is made on the basis of
subject's feelings of care and affection, openness and
self-disclosure (of personal matters and interpersonal
issues, feelings) and sensitivity and genuine interest in
friends. The Isolate status is defined by the first
criterion, and the non-Isolate statuses with respect to the
second and third criteria. Intimates and Pseudointimates
have entered into a committed heterosexual relationship, but
not Preintimates or Stereotyped Relationships subjects.

<u>Intimates</u> and <u>Preintimates</u> form "deep" relationships characterized by openness, mutual disclosure and care, etc. By contrast, <u>Pseudointimates</u> and Stereotyped subjects have relatively superficial relationships.
SAMPLE ITEM. What kinds of things do you discuss with him (her)?
LENGTH. 30 minute semi-structured interview.
AVAILABILITY. From NAPS-2.
ABSTRACTED BY: Jacob L. Orlofsky
REFERENCES.
    Marcia,J.E. Identity six years after: a follow-up study. Journal of Youth and Adolescence, 1977, 5, 145-160.
    Orlofsky,J.L. Intimacy status: relationship to interpersonal perception. Journal of Youth and Adolescence, 1976, 5, 73-88.
    Orlofsky,J.L. The relationship between intimacy status and antecedent personality components. Adolescence, in press.
    Orlofsky,J.L. and Ginsburg,S.D. Intimacy status: relationship to affect cognition. Adolescence, in press.
    Orlofsky,J.L. Marcia,J.E. and Lesser,I.M. Ego identity status and the intimacy versus isolation crisis of young adulthood. Journal of Personality and Social Psychology, 1973, 27, 211-219.

OTTO,H.A. Premarital Counseling Schedules

VARIABLE MEASURED. Interaction patterns believed relevant for marital success.
TEST DESCRIPTION. Three schedules used in counseling engaged couples, who inventory their opinions and actions in various areas. Beside each item are three columns: "How do we feel about this," "We have worked this out pretty well," and "We need to talk about this more." One of the two latter columns is checked for each item. The three schedules are: (1) Premarital survey covering 12 areas: housing, money matters, our relationship, education, employment, health, religion, in-laws, children, sex, leisure time, and wedding plans; (2) Sexual adjustment survey; (3) Family finance survey. Each area has 3-6 subtopics as well as space for additional topics.
SAMPLE ITEM. (Our relationships:) Expressing ourselves freely to each other.
LENGTH. Time: 60 minutes.
AVAILABILITY. From Consulting Psychologists Press, 577 College Avenue, Palo Alto, California 94305.
REFERENCES.
    Buros,O.K. (Ed.) Personality Tests and Reviews. Highland Park, N.J.: Gryphon Press, 1970.
    Otto,H.A. The use of inter-action centered schedules in group work with pre-marital couples. Group Psychology, 1952, 12, 223-229.
    Otto,H.A. The development, application, and appraisal of pre-marital counseling schedules. Ph.D. dissertation,

Florida State University, 1956.
     Otto,H.A. The use of inter-action centered schedules
in group work with pre-marital couples. Group
Psychotherapy, 1959, 11, 223-228.

SPORAKOWSKI,M.J. Marital Preparedness Instrument

VARIABLES MEASURED. Marital preparedness defined as the
readiness or degree of preparedness for marriage, perceived
by the individual, as evidenced by a number of factors
identified to be relevant in assessing marital adjustment.
TEST DESCRIPTION. The person taking the M.P.I. rates
himself/herself on 30 items relevant to various adjustment
factors related to the courtship and marital adjustment
processes. The 31st item asks the individual to rate
his/her preparedness for marriage as a whole. Each item is
rated on a five-point scale from Very well to Very poorly
prepared. Depending on the usage intended, total or item
scores may prove useful. The scale was developed for use
primarily in counseling and educational settings.
SAMPLE ITEM. Living with a person of the opposite sex.
LENGTH. Time: 10 minutes. Items: 31.
AVAILABILITY. In Sporakowski, 1968.
ABSTRACTED BY: Michael J. Sporakowski.
REFERENCE.
     Sporakowski,M.J. Marital preparedness, prediction and
adjustment. The Family Coordinator, 1968, 17, 155-161.

STUART,R. and STUART,F. Premarriage Counseling Inventory

VARIABLES MEASURED. Strengths and weaknesses of planned
marriages.
TEST DESCRIPTION. This instrument covers past marital
history, relevant aspects of family of orientation,
perception of interpersonal space, immediate relationship
history, basic attitudes toward marriage, specific
expectations for the planned marriage and general commitment
to or confidence in the relationship. It is premised on the
notion that one of the predictors of effective marital
interaction is the accuracy of prenuptial agreements, many
of which are implied rather than explicit. The Inventory is
intended to review these expectations, to measure the
consensus on important attitudes about marriage and to
assess the similarity of the interpersonal constructs
(Kelly, 1955) shared by each partner.
SAMPLE ITEM. The Inventory includes a modified REP Test
(Kelly, 1955) and a series of open-ended and Likert-type
scalar items. A sample of the latter type of item is:
Religion is important in the lives of men and women.
Strongly agree = 1...Strongly disagree = 5.
LENGTH. Nine pages.

AVAILABILITY. Research Press, 2612 North Mattis Avenue, Champaign, Illincis 61820.
ABSTRACTED BY: Richard B. Stuart (modified).
REFERENCES.

Kelly,G. The Psychology of Personal Constructs. New York: Norton, 1955.

Stuart,R.B. and Stuart,F. Premarriage Counseling Inventory. Champaign, Illinois: Research Press, 1975.

TERMAN,L.M. Terman Marital Prediction Test

VARIABLES MEASURED. Social background and personality factors predictive cf marital success.
TEST DESCRIPTION. Composed of two main types of items; (1) 140 personality test items (largely from the Bernreuter (1938) and the Strong (Strong et al., 1966) inventories), and (2) 29 items concerning experiences before marriage especially those within the family of orientation (such as religious training received, extent of conflict with parents, age at marriage).
SAMPLE ITEM. (Personality:) Do you daydream frequently? Yes, No. (Backgrcund:) Amount of conflict (before marriage) between you and your father. None, Very little, Moderate, A good deal, Almost continuous conflict.
LENGTH. Items: 159.
AVAILABILITY. In Terman, 1938.
REFERENCES.

Bernreuter,R.G. The Personality Inventory. Palo Alto, California: Consulting Psychologists Press, 1938.

Edmonds,V.H. Withers,G. and Dibatista,B. Adjustment, conservatism, and marital conventionalization. Journal of Marriage and the Family, 1972, 34, 96-103.

Strong,E.K.Jr. Campbell,D.P. Berdie,R.F. and Clark,K.E. Strong Vocational Interest Blank. New York: Psychological Corporation, 1966.

Terman,L.M. assisted by Buttenwieser,P. Ferguson,L.W. Johnson,W.B. and Wilson,D.P. Psychological Factors in Marital Happiness. New York: McGraw-Hill, 1938.

Terman,L.M. and Wallin,P. The validity of marriage prediction and marital adjustment tests. American Sociological Review, 1949, 14, 497-504.

Indexes

Author Index

593

Test Title Index

Subject Index

629

in dating, 571
parental, 346
Association: enjoyment of family, 36
  family vs peers, 288, 314, 315
  mother vs father, 316
Attachment: emotional, 577
  excessive, parent attitudes toward, 379
  mother-child, 196, 287, 348
  See also: closeness
Attention: husband-wife, 161
  in family interaction, 496
  in mother-child interaction, 199, 336, 367
  maternal handling of child's dependency in, 301
Attitudes: concerning ideal and real family, 418
  degree of self-disclosure about, 467
  generational differences in, 412
Attractive: images of parents as, 379
Authoritarian: child-rearing, 217, 225, 229, 242, 254, 261,
    369, 380, 534
  child-rearing, child's reaction to, 242
  ideology, family, 63
  power, 487
  submission, 521
Authority: child's cooperation with, 383
  father's, traditional standards in, 520
  husband-wife, 74, 84, 166, 522
  importance of each parent in, 259
  inhibiting parental, child's reaction to, 242
  mother's, 511
  parent-child, democratic vs autocratic, 232
  parental, 238, 243, 270, 300
  traditional vs liberal, 152
  See also: power
Automobile and transportation: husband-wife satisfaction
    in, 68
Autonomy: adolescents', 215, 303
  child's, 233, 251, 292, 300, 353, 355
  child's, parental acceptance of, 180, 248
  encouragement vs restriction of, 346
  family, 305, 402
  husband-wife, perceptions of, 158
  in interpersonal relations, 120
  of college students from parents, 301
  parental attitudes toward, 295, 302
  parents' expectations for child's, 296
  parents' respect for child's, 340
  women's, attitudes toward, 107
Avoidance: child's, 383
  father, 170
  in family, 187
  mother, 170
  of child by parents, 255
  See also: rejection

Shame: parents' use of, 206
Sharing: family, 478
  in child-rearing, 229
  marital role, 160
  parent-child, 353
  parental attitudes toward, 239
Siblings: ability to understand and deal with, 277
  child's problems with, 213
  differences, 344
  differences, in discipline and rapport, 243, 485
  expectations for child by parents, 373
  relations between, 367, 380, 384, 432
Similarity: couple, 581
  family member, 460, 462, 498
  husband-wife, in role tension, 57
  husband-wife, in self perception, 31
  mother-child, 312
  parent-child, in opinions, 327
  parent-child, perceived, 270, 314, 316, 322, 332
  sibling, 344
Sleeping: child's problems in, 213
  of child, flexibility of mother, 281, 365
Sociability: child's, 220
  child's, mother's concern about, 355
  encouraging by parents, 353
  parent-child, 332
Social: desirability, 153, 348
  development, infant, 339
  isolation, maternal, 355
  participation, husband-wife, satisfaction in, 25
  participation, parents', lack of, 206
  participation, wife's post-hospital, 95
  relations, husband-wife problems in, 63
Social-emotional behavior: family, 471
  husband-wife, 158
  satisfaction in, 172, 209
Social worker: family relation with, 152
Socialization: see child-rearing
Sociopathic traits: husband-wife, 41
Soiling: child's problems in, 213
Solicitousness: family, 475
  parent attitudes, 379
  parent-child, 332
  See also: support
Solidarity: family, 36, 400, 401, 432, 452, 471, 533
  husband-wife role expectations and role enactments, 166
  with family of orientation and procreation, 390
  See also: closeness, cohesiveness, integration, support
Spatial: relationships, family, 514
  setting, family, 547
Spoiled child: maternal child-rearing, 383
Spouse: feelings toward, 151
  ideal and actual, 530
  independence, happiness in, 25